Mexican American Religions

Mexican American Religions

Spirituality, Activism, and Culture

edited by GASTÓN ESPINOSA *and* MARIO T. GARCÍA

DUKE UNIVERSITY PRESS

Durham & London 2008

© 2008 Duke University Press
All rights reserved
Printed in the United States of America on acid-free paper ∞
Designed by C. H. Westmoreland
Typeset in Carter & Cone Galliard by Achorn International
Library of Congress Cataloging-in-Publication Data appear on
the last printed page of this book.

frontispiece photo: 17 November 2004.
courtesy of Ann E. Robson.

This book is dedicated to

our hardworking Mexican American fathers—

RAFAEL JIMÉNEZ ESPINOSA (1931–78) AND

AMADO GARCÍA RODARTE (1909–86)

Contents

Preface

This book examines the important role that religion plays in the Mexican American/Chicano community in the United States. Although there is a growing literature on Black, Native American, and Euro-American religions, few books on Mexican American religions have been published from a pluralistic and nonsectarian perspective. This is remarkable given the fact that the vast majority of U.S. Latinos self-identify with some kind of religion, multiple religions, or a general belief in a transcendent power. Furthermore, many people outside of the Mexican American community are surprised to hear that Mexican American activists, authors, and artists such as César Chávez, Reies López Tijerina, Luis Valdez, Sandra Cisneros, Gloria Anzaldúa, Amalia Mesa-Bains, and many other prominent figures have been deeply influenced by their religious backgrounds or beliefs. This book will not only analyze these figures, but also important symbols, traditions, and icons, including Our Lady of Guadalupe, the Los Pastores Shepherds' play, utopian communities, Pentecostal and *curandera* healers, and pop culture music icons such as Selena.

This book would not have been possible without the generous support of our colleagues and sponsors. We thank the Claremont McKenna College (CMC) Department of Philosophy and Religious Studies, the CMC Benjamin Z. Gould Center for Humanistic Studies, the CMC's Dean's Office, Richard Hecht, Sarah Cline, Catherine Albanese, Wade Clark Roof, Philip Hammond, Inés Talamántez, and the University of California, Santa Barbara (UCSB), Provost's Office, the UCSB Departments of Religious Studies, History, and Sociology, the Northwestern University Department of Religious Studies, and the Andrew W. Mellon Postdoctoral Fellow Program for their support in the publication of this manuscript. We also thank Pamela Gann, William Ascher, Nicholas O. Warner, Eugene Lowe, Antonio Pravia, and student assistants Michelle Unzueta, Saskia van Gendt, Tess Mason-elder, Evan Rutter, Benji Rolsky, Robert

González, and especially Charles Geraci for their assistance in preparing this manuscript. Last, but not least, we thank our family, friends, and community, without whose support and patience this book would have never been completed.

Introduction

The purpose of this book is to examine the role of religion in the Mexican American/Chicano experience in the United States. Despite the fact that the vast majority of U.S. Latinos claim to be religious or spiritual, little has been written on Mexican American/Chicano religions from a multidisciplinary perspective.[1] Most scholars writing on religion have tended to focus on the larger U.S. Latino population, on theology, or on a specific denomination or tradition. However, the Mexican American community's rich history, large numbers, and variety of religious experiences warrant specific attention. Mexican Americans trace their roots back 400 years to the founding of New Mexico in 1598, and make up almost two-thirds of all U.S. Latinos.

There are external and internal reasons why no systematic attempt has been made to create and define the field of Mexican American religions in the United States. First, prior to the Chicano cultural renaissance of the 1960s, there were relatively few Mexican Americans with PhDs in the United States and in a position to conduct such scholarship. When theses, dissertations, and books did touch on Mexican American religions, they almost always did so in a field outside of religious studies, such as history, sociology, and anthropology.[2] Second, prior to the 1990s, few academic institutions and tenure-review committees considered Mexican American religions a serious and credible intellectual topic of inquiry.[3] Third, most scholars assumed that the study of Mexican American religions was essentially the study of Catholic theology and the institutional church, two subjects that were politically incorrect to study and perceived as largely unimportant at secular research universities. This attitude is still prevalent.[4] Fourth, the field of religious studies was largely in its infancy and did not really begin to take shape until after the *School District of Abington v. Schempp* (1963) Supreme Court decision made explicit the constitutional right to teach religion in public colleges and universities.[5]

In addition to the external factors that retarded the growth and study of Mexican American religions, there were also internal factors. First, many Mexican Americans internalized the negative attitude toward their history, culture, and religious traditions and were thus anxious to avoid studying religion lest they be stereotyped as religious or nonacademic. This prompted many potential scholars of Mexican American religions to shift their focus to other more "respectable" and "legitimate" fields of inquiry—such as history, sociology, political science, education, anthropology, and literature. Still others made the religious component of their work subsidiary to another acceptable field of inquiry. Second, during the Chicano Civil Rights Movement of the 1960s, a number of Mexican American intellectuals embraced or dabbled with Marxist, Socialist, or leftist social theories, many of which were critical of religion and suggested that it functioned as an agent of oppression, assimilation, or disempowerment. This prompted many scholars during the 1960s and 1970s to either avoid the topic altogether or use it only instrumentally in order to make a larger point.

Third, many Chicano intellectuals had negative experiences in the institutional church or practiced non-Catholic or non-Christian religious traditions. This has fueled a kind of de facto and de jure anti-institutional (though not antispiritual) Catholic and Christian sentiment in some Chicano, Latino, and Latin American studies programs that exists largely to this day. Still others treat the study of religion as largely irrelevant. Although for some this bias is driven by a kind of disciplinary and methodological imperialism, for others it is based on negative personal experiences with the institutional church. In fact, the authors cannot think of a single major Chicano, Latino, or Latin American studies program at a major secular university that has to date made a conscientious decision to hire someone in Mexican American or Latino "religions" because of the important role that religion (both popular *and* institutional) itself plays in the community. In most cases, Latino hires that deal with religion do so under the disciplinary rubric of Chicano/Latino "culture," "society," or "history," and often have a joint appointment in a department *other* than religious studies.[6]

Despite these historical obstacles today, the study of Mexican American religions is attracting increasing attention. There are a number of reasons for this development. First, a new generation of post–Cold War and post–Chicano Movement scholars found Mexican American religions understudied. Given the practical need for MA and PhD students to find original subjects of inquiry, religious topics are plum for the picking.

Second, the rise of the academic study of religion within the social sciences created alternative ways of thinking about, talking about, and interpreting religion, ways that were generally nontheological, nonsectarian, nonnormative, and non-value-laden. This has helped to legitimize the study of Mexican American religions in the academy. The field of religious studies and study of Mexican American and Latino religions received a boost in the academy after the *Schempp* decision opened the door to the academic study of religion in American public higher education. It had a threefold effect on the study of religious studies in general and Mexican American and Latino religions in particular. First, it encouraged the academic study of religion in public and private schools, colleges, and universities across the United States. Second, it encouraged a nonsectarian, pluralist, and comparative approach to the study of religion. And third, by encouraging the academic, nonsectarian study of religion, it stimulated the study, growth, and patronage of religious studies in colleges and universities—including those that served the growing Mexican American and Latino population, such as the California State University, University of California, and University of Texas systems. Given the fact that most Mexican Americans and Latinos attend state rather than private universities, this in turn afforded greater opportunities for Latinos to study religion at the undergraduate and graduate levels.

However, a large number of Mexican American and Latino scholars of religion have historically received their methodological training and PhDs at religiously affiliated universities, largely Catholic (e.g., University Notre Dame, Boston College) and/or Mainline Protestant affiliation (Union Seminary, New York, Harvard, Yale, Princeton, Boston University, Graduate Theological Union, Drew University). To this day, many of them take a decidedly theological approach (normally influenced by liberation theology) to the study of religion, while those scholars trained at secular private or state universities tend to take a nontheological, humanities or social-science approach to the study of religion, although still often influenced by liberation theology. There are clearly exceptions to this pattern, but it remains largely true to this day. This has led to minor disagreements over whether or not scholars should take a secular approach to the study of Latino religions and whether or not they should use only secular social and humanistic theories to frame their scholarship.

This conflict is largely generational and can in part be explained by the fact that many Latino scholars of religion were trained in PhD programs that did not expose them to the history and theories of secular religious studies in graduate school.[7]

The chapters in this book are the fruit of an intellectual dialogue on Chicano religions that has been going on with the Chicano/Latino intellectual community for many years. Although talk about Mexican American religions can be traced back to the conquest of the American Southwest during the war between the United States and Mexico (1846–48), a concerted effort was not made to begin delineating Mexican American religions until the 1970s and 1980s, with the work of theologians and writers including Virgilio Elizondo, Moises Sandoval, Andrés Guerrero, Anthony M. Stevens-Arroyo, Yolanda Tarango, and many others.[8] Their work was marked by a generally theological, liberationist, and Christian (almost exclusively Roman Catholic) orientation, which invariably led them to frame their work from a Christian theological perspective that sought to challenge and change the institutional Catholic Church and field of religious studies and carve out an academic niche. Although this book is indebted to their work, it also builds upon and expands their scholarship by taking a decidedly nonsectarian, noninstitutional, and nonnormative approach to the study of religion by exploring religious sentiments in literature, art, politics, and pop culture.

Taken as a whole, these chapters suggest that contrary to stereotypes, Chicano religions have played and continue to play critical, defining roles in the Mexican American community. Furthermore, the chapters also suggest unique religious expressions that have been shaped by the Mexican American experience. It is precisely the Mexican American blending, reexamination, and rearticulation of Mexican and American traditions, customs, practices, symbols, and beliefs that we call Chicano/a religious expressions or Chicano/a religions.

This blending becomes clearly evident in the interdisciplinary scholarship in this volume. In particular, the chapters on religion and literature and pop culture problematize any kind of essentialist methodological interpretations of Mexican American religions as being limited to institutional and/or organized religion. As the authors show, some of the most important insights into Mexican American religions are found in unexpected places: novels, political protests, art, poetry, pop music icons, and the like. Despite this fact, we believe that a historical framework is critical in helping delineate the trajectory of Mexican American religions in the United States. To this end, this book is broken down into six sections:

(1) History and Interpretations of Mexican American Religions, (2) Mexican American Mystics and Prophets, (3) Mexican American Popular Catholicism, (4) Mexican American Religions and Literature, (5) Mexican American Religions and Healing, and (6) Mexican American Religions and Pop Culture. Espinosa, in addition to his original chapter on Selena (chapter 15), contributed chapters on Pentecostal healing (chapter 11) and the history and theory in the study of Mexican American religions (chapter 1) at the request of the external reviewers. They had indicated that the volume needed at least one chapter on Pentecostal Protestantism, given its seismic growth in the community, and one chapter on the historical development of the field of Mexican American religious studies. The editors also added chapters by Luis D. León on *curanderismo* (chapter 12), Kay Turner on home altars (chapter 7), and María Herrera-Sobek and Laura E. Pérez on Mexican American religions, art, and popular culture (chapters 13 and 14, respectively)—all at the recommendation of the reviewers.

In part I, "History and Interpretations of Mexican American Religions," Gastón Espinosa (chapter 1) examines the historical development of Mexican American religions over the past 100 years, with particular focus on the field since 1960. He argues that the modern academic study of Mexican American religions was birthed in 1968, although writing on the subject from various disciplines stretches back more than a century. The writings by César Chávez, Virgilio Elizondo, Gustavo Gutiérrez, Enrique Dussel, and others served as major catalysts in the future methodological and theoretical development of the field. Espinosa proposes an ethno-phenomenological method as one of the many alternatives to interpreting Mexican American religions at secular colleges and universities, which are required by law not to teach or promote a theological worldview. This nonsectarian methodology combines race, class, gender, and phenomenological analyses and grounds them in their historical, social, theological, and political contexts.

Anthony Stevens-Arroyo, in chapter 2, draws on the Chicano theorist Mario Barrera's internal colonialism theory to explore the various ways Mexican Americans have used their faith traditions to resist a kind of religious internal colonialism imposed upon them by Anglo-American secular society and the institutional church. In fact, Stevens-Arroyo argues that one of the reasons why alternative Latino religious traditions have been overlooked is that the institutional Catholic and Protestant churches engaged in a kind of pious colonialism in their treatment of Mexican Americans in the Southwest. Drawing on Barrera, he argues that in contrast to Spanish colonialism, which led to acculturation and cultural mixing or *mestizaje* through intermarriage, Anglo-American colonialism did not lead to transculturation, because it sought to suppress and "despoil" Latino identity. Mexican Americans in the Southwest after the U.S.-Mexico war ended in 1848 were "subjugated" and treated as a conquered people. This subjugation took place simultaneously in Anglo-American secular society and the institutional church. Together Anglo-American society and churches attempted to impose the English language, repress many native popular religious traditions and practices, inferiorize Latino clergy, and stigmatize Latino culture. In reaction to this pious colonialism, Mexican Americans drew upon their popular religious traditions, which served as collective sites and symbols of resistance. However, they were not able to overcome the subjugation and marginalization until the Latino religious resurgence between 1967 and 1983. The emergence of a growing number of Latino/a priests, nuns, clergy, and lay leaders challenged and put an end to most of the pious paternalism in the churches, although vestiges continue in certain corners of the church even to this day.

The political struggle of Mexican Americans to define their own lives and future is evident in part II, "Mexican American Mystics and Prophets." Rudy V. Busto, Stephen R. Lloyd-Moffett, and Mario T. García explore how religious ideology, symbols, values, moral teaching, and rhetoric empowered grassroots leaders and organizations. They analyze how Reies López Tijerina, César Chávez, and Ricardo Cruz and Católicos Por La Raza carved out a space of dignity and human rights for Mexican Americans living in the shadows of the U.S.-Mexico borderlands. Tijerina and Chávez drew upon their mystical experiences to justify their political, social, and religious activities. Rudy Busto, in chapter 3, explores the link between religion and utopian communities in his analysis of Reies López Tijerina, one of the principle leaders in the Mexican American Civil Rights Movement. Busto analyzes Tijerina's decision to create the Valle de Paz utopian underground community in the Arizona desert and subsequent political activism. This is one of the first religious Mexican American utopian community in the United States. He points out how intrinsic Tijerina's religion was to his vision of society and that his visions, dreams, and altered states of consciousness shaped his subsequent activism.

In like manner, Stephen Lloyd-Moffett argues in chapter 4 that César Chávez fused his mystical religious experiences with his United Farm Workers political and social activism to rally the masses to his cause, or *la causa*. Like Father Antonio José Martínez in nineteenth-century New Mexico, Chávez drew inner strength and resolve from his Catholic faith and popular traditions, symbols, and rhetoric. Lloyd-Moffett argues that his fasts, pilgrimages, and activism were inspired by Jesus, Saint Francis of Assisi, Mohandas Gandhi, Martin Luther King Jr., and the African American Civil Rights Movement. He suggests that we do not hear more about the spiritual dimension of Chávez's activism because the liberal intelligentsia and militant Chicano activists have deliberately secularized his image to suit their own political and ideological goals.

Chávez not only influenced the outcome of the UFW, but also of student political and social activism. Mario T. García argues that Chávez inspired a new generation of Mexican American college students to engage in faith-based political activism through Catholic student organizations such as Católicos Por La Raza. He challenges the notion that the Chicano Movement was a largely secular affair, arguing that Católicos illustrates the critical role religion played in student activism and that students targeted religion in their focus on social justice and community organizing. The founder of the movement, Ricardo Cruz, who had protested with Chávez on the picket line, took the struggle for Chicano civil rights into the Roman Catholic Church. García explores the movement's attempted takeover of Cardinal Frances McIntyre's St. Basil's Church on Christmas Eve, 1969, and the conflict that erupted as a result. He also analyzes the list of student demands, and the subsequent impact their protest made on the Archdiocese of Los Angeles.

Part III, "Mexican American Popular Catholicism," explores how popular religious symbols, traditions, and practices can function as vehicles for personal, social, and political empowerment and resistance. This is evident in the work of Socorro Castañeda-Liles, Kay Turner, and Richard R. Flores. Castañeda-Liles, in chapter 6, argues that the symbolic significance of Our Lady of Guadalupe is hotly debated. Interpretations of Our Lady of Guadalupe in the Mexican American community can be classified into at least four approaches. The first is theological and is exemplified in the work of Virgilio Elizondo and Jeanette Rodríguez. They affirm the apparition of Our Lady of Guadalupe, which according to Catholic tradition, appeared on 9 December 1531 to Juan Diego on Tepeyac Hill outside present-day Mexico City. They argue that the story and subsequent veneration are an authentic and collective expression of faith rooted in the needs of the people. In contrast, Louise Burkhart and Stafford Poole offer decidedly historical analyses of Our Lady of Guadalupe. They argue that the tradition has no basis in fact or history. Rather, the image was probably a pious invention by the criollo elite in the 1650s out of jealousy and disgruntlement at their treatment by the Spanish *peninsulares*, who thought they were better than the criollos because they were born in

Spain rather than the New World. Despite these authors' factual reading of the Guadalupe "legend," they recognize that for the pious believer, her historicity is largely irrelevant because she has become a symbol of Mexican identity, pride, and nationality. The Chicana feminist writers, such as Ana Castillo and Sandra Cisneros, in turn, interpret her as a symbol, which can be manipulated by men to oppress women or by women to liberate themselves. More often than not, however, Guadalupe functions as a symbol of sexual empowerment for Mexican American women. This is especially true in the work of Chicana artists, Esther Hernández and Yolanda López for instance, who almost always reinterpret Guadalupe in the guise of the modern Chicana. Drawing on feminist notions of empowerment, Hernández, López, and others see Guadalupe as a source of social, cultural, and political empowerment and an agent of resistance to machismo and patriarchy.

Kay Turner, in chapter 7, further analyzes the symbolic significance of gender in the Mexican American community by exploring the ancient home altar tradition. She argues that the home altar practice is a women's tradition passed on from one generation to the next and that these altar practices build maternal and relational values. She interprets the home altar as an instrument of empowerment. At the most fundamental level, Turner argues that the creation and manipulation of this symbolic system validates the sacred tradition of mothering.

While Kay Turner analyzes the role of popular religiosity in the private sphere of the home, Richard Flores analyzes it in the public sphere. In chapter 8, he argues that scholars tend to interpret popular religion as either the result of "increased secularization" or as a reaction to "dislocation associated with modernity." He challenges this interpretation along with Marxist and feminist analyses, which claim that popular religious practices are associated with prescientific practices and patriarchal ideologies. Rather, gender roles in Mexican American plays such as Los Pastores need to be reread as sites of liberation and empowerment of the "gathered collective." Thus ritual practices such as Los Pastores serve as collective enterprises that can both oppress and liberate Mexican Americans living in contemporary society.

The role that women, gender, and sexuality play in Mexican American religion and culture is further analyzed in part IV, "Mexican American Religions and Literature." Davíd Carrasco and Roberto Lint Sagarena, and Ellen McCracken explore the religious impulse in Chicana/o literature. Carrasco and Sagarena, in chapter 9, argue that Gloria Anzaldúa's borderlands is a religious vision and vibrant mythic consciousness and shamanic space where empowerment is achieved through ecstatic trances that enable her to cast a vision of a new mestiza reality. They argue that personal suffering, conflict, ecstatic experiences, reported visitations by the spirit world, journeys to the underworld, and moments of illumination and healing fuel this shamanic space. Anzaldúa engages in "*loca-centered*" thought, which enables her to reveal the oppression, evil, and madness of the dominant, racist cultural narratives that have oppressed Chicanos/as. They contend that loca-centered thought highlights the important contributions of the contentious and melodious narratives and ignored histories and peoples of the borderlands. For this reason, one can interpret Anzaldúa as using ecstatic experiences and language to "challenge authority—white, brown, male—even her own as a writer."

Similarly, Ellen McCracken argues that Chicana writers such as Mary Helen Ponce, Denise Chávez, and Sandra Cisneros use religious symbols, rhetoric, and values to reverse the melting-pot paradigm of integration and to resignify the Mexican American community. In so doing, they create a new moral vision and a new ethic that part company with institutional orthodoxy and instead spotlight the themes of social justice, immigrant concerns, feminists, the landless, and other marginalized groups. Although sometimes these authors juxtapose popular religious practices against official practices, in most cases popular religious practices are used to reread official doctrines and rites. Rather than simply reject official Anglo-American institutional Catholicism, McCracken argues, Chicana writers engage in a rearticulation of Catholic beliefs, rituals, and behaviors. In one sense, they employ forbidden practices, speeches, and visions as a way to reclaim religion in their fight for social justice.

The critical role that religion plays in Mexican American culture is not only evident in literature, but also in part V, "Mexican American Religions and Healing." Gastón Espinosa, in chapter 11, argues that healing is not only a widespread theme in Latino popular Catholicism but also in Latino Protestant Pentecostalism. His chapter points out that the Protestant Pentecostal movement has a healing tradition over 100 years old. Despite this fact, we know surprisingly little about it. The key to Pentecostal growth has been its practice of blending healing and evangelism. Healing-evangelists such as Francisco Olazábal conducted large-scale healing campaigns in barrios and *colonias* throughout the 1920s and 1930s in East Los Angeles, El Paso, San Antonio, Houston, Chicago, Spanish Harlem, and Nogales, Arizona. He preached to over 250,000 people throughout his ministry in the United States, Mexico, and Puerto Rico. After participants were converted, he used them to help form new congregations, which institutionalized and carried on the practice of mixing healing and evangelism. This religious practice might have been kept localized and marginalized had it not been for his emphasis on planting indigenous Latino churches in every location where he conducted large-scale evangelistic services. Contrary to the claim of some sociologists of religion, Mexican American Pentecostals such as Francisco Olazábal created large independent, indigenous, and autonomous Protestant churches as early as the 1920s.[9]

One of the reasons healing has been such an important factor in Catholic conversion to Pentecostalism is because of the long-standing practice of popular Catholic healing in the Mexican and Mexican American community. Luis León, in chapter 12, analyzes the central role of healing in the Mexican American Catholic community in Los Angeles. He argues that the healing tradition known as curanderismo illuminates the various ways Chicanos and Mexicans seek to heal themselves and their loved ones and to negotiate suffering and injustice. He argues that it provides a way to "overcome the limitations of the material world" and to heal the injuries inflicted upon them in a capitalist society. His ethnographic study examines one contemporary site of curanderismo in East Los Angeles—the Sagrado Corazón botánica and proposes directions for further investigation. It is based on over a dozen interviews with women and men who came to the *botánica* seeking divine healing.

The pervasive role of religion is not only evident in the above leaders and traditions, but also in Mexican American pop culture. In part VI, "Mexican American Religions and Pop Culture," María Herrera-Sobek, Laura Pérez, and Gastón Espinosa explore the fusion of religion and culture in their work on Chicano theater, art, and pop music icons. Focusing on the fusion of religion, political protest, and satire in Mexican American theater during and after the Chicano Movement, Herrera-Sobek, in chapter 13, examines the history of the *pastorela* and the critical role that religious symbols, metaphors, and art have played in Chicano theater, particularly Luis Valdez's La Pastorela: *"The Shepherds' Play."* She argues that Luis Valdez used his play to engage in a savvy and shrewd form of political and social protest. His strategic use of theater and comedy made his Chicano militancy appear less threatening and subversive than it really was. He used four major strategies to subvert the traditional pastorela structure in order to promote an ideology that was congruent with Chicano politics and social justice: (1) portraying farmworkers as protagonists, (2) using Chicano jargon and linguistic code-switching, (3) drawing upon musical genres to drive home his points, and (4) representing the devil as wealthy white California growers, Anglo-American Hell's Angels motorcycle bikers, and Middle Eastern Sultans. Thus far from serving as mindless entertainment, Valdez's *La Pastorela* was both transgressive and subversive because it empowered the poor and oppressed through an artistic production. Despite this fact, Valdez's play does affirm many traditional beliefs and values, such as love for one's family, respect for parents, and belief in the traditional teachings of the Catholic Church.

In contrast to Valdez, Laura Pérez, in chapter 14, argues that Chicana artists created a political spirituality after the Chicano Movement of the 1960s and 1970s that challenged the oppressive Western Christian patriarchal and traditional modes of religious expression. Chicana artists have attempted to decolonize the West through their political art by trying to re-create an egalitarian world that fights for justice against race, class, gender, sexuality, and environmental exploitation. In contrast to Western elite culture, which tends to trivialize spirituality, Chicanas engage in a kind of "cultural *susto*," which attempts to displace the spirit of Euro-American colonialism that has oppressed Mexican Americans. Chicana artists such as Amalia Mesa-Bains often structure their work like the painter-scribes of Mesoamerica. They create oppositional views of art and spirituality that are cross-cultural, interdisciplinary, and beyond sexist and heterosexist myopias. They create alternative paths to wholeness, community, purpose, and meaningfulness. This art often leads to the creation of hybrid spiritualities and decolonizing cultural appropriations that can empower Mexican Americans. Postsixties Chicana feminist artists use spiritual beliefs and practices to fight for social and political effects that matter. Pérez argues that their "hybrid spirituality" is a " 'politicizing spirituality.' "

Like Herrera-Sobek and Pérez, Gastón Espinosa (in chapter 15) explores the symbolic connection between religion and pop music stardom. He discusses the reaction of the masses to Selena Quintañilla Pérez's death in 1995, and argues that Selena has become more popular in death than in life largely because of the timing of her death; her reconstruction by the Mexican American/Chicano intelligentsia, media, and youth culture; and because she functions as a collective and a symbolic counternarrative and as an agent of cultural redemption and resistance for some working-class Mexican American youth. She provides cultural redemption in the areas of race, gender, class, transnational cultural hybridity, and the U.S.-Mexico borderlands. Selena's reconstruction and pop culture beatification reveal the important function of religion in Mexican American and Latino pop culture. It also reveals, Espinosa notes, "the Mexican American penchant for transforming its seemingly secular cultural heroes into pop culture saints" and its grounded aesthetic practices of materializing the sacred and sacralizing the profane in everyday life.[10]

Taken as a whole, these chapters represent the first attempt to explore Mexican American religions from a multidisciplinary perspective. The authors generally take a nonsectarian, nonnormative, nontheological, and social-science or humanistic perspective, although theological perspectives and frameworks are also included. Many break new ground because they are among the first essays to explore the critical intersection between Mexican American religions and literature, art, politics, and pop culture. It is hoped that this book will spur on a new generation of scholars to explore the dynamic relationship between religion and Mexican American culture and society in the twenty-first century.

Notes

1. The Hispanic Churches in American Public Life (HCAPL) National Survey (n = 2,060) found that fewer than one-half of 1 percent (.37 percent) of all U.S. Latinos self-reported being atheist or agnostic. Ninety-three percent self-identified with an existing Christian denomination or tradition, as Born-Again Christian, or as both. Fewer than 1 percent self-reported affiliation with a world religion (e.g., Buddhism, Islam, Judaism, Hinduism, etc.) and slightly fewer than 6 percent reported having no particular religious preference. Some reports on Latino religious affiliation differ because they count those who state they have "no religious preference" as having "no religion." However, this is problematic, for example, because the majority of those in this category also self-identified with a Christian tradition or as a Born-Again Christian on other questions later in the HCAPL survey. For this reason, it is more likely that respondents in this category have no single religious preference (rather than no religion) or have multiple religious preferences. Gastón Espinosa, Virgilio Elizondo, and Jesse Miranda, *Hispanic Churches in American Public Life: Summary of Findings* (Notre Dame, Ind.: Institute for Latino Studies, University of Notre Dame, 2003), 14. Gastón Espinosa, "Methodological Reflections on Latino Social Science Research," in *Rethinking Latino Religions and Identity*, ed. Miguel de la Torre and Gastón Espinosa (Cleveland, Ohio: Pilgrim Press, 2006), 13–45.

2. This is evident in even a cursory review of masters and doctoral dissertations that touch on Mexican American religions between the 1960s and 1980s.

3. We know of at least three recent instances in which a Latino/a scholar of religion was denied tenure because he or she wrote a book on Latino religious topics that were not deemed "mainstream" by their departments. We are intentionally withholding the names of the people denied tenure to protect them from recrimination.

4. This sentiment was evident when the lead author of this book asked a U.S. history and women's studies professor why the colonial American history course he was a teacher-assistant for had no assigned readings on Latino history. She dismissively said it was "simply the study of Spanish missions" and was "largely unimportant given their time constraints."

5. For a history of the discipline of religious studies, see Eric J. Sharpe, *Comparative Religion: A History* (La Salle, Ill.: Open Court, 1994); Walter Capps, *Religious Studies: The Making of a Discipline* (Minneapolis: Fortress Press, 1999). The most insightful book in delineating the difference between a theological and a religious studies approach to the study of religion is Donald Wiebe, *The Politics of Religious Studies: The Continuing Conflict with Theology in the Academy* (New York: St. Martin's Press, 1999).

6. The stories and anecdotes in this chapter are based on the personal observations of the authors and their conversations with Mexican American and Latino scholars. Names have been withheld to protect their anonymity.

7. Sharpe, *Comparative Religion*; Capps, *Religious Studies*; Wiebe, *The Politics of Religious Studies*. The comments and observations in this chapter are based on personal observations and conversations with Mexican American and Latino scholars and graduate students. The names of the persons have been withheld to protect their anonymity.

8. One of the first academically trained Mexican American historians to discuss Mexican American Catholicism was Carlos Castañeda, who wrote a monumental multivolume history of the Mexican American Catholic Church in Texas in the 1930s. That same decade, the Mexican anthropologist Manuel Gamio published a monograph on Mexican immigration to the United States and a book of documents, both of which include attention to religion. Moises Sandoval edited the first comprehensive history (largely liberationist in approach) of U.S. Latino Christianity in the United States in 1983, entitled *Fronteras: A History of the Latin American Church in the USA since 1513* (San Antonio: Mexican American Cultural Center, 1983), and a shorter version of the book, *On the Move: A History of the Hispanic Church in the United States* (Maryknoll, N.Y.: Orbis Books, 1991). Since then, Jay P. Dolan edited a three-volume series on Hispanic Catholicism in the United States in the 1990s: Jay P. Dolan and Allan Figueroa Deck, SJ, eds., *Hispanic Catholic Culture in the U.S.: Issues and Concerns* (Notre Dame, Ind.: University of Notre Dame Press, 1994); Jay P. Dolan and Gilberto M. Hinojosa, eds., *Mexican Americans and the Catholic Church, 1900–1965* (Notre Dame, Ind.: University of Notre Dame Press, 1994); Jay P. Dolan and Jaime R. Vidal, eds., *Puerto Rican and Cuban Catholics in the U.S., 1900–1965* (Notre Dame, Ind.: University of Notre Dame Press, 1994). All of these volumes focus exclusively on Hispanic Christianity in the United States. The vast majority of the attention is focused on Catholicism, with just a chapter or in most cases a few paragraphs to Mainline Protestant and Evangelical Christianity. No attention is given to Mormonism, Jehovah's Witnesses, the Seventh-Day Adventists, metaphysical and occult traditions, Native American traditions, or world religions.

9. When comparing Latinos to African Americans, they write in 1993, "There is no tradition of a separatist or autonomous Hispanic church" in the United States. Barry Kosmin and Seymour Lachman, *One Nation under God: Religion in Contemporary Society* (New York: Harmony Books, 1993), 138.

10. For a discussion of material Christianity, see Colleen McDannell, *Material Christianity: Religion and Popular Culture in America* (New Haven, Conn.: Yale University Press, 1995). Also see David Morgan, *Visual Piety: A History and Theory of Popular Religious Images* (Berkeley: University of California Press, 1998).

I

History and

Interpretations of

Mexican American Religions

I

History and Theory in
the Study of Mexican American Religions

The contemporary academic study of Mexican American religions traces its origins to 1968, although important historical, sociological, and anthropological writing on the topic stretches back throughout the twentieth century. That year the writings and intellectual foment stimulated by César Chávez, Virgilio Elizondo, Gustavo Gutiérrez, Enrique Dussel, and others served as major catalysts in the future methodological and theoretical development of the field.[1] Between 1970 and 1975, some of the first major academic books, articles, and centers were written, created, and organized by scholars such as Elizondo, Dussel, Moises Sandoval, Juan Romero, Juan Hurtado, Patrick McNamara, Joan Moore, and others.[2] The Mexican American Cultural Center (MACC), which was cofounded and directed by Elizondo in San Antonio, Texas, in 1972, played a decisive role by publishing many of the first academically oriented biographies, histories, and studies in the emerging field. The field of Mexican American religions received a boost in 1987–88 with the publication of the work of feminist-informed Chicana/o literature and theologies by Gloria Anzaldúa, Andrés Guerrero, and Ada María Isasi-Díaz and Yolanda Tarango.[3] The next major turning points came in 1994–96, when Jay P. Dolan and the University of Notre Dame Press published the three-volume series on Latino Catholicism (1994), Anthony Stevens-Arroyo and the Program for the Analysis of Religion Among Latinos (PARAL) published the four-volume series on U.S. Latino religions (1994–95). In 1997, Rudy V. Busto and Daniel Ramirez organized a conference at Stanford on U.S. Latino evangelism, and in 1996 Gastón Espinosa and Mario T. García attempted to help define the field at their "New Directions in Chicano Religions" conference at the University of California, Santa Barbara (1996).[4] This book is part of the fruit of that conference.

Over the past thirty-five years, scholars have often taken one of five approaches to the study of Mexican American religions: (1) traditional church history (e.g., Brackenridge and García-Treto, Dolan, and Hinojosa), (2) interdisciplinary liberation theology church history (e.g., Sandoval, Romero), (3) interdisciplinary popular theology and religion (e.g., Elizondo, Guerrero, Rodríguez, Tarango), (4) anthropology, psychology, and sociology (e.g., Madsen, Kiev, McNamara, Moore), and (5) interdisciplinary phenomenological religious studies (e.g., Carrasco, León, Espinosa).[5] Still other scholars have blended approaches or taken a Chicano studies/ethnic studies approach (e.g., Busto, Aquino).[6] Some scholars have drawn on Chicano literature and poetry (Carlos Castañeda, Luis Valdez, Rodolfo "Corky" Gonzáles, Rudolfo Anaya, and Gloria Anzaldúa), the writings of Reies López Tijerina, the Chicano Student Movement, Chicana feminism, Black studies, secular religious studies, and the emerging scholarship on postcolonialism, transnational studies, critical theory, ethnic studies, and race, class, gender, and sexuality.[7]

After sketching the historical development of the field of Mexican American religions, I will propose that a *nepantla*-informed, ethnophenomenological method is one of many possible alternatives for studying and interpreting Mexican American religions at secular colleges and universities, which are required by the state or college mission statement not to promote or endorse a normative theological worldview.[8] This approach blends race, class, gender, and phenomenological analyses grounded in their historical, social, theological, and political contexts. It identifies, recognizes, and interrogates religious leaders and structures, traditions, movements, and experiences on their own plane of reference. Such an approach is taken in order to understand how such leaders and structures provide hope and meaning to practitioners and contribute to their larger culture. It also seeks to bridge the growing chasm that separates secular religious studies from theology as described in Donald Wiebe's book *The Politics of Religious Studies: The Continuing Conflict with Theology in the Academy* (1999). It does so by listening to, dialoging with, and drawing upon the important insights from theology and the above-noted influences. While Mexican American and U.S. Latino religions are organically connected, due to time, space, and regional limitations I will focus on the historical development of Mexican American religions in the Southwest. The best place to review the literature on Mexican American religious historiography are the bibliographies and essays edited or written by

Anthony M. Stevens Arroyo and Segundo Pantoja, Paul Barton and David Maldonado, Justo L. González, and Daisy Machado.[9] Although beyond the scope of this study, there are also a number of overviews on U.S. Latino theology and history by Alex Saragoza, María Pilar Aquino, Lara Medina, Eduardo Fernández, Orlando Espín, Miguel de la Torre and Edwin Aponte, and Miguel H. Díaz.[10]

Why Mexican American Religious Studies?

Despite the growing scholarship on Mexican American religions, no one has attempted to systematically map out its historical development over the last 100 years. This is largely because it has been subsumed under the rubric of U.S. Latino religions. However, there are a number of reasons why it should itself be an academic field of intellectual inquiry. People of Mexican ancestry have lived in the Southwest for over 400 years—since 1598. Their history in the American Southwest predates that of the Pilgrims and Puritans at Jamestown in 1607 and Plymouth Rock in 1620. People of Spanish and Mexican ancestry have a number of rich and unique religious traditions (e.g., New Mexican popular Catholicism, the *santero* tradition, the Chimayó Pilgrimage site, Día de los Muertos), saints and spiritual healers (e.g., Our Lady of Guadalupe, El Niño Fidencio, María Teresa Urrea, Don Pedrito Jaramillo, Juan Soldado, Francisco Olazábal), brotherhoods and social-spiritual movements (e.g., the Penitente Brotherhood, the Cursillo, PADRES, Las Hermanas, La Raza Churchmen), political leaders (e.g., Padre Antonio José Martínez, César Chávez, Reies López Tijerina, Dolores Huerta), and religious leaders (e.g., Junipero Serra, Eusebio Kino, Francisco Olazábal, Archbishop Patricio Flores), all of which have influenced U.S. Latino and American religious history.[11] People of Mexican ancestry have shaped the history, architecture, politics, culture, and cuisine of the Southwest for over 400 years.

The 2006 U.S. Census Bureau noted that people of Mexican ancestry made up 64 percent (28 million) of the nation's 44.3 million Latinos. They are now more numerous than all Asian Americans (14.9 million), Jewish Americans (6 million), and Native Americans (4.5 million) combined, all of which have their own discrete intellectual fields of study. They are also the fastest growing Latino subgroup in the United States and account for 52 percent (8.2 million) of all Latin American immigrants to the United States (16 million).

The Mexican American community is also becoming more religiously diverse. The Hispanic Churches in American Public Life (HCAPL) National

Survey, which surveyed more than 2,060 Latinos across the country (1,103 of whom were of Mexican ancestry), found that 79 percent of all Latinos of Mexican ancestry were Roman Catholic and 21 percent were Protestant and other Christian. Of this population, 27 percent self-identified as Catholic Charismatic. When the figures are broken down by five religious family groupings, 79 percent of people of Mexican ancestry self-reported Roman Catholic affiliation, 7.2 percent Pentecostal, 6.9 percent Evangelical non-Pentecostal, 4 percent Mainline Protestant, and 3 percent Alternative Christian, such as Jehovah's Witnesses, Mormon, and other. All combined, 14 percent (almost 1 in 6) of all Mexican Americans self-identify as Pentecostal/Evangelical. Furthermore, over 30 percent of those who self-identified as Mainline Protestant also self-identified as a Born-Again Christian, thus indicating that the actual percentage of Mexican-ancestry Evangelical Protestants is larger than the figures above indicate. An analysis across all denominations and religious traditions shows that 35 percent of all people of Mexican ancestry self-reported being a Born-Again Christian, slightly less than the overall U.S. Latino population at 37 percent. This number is shaped by the influence of the trans-denominational Pentecostal/Charismatic movement as 36 percent of all those of Mexican ancestry also reported being both Born-Again Christian and Pentecostal/Charismatic/Spirit-Filled. Other spirit-led metaphysical religious traditions are also active. The HCAPL survey found that 18.3 percent of all people of Mexican ancestry said they "believe in the practice of" *espiritismo, curanderismo, brujería,* or all of the above. All of these figures point to a very vibrant and diverse religious community.[12]

Genealogy of Mexican American Religious Studies

The exact origin of the academic study of Mexican American religions is difficult to determine. The most important systematic records of Mexican American religious experiences in the Southwest were written from the sixteenth to the nineteenth centuries by Catholic Franciscan and Jesuit missionaries, diocesan priests, lay leaders, and American and European clergy, missionaries, and traders such as Father Alonso de Benavides, Father Eusebio Kino, Father Junipero Serra, Richard Henry Dana, and others.[13] In the late nineteenth century and early twentieth, we see the rise of slightly more formal institutional church histories, such as Jean-Baptiste Salpointe's *Soldiers of the Cross: Notes on the Ecclesiastical History of New Mexico, Arizona, and Colorado* (1898) and Thomas Harwood's *History of Spanish and English Missions of the Methodist Episcopal Church from 1850 to 1910*, 2 vols. (1908, 1910). However, these were written almost exclusively by clergy about their own institutional churches and for a Christian audience.

In the wake of the first massive wave of Mexican immigration to the United States from 1880 to 1920, we begin to witness in the 1920s and 1930s a number of church-sponsored or affiliated Catholic and Protestant books, reports, and articles on Mexican Americans in the Southwest. The most important books include Jay S. Stowell's *A Study of Mexicans and Spanish Americans in the United States* (1920), Vernon M. McCombs's, *From Over the Border: A Study of the Mexican in the United States* (1925), Linna Bresette's, *Mexicans in the United States: A Report of a Brief Survey* (1929), Robert N. McLean's, *The Northern Mexican* (1930), Robert C. Jones's and Louis R. Wilson's, *The Mexican in Chicago* (1931), and Theodore Abel's, *Protestant Home Missions to Catholic Immigrants* (1933). Many other articles, reports, and books were also published.

In the early twentieth century we also note a growing number of university-affiliated humanistic and social-science theses, books, reports, articles, and studies on Mexican Americans that include attention to religion.[14] One of the first major social-science studies on Mexican American religions was the Methodist bishop G. Bromley Oxnam's article "The Mexican in Los Angeles from the Standpoint of Religious Forces of the City" (1921).[15] This research was more social-science oriented than the previous church-sponsored literature. It was soon augmented by a number articles, folklore and museum studies, and histories on religion and culture in New Mexico and elsewhere.[16]

One of the first set of significant humanistic interpretations of Mexican American religiosity were Manuel Gamio's classic anthropological studies *Mexican Immigration to the United States: A Study of Human Migration and Adjustment* (1930) and *The Mexican Immigrant: His Life-Story* (1931). Gamio, who was a highly respected anthropologist from Mexico, conducted his field research in the United States over a two-year period from 1926 to 1927. His books were among the first to examine the role that religious beliefs played in helping Mexican immigrants transition into American society. Unlike the approach of previous church-sponsored work, the methodological orientation of his work is almost entirely secular, humanistic, and anthropological. His work touches on anti-clericalism, church attendance, popular-Catholic practices, and why many Catholics were switching over to Protestantism. Perhaps more important for the future methodological development of Mexican American religions, his pluralistic and nonsectarian work notes the importance of Evangelical

Protestantism and other religious traditions such as Spiritualism, Spiritism, and brujería.[17]

Oxnam's and Gamio's work influenced Robert C. Jones' report on "The Religious Life of the Mexican in Chicago" (1929) and his subsequent book *The Mexican in Chicago* (1931).[18] Similarly, American Baptist Samuel M. Ortegón drew upon Oxnam's and Gamio's work for his MA thesis at USC entitled "Mexican Religious Population of Los Angeles" (1932).[19] Like Gamio and Jones, Ortegón's work was pluralistic in scope and included brief mention of Mainline Protestants, Evangelicals, Pentecostals, Seventh-Day Adventists, Spiritualists, Theosophists, Jehovah's Witnesses, and Roman Catholics. His study was perhaps the first significant qualitative and quantitative ethnographic study of Mexican American religions in Los Angeles. Gamio's work was later picked up with vigor by Chicano Movement scholars hungry for Mexican authors and cultural interpreters.[20]

The flurry of scholarship on Mexican American religions in the late 1920s and early 1930s continued in a steady stream throughout the 1940s,[21] and especially the 1950s in the wake of the bracero guest-worker program agreement between the U.S. and Mexican governments.[22] The two most notable book-length manuscripts were Samuel M. Ortegón's massive USC PhD dissertation, "Religious Thought and Practice among Mexican Baptists of the United States, 1900–1947" (1950), and Carlos Eduardo Castañeda's (1896–1958) seven-volume history, *Our Catholic Heritage in Texas, 1519–1950* (completed in 1958).[23] Although both works were clearly rooted in their respective theological and ecclesiastical traditions, they mark a major leap forward in the academic study of Mexican American religions because they also included social-science interpretations and explanations that were not strictly shaped by a theological method. Perhaps more important, they represent two of the first major histories of Mexican American Protestantism and Catholicism written by, about, and for the Mexican American and Anglo-American communities. A number of scholars cited their work in the wake of the Chicano Movement.[24]

Ortegón and Castañeda were part of what Mario T. García has called the Mexican American GI Generation (1930s–50s), which sought to uncover and reclaim a Mexican American historical consciousness and fight for civil rights by working within the existing political and social system.[25] Although they were professionally trained intellectuals and church historians living in the American Southwest that were engaged in a process of historical retrieval, their work does not mark the birth of the field, because they (like Gamio before them) did not see themselves as scholars of Mexican American religions per se and because they did not seek to self-consciously define or construct a field as such.

César Chávez and Birth of the Study of Mexican American Religions

The key turning point in the development of Mexican American religious studies took place in 1968. That year the writings and intellectual foment stimulated by César Chávez, Reies López Tijerina, Virgilio Elizondo, Gustavo Gutiérrez, Enrique Dussel, Carlos Castañeda (1925–98), and others served as major catalysts in the future methodological and theoretical development of the field. The spark that helped ignite the field came from an unlikely source—a former community service organizer (cso) named César Chávez.[26] Inspired by Father Donald McDonnell to fight for social justice and to unionize Mexican American migrant farmworkers, in 1965 Chávez and Delores Huerta organized the United Farm Workers organization in Our Lady of Guadalupe Church in Delano, California, to fight for better wages, housing, and civil rights. In March 1968, during his first major fast for social justice, Chávez penned one of the first significant historical, social, political, and theological critiques of the Catholic Church by a Mexican American titled "Mexican Americans and the Church."[27] Echoing other Latinos throughout the Americas struggling for justice, he criticized the institutional Catholic Church's lack of support for the Mexican American people and called on it to sacrifice with the people for social change and political and economic justice. His critique differed from Gamio's and Castañeda's (d. 1958) because it asked the Catholic Church to takes sides, affirmed indigenous popular Catholicism, and blended faith, writing, and activism. Chávez and Chicano Movement activists differed from the Mexican American GI Generation activists because he was willing to work outside of the system and because he drew on his faith in his activism.

Chávez's critique and faith-based activism had a profound influence on the future development of Mexican American religious studies. His essay and activism were widely cited and followed in Chicano periodicals such as El Grito del Sol (1968) and by a number of Chicano and Latino scholars such as Rodolfo Acuña, Octavio I. Romano, Francisco García-Treto, Virgilio Elizondo, Juan Hurtado, Antonio Soto, Moises Sandoval, Anthony M. Steven-Arroyo, and later by Andrés Guerrero, Gilberto Hinojosa, and others.[28] Chávez's critique and faith-based activism along with that of the African American, Chicano, American Indian, feminist, and liberation theology movements inspired an emerging generation of Mexican Americans and U.S. Latino scholars to use their scholarship to fight for social, political, and economic justice on behalf of their communities. It also inspired many religious clergy and laity to participate in the Chicano cultural renaissance, which sought to celebrate their Mexican and indigenous cultural and religious identity.[29]

The struggle in California experienced by Chávez's United Farm Workers organization was important because it also helped spotlight the struggle of other Mexican American activists, such as former Assemblies of God Pentecostal evangelist-turned-activist Reies López Tijerina. His *aliancista* land grant struggle in New Mexico along with his Poor People's March in 1968 inspired many Mexican Americans to fight for civil rights and social justice. However, his activism and writings were largely overlooked by scholars writing on Mexican American religions because most of them had Catholic backgrounds and they tended to find more resonance with Chávez's openly ecumenical Catholic pacifism than with Tijerina's magical-literalist militant activism.[30]

The critical role that popular Catholicism and indigenous religious symbols played in the Mexican American Civil Rights Movement was influenced by Chávez's fasts, pilgrimages, and decision to march behind the colorful banner of Our Lady of Guadalupe. They were also influenced by Reies López Tijerina's land grant struggle; by the religious themes in Luis Valdez's *Plan of Delano* and *La Pastorela* play; by Rodolfo "Corky" González's epic poem, *I am Joaquín*, and his call for a national Chicano homeland (Aztlán); and by hundreds of barrio wall murals, poems, songs, theater troops, and student movements sprouting up across the Southwest and nation in the early 1970s.[31] This first generation of Mexican American activists provided *el movimiento* with a spiritual impulse and a sacred set of symbols (Our Lady of Guadalupe, Aztec Eagle), a sacred genealogy (*la raza cósmica*—a cosmic racial heritage going back to the "brilliant" civilizations of the Aztecs and Mayas), a set of sacred traditions (pilgrimages, fasts, and penance, ecclesiastical history), and a sacred homeland (Aztlán—the American Southwest) that gave ordinary Mexican Americans a "Chicano" identity and a sense of collective mission that they could understand, appreciate, and rally behind.

Their grassroots activism contributed to the birth of a Mexican American/Chicano cultural renaissance that promoted cultural nationalism and a sense of ethnic pride that manifested itself in art, music, poetry, theater, politics, and historical recovery. Chicano cultural nationalists argued for an oppositional "us versus them" attitude toward Anglo-American society. "Corky" González called for the creation of a national Chicano homeland in the Southwest, which he named Aztlán after the mythical homeland of the Aztecs and Mexican people. Drawing upon the work of Paulo Freire, Acuña argued that Chicanos were an internal colony suffering oppression like other "Third World peoples."[32] This led many Chicano scholars, such as Juan Gómez-Quinones, to argue that in their struggle for liberation there could be no neutrality because "to acculturate is not merely to exercise a cultural preference but to go to the other side."[33] Acuña's vision of internal colonialism was further refined in Mario Barrera's essay "Barrio as an Internal Colony" and in his 1979 landmark study on internal colonialism, *Race and Class in the Southwest: A Theory of Racial Inequality*, which were later picked up by U.S. Latino scholars of religion.[34]

Despite their important contributions, the Chicano historian Alex M. Saragoza argues that the work of Acuña and others led to a kind of nationalist romanticization and mythologization of Mexican American history that painted an us-versus-them struggle. This approach minimized internal conflict and dissension, focused on local community studies rather than comparative analyses, and exaggerated the continuities and downplayed discontinuities in Chicano and *mexicano* cultures. Seeking to create a collective history and identity, Saragoza argues that authors such as Acuña tended to project normative value judgments in a world where there were good people (largely Mexican American, Latina/o, ethnic minority, poor, women, etc.) and bad people (largely white males or ethnic minorities that sought to accommodate and/or transform society within the existing social and political system). Furthermore, there was a certain moral urgency and rightness to their scholarship; they assumed that because they were either describing or promoting tolerance, pluralism, diversity, or social justice, they were justified in offering an otherwise explicitly and unapologetically negative ideological interpretation of their opponents all the while purporting to be engaging in critical, fair-minded academic scholarship.[35]

Latin American Influences on Mexican American Religious Studies

At the same time Chávez, Huerta, Tijerina, and others were fighting for social justice, civil rights, land rights, and human liberation, Catholics and Protestants in Latin America were engaged in a similar struggle. The same year that Chávez penned "The Mexican American and the Church," hundreds of Catholics met at the Second General Conference of Latin

American Bishops (CELAM) in Medellín, Colombia, where they began to articulate a theology of liberation.[36] The critical development of liberation theology took place when the Peruvian priest and theologian Gustavo Gutiérrez asked his colleagues if their theology of socioeconomic empowerment would "be a theology of development [i.e., capitalism] or a theology of liberation?"[37] Blending conviction with academic precision, Gutiérrez penned Latin America's most important contribution to the global Christian theology, *Teología de la liberación* (1971), which was subsequently translated into English as *A Theology of Liberation* (1973). In this book he argues that Jesus was a scorned suffering servant and revolutionary who preached a Gospel of liberation to the poor and oppressed, who fought for spiritual, political, social, and economic justice against the religious and political establishments, and was as a result martyred on behalf of his people in order to help usher in the kingdom of God.[38]

Liberation theologians such as Ruben Alves, Gustavo Gutiérrez, Hugo Assmann, Leonardo Boff, Clodovis Boff, Juan Luis Segundo, José Miguel Bonino, Enrique Dussel, and many others in Latin America argue that their movement is a theological and practical movement that emphasizes present deliverance of the oppressed from their sinful oppressors. The authentic starting point for any Christian theology is commitment to the poor, the "nonperson."[39] The Christian message, they suggest, has to be interpreted out of the context of the suffering, struggle, and hope of the poor. Drawing on the story of Moses leading his people out of slavery in Egypt, they preach a revolutionary and prophetic praxis-based message that maps the trajectory of human history from "captivity" to "exile" to divine hope and human liberation. "Conscientization" (consciousness-raising), contextualization, and praxis are the keys to realizing this liberation, they teach. They believe God is on their side—and the side of the poor against the symbolic pharaohs of this life. They tend to focus on the importance of economic factors in oppression, pay close attention to class struggle, argue for the mystifying power of ideologies, including religious ones, emphasize the role that society plays in oppression of individuals and communities, and argue that suffering is also the result of unjust social and political structures. Liberation theologians have been unfairly criticized as being Marxists. However, they tend to use Marxism in a purely instrumental way.[40] Today most have distanced themselves from any Marxist influence.

Latin American liberation scholars such as Enrique Dussel also influenced the rise and methodology of Mexican American religious history. He formulated a praxis-based historical methodology that reframed history as a struggle for liberation from neocolonial dependency on Anglo-Saxon English and American industrial capitalism. Echoing Marxist, leftist, and social historians, Dussel argued that no description of a historical fact is obvious or neutral. Every historical account presupposes an "interpretation" based on one's ideological and theological worldview that either upholds the capitalist structure of society, or promotes a revolutionary movement toward human liberation and freedom. For this reason, he argued that scholars must create a Christian faith-based interpretation of history and society that blends the rigors of a critical scientific methodology with an equally rigorous contextual and praxis-oriented commitment to the suffering, aspirations, and perspectives of the poor and the oppressed.[41]

Dussel's methodological influence is clearly evident in Moises Sandoval's groundbreaking history, *Fronteras: A History of the Latin American Church in the USA since 1513* (1983). In the preface, Bishop Ricardo Ramírez states that the idea for Sandoval's book came from Dussel, who was then president of the Commission for the Study of the History of the Church in America (CEHILA).[42] This influence is also noticeable in Virgilio Elizondo's introduction to the book, where, echoing the language of Paulo Freire's conscientization, he states that one of the reasons so many Latinos were confused and divided over their ethnic identity was because they have been deprived of a "real consciousness of . . . [their] historical becoming." The best way to address this problem was to follow the examples of Dussel and especially of Acuña, whose work "beautifully brings out the Chicano struggle for liberation." Far from being a dead and fossilized past, Mexican American history and religion were very much alive in the dynamic and creative imagination of *corridos, leyendas, cuentos, murales, pinturas* (songs, legends, stories, murals, paintings) and religious celebrations of the saints and cultural heroes such as Our Lady of Guadalupe, Elizondo writes. After thanking Enrique Dussel and CEHILA for inviting them to write the book, he ends his introduction by stating that it filled him with great joy that MACC was able to publish this first general history of Latino Christianity in the United States.[43]

Virgilio Elizondo and the Birth of Mexican American Religious Studies

Virgilio Elizondo (figure 1) played a pivotal role in the birth of Mexican American theology and religious studies. A native of San Antonio, Elizondo stated to me that his praxis-oriented scholarship wove together a Mexican American/Chicano theology that reflected the influences of his

1. Virgilio Elizondo, 2000. Courtesy: Virgilio Elizondo.

seminary training's emphasis on social justice; Archbishop Robert Lucy's grassroots work on the war on poverty and farmworkers' movement; and Vatican II's insistence on incarnational theology, the need for "inculturation," and the dynamic notion of divine revelation. He further noted that he was influenced by the Dogmatic Constitution on Divine Revelation, "Dei Verbum"; the Decree on the Missionary Activity of the Church, "Ad Gentes"; and the Pastoral Constitution on the Church in the Modern World, "Gaudium et Spes." In addition, his thought and method were directly shaped by Chávez, Gutiérrez, Dussel, Acuña, and others in the Chicano cultural renaissance. Perhaps his most important influences were Johannes Hoffinger and Alfonso Nebreda of the East Asian Pastoral Institute because they argued that he needed to draw on cultural anthropology for any kind of Christian theological reflection. These influences were clarified and deepened by Jacques Audinet of the Institut Catholique de

Paris's insistence on using the social sciences in the task of creating local theologies. Elizondo not only knew Chávez firsthand and learned about the promulgations of Vatican II from Archbishop Robert Lucy who had attended the event, but he also accompanied Lucy to the preparatory meetings of the now historic CELAM conference in Medellín, Colombia, in 1968, where he met and conversed with Gustavo Gutiérrez, Enrique Dussel, and many other Latin American liberation theologians. These influences are evident in his groundbreaking 1968 essay, "Educación religiosa para el méxico-norteamericano," published in the Mexican journal, *Catequesis Latinoamericana* and other articles from this period.[44] He was also later influenced by the Chicano historian Jesús Chavarría at the University of California, Santa Barbara, who said that "As long as you do not write your own story and elaborate your own knowledge, you will always be a slave to another's thoughts."[45] These influences were later refined in his *Anthropological and Psychological Characteristics of the Mexican American* (1974) and in his classic study *Christianity and Culture* (1975). They came to their intellectual maturity in his germinal works *Mestizaje: The Dialectic of Birth and Gospel* (1978), *La Morenita: Evangelizer of the Americas* (1980), and especially *Galilean Journey* (1983) and *The Future Is Mestizo: Life Where Cultures Meet* (1988).

Elizondo's writings signal the academic birth of Mexican American theology and history.[46] Drawing upon the methodology of Gutiérrez, Dussel, Acuña, and others, he argued that Mexican American scholars should create and publish collective revisionist scholarship on Mexican American theology and religious history from the perspective of the poor and marginalized that is also "objective" and academically rigorous.[47] He brought this vision to fruition by publishing not only theological works but also some of the foundational historical, biographical and sociological books on Mexican American religions through MACC. In addition to three of his own books, under his influence MACC also published Juan Romero and Moises Sandoval, *Reluctant Dawn: Historia del Padre A. J. Martínez, Cura de Taos* (1976), Juan Hurtado, *An Attitudinal Study of Social Distance between the Mexican American and the Church* (1975), Sandoval, *Fronteras*, and many other books, reports, and articles.

Although Elizondo was proactive in publishing the work of other scholars and writers, it was his own aforementioned books that challenged and revised the theological agenda of the day. His mestizo paradigm contended that Mexican Americans are like Jesus because they are religious outsiders who are rejected by the racial and religious establishment for being from a racially and theological impure (meaning mixed blood—a popular Jewish counter-tradition taught that Jesus's father was a Roman soldier) bloodline from the scorned region of Galilee. For this reason, Elizondo called on all Mexican Americans to be proud of their mixed racial and hitherto-scorned Mexican popular-Catholic heritage. The work of Elizondo and other U.S. Latinos contributed what Ana María Díaz-Stevens and Anthony M. Stevens-Arroyo have called a resurgence in the study of U.S. Latino religions (1988).

The work of Elizondo, Chávez, Gutiérrez, Tijerina, and others in the 1960s and 1970s influenced, to varying degrees, the work of later Mexican American and U.S. Latino/a scholars in the 1980s and 1990s, including Andrés G. Guerrero, *A Chicano Theology* (1987), Ada María Isasi-Díaz and Yolanda Tarango, *Hispanic Women: Prophetic Voice in the Church* (1988), and Jeanette Rodriguez, *Our Lady of Guadalupe: Faith and Empowerment among Mexican-American Women* (1994). Whereas in the United States, Elizondo and Isasi-Díaz and Tarango's work exerted tremendous influence in the study of Mexican American and U.S. Latino religions, Guerrero's book was, by comparison, largely overlooked despite the fact that he cites Chávez, Tijerina, Gutiérrez, and Elizondo.[48] Guerrero's theology (based on a set of nine interviews with Chicano Catholic and Protestant leaders) stated that the Christian Church was the last hope of Chicanos. However, he also accused it of working against Chicano liberation, practicing sexism, preaching the inferiority of women, and using Our Lady of Guadalupe to both liberate and oppress Chicanos. Some interviewees promoted fighting for communal lands taken by Anglos in the wake of the 1848 war between the United States and Mexico and to use whatever means was necessary (including violence) to achieve liberation—a position that the pacifist Guerrero did not support. Despite his rejection of violence in the struggle for liberation, his book has been largely overlooked by scholars because it is seen as romanticizing the Chicano struggle, being too academic and too militant, falling into a simplistic us-versus-them binary, and perhaps because it was too quick to condemn the institutional Church, which, love it or leave it, was, and still remains, the religious home of most Mexican Americans.[49]

Mexican American and U.S. Latino scholars have promoted a largely liberationist methodological outlook and praxis-based orientation through a number of pan-Latino interdisciplinary associations, organizations, and journals such as the Association of Catholic Hispanic Theologians of the United States (ACHTUS—1988), the Program for the Analysis of Religion Among Latinos (PARAL—1988), La Comunidad of Hispanic Scholars of Religion (1989), the Hispanic Fund for Theological Education, the Hispanic Theological Initiative (HTI—1995), and interdenominational journals such as the United Methodist–affiliated *Apuntes: Reflexiones teológicas desde el margen hispano* (1981), and the Roman Catholic–affiliated *Journal of Hispanic/Latino Theology* (1994). These organizations and forums have trained and funded many Mexican American and U.S. Latino/a scholars of religion. In 1992, Rudy V. Busto and Daniel Ramírez secured grant money to hold a conference entitled "Nuevas Fronteras / Reconsidering Borders: U.S. Latino Evangelicalism," at Stanford University. Through these endeavors, Mexican American and U.S. Latino/a theologians and scholars have been able to keep alive, institutionalize, and mainstream their largely Christian, liberationist-theological, praxis-based methodology. For these reasons and others, Mexican American theology and, to a lesser degree, religious studies and Chicana feminist theology, has largely been a footnote to liberation theology—in one manifestation or another.

Chicana Feminism and Women in Religion

Gustavo Gutiérrez and Virgilio Elizondo directly influenced (along with other Chicana/Latina women) the rise of Chicana feminism and later *mujerista* theology through the Chicana Yolanda Tarango and Cuban-born Ada María Isasi-Díaz's pioneering work, *Hispanic Women: Prophetic Voice in the Church* (1988). Their Latina, feminist liberation theology was based on a series of interviews with Hispanic women. It also drew upon the insights and writings of Rosemary Radford Reuther, Margaret Farley, Elizabeth Schüssler Fiorenza, Mary Elizabeth Hunt, Clifford Geertz, Antonio Gramsci, Paul Tillich, José Míguez Bonino, Paulo Freire, and others. They sought to create a Hispanic cultural, feminist, and liberation theology that captured the sentiment and struggles of ordinary women. They saw themselves first and foremost as activists struggling for justice and peace and saw no conflict in combining theology and activism. They sought to "militantly" fight against both Anglo-American and Latino multilayered sexism, patriarchy, classism, and economic oppression. Some of their work, especially as articulated by Isasi-Díaz, was methodologically important because it (a) provided a sharp critique of Latino sexism, classism, elitism, and patriarchy, (b) called on Latino men to share leadership and the theological enterprise with women, (c) called for more inclusive theologies, and (d) gave voice to Latina women and sought to shift the focus away from "orthodoxy" (right belief) to "orthopraxis" (right practice).[50]

Despite the pivotal role that Tarango's and Isasi-Díaz's book played in the development of a Latina, feminist liberation theology, María Pilar

Aquino has warned scholars to be careful not to assume that their work represents all Chicana and U.S. Latina feminist theologians. In fact, Chicana and Latina feminism is much broader, pluralistic, and effusive than the work of Isasi-Díaz and Tarango, Gutiérrez, and Elizondo, despite their important influences, Aquino argues. Furthermore, Aquino suggests that Isasi-Díaz's mujerista theological perspective is in fact a creative fiction because "there are no *mujerista* sociopolitical and ecclesial subjects in the United States or Latin America." The problem with Isasi-Díaz's work, Aquino continues, is that she created a theology that "glorifies difference" and produces "'discursive . . . locations . . . and false oppositions' that weaken the political force of feminism." For these reasons and others, she suggests that Chicana/Latina "theology must be clearly characterized by a *non-mujerista* orientation."[51] Furthermore, she calls on Chicana and U.S. Latina feminist theologians to draw on the work of Chicana feminist writers and thinkers such as Norma Alarcón, Ana Castillo, Gloria Anzaldúa, Cherrie Moraga, Vicki Ruiz, Chela Sandoval, Dena González, Olga Villa-Parra, Alma García, and Cynthia Orozco, and on other feminist voices.[52]

Pilar Aquino equally distances Chicana feminist scholarship on religion from Loida Martel Otero's important 1994 work on Latina *evangélicas* because of her subject's perceived lack of commitment to social transformation.[53] Espinosa's work on Latina Pentecostal women in ministry, along with that of Elizabeth Ríos and Arlene Sánchez-Walsh, argues that there is in fact a long tradition of Latina Pentecostal women engaging in social action ministry.[54] Mexican American Pentecostal women have been engaging in social ministry since 1906, and most have historically voted for Democratic Party candidates, despite their very conservative position on abortion and same-sex marriage—which they reject as unbiblical. In fact, 69 percent of Latino Pentecostals voted for Bill Clinton in the 1996 presidential election and in 2000, 67 percent of Latino Protestants voted for Al Gore.[55] However, although Latina Pentecostal women are morally conservative, women such as Aimee García Cortese engaged in a kind of feminist discourse and protest (although she was uncomfortable with the word *feminist*) as early as the late 1950s in their struggles against sexism within the Latino Assemblies of God.[56] Despite this fact, Cortese and others rejected feminism because of its association with a "pro-abortion" position and "the gay movement."[57]

Chicana feminist interpretations of religion are critical to understanding and interpreting the Mexican American religious experience. Every effort should be made to support feminist scholarship and scholars. Building on their work, there is also a great need to uncover, discover, and analyze the stories of millions of other nonfeminist women from new and hybrid theoretical and methodological interpretive frameworks. They can include new and hitherto-overlooked voices of women from diverse religious traditions, such as Catholic Charismatics, Mainline Protestants, non-Pentecostal Evangelicals, Pentecostals, Muslims, Jews, Jehovah's Witnesses, Mormons, Spiritualist/Spiritists, adherents of brujería, Buddhists, Hindus, atheists, agnostics, Native Americans, practicers of mixed religion, New Agers, and others. This pluralistic framework is important in light of the growing religious diversity within the Mexican American and U.S. Latino communities.[58]

As the research above indicates, there is also a great need for research on non-Christian and hybrid Mexican American and U.S. Latino religions and spiritualities. The religious boundaries are as porous as the country's border.[59]

Secular Interpretations of Mexican American Religions

Like the work of Gamio, Jones, and Ortegón forty years earlier, Anglo-American scholars such as Patrick McNamara and Joan Moore also published important sociological and historical essays on Mexican American religions in Leo Grebler, Joan W. Moore, and Ralph C. Guzman, *The Mexican American People: The Nation's Second Largest Minority* (1970), which included brief attention to Presbyterians, Methodists, Baptists, Evangelicals, Pentecostals, and Mormons. Their essays sketched the role that churches played in assimilation, socialization of values, and furthering social change, which together contributed to socioeconomic advancement and social justice. McNamara argued that "folk" Catholicism combined "normal" Catholic practices with "pagan (Indian) rites."[60] Unlike the "ideologically-tinged ethnic spokespersons and activists who as insiders had their own agendas," he claimed, his survey research findings could "influence the objectivity of outsiders."[61] He further states that his essay provided data for a new generation of Chicano scholars such as Acuña, who were "bent upon rewriting the history of the Southwest in a conflict/internal colonialism framework."[62] Although his study was cited by Mexican American scholars for hard facts, it does not mark the birth of the field, because McNamara stated that his sociological focus was *not* on Mexican American religiosity and because he did not attempt to define or construct a field as such.[63] However, McNamara's and Moore's research is methodologically important because of its social-science approach and because it clearly built on the previous writings of Jean-Baptiste Salpointe,

McCombs, Abel, Ortegón, Castañeda, Delbert Lee Gibson, Soto, Chávez, and others.

In addition to the rise of secularly oriented social-science research, we also see humanistic anthropological research on Mexican American religions. From the 1930s through the 1960s, we saw the rise of secular anthropological, historical, psychological, and folklore research and literature both on Mexican American Christian healing traditions, such as Pentecostalism and Catholic *curanderismo*, and on metaphysical traditions, such as Spiritualism, Spiritism, and brujería.[64] This literature has continued to grow from the 1970s through the present thanks to the work of Juan Castañon García, June Macklin, Marc Simmons, Robert T. Trotter II and Juan Antonio Chavira, Beatrice A. Roeder, Davíd Carrasco, Luis León, Gastón Espinosa, Lara Medina, Inés Hernández-Avila, and many others.[65] Little, by contrast, was written on Latino Mormonism, Jehovah's Witnesses, Seventh-Day Adventists, and world religions, with the exception of brief references by Ortegón, Moore, and Espinosa.[66]

During this period from 1965 through the publication of *Fronteras* in 1983, we also see the rise in number of histories, biographies, and other works about Mexican American and U.S. Latino Mainline, Evangelical, and Pentecostal Protestants.[67] They were not explicitly liberationist in orientation.[68] This church-based scholarship was supplemented by a number of books by Chicano historians such as Ramón Gutiérrez, Mario T. García, Vicki Ruiz, George Sánchez, and others. They provided alternative theoretical and methodological frameworks for interpreting Mexican American history and religions that clearly went beyond the purview of traditional church history and liberation theology.

The work of these Chicano historians is important because they moved away from the static us-versus-them oppositional approach of the 1970s and instead argued for more complicated, contradictory, and nuanced histories of the Mexican American experience.[69] Mario T. García, for example, wrote that the "Mexican border culture [was] neither completely Mexican nor American, but one revealing contrasting attractions and pressures between cultures."[70] Sánchez similarly wrote that "any notion that individuals have occupied one undifferentiated cultural position—such as 'Mexican,' 'American,' or 'Chicano'—has been abandoned in favor of the possibility of multiple identities and contradictory positions."[71] Their work has in turn shaped an emerging generation of Mexican American religious studies historians and scholars such as Rudy Busto, Gastón Espinosa, Luis León, Arlene Sánchez-Walsh, Alberto Pulido, Lara Medina, Roberto Lint Sagarena, Paul Barton, Laura Pérez, Daniel Ramírez, and others.

Chicano Literature, History, and Mexican American Religious Studies

The field of Mexican American religions has not only been shaped by the faith-based activism of Chávez and Tijerina, the Chicano Movement, liberation theology, denominationally sponsored church histories and theologies, and social scientific and humanistic scholarship, but also by Chicano literature. Although writing outside of the academy, literary works—Carlos Castañeda's *The Teachings of Don Juan: A Yaqui Way of Knowledge* (1968), Rudolfo Anaya's *Bless Me, Ultima* (1972), Gloria Anzaldúa's *Borderlands / La Frontera: The New Mestiza* (1987)—have also contributed to the interdisciplinary and canon-busting movement away from institutional theology. They focus on noninstitutional forms of religiosity and theology and treat the U.S.–Mexico borderlands as a hybrid shamanic space that challenges traditional Catholic and Protestant hegemony, traditions, and way of life.[72]

Castañeda's anthropological foray into the world of Don Juan, a *diablero*, or satanic sorcerer from northern Mexico then living in Los Angeles, explores shamanistic cognition and ways of knowledge and power that challenge modern Western categories, medicine, religion, and epistemology. Like Castañeda's emphasis on Mexican American healing traditions, Anaya's novel analyzes the influence of Native American indigenous history, spirituality, and mythology on the magical-realist outlook on life and the world in popular Catholicism. It does so through the life and work of a *curandera*, or folk healer, named Ultima. She teaches her coming-of-age grandson and apprentice, Antonio, that life cannot be reduced to a simple binary of good versus evil. Knowledge, like the world, is fragmented and yet one can find liberation and hope through moving beyond one's individual identity.[73] This magical-realist outlook has been shaped by a number of other writers and has influenced the writing of Mexican American scholars such as Rudy Busto.[74]

Castañeda's and Anaya's work inspired and influenced Gloria Anzaldúa's new mestiza paradigm, which calls for the celebration of a shamanic state of consciousness that challenges traditional Western conceptualizations of religion, gender, sexuality, and identity. Her work explores in prose and poetry the ambivalence of Chicanos/as in Anglo culture, women in Latino culture, and lesbians in the straight world. She criticizes anyone who oppresses people considered culturally or sexually different. Although her work has been overlooked by some Mexican American scholars of religion who have strong ties to the institutional church or who were trained in seminaries and divinity schools, she has found vibrant sponsorship by many Chicano/a scholars of religion trained in secular Chicano, ethnic, and religious studies programs, and Latina feminist theologians with strong interests in borderlands studies, gender, race, ethnicity, or sexuality.[75]

Davíd Carrasco, Chicano Literature, and the Decentering of Mexican American Religious Studies

The intellectual and methodological development of the emerging field of Mexican American religious studies comes to its fullness in the work of Davíd Carrasco. His work marks the methodological crystallization of a Mexican American religious studies paradigm that expanded the methodological and theoretical boundaries beyond the field and scope of liberation theology. His work in the early 1980s, along with that of Chicano/a writers such as Gloria Anzaldúa and others, contributed to the decentering of the scholarship on Mexican American religions. This movement away from the orbit of liberation theology and church histories to increasingly pluralistic religious and Chicano studies analyses no longer privileged a liberationist or institutional methodological approach to religion. Perhaps the best example of this shift is Carrasco's analysis of Rudolfo Anaya's novel *Bless Me, Ultima* published in *Aztlán: A Journal of Chicano Studies*, his groundbreaking books *Quetzalcoatl and the Irony of Empire: Myths and Prophecies in Aztec Traditions* (1982) and *Religions of Mesoamerica: Cosmovision and Ceremonial Centers* (1990), and in his work in this volume on Gloria Anzaldúa (chapter 9).

Unlike most contemporary scholars who were writing on liberation theology, Carrasco took many of his main theoretical and methodological cues from Mircea Eliade, Charles Long, Paul Wheatley, the Chicago School of the History of Religions, cultural anthropology, and Virgilio Elizondo's theological anthropology of *mestizaje*. He also uses Chicano literature as primary source texts to illustrate the native indigenous elements in Mexican and Mexican American religions. Drawing upon the work of phenomenologist Mircea Eliade and the urban ecologist Paul Wheatley in particular, Carrasco's work applied and reimagined a series of potent interpretive categories within the context of Mesoamerican and Mexican American history. These interpretive categories included sacred time, sacred centers, sacred spaces, world-making, world-centering, world-renewing, and what Carrasco calls "center/periphery dynamics."[76]

Unlike Gamio, who had a negative view of Mexican Indian influences on religion, Carrasco celebrates the cultural and religious hybridity of the

Mexican American religious experience. He explores the benefits of using both the categories of syncretism and transculturation in attempting to capture the rich texture of Mexican American religious hybridity in that most important symbol of Mexican American identity—Our Lady of Guadalupe. Carrasco writes: "In Guadalupe we see a curious and even furious syncretistic mixture. She is Indian and Spaniard. She is an Earth Mother and Holy Mother. She is a comforter and a revolutionary. She is the magnet for pilgrimages and she is a pilgrim herself, traveling in front of the rebel soldiers and entering every heart who needs protection and comfort."[77] Carrasco inadvertently challenges and transforms McNamara's relatively negative depiction of Mexican popular Catholicism as rooted in "pagan Indian rites" by shifting the locus of Mexican American religions away from institutional Catholicism and concerns about the theological orthodoxy of religious practices.[78]

However, Carrasco's work does not necessarily represent an ideological or a theoretical break with the goals and aims of the Chicano Movement or even with liberation theology's commitment to the poor and marginalized. Instead, it represents a methodological break with the largely theological orientation of some of his colleagues. His interest in a phenomenological approach to Mexican American religions is largely the result of his training in the history of religions at the University of Chicago and because of his pluralist interest and experiences in non-Christian Mexican, metaphysical, and Mesoamerican and U.S. Native American religious traditions. At Chicago, Carrasco was influenced by Long and Wheatley, both of whom taught him the value of the comparative study of religion and the importance of putting phenomenology in constant dialogue with the study of social stratification and literary expressions. Carrasco's current work argues that we are entering a "Brown Millennium" that will forever change the course of events and the study of religion both in the United States and around the world. This transformation will occur because Chicano/Latino growth in our megacities represents a new mestizo aesthetic that will reorient and rejuvenate our understanding of how the current *"cultural and religious change"* will radically change "the *religious, economic, civic and social ordering* of our socially stratified societies."[79]

History and Theory of Religious Studies

Carrasco's phenomenological approach to religious studies has a distinct genealogy and method that trace their recent origins back through Eliade, Rudolf Otto, and Geradus van der Leeuw to Enlightenment philosophers such as David Hume, Immanuel Kant, John Locke, and nineteenth-century anthropologists such as Max Müller and E. B. Tylor.[80] It purports to be entirely naturalistic in orientation and does not assume an a priori belief in the existence of God. This naturalistic approach developed slowly into the field of religious studies until the 1963 *Schempp* decision along with the work of Mircea Eliade and the Chicago School of the History of Religions led to four decades of unprecedented expansion, from the 1960s to the present.[81] Although some variation of this religious studies approach has been embraced by almost all of the major secular PhD-granting institutions in the United States, most Catholic, Mainline Protestant, and Evangelical PhD-granting institutions and seminaries have not strictly embraced this secular approach. They see it as running contrary to their Christian roots—theologically and professionally oriented seminaries and divinity schools—and many of their faculty's a priori beliefs in God.

Some religious studies scholars (also known as historians of religion and scholars of comparative religions) trained in the classical and contemporary theoreticians in the history of comparative religions as described in Eric Sharpe, Walter Capps, and Donald Wiebe distinguished themselves from their theological counterparts in their attempt to (1) take a scientific, nonapologetic, non-value-laden (good vs. bad theology or morals), and nonsectarian pluralistic approach to the study of religion; (2) suspend or bracket belief in God and the divine origin of religion in their writings; (3) compare two or more religious traditions, regions, and/or religious phenomena; (4) identify religious rituals, myths, and social patterns and phenomena that transcend many religious traditions; (5) offer nontheological interpretations and explanations of religious rituals, traditions, beliefs, and events; (6) take an interdisciplinary and often humanistic and/or a social scientific approach to interpreting religion; and (7) seek to interpret the meaning, purpose, and function of religion in culture and society.

In the words of William Paden, religious studies attempts to "create a language that explains what is otherwise expressed only by the language of religious insiders."[82] What generally differentiates a history of religions or religious studies scholar from a theologian or ethicist is the former's comparative emphasis and attempt to avoid writing normative theological, ethical, and political faith statements about what society should believe or look like. This job they leave primarily to their colleagues in ethics and theology.

Mircea Eliade, perhaps the most famous exponent of religious studies, argued that the phenomenological approach to the study of religion assumes that the sacred is "an element in the structure of [human] consciousness, not a stage in the history of consciousness." In so doing, he rejects the modernist assumption that religion is a cultural artifact restrictred to bygone ages. He suggested that religion is important because it helps people make meaning out of life by imitating paradigmatic experiences with the sacred. Phenomenologists identify and decipher religious structures in society to better understand and interpret the meaning behind these private worlds and imaginary universes. Eliade believed that the historian of religions must make an effort to understand religious experiences and movements on their own plane of reference in order to gain insight into their deeper meaning. Finding this deeper meaning is not an end in and of itself, but rather a means to understanding its contribution to the *"entire culture."*[83]

As important as Eliade's theories are to the study of comparative religions, they tended to be, in the words of Richard Hecht, of the University of California, Santa Barbara, ahistorical, apolitical, and consensual, and assume what Donald Wiebe has identified as a theological a priori.[84] Furthermore, some might argue that some religious studies scholars engage in a modernist intellectual and ideological program whose findings are described as objective truth but in fact are projections of a neocolonial and neo-Orientalist enterprise. Recognizing these limitations, recent historians of religion such as Jonathan Z. Smith have emphasized the need to ground one's study of religion in their historical, social, and political contexts. Furthermore, Smith argues that "there is no data for religion [*sic*]," only the scholar's creative imagination. For this reason, it is incumbent upon scholars to be "relentlessly self-conscious" of their subject and subjectivities. The scholar must gain mastery of the primary sources and secondary interpretations, select an appropriate methodology for interpreting the data, and then argue for a new paradigm, theory, or some fundamental question. This approach, along with what Eliade calls the perspective of the critical but sympathetic outsider, may yield one of many useful interpretive frameworks for analyzing religion.[85]

Toward a Mexican American Religious Studies Framework

The years 1994–96 proved the next critical turning point in the field of Mexican American religions, with the publication of a number of important historical, social-science, and theological works, including the Jay P. Dolan three-volume Notre Dame History of Hispanic Catholics in the U.S., and Anthony M. Stevens-Arroyo's four-volume Program for the

Analysis of Religion Among Latinos (PARAL) series on Latino popular religiosity, identity, syncretism, and bibliography, both of which offered sustained attention to Mexican American religiosity. These multivolume works were joined by a number of other important books, published from 1990 to 2000, that focused exclusively or in part on Mexican American religions.[86]

The next critical turning points in the development of the general field of Mexican American religions took place in 1992 with the Busto and Ramíres Conference at Stanford and then in 1996 with the "New Directions in Chicano Religions" conference held at the University of California, Santa Barbara. The latter conference focused almost exclusively on Mexican American religions. It was initiated by Gastón Espinosa and codirected with Mario T. García. Sixteen scholars were invited to come together to reflect on and help define the emerging field of Mexican American/Chicano religions.[87] This was the first academic conference to explore and map out the field of Mexican American/Chicano religious studies from a denominationally pluralistic and scholarly perspective that was largely shaped by a religious studies methodology and discourse. It was largely pluralistic, humanistic, nonsectarian, and nontheological in its basic framework and orientation. Although several authors drew upon liberation theology to frame their work, most engaged in theoretical and methodological approaches from anthropology, sociology, religious studies, history, literature, ethnic studies, and political science. The conference included essays that examined the role of religion in both Chicano literature and gay liberation theology, perhaps the first conference on Mexican American and U.S. Latino religions to do so. It helped stimulate the creation of a two-year-long UCSB Chicano religions evening colloquium that met in Mario T. García's home, the short-lived National Association for the Study of Chicano Religions (NASCR) (1996), and the UCSB Religions of Aztlán course designed by Luis Léon. It also served as a catalyst in the creation of this volume and in many other subsequent articles and books.

Toward a Working Definition of Chicano Religions

At the conference, the religious studies scholar Charles Long challenged the participants to define what they meant by Mexican American/Chicano religions and to then show how they were different from any other kind of religious phenomena. While no immediate or systematic response was given at the time, I argue that it is precisely the Mexican American blending and combinative reconstruction of Mexican and "American" traditions, customs, practices, symbols, and beliefs in the United States that we call the distinctively Mexican American/Chicano religious expressions or Mexican American/Chicano/a religions. To be sure, religious rituals found in Mexican American religions can also be found in other non-Mexican American religions. However, Mexican American cultural reimagination, blending, rearticulation, and poetic reconstruction and aesthetic of "Mexican" and "American" religious rituals, customs, traditions, practices, beliefs, and symbols give them a Mexican American or "Chicano" inflection that sometimes differentiates them in application and form, though not necessarily in function, from non-Mexican American religious practices. Thus while because of this blending, Mexican American religions share common ritual functions with some other African American, Asian American, Native American, and Euro-American religious practices, their application, inflection, and expression are also noticeably and often qualitatively different in their execution. Chicano religious practices and traditions both resonate with their Mexican counterparts while at the same time exhibiting a blending, a combining, a fusing, or a mixing with non-Mexican U.S. practices and traditions to create a new hybrid reality that is neither entirely Mexican nor entirely American but is in fact Mexican American or Chicano. Some of these practices have combined and blended Mexican and American religious and cultural traditions and have in turn transformed themselves into a new hybrid combinative realities, such as New Mexican popular Catholicism, curanderismo, and U.S. Latino liberation theology. This combinative hybrid spirituality has given birth to the predicament of nepantla, or of being located in the middle, on the border—"en La Frontera."[88]

Ethno-Phenomenological Approach to the Study of Religion

One approach to interpreting Mexican American religions at secular public colleges and universities is an ethno-phenomenological approach and methodology that seeks to bridge the open hostility between religious studies and theology through an interdisciplinary, transnational, and phenomenological religious studies method. Such a method listens to, dialogues with, and, when appropriate, draws upon the important discoveries and insights from theology and the above-noted disciplines. This approach should also seek to enter into and analyze the world of its historical and contemporary subjects on their own plane of reference through a methodology that respects and holds in balance both the perspective of the committed religious insider and that of the skeptical, noncommitted secular outsider. An ethno-phenomenological approach to the study of Mexican American religions should offer a scholarly framework that engages in what Ninian Smart has called "bracketed realism," whereby the scholars' own religious beliefs (or lack thereof) and ideological political positions are bracketed or suspended and not superimposed on their subjects in order to try to understand, analyze, and interpret a religious leader, tradition, movement, practice, belief, or phenomena on its own plane of reference.[89] While personal subjectivities and values are unavoidable, a scholar should nonetheless try to fairly present the community in a way that is both critical and yet recognizable to the insider.

Although scholars taking this approach should (in their scholarship and classroom teaching) seek political and theological neutrality regarding the value, truth, or falsity of their subject's theological beliefs and moral behavior—out of consideration for the religion itself and the diverse student body at secular institutions—this does not mean that the scholars cannot engage in advocacy on behalf of their community or religious and political beliefs outside of these forums. Scholars should be free to advocate their own educational, social, racial, political, and religious views provided that they do not intentionally seek to use their classroom lecterns and scholarship as a bully pulpit to force, coerce, or manipulate their students or colleagues into adopting their position as the one and only legitimate approach to their subject for all truly "open-minded" and "tolerant" people. Given that all knowledge and truth are provisional, relative, and perspectival, any attempt to force, coerce, or manipulate someone to embrace one's own position represents a kind of intellectual violence and neocolonialism that can silence, oppress, or marginalize dissenting voices and points of view even among their own people, all the while demanding freedom, tolerance, liberation, and empowerment for themselves in the Euro-American-dominated academy. This kind of ideological proselytizing can have a chilling effect in the classroom and in the field because it may stifle the introduction of new and creative ideas, theories, methodologies, and points of view out of fear of reprisal and retribution for not towing the ideological and methodological "party line."

An ethno-phenomenological approach to the study of Mexican American religions should also strive to be politically and methodologically pluralistic, multidisciplinary, humanistic, social-science-based, comparative, and transnational in its orientation, assumptions, and use and evaluation of evidence. Ideally, scholars should not only be trained in Mexican American religions, but also in U.S. Latino, Mexican, Mesoamerican, and

Latin American; and American, Ethnic, and Native American religions and theology, both historical and contemporary. They should also be at home working in archives and, when possible, in conducting quantitative and qualitative ethnographic and oral history or *testimonio* research.

Conclusion

I have suggested that the contemporary academic study of Mexican American religions stretches back at least a century. The field of Mexican American theology traces its foundational origins back to the period from 1968 through 1975 through the writings of César Chávez, Gustavo Gutiérrez, Enrique Dussel, and Virgilio Elizondo. They pioneered the field of Mexican American/Chicano theology. Their work was joined by scholarship from writers in history, sociology, anthropology, Chicano studies, and literature. All of these forces along with the contributions of the Chicago School of the History of Religions helped shape and give rise to the methodologically pioneering work of Davíd Carrasco and others in the 1980s. The field went through a period of tremendous growth and refinement throughout the 1990s. I have proposed that an ethno-phenomenological method and approach is one of many possible alternatives and ways to rethink how they go about studying and interpreting Mexican American religions at secular colleges and universities where they are required by the state and/or college mission statement not to promote or endorse a theological worldview. This methodology seeks to bridge the chasm that often separates religious studies from theology by maintaining dialogue with theologians and religious studies scholars. I hope that this approach will help generate new social-science, ethnic, pluralistic, comparative, and transnational scholarship that examines the way ordinary people find hope and interpret their very real and imaginary universes.

Notes

We wish to thank Virgilio Elizondo, Davíd Carrasco, Rudy V. Busto, Miguel de la Torre, and Ulrike Guthrie for their critical feedback on early drafts of this chapter. Any shortcomings in this essay are, of course, our own.
1. César Chávez, "The Mexican American and the Church," *El Grito del Sol* 1, no. 4 (summer 1968): 9–12; "The Mexican American and the Church," in *Voices: Readings from El Grito. A Journal of Mexican American Thought, 1967–1973*, ed. Octavio I. Romano V. (Berkeley, Calif.: Quinto Sol Publications, 1973), 215–18; Virgilio Elizondo, "Educación religiosa para el méxico-norteamericano," *Catequesis latinoamericana* 4, no. 14 (1972): 83–86; Elizondo, *Anthropological*

and Psychological Characteristics of the Mexican American (San Antonio: Mexican American Cultural Center, 1974); Elizondo, *Christianity and Culture: An Introduction to Pastoral Theology and Ministry for the Bicultural Community* (Huntington, Ind.: Our Sunday Visitor, 1975); Elizondo, *Mestizaje: The Dialectic of Birth and Gospel* (San Antonio: Mexican American Cultural Center, 1978); Elizondo, *La Morenita: Evangelizer of the Americas* (San Antonio: Mexican American Cultural Center, 1980); Elizondo, *Galilean Journey: The Mexican-American Promise* (Maryknoll, N.Y.: Orbis Books, 1983 [1994]); Gustavo Gutiérrez, *Teología de la Liberación* (Lima: CEP, 1971); Gutiérrez, *A Theology of Liberation: History, Politics and Salvation* (Maryknoll, N.Y.: Orbis Books, 1973); Enrique Dussel, *A History of the Church in Latin America: Colonialism to Liberation (1492–1979)*, trans. Alan Neely (Grand Rapids, Mich.: Wm. B. Eerdmans Publishing Company, 1981); Dussel, ed., *The Church in Latin America, 1492–1992* (New York: Orbis Books, 1992).

2. See above works by Elizondo and Dussel; Juan Romero and Moises Sandoval, *Reluctant Dawn: Historia del Padre A. J. Martínez, Cura de Taos* (San Antonio: Mexican American Cultural Center, 1976); Moises Sandoval, ed., *Fronteras: A History of the Latin American Church in the USA since 1513* (San Antonio: Mexican American Cultural Center, 1983); Sandoval, *On the Move: A History of the Hispanic Church in the United States* (Maryknoll, N.Y.: Orbis Books, 1991); Juan Hurtado, *An Attitudinal Study of Social Distance between the Mexican American and the Church* (San Antonio: Mexican American Cultural Center, 1975); Patrick McNamara, "Dynamics of the Catholic Church from Pastoral to Social Concerns," in *The Mexican American People: The Nation's Second Largest Minority*, ed. Leo Grebler, Joan Moore, and Ralph C. Guzman (New York: Macmillan Free Press, 1970), 449–85; McNamara, "Catholicism, Assimilation and the Chicano Movement: Los Angeles as a Case Study," in *Chicanos and Native Americans*, ed. Rodolfo O. de la Garza, Z. Anthony Kruszewski, and Tomás A. Arciniega (Englewood Cliffs, N.J.: Prentice Hall, 1973), 124–30; McNamara, "Assumptions, Theories and Methods in the Study of Latino Religion after 25 Years," in *Old Masks, New Faces: Religion and Latino Identities*, ed. Anthony M. Stevens-Arroyo and Gilbert R. Cadena (New York: Bildner Center for Western Hemisphere Studies, 1995), 23–32; Joan Moore, "Protestants and Mexicans," in Grebler, Moore, and Guzman, *The Mexican American People*, 486–512.

3. Gloria Anzaldúa, *Borderlands/La Frontera: The New Mestiza* (San Francisco: Aunt Lute Books, 1987); Andrés G. Guerrero, *A Chicano Theology* (Maryknoll, N.Y.: Orbis Books, 1987); Ada María Isasi-Díaz and Yolanda Tarango, *Hispanic Women: Prophetic Voice in the Church* (Minneapolis: Fortress Press, 1988); Isasi-Díaz, *En La Lucha, In the Struggle: Elaborating a Mujerista Theology* (Minneapolis: Fortress Press, 2004).

4. The three-volume Notre Dame History of Hispanic Catholics in the U.S. series includes Jay P. Dolan and Gilberto Miguel Hinojosa, *Mexican Americans and the Catholic Church, 1900–1965* (Notre Dame, Ind.: University of Notre Dame Press, 1994); Jay P. Dolan and Allan Figueroa Deck, SJ, eds., *Hispanic Catholic*

Culture in the U.S.: Issues and Concerns (Notre Dame, Ind.: University of Notre Dame Press, 1994); Jay P. Dolan and Jaime R. Vidal, eds., *Puerto Rican and Cuban Catholics in the U.S., 1900–1965* (Notre Dame, Ind.: University of Notre Dame Press, 1994). The four-volume Program for the Analysis of Religion Among Latinos (PARAL) series includes Anthony M. Stevens-Arroyo and Ana María Díaz-Stevens, eds., *An Enduring Flame: Studies on Latino Popular Religiosity* (New York: Bildner Center for Western Hemisphere Studies, 1994); Stevens-Arroyo and Cadena, *Old Masks, New Faces*; Stevens-Arroyo and Andrés I. Pérez y Mena, eds., *Enigmatic Powers: Syncretism with African and Indigenous Peoples' Religions among Latinos* (New York: Bildner Center for Western Hemisphere Studies, 1995); Stevens-Arroyo with Segundo Pantoja, eds., *Discovering Latino Religion: A Comprehensive Social Science Bibliography* (New York: Bildner Center for Western Hemisphere Studies, 1995).

5. In addition to the previously cited work, see R. Douglas Brackenridge and Francisco O. García-Treto, *Iglesia Presbiteriana: A History of Presbyterians and Mexican Americans in the Southwest* (San Antonio: University of Texas Press, 1987); Jeanette Rodriguez, *Our Lady of Guadalupe: Faith and Empowerment among Mexican-American Women* (Austin: University of Texas Press, 1994); Claudia Madsen, *A Study of Change in Mexican Folk Medicine* (New Orleans: Tulane University Middle American Research Institute, 1965); William and Claudia Madsen, *A Guide to Mexican Witchcraft* (Claremont, Calif.: Ocelot Press, 1977); Ari Kiev, *Curanderismo: Mexican-American Folk Psychiatry* (New York: Free Press, 1968); Ada Isasi-Díaz and Tarango, *Hispanic Women*; Davíd Carrasco, *Quetzalcoatl and the Irony of Empire: Myths and Prophecies in the Aztec Tradition* (Chicago: University of Chicago Press, 1982); Carrasco, "A Perspective for the Study of Religious Dimensions in Chicano Experience: *Bless Me, Ultima* as a Religious Text," *Aztlán: A Journal of Chicano Studies* 13 nos. 1 and 2 (1982): 195–221; Carrasco, *Religions of Mesoamerica: Cosmovision and Ceremonial Centers* (San Francisco: HarperSanFrancisco, 1990); Carrasco, "The Myth of the Chicano Borderlands: Shamanism and the Loco-Centric Imagination in the Work of Gloria Anzaldúa and Dr. Loco," an earlier draft of Carrasco's and Sagarena's essay (chapter 9) in this volume; Carrasco, "'Cuando Dios y Usted Quiere': Latinos Studies between Religious Powers and Social Thought," in *Blackwell Reader on Latino Studies*, ed. Juan Flores and Renato Rosaldo (Oxford: Blackwell Publishers, 2007); Luis León, *La Llorona's Children: Religion, Life, and Death in the U.S.-Mexican Borderlands* (Berkeley, Calif.: University of California Press, 2004).

6. Rudy V. Busto, *King Tiger: The Religious Vision of Reies López Tijerina* (Albuquerque: University of New Mexico Press, 2005); María Pilar Aquino, "Perspectives on Latina's Feminist Liberation Theology," in *Frontiers of Hispanic Theology in the United States*, ed. Allan Figueroa Deck (Maryknoll, N.Y.: Orbis Books, 1992); María Pilar Aquino, "Directions and Foundations of Hispanic/ Latino Theology: Toward a Mestiza Theology of Liberation," *Journal of Hispanic/Latino Theology* 1, no. 1 (1993): 5–21.

7. For example, see the above-cited work of León and Busto.

8. Denominational and religiously affiliated institutions are often not bound by the Supreme Court decision on the separation of church and state and are thus free to follow any methodology they desire. I do not use *secular* and *atheistic* interchangeably. A person can take a secular social-science approach to the study of Mexican American and U.S. Latino religions and at the same time be a devout practitioner of a particular religion in his or her private or nonacademic public life. By "nepantla-based" I mean a methodological position that seeks to be in the balanced middle and that serves as a bridge between different methodologies and ideological perspectives. *Nepantla* is an Aztec Nahuatl term that means to be in the middle or in between. When the Spanish padres asked why the Aztecs did not renounce their religion and culture and convert exclusively to Catholicism and Spanish culture during the spiritual conquest of Mexico in the early 1500s, the Aztecs responded with the metaphor that they were nepantla or in the middle. They stated that they would answer exclusively neither to one faith nor the other, and that they were going to embrace aspects of Spanish culture while at the same time retaining some of their ancient customs, values, and traditions. This middle or in-between status can also be applied to a sociopolitical location. This nepantla location is not a stage en route to another position. In short, many Mexican American mestizos are nepantla. In many respects, Latinos represent a nepantla community—racially, socioculturally, politically, and religiously—in that they accommodate and resist certain aspects of U.S. culture, while at the same time retaining some aspects of their Latin American heritage and worldview. Furthermore, they also tend to share similar attitudes with whites and especially with Blacks on certain political, economic, moral, social, and cultural issues and values. For the original use of the term *nepantla*, see the work of Miguel León-Portillo, *Broken Spears: The Aztec Account of the Conquest of Mexico* (Boston: Beacon Press, 1992).

9. In addition to the above-cited works, see Paul Barton and David Maldonado Jr., *Hispanic Christianity within Mainline Protestant Traditions: A Bibliography* (Decatur, Ga.: AETH [*Asociación para la Educación Teológica Hispana*], 1998); Justo L. González, "Characteristics of Latino Protestant Theology"; and Daisy Machado, "The Writing of Religious History in the United States: A Critical Assessment," in Barton and Maldonado, *Hispanic Christianity within Mainline Protestant Traditions*, 11–13, 83–86.

10. Alex M. Saragoza. "Recent Chicano Historiography: An Interpretive Essay," *Aztlán: A Journal of Chicano Studies* 19, no. 1 (1999): 1–77; Aquino, "Directions and Foundations of Hispanic/Latino Theology"; Lara Medina, "Broadening the Discourse at the Theological Table: An Overview of Latino Theology 1968–1993," *Latino Studies Journal* 5, no. 3 (September 1993): 10–36; Eduardo Fernández, *La Cosecha: Harvesting Contemporary United States Hispanic Theology (1968–1998)* (Collegeville, Minn.: Michael Glazier Books, 2000); Miguel de la Torre and Edwin Aponte, *Introducing Latino/a Theologies* (Maryknoll, N.Y.: Orbis Books, 2001); Miguel H. Díaz, *On Being Human: U.S. Hispanic and Rahnerian Perspectives* (Maryknoll, N.Y.: Orbis Books, 2001).

11. For a discussion of some of these key themes, movements, and leaders, see Sandoval, *Fronteras*; Gastón Espinosa, Virgilio Elizondo, and Jesse Miranda, eds., *Latino Religions and Civic Activism in the United States* (New York: Oxford University Press, 2005).

12. ArriveNet Politics Press Release, "Census Bureau: Hispanic Population Passes 40 Million; Number of Elementary School-Age Children in Nation Totaled 36.4 Million," 9 June 2005; 2004 U.S. Census Bureau, available at http://press.arrivenet.com/pol/article.php/650602.html and http://www.census.gov/popest/.

13. Sandoval, *Fronteras*; Ramón A. Gutiérrez, *When Jesus Came, the Corn Mothers Went Away: Marriage, Sexuality, and Power in New Mexico, 1500–1846* (Stanford, Calif.: Stanford University Press, 1991).

14. John E. Kienle, "Housing Conditions among the Mexican Population of Los Angeles" (MA thesis, University of Southern California, Los Angeles, 1912); William M. McEuen, "A Survey of the Mexicans in Los Angeles" (MA thesis, University of Southern California, Los Angeles, 1914); Alice Bessie Culp, "A Case Study of the Living Conditions of Thirty-five Mexican Families of Los Angeles with Special Reference to Mexican Children" (MA thesis, University of Southern California, Los Angeles, 1921); Evangeline Hymer, "A Study of the Social Attitudes of Adult Mexican Immigrants in Los Angeles and Vicinity" (MA thesis, University of Southern California, Los Angeles, 1923).

15. Bromley G. Oxnam, "The Mexican in Los Angeles from the Standpoint of Religious Forces of the City," *Annals of the American Academy* 93 (1921): 130–33.

16. Aurelio M. Espinosa, "Spanish Folk-lore in New Mexico," *New Mexico Historical Review* 1 (1926): 135–55; Aurelio M. Espinosa, *España en Nuevo Méjico* (New York: Allyn and Bacon, 1937); France V. Scholes, "Documents for the History of New Mexican Missions in the Seventeenth Century," *New Mexico Historical Review* 4 (1929): 195–99; Scholes, "The First Decade of the Inquisition in New Mexico," *New Mexico Historical Review* 10 (1935): 195–241; Scholes, "Church and State in New Mexico, 1610–1650," *New Mexico Historical Review* 11 (1936): 9–76 and (1940): 78–106; Scholes, *Troublous Times in New Mexico, 1659–1670* (Albuquerque: University of New Mexico Press, 1942); B. A. Hodges, *A History of Mexican Mission Work Conducted in Synod of Texas* (Waxahachie, Tex.: n.p., 1931); Lucero-White, "Los Pastores de Las Vegas" (MA thesis, New Mexico Normal University, Las Vegas, 1932); Lucero-White, *The Folklore of New Mexico* (Santa Fe, New Mexico: Seton Village Press, 1947); Geary J. Gerald, *The Secularization of the California Missions* (Washington, D.C.: Catholic University of America, 1934); Una Roberts Lawrence, *Winning the Border: Baptist Missions among the Spanish-Speaking Peoples of the Border* (Atlanta, Ga.: Home Mission Board, Southern Baptist Convention, 1935); Manuel J. Espinosa, "The Virgin of the Reconquest of New Mexico," *Mid-America* 18 (1936): 79–87; Yong Hak Park, "A Study of the Methodist Mexican Mission in Dallas," MA thesis, Southern Methodist University, Dallas, 1936; Charles W. Hackett, *Revolt of the Pueblo Indians of New Mexico and Otermín's Attempted Reconquest, 1680–1682*, 2 vols.

(Albuquerque: University of New Mexico Press, 1942); Inez Tatum, "Mexican Missions in Texas" (MA thesis, Baylor University, Waco, Tex., 1939); Arthur L. Campa, *Spanish Religious Folktheatre in the Southwest* (Albuquerque: University of New Mexico Press, 1943); Angélico Chávez, *The Old Faith and Old Glory: Story of the Church in New Mexico since the American Occupation, 1846–1946* (Santa Fe, N. Mex.: privately printed, 1946); Angélico Chávez, *Our Lady of the Conquest* (Albuquerque: Historical Society of New Mexico, 1948).

17. Manuel Gamio, *Mexican Immigration to the United States: A Study of Human Migration and Adjustment* (Chicago: University of Chicago Press, 1930; repr. Dover Publications, 1971); Gamio, *The Mexican Immigrant: His Life-Story* (Chicago: University of Chicago Press, 1931; repr. Dover Publications, 1971). Gamio made specific references (1930 [1971]) to Protestants (55, 195–207, 201–207, 264), Spiritualism (p. 197), witchcraft (25, 46, 78, 85, 232), and satanic witches (78), and general references to religion through his first book (288).

18. Robert C. Jones, *The Religious Life of the Mexican in Chicago*, self-published report, Chicago, 1929; Robert C. Jones and Louis R. Wilson, *The Mexican in Chicago* (Chicago: Comity Commission of the Chicago Church Federation, 1931).

19. Samuel M. Ortegón, "Mexican Religious Population of Los Angeles" (MA thesis, University of Southern California, Los Angeles, 1932); Ortegón, "Religious Thought and Practice among Mexican Baptists of the United States, 1900–1947" (PhD diss., University of Southern California, Los Angeles, 1950).

20. Rodolfo Acuña, *Occupied America: A History of Chicanos* (San Francisco: Canfield Press, 1972), 151; Mario T. García, *Desert Immigrants: Mexicans and the Making of El Paso* (New Haven, Conn.: Yale University Press, 1981), 306; Ricardo Romo, *East Los Angeles: History of a Barrio* (Austin: University of Texas Press, 1983), 215; Sandoval, *Fronteras*, 237, 253, 266; Mario T. García, *Mexican Americans: Leadership, Ideology, and Identity, 1930–1960* (New Haven, Conn.: Yale University Press, 1989), 356; George Sánchez, *Becoming Mexican American: Ethnicity, Culture and Identity in Chicano Los Angeles, 1900–1945* (New York: Oxford University Press, 1993), 356; Dolan and Hinojosa, *Mexican Americans and the Catholic Church*, 368; David G. Gutiérrez, *Walls and Mirrors: Mexican Americans, Mexican Immigrants, and the Politics of Ethnicity* (Berkeley: University of California Press, 1995), 313.

21. Lela Weatherby, "A Study of the Early Years of the Presbyterian Work with the Spanish Speaking People of New Mexico and Colorado and Its Development from 1850–1920" (MA thesis, Presbyterian College of Christian Education, 1942); National Catholic Welfare Conference, *The Spanish-Speaking of the Southwest and West* (Washington, D.C.: National Catholic Welfare Conference, 1943); Abraham Fernández, "History of the Presbyterian Church, U.S.A. among the Spanish-Speaking People of the Southwest" (BD thesis., San Francisco Theological Seminary, 1943); Angélico Chávez, *The Old Faith and Old Glory*; Angelico Chávez, *Our Lady of the Conquest*; Pauline R. Kibbe, *Latin Americans in Texas* (Albuquerque: University of New Mexico, 1946); Beatrice Griffith, *American Me* (Boston: Houghton Mifflin Company, 1947).

22. Joshua Grijalva and Dorothy Grijalva, *Heirs of the Soil* (Atlanta: Home Mission Board, Southern Baptist Convention, 1950); David C. Harrison, "A Survey of the Administrative and Educational Policies of the Baptist, Methodist, and Presbyterian Churches among Mexican American People in Texas" (MA thesis, University of Texas, Austin, 1952); Albeus Walsh, "The Work of Catholics Bishops' Committee for the Spanish-Speaking in the United States" (MA thesis, University of Texas, Austin, 1958); David H. Stratton, "A History of Northern and Southern Baptists of New Mexico 1849–1950" (MA thesis, University of Colorado, 1953); Isidro Garza, "The Development of the Southern Baptist Spanish Speaking Work in California" (PhD diss., Golden Gate Baptist Theological Seminary, San Francisco, 1954); John Burma, *Spanish-Speaking Groups in the United States* (Durham, N.C.: Duke University Press, 1954); Ernest Stapleton, "The History of the Baptist Missions in New Mexico, 1849–1866" (MA thesis, University of New Mexico, Albuquerque, 1954); Rosemary E. Smith, "The Work of Bishops' Committee for the Spanish-Speaking on Behalf of the Migrant Worker" (MA thesis, Catholic University of America, Washington, D.C., 1958); Delbert Lee Gibson, "Protestantism in Latin American Acculturation" (PhD diss., University of Texas, Austin, 1959).

23. Ortegón, Religious Thought and Practice among Mexican Baptists of the United States; Carlos Eduardo Castañeda, *Our Catholic Heritage in Texas, 1519–1950*, 7 vols. (Austin, Tex.: Von Boekmann-Jones, 1936–58).

24. For example, see above-cited McNamara, "Dynamics of the Catholic Church from Pastoral to Social Concerns"; Moore, "Protestants and Mexicans"; Sandoval, *Fronteras*, 168, 194, 237; Mario T. García, *Mexican Americans*, 356; Dolan and Hinojosa, *Mexican Americans and the Catholic Church*, 363.

25. Mario T. García, *Mexican Americans*, 13–22.

26. Espinosa, Elizondo, and Miranda, *Latino Religions and Civic Activism in the United States*, 8–9, 35–64; Frederick John Dalton, *The Moral Vision of César Chávez* (Maryknoll, N.Y.: Orbis Books, 2003).

27. César Chávez, "The Mexican American and the Church," *El Grito del Sol* 1, no. 4 (summer 1968): 9–12.

28. Acuña, *Occupied America*; Octavio I. Romano, *Voices: Readings from El Grito* (Berkeley, Calif.: Quinto Sol, 1973); Brackenridge and García-Treto, *Iglesia Presbiteriana*; Elizondo, *Christianity and Culture*; Elizondo, *La Morenita*; Hurtado, *An Attitudinal Study of Social Distance between the Mexican American and the Church*; Antonio Soto, *The Chicano and the Church: Study of a Minority within a Religious Institution* (Denver: Marfel Associates, 1975); Sandoval, *Fronteras*; Sandoval, *On the Move*; Stevens-Arroyo and Díaz-Stevens, *An Enduring Flame*; Díaz-Stevens and Stevens-Arroyo, *Recognizing the Latino Resurgence in U.S. Religion: The Emmaus Paradigm* (Boulder, Colo.: Westview Press, 1998); Andrés Guerrero, *A Chicano Theology*; Dolan and Hinojosa, *Mexican Americans and the Catholic Church, 1900–1965*.

29. See Espinosa, Elizondo, and Miranda, *Latino Religions and Civic Activism in the United States*.

30. See Busto, *King Tiger*; Busto in Espinosa, Elizondo, and Miranda, *Latino Religions and Civic Activism in the United* States, 65–75.

31. Espinosa, Elizondo, and Miranda, *Latino Religions and Civic Activism in the United States*; F. Arturo Rosales, *¡Chicano! The History of the Mexican American Civil Rights Movement* (Houston: Arte Público Press, 1997).

32. Acuña, *Occupied America*, iii, 1–5; Paulo Freire, *Pedagogy of the Oppressed, New Revised 20th-Anniversary Edition*, trans. Myra Bergman Ramos (New York: Continuum Books, 1972 [1994]).

33. Juan Gómez-Quiñones, "On Culture," *Revista Chicano-Riquena*, 5, no. 2 (1977): 29, 33, 35, 39; George Sánchez, *Becoming Mexican American*, 6.

34. Mario Barrera, Carlos Muñoz, and Charles Ornelas, "The Barrio as an Internal Colony," in *La Causa Política: A Chicano Politics Reader*, ed. F. Chris García (Notre Dame, Ind.: University of Notre Dame Press, 1972 and 1974); Mario Barrera, *Race and Class in the Southwest: A Theory of Racial Inequality* (Notre Dame, Ind.: University of Notre Dame Press, 1979); Díaz-Stevens and Stevens-Arroyo, *Recognizing the Latino Resurgence in U.S. Religion*.

35. Saragoza, "Recent Chicano Historiography," 5, 8–11.

36. Enrique Dussel, *Método para una filosofía de la liberación: Superación analéctica de la dialéctica hegeliana* (Salamanca, Spain: Ediciones Sígueme, 1974); Dussel, *A History of the Church in Latin America: Colonialism to Liberation* (1981); Dussel, *The Church in Latin America, 1492–1992* (1992). See especially Dussel (1981), 244–47; Dussel (1992), 391–96.

37. Dussel, *A History of the Church in Latin America* (1981), 327.

38. Dussel, *The Church in Latin America* (1992), 1–2.

39. Rubem Alves, *A Theology of Human Hope* (Washington, D.C.: Corpus, 1969); Hugo Assmann, *Teología desde la praxis de liberación: Ensayo teológico desde América Latina dependiente* (Salamanca, Spain: Sígueme, 1973); Assmann, *A Theology for a Nomad Church*, trans. Paul Burns (Maryknoll, N.Y.: Orbis Books, 1975); Leonardo Boff and Clodovis Boff, *Introducing Liberation Theology* (Maryknoll, N.Y.: Orbis Books, 1987); Juan Luis Segundo, *The Liberation of Theology*, trans. John Drury (Maryknoll, N.Y.: Orbis Books, 1976); Jon Sobrino, *Christology at the Crossroads: A Latin American Approach*, trans. John Drury (Maryknoll, N.Y.: Orbis Books, 1978); Jon Sobrino and Juan Hernández Pico, *Theology of Christian Solidarity*, trans. Philip Berryman (Maryknoll, N.Y.: Orbis Books, 1985); José Míguez Bonino, *Doing Theology in a Revolutionary Situation* (Philadelphia: Fortress Press, 1975).

40. Gutiérrez, *A Theology of Liberation*; Boff and Boff, *Introducing Liberation Theology*, 28; Humberto Belli and Ronald Nash, *Beyond Liberation Theology* (Grand Rapids, Mich.: Baker Book House, 1992).

41. Dussel, *A History of the Church in Latin America* (1981), 293–333.

42. Sandoval, *Fronteras*, vii.

43. As cited in Elizondo's introduction to Sandoval's *Fronteras*, xi–xiv.

44. Virgilio Elizondo and Alan Oddie, "San Antonio International Study Week of Mass Media and Catechetics: A Report," *Living Light* 6 (winter 1969): 67–74; Virgilio Elizondo, "Crisis of Our Times," *Good Tidings* 9 (July–August

1970): 83–90; Virgilio Elizondo, *A Search for Meaning in Life and Death* (Manila: East Asian Pastoral Institute, 1971). This was subsequently published as *The Human Quest: A Search for Meaning through Life and Death* (Huntington, Ind.: Our Sunday Visitor, 1978), and in Spanish as *Hombre quién eres tú? El enigma del hombre en el tiempo y en el más allá* (Mexico City: Instituto de Pastoral Catequé-tico, 1971); Virgilio Elizondo, "Educación religiosa para el méxico-norteameri-cano," *Catequesis latinoamericana* 4, 14 (January–March 1972): 83–86; Elizondo, *Anthropological and Psychological Characteristics of the Mexican American* (San Antonio: Mexican American Cultural Center, 1974); Elizondo, *Religious Prac-tices of the Mexican American and Catechesis* (San Antonio: Mexican American Cultural Center, 1974); Elizondo, *Christianity and Culture*; Elizondo, "A Cat-echetical Response for Minorities," in *Colección Mestiza Americana* (San Anto-nio: Mexican American Cultural Center, 1975), 92–109; Elizondo, "A Challenge to Theology: The Situation of Hispanic Americans," *Catholic Theological Society of America Proceedings* 30 (1975): 163–76; Elizondo, "Theological Interpretation of the Mexican American Experience," *Perkins School of Theology Journal* 29 (fall 1975): 12–21; Virgilio Elizondo, "Politics, Catechetics, and Liturgy," *Religion Teacher's Journal* 10 (November–December 1976): 30–32.

45. This discussion of Elizondo's intellectual, cultural, and theological influ-ences, along with the quotation, is based on the author's e-mail correspondence with Virgilio Elizondo, September 2005.

46. Medina, "Broadening the Discourse at the Theological Table," 13; Espi-nosa, Elizondo, and Miranda, *Latino Religions and Civic Activism in the United States*, 88.

47. As cited in Elizondo's introduction to Sandoval's *Fronteras*, xiii.

48. Andrés Guerrero, *A Chicano Theology*, 166–81.

49. Ibid., 156–65.

50. Isasi-Díaz and Tarango, *Hispanic Women*, 116–23.

51. Aquino, "Perspectives on Latina's Feminist Liberation Theology"; Aquino, "Directions and Foundations of Hispanic/Latino Theology," 5–21; Aquino, "Latin American Feminist Theology," *Journal of Feminist Studies in Religion* 14 (spring 1998): 94; Aquino, Daisy L. Machado, and Jeanette Rodríguez, "Intro-duction," in *Religion and Justice: A Reader in Latina Feminist Theology* (Austin: University of Texas Press, 2002), 138–39.

52. Vicki Ruiz, *From out of the Shadows: Mexican Women in Twentieth-Century America* (New York: Oxford University Press, 1998).

53. Loida Martell-Ortero, "Women Doing Theology: Una Perspectiva Evan-gélica," *Apuntes* 14 (1994): 67–85; Pilar Aquino, Machado, and Rodríguez, "In-troduction."

54. Gastón Espinosa, "'Your Daughters Shall Prophesy': A History of Women in Ministry in the Latino Pentecostal Movement in the United States," in *Women and Twentieth-Century Protestantism*, ed. Margaret Lamberts Bendroth and Virginia Lieson Brereton (Chicago: University of Illinois Press, 2002), 25–48; Arlene M. Sánchez-Walsh, *Latino Pentecostal Identity: Evangelical Faith, Self, and Society* (New York: Columbia University Press, 2003); Elizabeth Ríos,

"'The Ladies are Warriors': Latina Pentecostalism and Faith-Based Activism in New York City," in Espinosa, Elizondo, and Miranda, *Latino Religions and Civic Activism in the United States*, 197–217.

55. Espinosa, cited in Espinosa, Elizondo, and Miranda, *Latino Religions and Civic Activism in the United States*, 298–300.

56. Gastón Espinosa, "'Your Daughters Shall Prophesy,'" 25–48.

57. Ibid., 24–48; Gastón Espinosa, Virgilio Elizondo, and Jesse Miranda, *Hispanic Churches in American Public Life: Summary of Findings* (Notre Dame, Ind.: Institute for Latino Studies, University of Notre Dame, 2003), 28; Sánchez-Walsh, *Latino Pentecostal Identity*, 125.

58. Milagros Peña (sociologist), Daisy Machado (historian), Elizabeth Conde-Frazier (theologian and Christian educator), and María Elena González, RSM (Religious Order of the Sisters of Mercy) (theologian) served on the advisory board and helped shape the framework, language, and questions on the Hispanic Churches in American Public Life National Survey instrument.

59. Gastón Espinosa, "Changements démographiques et religieux chez les hispaniques des Etats-Unis," *Social Compass: International Review of Sociology of Religion* 51 (2004): 303–20; Gastón Espinosa, "The Pentecostalization of Latin American and U.S. Latino Christianity," *Pneuma: The Journal of the Society for Pentecostal Studies* 26, no. 2 (fall 2004): 262–92; Espinosa, Elizondo, and Miranda, *Latino Religions and Civic Activism in the United States*, 6.

60. McNamara, "Dynamics of the Catholic Church from Pastoral to Social Concerns," 450.

61. McNamara, "Assumptions, Theories and Methods in the Study of Latino Religion after 25 Years," 25.

62. Ibid., 27.

63. Ibid., 25.

64. Jones, *The Religious Life of the Mexican in Chicago*; Gamio, *The Mexican Immigrant*, 78–81, 197; Ruth Dodson, *Tone the Bell Easy* (Dallas: Southern Methodist University, 1932); Dodson, *The Healer of Los Olmos* (Austin: Texas Folklore Society, 1951); Norman McNeil, *Curanderos of South Texas and Horns on the Toads* (Dallas: Southern Methodist University, 1959); Claudia Madsen, *A Study of Change in Mexican Folk Medicine*; William and Claudia Madsen, *A Guide to Mexican Witchcraft*; Kiev, *Curanderismo*.

65. Juan Castañon García, "Healer Roles, Society and Healing Efficacy: An Anthropological Essay," *El Grito del Sol* 4, no. 1 (winter, 1979): 80–82; June Macklin, "Curanderismo and Espiritismo: Complementary Approaches to Traditional Health Services," in *The Chicano Experience*, ed. Stanley A. West and June Macklin (Boulder, Colo.: Westview Press, 1979); Marc Simmons, *Witchcraft in the Southwest: Spanish and Indian Supernaturalism on the Rio Grande* (Lincoln: University of Nebraska Press, 1980); Robert T. Trotter II and Juan Antonio Chavira, *Curanderismo: Mexican American Folk Healing* (Athens: University of Georgia Press, 1981); Beatrice A. Roeder, *Chicano Folk Medicine from Los Angeles, California* (Berkeley: University of California Press, 1988); Carrasco, "A Perspective for the Study of Religious Dimensions in Chicano Experience";

Carrasco, *Religions of Mesoamerica*; Luis León, "'Soy una Curandera y Soy una Católica': Poetics of a Mexican Healing Tradition," in *Horizons of the Sacred: Mexican Traditions in U.S. Catholicism*, ed. Timothy Matovina and Gary Riebe-Stressa, SVD (Society of Divine Word) (Ithaca, N.Y.: Cornell University Press, 2002); Luis León, *La Llorona's Children*; Gastón Espinosa, "Changements démographiques et religieux chez les hispaniques des Etats-Unis"; Gastón Espinosa, "The Pentecostalization of Latin American and U.S. Latino Christianity"; Gastón Espinosa, "'God Made a Miracle in My Life': Latino Pentecostal Healing in the Borderlands," in *Religion and Healing in America*, ed. Linda L. Barnes and Susan S. Sered (New York: Oxford University Press, 2005), 123–38; Lara Medina, "Communing with the Dead: Spiritual and Cultural Healing in Chicano/a Communities," in Barnes and Sered, *Religion and Healing in America*, 205–15; Inés Hernández-Avila, "La Mesa del Santo Niño de Atocha and the Conchero Dance Tradition of Mexico-Tenochtilán: Religious Healing in Urban Mexico and the United States," in Barnes and Sered, *Religion and Healing in America*, 359–74.

66. Ortegón, "Mexican Religious Population of Los Angeles," 15, 40–44, 50; Moore, "Protestants and Mexicans," 505–7; Gastón Espinosa, "The Impact of Pluralism on Trends in Latin American and U.S. Latino Religions and Society," *Perspectives: Occasional Papers*, no. 7 (fall 2003): 33–35; Espinosa "Changements démographiques et religieux chez les hispaniques des Etats-Unis"; Espinosa, Elizondo, and Miranda, *Latino Religions and Civic Activism in the United States*, 282–302.

67. Adam Morales, *American Baptists with a Spanish Accent* (Los Angeles: Judson Press, 1964); Jorge Lara-Braud, "Our Spanish-American Neighbors," *Christian Century* 85, no. 2: (1968): 43–45; José Moreno Fernández, "The History and Prospects of Hispanic Methodism in the Southern California–Arizona Conference of the United Methodist Church" (PhD diss., Claremont School of Theology, 1973); Ruben Reyes, "Prolegomena to Chicano Theology," DM in project, Claremont School of Theology, Claremont Calif., 1974; Clifton J. Holland, *The Religious Dimension of Hispanic Los Angeles: A Protestant Case Study* (South Pasadena, Calif.: William Carey Library, 1974); Leo D. Nieto, "The Chicano Movement and the Churches in the United States," *Perkins Journal* 29, no. 1 (1975): 32–41; Alfredo Nañez, *History of the Rio Grande Conference of the United Methodist Church* (Dallas: Bridwell Library, Southern Methodist University, 1980); Ernest E. Atkinson, *A Selected Bibliography of Hispanic Baptist History* (Nashville: Historical Commission, Southern Baptist Convention, 1981); Joshua Grijalva, *A History of Mexican Baptists in Texas 1881–1981* (Dallas: Office of Language Mission, Baptist General Convention of Texas in cooperation with the Mexican Baptist Convention of Texas, 1982); Joshua Grijalva, "The Story of Hispanic Southern Baptists," *Baptist History and Heritage* 18, no. 1 (1983): 40–47; Edwin E. Sylvest Jr., "The Hispanic American Church: Contextual Considerations," *Perkins Journal* 29, no. 1 (1975): 22–31; Edwin E. Sylvest, "Hispanic American Protestantism in the United States," in Sandoval, *Fronteras*, 279–338; Jane Atkins-Vasquez, ed., *Hispanic Presbyterians in Southern California: One Hundred*

Years of Ministry (Los Angeles: Hispanic Commission, Synod of Southern California and Hawaii, 1988).

68. Ernesto S. Cantú and José Ortega, *Historia de la Asamblea Apostólica de la Fe en Cristo Jesús* (Mentone, Calif.: Sal's Printing Press, 1966); Elias Gabriel Galvan, "A Study of the Spanish-Speaking Protestant Church and Her Mission to the Mexican American Minority" (PhD diss., Claremont School of Theology, Claremont, Calif.,1969); Victor DeLeón, *The Silent Pentecostals* (Taylors, S.C.: Faith Printing Company, 1979); A. C. Valdez with James F. Scheer, *Fire on Azusa Street* (Costa Mesa, Calif.: Gift Publications, 1980); Miguel Guillén, *La Historia del Concilio Latino Americano de Iglesias Cristianas* (Brownsville, Tex.: Latin American Council of Christian Churches, 1982); Nellie Bazán with Elizabeth B. and Don Martínez Jr., *Enviados de Dios: Demetrio and Nellie Bazán* (Miami, Fla.: Editorial Vida, 1987); Josue Sánchez, *Angels without Wings: The Hispanic Assemblies of God Story* (New Braunfels, Tex.: Atwood Printing, n.d.); José Vicente Rojas, *José Vicente Rojas: God Found Me in Los Angeles* (Hagerstown, Md.: Review and Herald Publishing Association, 1999).

69. See Saragoza, "Recent Chicano Historiography."

70. García, *Desert Immigrants*, 231.

71. Sánchez, *Becoming Mexican American*, 8.

72. Carlos Castañeda, *The Teachings of Don Juan: A Yaqui Way of Knowledge* (Berkeley: University of California Press, 1968 [1998]); Rudolfo A. Anaya, *Bless Me, Ultima* (New York: Warner Books, 1972; repr. Warner Books, 1994); Anzaldúa, *Borderlands/La Frontera*.

73. Angelika Köhler, "The New World Man: Magical Realism in Rudolfo Anaya's *Bless Me, Ultima*," in *U.S. Latino Literatures and Cultures: Transnational Perspectives*, ed. Francisco A. Lomelí and Karin Ikas (Heidelberg, Germany: Universitatsverlag C. Winter, 2000).

74. See previously cited Busto, *King Tiger*, and Busto's essay in Espinosa, Elizondo, and Miranda, *Latino Religions and Civic Activism in the United States*.

75. See Pilar Aquino, Machado, and Rodríguez, "Introduction"; Luis León, *La Llorona's Children*; Busto, *King Tiger*; Laura Pérez, "Spirit Glyphs: Reimagining Art and Artist in the Work of Chicana *Tlamatinime*," *Modern Fiction Studies* 44, no. 1 (spring 1998): 37–76; Laura Pérez, "El Desorden, Nationalism, and Chicana/o Aesthetics," in *Between Woman and Nation: Nationalisms, Transnational Feminisms, and the State*, ed. Caren Kaplan, Norma Alarcón, and Minoo Moallem (Durham, N.C.: Duke University Press, 1999); Ada María Isasi-Díaz, *En la Lucha, In the Struggle*; Isasi-Díaz, *La Lucha Continues: Mujerista Theology* (Maryknoll, N.Y.: Orbis Books, 2004); Carrasco, "'*Cuando Dios y Usted Quiere.*'"

76. This information is based on an e-mail dialogue with Carrasco, September 2005.

77. Carrasco, "'*Cuando Dios y Usted Quiere,*'" 124–57.

78. McNamara, "Dynamics of the Catholic Church from Pastoral to Social Concerns," 450; Stevens-Arroyo and Díaz Stevens, *An Enduring Flame*, 9–36.

79. Carrasco, "'*Cuando Dios y Usted Quiere,*'" 60–76.

80. Wiebe, *The Politics of Religious Studies: The Continuing Conflict with Theology in the Academy* (New York: St. Martin's Press, 1999), 31–50.

81. Kathryn Alexander argues that the *Schempp* decision "altered the total picture of the study of religion in America by introducing the language which has governed its subsequent development in secular public colleges and universities." Donald Wiebe further noted: "The distinction it [*Schempp*] introduced into the field was that between the teaching *of* religion and the teaching *about* religion, with the former being excluded from public institutions by the Constitution, and it opened a window for the inclusion of the academic study of religions in the curriculum of the modern public university" (emphasis in original). Alexander and Wiebe, cited in Wiebe, *The Politics of Religious Studies*, 86, 107, 110, 297; Eric Sharpe, *Comparative Religion: A History* (Peru, Ill.: Open Court, 1994); Walter Capps, *Religious Studies: The Making of a Discipline* (Minneapolis: Fortress Press, 1995).

82. Sharpe, *Comparative Religion*; Capps, *Religious Studies*; Wiebe, *The Politics of Religious Studies*. William E. Paden, "A New Comparativism: Reply to Panelists," *Method and Theory in the Study of Religion* B-1 (1996): 37–49.

83. Mircea Eliade, *The Quest: History and Meaning in Religion* (Chicago: University of Chicago Press, 1984), preface, 4, 7–9.

84. Wiebe, *The Politics of Religious Studies*, 59–61, 100–101; Richard Hedit, "Eliade and the History of Religion," lecture delivered at Santa Barbara, Calif., Winter 1995.

85. Ibid., 59–61, 100–101; Jonathan Z. Smith, *Imagining Religion: From Babylon to Jonestown* (Chicago: University of Chicago Press, 1988), xi, xii.

86. Sandoval, *Fronteras*; Sandoval, *On the Move*; Justo L. González, ed., *Each in Our Own Tongue: A History of Hispanic United Methodism* (Nashville: Abingdon Press, 1991); Elizondo, *Galilean Journey*; Elizondo and Timothy M. Matovina, *Mestizo Worship: A Pastoral Approach to Liturgical Ministry* (Collegeville, Minn.: Liturgical Press, 1998); Elizondo, *Beyond Borders: Writings of Virgilio Elizondo and Friends*, ed. Timothy Matovina (Maryknoll, N.Y.: Orbis Books, 2000); Allan Figueroa Deck, *The Second Wave: Hispanic Ministry and the Evangelization of Culture* (New York: Paulist Press, 1989); Jeanette Rodriguez, *Our Lady of Guadalupe*; Daniel R. Rodríguez-Díaz and David Cortés-Fuentes, *Hidden Stories: Unveiling the History of the Latino Church* (Decatur, Ga.: AETH [Asociación para la Educación Teológica Hispana], 1994); Roberto Goizueta, *Caminemos con Jesús: Toward a Hispanic/Latino Theology of Accompaniment* (Maryknoll, N.Y.: Orbis Books, 1995); Timothy Matovina, *Tejano Religion and Ethnicity: San Antonio, 1821–1860* (Austin: University of Texas Press, 1995); Timothy Matovina and Gerald E. Poyo, eds., *¡Presente! U.S. Latino Catholics from Colonial Origins to the Present* (Maryknoll, N.Y.: Orbis Books, 2000); Timothy Matovina, *Guadalupe and Her Faithful Latino Catholics in San Antonio, from Colonial Origins to the Present* (Baltimore: Johns Hopkins University Press, 2005); Arturo J. Bañuelas, *Mestizo Christianity: Theology from the Latino Perspective* (Maryknoll, N.Y.: Orbis Books, 1995); José David Rodríguez and Loida I. Martell-Otero, eds., *Teología en Conjunto: A Collaborative Hispanic Protestant Theology* (Louisville,

Ky.: Westminster, 1997); Orlando Espín, "Popular Religion as an Epistemology (of Suffering)," *Journal of Hispanic/Latino Theology* 2, no. 2 (November 1994): 66; Orlando Espín, "Tradition and Popular Religion: An Understanding of the *Sensus Fidelium*," in Bañuelas, *Mestizo Christianity*; Orlando Espín, *The Faith of the People: Theological Reflections on Popular Catholicism* (Maryknoll, N.Y.: Orbis Books, 1997); Orlando Espín, "The State of U.S. Latino/a Theology: An Understanding," *Perspectivas: Occasional Papers*, Hispanic Theological Initiative 3 (fall 2000): 15–55; Orlando Espín and Miguel Díaz, ed., *From the Heart of Our People: Latino/a Explorations in Catholic Systematic Theology* (Maryknoll, N.Y.: Orbis Books, 1999); Alberto Pulido, *The Sacred World of the Penitentes* (Washington, D.C.: Smithsonian Institution Press, 2000); David J. Maldonado, ed., *Protestantes/Protestants: Hispanic Christianity within Mainline Traditions* (Nashville: Abingdon Press, 1999); Eduardo Fernández, *La Cosecha*.

87. In 1994, Gastón Espinosa initiated a discussion with Mario T. García about creating an academic, nonsectarian, noninstitutional yet theologically informed approach to the study of Mexican American and Chicano religions at the University of California, Santa Barbara (UCSB). Over the next two years critical conversation partners who also shared this view were Luis Léon, Alberto Pulido, Richard Hecht, and others. This dialogue led to the UCSB "New Directions in Chicano Religions" conference. The sixteen scholars invited to present original papers were Gastón Espinosa, Mario T. García, Davíd Carrasco, Anthony M. Stevens-Arroyo, Luis Léon, Deborah Baldwin, Ellen McCracken, Lara Medina, Rudy V. Busto, Daniel Ramírez, Alberto Pulido, Daryl Caterine, Allan Figueroa-Deck, Gilbert Cadena, Ines Talamántez, and Alma García. Catherine Albanese, Charles Long, Wade Clark Roof, Phillip Hammond, and Richard Hecht served as the five panel respondents. The UCSB Department of Religious Studies was perhaps the first doctoral-granting university to create a *permanent* course on Chicano/Mexican American Religions (Religions of Aztlán) in a religious studies department in the United States. Luis León, Alberto Pulido, Mary Rojas, Inés Talamántez, Gastón Espinosa, and Rudy V. Busto have all taught courses on Chicano/Latino religions for the UCSB Department of Religious Studies. Busto is presently professor of Chicano/Latino and Asian American Religions at UCSB.

88. See note 8.

89. Ninian Smart, *The Phenomenon of Religion* (London: Macmillan Press, 1973), 31–34, 60; Wiebe, *The Politics of Religious Studies*, 53–67.

ANTHONY M. STEVENS-ARROYO

2

Pious Colonialism

Assessing a Church Paradigm for Chicano Identity

Analysis of religion's role in American minority history reveals major contradictions. On the one hand, religion is part of the oppressive mechanism of state and politics; on the other, it is the wellspring of collective memory and communitarian belonging. I believe these opposing functions can be understood by use of the concept of "pious colonialism" to interpret specifically Chicano and Latino history in the United States. I will not rehearse here the theory of "internal colonialism,"[1] which is the secular soul mate of Pious Colonialism. Let me only stress that both internal and "classical colonialism" have been used against Latinos;[2] and second, that Mario Barrera,[3] who developed internal colonialism in his analysis of the Chicano reality, has not offered much of a description of colonialism within religious institutions and church policies. This means that systematic application of the concept of colonialism to the churches is a relatively new area of investigation.[4]

I believe that a sober assessment of colonialism is a long-overdue step toward a better understanding of Latinos and of their religious expressions. Colonialism has a visible political face: it is the denial of complete democratic rights of citizenship to the people of a region where alien rule has been imposed by force.[5] The United States is not the only country in history to have expanded its borders by imperialist wars, of course. Indeed, the further back one turns the pages of history, the more common this experience. The settlers of Teotihuacán eclipsed the Olmecs in Mesoamerica and then were themselves conquered by the Toltecs, who were later conquered by the Aztecs. This process on the continent differs little from the way the Assyrians conquered the Sumerians and then were later replaced by Persians, who gave way to the Greeks, who were supplanted by the Romans. Examples of colonial subjugations by force can be found in abundance, so the question to be asked is not about the *existence* of colonialism; it is about salience.

What difference does it make to the Irish today that the history of their island mixes conquering waves of Celts, Romans, and Vikings? Have not the particularities of each of these groups been lost in the creation of today's Irish cultural identity? At a certain point, it might be argued, the colonial experience is so far removed from everyday reality as to have lost its salience for social science. But not all colonialisms end with the conquered people merging with the conquerors, and not every nation is today populated by a new people that resulted from the merging of both conqueror and conquered. The same Irish cited in the example above would be likely to have strong opinions about the British invasions, even if they had been indifferent to all the others.

The British, colonizers of the Irish, have also been colonized. The romantic novels of Sir Walter Scott paint for us the pain and the glory of this process of merging that took place in medieval England between Saxon and Norman. A less dramatic side of this tale centers on a host of small struggles over language, symbols, law, and religion. But if the Hollywood image of Ivanhoe dashingly defending damsels in distress and preserving the kingdom is too rosy, television today gives us a harsher reminder that in many countries this merging of populations has encountered failure. The term Balkanization has the pejorative meaning of nation-states that instead of "merging" have been fragmented by ethnic and religious differences.

Are Latinos going to "merge" with the Euro-American population, much as Saxon with Norman in England, so that both groups grow more like each other? If such merging seems quixotic, then is the alternative Balkanization?[6] When Latinos became more numerous than African Americans in 2003,[7] did the cultural and linguistic fault lines that divide Euro-American and Latino change? And what will be the role of religion in the United States in these scenarios?

Although the word *mestizaje*'s biological meaning is primary, with the cultural meshing seen as a side-effect, some Latino theologians use this Spanish term as the equivalent of the social process of merging.[8] In social science circles, *transculturation* has been utilized to emphasize the change on both sides of the cultural equation, and that is my preferred term. First developed through the collaboration of Fernando Ortiz, the Cuban *homme de belles lettres*, and the anthropologist Bronislaw Malinowski, it is our preferred way to speak of a symmetrical exchange between groups. Transculturation describes acquisition of new cultural traits as mutual enrichment, independently of power relations. From the transculturation perspective, common property is common gain. As Malinowski defines it in his introduction to Ortiz's *Cuban Counterpoint*, rather than a "mosaic" or a "conglomeration" it is "an original and independent phenomenon."[9]

Without romanticizing the process of transculturation or overlooking its colonist nature, I believe that transculturation is what took place during Spanish colonialism. It is my premise that upon conquest of the Latino homelands, the United States encountered a people different from both the Amerindian population and the Iberian settlers. During the centuries under Spain, the dynamics of religious traditions gradually forged a new identity for today's Latinos—a successful mestizaje—that created a new people by erasing most of the distinctions between the conquered and the conqueror.

When discussing transculturation—a term more common in European and Latin American scholarship than in U.S.-based studies—certain cautions must be expressed. Transculturation does not undo the pain, the injustice, or the dislocation caused by invasions, such as the Iberian conquest. The superiority of one group's technology—the Spanish had writing, for instance—does not constitute a denial that the other groups also possessed a culture with segments superior to those of the conquerors. Transculturation, in fact, implies some form of successful native resistance to the invasion, because it constitutes the subversion of the hegemonic system. And finally, transculturation usually takes place over long periods of time, because it requires that generations of people have forgotten the particular (and divisive) origins of the tools, concepts, and practices they have adopted. This centuries-long process can be speeded up if the reminders of who is inferior and superior are removed from society, if there is significant intermarriage, if the religion is the same, and so on.[10]

But the relations between Latinos and Euro-Americans today do not meet most of the criteria for transculturation. The Bolton School's concept of "borderlands" approximates a notion of transculturation, but with significant analytical flaws.[11] More frequently, U.S. social science treats contact between the two groups in the context of some expected or anticipated assimilation of Latinos into Euro-American culture. There are those who are hostile to any vestige of Latino identity and others who soften assimilation with reference to a "melting pot" that justifies the despoiling of Latino identity by recalling that Euro-American immigrants have already lost their distinct cultures.[12] It could be argued, of course, that Latino resistance to assimilation is comparable to the nostalgia immigrant groups have experienced after arriving in the United States from their homelands. In this view, time helps erase attachment to the "old country" until it finally melts into a ritualistic ethnic identity—one that can be "put on or off like a set of clothes."[13] But this comparison with Euro-American immigrant groups ignores the significant difference between migration and conquest. In the former, individuals choose to leave their homeland and travel to another country; in the latter, military force comes into the homeland and, by hoisting a new flag, makes the inhabitants strangers in their own land.[14]

Thus, it may be said, Latinos are more like the Irish Catholics in Belfast than like the Irish Americans in Boston.[15] We have been subjugated in our own lands, not in an adopted country where we are the guests. The persistence of Latino identity, especially in the use of the Spanish language, seems to exceed the linguistic loyalty of virtually all Euro-American groups to a language other than English,[16] a loyalty that may be ascribable to the colonial experience and its significance, which are harsher than immigration.[17]

Catholicism in the Latino homelands was initially shaped by the peripheral status of these colonies to the Spanish empire.[18] Loyalty to religion rather than to institution was a by-product of belonging to the periphery, as was a softer configuration of racial relations than what characterized most of Latin America.[19] Most important was the evolution of specific traits for Latino Catholicism prior to conquest by U.S. troops. Unlike Euro-American Catholicism, which migrated with the immigrants, Catholicism was already established in parishes and dioceses in America when the lands of Florida (1821), Texas (1845), New Mexico–California (1848), and Puerto Rico (1898) were annexed.[20]

Thus, I would say, the presence of Latinos within the United States is radically different from the arrival of immigrants from Europe. Whereas Euro-Americans left Europe by conscious decision, Latinos became foreigners in their own homeland by force of military might. Rather than immigrants, Latinos are conquered peoples. It would be impossible to explain the Palestinian and Israeli conflicts without recognizing that neither group considers itself "immigrant" and that both claim the territory as "homeland." And the conflicts in the Balkans are intensified because the conflicted parties all claim to defend their homeland. Similarly, the conquest of Latino homelands is the foundation for an accurate appraisal of Latino religion.[21] The immigrant operates with clear distinctions between the "old country" as the place of origin and the "new country" as the selected homeland. Equal treatment or immediate success can be deferred, because the immigrant is a guest in someone else's country. But inferiorization in one's own homeland constitutes an attack upon cultural identity, social location, and self-worth.[22] This attack is repulsed over and over again in the assertion of our Latino and Latina cultural identity. Certainly, that is the best context in which to understand the passionate eloquence about homelands and borderlands in the writing of the Chicana author Gloria Anzaldúa in the analysis provided by Davíd Carrasco and Roberto Lint Sagarena in chapter 9 of this volume.

But poets such as Anzaldúa are not the only defenders of homeland. Religious traditions serve as collective memory for the colonized and preserve a cultural identity that cannot be easily destroyed, even by military conquest. In what may seem a paradox to those who have not studied this issue in depth, colonialism destroys the nation-state but not the nationality. Using a nineteenth-century definition of *nation* to view the Latino social cohesiveness via a common language, history, and set of sustaining religious traditions makes it more precise to describe us as a "people" than as a "minority group."[23] We Latinos and Latinas possess traits that would have entitled us to the establishment of our own nation-state had there not been intervention from the United States. In fact, military invasion was pressed, according to some historians, precisely because some in Washington considered it easier to annex the Latino homelands while they were still Spanish colonies,[24] or while they were the fringes of nineteenth-century Mexico.[25]

Language is only one of the important traits of peoplehood that has endured until the present day. Latino culture cannot be defined convincingly as a vestige derived from the "old country." Latinos continue to be vitally connected to the roots of national identity and possess religious traditions as vigorous as they are particular. Perhaps most important, Latino identity responds to cultural patterns that constitute a New World reimaging of Iberian civilization.[26] In a certain sense, Latinos march to a drumbeat that does not correspond to the rhythms of an Anglo-American core, but resonates instead with Latin America.[27] Thus, the conquests that placed the Latino homelands under the U.S. flag represented a set of problems that had no exact parallel with Euro-American immigration, or even with the forced importation of slaves from Africa.[28] More apt comparison of the Latino condition as conquered nations lies with the Native Americans in the Americas and with the Russian annexation of Ukraine, Lithuania, Latvia, and Estonia.

The literature on the causes and purposes of the wars that annexed the Latino homelands to the United States is extensive and demonstrates a diversity of interpretations.[29] But colonialism is an institution, and studies of slavery in the United States have offered a useful distinction. The institution of slavery was racist, but there was a wide variance among the attitudes of individual slaveholders toward Black slaves. Just as some white slaveholders nonetheless demonstrated benignity toward their slaves despite the vicious nature of nineteenth-century slavery, we recognize that not every Euro-American who profited from the colonialism imposed on the Latino homelands was an imperialist.

There can be no denying, however, that with the exception of the Texas Republic, these wars transferred the governance of the conquered Latino homelands to the territorial clause of the U.S. Constitution (art. IV, sec. 3, 2). In a technical sense, this territorial clause constitutes colonialism because it bestows the sovereign power of government upon the U.S. Congress, in which the territories have no voting representative. Residents in a territory—even if they hold U.S. citizenship—are denied the most basic freedom of a democracy: no political power of self-determination in the nation-state. The U.S. Congress was not adverse to initiating its rule by placing total governmental power in the hands of the conquering military general, ignoring completely any civil governance and relying on the territorial clause for authority.

The Texas Republic avoided categorization as a territory, since it was admitted to the federal union as a sovereign state in 1845. However, during the interim between the establishment of the Texas Republic and Texas's admission into the United States, the native Spanish-speaking Texan people had been denied equal status with Euro-American settlers. The Texas War of Independence was embraced by several native Tejano leaders on the expectation of a bilingual and bicultural nation, representing the mestizaje of two separate groups; instead it ended with a society of white, Anglo, Protestant hegemony.[30] To its credit, the Catholic Church respected the Tejano nationality by creating a new Diocese of Galveston in 1847, which was directly under the Holy See rather than affiliated with the U.S. bishops. A French national, Jean Marie Odin, rather than a U.S.-born prelate or native Spanish-speaking Tejano, was placed in charge. Unfortunately, this halfway measure was precisely that: halfway, and it ultimately brought as many problems to Catholicism as it avoided, not only in Texas but also in Puerto Rico a half century later.

While Texas avoided the legality of a colonial status under the U.S. flag, it became a model for the effects of colonialism that were imposed on the Latino populations elsewhere. In this process, the natives of each of the territories—Tejanos, New Mexicans, Californians, and Puerto Ricans—were treated as if they were the same. Ironically, the concept of "Chicano" or "Latino"—which for us is a proud badge of unity—has a counterpart in the imperialist desire to subordinate all of us with the same policies. I would argue that introducing Puerto Rico (and Cuba and the Philippines) into an analysis of Chicanos is necessary to make the case for colonialism. If the measures used in Texas, the Southwest, and California in the middle of the nineteenth century are also invoked fifty years later in the subjugation of the Spanish speaking in the islands, then these measures can be considered to have been policies, and not merely improvised modes of discrimination. By referring to works on both Chicano experience and Puerto Rican history, I hope to highlight in this chapter that the policies imposed upon our people were similar.

The five measures that have direct relevance to our study of religion among Latinos and Latinas are (1) the imposition of the English language for official transaction; (2) the replacing or superseding of existing legal codes with the law of the United States as the supreme law of the land; (3) the declaration of opposition to the above measures as illegal activity, ranging from the political charge of treason to violations of the criminal code; (4) control of the public schools and educational curriculum in order to foster Americanization and accord inferior status to Latino contributions; and (5) the demographic diminution of the native Spanish-speaking population. In this last instance, the conquering government stimulated Euro-American migration to the Latino homelands so that there would be more English speakers than Spanish speakers. When this strategy was transferred to Puerto Rico some fifty years later, it had to be modified because Puerto Rico was already heavily populated and massive Euro-American immigration was not possible. Rather than the immigration of English speakers, the native demographics were altered by government-sponsored programs of population control,[31] and by massive out-migration of Puerto Ricans.[32]

The principal difference between what North Americans did in the nineteenth century and what Spaniards had done in the sixteenth lies in the different purposes of these types of colonialism. Spain had maintained the imbalance of power between the colonies and the mother country as a means of maintaining control, so that not only the people but also the political territory were treated as inferior. This is classic colonialism. The United States, on the other hand, sought to absorb the conquered lands totally as acquired territory, juridically indistinct from the rest of the country and on the march toward statehood. This policy required equal rights for the inhabitants of the territories. If this norm had been applied fairly, the conquered Latino natives would have been politically strong enough to oppose the incoming North American immigrants who followed the invading troops. Instead, the conquered Latinos were effectively denied equality by collusion. Barriers were constructed that disenfranchised Latino language, customs, economic systems, educational values, and religious faith, allowing the invaders to usurp social, political, and economic power.[33]

I want to extend this paradigm to the ways U.S. churches operated in the Latino homelands from the nineteenth century until the New Deal. Like Spanish colonialism before it, which replaced native religions with Catholicism as a means of subjugating the population, the invasion of Latino homelands by the United States during the nineteenth century used North American religious institutions to achieve the subjugation of Latinos. Religious institutions were intended to serve as means of Americanization, in tandem with other institutions brought by the U.S. invaders, such as civil service, public education, health services, hospitals, and political organizations.[34] These Americanizing religions could not differentiate between the colonized and the colonizer without direct violation of Gospel values, but they could privilege the conqueror's modes of expressing the faith. This is the important conceptual contribution of "internal colonialism" introduced by Barrera and his colleagues.[35] It has direct application to the religious institutions established in the conquered Latino homelands.[36] The religious hegemony enjoyed by the invaders stigmatized the ways native Latinos worshiped, and it lessened the prestige of their local churches, much as Barrera's model had shown to have occurred in labor-force segmentation.

Religion supplied legitimization both for the invasion as well as for the colonial treatment of the Latinos. There is a considerable literature on Manifest Destiny and its connection to various Protestant clergymen, such as Josiah Strong.[37] The United States and its religion were exalted as more modern than Catholicism or Hispanic culture. Anglo-Saxon Protestantism, it was claimed, was destined to supplant the weak and inferior religion with the strong and superior one. Often enough, U.S. victory in war became evidence for the excellence of Anglo-American Protestantism. The native religion (Catholicism) and native language (Spanish) were made targets for elimination, or at least, for marginalization. Such was the inevitable and providential result of God's destiny for the United States.[38] Essentially, the English-speaking conquerors were scarcely different from the Spanish Catholics who centuries before had done the same with the indigenous peoples. The modes of subjugation, however, were more controlled and complex.

Protestant missionary work in all of the conquered lands assumed three basic patterns.[39] First, there was the conversion of natives to the Protestant faith.[40] The new converts from Catholicism were more proficient than the U.S. missionaries in preaching in the Spanish language and sometimes included resigned priests, who already had pastoral experience. Second, money came from the church mission board controlled by English speakers, while the preaching and administration of the new churches came from Spanish-speaking converts. Such arrangements were not contradictory, but they did produce conflicts. Given the gradual impoverishment produced by the U.S. takeovers, the viability of self-financing of the new Latino Protestant congregations grew less, rather than greater. This lack of funds meant that the effective work of the converts was usually subordinated to the control of non-Latino missionaries. Put in other terms, positions of power were given to native speakers of English to a degree much greater than to their Spanish-speaking counterparts, even though the churches depended on the Latino converts for their early effectiveness.

Third, the public school system was used as a vehicle for eliminating the Spanish language, for stigmatizing Latino culture, and for alienating children from their history. The public school system also was a prime employer of English-speaking Protestant missionaries and played a major role in attacking Catholic customs.[41] The United States fostered a civil religion that systematically favored Protestantism and cast in an inferior light Latino Catholicism well into the first half of the twentieth century. Ironically, the Catholic schools operated with almost identical results.[42]

Protestantism legitimated the U.S. conquests and perpetuated the colonialism imposed on Latinos in their homelands. Doubtlessly the Protestants viewed the replacement of Catholic tradition as part of their apostolic task, and they set themselves to preach the faith with intrepid zeal. But in this process they mixed politics and religion so as to reinforce within the Latino homelands the negative effects of colonialism that were listed above.[43] English was installed as the official language in worship as well as in politics, local law was relegated to elimination as "superstition" and "Romanism," organized resistance was outlawed with God's thunder to back up frontier pistols, and the English speaking—even when they were not more numerous than the Spanish speaking—became the hegemonic majority. All these changes were inaugurated with an infallible sense of knowing God's will and was backed by force of arms. What may be less obvious is the role of U.S. Catholicism in reinforcing the same results as U.S. Protestantism.

The official policies imposed by U.S. Catholicism, when it assumed ecclesiastical jurisdiction over the conquered Latino lands, reinforced colonialism and its effects. But nurture of traditional Catholic practices of the conquered peoples would have left the church open to charges of fomenting an irredentist nationalism, antagonistic to the Protestant majority in the United States. Rather than serve Latinos in the United States as the church in Poland and Ireland had served its conquered peoples, the Catholic Church fostered an immigrant's view of the United States as a substitute for historical reality. Although Latinos were peoples conquered in war, the church undermined awareness of that fact. At times unwittingly and at others deliberately, Catholicism's representatives told Latinos that they should imitate an immigrant's gratitude for opportunity in a new home rather than nurture resentment against an invading U.S. imperialism.

The historical accounts in the Notre Dame History of Hispanic Catholics in the U.S. series offer many examples of how clergy, particularly the U.S.-appointed bishops of the newly conquered lands, suppressed the existing Latino Catholicism.[44] Some, like Joseph Sadoc Alemany, named bishop of Monterey in 1850 and archbishop of San Francisco in 1853, were benign toward the native Spanish-speaking Californians; others, like Alemany's successor in Monterey, Thaddeus Amat (who transferred his residence to Los Angeles, renaming the diocese) were antagonistic to the Spanish speaking and the Mexican clergy who served them.[45] But although they differed in attitude, neither bishop opposed U.S. rule over the newly appended lands and both strove to remake the existing Catholicism into the image and likeness of European immigrant Catholicism on the East Coast. This was the special perniciousness of U.S. Catholicism toward the already vigorous Latino Catholicism in the new colonies.

East Coast Catholicism had used canon law to create national parishes which served non-English-speaking persons within an established jurisdiction. National parishes were not located in remote mission territories, but were more often found in city neighborhoods that had become ethnic immigrant enclaves. The principle that regulated these national parishes was assimilation.[46] Once the English language was learned, the parishioners of the national parish were expected to join the territorial parish, which conducted services in English (often English only). Canon law maintained the subordination of the national parish to the local ordinary, or bishop. On the East Coast, the bishops viewed the national parishes as a temporary measure. In practice, the national parishes were assigned to religious orders, often ones which were supplied with clergy from the immigrants' native land. One of the advantages to the bishop of this arrangement was that the finances of the national parish as well as the salary for the clergy could be shifted away from the diocese and onto the shoulders of religious order and the immigrants.[47] Once the immigrant community became established and prosperous, however, the bishop was empowered to reassert his jurisdiction. It was common for this to happen, and conflicts frequently arose when the bishop was viewed as abusing his prerogatives.[48]

In California, New Mexico, and Texas, the bishops installed with U.S. rule often treated the existing Mexican parishes as national parishes, concentrating diocesan funds and interest on new churches to be built for the English speaking.[49] This inverted the function of the East Coast system, where the national parishes were for newcomers and the existing churches for the English speaking. Yet the application of canon law was used with the same edge that gave financial and legal advantages to the conquerors.

In Southern California, Bishop Amat's policies were decidedly antagonistic to traditional Latino Catholicism in ways that paralleled the political and economic eclipse of native social status. By the turn of the century in Los Angeles, not only had the original Spanish-speaking people lost political power and economic prosperity; the diocese was effectively segregated into one set of churches for poor, Spanish-speaking Catholics, and another for the middle-class, English-speaking Catholics. Bishop Amat's confiscation of Mexican Franciscan foundations and threats of excommunication added to the alienation of the Spanish speaking from institutional Catholicism. Bishop Amat demanded that the already-established Spanish speaking adapt to the English-speaking newcomers. The bishop and his successors used financial resources to imitate the kind of diocesan and parish structures common to the major ethnic sees of New York, Chicago, and Philadelphia.[50] California witnessed the building of Catholic schools, hospitals, convents, and seminaries that provided services for the English speaking. The Spanish speaking were generally expected to raise their own funds, because they were in parishes administered by religious orders.[51]

Catholic discrimination toward Latinos was tolerated, when not also encouraged, by bishops sent by the U.S. episcopate into the conquered territories. The most outrageous of these prelates may have been Jean-Baptiste Lamy (1850–85), who became the first archbishop of Santa Fe,

1. Padre Antonio José Martínez (1793–1867). Courtesy: Palace of the Governors (MNM/DCA), Neg. No. 174508.

New Mexico. French-born, trained in a Gallic Catholicism antagonistic to the spontaneity of popular religiosity, Archbishop Lamy set about extirpating Latino Catholicism by depriving the native clergy of leadership in New Mexico. He spied on, publicly humiliated, and in 1857 defrocked the native clergy leader, Father José Martínez of Taos (figure 1), New Mexico.[52]

This conflict is a highly visible example of similar confrontations with native clergy by the hierarchy in Latino homelands after the conquest. The archbishop justified his extreme actions chiefly by citing sexual lapses by Father Martínez, who was accused of concubinage while a priest. But concubinage was not a deviance encountered only with Martínez and other native Latino clergy. This is a condition that has been a constant concern throughout the history of Catholicism.

Martínez held a high public profile, once serving in the Territorial Congress, and was admired by the native New Mexican clergy. In plain terms, he was a rival of the archbishop as leader of New Mexico's Catholics, and it would be naive not to attribute a political motive to the Archbishop Lamy's actions that humiliated Martínez. In fact, Father Martínez had challenged the wisdom of the archbishop's policies, leveling charges of his own against the archbishop and the French clergy brought into New Mexico. Martínez accused the archbishop of simony because the schedule of fees imposed by the chancery in 1854 effectively put the sacraments and masses up for sale. He warned him that blanket restrictions on traditional celebrations of popular religiosity would drive Latino people from the church. In Martínez's frequent correspondence with the archbishop, he also complained of incidents when prejudice against native new Mexican priests reared its ugly head in matters such as clerical appointments and the assignment of space in rectories, which invariably went to French clergy. Finally, he questioned the archbishop about hobnobbing with public figures such as Kit Carson, who symbolized to the New Mexican people the excesses of the U.S. military.

None of the charges made by Martínez and other Latino Catholics against Archbishop Lamy were considered as threatening to ecclesiastical good order as sexual lapses by the native clergy. So while the zeal for personal morality on the part of the archbishop may have been laudable, his insensitivity to local customs eroded his credibility with Latino Catholics. Father Juan Romero,[53] who has studied the case carefully, considers Archbishop Lamy's excommunication of Father Martínez of Taos as part of the archbishop's general disdain for Latinos and their brand of Catholicism. Moreover, the weakening of Latino religion through the punishment of clerical defenders for their lapses, both real and supposed, continues up to the present day.

It is my contention that the policies outlined above were not haphazard or occasional. In comparing the entry of U.S. Catholicism into Puerto Rico some fifty years after the invasion and annexation of Mexican homelands, I have found that the same policies of pious colonialism are operative. In other words, the Chicano experience was extended to other groups, thus becoming the basis for the Latino experience. Partially because English-speaking colonists never accounted for more than a fraction of the total island population, favoritism for the English speaking has never made much sense in Puerto Rico. Yet, when the United States annexed Puerto Rico in 1898, the U.S. episcopate looked upon the island as if it were one of the Latino homelands such as Texas or New Mexico. Puerto Rico, like the Diocese of Galveston, Texas, in 1847, was placed directly under the Holy See. One of Archbishop Lamy's successors in Santa Fe, Placide Louis-Chapelle, named archbishop of New Orleans in 1897, used his influence to have a protégé (James Blenck, a native of Bavaria) appointed bishop of Puerto Rico rather than a native Puerto Rican priest.[54] Once again, the premise of Spanish colonialism that no native could be bishop among his own people for fear of inciting rebellion, was echoed by U.S. Catholicism in Puerto Rico as it had been in the Southwest.

Bishop Blenck (1898–1907) banned the Christmas Midnight Mass (*misa de gallo*) in the San Juan Cathedral in 1898, considering it too rowdy and offensive to U.S. culture, in much the same way that Lamy had outlawed many traditional New Mexican religious celebrations. Eventually Bishop Blenck proved less antagonistic to Puerto Rican Catholicism than his successor, Bishop Ambrose Jones (1907–21), would be. Jones disbanded the centuries old *cabildo*, or synod of cathedral canons, that could have supplied a native clergy voice in formulating church policy, much as happened in Archbishop Lamy's New Mexico. In his ecclesiastical appointments, the bishop often placed English-speaking pastors over native Puerto Rican priests many years their senior, much as the French clergy had been favored in Santa Fe. Bishop Jones actively promoted the massive displacement of local clergy in favor of "missionaries" from New York and Philadelphia to found parish schools that still teach only in English.[55] Americanizing lay organizations, such as the Knights of Columbus, were established among the wealthy, who became the principal clients of these Catholic schools, which were seldom affordable for working-class Puerto Ricans.[56] These were just some of the measures used to reinforce colonialism, and they are clearly resonant with the policies of Archbishops Lamy in New Mexico and Amat in Southern California. In fact, just as Bishop Blenck had been a protégé of one of the French Bishops who succeeded Archbishop Lamy in New Mexico, Bishop Jones was from Philadelphia, where Archbishop Amat had been a seminary professor.

Pious colonialism among both Catholics and Protestants always included forcing native religious leaders into inferior positions; to maintain the hegemony of U.S. religion in concert with the imposed political power, church officials—whether Catholic or Protestant—had to confront the issue of native clergy. The problem had different contours, of course, depending on the denomination. The social distance between a Catholic priest and his flock was considerable. To be a priest one had to be highly educated, speak English and live without family in celibacy. The Protestant minister was not required to live outside of family, but other demands, especially in formal education, were virtually the same.

The dilemma of Protestant Latinos, however, was that in conversion to a faith that held hegemony with U.S. civil religion, they had to turn their back upon centuries of Catholic liturgy and traditions that were interwoven with native Latino culture. Moreover, rather than encourage an accommodation with a Catholic culture, Protestant churches among Latinos often adopted a hostility toward Catholicism matched only by the hostility Catholicism held toward Protestantism in Catholic countries.

From Puerto Rico to California, pious colonialism depreciated the traditions of Latino Catholicism and subordinated the maintenance or recruitment of native vocations to the goals of using Catholicism as a vehicle for Americanization.

There were exceptions to this general pattern. Individual Euro-American clerics identified with the needs of the Latinos and fostered the preservation of Latino religious traditions.[57] There were even priests, such as Father Laurence Forristal, who seemed to recognize the evils of colonialism. After sixteen years among Latinos in San Diego, the Irish-born Father Forristal emphasized the permanent importance of the Spanish language as the language of the people and warned against Americanization:

> If it means that every Mexican must be recast in a special American mold, the proposal is immense and impossible of accomplishment . . . There is no more contemptible creature than the Mexican who is ashamed of his blood and face. Invariably he is also ashamed of his religion.[58]

There were many clergy, Protestant and Catholic, who faithfully fulfilled the call of ministry. They remained loyal to their ministerial obligations despite a climate that permitted discrimination against Latinos and their religious traditions. One of these sympathetic Catholic priests, Father John J. Cantwell, eventually became bishop and then archbishop in California and used his authority to bring awareness of Mexican culture into Catholic ministry. But this dedication to apostolic service did not threaten the structures of colonialism that had been imposed upon the Latinos by force of arms. Much of the openness toward incorporating Latino cultural values in the ministry flowed from the premise that Latinos were an ethnic group on the way to eventual assimilation. Seldom did church leaders take any initiative that might have been interpreted as an effort to lift up a conquered people with the right to establish their own nation. The dedicated clergy, in effect, sought to lessen the evil effects of colonialism, but they seldom challenged colonialism itself.

To describe this religious version of internal colonialism, then, I prefer the word *pious* to describe this participation of the churches. From Latin, *pious* means "loyal." In order to fulfill the religious obligations of the sacraments—liturgy and prayer—every believer must have recourse to the official church and its clergy and its structures. Put in the terms of Otto Maduro, the "religious production" of Latinos required legitimization from official religion.[59] For instance, Catholics in the conquered Latino homelands needed the clergy to marry them, baptize their children, bury the dead, and provide everything from holy water to blessed statues for the exercise of traditional Catholic piety. Latinos who did not like the Americanizing cost of the newly installed bishop and clergy could leave Catholicism and become Protestants. But the Mainline Protestant churches were no less Americanizing, and perhaps even more so, than the U.S. Catholic Church.[60] Moreover, as suggested above, Protestant leaders reserved control over denominational resources even while they encouraged native Latinos to organize and serve in local congregations. While Protestantism differed from Catholicism in the type of religious production, the pattern of control over the means of religious production was much the same whether the controls were Protestant supervisors or Catholic bishops. Religion in the conquered Latino homelands was regulated by U.S. administration, much as civil authorities controlled most transactions in the public sphere. Hence, the name *pious colonialism* refers not only to the mindset of the U.S. missionaries but also to the target of their control.

Of course, all Latinos were not passively submissive to pious colonialism. While some Latino Catholics accepted the stigmatization of their traditional piety and assimilated to Euro-American values, Latinos more frequently rejected this course. However, although some voices were raised against the manipulation of institutional Catholicism for colonial purposes,[61] maintenance of traditional ways was largely absent the conscious choice of resistance. These religious experiences were like other practices that sowed the seeds of collective consciousness, and that emerged as a political movement in the 1960s. But if secular modes of cultural affirmation—such as literature, arts and music—can be viewed as inchoate forms of resistance to imperialism,[62] then home-centered religions deserve the same classification. Popular religiosity, as reminded in scholarly work today, often becomes political and social resistance. Indeed, transculturation after more than 300 years of Spanish colonialism had created mestizaje.[63]

Protestantism had always offered a close link between clergy and laity. One of the attractions for Latinos to become Protestants was a wider accessibility to clerical and leadership roles. To the degree that Protestantism flourished in urban centers in the Latino homelands, it produced a significant cohort of Latino leaders; it accomplished this feat virtually overnight, often with the help of Latino Catholic priests who had converted. Protestantism also placed great emphasis on individual responsibility to reform one's life. Self-destructive habits of drinking and gambling were special targets of concern. But more significant than those appeals, the more successful denominations among Latinos were those that maintained a family or fictive family support system to confirm the convert in the resolve to live by the Gospel.

Catholic traditions derived from the Spanish experience tended to thrive most in small villages and remote rural areas, where a North American clergy could not interfere with the established Catholicism of centuries.[64] While the parish church and its sacramental distribution were always a part of such traditional Catholicism, the power of belief in the setting of home altar, of local processions, and of village customs coexisted with the institutional changes. Social distance, which made Latinos less important to the official churches, had the simultaneous effect of making the official churches less important to Latinos. These patterns were interrupted by the mass migrations to urban centers of the United States, which occurred after the two World Wars.[65]

But the period from conquest until the New Deal demonstrated remarkable consistency in the policies directed by the churches toward Latinos. Pious colonialism, I contend, is the underlying explanation of why evangelization was also Hispanicization under Spain and Americanization under the United States. Both empires privileged the language of the conqueror (first Spanish, then English), repressed native religious traditions, cast Latino clergy into an inferior position, and stigmatized the culture of the people in the Latino homelands. Ironically, the "pious" part of pious colonialism also motivated the setting aside of denominational resources to the Latino ministry for the struggle against social injustice and for dedicated missionaries.

Pious colonialism under Spain changed during some 300 years, so that when the Spanish empire began to break apart, the indigenous peoples and the Spanish conquerors had been merged into a new people that was different from either of its components. On the other hand, the colonialism of the United States over Latino homelands has lasted only about half as long as the Spanish experience. We do not know yet how or if there will be a similar transculturation of Euro-Americans and Latinos.

I maintain that under the U.S. flag the Catholic and Protestant churches attended to the religious concerns of Latinos, but virtually never in ways that confronted the morally evil institution of colonialism. Colonialism after the wars of conquest, like slavery before abolition, was often viewed as a social reality the church ought to ameliorate rather than challenge. Like slavery, colonialism persisted in its effects even after it had technically disappeared because of statehood, or in the case of Puerto Rico, because of commonwealth status. Among Latinos, these effects could be measured by gradual impoverishment. Despite laudable efforts to combat the pernicious effects of colonialism, Latinos lacked the material resources, the intercommunication, and the leadership necessary to reverse these circumstances.

The thirty-five years from the New Deal to 1967 witnessed unprecedented socioeconomic changes. They reconfigured the Latino reality: a mostly rural, agricultural people became urban and proletarian, education attainments increased, new class divisions were created, a more complex labor force segmentation appeared, and a wider religious diversity was manifested among Latinos. The changes from 1932 until 1967 did more to alter the everyday life of Latinos than had the political transfer of power from Mexico and Spain to the United States after the wars of conquest. But although there was less segregation, a larger number of educated people, and a growing middle class, city life brought a host of new problems and challenges.

Latino religion, with its reliance on tradition, had carved out a niche for itself within Pious colonialism. But as the agricultural base of Latino religion was kicked out from under it, there was a drastic need for rapid adaptation to the new circumstances.[66] Nowhere was this more evident than among the Latino migrants to big cities. As the Spanish-speaking urban population swelled in the decade after World War II, many churches adopted policies to attract Latinos to city parishes and congregations.[67] Although programs such as the Bishops' Committee for the Spanish-Speaking differed from pious colonialism by introducing a more solid institutional commitment by churches to social justice backed up with higher levels of economic support, the programs shared the essential characteristic of the previous approach that viewed Latinos as another episode of the assimilationist pattern of the Euro-American groups.[68] Protestant settlement houses continued this dual task of the social and the pastoral, albeit with denominational differences, as they ministered to Latino migrants to the cities. Although their numbers were significantly smaller than in the Catholic effort, the quality of professionalism was undeniable. Often, Protestant Latino leadership sat at the table as equals with Catholic clergy in civic and political associations. While their churches did not have the clout of big-city Catholicism, these pastors often enjoyed the advantage of being Mexican American or Puerto Rican, while the Catholic clergy were frequently Irish Americans.

For all effects, by 1960 the "benign neglect" toward Latinos that once characterized pious colonialism had been replaced by a zealous apostolate to repeat for Latino religion the familiar patterns of parish and congregational participation that had Americanized Euro-American groups. For instance, within Catholicism national parishes that had been relatively autonomous precisely because they were colonial, were downgraded. Latinos in New York, Chicago, and Los Angeles were pushed into "integrated parishes" where they shared facilities with the Euro-American groups. It was argued that this was a middle way to preserve both unity and diversity within the Catholic Church.[69]

However, these integrated parishes easily became two autonomous parishes, sharing the same facilities. The Euro-American congregation continued to assume a lion's share of attention within most New York parishes, while Puerto Ricans were shunted to the basement church facility. The "basement" church of the Puerto Ricans, notes Ana María Díaz-Stevens, stigmatized the Spanish speaking even while supposedly offering equality by integration. Yet, with their self-generated creativity, the basement churches often functioned for Puerto Ricans much as a national parish. In many urban settings of Mexican American migration, a similar pattern took shape. During the decade of the 1950s, this policy of integration began to show effects in the vitality of religious practice and in the disposition to participate in other areas of Catholic parish life. The parochial schools began to find more Latino pupils, while seminaries and convents experienced a gradual increase of Latina and Latino candidates after 1955. Within Protestantism, a cohort of capable Latino pastors and seminary professors began their journeys to leadership positions.

The presence of Latinos in small but significant numbers among the clergy ranks was often interpreted as proof that Americanization would work and that assimilation was a desirable goal. Yet abruptly, these trends ended and reversed course. In what I have chosen to call "the Latino Religious Resurgence," a new role for Latino religion was proclaimed, elaborated, and implemented.[70] Latino church leaders redefined their ecclesiastical roles. They announced a mission of restoring and redeveloping Latino religion because it was distinct and nonassimilable to the Euro-American experience. This phenomenon produced many documents that, with considerable theological sophistication, explained the new trend, thus inoculating it from ecclesiastical condemnation. There was considerable emphasis upon education and leadership formation so that the new vision of Latino religion was rapidly diffused through agencies, organizations, and institutions that previously served an assimilationist function.[71] Perhaps more important, a new identity that transcended specific nationality groups was created. Although the road to a Latino or Hispanic transnational identity was not always smooth,[72] it was more successful than secular efforts in the same direction, with the notable exception of Chicago.[73] In effect, Latino religion dissolved the last bonds of pious colonialism by subverting the very institutions that had been used for Americanization and reconfiguring them into vehicles for Latino reaffirmation. Finally, these changes were tied to militancy on social justice issues.[74] Parishes and congregations became the core membership and meeting rooms as the local church became the assembly point for neighborhood organizations and agencies, many of which received government funds. These new political roles were matched by effective—and sometimes spectacular—ritual celebration in Latino cultural idioms. The liturgy in local churches often assembled musicians and singers who regularly produced worship services that entertained as well as inspired. At times, people came to church due to these services. In other words, the substantial and dramatic changes formulated by leadership were transmitted to Latino churchgoers in ways that were both pragmatically beneficial and culturally popular.

This chapter concludes, therefore, on a positive note. Pious colonialism has been brought to an end, even if vestiges remain in certain corners as constant reminders of these black chapters of history. A new generation of leadership appeared within the churches, just as it did in the secular quarter.[75] The end was brought about by a radically new mentalité that was forged by a generation of Latino religious leaders during the tumultuous years 1967–83. It is a measure of this victory that a conservative Catholic pope extolled cultural resistance to colonialism from the global forum of the United Nations:

> Its [a nation's] right to exist naturally implies that every nation also enjoys the right to its own language and culture, through which a people expresses and promotes that which would call its fundamental spiritual sovereignty. History shows that in extreme circumstances (such as those which occurred in the land where I was born) it is precisely its culture that enables a nation to survive the loss of political and economic independence.[76]

In conclusion, I would classify pious colonialism as a necessary hermeneutic for understanding religion among Latinos and Latinas in general and Mexican Americans in particular. But it is also a key matter to be analyzed in secular terms. Current political trends have challenged the hard-won achievements of a generation of Latino leaders, and there is a sad but likely prospect that much of the progressive legislation of the 1960s will be rewritten, if not abolished. How the churches respond to this hateful turn against Latinos will shape much of the twenty-first century.

Notes

1. Robert Allen, *Black Awakening in Capitalist America* (Garden City, N.Y.: Doubleday Anchor, 1970); Robert Blauner, "Internal Colonialism and Ghetto Revolt," *Social Problems* (spring 1969): 393–408; *On Racial Oppression in America*, ed. Robert Blauner (New York: Harper and Row), 1972.

2. Ronald Bailey and Guillermo V. Flores, "Internal Colonialism and Racial Minorities," in *Structures of Dependency*, ed. Frank Bonilla and Robert Girling (Palo Alto, Calif.: Nairobi Press, 1973), 149–60.

3. Mario Barrera, Carlos Muñoz, and Charles Ornelas, "The Barrio as an Internal Colony," in *La Causa Política: A Chicano Politics Reader*, ed. F. Chris Garcia (Notre Dame, Ind.: University of Notre Dame Press, 1974), 281–301; repr. from *Urban Affairs Annual Reviews*, ed. Harlan Han, Sage Publications, 6 (1972): 465–98.

4. Pentecostalism will be omitted from this study for three reasons: first, as a sociological construct, Pentecostalism is a "sect" and is not the kind of institution that is governed by policy from a hierarchical center; second, as Gastón Espinosa has shown, the origins of Puerto Rican Pentecostalism differ from those of Chicano Pentecostalism, and the comparison possible with the other denominations is much too complicated for the space limitations of this chapter; third, and perhaps most important, the chapter by Espinosa in this book (chapter 11) treats the Pentecostal experience with insights more telling that what I could provide here. I leave it to future study to explore the question of whether or not Pentecostalism has historically legitimated U.S. colonialism.

5. Rodolfo Acuña, *Occupied America: A History of Chicanos* (San Francisco: Canfield Press, 1972); Richard Griswold del Castillo, *The Los Angeles Barrio, 1850–1890: A Social History* (Berkeley: University of California Press, 1979); Manuel Maldonado-Denis, *Puerto Rico: A Socio-historic Interpretation* (New York: Vintage Books, 1972.

6. Nathan Glazer, *Ethnic Dilemmas, 1864–1982* (Cambridge, Mass.: Harvard University Press, 1983).

7. Justo González, *The Theological Education of Hispanics* (New York: Fund for Theological Education, 1988), 9–12.

8. Virgilio Elizondo, *The Future Is Mestizo: Life Where Cultures Meet*, 2nd ed. (New York: Crossroads Publishing, 1992).

9. Malinowski in Fernando Ortiz, *Cuban Counterpoint: Tobacco and Sugar* (New York: Knopf, 1947). See also the reference in this concept to archetypes in Anthony M. Steven-Arroyo, "The Persistence of Religious Cosmovision in an Alien World," in *Enigmatic Powers: Syncretism with African and Indigenous Peoples' Religions among Latinos*, ed. Anthony M. Stevens-Arroyo and Andrés I. Pérez y Mena, eds., vol. 3 in Program for the Analysis of Religion Among Latinos (PARAL) series (New York: Bildner Center for Western Hemisphere Studies, 1995), 113–35.

10. Although he does not use the word *transculturation*, Nathan Glazer in *Ethnic Dilemmas, 1964–1982* (Cambridge, Mass.: Harvard University Press, 1983)

cites the development of all these conditions throughout world history, and with reference to the particularities of the United States.

11. David J. Weber discusses these issues with consideration for the nuances of the different sides of the argument in *The Spanish Frontier in North America* (New Haven, Conn.: Yale University Press, 1992), 353–60. Many of his insights ring true to similar debates in Caribbean history. See Anthony M. Stevens-Arroyo, "Juan Mateo Guaticabanú, September 21, 1946: Evangelization and Martyrdom in the Time of Columbus," *Catholic Historical Review* 82, no. 4 (October 1996): 614–37.

12. Nathan Glazer, *Ethnic Dilemmas*; Andrew Greeley, *The American Catholic* (New York: Basic Books, 1977).

13. Greeley, *The American Catholic*.

14. David F. Gómez, *Somos Chicanos: Strangers in Our Own Land* (Boston: Beacon Press, 1973).

15. Anthony M. Stevens-Arroyo, "Jaime Balmes Redux: Catholicism as Civilization in the Political Philosophy of Pedro Albizu Campos," in *Bridging the Atlantic: Iberian and Latin American Thought in Historical Perspective*, ed. Marina Pérez de Mendiola (Albany: SUNY [State University of New York] Press, 1966), 129–51.

16. Glazer, *Ethnic Dilemmas*, 238ff.

17. Mario Barrera, *Beyond Aztlán* (Notre Dame, Ind.: University of Notre Dame Press, 1988).

18. Anthony M. Stevens-Arroyo and Ana María Díaz-Stevens, "Religious Faith and Institutions in the Forging of Latino Identities," in *Handbook for Hispanic Cultures in the United States*, ed. Felix Padilla (Houston: Arte Público Press, 1993), 257–91.

19. Weber, *The Spanish Frontier in North America*; Anthony M. Stevens-Arroyo, "The Inter-Atlantic Paradigm: The Failure of Spanish Medieval Colonialism of the Canary and Caribbean Islands," *Comparative Studies in Society and History* 35, no. 3 (July 1993): 515–43.

20. Jeffrey M. Burns, "The Mexican American Community in California," in *Mexican Americans and the Catholic Church, 1900–1965*, ed. Jay P. Dolan and Gilberto M. Hinojosa, vol. 1 of the Notre Dame History of Hispanic Catholics in the U.S. series (Notre Dame, Ind.: University of Notre Dame Press, 1994), 9–125; Richard Santos, "Missionary Beginnings in Spanish Florida, the Southwest and California," in *Fronteras: A History of the Latin American Church in the USA Since 1513*, ed. Moises Sandoval (San Antonio: Mexican American Cultural Center, 1983), 3–54; Samuel Silva Gotay, "The Ideological Dimensions of Popular Religiosity and Cultural Identity in Puerto Rico," in *An Enduring Flame: Studies of Latino Popular Religiosity*, ed. Anthony M. Steven-Arroyo and Ana María Díaz-Stevens, vol. 1 (New York: Bildner Center Books, 1994), 133–70.

21. Anthony M. Stevens-Arroyo, with Segundo Pantoja, "Discovering Latino Religion," in *Discovering Latino Religion: A Comprehensive Social Science Bibliography* (New York: Bildner Center for Western Hemisphere Studies, 1995), 13–40.

22. Alvin R. Sunseri, *Seeds of Discord: New Mexico in the Aftermath of the American Conquest, 1846–1861* (Chicago: Nelson Hall, 1979).

23. Antonio M. Stevens-Arroyo, *Prophets Denied Honor: An Anthology on the Hispanic Church in the United States* (Maryknoll, N.Y.: Orbis Books, 1980); Anthony M. Stevens-Arroyo, "The Emergence of a Social Identity among Latino Catholics: An Appraisal," in *Hispanic Catholicism in the U.S.*, vol. 3, ed. Jay Dolan and Alan Figueroa Deck SJ (Notre Dame, Ind.: University of Notre Dame Press, 1994), 77–130.

24. Denis, *Puerto Rico*, 54–56.

25. Acuña, *Occupied America*, 19–27.

26. Stevens-Arroyo, "The Inter-Atlantic Paradigm."

27. Jorge Klor de Alva, "Aztlán, Borinquen and Hispanic Nationalism in the United States," in *Aztlán: Essays on the Chicano Homeland*, ed. Rodolfo Anaya and Francisco Lomelí (Albuquerque: University of New Mexico Press, 1991), 135–77.

28. Acuña, *Occupied America*; Gordon K. Lewis, *Puerto Rico: Freedom and Power in the Caribbean* (New York: Monthly Review Press, 1963).

29. Acuña, *Occupied America*; Lewis, *Freedom and Power*; Maldorado-Denis, *Puerto Rico*; Griswold del Castillo, *The Los Angeles Barrio, 1850–1890*.

30. Acuña, *Occupied America*; Jay P. Dolan and Gilberto Miguel Hinojosa, ed., *Mexican Americans and the Catholic Church, 1900–1965* (Notre Dame, Ind.: University of Notre Dame Press, 1994); Carmen Tafolla, "The Church in Texas," in Sandoval, *Fronteras*, 183–94.

31. Annette B. Ramírez de Arellano and Conrad Seipp, *Colonialism, Catholicism, and Contraception: A History of Birth Control in Puerto Rico* (Chapel Hill: University of North Carolina Press, 1983).

32. Anthony M. Stevens-Arroyo and Ana María Díaz Ramírez, "Puerto Ricans in the United States," in *The Minority Report*, 2nd ed., ed. Gary and Rosalind Dworkin (New York: Holt Rinehart and Winston, 1982), 196–232.

33. José Hernández, "Hispanics Blend Diversity," in *Handbook of Hispanic Cultures in the United States: Sociology*, ed. Felix Padilla (Houston: Arte Público Press, 1994), 20–21.

34. Acuña, *Occupied America*, 147–49; Gotay, "The Ideological Dimensions of Popular Religiosity and Cultural Identity in Puerto Rico."

35. Mario Barrera, Carlos Muñoz, and Charles Ornelas, "The Barrio as an Internal Colony," 281–301.

36. Sunseri, *Seeds of Discord*, 125–41; Lewis, *Freedom and Power in the Caribbean*, 103–19.

37. Gotay, "The Ideological Dimensions of Popular Religiosity and Cultural Identity in Puerto Rico," 133–70.

38. Evidence of this indoctrination can be found with different perspectives in much of the literature. I suggest examining the following works, each distinct in its approach to Protestant missions and missionaries: Sarah Deutsch, *No Separate Refuge: Culture, Class, and Gender on an Anglo-Hispanic Frontier in the American*

Southwest, 1880–1940 (New York: Oxford University Press, 1987); Justo González, *The Theological Education of Hispanics*; Edwin Sylvest Jr., "Hispanic American Protestantism in the United States," in Sandoval, *Fronteras*, 279–338.

39. Sylvest, "Hispanic American Protestantism in the United States"; Gotay, "The Ideological Dimensions of Popular Religiosity and Cultural Identity in Puerto Rico."

40. Sylvest, "Hispanic American Protestantism in the United States," 279–338.

41. Aida Negrón Montilla, *Americanization in Puerto Rico and the Public School System, 1900–1930* (Río Piedras, Puerto Rico: Editorial Edil, 1970).

42. Charles J. Beirne SJ. *The Problem of Americanization in the Catholic Schools of Puerto Rico* (Río Piedras, Puerto Rico: Editorial Universitaria de la Universidad de Puerto Rico, 1975).

43. Alberto López Pulido, "Searching for the Sacred: Conflict and Struggle for Mexican Catholics in the Roman Catholic Diocese of San Diego, 1936–1941." *Latino Studies Journal* 5, no. 3 (September 1994): 37–59.

44. Jaime R. Vidal, "Puerto Rican Catholicism," in *Puerto Rican and Cuban Catholics in the U.S., 1900–1965*, ed. Jay P. Dolan and Jaime Vidal (Notre Dame, Ind.: University of Notre Dame Press, 1994), 11–134.

45. Burns, "Mexican Americans and the Catholic Church in California, 129–33.

46. Joseph P. Fitzpatrick, SJ. *Puerto Rican Americans: The Meaning of Migration to the Mainland* (Englewood Cliffs, N.J.: Prentice Hall, 1971).

47. Anthony M. Stevens-Arroyo, "Cahensly Revisited? The National Pastoral Encounter of America's Hispanic Catholics," *Migration World* 15, no. 3 (fall 1987): 16–19.

48. Pulido, "Searching for the Sacred."

49. Sandoval, *On the Move: A History of the Hispanic Church in the United States* (Maryknoll, N.Y.: Orbis Books, 1991).

50. David A. Badillo, "The Catholic Church and the Making of Mexican-American Parish Communities in the Midwest," in *Mexican Americans and the Catholic Church, 1900–1965*, ed. Jay P. Dolan and Gilberto M. Hinojosa (Notre Dame, Ind.: University of Notre Dame Press, 1994), 237–308.

51. Burns, "The Mexican American Community in California."

52. Lamy's refashioning of New Mexican Catholicism to conform to the values of North American society was described by the novelist Willa Cather in *Death Comes for the Archbishop*, and the image of Martínez, like that of all Latinos, suffered from her bias. Sandoval's *On the Move* summarizes some of the recent efforts at rehabilitation. See also Stevens-Arroyo, *Prophets Denied Honor*, 81–84.

53. Juan Romero and Moises Sandoval, *Reluctant Dawn: Historia del Padre A. J. Martínez, Cura de Taos* (San Antonio: Mexican American Cultural Center, 1976).

54. Vidal, "Puerto Rican Catholicism."

55. Beirne, *The Problem of Americanization in the Catholic Schools of Puerto Rico.*

56. Silva Gotay, "The Ideological Dimensions of Popular Religiosity and Cultural Identity in Puerto Rico."

57. Patrick H. McNamara, "Dynamics of the Catholic Church from Pastoral to Social Concerns," in *The Mexican American People: The Nation's Second Largest Majority*, ed. Leo Grebler, Joan W. Moore and Ralph C. Guzman (New York: Macmillan Free Press, 1970), 449–85.

58. Cited by Burns, "The Mexican American Community in California," 150, nn. 10, 11, 12.

59. Otto A. Maduro, *Religion and Social Conflicts* (Maryknoll, N.Y.: Orbis Books, 1982).

60. González, *The Theological Education of Hispanics*, 62; Stevens-Arroyo and Díaz-Stevens, *An Enduring Flame*, 140–46; 153–65.

61. Stevens-Arroyo, *Prophets Denied Honor*, 50–64; 58–63; 85–99.

62. Acuña, *Occupied America*, 8.

63. Elizondo, *The Future Is Mestizo*; Stevens-Arroyo and Díaz-Stevens, *An Enduring Flame*.

64. Ana María Díaz-Stevens, *Oxcart Catholicism on Fifth Avenue* (Notre Dame: University of Notre Dame Press, 1993); Ana María Díaz-Stevens, "The Matriarchal Core of Latino Catholicism," *Latino Studies Journal* 4, no. 3 (September 1993): 60–78.

65. The Mexican American Catholic experience is described in its various regional manifestations in *Mexican Americans and the Catholic Church, 1900–1965*; for Puerto Rican migration see Stevens-Arroyo and Díaz-Stevens Ramírez, "Puerto Ricans in the United States," 196–232. Also very useful is Joan Moore, "The Social Fabric of the Hispanic Community since 1965," in *Hispanic Catholic Culture in the U.S.: Issues and Concerns*, ed. Jay P. Dolan and Allan Figueroa Deck, SJ (Notre Dame, Ind.: University of Notre Dame Press, 1994), 6–49.

66. Patrick Hayes McNamara, "Bishops, Priests and Prophecy: A Study in the Sociology of Religious Protest" (PhD diss., University of California, Los Angeles, 1968). By the same author see also "Dynamics of the Catholic Church from Pastoral to Social Concerns," in Grebler, Joan Moore, and Ralph C. Guzman, *The Mexican American People*, 449–85; "Catholicism, Assimilation and the Chicano Movement: Los Angeles as a Case Study," in *Chicanos and Native Americans*, ed. Rudolfo de la Garza, Z. Anthony Kruszewski, and Tomás A. Arciniega (Englewood Cliffs, N.J.: Prentice Hall, 1973), 124–30.

67. There was considerable variance in the shape of the outreach. Within Catholicism, for instance, pastoral care and social concerns often competed for hegemony. The first approach emphasized the administration of sacraments, church attendance, and piety; the other viewed the church's mission in terms of aid in matters such as housing, clothing, job opportunities, and social organization. Generally, the two emphases coexisted, as for instance in the inter-diocesan initiative of the Bishops' Committee for the Spanish-Speaking. Established in 1945, this was an effort funded and coordinated at a national level to address the religious and social needs of Mexican American migrant workers who traveled annually from Texas and California northward toward Illinois, Michigan, and

Ohio in search of seasonal work. See Sandoval, *On the Move*, 46–48. In this program, clergy were trained to speak Spanish and to provide services to the workers as they traveled from one place to another. Those who chose pastoral care as their primary duty devoted their energies to administering the sacraments. But alongside them were still others who struggled against poor wages and miserable living conditions by taking political action. Although ostensibly for all Latinos in the United States, the Bishops' committee really targeted Mexican Americans. That appears to be the reason that Cardinal Spellman of New York inaugurated a similar program with both pastoral and social concerns that linked New York and the northeast with Puerto Rico, thus providing religious attention to migrants from Puerto Rico. See Díaz-Stevens, *Oxcart Catholicism on Fifth Avenue*.

68. Stephen A. Privett, SJ, *The United States Catholic Church and Its Hispanic Members: The Pastoral Vision of Archbishop Robert E. Lucey* (San Antonio: Trinity University Press, 1988).

69. Joseph P. Fitzpatrick, SJ, *One Church, Many Cultures* (Kansas City, Kans.: Sheed and Ward, 1987).

70. This is the subject of a book coauthored with Ana María Díaz-Stevens: *Recognizing the Latino Resurgence in U.S. Religion: The Emmaus Paradigm* (Boulder, Colo.: Westview Press, 1998).

71. Anthony M. Stevens-Arroyo and Ana María Díaz-Stevens, "Latino Church and Schools as Urban Battlegrounds," in *Handbook of Schooling in Urban America*, ed. Stanley Rothstein (Westport, Conn.: Greenwood Press, 1993), 245–70.

72. Ana María Díaz-Stevens, "From Puerto Rican to Hispanic: The Politics of the *Fiestas Patronales* in New York," *Latino Studies Journal* 1, no. 1 (January 1990): 28–47.

73. Felix Padilla, *Latino Ethnic Consciousness: The Case of Mexican Americans and Puerto Ricans in Chicago* (Notre Dame, Ind.: University of Notre Dame Press, 1985).

74. Armando Rendon, *Chicano Manifesto* (New York: Collier Books, 1971).

75. Mario T. García, *Mexican Americans: Leadership, Ideology, and Identity, 1930–1960* (New Haven, Conn.: Yale University Press, 1989).

76. Pope John Paul II, Address to the Fiftieth General Assembly of the United Nations, New York, 5 October 1996, 14, *Insegnamenti* 18, no. 2 (1995): 741.

II

Mexican American Mystics

and Prophets

3

Sacred Order, Sacred Space

Reies López Tijerina and the Valle de Paz Community

In February 1957, a small group of Mexican American farmworkers clad in white robes emerged from the Arizona desert and arrived in the snow-covered landscapes of northern New Mexico. Wary of these outsiders, the New Mexican *vecinos* warned their neighbors, "¡Los barbones aquí andan!" (Here come the bearded ones!). The leader of the group, a young, brash ex–Assemblies of God preacher named Reies López Tijerina (figure 1), had months earlier received a spectacular vision from heavenly messengers and was now making his way toward its fulfillment in the pine-covered mountains and valleys of northern New Mexico's Río Arriba County. At the time no one could predict that in ten years' time this Pentecostal evangelist would throw the political landscape of New Mexico into utter chaos, becoming one of the legendary heroes of the Chicano Movement. But in 1957, Tijerina and his followers had come to New Mexico as a be-draggled and homeless group of religious sectarians.

Through the mediation of acquaintances Tijerina began meeting with community elders and the aged members of the secretive Catholic Peni-tente Brotherhood, systematically educating himself in the history of New Mexico Hispano land loss in the decades following the end of the Mexi-can-American War in 1848. At public meetings with the descendants of land grant families, some older members of the community approached him on their knees to kiss his feet, proclaiming him to be the prom-ised leader of local legends who would turn back the white man.[1] Over time Tijerina would employ the oral testimonies he had gathered and, later, original land grant deeds and legal documents he collected to fuel an organized struggle to regain lands that many Spanish-speaking New

1. Reies López Tijerina speaking on behalf of the Poor People's
March, 1968. Courtesy: Karl Kernberger Collection, Center for
Southwest Research, University of New Mexico.

Mexicans considered to be stolen. In 1963, Tijerina organized the Alianza
Federal de Mercedes Reales (Federal Alliance of Land Grants) as a strategy to combine the efforts of land grant activists who had struggled for
land use rights, with the adjudication of disputed Spanish and Mexican
land grant deeds. For over a century resistance by Hispanos to the loss
of land and access to grazing and timber had taken the forms of threat,
outright violence, fence cutting, and litigation.

Tijerina's advocacy work in the rough-and-tumble world of New Mexican land grant politics eventually led to direct action by the *alianza*, including the 1966 reoccupation of the San Joaquín del Río de Chama land
grant—which happened to be within the boundaries of the U.S. National
Forest lands—and the spectacular June 1967, armed assault on the Tierra
Amarilla County Courthouse. The "courthouse raid," a signature event in
Chicano history that helped launch the Chicano Movement, also forever
changed the way that politicians, policy makers, activists, and scholars
think about issues of land and water rights, economic development, and
cultural preservation throughout the American Southwest. The alianza's
attack on the courthouse, intended to arrest the New Mexico district at-

torney, Alfonso Sánchez, had been provoked by Sánchez's attempt to keep the organization from holding a meeting. As a result of the courthouse raid and the massive manhunt for the raiders that followed, Tijerina and the alianza grabbed headlines across the nation. In 1972 an NBC documentary dubbed him "The Most Hated Man in New Mexico." Chicano activists celebrated him as a bona fide revolutionary—some referring to him as the "Che Guevara" of northern New Mexico—while his critics feared his land grant organization would lead to the "Cubanization" of New Mexico.[2]

Tijerina's success at galvanizing Spanish-speaking Americans in poverty-stricken northern New Mexico into an organized and formidable defense of contested land grants was all the more remarkable given that he was an outsider from Texas and had arrived in Catholic New Mexico as a Pentecostal schismatic. Born and raised a migrant farmworker in South Texas, Tijerina had come into contact with Evangelical Christianity in his teen years and had received the call to preach the Pentecostal version of the Gospel at age eighteen. Although he had only a partial grade-school education, he entered the Assemblies of God Instituto Bíblico Latino Americano, in Saspamco, Texas, in 1944 to train as a minister. Between 1946, the year he was expelled from the Bible Institute, and his arrival in New Mexico in 1957, Tijerina wandered the countryside preaching a puritanical fundamentalist theology that chastised the complacency of American Christianity and condemned the evils of post–World War II American culture. This powerful religious worldview, which continued to inform his land grant politics even at the height of his notoriety in the 1960s, however, has not been fully acknowledged in the historical narratives of the Chicano Movement.

Since the late 1960s Chicano history has characterized Tijerina as one of the "Four Horsemen" of the Chicano Movement (along with César Chávez, Rodolfo "Corky" Gonzáles, and José Angel Gutiérrez). Jesús Treviño's film *Yo soy chicano* (1972), for example, depicts Tijerina as the reincarnation of turn-of-the-century Mexican "bandido" armed guerrilla resistance against Anglo hegemony. Similarly, but with scarcely less subtlety, the 1996 documentary *¡Chicano! The History of the Mexican American Civil Rights Movement* (episode 1, "Quest for a Homeland"), wrapped Tijerina in a cultural nationalist sentimentality focused on the inexorable quest for a Chicano homeland.[3]

This view of Tijerina as the consummate Chicano *movimiento* activist, however, has foreclosed other interpretations of him and ignores crucial religious aspects of his remarkable, controversial, and robust life. When

Tijerina was released from federal prison in 1971 after serving twenty-one months of concurrent prison sentences for his land grant activities, his supporters expected "King Tiger" to come roaring out of his cage and reinvigorate the flagging Chicano Movement. Instead, Tijerina emerged from his confinement preaching a new conciliatory and coalition politics based on a platform he called "Brotherhood Awareness." Such a dramatic shift in Tijerina's political perspective led to rumors about involuntary lobotomies and forced experimental drug trials at the hands of the U.S. government while he was in prison. These conspiratorial explanations were in fact the only ones that made any sense to Chicano activists unaware of, or refusing to acknowledge, the religious motor driving Tijerina's life and thought. When Tijerina no longer played the part of the Chicano revolutionary nationalist, he was written out of the trajectory of Chicano history and locked inside the narratives of the 1967 courthouse raid image.

Yet Tijerina did in fact continue a vigorous and contentious public life after 1971, though that part of his biography is beyond the scope of this essay. However, if we are to make any sense of Tijerina's life, we must first ask, "What happened to Tijerina before he began his land grant work in New Mexico in 1957?" Or better perhaps, "What does Tijerina's life look like between the lines of standard interpretations of him in Chicano history?" This chapter examines two years in Tijerina's extraordinary life prior to his land grant politics: his experiment in sectarian communalism, the Valle de Paz (1955–57).

The Valle de Paz Experiment

The story of the Valle de Paz (Valley of Peace) community has yet to be told. Most of what we know about this short-lived communitarian experiment comes from a short description in Tijerina's memoir, *Mi lucha por la tierra*, and a few summarizing paragraphs in Richard Gardner's and Peter Nabokov's books on the courthouse raid.[4] Tijerina's own account, retold through the hindsight advantage of two decades, remains the only insider glimpse we have. The lack of collected and documented evidence, however, in no way diminishes the importance of the Valle de Paz as the only known Mexican American religious utopia in the United States. In fact, the elusiveness and disappearance of the Valle de Paz in Chicano history's imagination, scholarship on American utopias, and the physical geography itself are very much evidence of the erasure and invisibility of Mexican American labor and religion in the U.S. Southwest. Arising within the context of a bureaucratic agricultural economy dependent upon Mexican labor in the irrigated desert, the short-lived Valle de Paz was eventually swallowed up by the outcomes of regional Sunbelt development.

After his expulsion from the Instituto Bíblico in 1946, Tijerina spent almost a decade as a wandering evangelist. By 1955 he headed a band of *valientes* (brave ones): men, women, and children drawn to him by their religious conviction and faith in his leadership. His wife, María, who had also been a student at the Bible Institute, accompanied him throughout his ministry and managed to raise their first children on the road. During his itinerancy Tijerina wrote and privately published a collection of apocalyptic sermons, *Hallará fe en la tierra . . . ?*; it served as the theological blueprint for his community. These short sermons, full of wrath and contempt for false Christianity, reveal that Tijerina anticipated the imminent destruction of corrupt American society.[5] Between his exile from the Assemblies of God Bible Institute, and his arrival in the Arizona desert, Tijerina and his family wandered the entire width and breadth of the nation on the edge of abject but spiritually purifying poverty. At times he would leave his family and wander off on his own,

> teaching, talking to the other people . . . farm workers, in the towns going from one church to another where I was invited. I would sleep under bridges, or in the open. Drunkards and poor people would invite me to their homes to eat. It was a training period. My beliefs were greater than my experience.[6]

Eventually the years on the road and watching his family live from hand to mouth wore him out. He decided it was time to put into practice what he had, up to now, only known was right in his heart. With his closest followers he began to look for a suitable location for his experiment in truth, ready to see himself and his followers through the impending holocaust as the truly chosen spiritual Israel. After years of provoking congregations to admit their hypocrisy and reform their lives, he was ready to brush the dust of their complacent faith from his shoes and withdraw with his followers from the corruption of the world: "I saw and heard so many things in those years that I was preaching from place to place that I can't remember them all, only the ugliness and hopelessness," he told one of his early biographers, "a man could preach the word of God forever and never change a thing."[7]

Tijerina lists nine men and their families as loyal followers coming out of the shadowy first half of the 1950s.[8] Calling themselves the Heralds of Peace, Tijerina and his followers purchased a tract of Arizona desert for less than $9 an acre between a triangle bounded by the small towns of Casa

Grande, Eloy, and Coolidge, approximately fifty miles south of Phoenix. Tijerina tells us that his first choice for the community had been somewhere in Texas near where his mother was buried but the land prices there were prohibitive. Gardner records that Tijerina chose "the wildest spot I could find so that we wouldn't trouble others and wouldn't be bothered ourselves." Tijerina remembers that the Valle de Paz was a way to rescue his family and those who wanted to "withdraw from the system of the 'church' and corrupt society." In 1955 he and his followers spent a back-breaking summer thinning, weeding, and blocking sugar beets in Fruita, Colorado. At the end of the season they pooled their wages and bought 160 acres of forbidding chaparral. "I had fought with the 'church' (with all religion) for ten long years, trying to get them to take the side of the poor in their struggle against the rich, but had failed," he remembers. The Assemblies "threw me out and I was convinced that my struggle (against them) was useless." However, "here in the desert my soul found the peace and safety that I longed for"; "We decided to call this virgin land, Valle de Paz. Here neither the church nor the school would be able to condition the minds of our children. We were far from danger, from temptation, from the influences of the monopolies, and we would be happy."[9]

The Heralds of Peace sought refuge in the dramatic Santa Cruz Valley desert flatlands surrounded by sawtooth mountains, far from the corrosive influences of the wicked cities. Constructing dwellings appropriate to their poverty and sense of simplicity, Tijerina recalls: "Like ants, we began to remove the earth. Each family settled temporarily beneath a tree while each *valiente* dug a pit. From the city dumps of Casa Grande and Eloy, Arizona, we obtained car hoods and trunks for roofing our subterranean homes."[10]

In addition to the subterranean homes, the Heralds built a church, school, and small common storage facility. To keep the settlement viable, the utopians worked in local agricultural during the day, returning in the evenings to continue excavating and constructing their homes.[11] The small settlement appears to have started out replicating traditional Mexican patriarchal family life under Tijerina's charismatic leadership. Life was simple. The women made all of the clothing and cooked in converted gas tanks retrieved from local dumps. Food was shared in common, and parents were held responsible for their children's socialization and education. "We created what we considered to be a paradise," Tijerina recalls. "Everyone was happy. No one spoke of returning to his or her previous lives. For the first six months we enjoyed the peace and freedom that we had been looking for." Outside the community, there seems to have been only marginal interest at first in the "gypsy camp over at Peter's Corner" during the first fall and winter spent in the mild desert climate.[12] A long growing season translated into plentiful work, and nearby towns would supply any necessities the Heralds of Peace might need to buy.

Initially the Valle of Paz community was self-sufficient and isolated, but eventually it attracted notice among local farmworkers and other minorities. Tijerina's reputation as someone knowledgeable about legal matters and willing to mediate on behalf of the poor had followed him.

> Blacks, Indians, and Mexicans from the surrounding area began to visit us. Many of them revealed to us their problems and grievances: soon after helping the first one out of jail I was unable to handle them all. Mothers, fathers, spouses and other relatives came to see me in order to get their loved ones out of jail.[13]

The Valle de Paz experiment is the first event Tijerina records in his memoir. As with all of his writing, there is an overpowering relationship to the Bible in the memoir and especially in his narration about the Valle de Paz settlement. Here Tijerina constructs the Valle de Paz narrative to reenact the important events of Old Testament patriarchs and prophets, choosing Moses as his framing figure (leading his followers into and out of the desert). The intervening episodes between when the Valle de Paz was established in 1955, and early 1957 when the community collapsed, recapitulate dramatic events from the lives of Adam, Noah, Jacob, and Zechariah interpreted through a fundamentalist cosmovision of divine good struggling to overcome powerful evil. This cosmic battle he sets into motion through the account of María's delivery of a daughter in the spring of 1956.

> On the 18th of April, the first inhabitant of Valle de Paz was born. I helped my wife with the birth, the child was born in the subterranean home that I had built with my own hands. I was thirty years old and this was the first house that I had ever built. It cost me sixty days of work, but not a single cent. When my wife gave birth, I took into my hands the child I named Ira de Alá. And when I stood up, I saw a rattlesnake tangled around the headboard of the bed where my wife lay. I moved my daughter and wife away and killed the snake.

> It had been 10 years since the United States had started to manufacture atomic bombs; continuing day and night without ceasing. And I had been convinced that the Church had damaged humanity more than any other organization on the Earth.

I knew that if there was a God of Justice, he had to be angry and very unhappy with those who ran the government and religion here on the earth.

And for this reason I gave my daughter the name Ira de Alá [wrath of God]; I was also very unhappy with the way men were running things.[14]

On the surface, the mythic themes of creation, the combat between good and evil, and theogony are compelling. Here Tijerina inserts the actors of Ira de Alá's birth into the framework of the biblical creation myth, infusing it with his fundamentalist preacher's anger ("I was also very unhappy with the way men were running things").

The snake, the biblical symbol for evil (Gen. 3:14–16), appears here in opposition to the birth of a female child later named "Wrath of God," reminding the reader of the enmity placed by God between Eve and the serpent in Genesis 2. Tijerina writes himself into the role of creator or protector in the narrative and brings to this primordial chaos and antagonism Satan's defeat as promised in the New Testament. However, Tijerina's subterranean narrative is more than a rehearsal of Biblical cosmogony, reflecting a deep Mexican connection to the physical earth, traditional Mexican family values of patriarchal control, and gestures toward indigenous concepts of genesis and emergence. Beneath the profane surface world of humanity, outside of the measurements of time and history, Tijerina forges his own version of the creation: the incarnate "Wrath of God" is born out of the union between father/Adam/King (*Reies*), and the mother of God/Eve/Mary (*María*). There are two simultaneous acts of creation or salvation here: the mythological one in the Bible and the one that creates the Valle de Paz. The magic realist quality in Tijerina's recounting of his daughter's birth is not merely allegory or origin myth, but the material unfolding of a triumphant divine justice in the world—expressed here on the microcosmic, personal, one might say daily level of humble human existence.

"I the Lord will make myself known unto him in a vision" (Num. 12:6)

Seven days after Ira de Alá's birth, Tijerina left the Valle de Paz for Southern California. He was still pulled to his evangelist calling, and a church in Visalia had invited Tijerina to preach. While he was away in California a torrential rainstorm swept over the tiny Valley of Peace, flooding out many of its residents. Guadalupe Jáuregui, the *valiente* who had been left in charge of the community, called Tijerina in California to relay the extent of the storm's damage. "Your wife is living under a tree because your home is under water," Jáuregui reported. Forced to rethink the wisdom of his withdrawal into the desert now that his family was homeless, Tijerina was thrown into despair, afraid that he had led his followers into disaster. That evening, tired and distraught, he spent the night outside his host's house. "All night I spent outside. That night I had a vision."[15] Tijerina's vision, or *supersueño* (superdream) as he refers to it, changed the course of his life and has ever since led him to search out its possible meanings.

The "superdream," vivid and full of biblical and archetypal images, involved being caught up in a cloud/machine by three angels and taken to a dark forest. There Tijerina came across a herd of frozen horses, who came to life when he and his angelic companions mounted them. Eventually the group arrived at the gates of an ancient kingdom, where Tijerina was held aloft by a great crowd and then ushered forward to meet with the aged "chiefs," who offered him a silver key and dominion over a large stretch of territory.[16]

Tijerina explains that at the time he was still unsure about the meaning of the dream. At first he told only his two trusted traveling companions because he was afraid of what the others might have thought of him. Later, when discussing with several of his valientes the possible implications that the dream had for the entire Valle de Paz community, he reviewed the events of his life and concluded that the dream was responding to "the invitations that the people of Tierra Amarilla had made in 1945, 1951 and 1952" for him to settle among them. Eventually he was convinced that the ancient kingdom in the dream was in fact New Mexico, and the frozen horses the dormant Spanish land grants. As in the dream, Tijerina would be the agent of their reanimation.[17]

Awakened from his extraordinary dream, he began "to see new things and to understand other things" that earlier he "could not have understood." Later that morning he and his companions bid farewell to their hosts and drove back to Arizona. Later, when he was leading the valientes to Colorado to work the sugar beets a brilliant rainbow arched across the sky, confirming for him that he was following the right path.

The Collapse of Valle de Paz

Believing, but not fully understanding the commission revealed to him in the superdream, Tijerina's enthusiasm for his world-renouncing experiment in the desert faded, with trouble coming from his rancher neighbors, local and federal officials, and a series of events he assumed foreshadowed the Valle de Paz's doom. Vandalism by neighborhood teens on horseback went uninvestigated by the local sheriff; one of the community's children was abducted and raped while walking down a road adjacent to the colony; and a U.S. Air Force jet crashed on the property. An old woman in the community went insane, and a pregnant girl lost her child. Eventually, multiple charges of theft against Tijerina and his brothers forced the leadership to consider abandoning the settlement.

The financial condition of the community began to deteriorate, and by May of 1956 the entire community was forced to return to the Colorado beet fields. In June, Tijerina was in New Mexico with a handful of his male followers, drawn by a connection between his dream and memories of earlier trips he made there as an evangelist. An acquaintance, Zebedeo Martínez, began to explain to Tijerina the loss of the Tierra Amarilla land grant. He introduced him to the aging members of the Penitente Brotherhood, who related stories of how Spanish Americans had been cheated out of their lands, convincing Tijerina that perhaps Mexico's history held answers to questions about the land grants. Three months later he traveled alone to Mexico on his thirtieth birthday.

Tijerina spent three inspired months in Mexico visiting archives and touring historical sites. It was there that he learned about Spanish colonial administrative documents, and held in his hands a fragile copy of the *Recopilación de leyes de los Indias*, the first codified laws for Spanish America. Along with the Bible, the "Laws of the Indies" would later serve as a "sacred" text for Tijerina in his land grant research. He thrice visited the pyramids at Teotihuacán, the last time climbing to the summit of one of them and meditating on recent events. "I felt like a stranger on this planet" he recalls, "[a planet] so old and yet I don't even know the history of my own people, much less the world." That night Tijerina had another dream whose meaning he pondered for days: "I found myself among the magnates of Mexico and the continent. But the way we treated each other was with the trust that can only exist between brothers of the same family." He was now certain that his mission was to work in New Mexico among the disinherited land grant heirs.[18]

The final blow to the Valle de Paz came in the form of the U.S. Department of Education, whose agents had arrived to investigate truancy among the children. Tijerina claims to have obtained permission from the Arizona Department of Education to homeschool the children, and the community had devoted three months to building a one-room schoolhouse. But along with the vandalism of the subterranean homes, the school had been damaged and burned by neighboring teens. Tijerina writes that he argued forcefully with the state for an exemption under the First Amendment, citing the Mennonite, Quaker, and Amish exemptions to mandatory public schooling. But this final attempt to salvage the integrity of the community's sovereignty failed. Even attempts to gain public sympathy for the community by getting his side of the story told in the Arizona press were unsuccessful. "We had left our home states, sacrificed our families and left the world in search of peace. And now they denied us the right to educate our children," he complained. "We were forced by threat of jail and guns to accept a foreigner's education. . . . They closed all of the doors. I asked for counsel from the invisible forces, but there was no solution or alternative to the Anglo threats and violence." The ultimatum from the Education Department was an obstacle the Heralds of Peace were unable to overcome. "They didn't bother us about religion, invite us to their churches or force us to their gatherings. But they wanted our children in their school. And they decided to teach them by force."[19]

Besieged by forces beyond their control, the Heralds decided to flee the Valley of Peace rather than meet a prescribed deadline for placing the children in local public schools. Conveniently, pressing difficulties with the local Pinal County sheriff's office over charges of stolen property found in the community made the decision to abandon the property expedient. Leaving behind a few members of the community to safeguard the property, Tijerina led a caravan out of the Valley of Peace and headed northeast toward New Mexico in the cold first days of February 1957. The community had collapsed.

Larger Landscapes

Notwithstanding Tijerina's later claims that the community was not religious, the model and principles directing his leadership were undeniably the outcome of his Pentecostal or fundamentalist suspicion of the secular world, propelled by a dark apocalypticism. By the end of the communal experiment Tijerina's religious worldview remained intact, but the changing world around him forced him to accommodate his beliefs to the immediate needs of his followers. It is here in the desert crossroads between the metropolitan areas of Phoenix and Tucson, amidst a patchwork of Native American reservations and the northward migration of Mexican nationals, that race difference and class antagonisms began to erode the spiritual vision of a separate community based on an exclusivist Christianity.

Tijerina's move into the Arizona desert had been in large part motivated by the growing nativism and Cold War fears of the period. Chicano scholars have summarized the crushing effects postwar changes in the American economy and culture had on Mexican Americans and how Mexican American labor became trapped in the secondary-labor market sector.[20] Tijerina's wanderings through the Southwest and Midwest and across the U.S.-Mexican border brought him into contact with an endless cross-stream of bracero and *mojado* ("wetback") labor under constant threat by Anglo labor unions and deportation programs of the Immigration and Naturalization Service (INS). Tijerina's suspicion of the secular world was everywhere confirmed as he watched Mexican Americans moving into urban areas, where they encountered the corrosive effects of "white flight," job discrimination, and de facto racial segregation.

Economic life in rural Pinal County during the late 1950s provides insight into the context for how the Valley of Peace was able to survive on a day-to-day basis. Situated in the western, agricultural area of the county, the Valle de Paz colonists took advantage of the rapidly growing cotton production in the long growing season climate of the central Arizona desert. The miracle of modern irrigation initiatives had transformed the chaparral-covered county into one of the nation's top cotton-growing regions. In 1956, the first year of the Valle de Paz settlement, Pinal County ranked third in the nation for cotton production. Ample agricultural labor opportunity was just outside the Valle de Paz, with some 350,000 irrigated acres within the Casa Grande, Eloy, and Coolidge triangle.

As with other western agricultural paradises, more than half of the cultivation and harvesting of cotton at the time was performed by seasonal workers supervised by labor contractors and crew leaders. The majority of laborers, or "Drive Out" crews as they were called, were strategically housed at a labor camp aptly named 11 Mile Corner, because it was a convenient eleven miles or so to any of the three cities in the agricultural triangle. The Arizona State Employment Office notes that at the time this farm labor force was "comprised of Negroes, Spanish-Americans, Anglo-Americans, Pima and Papago Indians." To supplement the fall cotton harvest, an additional multiracial labor force was hired. Augmenting this already large workforce in 1956 was a population of 3,794 bracero Mexicans vulnerable to the vicissitudes of local and national labor markets and xenophobia. Incoming bracero labor, welcomed as temporary workers after World War II, was cresting at an all time high nationally the same year Tijerina set up his community.[21]

Arizona become dependent upon bracero labor for the agricultural boom in the 1950s. Unfortunately, the weaknesses in a system which denigrated Mexican labor but was almost completely reliant upon large numbers of these workers allowed for the abuse and exploitation of these men and women. It is no surprise then that the Valle de Paz, a Spanish-speaking community suspicious of the world beyond their 160 acres, provided welcome sanctuary for undocumented laborers making their way through the desolate Sonora desert along the lifelines of Highway 84 or the Southern Pacific Railroad tracks that passed the northeast corner of the community's property. Making their way northward, migrant and undocumented workers and their families not only had to contend with searing heat in the long summers and bone-chilling nights in the winter and lack of water; they also had to hide from an increasingly militarized INS, and avoid falling into the hands of local Native American bounty hunters with "Operation Wetback," who were paid $2.50 to $3.00 per person caught on surrounding reservation lands.[22] At one point, the Valle de Paz community sheltered a group of braceros who complained to Tijerina about the withholding of wages by ranchers and the commonplace violence that Mexican laborers had to endure.[23]

The centrality of a racialized agricultural labor force in the American West, and the process of taming wild desert landscapes into disciplined and productive rows of crops both set the larger context for the Valle de Paz. These factors were simultaneously responsible for the physical survivability of the community as well as its inevitable doom. Fueled by the power of Tijerina's charisma and the sheer determination of its members, the Valle de Paz upset both the need for a deportable, migratory ethnic Mexican labor force, and the encroaching sightlines of the surveyor's vision of well-ordered highways, tract houses, and city streets.

For as briefly as it stood, the Valle de Paz challenged the secular ideologies that eventually crushed it. Compelled by religious vision and faith, the community was in direct opposition to the economic and political realities surrounding it. It was also hampered by its religious differences with local Mexican American communities that might have otherwise offered them assistance. The Heralds of Peace were from neither the closely knit communities in the area, nor part of the mobile transient Mexican national agricultural labor force.[24] Their middle position between these two sets of ethnic Mexican populations (the ones that are usually the focus of study) no doubt worked against them at times, but assured them their isolation and served to reinforce group bonds and tie them closer to their leader. This isolation, as well as a basic misunderstanding of the desert ecology, could not, however, be overcome even by their intrepid leader's resourcefulness.

Valle de Paz as Frontier Utopia

The Valle de Paz colony has been ignored or regarded as an odd footnote in the story of Tijerina's personal transformation from doomsday Pentecostal prophet to fiery land rights activist. This omission by his biographers and Chicano history, misses the power of Tijerina's religious vision and his community's spiritual ideology. The uprooting of families from their traditional kinship networks in response to Tijerina's millennialist call required not only the courage of conviction, but a transcending of cultural identities and values in favor of citizenship in a fragile earthly fellowship. If at any point in his religious life Tijerina fit the classical model of sectarian religious leadership, it was here at the head of the short-lived Valle de Paz community. The power of his vision of a restored, original Christianity amplified through his overwhelming personal magnetism goes a long way toward explaining how he was able to attract and convince a sizable number of believers into following him into a future visible only to those with the eyes of faith. Withdrawing from a world they had come to see as already judged and consigned to God's refining fire, they awaited the inevitable apocalyptic end their leader predicted would soon come.

Like so many other religious visionaries in American Christianity, Tijerina pursued what he thought to be a better way for Christians to live in the world as inspired by the triumph of ancient Israel (as a model of God's chosen people) and the first-century Christians. These ideas and principles we see in his writing and in the Valle de Paz community experiment. What is less accessible through Tijerina's writing and scholarship about him is his overwhelming charisma; a force more than the sum of his physical stature, religious zeal, piercing hazel eyes, animated gestures, and electrifying public speaking. This sacred "*extraordinary* quality" of Tijerina's leadership, however, is different from the symbolic, political leadership imposed on him later by Chicano Movement historians.[25] Unwilling to abide by any other authority than God's—whether in dreams, or in the ancient texts of the Bible—Tijerina's confidence in the God of justice meant rejecting American Christianity; insulating his followers from the corrupt churches and isolating them from the corrupting Americanization occurring around them.

Ultimately the Heralds of Peace were unable to completely disconnect from the world, owing to the hard facts of race and the labor market. Despite their valiant efforts and physical seclusion from the secular world, the realities of daily survival must have been rude reminders for them that the Kingdom of God on earth would be long in coming. And even though the victorious theology of Pentecostalism might have compensated the colonists for their structural location in the real world as migrant laborers, there were no real world gains to be had in the Arizona desert: outside of their enclave, the chosen of God were valued by the world only as cheap Mexican labor. Clinging to their convictions, they found the forces of the world literally come crashing down on them as neighboring youth on horseback rode over their homes, thunderstorms washed them out, and state and local governments began pressuring them to assimilate. The combined chaos and hostility of the world overcame even the power of Tijerina's strong leadership.

The other part of the Valle de Paz story is the physical context, of which corporate agriculture is only one facet. The vastness of the central Arizona desert is itself integral to the narrative of the Valle de Paz as it struggled at the edge of a rapidly transforming Sunbelt geography. A reading of the Valle de Paz landscape—with its subterranean pit houses, rustic above-ground structures, and human interactions—requires a type of salvage archaeology or hermeneutic of space for analyzing the relationships between geography, built environment, race relations in industrial agriculture, and a people transformed through religious ideology. The Valle de Paz offers us an opportunity to understand how this desert space was simultaneously "a social product (or outcome) and a shaping force (or medium) in social life." Nigel Thrift's notion of ephemeral historical spaces as "lost wor(l)d's" speaks to the elusiveness and eventual loss and erasure of the Valle de Paz as a once viable, but now lost "living set of social relations" in that small tract of land.[26]

In 1960, while preoccupied with learning about the New Mexico land grant situation, Tijerina had been contacted by interested parties offering to buy the Valle de Paz property. Learning that Rockefeller money was being poured into the planning of Arizona City, a model community less than three miles from the now defunct colony, Tijerina paid the back taxes on the property and waited for a better offer. While in its brief and troubled life the Valle de Paz signified a utopia of nature and escape, the retirement and leisure development, Arizona City, replaced it as a utopia of technology, bureaucracy, and reconstruction—what Dolores Hayden refers to as a "Fat City:" a "suburb which instead of synthesizing the best of both an urban and rural life has denied itself the quality of either in exchange for the material benefits of both." As such, Arizona City would become a Fat City heaven that could boast: "a low crime rate," "a wide choice of recreation," an "18-hole championship golf course," "over 90 miles of paved wide congestion free streets," and easy access to "two factory malls, over 85 stores" located in the heart of the "golden corridor" midway between Tucson and Phoenix.[27] The final obliteration of the tiny community by the construction of Interstate Highway 10 in the 1960s, and the promises of "golden corridor" boosters, does in fact speak wor(l)ds to the capitalist development and cartographic control of the landscape by regional planners in the booming 1950s Arizona Sunbelt economy.

But the Arizona desert has always been a stage for utopian dramas. The same year that the Heralds of Peace were digging into the desert earth, 125 miles to the north the Italian visionary architect, Paolo Soleri, was carving out an earth house prototype of his futuristic community of Arcosanti into the high desert. Inspired by a philosophy of "Arcology," Soleri imagined urban architecture and ecology as a single interwoven process. And like the Valle de Paz, Soleri's vision of utopia would also fall prey to the necessities of capitalism and consumerism—as the project's survival became dependent upon optimistic volunteers, the proceeds from tourist visits, and the sale of expensive ceramics and wind chimes. Only miles from the Valle de Paz the remnants of the U.S. government's experiment in farming, Valley Farms, had also been drawn to the promises of the open landscape and the miracles of desert irrigation. Initiated by no less than Eleanor Roosevelt, Valley Farms was imagined to be a modern agricultural utopia, a witness to the blooming desert and the ingenuity of technology, but completely held hostage to the availability of cheap migrant labor. The nearby remains of the Poston Relocation Center, housing hundreds of Japanese Americans in the 1940s, and the quilt of surrounding Native American reservations are also part of this desert "heterotopia," posing the rhetorical question, "Whose utopia?"[28]

Decades after the rapid suburbanization of the so-called golden corridor and eighty miles east of where the Valle de Paz stood, the scientific visionary community Biosphere 2 attempted to defy the desert by collapsing the opposing utopias of garden and city in a postmodern encapsulation of nature within the bubble of technology—protecting it, ironically, from the natural world itself. Like the Valle de Paz, Biosphere 2's origins lay in the powerful visions of John Polk Allen, who placed his faith in ideas at the margins of scientific inquiry. Eventually, ringing both Phoenix and Tucson in ever expanding concentric circles arose the "edge cities" of retiring workers flocking to the desert Eden's of Sun [City] and Leisure [World].[29]

Valle de Paz, Dreaming, Landscape, and Memory

Cultural geographers have compared the social construction of space with the creation and interpretation of texts and theatrical production, metaphors applicable to what happened at the Valle de Paz. What is less often described in the "new geography" is the alternate script that sectarian religious vision has played out on the stage of landscape. Even though it was viable for only a year or two, the Valle de Paz was charted by an eternal, heavenly geography, a theological cartography superimposed upon the county registrar's meticulously measured maps.[30]

In his memoir Tijerina is imprecise about the exact location of the settlement, hinting only at nearby roads and locations as backdrops to the drama of the landscapes that occurred beneath the visible desert surface and in the nighttime forest and kingdom of his superdream. In ways equally important to the daily economic struggle of the Heralds of Peace, Tijerina's heavenly landscape—full of promise and salvation—was simultaneously dependent upon and yet floated above the worldly concerns of agribusiness, regional planning, and the demands of government education bureaucrats. The texts that ordered and instructed the Valle de Paz were ancient Greek and Hebrew ones that did not necessarily translate into the articulations of capitalism and the post–World War II consumerist environment being set up around them. In 1956 biblical narratives produced the dreamscapes upon which Tijerina built his future. Laid over the narrative of the Valle de Paz's rise and fall, the religious impulse of dreams and prophecy remained at the core of the Heralds of Peace's entry into and exit out of the wilderness. In Tijerina's textual reconstruction of what happened at the Valle de Paz, he interiorized the texts of Genesis and Exodus and scripted the desert with his reenactments of Adam in the Garden, Noah escaping the flood, Jacob's dream and struggle with the angel, Zechariah's vision of men on horses, and Moses leading his people into the wilderness, and then to the edge of the promised land.[31]

When the last car carrying the Heralds of Peace turned off the dirt road onto the highway pointed toward New Mexico, they left behind a palimpsest upon which ideologies of various sorts had inscribed themselves for more than a thousand years. Less than five miles away, the ancient and mysterious Hohokam had built the multistoried Casa Grande fortress against the encroachments of Mexican cultures from the south. The

Spanish had bypassed the hostile region in search of Cíbola, but left missionaries with the people there. In 1862, conflicts that were meaningless to nearby residents erupted at Picacho Pass in the only Civil War battle fought in Arizona. And in 1883 James Addison Reavis, who was settling into his mansion in nearby Arizola, had just filed fraudulent documents proving ownership of the whole of central Arizona and part of eastern New Mexico. In the twentieth century the success of cotton production brought with it the accouterments of American civilization, but at the price of what geographer Don Mitchell refers to as the "ugly process" of agricultural production that ignores the presence of Mexican American labor on the land. Like other farmlands in the late twentieth century, the fertile cotton fields eventually gave way to numbing suburban development. The fragile sacred geography of Tijerina's religious vision was swept away by the utopianism of planned development and economic progress. In the scheme of such overweening designs, the Valle de Paz's presence and impact on the land are negligible but it remains, as Tijerina prefers to remember it, a "monument of our rebellion against the corruption of this nation."[32]

The Valle de Paz experiment was the first of several efforts Tijerina undertook to create bounded and sovereign communities. A decade after the collapse of the Valle Paz, he attempted to reclaim the San Joaquín del Río de Chama land grant. Even the famous 1967 Tierra Amarilla Courthouse raid needs to be understood as Tijerina's search for community, not as bravado for the glory of a nascent Chicano Movement, or the return to the gun-slinging frontier West. Rather, Tijerina's most infamous action occurred as his frustration over bureaucratic obstacles to Spanish-speaking persons' claims to historical communities and land uses boiled over. What is missing in the Chicano historical narratives is that Tijerina eventually found his valley of peace. In the 1980s and 1990s Tijerina and his followers successfully resurrected a portion of the San Joaquín land grant as the "Republic of San Joaquín."

Erased from historical memory for more than half a century, the Valley of Peace remains hidden beneath the desert, its borders on topographical maps forming a diamond set between the old two-lane highway and the newer six-lane interstate cutting diagonally across the desert. To the northwest and southeast, numbered freeway exits with self-serve gas stations and fast-food chain restaurants add to the anonymity of that particular stretch of desert. There is nothing left to see of the Valley of Peace, only burned-out, collapsed shells of the homes that once witnessed the birth of a promised better world.

Notes

This chapter is an earlier conference version of chap. 3 of Rudy V. Busto, *King Tiger: The Religious Vision of Reies López Tijerina* (Albuquerque: University of New Mexico Press, 2005).

1. Nancie L. González, *The Spanish-Americans of New Mexico: A Heritage of Pride* (Albuquerque: University of New Mexico, 1969), 99.

2. The best account of the raid, its background, and consequences remains Peter Nabokov, *Tijerina and the Courthouse Raid* (Berkeley, Calif.: Ramparts Press, 1969). Tijerina's version is recorded in his memoir, *Mi lucha por la tierra* (Mexico City: Fondo de Cultura Económica, 1976). Tijerina eventually spent time in prison for the courthouse raid, for a scuffle with rangers at the occupation of the National Forest in 1966, and for helping his wife, Patricia, set fire to a U.S. National Forest sign in 1969. Clark Knowlton, "Violence in New Mexico: A Sociological Perspective," *California Law Review* 58 (1970): 1053–84.

3. Alejandro Morales, "Expanding the Meaning of Chicano Cinema: Yo Soy Chicano, Raíces de Sangre, S. Shumate Morrison, Susan Seguin," *Bilingual Review/La Revista Bilingüe* 10, nos. 2–3 (May–December 1983): 121–37; Arturo F. Rosales, *¡Chicano! The History of the Mexican American Civil Rights Movement* (documentary film, episode 1, "Quest for a Homeland") (Los Angeles: National Latino Communications Group, 1996).

4. Reies López Tijerina, *Mi lucha por la tierra*, 27–45; Richard Gardner, *¡Grito! Reies Tijerina and the Land Grant War of 1967* (Indianapolis: Bobbs-Merrill, 1970), 45–47; Nabokov, *Tijerina and the Courthouse Raid*, 200–205.

5. Reies López Tijerina, *Hallará fe en la tierra . . . ?* N.p., [1954?].

6. Michael Jenkinson, *Tijerina: Land Grant Conflict in New Mexico* (Albuquerque: Paisano Press, 1968), 21.

7. Gardner, *¡Grito!*, 44.

8. The published memoir lists seven men and their families besides his own. Other sources vary in the number of families that followed him into Arizona.

9. Tijerina, *Mi lucha por la tierra*, 27.

10. Ibid.

11. The remains of the settlement indicate that the subterranean homes were arranged in a roughly circular pattern around central community structures that have since been destroyed.

12. Gardner, *¡Grito!*, 45.

13. Tijerina, *Mi lucha por la tierra*, 28.

14. Ibid.

15. Ibid., 139–40.

16. Busto, *King Tiger*, 122–24.

17. Tijerina, *Mi lucha por la tierra*, 35–36, 139–40.

18. Ibid., 35–36.

19. It is unclear to which U.S. Supreme Court cases he is referring. The Amish case, *Wisconsin v. Yoder*, 406 U.S. 205 (1972), was decades away. He may be conflating the issue of taxation exemption for Quakers and Mennonites with

the education issue in his reconstructed memory. Tijerina, *Mi lucha por la tierra*, 37–38.

20. See, for example, Mario Barrera, *Race and Class in the Southwest: A Theory of Racial Inequality* (Notre Dame, Ind.: University of Notre Dame Press, 1979), 113–49.

21. Employment Security Commission of Arizona, "Pinal County Agricultural Employment Study, September 1956–August 1957," (Phoenix: Arizona State Employment Office, 1957), 3, 5–6; "Pinal County Arizona: An Industrial and Commercial Summary" (Florence, Ariz.: Pinal County Development Board, 1957), 8.

22. Rodolfo Acuña, *Occupied America: A History of Chicanos*, 4th ed. (New York: Addison Wesley Longman, 2000), 304.

23. Tijerina, *Mi lucha por la tierra*, 41.

24. See James Officer, "Sodalities and Systemic Linkage: The Joining Habits of Urban Mexican Americans" (PhD diss., University of Arizona, Tucson, 1964); David Gutiérrez, *Walls and Mirrors: Mexican Americans, Mexican Immigrants, and the Politics of Ethnicity* (Berkeley: University of California Press, 1995).

25. Max Weber defines *charisma* at one point as "an extraordinary quality of a person, regardless of whether this quality is actual, alleged, or presumed. 'Charismatic authority,'" hence, he writes, "shall refer to a rule over men, whether predominantly external or predominantly internal, to which the governed submit because of their belief in the extraordinary quality of the specific person." *From Max Weber: Essays in Sociology*, 2nd ed., trans. Hans Gerth and C. Wright Mills (New York: Oxford University Press, 1949), 295.

26. Edward Soja, *Postmodern Geographies: The Reassertion of Space in Critical Social Theory* (London: Verso Books, 1989), 7. Nigel Thrift, quoted in Allan Pred, *Lost Words, Lost Worlds: Modernity and the Language of Everyday Life in Late Nineteenth-Century Stockholm* (Cambridge: Cambridge University Press, 1990), 7–8, 246, 251 n. 41.

27. Dolores Hayden, *Seven American Utopias: The Architecture of Communitarian Socialism, 1790–1975* (Cambridge, Mass.: MIT Press, 1976), 323; Philip W. Porter and Fred E. Lukermann, "The Geography of Utopia," in *Geographies of the Mind: Essays in Historical Geography* (New York: Oxford, 1976), 197–223; visitor's guide, *Sunland Visitor Center* 5, no. 2 (spring/summer 1996): 4.

28. Paolo Soleri, *The Bridge between Matter and Spirit Is Matter Becoming Spirit: The Arcology of Paolo Soleri* (Garden City, N.J.: Anchor, 1973); Arcosanti promotional brochure (Scottsdale, Ariz.: Cosanti Foundation, n.d.). The Poston internment camp was built by Del Webb, Arizona's foremost developer best known for building the Sun City retirement community. Webb considered the Poston camp his proudest achievement: "I think the greatest thing our company ever did was move the Japs out of California. We did it in 90 days back in the war." John M. Findlay, *Magic Lands: Western Cityscapes and American Culture after 1940* (Berkeley: University of California Press, 1992), 177. Michel Foucault defined heterotopias as spaces "capable of juxtaposing in a single space several

spaces, several sights that are in themselves incompatible." Foucault, "Of Other Spaces," *Diacritics: A Review of Contemporary Criticism* 16, no. 1 (1986): 25.

29. Laurence Veysey, *The Communal Experience: Anarchist and Mystical Counter-cultures in America* (San Francisco: Harper and Row, 1973), 279–406. Carl Abbott, *The Metropolitan Frontier: Cities in the Modern American West* (Tucson: University of Arizona Press, 1993), 68. See also David Jeffrey, "Arizona's Suburbs of the Sun," *National Geographic* 152, no. 4 (October 1977): 487–517.

30. See the essays in James Duncan and David Ley, *Place/Culture/Representation* (London: Routledge, 1993).

31. Soja comments that "every ambitious exercise in critical geographical description, in translating into words the encompassing and politicized spatiality of social life provokes . . . linguistic despair. What one sees when one looks at geographies is stubbornly simultaneous, but language dictates a sequential succession, a linear flow of sentential statements bound by that most spatial of earthly constraints, the impossibility of two objects (or words) occupying the same precise space (as on a page). All that we can do is re-collect and creatively juxtapose, experimenting with assertions and insertions of the spatial against the prevailing grain of time." *Postmodern Geographies*, 2.

32. Tijerina, *Mi lucha por la tierra*, 76, 120. During Tijerina's 1959 visit to the Guadalajara archives, he would discover the theft of documents by Reavis in 1880. See also Rosanna Miller, "The Peralta Land Grant," *Western Association of Map Libraries* 22, no. 2 (March 1991): 121–26; Don Mitchell, *The Lie of the Land: Migrant Workers and the California Landscape* (Minneapolis: University of Minnesota Press, 1996), 202.

4

Holy Activist, Secular Saint

Religion and the Social Activism of César Chávez

The frail, humble man lies peacefully under a crucifix in a dark, small "monastic cell." Like Christ, Saint Francis of Assisi, and Mohandas Gandhi, whose lives he seeks to emulate, he is engaged in an extended fast to gain spiritual strength and discernment. Inspired by a vision of a new world, he denounces the injustices of the current one with a message that is as powerfully spoken as it is inscribed on his body. It was seen as a Second Coming to the groups of men, women, and children of various races and faiths who come like devotees on a sacred pilgrimage. Twenty thousand pilgrims will come over twenty-five days, many of whom will crawl on their knees from the highway to his cell, like the penitent to a holy man. They bring him religious items, crucifixes, and images of saints. They huddle around makeshift shrines to the Virgin of Guadalupe, keeping vigil for the duration of his fast. Priests, with vestments cut from the man's symbolic flag, administer communion from a chapel constructed in a small room across from his bed. The common people fight to merely touch him or kiss him. Some call him a messenger of God sent to deliver the poor from their life of misery, while others call him a shaman, with superhuman hearing abilities and clear visions of the will of God. As he walks outside to receive communion, a prominent statesman awaits. Civic and religious leaders from around the globe send their prayers as he breaks the fast and celebrates his movements and his own personal resurrection with the blood and body of Christ. Five hundred years ago, this man would be seen as a living saint. Today, César Chávez is political activist.

César Chávez (figure 1) is both the most celebrated Latino in American history and one of the most recognizable social activists of the modern

1. César Chávez leading 250-mile pilgrimage march from Delano to Sacramento, California, in 1966. Courtesy: The Walter P. Reuther Library, Wayne State University.

era. Before and especially since his death in 1993, a battle has emerged to define his legacy. The image that has emerged and come to dominate the public discourse is unbalanced. He has been championed as a social and political activist driven by a secular ideology of justice and nonviolence. Yet, contrary to common historical record, it was his *personal spirituality* and not a secularized "ideology" that informed his activism. A careful reading of the historical sources, particularly the words of Chávez himself, reveals that he routinely had direct, extraordinary, and profound encounters with God during his extended fasts. These mystical experiences grounded, directed, and infused his program of social reform by serving as the basis for his decisions. Furthermore, these direct encounters with God were part of a lifelong pattern that was continually shaped by his religious life. Once his actions are read through the prism of his religious life, Chávez emerges as a classical Catholic saint whose closeness to God led him to be seen as a Prophet by his people.

This "sanctified" Chávez is recognized by many in "his" Latino community—especially among farmworkers—but is surprisingly rare outside of it. Seeking to co-opt Chávez and his cause, those who defined his early legacy—the liberal intelligentsia and some Chicano activists— embarked on a conscious, consistent, and comprehensive agenda to secularize Chávez and substitute their own values for his stated motivations.

In the process, they erased the spiritual basis of his public record, thereby creating the "Christ-less" Chávez of popular perception. As the Latino community gains exposure and influence in our society, the difference between the common Latino image of Chávez and the popular media will increasingly become apparent. Will Chávez remain a secular activist, or can he emerge in the public square as a new universal type who can transcend the traditional American boundaries between social activist and popular saint?

The Mysticism and Social Action of César Chávez

Throughout his life, Chávez was a devout Catholic. He spent usually an hour a day in prayer and attended Mass almost daily.[1] As will be apparent in this chapter, elements of his Catholic faith were standard practices of union activities: masses on the picket lines, prayers before meetings, and pilgrimages led under the banner of Our Lady of Guadalupe. During moments of crisis, however, Chávez consistently turned to the particular mystical vehicle of fasting. He made all of his major decisions while engaged in extended fasts. These periods of fasting propelled Chávez to have direct and extraordinary encounters with God—mystical experiences[2]— which he employed as the basis for his major decisions about the life of the United Farmworkers of America (UFW) union. Thus, one can make a direct link between his mystical experiences and his program for social reform. This link is evident throughout the historical sources.

While concerning himself with the everyday business of running a union, Chávez routinely fasted. He fasted "about eight to twelve days every forty-five to sixty days . . . [and] every day between midnight and noon the following day."[3] As a result, his state of mind was continually being shaped by his fasting experience. This is acutely evident in his three public fasts, which came at critical times in his life and the life of his union.[4] For example, the conditions of his 1968 fast were so dire that he even questioned his will to continue.[5] For the popular press and many scholars, the extended fasts were assumed to be protest fasts: hunger strikes to call attention to a specific injustice.[6] Chávez consistently and categorically stated otherwise.[7] His goal was not to incite change in others—which would be consistent for a protest fast—but a personal spiritual transformation.[8] Chávez explained this spiritual goal explicitly in a letter to the National Council of Churches during his 1968 fast: "My fast is informed by my religious faith and by my deep roots in the church. It is not intended as a pressure on anyone but only as an expression of my own deep feelings and my own need to do penance and to be in prayer."[9] By fasting, he was not "demanding something" but "giving" of himself under God.[10]

For Chávez, extreme fasting was a personal spiritual exercise. He stated that his fasts were "a very personal form of self-testing and prayer,"[11] and were primarily "a very personal spiritual thing."[12] Thus, the goal was internal transformation. He said, "The fast was first and foremost directed at myself. It was something I felt compelled to do to purify my own body, mind, and soul."[13] Thus, his motivations were personal, not social, and he sought to make this explicit to the public. An open letter issued by the UFW Organizing Committee at the time of his 1968 fast states, "César Chávez is engaged in a prolonged religious fast which is first and foremost a deeply personal act of penance and hope."[14] He was hoping for a profound spiritual encounter with God that would transform how he viewed the world.

The design of his fast followed a classical mystic model for preparing for a spiritual encounter with God. Chávez felt called by God to fast. He describes this dynamic in regard to his 1988 fast: "A powerful urge has been raging within me for several months," one that he could no longer resist and that led him to fast.[15] Fasting was the medium through which he discovered authentic existence. He once revealed, "I can't live without fasting anymore."[16] Next, he surrounded himself in an environment conducive to a profound religious experience. In the 1968 fast, he transformed a small storage room in a service station into his "monastic cell."[17] He surrounded himself with simple, religious paraphernalia, such as a crucifix and images of the saints and the Virgin of Guadalupe. Like many of the medieval female mystics, he was sustained solely by the Eucharist.[18]

In time, he began to receive spiritual gifts and a wholly new perspective. He claims to have developed extrasensory hearing capabilities.[19] Chávez often spoke of his enhanced powers of the mind gained through fasting: "After seven days it was like going into a different dimension. I began to see things in a different perspective, to retain a lot more, to develop tremendous powers of concentration."[20] Finally, he was granted a fearless and unifying vision of the world. He said, "Once I am on a fast, I am on a different level. Patience is infinite. . . . Maybe what happens is you go on a fast, and get feelings so great you're not even afraid of death."[21]

Like many traditional mystics, Chávez found this experience ultimately ineffable. Commenting about his 1968 fast, Chávez told his biographer Levy, "There is . . . there is a force there. I don't quite know what it is."[22] Furthermore, he received this reward of fasting—a higher vision of reality—*every* time he fasted.[23] Chávez stated,

About the third or fourth day—and this has happened to me every time I've fasted—it's like all of a sudden you're up at a high altitude, and you clear your ears; in the same way, my mind clears, it is open to everything. After a long conversation, for example, I could repeat word for word what had been said. That's one of the sensations of the fast; it's beautiful. And usually I can't concentrate on music very well, but in the fast, I could see the whole orchestra and everything, that music was so clear.

Given the frequency of his fasting, this perception must have become common to his everyday frame of mind. Most important for this study, he received a new and higher vision of the world through these experiences by which to make decisions about his life and union. He explained,

You are able to see things in a different light—see other people and yourself in a different light. . . . It is easier to find solutions and be able to detach yourself much, much more completely . . . vastly more profound and yet more removed. . . . You speak from then from that experience of fasting while you are fasting. . . . You are really talking about nonviolence in a different light, in a different authority, with a lot of authority.[24]

There haven't been in the last four or five years any major decision that I didn't make while I was fasting. I wouldn't unless it was an emergency, but I would prepare for it by going into a fast and then look at it from that perspective, which is a completely different matter—fasting—I doubt if you can make mistakes when you are fasting. I really seriously doubt it because you are able to look at things in a very special way. You are ready to look at them when you are in a different mental and physical plane.[25]

On this "different plane," Chávez directed the critical movements of his social activism. His program of social change was guided by his encounters with God. In this process, he was directly placing his faith at the base of his social action. He seems aware of this dynamic when discussing prayer, which with penance was one of his two stated goals of fasting: "Prayer is for you, for one's self. . . . Your prayer then translates into action and determination and faith."[26] It is this "translation" of his mystical encounters into action that places him squarely within the mystical-reformer heritage of the Catholic tradition.

Chávez's own recognition of his place within this tradition is evident in the public speeches he gave following his fasts. They were decidedly religious in tone, content, and style. He spoke with the moral authority of a prophet, denouncing the kingdom of this world and proclaiming a new one under God. One should note the numerous biblical allusions—especially self-crucifixion in selfless love for others—in his 1968 speech:

> Our struggle is not easy. Those who oppose our cause are rich and powerful, and they have many allies in high places. We are poor. Our allies are few. But we have something the rich do not own. We have our own bodies and spirits and the justice of our cause as our weapons. When we are really honest with ourselves we must admit that our lives are all that really belong to us. So it is how we use our lives that determine what kind of men we are. It is my deepest belief that only by giving our lives do we find life. I am convinced that the truest act of courage, the strongest act of manliness is to sacrifice ourselves for others in a totally non-violent struggle for justice. To be a man is to suffer for others. God help us to be men![27]

This imagery could not be lost on the audience as they faced his emaciated body. Chávez was the one who suffered for his people; he sacrificed *his* body so that his people would live. The transparent reference to the saints' goal of *imitatio Christi* (imitation of Christ) appears likewise in his 1972 public pronouncement. "The greatest tragedy is not to live and die, as we all must. The greatest tragedy is for a person to live and die without knowing the satisfaction of giving life for others."[28] Perhaps consciously linking himself to prophetic tradition of the church, he harkens to the prophet Micah to conclude his first major speech after breaking his fast in 1988: "What does the Lord require of you, but to do justice, to love kindness, and to walk humbly with your God."[29] By the words and imagery Chávez chose to employ, he transmitted the character of his experience of God to the people around him. He proclaimed God's message for civic engagement and thus united the two realms in a manner unique in America.

The people around Chávez also seemed to instinctively place him within the tradition of the Catholic mystic-reformer by responding to him in a manner consistent with how generations of Christians have treated their holy mystics and saints. Although his initial fast angered some of his followers, most felt impelled to visit, which took the form of a pilgrimage. The description at the beginning of this essay captures the scene of the gas station transformed into a hermitage of a living beacon of the faith. One observer at the time noted of the 1968 fast, "there is a strength of spirit emanating from him that obviously touches those who see him."[30] When he had to go to Bakersfield to have a court date during his fast, over 1,000 farmworkers and priests sang and prayed on their knees around the courthouse. They kneeled before a man they wholeheartedly believed was touched by God. In doing so, they instinctively acted in the same spirit as generations of Christian communities have reacted toward a living saint.

A Spiritual Context for Chávez's Social Action

César Chávez's spiritual fasts do not represent an isolated eruption of spirituality onto an otherwise secular existence. On the contrary, the life of César Chávez is a religious story in which his Catholic faith and a dedication to God are central. While not blind to political realities, Chávez saw the world through a spiritual lens which was honed and focused by his upbringing, education, and social activism. In this way, his life resembles many of great saints of the Catholic faith, whose lifelong dedication to the spiritual life culminates in spiritually heroic acts. While Chávez's whole life can be seen in this way, an examination of the early period of the farmworker movement makes it readily apparent.

The beginning of Chávez's active participation in social activism can be traced to the period when he and his wife lived in a shack in a barrio named "Sal Si Puedes" (Get Out If You Can). Chávez was working as a lumber handler in a San Jose mill in 1952 when an encounter with a Catholic priest named Father McDonnell changed his life. Father McDonnell introduced Chávez to a new way of looking at the world, grounded in both his community and the ancient traditions of the church. Through McDonnell, Chávez began to see a systematic social injustice in the farming system and in their fragmented experiences of pain and constant hardship. Furthermore, McDonnell gave Chávez hope by introducing him to a form of Catholicism that was sharpened and reformulated to address the pain and injustices of the farmworkers. This vision ultimately drew Chávez back toward the church, from which he had drifted in the previous decade. Chávez recalls, "While most people drawn toward liberalism or radicalism leave the church, I went the other way. I drew closer to the church the more I learned and understood."[31] Chávez's education in social justice coincided with his education about the church. From that time onward, the two could never be separated for him. He carried this connection throughout his career. Later, he would define his mission in terms of church teaching: "Everything they [the church] had taught for two thousand years was at stake in this struggle."[32] For him, the struggle for social justice was informed by the teaching of the church, and the teachings of the church had to be harnessed for the struggle against social injustice.

According to Chávez, his turn toward social activism began by reading the papal encyclicals of Pope Leo XIII concerning the rights of workers and the works of Saint Francis of Assisi on the poor.[33] He began to see not only the systematic injustices of his culture but also his Catholic faith as a vehicle for social change. He found himself drawn to the leadership models of St. Paul and particularly Saint Francis of Assisi.[34] Chávez recalls,

> When I read the biography of St. Francis of Assisi, I was moved when he went before the Moslem prince and offered to walk through fire to end a bloody war. And I still remember how he talked and made friends with a wolf that had killed several men. St. Francis was a gentle and humble man.[35]

Chávez recognized in Saint Francis a form of devotion that did not separate the believer from the plight of those on earth, but compelled him to better it. It was a model whose impact was not measured by church attendance but social transformation. This model was exemplified in the modern world by the Indian ascetic and liberator Gandhi, to whom Father McDonnell also introduced him. Chávez stated, "Gandhi was the most perfect man, not including Christ. . . . I said he was perfect in the sense that he wasn't afraid to move and make things happen. And he didn't ask people to do things he couldn't do himself."[36] For Chávez, Saint Francis and Gandhi represented the active quest for social transformation founded upon the total self-sacrifice of the leader. This new vision of the church and holiness ultimately refocused his understanding of Christ. He began to see Christ as "extremely radical" and as an agent for social change.[37]

Furthermore, he discerned in Gandhi, Saint Francis, and Christ a unique mode for social change: self-inflicted suffering as a means to discern God's will and vindicate justice. He writes of Gandhi,

> Then, of course, there were more personal things, the whole question of the spirit versus the body. He prepared himself for it by his diet, starving his body so that his spirit could overtake it. . . . He was very tough with himself. He believed that truth was vindicated, not by infliction of suffering on the opponent, but on oneself. That belief comes from Christ himself, the Sermon on the Mount, and further back from Jewish and Hindu traditions. . . . That's what separates ordinary man from great men."[38]

This model of vicarious suffering lies at the root of Chávez's later fasting. Thus, Chávez formulated both his view of the fundamental *problem* facing the farmworkers (structural injustice) and the *solution* within a profoundly religious environment whereby fasting was uplifted as a means to discernment of God's will and a mechanism for embodying justice and truth. Contrary to most biographies, herein lies the genesis of Chávez's social action. Furthermore, although Chávez may have dropped out of school in the ninth grade, this fact does not mean he was uneducated; rather, he developed a sophisticated and profound lens through which to filter his experiences, in his relations with a Catholic priest and through his study of saintly religious reformers.

Chávez's "call" came a decade later. After working for Latino social issues, Chávez began to see himself as "literally commanded to do something."[39] In the words of John C. Hammerback and Richard J. Jensen, Chávez saw "himself as an agent of God's will."[40] God called him to his life's mission, and its eventual triumph was manifest destiny. Chávez once told a group of mourners at the funeral of a slain farmworker: "We are here because his service and sacrifice has touched and moved our lives. The force that is generated by that spirit of love is more powerful than any force on earth. It cannot be stopped."[41] For Chávez, God was directing his struggle and ensuring its final victory.

As with many classical reformers, Chávez experienced a particular moment in which he had to choose to respond to his calling. This choice occurred during an early rally. After hearing numerous cries of "Viva César Chávez," Chávez is reported to have turned to another Catholic priest who had come to help the movement, Father McCullough, and said, "I don't want to be an indispensable man. I want to be able to leave and know that the union will go on." Father McCullough reportedly responded by saying:

> You have told the members that they would have to sacrifice greatly. Maybe that's what you are now called on to do: sacrifice your privacy, to do things you feel very uncomfortable doing, for the good of the group. Maybe in a couple of years you can step out of the spotlight. But right now, this is just something you have to accept—a cross you have to bear.[42]

By leading the union, Chávez responded to his call; he picked up his cross, in the words of Father McCullough, by taking upon his shoulders the burdens of the farmworkers.

Accepting his call, Chávez's presence in the eyes of union members began to attain nearly superhuman dimensions.[43] Chávez led his first strike in 1965 against grape growers in order to improve the working conditions for pickers. At the inception of this strike, Chávez spoke to the farmworkers about the forthcoming struggle. He said,

A 155 years ago in the state of Guanajuato in Mexico, a padre proclaimed the struggle for liberty. He was killed, but ten years later Mexico won its independence. We are engaged in another struggle for the freedom and dignity which poverty denies us. But it must not be a violent struggle, even if violence is used against us.[44]

In this speech in the hall of Our Lady of Guadalupe (the patron saint of the Mexican people) in Delano, Chávez becomes a *new* "padre" calling for a *new* revolution. By consciously and directly connecting himself with the famous Mexican priest, Chávez set himself up as the Prophet proclaiming a new kingdom, a promised land based on God's Providence. Chávez recalls, "We said, 'God will provide,' and we struck . . . There was absolutely no way that I could [do it without divine help.]"[45] He had accepted his call and begun his period of prophecy.

Chávez became the one sent by God to give hope to his people and lead them to the promised land. Luis Valdez, employing language that can equally be applied to any of the Hebrew prophets, says, "We didn't know it until we met him, but he was the leader we had been waiting for."[46] For later interpreters, this prophetic crowning would seem largely metaphorical, such as when Matthiessen deemed him as "Messenger from God"[47] or President Clinton called him a "Moses of his people" when honoring him posthumously with the Congressional Medal of Freedom. However, to many farmworkers, he was a new Moses and a new Christ in their midst. A small gesture by the farmworkers after a union victory captures this widespread sentiment: "A field worker, her face lit with emotions, handed him [Chávez] a statue of Christ dressed in green and white robes. Slowly Chávez raised the statue above his head. '*Viva!*' they shouted. '*Viva la huelga!*' '*Viva la causa!*' '*Viva César Chávez!*'"[48] For those in the room, the symbolism could not have been more obvious. Chávez had become more than a social leader; he had become a prophet. Like Christ before him, God had operated through this small humble man. He would lead his people to the promised land.

When his first major strike continued without hope of a settlement, Chávez decided the farmworkers would march from Delano to Sacramento in the spring of 1966. Once again, he saw the march not in political terms, but in religious ones. In the tradition of the Lenten *peregrinaciones* of Mexico, the pilgrimage to Sacramento (translated as "the city of the Sacrament") would be primarily penitential, having the theme "Penitence,

Pilgrimage, and Revolution." It was "an atonement for past sins of violence on the part of the strikers, and a kind of prayer."[49] Chávez recalls, "This was penance more than anything else—and it was quite a penance, because there was an awful lot of suffering involved in this pilgrimage, a great deal of pain."[50] The aura was decidedly religious—a fact that was not lost on even the most nonreligious of the group[51]—and occurred throughout Lent to reach its pinnacle on the day of the Resurrection. At the front of the pilgrims was the Virgin of Guadalupe.[52] Mass was said each day. At night, hymns were sung and prayers were said. A reporter along the route called it "a Passover March to the Promised land,"[53] and Luis Valdez called it "a truly religious act."[54] Thus it became an authentic religious pilgrimage carried out during the days of Lent, with a goal not of a place but a state, a state of justice for all. Although Chávez was in intense pain, he refused to take painkillers in order to experience the full weight of the penitent walk. When the pilgrimage ended on Easter Sunday, 10,000 people celebrated the miracle of the Resurrection on the step of the capital. The first contract with a grape grower had been signed. The result of the Easter pilgrimage was victory over an instrument of the culture of death. Chávez likely saw this as the beginning of a second resurrection.

Upon his return, Chávez began to transform the picket line from a place of confrontation and publicity to a place of prayer. In the ongoing battle with the DiGiorgio Corporation, Chávez fixed an altar to the back of his station wagon. Hundreds of farmworkers prayed at the shrine, which was adorned nightly with votive candles, flowers, and images of the Virgin of Guadalupe. Even strikebreakers would often brave the wrath of their supervisors and come to pray alongside the strikers.[55] For Chávez, it was these prayer sessions that were the "decisive factor in winning the DiGiorgio campaign."[56] Chávez recalls:

> Every day we had a mass, held a meeting, sang spirituals, and got them to sign authorization cards. Those meetings were responsible in large part for keeping the spirit up of our people inside the camp and helping our organizing for the coming battle. It was a beautiful demonstration of the power of nonviolence.[57]

For Chávez, public prayer became an instrumental aspect to success in his struggle. Prayer became a part of every action. Dalton aptly describes this role: "Farm workers prayed to get out of jail, they prayed to get into jail, and they prayed while being beaten by police who would take them to jail."[58] It is no coincidence that the only widely disseminated piece of writing attributed to Chávez is a prayer, "Of the Farm Workers' Struggle." For those in the union, prayer was not a mere "ingenious organizing technique," as later interpreters would be inclined to see it,[59] but an active working of the Spirit.

Herein lies the context for Chávez's fasts. His fasts were not protest tools, as many have claimed, but rather deeply imbedded within a profoundly religious worldview. They were the natural product of a personal theology that linked self-sacrifice and suffering with a personal call from God to transform the world into a more humane and just place. Without doubt, Chavez was a social activist but not *only* a social activist. Rather, he was a unique breed of social reformer whose basis for action is derived from his direct encounters with God.

The Secularization of Chávez

Despite Chávez's claims to the contrary, the analysis of fasts by the mass media has been primarily defined in terms of the labor struggle; they have been seen as calculated hunger strikes aimed to raise public opinion.[60] This portrayal of his motivations for fasting is part of a much broader secularization of Chávez's persona within popular history. Sanitized of all religious referent, Chávez becomes a modern humanist, driven by philosophical ideals of justice and nonviolence. His faith is usually presented as merely incidental to his action. The diffusion of this caricature is widespread and ingrained.[61]

The secularization project was initially engineered by two separate groups—the liberal intelligentsia and Chicano activists—which sought to mold Chávez in variant forms. The liberal intelligentsia saw in Chávez a minority leader who shared their goals of social justice and who had gained the moral capital from his people to enact their vision. They sought to co-opt Chávez and his Cause. Yet, their humanist basis for social justice was largely incommensurate with that of Chávez's religious basis.[62] Chávez became a "guerrilla leader" engaged in a "power struggle" and "social revolution."[63] His life work was "conflict organizing."[64] In this way, they created a symbol out of Chávez that matched their own secular ideology and erased Chávez's own religious referent. The Chicano activists carried out a similar secularization plan. They saw in Chávez a figure that united their race and had widespread support in the larger culture. As a result, they created a Chávez that could fit within their model. For them, he was not motivated by a social ideology for justice or by a desire for nonviolence, but by a Chicano manifesto to liberate his people. Thus, Acuña in *Occupied America* presents Chávez as a social revolutionary and the essence of La Raza (the Hispanic race).[65] In this way, his religious basis was sanitized, and Chávez became another tool by which the activists sought their goals. This transformation meant that both the activists and the liberal intelligentsia ascribed to Chávez their motivation in order to capitalize on his public goodwill.

But one must recall that the American public warmly received this secularized Chávez, for this image of Chávez was the *only* image to which most Anglo-Americans were exposed.[66] Their secularized Chávez *is* the Chávez that many in America came to respect. How popular would Chávez have been if his deep religious convictions and routine encounters with God were exposed and widely reported? Rather, it seems that the resultant image of a humanist and peaceful Che Guevara was seen as more palatable to the American public than a radically political Saint Francis of Assisi. Few recognize how contrary this secularized portrayal is to how Chávez saw himself and the decision process he used to guide his social action as was presented above.

Recognizing this secularizing tendency, Chávez continually reaffirmed the religious basis for his action. Chávez states, "I was convinced [that my ideology was] . . . very Christian. That's my interpretation. I don't think it was so much political or economic."[67] He told others that he was motivated by his "faith in God and our choice to follow His son."[68] A purely secular ideology was ultimately unsatisfying to Chávez. He states, "Today I don't think I could base my will to struggle on cold economics or some political doctrine. I don't think there would be enough to sustain me. For me the base must be faith."[69] For Chávez, the connection to God was clear and direct; he saw himself doing "Christ's work on earth" and carrying out God's will.[70] Chávez describes it as "a fire—a consuming, nagging everyday and every-moment demand of my soul to just do it. It's difficult to explain. I like to think it's the good Spirit asking me to do it."[71] Furthermore, he was cognizant of the dangers of divorcing his politics from his spirituality. He said in a 1969 interview,

> I don't think we can find total happiness in a purely economic struggle, regardless of how many benefits we may get. Not that these aren't important—I'd be the first to say they are important—but I think that if we divorce the struggle from religion we would not be totally happy, even though we may make great gains.[72]

Despite his plea, this divorce of Chávez's spirituality from his social activism is the distinctive mark of presentations of Chávez. The image is firmly entrenched.

The Sanctification of Chávez

The story of the life of César Chávez ends like many of the hagiographies of old. Chávez died while in the midst of yet another fast in 1993 at the age of sixty-six. His body finally gave out after years of severe fasting. The official UFW biography states that when they found his body, there was a peaceful smile on his face.[73] He immediately came to be seen as a martyr for his people.[74] At the funeral, Cardinal Mahoney called him "a very special prophet for the farm workers of the world." Then, more than 35,000 people followed his casket for three miles in a final penitent procession. It was characterized as the loss of a messenger of God. Manuel Amaya said, "God has taken the strongest arm that we have, but we will continue."[75] Griswold del Castillo and García called it a "resurrection of Chávez's spirit: a *día de los Santos*, and a *día de los Muertos.* . . . We were one with César Chávez."[76] As the people processed, followers solemnly chanted the words that characterized his vision of hope: "*Se puede; si se puede* — It can be done, yes it can be done." A final Mass was held, and the pope and the presidents of Mexico and the United States sent their personal condolences. In the decade of the 1990s, only Mother Theresa's funeral Mass could be characterized as being equally conscious of the spiritual magnitude of the saint who was being buried. Luis Valdez paid the final tribute that is the beacon call for future saints: "You shall never die."

As the bodily Chávez died, a new spiritual Chávez has emerged among "his" people. The Latino community — especially the farmworkers — look to him not as a deceased secular social leader but living savior still in their midst. Icons and church murals have been produced bearing his image. Vigils are held all over the American Southwest on the anniversary of his death. People fast in preparation for that day and prayers go long into the night, culminating in a celebration. This transformation of Chávez is most evident when one visits his grave in La Paz, outside of Bakersfield. Over the past several years, his grave and surrounding garden have become a pilgrimage site for Latinos and non-Latinos alike. Many come to pray by the simple wooden cross that marks his grave. They come with candles, pictures, and symbols of the movement, such as a short-handle hoe or worn UFW flags. When the author was last there in the spring of 2005, someone had placed a crown of thorns over the cross. They come often with tear-filled eyes, sharing their suffering with Chávez in death as they had in life. To those who journey to Chávez's "abode of *la paz*," he is much more than just a secular social activist. He is still their leader and, indeed, friend among the saints.

If Chávez had lived 500 years ago, he would have been readily identified as an ascetic, mystic, and saint. The fact that our contemporary society does not recognize him as such speaks to the values and biases of our cultural environment. Our modern society is uncomfortable with the confluence of religion and social action. America may want a social and political Messiah, but only a Messiah without any obviously religious traits.[77] In the process of secularizing Chávez, his biographers transposed this stark division unnaturally to Chávez. The American public embraced this divided Chávez. For Chávez, however, the two realms were fused.[78] It was his direct encounters with God that drove his action, *and* his political realities drove him increasingly toward God. At the center of his life were the direct experiences of God that he gained while fasting. It is through this prism that all his other actions must be understood and his story told. According to Chávez, these encounters infused the core of his being and motivated his actions. Generations past would likely have seen Chávez as a religious ascetic and mystic with particularly far-ranging reach. Today, Chávez is popularly known as a secular sociopolitical activist. His spiritual life has been intently buried for all—or nearly all. Despite this, many in the Latino community will turn to him in death for the same reasons that countless communities over the ages have turned to their saints: because their love for him is not bounded by death. A reporter once asked Chávez why the farmworkers love him so much. His reply may reveal why many within the Latino community believe that Chávez will one day emerge as a religious figure in American society: he simply said, "Because the feeling is mutual."

Notes

1. According to Pat Henning in Arthur Jones, "Millions Reaped What César Chávez Sowed," *National Catholic Reporter*, 7 May 1993, 7.

2. For more detailed analysis on the mysticism of César Chávez, see Stephen R. Lloyd-Moffett, "The Mysticism and Social Action of César Chávez," in *Latino Religions and Civic Activism in the United States*, ed. Gastón Espinosa, Virgilio Elizondo, and Jesse Miranda (New York: Oxford University Press, 2005), 35–52.

3. Paul Anthony Hribar, "The Social Fasts of César Chávez" (PhD diss., University of Southern California, Los Angeles, 1978), 332. See also Susan Ferriss

and Ricardo Sandoval, *The Fight in the Fields* (New York: Harcourt Brace, 1997), 254. Additionally, he confided to Peter Matthiessen that he often fasted without people knowing. Matthiessen, *Sal Si Puedes: César Chávez and the New American Revolution* (New York: Random House, 1969), 139–40.

4. These fasts took place February–March 1968, amidst the strike and boycott of Giumarra Corporation; May 1974, while lobbying for a law in Arizona guaranteeing farmworker elections; July–August 1988, while battling for pesticide reduction.

5. Chávez wrote in his journal, "It's very tough. I don't know if I can continue." Quoted in Ferriss and Sandoval, *The Fight in the Fields*, 140.

6. See, for example, *Cambridge Dictionary of American Biography*, ed. John S. Bowman (Cambridge: Cambridge University Press, 1995), 129; *The Encyclopedia Americana*, 2000; "Grapes of Wrath," *Economist*, 20 August 1998, 25.

7. The one exception was his 1970 fast in response to the Teamsters' insurgence. This self-proclaimed "protest fast" was a failure at every level, in Chávez's own opinion. See Levy, *César Chávez: Autobiography of La Causa* (New York: Norton, 1975), 340.

8. "Now this is a fast which means that I'm not doing it to put pressure on anybody. . . . This is not a hunger strike." Chávez in Levy, *César* Chávez, 274. Referring to his 1968 fast, Chávez states, "It was not a hunger strike because its purpose was not strategic; it was an act of prayer and love." Matthiessen, *Sal si puedes*, 180.

9. Chávez, "Letter to the National Council of Churches," 20 February 1968; repr. in Winthrope Yinger, *César Chávez: Rhetoric of Nonviolence* (Hicksville, N.Y.: Exposition Press, 1975), 108.

10. Hribar, "The Social Fasts of César Chávez," 372.

11. César Chávez, "Non-Violence Still Works," *Look*, 1 April 1969, 52.

12. Levy, *César Chávez*, 465.

13. Chávez, "Address by César Chávez, President United Farm Workers of America, AFL-CIO," Pacific Lutheran University, Tacoma, Washington, March 1989. Available at www.ufw.org/fast.html.

14. "Statement of the Fast for Non-violence," United Farm Workers Organizing Committee, 25 February 1968.

15. John C. Hammerback and Richard J. Jensen, *The Rhetorical Career of César Chávez* (College Station: Texas A&M University Press, 1998), 186.

16. Hribar, "The Social Fasts of César Chávez," 378.

17. Richard Griswold del Castillo and Richard García, *César Chávez: A Triumph of Spirit* (Norman: University of Oklahoma Press, 1995), 85.

18. Levy, *César Chávez*, 464. Hribar, "The Social Fasts of César Chávez," 264.

19. He reportedly heard music from across the street through an almost soundproof concrete wall, to the amazement of all those around him. Matthiessen, *Sal Si Puedes*, 187–88.

20. Levy, *César Chávez*, 276.

21. Ibid., 350.

22. Ibid., 350.

23. Matthiessen, *Sal Si Puedes*, 187.

24. Hribar, "The Social Fasts of César Chávez," 368–69.

25. Ibid., 379.

26. John Dear, "César Chávez on Voting in the Marketplace," *Pax Christi USA* (winter 1992): 21.

27. Levy, *César Chávez*, 286.

28. Ibid., 465.

29. "Address by César Chávez, President, United Farm Workers of America, AFL-CIO."

30. Levy, *César Chávez*, 465.

31. Ibid., 27.

32. Hammerback and Jensen, *The Rhetorical Career of César Chávez*, 66.

33. The encyclicals of Pope Leo XIII would later be quoted often in the official newspaper of the union, *El Malcriado*. For example, see nn. 14, 19, and 20 and Frederick John Dalton's discussion in "The Moral Vision of César E. Chávez: An Examination of His Public Life from an Ethical Perspective" (PhD diss., Graduate Theological Union, Berkeley, 1998), 302–3.

34. Chávez once commented, "St. Paul must have been a terrific organizer, as he would go and talk with people right in their homes, and sit with them and be with them" (Hammerback and Jensen, *The Rhetorical Career of César Chávez*, 17). Chávez began to follow this model precisely through his involvement in the Community Service Organization (CSO), in which he literally walked door to door to talk with people in their homes.

35. Levy, *César Chávez*, 91.

36. Ibid., 92.

37. Ibid., 27.

38. Ibid., 92.

39. Hammerback and Jensen, *The Rhetorical Career of César Chávez*, 30.

40. Ibid., 44.

41. Ibid., 109.

42. Joan London and Henry Anderson, *So Shall Ye Reap* (New York: Crowel, 1970), 182.

43. Jim Drake recalls, "He was the mystical guy who was around, but he was not exerting leadership . . . but it was weird because things were happening where he was." Ronald B. Taylor, *Chávez and the Farm Workers* (Boston: Beacon Press, 1975), 114.

44. Levy, *César Chávez*, 184.

45. Hammerback and Jensen, *The Rhetorical Career of César Chávez*, 68.

46. Luis Valdez, "The Tale of the Raza," in *Chicano: The Beginnings of Bronze Power*, ed. Renato Rosaldo, Robert A. Calvert, and Gustav L. Seligmann (New York: William Morrow, 1974), 54.

47. In Griswold del Castillo and García, *César Chávez*, 106.

48. John Gregory Dunne, *Delano: Revised and Updated* (New York: Farrar, Straus, and Giroux, 1971), 167.

49. Matthiessen, *Sal Si Puedes*, 127–28.

50. Levy, *César Chávez*, 207.

51. Bill Kircher tells Taylor, "The whole thing had a strong cultural religious thing, yet it was organizing people." Taylor, *Chávez and the Farm Workers*, 168.

52. She was also present at every meeting.

53. Mark Day, *Forty Acres: César Chávez and the Farm Workers* (New York: Praeger, 1971), 75.

54. Valdez, "The Tale of the Raza," 55.

55. Ferriss and Sandoval, *The Fight in the Fields*, 128.

56. Day, *Forty Acres*, 117.

57. Levy, *César Chávez*, 227.

58. Dalton, "The Moral Vision of César E. Chávez," 318.

59. Ferriss and Sandoval, *The Fight in the Fields*, 128.

60. For example, a recent article in the *San Diego Union Tribune* states without qualification that the "labor leader" César Chávez went on a twenty-five-day "hunger strike" in 1968 (8 November 1998), A-1.

61. The evidence for this project can be found in Lloyd-Moffett, "The Mysticism and Social Action of César Chávez," 41–44.

62. The two major early and influential biographies by Levy and Matthiessen were written by established authors intimately connected with the wider liberal ideology. Similarly, the other major early works—Nelson, Day, Dunne, Taylor, Kushner, London and Anderson, Young, and Horowitz—were all written by individuals with social rather than religious objectives.

63. For example, see Taylor, *Chávez and the Farm Workers*, 181–82. Levy's "autobiography" of Chávez—which is the single most influential book—was instigated as an attempt to record the struggles of the union against the powerful agribusiness. Levy, *César Chávez*, xv. Thus, despite consisting largely of Chávez and his coworkers' own statements, it is framed in terms of oppression, struggle, and revolution. Yet, one must recognize these elements as better representing Levy's social Marxism than the Chávez of faith described above. Similarly, the very title of Matthiessen's book—*Sal Si Puedes: César Chávez and the New American Revolution*—relays his political outlook.

64. Taylor, *Chávez and the Farm Workers*, 85.

65. Rodolfo Acuña, *Occupied America: A History of Chicanos* (New York: Harper and Row, 1988).

66. This is true to a lesser extent for the influence of radical Chicanos on the Latino population.

67. Griswold del Castillo and García, *César Chávez*, 111.

68. Hammerback and Jensen, *The Rhetorical Career of César Chávez*, 153. When challenged by an interviewer who asked if he was a communist, Chávez responded, "No, I am not a communist. . . . I'm saying this because I am a Christian and I'm proud of that." Day, *Forty Acres*, 67.

69. Levy, *César Chávez*, 27.

70. Chávez, as cited in "Love Thy Neighbor," *U.S. Catholic* 50, no. 10 (October 1985): 38. See also Hammerback and Jensen, *The Rhetorical Career of César Chávez*, 99.

71. Chávez, cited in Dalton, "The Moral Vision of César E. Chávez," 353.

72. Chávez, "Our Best Hope," *Engage* 2, no. 5 (11 November 1969).

73. Web page of UFW, biography.

74. At the UFW's Twelfth Constitutional Convention, in 1994, Chávez was honored as one of the six martyrs of La Causa.

75. Griswold del Castillo and García, *César Chávez*, 174.

76. Ibid., 177.

77. The opposite is also true: America tends to depoliticize its religious heroes. For example, the Trappist monk Thomas Merton has emerged as a widespread spiritual hero and is considered by many to be a modern Catholic mystic. In the process of this image emerging, Merton's social activism—which was extremely prevalent in his writings and speaking—has largely been erased from the popular historical record. Today, he is usually depicted solely as a deeply spiritual Catholic man. In this way, he is the reverse coin of Chávez: history has forgotten his social activism and formed him into a classical mystic model. Clearly, this dynamic reveals America's uncertainty about its political mystics.

78. "If I'm going to save my soul, it's going to be through the struggle for social justice." Chávez in Levy, *César Chávez*, 276.

MARIO T. GARCÍA

5

Religion and the Chicano Movement

Católicos Por La Raza

The study of religion is one of the most neglected areas in Chicano studies. Yet religion is one of the central forces in the life of any community. This has certainly been true within the Mexican American experience. Perhaps one explanation for this neglect lies in the relationship between the Chicano Movement of the late 1960s and the early 1970s and the origins of Chicano studies.

The Chicano Movement represented the most significant and widespread protest by Mexican Americans in the history of the United States. Reacting to a legacy of conquest in the Southwest in the nineteenth century, to a history of labor exploitation, and to experiences as second-class citizens characterized by various forms of discrimination and segregation, including lack of access to quality education, Mexican Americans by the 1960s challenged the system as never before. The movement was a Chicano "intifada."

As part of its agenda, the movement gave birth to Chicano studies, defining it in strong ethnic and nationalist terms. In turn, Chicano nationalism was largely portrayed as an expression of secular values and goals. The role of religion, especially Catholicism, was not perceived by early students of Chicano studies to have played a major role in the movement. And yet while secularization characterized a good deal of the movement's politics, religion was not absent. Religion, primarily but not exclusively Catholicism, played a role in the formation of a movement value system focused on social justice. Religion in some cases also proved to be the basis for community organization.

1. Católicos Por La Raza, 1970. Courtesy: Ricardo Cruz and Católicos Por La Raza and Special Collection, University of California, Santa Barbara.

This chapter is a case study of the role of Catholicism in the Chicano Movement in Los Angeles as exemplified by Católicos Por La Raza (figure 1). It began as an extension of some of the early movement activities in Los Angeles that had sprung up first in reaction to the inspirational struggle of César Chávez and the farmworkers when they struck for union recognition in 1965. Many movement activists in urban locations such as Los Angeles first received their political baptism by making their pilgrimage to Delano, the headquarters of the union, to take food to the striking farmworkers and by supporting the initial grape boycott when it was launched in 1967 as a way of pressuring the growers to negotiate with the union.

The 1968 school "blow-outs" in East Los Angeles during the spring of that year, when several hundred Mexican American students walked out of their schools to protest inferior education, likewise helped to ignite the movement in Los Angeles.

Católicos Por La Raza (abbreviated in this chapter as Católicos) was one of many offshoots of these early protests and interacted with still many others. The movement, at least in Los Angeles, was never fragmented into separate independent parts. Many activists wore many hats. It was not unusual for a movement activist to be involved as a student leader, as a supporter of the farmworkers, or as an organizer against the

Vietnam War as well as other later manifestations, such as the creation of La Raza Unida Party, an independent Chicano political party.

In retrospect, this interrelationship characterized both the rise and fall of groups such as Católicos. For while much energy could quickly flow into one protest activity, it could just as easily flow out of that effort into another thus undermining the permanent organization of one form of protest.

Católicos was organized as the result of the coming together of three groups: the Chicano Law Students Association at Loyola Marymount College (a Jesuit institution in Los Angeles), *La Raza* newspaper (a community-based Chicano publication), and United Mexican American Students (UMAS), a Chicano student group at Los Angeles City College. Richard Martínez, who at the time was the head of UMAS (later to be re-named MEChA [Movimiento Estudiantil Chicano de Aztlán]), recalls that he and other Chicano students were inspired by learning about African Americans in the eastern part of the United States protesting against of the Mainline Anglo Protestant churches, whom they believed were making few if any commitments to the Black struggle for self-determination. Martínez began to question the role of the Catholic Church in Los Angeles with respect to Chicanos. "If you have the Church standing with you in making a demand," Martínez remembers thinking, "it's a hell of a lot more powerful than you standing by yourself. If the Bishop is next to me, I'm in good shape."[1]

Martínez convinced other UMAS students at his school that they should make the relevance of the church to the Chicano community one of their top priorities. At Loyola, the Chicano Law Students Association appears to have started when some of the Chicano students protested what they claimed was the failure of the school to support, financial and otherwise, the Chicano law students. This local grievance soon expanded to include the church's general neglect of the Mexican American community. At *La Raza*, Joe Razo, one of the organizers of the newspaper, seems to have already been involved with various dissident Chicano priests in Los Angeles, who less than a year later formed a branch of PADRES (Priests Associated for Religious, Educational, and Social Rights), an association of Chicano priests in the Southwest who likewise wanted to make the church more sensitive to the conditions of Mexican Americans. Razo, himself, was not a priest.[2]

At some point, around November 1969, Martínez recalls meeting with Richard (Ricardo) Cruz, the chair of the Loyola group, to discuss their common concerns. Martínez believes that it may have been Razo who arranged the meeting. Cruz, whom Martínez characterizes as thought-ful, intelligent, quick-minded, determined, and possessing clear organi-zational thinking along with a high intensity level, was part of what was referred to as the "Cathedral Mafia"—a group of graduates from Cathe-dral High School in Los Angeles, a Catholic school just north of China Town and bordering the east side of the city. Members of the "mafia" went on to college and to become activist in the Chicano Movement. Because members of the Cathedral Mafia, including Cruz, were graduates of parochial schools during the period of the liberal reforms of Vatican Council II championed by Pope John XXIII, they knew much more— according to Martínez—about the politics of the church than those, such as Martínez, who had been raised Catholic but who had not gone to Catholic schools.

Shortly after the meeting between Martínez and Cruz, Católicos Por La Raza was formed to launch a Chicano Movement assault on the church in Los Angeles. According to Raúl Ruiz, the editor of *La Raza*, Católicos was the brainchild of Richard Cruz. The name of the group, especially the term Católicos, was deliberately chosen in order to stress that the members were not anti-Catholic.[3]

As it prepared to protest against the church, Católicos moved from be-ing strictly a student effort to an off-campus one as a way of expanding its base. Raúl Ruiz stresses that Católicos was a good example of how the movement was always a mixture of students and community, and not just students as one recent study of the movement contends.[4] Still, the three key pillars of Católicos were the Loyola law students, *La Raza* newspaper and later magazine, and UMAS at Los Angeles City College, but which in a short time also included UMAS students from other schools, such as Long Beach State.[5] Functioning primarily in Los Angeles, Católicos, as Alberto Pulido has noted, inspired the formation of at least one other Católicos' group in San Diego.[6]

While Católicos was inspired by the individual and group views of the activists who formed it, it was at the same time influenced by other expres-sions of religiosity in the movement that likewise questioned the Catholic Church's role in the Chicano community. César Chávez and the farm-workers' struggle stands as one such influence on Católicos.

In his efforts to organize a largely Mexican American force of farm laborers in California, Chávez brilliantly combined basic labor-union or-ganizing strategies with ethnic and religious ones. As a result, the farm-workers' cause came to represent not just a union but a movement for social justice. Chávez understood that for his effort to succeed, he needed to appeal to a wider array of supporters. He also understood that just as in past labor struggles in this country, the antiunion forces would attempt to stigmatize the farmworkers' union as being communist or communist influenced. Internally, Chávez further understood that he needed to appeal to farmworkers not just at the level of material needs, but at a cultural and spiritual level as well. For all of these reasons and due to Chávez's own deep ethnic, religious, and spiritual beliefs, he clothed the farmworkers' movement beginning with the Delano strike in 1965 with the mantle of a Mexican American Movement.[7]

Chávez and the farmworkers' union employment of Mexican Catholic symbols, spiritual appeals, and a critique of the church undoubtedly formed part of the backdrop and inspiration for the formation of Católicos. Indeed, Ricardo Cruz, and possibly other members of Católicos, had first become politically involved by making their pilgrimages to Delano to support the farmworkers.

Still another inspiration for Católicos must have come from the organization of the initial and historic Denver Youth Liberation Conference sponsored by the Crusade for Justice led by one of the major political figures of the Movement: Rodolfo "Corky" Gonzales. Following the publication in 1967 of his epic poem *I am Joaquín*, which began to plot out the cultural nationalist ideology of the Chicano Movement, Gonzales called for a national gathering of all Chicano activists in Denver in March 1969 for a conference to set out a plan of action for expanding the movement.

Future Católicos, such as Joe Razo and Raul Ruiz of *La Raza*, made the pilgrimage to Denver and returned even more committed to the movement. That commitment was strengthened by the drafting of *El Plan de Espiritual de Aztlán*, a virtual declaration of independence for the Chicano Movement.[8] Its preamble, drafted by the young Chicano poet Alurista (a single-name pseudonym), invented a political, cultural, and spiritual homeland for Chicanos—Aztlán—the pre-Columbian Southwest. Aztlán was to become the battleground for the movement's effort at not only cultural rebirth and ethnic revitalization, but also the establishment of what some envisioned as a nation within a nation.

While the *Plan* did not specifically refer to religion or to the Catholic Church, it nevertheless can be interpreted not only as a political document, but as a Chicano version of the Ten Commandments, with Corky Gonzáles as Moses, Rocky Mountain high Denver, Colorado, as Mount Sinai, and the *Plan de Aztlán* as the Ten Commandments. The *Plan* called on Chicanos to abandon gringo values based on the dollar system and instead embrace a nonmaterial creed of "love and brotherhood." The *Plan* inspired Chicano activists like Oscar Zeta Acosta, Raul Salinas, and Eduardo Quevedo Jr. to fight for civil rights and change inside and outside of the church. Quevedo Jr. wrote an essay entitled "The Catholic Church in America." In this essay, Quevedo although never specifically referring to liberation theology—which was at that very moment being conceptualized and developed in Latin America—did provide some evidence of either the influence of liberation theology on some Chicanos or the parallel development of an organic Chicano liberation theology, or both.[9]

Quevedo criticized the church, as did liberation theologians, for losing its commitment to the poor and the disempowered and instead pacifying them by what Quevedo referred to as "the static and death-wish philosophy and theology of a Thomas Aquinas" through the church's concentration on salvation in an afterlife in heaven. "Moral betterment and religious goodness, the child has been told," Quevedo added, "is all that matters." No better example of this "other-worldly" theology could be found than in Latin America where, Quevedo pointed out, the church built magnificent cathedrals to direct the countless poor upward while at the same time neglecting their cries of poverty and despair. For Quevedo this represented neither true Catholicism nor true Christianity. "Catholic Church as an institution," Quevedo lamented, "has lost all sense of itself as a pilgrim institution, or better, simply as a Christian experience."

By contrast, Quevedo concluded, in observing the growing clamor for social justice by Mexican Americans in the United States and the church's aloofness from this movement, within that relationship and process Mexican Americans were emerging as more Christian than the church itself. "It is totally possible," he wrote, "that a Christian people has suddenly emerged more Christian than the Mother that brought it forth, and that the reaction of the Mother at the sight of this 'monster' is to go back on herself and remain astonished at the revolt on her hands."

It is not clear whether liberation theology, as it emanated from the historic Medellín conference held in Colombia in 1968, had a direct influence on the organization of Católicos. As noted in the Quevedo essay, certain tendencies of liberation theology—particularly the stress on a renewed commitment of the church to the alleviation of the temporal sufferings of the poor and the church's further commitment to the empowerment of the poor—are visible. Ricardo Cruz and other members of the Chicano Law Students Association at Loyola, a liberal Jesuit institution, would have undoubtedly encountered liberation theology in some form. Raul Ruiz recalls that the idea behind Católicos was in part to propose a "theology of liberation East L.A. style."[10]

Evidence of familiarity with at least some facets of liberation theology do surface in the *La Raza* magazine, edited by Ruiz sometime after Católicos was formed. Ruiz, who was studying Latin American history at California State University, Los Angeles, under radical professors such at Tim Harding, was quite aware of events in Latin America. At the end of 1969, Ruiz traveled to Cuba as part of a U.S. delegation to help celebrate the tenth anniversary of the Cuban Revolution.[11] *La Raza* consistently carried articles on Latin American revolutionary movements, including references to those progressive elements within the church which supported such movements for social change. One such story from Bogotá dated Christmas day, 1968, concerns a statement issued by the bishop of Buenaventura and forty-eight priests calling for "a revolution which will overthrow the ruling classes of our country, through whom our foreign dependence is maintained." The article notes that this statement was based on the findings of the Medellín conference. The statement further called on priests to commit themselves to humanity, which included becoming involved in revolutionary action against "imperialism and bourgeois neo-colonialism." The statement concluded: "We will work for the coming of a socialist organization of society which will eliminate all forms of exploitation."[12]

In addition, *La Raza* published articles extolling the exploits of Camilo Torres, the Colombian priest turned revolutionary who was killed by the Colombian military in 1966. In its first edition in early 1970, *La Raza* carried an essay on Torres entitled "The Brotherhood of Priestly Revolutionism," by the ex–Maryknoll priest Blase Bonpane of Los Angeles. Bonpane praised Torres's courage in taking up arms on behalf of the poor and the exploited in Latin America. Bonpane concluded that the worst violence was not in taking up arms but in allowing the people of Latin America to continue their suffering. Bonpane accused the church of being an accomplice in this oppression. As such, he questioned whether the church really represented Christianity. "It is rather a form of heresy," Bonpane argued.

As a priest I made a decision that I would never tell a destitute person to be patient. The religious people of Latin America do not eat. Should we ask them to be patient? Should we ask them to wait? To wait for what? Slow death? Shall we ask them to watch their children die of malnutrition?[13]

Fortunately, Bonpane added, some priests, such as Camilo Torres, would no longer tolerate these conditions. "Let it be understood that there is a new breed of religious people in Latin America," Bonpane concluded. "This breed is breaking with an ugly past. This breed is the catalyst of revolution." According to Bonpane, the poor of Latin America were also recognizing that they no longer needed to remain poor and that they did not have to accept their poverty as God's will. "These new people of God," Bonpane stressed, "will believe in a God who liberates as did the ancient Jews. The god that does not liberate is an idol."[14]

Influenced directly and indirectly by these various political and theological developments, Católicos, after its organization, put forward its own ideological views and critique of the church. First and foremost, members of Católicos made it very clear that they identified as Chicano Catholics. In its founding proclamation, Católicos stressed that it was precisely the Catholic background of its members that made them conscious of the contradictions of the church. "We have gone to Catholic schools and understand the Catholic tradition," Católicos pointed out. "Although Católicos was not a mass organization, it reminded the Church that Mexican-American as well as other Latino Catholics were predominantly Catholics and made up a large percentage of U.S. Catholics especially in the Southwest." While it appears that most members of Católicos were U.S.-born Catholics, some may have received their Catholic education in Mexico. For example, Pedro Arias, the oldest member (the *viejo*) of the group was forty-three, while most of the others were in their twenties and thirties. Born in Jalisco, Arias observed that he had embraced Catholicism as a young teenager and had been a member of the Catholic Association of Young Mexicans in Guadalajara. Exhibiting multiple identities—as Catholics, as Chicanos, and as self-proclaimed representatives of the poor—Católicos raised the cry "*Somos Católicos, somos pobres, somos Chicanos. Que Viva La Raza.*"[15]

As Catholics, members of Católicos stressed that one of the Catholic traditions that they embraced was an identity with the poor. This was an identity that Christ himself had established. "Because of our Catholic training we know," Católicos declared,

> that Christ, the founder of Catholicism was a genuinely poor man. We know that he was born in a manger because His compatriots refused Him better housing. We know that He not only worked and kissed the feet of the poor (Mary Magdalen) but did all in His power to feed and educate the poor.[16]

As Catholics and as Christians, members of Católicos believed that they had no option but to identify with the poor as Christ had done. "We have the duty," Católicos insisted, "to not only love the poor but to be as Christ-like as possible."[17]

Poverty for Chicanos, according to Católicos and other concerned Mexican American Catholics, was not a metaphor; it was a living reality. As a 1969 report by Andres Gallegos and Antonio Tinajero for the Division of the Spanish Speaking of the U.S. Catholic Conference pointed out, too many Mexican Americans remained poor and marginalized in the country. In the Southwest more than one-third of all Mexican Americans possessed twice the unemployment rate as did Anglo-Americans. Eighty percent of Mexican Americans employed worked in unskilled or low-skilled jobs. In Texas, 89 percent of Mexican Americans dropped out of school before completing a high school education. Forty percent of Mexican Americans in Texas were functionally illiterate. In California, Mexican Americans composed 14 percent of the public school population but fewer than one-half of 1 percent of students in the University of California.[18]

It was because poverty existed in the barrios—in the parishes—that Católicos, like liberationists in Latin America, called attention to the contradictions within the church concerning the poverty of the people and the wealth of the church. Católicos believed that this contradiction represented hypocrisy on the part of the church. It preached, on the one hand, that the poor through their devotion to Christ would acquire everlasting rewards ("Blessed are the poor"), while, at the same time, the church as an institution accumulated wealth beyond the imaginations of the poor. Part of this hypocrisy, Católicos charged, was the church's request each Sunday that poor Mexican Americans donate to the weekly collections while the church did little to alleviate the poverty of Chicanos.[19]

The contradictions between the poverty of the poor and the wealth of the church could especially be seen in housing conditions in the barrio and the church's ownership of property in Los Angeles. While most Chicanos lived in inadequate and deteriorating homes, the church, despite its own vast property holding, did nothing to reform barrio housing conditions. "I love going to Church," the *viejita* (old woman) said in a story published by Católicos. "It's so beautiful there, and my house is so ugly."[20]

Católicos deconstructed this story line to point out the contradictions of the church: "the Catholic Church gives the viejita a few hours of grace and beauty on Sundays. She is grateful, for it is a refuge from her living conditions on the other six days. But her gratitude and religious needs keep her from asking some crucial questions: Why must there be such contrast between the grandeur of the church and the squalor of home? If

the church were made a little less grand, couldn't the homes of parishioners be made a little less squalid?"[21]

Católicos noted that they were raising such questions because of the
church's dominant presence in East Los Angeles, and yet this part of the
city also represented among the worst living conditions. Católicos noted
that according to a Los Angeles County survey of housing, seventy-two
of the dwellings in East Los Angeles violated the building code. What this
meant, Católicos observed, was congestion, decay, and demoralization
for many Chicanos in that part of the city. "And how has the Los Angeles Archdiocese responded to Chicano housing needs? Católicos asked:
"We're not in the housing business," a church spokesman said. "And sure
enough, the archdiocese has not built a single unit of low-cost housing.
When the chancery claimed that their first responsibility is to serve the
Mexican American people, it apparently did not include their living conditions."[22]

To further document what Católicos claimed was the church's hypocrisy with respect to the poor, *La Raza* published a partial listing of church-
owned property acquired for the County Assessor's Office. According
to Católicos, these holdings amounted to a billion dollars. Moreover,
this amount only covered Los Angeles County and not the rest of the
archdiocese, which included Orange, Ventura, and Santa Barbara coun-
ties. *La Raza* further noted that this value might only cover part of the
church's property, since it did not include corporations owned by the
church. These properties listed, Católicos believed, did not just include
churches, schools, and rectories, but also private homes, apartments, and
businesses. According to Raul Ruiz, these holdings involved many slum
dwellings.[23]

Not only did the church possess such wealth in property, but it received
tax exemptions for these holdings. "You, *Raza*," Católicos pointed out
another contradiction, "are paying the property taxes the multi-billion
dollar Church is not paying. We do understand that the properties represent tremendous wealth which could be utilized for the betterment of
the barrios."[24]

If this disparity in property holdings between the poor and the church
was not enough, Pedro Arias of Católicos also noted the irony of this
wealthy church's requiring the poor to have to pay for the administration
of the sacraments. "Even after death one must keep paying in order that
these prayers 'may reach God,'" Arias concluded. This was not the way of
Christ, Arias reminded the church. "All those that have the least ideas of
what Christianity is," he noted,

know that Jesus Christ, during his existence in the world, spent his time combating the hypocrisy and the riches, and at the same time he preached and set an example of humbleness and love towards his fellowman. He demonstrated his first example of humility by his having been born in a manger and he wanted to be worshipped in the same manner.[25]

Part of the church's neglect of the poor, contended Católicos, included a lack of Chicano representation within the church's structure. Católicos noted that of the 12 million Spanish-speaking people in the United States, over 90 percent were Catholics. This made the Spanish speaking the largest single ethnic group within the church, constituting almost a quarter of all Catholics and 67 percent in the southwestern states. In addition, Católicos observed, the total population of "La Raza" exceeded that of some sixty nations. Latin American countries with smaller populations, including Puerto Rico, possessed their own native church hierarchy and institutions. By contrast, despite their numbers, Spanish-speaking Catholics in the United States had little representation. There was not a single Spanish-speaking bishop. Of over 720 priests in the Los Angeles Archdiocese, only fifty-one were Spanish speaking. This lack of representation, Católicos observed, in turn discouraged Mexican Americans and other Latinos from entering into vocations.[26]

This virtual exclusion, Católicos and other concerned Mexican American Catholics insisted, represented un-Christian and racist treatment. Gallegos and Tinajero in their report to the National Conference of Catholic Bishops observed that unlike the case with Latinos, the European-origin groups within the church had always possessed representation in their own priests and bishops. This representation insured that these ethnic groups would have their own Catholic colleges, labor unions, and civic and political organizations. "That has not happened to us," Gallegos and Tinajero lamented. Latinos, they explained, "are still in the shadows of the rectories, colleges, hospitals, agencies, seminaries, etc. and there is a reason."

We have been excluded, clergy and laity alike, from positions of influence and leadership in the American Catholic Church. . . . What would the Irish, the Italians and other European groups in New York have done if the Holy See had given them an Oriental or a Hispanic or an Indian Bishop? Is there any wonder why the Hispanic people across this land see the Church as an entity outside and away from themselves rather than to know and see themselves as an intimate and integral part of the Church?[27]

Católicos Por La Raza was even more specific about what it considered to be the ethnocentrism of the church. It believed that Irish American control of the church effectively barred Latino representation. "Not only was [the church] economically unable to talk to the poor, because of its holdings and comforts," Católicos charged, "but also because its hierarchy, as good Irishmen, have simply no sympathy for the struggle of our people for basic needs." At one point, Católicos observed that over 75 percent of all bishops and priests were Irish, although it did not specify if these figures pertained to the Los Angeles area or to the country as a whole.[28]

Católicos believed that the Spanish speaking had to be represented at all levels of the church and that both Latino clergy as well as laity needed to be part of the decision-making process of the church in order to give priority to the needs of the poor.

What needed to be done given the contradictions, hypocrisy, and insensitivity of the church was, according to Católicos, to transform the church from an elite institution to an agency of the people. Católicos stressed that this transformation was justified based on church doctrines and traditions themselves. "Saint Thomas says that concrete attribution of an authority is made by the people," Católicos noted. "When there is an authority opposed to the people, this authority is illegitimate and tyrannical. As Christians and Catholics, we can and must fight against the mismanagement of OUR Church." Quoting Saint Matthew (Matt.:20:28), Católicos reminded the church of Christ's mission: "I came not to be served, but to serve."[29]

Central to this transformation was reestablishing the church's identity with the poor. Here again Católicos reminded the church of its origins. Christ was born in poverty; he'd grown up with the poor, had washed their feet, and had died for them. He had loved the poor and now the church had to once again do the same. "We must return the Church to the poor," Católicos proposed, "or did Christ die in vain?"[30]

In this transformation, Católicos agreed with the Rev. Antonio J. Sclabassi, who, in his essay "The Catholic Church and *La Raza*," called for a distinction between the church as an institution and the church as people. The transformation of the church would not come from within the institution itself, but by the movement of the people themselves.[31] The people through grassroots organization or what liberation theologians called *comunidades de base* would become the church.[32] "This process has already begun," Sclabassi noted, "and there is much evidence that it is quickly growing."[33] Católicos added that part of its task was precisely to get other Chicanos to understand this distinction and, through a process of what liberationists also referred to as *conscientización*, mobilize a mass movement to regain the church.[34]

Transforming the church, Católicos further believed, would assure that the church likewise came to identify with the Chicano Movement. The movement would transform the clergy into "*La Raza* Churchmen."[35] "It is long overdue," Católicos observed, "that the Catholic Church in Los Angeles and throughout the Southwest have the moral integrity to identify with *el movimiento. Católicos Por La Raza* will not rest until that day has come."[36]

In their struggle to reconvert the church, members of Católicos believed that they had no better role model than Christ himself. Católicos as well as other Catholic activists in the movement reinterpreted Christ as a revolutionary. "Jesus Christ is being seen as the radical he really is," one New Mexican movement activist proposed. "He is seen as a revolutionist through the eyes of the revolutionaries, for it is from him that we draw strength."[37] As a revolutionary, Christ, as the Chicano poet Abelardo Delgado wrote, represented the "New Christ" bearing the "New Cross" that would establish the "New Church."[38]

In its call for a "New Christ," Católicos made it very clear that they were not attacking Catholic beliefs and doctrines, but the current leadership of the church, which had deviated from these beliefs and doctrines. "I think that we went to great length," recalls Raul Ruiz, "to explain every time we spoke or wrote that we were not writing about the ideology or the religion itself, but rather the human aspect of the church, which we felt was very defective."[39]

Católicos did not see itself as leading a schism from the church, but of leading it back to its own principles. "It is not the Church or more specifically the religious views that are inadequate to meet the needs of today's poor," Católicos pointed out, "but some of the men who help run the Church."[40] One of these men was Frances Cardinal McIntyre, who, according to Católicos, ran the Los Angeles Archdiocese with tyrannical hands; he was accused of suppressing both clergy and laity, especially those who identified with the poor. "Social action, to the Cardinal," Católicos stressed, "is regarded in the same vein as hell." Pedro Arias further emphasized the distinction between Catholic beliefs and wayward leaders of the church whom he had witnessed both in his native Mexico and in the United States:

Since . . . I have become aware of the corruption that exists among these elements and, also, I have understood and become closer to my Catholic faith, as I have come to the conclusion that if the Catholic religion continues to exist and to increase despite its bad leaders, it is because it is a pure and true religion. At the same time, I have come to the realization that is my duty and the duty of all Catholics to combat those bad elements because if they are not stopped, some day they shall destroy the Catholic faith. They are gradually betraying the Christ and fooling themselves and deceiving their flock.[41]

In its declaration of principles, Católicos concluded that the struggle for the soul of the church was critical for two basic reasons. One, it was foolish for the movement to neglect the church as a major institution that affected Chicanos. The church possessed vast wealth and power; if that could be converted toward the alleviation of poverty and the empowerment of Chicanos, then the movement would acquire a significant ally. Second, Católicos understood that in any social movement, such as the Chicano Movement, spirituality was essential to maintaining morale and commitment. Católicos believed that a liberated church would be able to provide this spiritual guidance. The movement and the poor needed not an unfriendly church but a friendly one. This is what Católicos aimed to achieve. "When poor people get involved in a long conflict, such as a strike, or a civil rights drive, and the pressure increases everyday," Católicos observed,

There is a deep need for spiritual advice. Without it families crumble, leadership weakens, and hard workers grow tired. In such a situation the spiritual advice must be given by a friend, not by part of the opposition. What sense does it make to go to mass on Sunday and reach out for spiritual help, and instead get sermons about the wickedness of your course? That only drives one to question and despair. We need a friendly spiritual guide. And this is true in every community where the poor face tremendous problems.[42]

Defining their beliefs and their objectives, members of Católicos shortly after organizing likewise drafted a list of demands which it hoped to present to Cardinal McIntyre. These demands reflected the philosophy of Católicos, but in a more concrete manner outlined the specific changes its members hoped to pressure the church into accepting. Key to the demands was acquiring a substantive input by the Chicano community into church decision-making. This would be achieved by the creation of a Commission on Mexican American Affairs within the hierarchy of the church in Los Angeles. The commission would be composed of representatives of Mexican American community organizations as well as of Mexican American priests and nuns. This commission would concentrate its efforts into reorienting church policy in the following areas:

1. Education. The commission would be authorized to make periodic accountings, for example, of church assets in order to determine the available funding for Chicano education programs.

2. Housing. This would involve church-provided housing loans for the purchase of homes or for repairs. The church would also built low-cost housing in the barrios.

3. Health. The commission would administer and control all church hospitals in the Mexican American community as well as provide free or low-cost health insurance for low-income Mexican Americans.

4. Shared governance. The commission would jointly share with the church hierarchy policy-making powers on all temporal affairs.

5. Leadership and orientation. The commission would oversee classes in all barrio parishes concerning leadership and Mexican American culture. The church would also provide orientation classes on Mexican American history and culture to its seminary students as well as to clergy assigned to barrio parishes.

6. Assignment of clergy to Chicano Movement. The church would see to it that concerned priests and nuns would be assigned on a full-time basis to work with Chicano community projects and organizations.

7. Freedom of speech for all priests and nuns. The church would guarantee such freedom of speech and would not retaliate against any member of the clergy for speaking out on secular issues.

8. Use of church facilities. The church would make available to Chicano community groups the use of church buildings for meetings and other events.

9. Public commitment to the Chicano Movement. The church would publicly support the struggles of the Chicano community in their varied manifestations, such as support for the farmworkers and for the anti–Vietnam War movement.[43]

By acceding to these demands, the church, according to Católicos, would "reflect the social condition of the people it serves." With demands in hand, Católicos in the fall of 1969 proceeded to devise a strategy to force the church in Los Angeles, specifically Cardinal McIntyre, to agree to them. Meeting at the headquarters of *La Raza* magazine, members of

Católicos (about twenty hard-core members) concentrated on devising the steps they would take. It does not appear that these meetings were the occasion for any philosophical discussions. Richard Martínez notes that the issue-oriented and pragmatic aspects of these meetings coincided with what he considered to be Católicos' more populist base as opposed to a philosophical one.[44]

Católicos devised a twofold but interrelated strategy. It would call for a meeting with the cardinal and at the same time commence picketing of the cardinal's residence at St. Basil's Church in order to force such a meeting. Católicos targeted Cardinal McIntyre because it understood that he held the power and the purse strings. "We pursued meetings with the Cardinal in our own inimitable way," Martínez stresses, "in your face." Picketing included a vigil on Thanksgiving Day in front of St. Basil's.[45]

After receiving no response from the cardinal, Católicos decided to raise the ante. On 18 December 1969, members of Católicos—between twenty and thirty—visited the cardinal's residence to demand a meeting. They had decided not to take no for an answer. Once inside the chancery, they were told that the cardinal was not available, but that one of his bishops would see them. Católicos agreed and three of them, including Richard Cruz and Richard Martínez, were escorted into another room. Unfortunately, this meeting came to naught, as the other member of Católicos proceeded to use the occasion to verbally attack the bishop for the church's neglect of the Chicano community.[46]

After the three representatives of Católicos returned to the rest of the group, a decision was made to barge into the cardinal's office. They forced open the door into the inner corridor in search of the cardinal's office. As startled priests emerged from their offices, they ran down the corridor and entered what appeared to be the cardinal's office. "That's it!" Richard Martínez recalls he and the other members of Católicos yelling out. Despite the priests' efforts to barricade the door, Martínez and the others pushed it open.[47]

There standing behind his desk was a red-faced and angry Cardinal McIntyre ordering his staff to call the police. "No, no, we don't need to call the police," Martínez remembers one of the staff responding. "Calm down, calm down."[48]

A livid cardinal agreed to meet with Católicos. He listened to the members' demands, but only promised to look into the issues presented to him. Martínez recalls that Richard Cruz did all of the talking for Católicos. Having forced their meeting with the cardinal, members of Católi-

2. Ricardo Cruz,
25 December 1969,
St. Basil's Church,
Los Angeles. Courtesy:
Ricardo Cruz and Católicos
Por La Raza, Special Collec-
tion, University of California,
Santa Barbara.

cos retreated, believing that they had at least won a moral victory. "We weren't very sophisticated," Martínez notes, "but that was our strength because with our energy and our enthusiasm we just charged ahead."[49]

A few days passed, and Católicos did not hear back from the cardinal. As a result, the decision was made to organize a large demonstration outside of St. Basil's on Christmas Eve and to disrupt the cardinal's Midnight Mass (figure 2). Since the Mass was also going to be televised, Católicos hoped to take advantage of the broadcast to publicize its demands. This more dramatic strategy may have been inspired by the actions of the Católicos group in San Diego, who on 30 November had taken over Camp Oliver, a Catholic youth camp in Descanso, just east of San Diego. The San Diego Católicos used the seizure to bring attention to their own demands. The takeover ended on 1 December.[50]

Richard Martínez recalls that at this point Católicos made increased contact with disaffected or ex-priests and nuns, such as Bias Bonpane. In the meantime, picketing and candlelight vigils outside of St. Basil's resumed. Raul Ruiz notes that large numbers participated in these protests, which included some sleepovers outside of the church.[51]

Additional preparation for the Christmas Eve demonstration involved recruiting additional Chicano student support. This was the task assigned to Martínez and the UMAS group at City College. Martínez remembers that while many other students responded positively to the planned demonstration, some raised doubts as to the correctness of the strategy of attacking the church. These students believed that this action would offend many Catholics. Moreover, they did not believe that the church was the real enemy.[52]

In addition to organizing students for the demonstration, Católicos—principally Joe Razo and Ricardo Cruz—concentrated on gathering community support and participation. They also arranged to have legal representation at the demonstration in case of encounters with the police. Since Católicos were not keeping their demonstration a secret, it assumed that the police would be present. Members arranged to secure the services of the movement's attorney, Oscar Zeta Acosta, the "Brown Buffalo." Acosta would later write about the St. Basil's demonstration as well as on other movement activities in his 1972 book, *The Revolt of the Cockroach People*. Additional support for the protest came from a group called the Coalition of Concerned Catholics, which was an organization of Anglo priests, nuns, and laypeople.[53]

The strategy for the intervention at the cardinal's Mass involved several steps. The assembled crowd would first have an alternative "people's Mass" outside of the church at the same time as the Mass inside of St. Basil's. Both Masses would actually commence at 11 p.m. and conclude at around midnight. The alternative Mass would be officiated by some of the ex-priests, including Bonpane. It would be timed to end a few minutes before the conclusion of the cardinal's Mass. The group would then line up in a candlelight procession and enter the church. Going through the vestibule, they would enter the sanctuary and proceed down the main aisle of the church. At the foot of the altar railing, they would spread out and face the congregation. Three of them, including Cruz and Martínez, would then take turns reading their demands. This strategy, according to Martínez, "sounded good."[54]

The events, however, did not quite turn out that way. It appears that somewhere between 200 and 350 people gathered to participate in the demonstration. They assembled at Lafayette Park, about a mile from the church, and then marched to St. Basil's. They grouped to the side of the main entrance and next to the large nativity scene. As people arrived for the Midnight Mass, some verbal altercations took place between those entering and members of Católicos. Bonpane said the alternative Mass in

Spanish, using a table for the altar. Instead of the regular wafers for communion, he used bits of tortilla. When their Mass ended, the Católicos group proceeded to form into a procession and prepared to enter the vestibule.[55]

At this point, the sequence of events is not perfectly clear. It appears, however, that discovering the front doors of the church shut, a small contingent proceeded to enter the church through a side door. They found themselves by the main altar and then walked down a side aisle to the vestibule at the back of the church. In the vestibule they encountered a number of "ushers," who later turned out to be undercover county sheriffs. Somehow the Católicos contingent managed to open one of the front doors, allowing those on the outside to come in. Either before this door was opened or after is when the conflict between the ushers and members and supporters of Católicos commenced.

Richard Martínez recalls that as he and other Católicos entered the vestibule, they realized that it was not going to be easy to go into the sanctuary or main part of the church. Blocking the doors to the sanctuary were the so-called ushers. Martínez notes that they were "not small." As Martínez and the others approached the ushers they started to chant, "Let the poor people in! Let the poor people in!" As they neared the ushers and attempted to open the sanctuary doors, as Martínez remembers, "All hell broke lose."[56]

As the melee broke out, additional ushers entered through the side of the vestibule. Fisticuffs, wrestling, and shouting filled the area. Raul Ruiz remembers that the congregation inside the church raised their voices in singing "O Come, All Ye Faithful" in an effort to drown out the calls of "Let the poor people in!" Although the Mass was being televised, viewers never saw the fighting although audio did pick up some of the shouting.[57]

Within a few minutes the ushers were reinforced by uniformed police, who, according to Católicos, had been waiting in close proximity to the church. Declaring the demonstration to be an "unlawful assembly," helmeted city police moved into the crowd, wielding their riot sticks and spraying mace both outside and inside the vestibule. "I felt a strong stream of something cold on my forehead," Pedro Arias later described being maced, "and almost immediately I felt my eyes sting. Because of this, I could hardly see."[58]

Inside the church as the Mass came to an end, an irate Cardinal McIntyre, aware of the disturbance in the vestibule, condemned the action of Católicos. "We are ashamed of the participants," he told the congregation, "and we recognize that their conduct was symbolic of the conduct of the rabble as they stood at the foot of the cross, shouting, 'Crucify Him!'" However, the cardinal asked the congregation to forgive the demonstrators: "for they know not what they do." The *Tidings*, the archdiocesan paper, later referred to the actions of Católicos as the "new barbarism."[59]

Outnumbered, the demonstrators retreated outside of the church and onto Wilshire Boulevard. In retreating, someone from the group smashed one of the main doors of the church. As the people inside the church began exiting, Martínez recalls seeing one of the churchgoers literally flatten a young student demonstrator, who had to be taken to the hospital. In addition, the police arrested four of the protestors, whom the *Los Angeles Times* the next day referred to as the "club-swinging mob." Those arrested were charged with conspiring to start a riot and assaulting an officer. Two of those arrested were Razo and Ruiz, who had to spend the rest of Christmas Eve in jail until bailed out the next day. Charges were later dropped at least for those arrested that night. Oscar Zeta Acosta would later refer to the events of that evening as a "police riot."[60]

The following day, Christmas Day, between 50 and 100 protestors returned to St. Basil's and held a vigil across the street from the church. Ricardo Cruz told a reporter, "We're not going to stop demonstrating. The Cardinal will have to kill us to get us to stop." The vigil was marred, however, by the actions of Gloria Chávez, a Católicos supporter, who entered St. Basil's during one of the Christmas Masses with a golf club in hand and proceeded to march down the main aisle before the ushers were aware of what was occurring. When she reached the altar, she waved the club, scaring the priest away, and then pulled the altar cloth off, spilling the items on it—including the chalice—onto the floor. Martínez recalls that Chávez's actions were disavowed by Católicos. A week later Católicos and supporters staged a three-day fast outside of St. Basil's.[61]

Although Católicos had only been in existence a couple of months, its demonstration at St. Basil's represented the climax of it short history. St. Basil's symbolized the differences and tensions between Católicos and the church in Los Angeles. The Christmas Eve protest led to a variety of repercussions. As far as the church was concerned, it denied the charges that it had been unresponsive to the Mexican American community. It pointed out its numerous educational and charitable services in East Los Angeles. Although rhetorically holding its ground, the church nevertheless moved to meet Católicos' challenge by instituting certain reforms or at least the appearance of reform.[62]

These moves on the part of the church were aided by the announced retirement of Cardinal McIntyre in early 1970. Whether the protests initiated against him by Católicos played a role in his retirement is hard to determine. One reporter believed that the cardinal's retirement was welcomed by the Vatican due to the cardinal's seeming inability to deal with what the reporter called a "theology of resistance" carried out not only by Católicos but by other discontented church sources.

With Cardinal McIntyre's departure, the church was in a better position to address the demands made on it by Católicos. McIntyre's successor, Timothy Manning, was more disposed to pursue a conciliatory policy within certain limits. Shortly after assuming office, Archbishop Manning met with representatives of Católicos and while the issue of shared governance was never conceded by Manning, he did proceed to meet some of the other issues of concern to Católicos. For one, he emerged as one of the leading Catholic bishops who helped end the grape boycott with the growers' agreeing to recognize the farmworkers' union. Manning authorized additional funds for the church's social and educational services in East Los Angeles. To deal with the issue of representation, Manning established an interparochial council of clergy and laypeople for the East Los Angeles parishes to serve as an advisory group to the archbishop. Cultural reforms included permission for Spanish-speaking parishes to include Latino music such as mariachi at Mass. Although it is not clear if Manning met again during the next several months with Católicos, he did visit the home of Ricardo Cruz later that September and met with members of Católicos. Outside of Los Angeles, similar changes also took place in other California and southwestern dioceses.[63]

At a larger level, the protests by Católicos—as well as a growing restlessness on the part of Chicano clergy—made an impression not only on the U.S. hierarchy but in Rome as well. In 1970, for example, the Vatican approved the appointment of the Reverend Patricio Flores of San Antonio as the first bishop of Latino descent in the United States. One year later, the Reverend Juan Arzube, a Latino of Ecuadorian origins, was appointed assistant bishop in Los Angeles, a clear concession to Católicos and other Chicano demands for more Latino representation in the Los Angeles church. By 1974 three additional Latino priests were appointed bishops in the United States. Moreover, within the U.S. church, working committees and conferences on the Spanish speaking were organized into the 1970s. This included the "Primer Encuentro Hispano de Pastoral" (First Hispanic Pastoral Encounter), which met in Washington, D.C., in 1972 under the U.S. Catholic Conference for the Spanish Speaking and which recommended a number of changes to make the church more relevant to the Latino communities.[64]

For its part, Católicos still believed that these concessions by the church were largely cosmetic. Through 1970 it continued to sponsor periodic vigils and picketing of the church. These additional protests were highlighted by a baptismal-certificate-burning vigil held in front of St. Basil's on 13 September 1970. This event was spearheaded by Pedro Arias, and his family who called on other Chicano Catholics to join them in burning their baptismal certificates as a way of protesting what Arias claimed was still a reluctance on the part of the church to become a church of and for the poor.[65]

Although Católicos continued its criticism of the church, it was significantly hampered by having to defend itself against new legal actions against it. One month after the St. Basil's demonstration, twenty-one members or supporters of Católicos were arrested for their participation in the Christmas Eve protest. Charges ranged from disturbing the peace to assaulting an officer. Oscar Zeta Acosta was retained as the attorney for the defendants, who were split into two separate trials, together lasting until June 1970. The trials were characterized by Zeta Acosta's theatrical antics, which questioned the legitimacy of the legal process especially with respect to the exclusion of Chicanos from the jury selection process. In the end, eight were found not guilty while twelve were found guilty. Some, like Martínez and Cruz, served from two to four months in jail. Others, such as Ruiz and Arias, received minor fines.[66]

The distraction of the trials clearly affected the ability of Católicos to maintain its momentum. In addition, Chicano activists, including members of Católicos—because they wore many hats in the movement—were further distracted by the growing buildup of the Chicano anti–Vietnam War movement during 1970. This buildup would itself climax on 29 August 29, when over 20,000, mostly Chicanos, demonstrated against the war in East Los Angeles. Like the St. Basil protest, but on a much larger scale, this example of growing Chicano discontent and militancy over the war was forcibly attacked and destroyed by the Los Angeles County sheriffs. That response in turn led to a full-scale riot in East Los Angeles. Three people were killed, including the *Los Angeles Times* reporter Rubén Salazar. By that tragic day and certainly into the fall, Católicos for all practical purposes had ceased to exist, as still other venues of social protest arose.

Notes

1. Interview with Richard Martínez, 21 January 1996, Los Angeles.
2. Interview with Raul Ruiz, 1 March 1993, Los Angeles.
3. Martínez interview.
4. Ibid. See also "Católicos Por La Raza," document, n.d., in possession of Pedro Arias.
5. Ruiz interview.
6. Ibid. See also Carlos Muñoz Jr., *Youth, Identity, Power: The Chicano Movement* (London: Verso Press, 1989). See Alberto L. Pulido, "Are You an Emissary of Jesus Christ? Justice, the Catholic Church, and the Chicano Movement," *Explorations in Ethnic Studies* 14, no. 1 (January 1991): 17–34.
7. Luis Valdez and Stan Steiner, *Aztlán: An Anthology of Mexican American Literature* (New York: Vintage Books, 1972), 384.
8. *The Spiritual Plan de Aztlán* was written by Mexican American civil rights activists in the late 1960s. It was a political and cultural manifesto that advocated Mexican American/Chicano pride, nationalism, and self-determination. It was endorsed and adopted by the First National Chicano Liberation Youth Conference in March 1969 hosted by Rodolfo Gonzáles's Crusade for Justice in Denver, Colorado. It is one of the pivotal documents of the Mexican American/Chicano Civil Rights Movement.
9. Eduardo Quevedo Jr., "The Catholic Church in America," *Con Safos* (fall 1968): 11.
10. Ruiz interview.
11. Ibid., 1 March 1993.
12. *La Raza* 1.1 (1970): 34. See also "The Revolutionary Church Is the Only Church of the People: The Church of the People Is the Revolution," *La Raza* 1.1 no.6, 71 and "Camilo Torres: Profeta de nuestro tiempo," Ibid., 63.
13. "*Católicos Por La Raza*," *La Raza* (February 1970); repr. in Valdez and Steiner, *Aztlán*, 391.
14. "Conference of Catholic Bishops," *La Raza* (n.d.): 29.
15. Statement of Pedro Arias, n.d., in possession of Arias.
16. "The Church: The Model of Hypocrisy," *La Verdad* (San Diego), December 1969, 22, in Valdez and Steiner, *Aztlán*, 391.
17. Ibid., 392.
18. "Conference of Catholic Bishops," *La Raza* 1 (1970): 39.
19. "Church Hypocrisy," *La Raza* (n.d.): 53.
20. "*Católicos Por La Raza* and Mexican Americans," *La Raza* (January 1970): 2.
21. Ibid., 2.
22. "Blessed Are the Poor," *La Raza* 1.1, no. 2: 55–65; Ruiz interview.
23. "Católicos Por La Raza," 390.
24. "Open Letter to Cardinal McIntyre," *La Raza* 1.1, no. 2: 51.
25. Statement of Pedro Arias, n.d., in possession of Arias.

26. Antonio J. Sclabassi, "The Catholic Church and *La Raza*," *La Raza* (January 1970).

27. "Conference of Catholic Bishops."

28. "Church Hierarchy," 53.

29. "Bautismo de fuego," flyer, in possession of Pedro Arias.

30. "Católicos Por La Raza" in Valdez and Steiner, *Aztlán*, 392.

31. "The Church: The Model of Hypocrisy," 9.

32. *LA Free Press*, 16 January 1970, 4.

33. "Church Hypocrisy," 65; "Católicos Por La Raza," 392.

34. See *La Voz del Pueblo* (Berkeley), February 1970.

35. "Church Hypocrisy," 54.

36. Ibid.

37. Dolores del Grito, "Jesus Christ as a Revolutionist," in Valdez and Steiner, *Aztlán*, 393–94.

38. Abelardo Delgado, "The New Christ," "The Organizer," and "A New Cross," poems in Valdez and Steiner, *Aztlán*, 394–97.

39. Ruiz interview, no date.

40. Sclabassi, "The Catholic Church and *La Raza*," 8.

41. Pedro Arias interview, n.d.

42. Ibid.

43. Sclabassi, "The Catholic Church and *La Raza*," 4.

44. See demands in *La Raza*," 1, no. 1 (1970): 25.

45. Martínez interview.

46. Ibid.

47. Martínez interview; *La Raza*, 1, no. 1 (1970): 24; *Tidings*, 2 January 1979, 3.

48. Martínez interview.

49. Ibid.

50. Ibid.; Pulido, "Are You an Emissary of Jesus Christ?" 25–27.

51. Martínez interview; Ruiz interview.

52. Martínez interview.

53. Martínez interview; Ruiz interview; *LA Free Press*, 16 January 1970, 4.

54. "Open Letter to Cardinal McIntyre," *La Raza* 1.1, no.2: 49; Martínez interview.

55. Martínez interview; *People's World*, 3 January 1970, 1, 12; *Los Angeles Times*, 25 December 1969 and 26 December 1969, 3; *Los Angeles Free Press*, 9 January 1970, 2 and 16 January 1970, 4; *Militant*, 23 January, 1970, 1; *La Raza* 1.1, no.1: 31.

56. Martínez interview.

57. Ibid.; Ruiz interview; *Los Angeles Times*, 26 December 1969, 3.

58. *Los Angeles Free Press*, 16 January 1970, 4; Arias statement, n.d., in possession of Arias.

59. *Los Angeles Times*, 26 December 1969, 32; *Los Angeles Free Press*, 16 January 1970, 4; *Tidings*, n.d., 1.

60. Martínez interview; Ruiz interview; *Los Angeles Times*, 25 December 1969 and 1 January 1970, 3; *La Raza* 1.1, no. 1 (1970): 31, 69; *People's World*, 3 January 1970, 12; *Los Angeles Free Press*, 16 January 1970, 2.

61. *Los Angeles Times*, 26 December 1969, 32; *People's World*, 3 January 1970, 12; Martínez interview.

62. *Los Angeles Free Press*, 23 January 1970, 4.

63. *Tidings*, 29 January, 1971, 1; *Los Angeles Times*, 14 September 1970, 18; Martínez interview.

64. *Los Angeles Times*, 28 July 1974, pt. II, 1; *La Voz Católica* (Oakland), July 1973.

65. "Bautismo de fuego"; *Los Angeles Herald-Examiner*, 14 September 1970, A-3.

66. *Los Angeles Herald-Examiner*, 6 June 1970, A-3.

III

Mexican American Popular

Catholicism

6

Our Lady of Guadalupe and
the Politics of Cultural Interpretation

During the Mexican Revolution in 1810, her image on a banner became Mexico's symbol of liberation as Father Miguel Hidalgo carried her into the battlefield. A century later, on the northern side of the U.S.-Mexico border in the Southwest, César Chávez did the same. He organized thousands of *campesinos* into what became a successful strike against grape growers who exploited their workers.[1] Her image knows no borders. She crosses *la frontera* undocumented every day as immigrants swim across the treacherous Rio Grande or walk through the scorching desert carrying her image on a chain around their necks, on an *estampita* in their wallets, or in their prayers.[2]

For centuries people of Mexican descent—regardless of class, gender, or sexual orientation—continue to see Our Lady of Guadalupe as the most influential Catholic symbol of Mexico. On her feast day in 2005, the Basílica de Nuestra Señora de Guadalupe of Mexico City, where the original image is housed, received approximately 8 million visitors.[3]

With such a disparate following, it might be expected that there are many interpretations and ways of experiencing Our Lady of Guadalupe. Indeed, when I searched for material on Our Lady of Guadalupe, I found at least 1,300 works. Yet, for the more traditional Guadalupanos such a multitude of readings is difficult to accept.[4] A Catholic religious sister whom I told of my research on Our Lady of Guadalupe responded, "What do you mean: different interpretations?" Her shocked response is not unique; instead it reflects what most believers in Our Lady of Guadalupe think. It also reveals the need, particularly today, for different voices to share their interpretations of Our Lady of Guadalupe.

For the purpose of this essay, I examine four scholarly approaches to Guadalupe: (1) Catholic apparitionist, (2) historical, (3) Chicana feminist literature, and (4) Chicana feminist art. Historical and theological approaches have dominated the study of Our Lady of Guadalupe. The work of the Catholic theologian Virgilio Elizondo represents an excellent starting point to look at how scholars sketch themes on the exaltation of ideal motherhood—a quintessential Catholic reflection of womanhood. Yet, I will also examine Jeanette Rodriguez's seminal empirical study of women's perceptions of Guadalupe. I will argue that her findings lead us away from the notion of the "submissive all-accepting mother," which, it can be argued, is connected to the Catholic Mexican patriarchy. Her work demonstrates that while cultural theology and memory play an essential role in the definition of motherhood, the theological and cultural meaning of Guadalupe is also continuously informed and shaped by the very people who find empowerment in her.

The historical research of Stafford Poole and Louise M. Burkhart will provide a suitable point of entry to the historical and what some devotees might call anti-apparitionist arguments. Though generally historians tend to belong to the anti-apparitionist school of thought, and theologians to the apparitionist school of thought, as I will demonstrate, there have been some exceptions. For example, the Mexican historians Fidel González Fernández, Eduardo Chávez Sánchez, and José Luis Guerrero Rosado contend that the Guadalupe account did take place and that Juan Diego was a historical figure. Finally, I will also examine how Chicana feminist literary writers—Ana Castillo, Sandra Cisneros, Carla Trujillo—and artists—Ester Hernández, Yolanda López, and Alma López—have contested the Mariology that envelopes the Guadalupe story, and the anti-apparitionist sweeping arguments that negate the influence of the Aztec goddess Tonantzin's apparition on Tepeyac hill.[5]

Synthesis of the *Nican mopohua*—"Here is told"

In 1521, Tenochtitlán, now known as Mexico City, fell to Hernán Cortés after Cuauhtémoc, the last Aztec ruler, surrendered. Spanish soldiers and a few missionaries used religion to justify the physical, emotional, and spiritual enslavement of the indigenous people. Women were raped. Thousands of men, women, and children were brutally killed and their sociopolitical and religious ways of knowing were shattered. The vanquished had lost all hope and desire to live, for the conquerors had stripped them of all dignity and self-worth, calling the indigenous people's very humanity into question. However, according to Catholic Mexican popular tradition, in the midst of this devastation, a great miracle took place—a miracle that was to return the people's dignity and restore their desire to live. As the Guadalupano poets recount, at early dawn on Saturday 9 December 1531 (a decade after the fall of Tenochtitlán), a Nahua Indian and recent convert to Christianity named Juan Diego was on his way to attend catechism classes. As he walked across the hill of Tepeyac (a sacred ancient worship site to the Aztec goddess Tonantzin), he heard birds singing at the hilltop. He then heard the sweet voice of a woman calling his name. He was astonished at what he saw at the top of the hill: A woman covered with a mantle as blue as the sky, golden sunrays gently branching out behind her (see figure 1). Her skin was cinnamon brown like his, her hands were together in the indigenous way of offering, "indicating that something is to come from her," and she spoke the Nahuatl language.[6] She identified herself as Mary, mother of God. She asked Juan Diego to go to the bishop of "New Spain" (Mexico), Juan Zumárraga, and tell him that she desired that a hermitage be built in her name on the hill of Tepeyac.[7] Juan Diego went to the bishop and delivered the heavenly Lady's message. In disbelief, the bishop responded that Juan Diego needed to come back a second time and tell about his vision again when he would be able to carefully listen to it.

Saddened, Juan Diego returned to the site where he had seen the apparition of the beautiful Lady and, finding her there once again, told her that the bishop did not believe him, since he was only a poor Indian. Juan Diego suggested that she consider sending another person, such as a respected noble, so that her message might be heard. With great compassion, the Lady told Juan Diego that she could have chosen anybody else but that she wanted him to deliver her message to the bishop. She told him to return to the bishop and tell him that the Ever-Virgin Mary, the Mother of God wanted a hermitage to be built on the hill of Tepeyac. On the next Sunday, he did as she directed. Upon questioning Juan Diego at length, the bishop told him that he remained unconvinced, and hence could not fulfill the wishes of the heavenly Lady. Juan Diego should go to the Lady and ask for a sign.

That day, Juan Diego found his uncle, Juan Bernardino, ill with smallpox. Juan Bernardino felt that his time had come, and he asked Juan Diego to fetch a priest from Tlatelolco to hear his confession. Going in search of the priest on the next day (Tuesday), Juan Diego decided to

1. Virgen de Guadalupe,
Basílica de Nuestra Señora
de Guadalupe in Mexico
City. Courtesy: Socorro
Castañeda-Liles.

avoid seeing the Lady by taking the route to Tepeyac that went around
the hill. To his surprise the heavenly Lady appeared to him nonetheless
and asked him what his hurry was. Mournful, Juan Diego told the Lady
about his dying uncle. With great love she told Juan Diego not to worry,
for his uncle was in good health. Juan Diego should go to the top of the
hill where he first saw her and pick some roses and bring them before
her. Her request confused Juan Diego, since this occurred in December,
in the dead of winter. He knew that no flowers would be growing at the
top of that hill.

Yet to his surprise when he went to the hill, he found beautiful and
fragrant Castilian flowers. Cutting them and placing them in his *tilma*,
he brought them before the Lady.[8] The heavenly Lady took the flowers,
but then placed them back in Juan Diego's tilma. She told him to return
to the bishop and show him the sign for which he had asked. At the Episcopal Palace, Juan Diego asked to see the bishop. When the doorkeepers,

friars, and servants noticed Juan Diego's ebullience, they demanded to see what he was hiding in his tilma. Fearing their disapproval, he nonetheless showed them a couple of flowers. To everyone's surprise, when the friars and the others tried to grab the flowers they disappeared into thin air. When he was finally brought before the bishop, Juan Diego unfolded his tilma. As the roses fell, the image of the heavenly Lady became imprinted on his cloak. Meanwhile, the Lady visited Juan Bernardino, and identified herself as the Ever-Virgin Holy Mary of Guadalupe. She told him that he, too, was to go to the bishop and tell him about his healing and all that he had seen. The bishop was finally convinced, and not long after La Virgen's apparition a hermitage was built in her honor.

This account is the most well known, and the one generally accepted by those who are familiar with Our Lady of Guadalupe. Its interpretation, however, is another matter, for ways of understanding the meaning of the *Nican mopohua*'s message (the *Nican mopohua* is the popular version of the Guadalupe account) vary anywhere between strictly indigenous to Catholic-centric indigenous readings of the text.

Theology: Guadalupe Theology in Lived Experience

For Mexican Americans, Our Lady of Guadalupe is a symbol of both cultural and religious identity. For people who were stripped of everything, she restores to them their dignity, their humanity, and their place in history. —RODRIGUEZ, *Our Lady of Guadalupe*, 45.

Scholars seek to interpret what they think they know; the people speak freely about what they experience. —VIRGILIO ELIZONDO, 1994, in Rodriguez, *Our Lady of Guadalupe*, xii.

Virgilio Elizondo is one of the many contemporary U.S. theologians of Our Lady of Guadalupe. In his book *Guadalupe: Mother of the New Creation* (1998), he takes the "*Nican mopohua* to develop a Catholic Guadalupe theology. Making an indigenous, Catholic analysis grounded in the Mexican experience, he develops a Guadalupe theology anchored in a mestizo reality.[9] From Elizondo's Catholic, indigenous interpretation, Guadalupe transcends everything human. She is seen as a higher being to whom people can turn to for comfort and affirmation. From this locality, Our Lady of Guadalupe becomes the mother who advocates for her children.

Elizondo maintains that Our Lady of Guadalupe is the beginning of a new creation—the mestizo people of Mexico—in which she is the "mother of a new humanity." Our Lady of Guadalupe, he says, is the feminine side of God: she represents the attributes of God that oftentimes are stripped away from what God represents. For Elizondo Guadalupe is "not a dogma of Christian faith," but represents a *mestizaje* (mixing) of faiths—"la azteca" and "la española." She embodies this continuity and transformation of faiths as lived and experienced by the people. In Elizondo's words: "she is constitutive of the faith-memory of the people." Why is she so powerful? What is it about her that attracts people? According to Elizondo, she is powerful because she represents liberation to the socially marginalized. People find her a safe and mystical "space" in the midst of the uncertainty, oppression, and violence in their lives.[10]

For Elizondo, Guadalupe is more than another Marian apparition; she is an original American Gospel, for she epitomizes the "narrative of a birth/resurrection experience at the very beginning of the crucifixion of the natives, the Africans, and their *mestizo* and mulatto children."[11] Elizondo's analysis of Our Lady of Guadalupe relies on liberation theology. He bases his arguments on the cultural memory of the people, maintaining that we must first understand what Guadalupe means in the lives of the people. How then is Our Lady of Guadalupe articulated by grassroots research on Mexican Americans?

Jeannette Rodriguez's book, *Our Lady of Guadalupe: Faith and Empowerment among Mexican-American Women* (1994), is the first scholarly attempt to empirically examine one aspect of what Elizondo proposes: understanding what Guadalupe means in the everyday lives of ordinary Mexican Americans.[12] The book then attempts to theologize from those social locations. Rodriguez represents what has come be the dominant theological interpretation. Her case study among Mexican American women is an important contribution to cultural theology because it places the voices of women at the center of Guadalupe theology. Significantly, her findings expose the variations that exist in how these women articulate Our Lady of Guadalupe.

Rodriguez insists that we place the lived experience of second-generation middle-class Mexican American women today in the larger context of their ancestral history of conquest and domination. Furthermore, religion was strategically used to reinforce women's marginality; and, from Rodriguez's perspective, this has had psychosocial effects on Mexican American women today. Like Chicana feminist intellectuals, she argues Our Lady of Guadalupe's image has been manipulated to encourage passivity in women. How a symbol that has been thus misused can have the potential to empower is a central question in Rodriguez's study. [13]

Like Elizondo, Rodriguez maintains that Our Lady of Guadalupe continues to live in the memory of the people. She is "a presence that exists for those who believe." Though she exercises scholarly caution about making any assumptions about Guadalupe, she nonetheless "effectively assert[s] that Our Lady of Guadalupe is of God." The women she interviewed also define Guadalupe: "although she is of primary importance to them, and they prefer to petition her before petitioning God, they understand that she is not God."[14]

The Mexican American women in Rodriguez's study struggle to live and survive in a predominantly white patriarchal society.[15] How then are these women able to retain their cultural and social values? Rodriguez's findings suggest that Our Lady of Guadalupe plays a pivotal role in the cultural renewal of these women. La Virgen is "a model that arises out of their own cultural living, a model of feminine strength that appears in both the secular and religious worlds."[16] Like Elizondo, Rodriguez maintains that Guadalupe is a source of strength for people, one who affirms their dignity.[17]

How exactly, then, do the women in this case study see La Morenita? One woman named Julia interviewed by Rodriguez said, "Our Lady of Guadalupe represents to me everything we as a people should strive to be: strong yet humble, warm and compassionate, yet courageous enough to stand up for what we believe in."[18] Still another named Monica argued that, "She is the Mother of our father Jesus Christ whom I also speak to for help and comforting."[19] Julia ascribes what seem contradictory attributes to Our Lady of Guadalupe and she is not the only one to do so. The women in Rodriguez's study see Guadalupe as kind, trusting, understanding, timid, humble, loving, courageous, strong, shy, sad, patient, gentle and helpful.[20] Many of these characteristics embody a patriarchal domination; however, at the same time, she is autonomous; Guadalupe is courageous and strong.

The contradictory duality of Guadalupe at first glance seems to make little sense. However, a closer analysis of what appear to be "inconsistencies" in the women's articulation of Our Lady of Guadalupe makes visible the patriarchal context in which these Mexican American women live and their struggle to affirm their self worth. When Rodriguez asked the women in her sample if they wanted to be like Guadalupe, many of them responded that they "might like to, but they could not," thus indicating that while they highly regard these characteristics, they know it is impossible to emulate Guadalupe.[21]

How then do these Mexican American women find empowerment in Guadalupe's paradoxical attributes? Rodriguez notes that a woman named Yolanda said, "She may look quiet and calm and everything, but that takes a lot to do. That's why I believe in her the way I do, because I think she's very strong."[22] Similarly, Carolina noted, "She is a strong woman, in a quiet sense," and in a "I don't have to tell the whole world that I'm strong, I know that I'm strong but I'm doing it for my very special reasons that if I told you about it you wouldn't understand."[23]

These women are able to see beyond the patriarchal ascriptions of passivity and disempowerment imposed on the image of Our Lady of Guadalupe. They find in her a source of empowerment in the way she is. But not all Guadalupe followers and intellectuals anchor their understanding of La Virgen in Catholic thought.

History: Our Lady of Guadalupe in History and the Historicity of Our Lady of Guadalupe

Guadalupe still remains the most powerful religious and national symbol in Mexico today. The symbolism, however, does not rest on any objective historical basis. — STAFFORD POOLE, *Our Lady of Guadalupe*, 225.

Those who do not believe the apparitionist theological interpretation have always posited a counternarrative. They have questioned the historicity of the apparition story and the miraculous authenticity of the image on the *tilma*. Burkhart's essay titled "The Cult of the Virgin of Guadalupe in Mexico" (1993) and Poole's book titled *Our Lady of Guadalupe: The Origins and Sources of a Mexican National Symbol, 1531–1797* (1995) illustrate two contemporary anti-apparitionist historical stances on this issue. Though they represent current historical perspectives on this subject, their interpretations stem from a legacy of complex accounts offered to counter the apparitionist theological interpretations of the story.[24] As mentioned earlier, not all historians belong to the anti-apparitionist school. Fidel González Fernández, Eduardo Chávez Sánchez, and José Luis Guerrero Rosado challenge anti-apparitionist arguments by contending that there is historical evidence that confirms the Guadalupe account and Juan Diego's existence.

Our Lady of Guadalupe—A Miraculous Event or a Prefabricated Story?

Initially some of the most prevalent counternarratives argued that the veneration of Our Lady of Guadalupe was a "pagan" invention with "demonic" underpinnings. What follows is a synopsis of these counterarguments as documented by Burkhart and Poole.

According to these historians, the missionaries were not only concerned with the growing devotion to Our Lady of Guadalupe among the indigenous people, but also with the increasing numbers of indigenous followers. The first Catholic missionaries who arrived in Mexico argued that Guadalupe was a "satanic" invention; one that probably had strong ties to Aztec goddesses—entities whom the missionaries considered to exercise an evil influence on the people. Francisco de Bustamante, a Franciscan friar, thought that "such excessive attention to a single image would confuse the Indians and counteract Franciscan efforts to direct their devotions not to images but to the figures represented by them." [25] Bustamante questioned the miraculous apparition of the image on the tilma. According to one witness, Bustamante referred in a sermon to the image as "a painting that Marcos, an Indian had made." Another person reported that Bustamante had said that it was an "image painted yesterday by an Indian." [26] Whether the image was painted or not, Bustamante was particularly concerned with the story's growing numbers of followers.

Missionaries considered Aztec religious thought and ritual to be satanic. Therefore, many had trouble accepting that the mother of God had appeared at an indigenous worship site. According to Poole, Bernardino de Sahagún, prominent Franciscan friar, was the first to ascertain that the hill of Tepeyac was indeed a preconquest site of worship. [27] The ancient shrine at the site was the place of worship to the Goddess Tonantzin. Unfortunately, according to Poole, there is little information about Tonantzin. What it is known is that the name Tonantzin meant "our revered mother" and "she was sometimes identified with two other mother deities, Coatlicue (serpent skirt) and Cihuacoatl (woman serpent)." [28] Moreover, both Poole and Burkhart question whether Tonantzin was the actual name of a goddess. According to Poole, Burkhart's findings indicate that "Tonantzin was not a proper name but rather a respectful form of address that was generally used in the sixteenth century not only for the Virgin Mary but also for the Church." [29]

Did the indigenous people see a relation between Tonantzin and Our Lady of Guadalupe? Or did they venerate the image of Guadalupe only to continue their worship of Tonantzin? Burkhart's findings about the indigenous people in the period following the conquest, and about the extent to which they worshiped the image, led her to conclude that Guadalupanismo was not simply a "merging of goddess and saint, or a Christian overlay upon native belief."[30]

Catholic preachers, for example, in their missionary efforts to Christianize indigenous people used the term Tonantzin to refer to Mary. Evidence demonstrates that while Christian indigenous people used the title Tonantzin to refer to Our Lady of Guadalupe, this was no indication of a specific connection to a particular Aztec goddess but was instead used generally to refer to Mary.[31] Indeed, the term Tonantzin was used to refer to other Marian images too.[32] Thus, "it is unlikely that, in 1576, Indians using this title for Mary were really thinking of any other sacred figure."[33] That the indigenous people's devotion to Our Lady of Guadalupe stemmed from worship to an ancient Aztec goddess therefore remains ambiguous. According to Burkhart, evidence demonstrates that the opposite was happening: indigenous people were using Christian interpretations to make sense of their religious pre-Christian past, thus "conceptualizing their ancient worship in terms of Mary."[34] Furthermore, Burkhart argues that according to Ciudad Real's report, it was Ixpuchtli (young woman) and not Tonantzin who was worshiped at Tepeyac.[35] The controversy over whom the indigenous people really worshiped when they paid tribute to Tonantzin is one that remains unclear. These are but few of the many roots of the argument regarding the historicity of Our Lady of Guadalupe. But what do contemporary counterarguments say about Our Lady of Guadalupe today? With the passing of time, the Guadalupe controversy has taken different forms. Generally, what at the beginning for many was a symbol with "satanic" attributes became a symbol whose apparitionist story had no historical roots.

Burkhart and Poole maintain that the lack of evidence in sixteenth- and seventeenth-century records indicates that the account of Our Lady of Guadalupe "as it has been known since 1648" has no historical foundation, for it "has no basis in the actual events of early post-conquest Mexico."[36] Therefore, the attempts to bring "authenticity" to Guadalupe's apparition before Juan Diego should be taken as "expressions of piety rather than of historical scholarship."[37] In fact, according to Burkhart, other scholars argue that at the beginning of the postconquest period, the Guadalupe story remained unfamiliar.[38] On the one hand, Burkhart argues that the origins of the Guadalupe account cannot be traced to 1531; on the other, she suggests that the priests who documented the event in 1648 and 1649 did not necessarily make up the story. Thus, Our Lady of Guadalupe as historical text is simply a myth, a legend, and nothing more than a national symbol. At the same time, like Elizondo (*Guadalupe*) and Rodriguez (*Our Lady of Guadalupe*), Poole and Burkhart maintain that Our Lady of Guadalupe is not simply another Marian devotion in popular Catholicism. As the "indulgent, affectionate, maternal, and intermediary" patroness of Mexico, she has also become the preeminent Mexican national symbol. Similarly, while Miguel León-Portilla neither admits nor denies the historicity of the Guadalupe account, he does recognize Guadalupe's impact on the religious and cultural reality of Mexico.[39]

Poole and Burkhart maintain that Our Lady of Guadalupe's apparition in 1531 to Juan Diego differs from what historians have documented about postconquest Mexico. They argue that once one views the story through a critical lens and divorces it from popular Catholicism, it becomes merely a legend with a national quality, lacking any historical underpinnings. What is known, according to Poole and Burkhart, is that in 1648 Miguel Sánchez wrote the first document on the Tepeyac event, and Luis Laso de la Vega wrote the *Nican mopohua* in 1649 "with the Indians as the intended audience." However, some scholars (Rodriguez; Elizondo; León-Portilla; González Fernández, Chávez Sánchez, and Guerrero Rosado) claim that Don Antonio Valeriano is the author of the *Nican mopohua*.[40]

Furthermore, Poole claims that whether or not the indigenous people were influenced by the apparition account is a question that remains unanswered. Based on their historical findings, Burkhart and Poole argue that indigenous people were not strong devotees of Guadalupe in the early colonial period. Instead, the publication of Miguel Sánchez's account coupled with the popularization of the story among criollos, and not indigenous people, are two important elements responsible for giving Our Lady of Guadalupe a national quality.[41] According to Poole, the story and the mysticism surrounding Guadalupe came at a crucial time.[42]

Criollos were not fully accepted by Spanish-born citizens of New Spain. They were seen as inferior and were thus discriminated against in various ways, including exclusion from high-level positions in New Spain's government. According to Poole, the Our Lady of Guadalupe account, as published by Sánchez, was thus a reaffirmation of the selfhood of criollos and became influential "in the development of a *Criollo* consciousness."[43] What about the indigenous element of the story? Poole's findings indicate that Miguel Sánchez strategically downplayed the indigenous component of the apparition story, and made it to be a celebration not of *indigenismo* but of *criollismo*.

> Criollo preachers took up the new devotion with enthusiasm, with a resulting wealth of published sermons in the period from 1660 to 1800. All these celebrated the Criollo nature of the devotion to the detriment of its Indian message. The apparitions themselves were infrequently described by these preachers and only occasionally did the figure of Juan Diego appear. The Criollos were the new chosen people; no other people had a picture of the Virgin that she had personally painted; God had not done the like for any other nation.[44]

Burkhart and Poole maintain that up until the eighteenth century, the criollos and not the indigenous people were more likely to be attracted to Our Lady of Guadalupe, and it was not until the beginning of the eighteenth century that indigenous people began to significantly venerate Guadalupe. They argue that no historical evidence exists of a vast and widespread conversion of indigenous people to Christianity immediately after 1531.[45]

Burkhart asserts that since 1556 the Tepeyac shrine had a new "miracle-working image painted by an Indian artist, possibly one named Marcos." Likewise, the maguey fiber that was used to paint the image could not possibly have been an Indian's cloak [tilma], due to "its excessive length." The painting, she argues, resembles the ones on cloth, called *lienzos*.[46] The image, Burkhart concludes, was painted on a maguey-fiber cloth that was longer than the cloaks used by indigenous men at the time; rendering the possibility that the image was imprinted on an indigenous man's cloak remains questionable.

Contrary to Burkhart and Poole, the Mexican historians Fidel González Fernández, Eduardo Chávez Sánchez, and José Luis Guerrero Rosado maintain that the Guadalupe account did take place.[47] The sources that these scholars used in their analysis came from three cultural backgrounds: (1) indigenous, (2) Spanish, and (3) mestiza. Cautious not to arrive at nationalist or ethnocentric conclusions, they emphasized that the object under examination determined the method of investigation, and it was not determined nor ideologically imagined by the researcher.

They also found that Don Antonio Valeriano, and not Luis Laso de la Vega, wrote the *Nican mopohua* in 1566.[48] They contend that it was during Alonso de Montúfar's ecclesiastical leadership that Valeriano wrote the *Nican mopohua*. According to León-Portilla it could have well been that Valeriano wrote the *Nican mopohua* either because Montúfar asked him to write the account, because Valeriano felt attracted to the topic, or for both reasons.[49]

Moreover, "the historical sources that they examined: oral tradition, written documents, representations (paintings, sculptures, etc . . .), and archaeological objects, demonstrate that there was a growing devotion that was closely associated with Juan Diego Cuauhtlatoatzin."[50] They also found that in indigenous iconography he is depicted with the symbols used to represent that which is sacred. Besides there had been a cult to Juan Diego in which he was understood to be the Virgin Mary's messenger.

However, anti-apparitionist scholars argue that Juan Diego is not a historical person, for his remains have never been found. The apparitionist scholars reply, "the fact that his burial site has not been found is not surprising for many of the burial sites of important indigenous figures (i.e., indigenous noblemen) and Spaniards (i.e., significant conquerors, bishops, and missionaries) remain anonymous."[51] Furthermore, one of the most contentious issues between apparitionists and anti-apparitionists is the lack of Spanish Guadalupan documents before 1548. Anti-apparitionists interpret the lack of evidence before 1548 as the strongest support against the historicity of the Guadalupe account, while apparitionists offer various hypotheses to explain this "silence."[52] For example, González Fernández and colleagues state that the researcher must take into account that the silence does not affirm nor deny anything. They further argue that the possibility cannot be discarded that Bishop Juan de Zumarraga's documents might be lost in the archives or libraries.[53]

One of the more recent, and significant findings is the *Escalada Codex* or the *Codex 1548*. The codex is a fragment of animal skin that depicts the apparition. It has the date 1531 and 1548 as the year of Juan Diego's death. It also shows Sahagún's signature and the glyph of Antonio Valeriano. After "rigorous photographic, chemical, graphological analysis," on Thursday 31 July 1997 Xavier Escalada, SJ, confirmed the authenticity of the codex.[54]

In summary, both Poole and Burkhart claim that when analyzing the historicity of the Guadalupe account and its aftermath, the story has no historical foundation. The Our Lady of Guadalupe account represents the faith of a people in an image that was painted by an indigenous artist possibly named Marcos. However, González Fernández, Chávez Sánchez, and Guerrero Rosado contend that in the indigenous context oral tradition was the main venue of cultural transmission. Thus, the importance of oral history among the indigenous population cannot be overlooked, because this was the main venue of transmission of the Guadalupe account.[55] Besides, if the image was indeed painted by an indigenous man named Marcos on a maguey-fiber cloth, why have some scientists who have examined the cloak concluded that it is impossible to determine the pigment's makeup as well as the how the tilma could have been preserved for more than 470 years? A close examination of the historicity of Our Lady of Guadalupe irons out many historical inconsistencies, but at the same time it leaves many questions unanswered.

David Carrasco, in his book *Religions of Mesoamerica: Cosmovision and Ceremonial Centers*, helps us to understand Our Lady of Guadalupe despite the historical inconsistencies that surround her image. For Carrasco, Our Lady of Guadalupe is a cultural symbol that transcends time and space:

> One of the most interesting responses to the changes of the modern West comes from the Chicano movement in the United States. This response includes the utilization and celebration of the pre-Hispanic past in the aesthetic and political expressions for Chicano liberation in the United States. Chicanos are Americans of Mexican descent who have formed a movement to liberate themselves from Anglo stereotypes, political oppression, poverty, unequal opportunity, and spiritual doubt.[56]

Thus, Chicanos in their search for liberation anchored their struggle in preconquest ways of knowing. Therefore, regardless of the historical validity of the apparitions of Our Lady of Guadalupe to Juan Diego, for Chicanas/os she is a symbol that incarnates an identity, a cultural and political consciousness. How exactly then does this "incarnation" manifest itself in the lives of Chicanas?

Our Lady of Guadalupe in Chicana Feminist Consciousness

> The experience of Guadalupe is not necessarily a somber one, even if it is always transcendental. There are lighter, extremely personal accounts of Guadalupe's meaning, which may place a frown on the conservative Guadalupanos, but we make no claim to represent the Catholic Church here. —ANA CASTILLO, *Goddess of the Americas*, xxiii.

Chicana feminist consciousness is the sociopolitical affirmation some Latina women choose to make. While one does not necessarily need to be of Mexican descent to claim a Chicana feminist consciousness, this type of "agentic" awareness does have specific ethnic and historical underpinnings—it is rooted in the Chicano Movement of the 1960s. Alma García in her anthology *Chicana Feminist Thought: The Basic Historical Writings* (1997) contextualizes Chicana feminist consciousness in the following way:

> Chicana activists traced the emergence of their feminist "awakening" to the internal struggles within the cultural nationalist Chicano movement. In the course of their political activism, directed at reforming the structures of social inequality embedded in American society and of proposing alternative structuring, Chicana activists turned part of their attention inward, embarking on a feminist journey that would change dramatically the course of El Movimiento.[57]

The Chicano Movement, while advocating emancipation for all Chicanas and Chicanos, re-created the patriarchal Mexican household social system by often relegating women to secondary roles.[58] Despite many barriers Chicanas faced in the movement, they were able to turn this contested space into one for Chicana feminist political action.

With the growth of the Chicana/o Movement, Chicana feminist scholarship began to emerge. In their quest to unveil the oppressive situations of Chicanas, Chicana scholars took anthropological (Patricia Zavella), sociological (Denise Segura and Beatriz Pesquera), or historical (Vicki Ruiz) approaches; while others took literary (Maria Herrera-Sobek, Ana Castillo, and Gloria Anzaldúa) or visual-arts (Ester Hernández and Yolanda López) approaches, among others. Chicana feminist scholarship focused on the liberation and empowerment of all Chicanas. In the case of Guadalupe studies, Chicana interpretations of La Virgen both contested or selectively celebrated traditional female roles articulated through patriarchal Catholicism and family configurations. Through their writings, paintings, and theory they recaptured Nahuatl oral history and religious imagery such as Tonantzin.

As Ellen McCracken will also show later in this book (chapter 10), this is the context from which Chicana feminist writers such as Ana Castillo Sandra Cisneros reenvision Our Lady of Guadalupe. In Chicana feminist consciousness Guadalupe is not Mary of Nazareth; she is the Aztec goddess Tonantzin. These scholars bring forth Our Lady of Guadalupe's indigenismo by emphasizing her kinship with her "ancestral sisters" Coatlicue (serpent skirt) and Cihuacóatl (woman serpent). Davíd Carrasco and Roberto Lint Sagarena also note in chapter 9 of this book that Gloria

Anzaldúa takes a similar approach. In this manner, they either partially (Ana Castillo) or completely (Sandra Cisneros and Gloria Anzaldúa) disassociate Our Lady of Guadalupe from traditional Catholic thought.

Ana Castillo, in her essay "Extraordinarily Woman," experiences the love of Our Lady of Guadalupe through the relationship she has with her grandmother: "I don't remember homemade soups like the ones grandmothers are credited with prescribing during fevers and colds. I was never taken to a hospital. No doctor was called in. But with her magic and with Our Mother's assistance, Abuelita rescued me from María Guadaña."[59] Her grandmother was a *curandera* and a devotee of Our Lady of Guadalupe.[60] Castillo's account of her own initiation as a curandera resonates with the story of Guadalupe. Juan Diego, a powerless indigenous man—who had been stripped of his identity, religion, culture, and humanity—became the messenger of Our Lady of Guadalupe. Of anyone she could have chosen as intermediary, she chose Juan Diego. According to Elizondo, in one of the conversations between La Virgen and Juan Diego, she told him:

> Listen, my most abandoned son, know well in your heart that there are not a few of my servants and messengers to whom I could give the mandate of taking my thought and my word so that my will may be accomplished. But it is absolutely necessary that you personally go and speak about this, and that precisely through your mediation and help, my wish and my desire be realized.[61]

Similarly, Castillo relates, "Abuelita—ancient crone *curandera*, disciple of Our Mother, Mexican matriarch—took her smallest, frailest offspring into her apprenticeship and taught me what she could until she died when I was ten years old."[62] In the *Nican mopohua*, Our Lady of Guadalupe's relationship is directly with Juan Diego. In Castillo's story, the relationship is triangular: Our Lady of Guadalupe, the protagonist's grandmother, and the protagonist herself. The emphasis on the triangular matriarchal relationship (Our Lady of Guadalupe, grandmother, and the protagonist) in Castillo's account gives precedence to Chicana feminist emphasis on sisterhood and relationality.

The theme of sexuality as it relates to Our Lady of Guadalupe has been documented by many Chicana intellectuals. A common thread in Guadalupe discourse in Chicana feminist consciousness is the juxtaposition of Our Lady of Guadalupe's potential to empower or suppress their own sexuality. This aspect of the Chicana feminist reenvisioning creates the most contention because female sexuality has always been and continues be a taboo subject among Latinas/os. Sandra Cisneros argues in her essay "Guadalupe the Sex Goddess" (which later inspired Alma López to paint "Our Lady") that female sexuality is more often than not treated with great modesty. Latina sexuality is robbed of any agency, constraining women to a "double chastity belt of ignorance and *vergüenza*, shame."[63] How then can Chicanas liberate themselves from their sexual oppression? For Cisneros, it is in Our Lady of Guadalupe that she finds her liberation. Yet, her encounter with Our Lady of Guadalupe was not liberating at first. In her childhood and on through her adult life, Cisneros rejected Guadalupe: "I saw *la Virgen de Guadalupe*, my culture's role model for brown women like me. She was damn dangerous, an ideal so lofty and unrealistic it was laughable."[64] Cisneros saw in Our Lady of Guadalupe a constraining role model her culture expected her to emulate. For Cisneros, nothing good could come from "*la Lupe*"(as she refers to Our Lady of Guadalupe) except a guaranteed life of unhappiness.[65]

However, with the passage of years the Guadalupe of Cisneros's childhood transcended the Catholic female role model from which she had always found herself running away.

> When I look at *la Virgen de Guadalupe* now, she is not the Lupe of my childhood, no longer the one in my grandparents' house in Tepeyac, nor is she the one of the Roman Catholic Church, the one I bolted the door against in my teens and twenties. Like every woman who matters to me, I have had to search for her in the rubble of history. And I have found her. She is Guadalupe the sex goddess, a goddess who makes me feel good about my sexual power, my sexual energy, who reminds me I must, as Clarissa Pinkola Estés so aptly put it, "[speak] from the vulva . . . speak the most basic, honest truth," and write from my *panocha*.[66]

For many Chicana feminists the ultimate liberation for women comes when they can publicly affirm, celebrate, and speak freely about their sexuality. Cisneros expresses her own freedom by engaging in a relationship with Our Lady of Guadalupe in which she relates to her not only as an indigenous goddess but also as a female sexual being—a Guadalupe that it is not ashamed to express her sexuality. The outcome of this process is thus the affirmation of not only Our Lady of Guadalupe's sexuality, but also that of her "daughters" here on earth.

Likewise, Chicana feminist lesbian reconfigurations of Guadalupe have also challenged conventional social constructions of this symbol. In 1998, Carla Trujillo in her essay "La Virgen de Guadalupe and Her Reconstruction in Chicana Lesbian Desire," imagines what it would be like to have Our

Lady of Guadalupe as her life partner.[67] She says: "First, we'd have to have sex." However, Trujillo does not want Guadalupe to be passive in the act. She adds: "I really hate having to do all the work."[68] She continues with satire intertwined throughout the piece. "I would be very kind to her and provide for her well-being. Although I'm sure she would make a lot more money than I would (since she gets all those donations and offerings from people)."[69] According to Trujillo, "never before, has La Virgen de Guadalupe been reconstructed in sexualized terms as Chicana lesbianas have done/are doing."[70] Consequently, their interpretations appear as sacrilegious by most Guadalupe followers. However, a careful reading and analysis of their works in the context of their histories of marginalization materializes the reasons that drive these Chicanas to reconstruct Guadalupe's sexuality and ascribe her a sexual preference. Guadalupe in Chicana lesbian thought represents a powerful yet palpable female subjectivity—a familiar social agent that advocates and accepts Chicana lesbian ways of knowing, caring, and loving.

Laura Pérez argues that notions of the spirit and spirituality tend to take place and shape within "socially controlled spaces."[71] Therefore, Chicana lesbian processes of understanding the complexity of Guadalupe challenge the prevailing notion of "Guadalupe the all-accepting mother" by arguing that if indeed she is all-accepting, then lesbians should share an equal spiritual space with their heterosexual counterparts.

Similarly Lara Medina, in her essay "Los Espíritus Siguen Hablando: Chicana Spiritualities," challenges conventional understandings of the spiritual. The women in Medina's study engage in an indigenous spirituality, which aims at "healing the split between the spiritual and the physical," simultaneously challenging patriarchy's division of spirituality and sexuality.[72] Her findings resonate with the literary reconfigurations by the Chicana scholars discussed above: the erotic and the spiritual are one and thus cannot be separated, for their *mezcla* (mix) is what brings forth a woman's energy, power, and creativity.

Our Lady of Guadalupe in Chicana Feminist Art—Sacred or "Profane"?

The patriarchal system in which we live, paralleled to the oppressive ascriptions imposed on women, also move Chicana feminist artists to creatively reconstruct Guadalupe. Chicana artists celebrate and affirm Guadalupe's womanhood in their representations. They accomplish this by taking her inner strengths and making them visual palpable expressions.

2. Etching—Ester Hernández, *La Virgen de Guadalupe Defendiendo los Derechos de los Xicanos*, 1975. *The Virgen of Guadalupe Defending the Rights of the Xicanos*, 1975. Courtesy: Ester Hernández.

Artists Ester Hernández and Yolanda López are two of the first Chicana feminists artists to reenvision Our Lady of Guadalupe. Ester Hernández was the first Chicana feminist to reenvision Guadalupe in her 1975 *La Virgen de Guadalupe Defendiendo los Derechos de los Xicanos*, which was published on the front cover of KBBF FM 89 Santa Rosa's programming guide (see figure 2). Hernández portrays La Morenita in a karate suit and wearing what could be interpreted as a karate black belt or the original black maternity band. Hernández's Guadalupe is ready to fight. Her veil hangs from her hair in a capelike form, and the angel at her feet has an expression of anger.

In 1978, Yolanda López painted a series of a "three-generation portrayal" of Our Lady Guadalupe. One is Guadalupe as a grandmother wearing glasses and sitting on her veil; her hair is black with thick gray streaks. The original black maternity belt is at her waist, and she has a knife in one hand and a snake's skin in the other. The second is Guadalupe as a working mother (see figure 3). She is sitting at a sewing machine station. She wears glasses, is heavyset, has short hair, and appears sewing her veil; there is an angel at her feet. The third Guadalupe is a self-portrait. This Guadalupe appears to be the youngest of the three; she wears the maternity band and has short hair. She appears to be running while gripping

3. Oil pastel on paper—Yolanda M. López, Margaret F. Stewart: *Our Lady of Guadalupe*, 1978. Courtesy: Yolanda López.

her veil with both hands and holding a snake by the neck. She is stepping over one of the angel's wings and has a smile of triumph. These artists' interpretations came at a high price: both Hernández and López where accused of committing a sacrilege against a sacred image, and their lives were threatened.

Alma López's *Our Lady*, a 1999 visual reconstruction of Guadalupe, is one of the most recent representations to have encountered a great amount of contention (see figure 4). López's Guadalupe is a computerized photo collage. Here Our Lady of Guadalupe is wearing a two-piece outfit made out of bright colorful roses, like the miracle roses of the apparition account. Her eyes and posture have a challenging expression. Her veil is the dismembered Aztec Goddess Coyolxauhqui (a moon goddess); the backdrop appears to be the color and design of Guadalupe's original dress. The angel carrying her is a bare-breasted female angel with butterfly wings.

During Holy Week, a museum in Santa Fe, New Mexico, exhibited *Our Lady*, as part of a larger exhibit titled Cyber Arte. "Our Lady's" ex-

4. *Iris/giclée* on canvas—Alma López, *Our Lady* (Lupe and Sirena series),
1999. Courtesy: Alma López.

hibit caused heated debates; on one side were the local city government, the Catholic Church hierarchy, and local parishioners; on the other were the museum, the artist, and her supporters. A city was divided, the opposition to remove the exhibit filed an appeal, and the lives of the artist and models were threatened. What led López to "undress" La Virgen? At age eighteen, Salinas, the model posing as "Our Lady" had been raped. Like many women who have been victims of rape, she did not find support in those closest to her. Instead, they blamed her. Accusing her of "precipitating her own rape, they made her feel humiliated and told her it was God's punishment." The humiliation was such that she rejected her femininity by covering herself up, and became an alcoholic. After more than ten years of therapy she slowly began to accept herself again, and posing for López as "Our Lady" became the culmination of her healing process. Thus, what for many was sacrilegious and blasphemous, became for Salinas the opportunity she had been waiting for to rid herself of the "shame and guilt" she had carried for so many years, "I feel good about my body. I carry no shame anymore."[73]

Aída Hurtado asserts that "Chicana feminist writers and artists have been at the forefront of the appropriation of religious and cultural rituals for the restitution of self that leads to individual 'empowerment' as well as to political mobilization."[74] And, as Salinas's story shows, the full meaning of these types of representations can only be understood within the context of conquest, patriarchy, and structural violence experienced by individual Chicanas/os. These three artists offer examples of the affirmation and celebration of Our Lady of Guadalupe's womanhood, empowerment, and sexuality in Chicana feminist thought.

Reflections on Interpreting Guadalupe

Apparitionist theologians have been among the first to write about the Our Lady of Guadalupe event. But along with their interpretations there has always existed a counterstory, one that has either demonized this spiritual symbol or simply negated its historical underpinnings. As we have seen, to this day many historians, such as the ones discussed in this essay, debate over whether the Guadalupe narrative is a historical account. Some maintain that an indigenous artist painted the image; yet others affirm that there is something mysterious about the image. True or not, her defenders argue that this does not necessarily mean that she is not from God.[75]

Regardless of the historicity and politics that surround her purported miracle, Our Lady of Guadalupe continues to be a significant religious, cultural, and national symbol—a symbol whose combined characteristics reflect the mestizo reality of the very people who continue to find empowerment in her image.

To understand why feminists reconstruct and continue to make visible the inner characteristics of Our Lady of Guadalupe to represent what we visually characterize as empowering, we must first consider the ways in which patriarchy penetrates even the most sacred symbols of our times. It has taken Chicana feminists to reenvision Our Lady of Guadalupe not that Chicana feminists have made La Virgen what she is not, but rather that Chicanas have extracted her inner strengths and made them visible. Thus, they demonstrate that Our Lady of Guadalupe is a strong woman who fights for justice and mirrors the women who find liberation in her.

In like manner, as demonstrated by Rodriguez's study, Chicana feminist ways of visually or textually reimagining Our Lady of Guadalupe do not necessarily reflect how Mexican-origin women see Our Lady Guadalupe. In fact, oftentimes Chicana feminists in their liberating processes run the risk of silencing the lived spirituality of the larger Mexican-origin female population who continue to find liberation in the original image and tradition of Our Lady of Guadalupe. At the same time, this does not mean that there is a disjuncture between Chicana feminist Guadalupe thought, and the ways grassroots women of Mexican origin understand her in their daily lives. Rather, it identifies the need for social-science research on the impact Guadalupe has on the daily lives of women of Mexican origin.

The Guadalupe theology of Elizondo and Rodriguez stems from the canonized version of the *Nican mopohua* story. For Elizondo, Our Lady of Guadalupe's story is one of cultural affirmation; her own mestizaje is a celebration of indigenous Catholicism—the Catholicism of a conquered people. Building on the intellectual tradition of Elizondo, Rodriguez's particular interest in the meaning of Guadalupe in the lives of Mexican American women leads her to explore her significance in the lives of the very conquered people Elizondo argues Guadalupe came to affirm. Her findings demonstrate that for the women in her study, Our Lady of Guadalupe is a mestiza—azteca and española. Yet they do not see her as an Aztec goddess, like many Chicanas do. Instead they see her as the Mother of Jesus Christ. Rodriguez's study is significant because it is the only empirical study to date on the views held by women of U.S.-Mexican origin about Our Lady of Guadalupe. Her study brings forth the ordinary voices of everyday Mexican American women who have inherited a Catholic Guadalupe devotion and have chosen to live it. And similar to what we shall read about Los Pastores in Richard Flores's work in chapter 8, Guadalupe becomes a cultural vehicle through which Chicanas and Latinas can inscribe and find their own meaning, voice, and cultural agency.

Conclusion

As we have seen in the selected works above, to get at a more accurate understanding of Our Lady of Guadalupe means stepping away from traditional linear conceptualizations of knowledge making. While historians continue to challenge the historicity of Our Lady of Guadalupe and theologians focus on the development of a Guadalupe theology that captures the lived reality of people, Chicana intellectuals and grassroots Mexican-origin women continue to reconfigure Guadalupe in a way that speaks to their realities.

Although the interpretations of Our Lady of Guadalupe are manifold and complex, this chapter provides a brief analysis of some of the most prominent interpretations of Our Lady of Guadalupe. The politics of interpretation that emerge as people attempt to understand her mystery are yet to be fully analyzed. What do Latina/o Protestants, Evangelicals, Jews, and Muslims think of Our Lady of Guadalupe? How do non-Mexicans and non-Latinos perceive Our Lady Guadalupe? Do Latina/o gays and lesbians at the grassroots find empowerment in her? What does she mean for young Latinas and Latinos today? These questions remain for future research on Guadalupe.

Even though Our Lady of Guadalupe's image continues to be contested, her potential to empower and unite knows no borders. Despite the counternarratives that have always accompanied her story, to this day she continues to be an important cultural, religious, and political symbol for millions of followers throughout the Americas.

Notes

1. Campesinos are farmworkers.

2. An estampita is a small religious card with the image of a saint on one side and a prayer on the other.

3. I use the terms Our Lady of Guadalupe, Guadalupe, La Virgen, and La Morenita interchangeably throughout the essay — these are the different ways in which people refer to this symbol.

4. Guadalupanas/os are people who are devotees of Our Lady of Guadalupe.

5. Interethnic identity politics is complex. I use the terms the scholars use in their works. Latina/o refers to all U.S.-born individuals whose origin can be traced to Latin America, regardless of their political ideology. Chicana/o refers

to U.S.-born Mexican origin individuals who for political reasons identify as such. The term Mexican American refers to Mexican-origin people born in the United States.

6. Virgilio Elizondo, *La Morenita: Evangelizer of the Americas* (San Antonio, Tex.: Mexican American Cultural Center, 1980), 1; Jeanette Rodriguez, *Our Lady of Guadalupe: Faith and Empowerment among Mexican-American Women* (Austin: University of Texas Press, 1994), 27.

7. The Spanish conquistadores named the conquered lands of the Aztecs New Spain.

8. *Tilma* was a cloak that indigenous people of that time used as part of their dress.

9. Virgilio Elizondo, *Guadalupe: Mother of the New Creation* (New York: Orbis Books, 1998), 17.

10. Elizondo, *Guadalupe*. According to Elizondo, mestizaje is "the process through which two totally different peoples mix biologically and culturally so that a new people begins to emerge."

11. Elizondo, *Guadalupe*, 134.

12. Rodriguez, *Our Lady of Guadalupe*. Rodriguez's model of acculturation has been criticized by a number of Chicana scholars.

13. Rodriguez, *Our Lady of Guadalupe*, 14.

14. Ibid., xix.

15. Rodriguez works from a psychosocial religious perspective. The sample consisted of the following characteristics: The women had to be (1) Mexican American; (2) Roman Catholic, with Our Lady Guadalupe as part of their religious experience; (3) English-speaking and acculturated into North American society; and (4) young married mothers. Rodriguez's sample consisted of 20 women between the ages of twenty-two and thirty with a median age of 23.5. The measuring scale of acculturation used by Rodriguez was that they must (1) be Mexican American, (2) be second-generation Mexican Americans, (3) be English speaking, (4) have a high school diploma, and (5) have been exposed to the image of Our Lady of Guadalupe. Rodriguez chose mothers because of their particular responsibility for the transmission of cultural and religious values in the family.

16. Rodriguez, *Our Lady of Guadalupe*, xxvi–xxvii.

17. Ibid., xxi.

18. Ibid., 107.

19. Ibid., 107.

20. Ibid., 137.

21. Ibid., 137.

22. Ibid., 124.

23. Ibid., 124–25.

24. Louis Burkhart, "The Cult of the Virgin of Guadalupe in Mexico," appears in Gary Gossen H., with Miguel León-Portilla, eds., *South and Meso-American Native Spirituality: From the Cult of the Feathered Serpent to the Theology of Liberation* (New York: Crossroad Publishing Company, 1993).

25. Burkhart, "The Cult of the Virgin of Guadalupe in Mexico," 205.

26. *Anales de Juan Bautista*, n.d., 16, cited in ibid., 205–6.

27. Burkhart, "The Cult of the Virgin of Guadalupe in Mexico," 207; Stafford Poole, *Our Lady of Guadalupe: The Origins and Sources of a Mexican National Symbol, 1531–1797* (Tucson: University of Arizona Press, 1995), 78.

28. Poole, *Our Lady of Guadalupe*, 78; Sahagún (*Historia general de las cosas de la Nueva España*, 1981), 3:352–54, cited in Burkhart, "The Cult of the Virgin of Guadalupe in Mexico," 207.

29. Poole, *Our Lady of Guadalupe*, 79; Burkhart, "The Cult of the Virgin of Guadalupe in Mexico," 208.

30. Burkhart, "The Cult of the Virgin of Guadalupe in Mexico," 198.

31. Poole, *Our Lady of Guadalupe*, 79.

32. Ibid., n. 12.

33. Ibid., 208.

34. Poole, *Our Lady of Guadalupe*.

35. Antonio de Ciudad Real (1976), 1:68, cited in Burkhart, *Our Lady of Guadalupe*, 208.

36. Burkhart, "The Cult of the Virgin of Guadalupe in Mexico," 200; Poole, *Our Lady of Guadalupe*, 33.

37. Burkhart, "The Cult of the Virgin of Guadalupe in Mexico," 200.

38. Lockhart (1992), cited in Burkhart, "The Cult of the Virgin of Guadalupe in Mexico," 200.

39. Burkhart, "The Cult of the Virgin of Guadalupe in Mexico," 198; Poole, *Our Lady of Guadalupe*.

40. Poole, *Our Lady of Guadalupe*, 1. See Rodriguez, *Our Lady of Guadalupe*; Elizondo, *Guadalupe*; León-Portilla, *Tonantzin Guadalupe*; Fidel González Fernández, Eduardo Chávez Sánchez, and José Luis Guerrero Rosado, *El encuentro de la Virgen de Guadalupe y Juan Diego* (Mexico City: Editorial Porrúa, 2001).

41. Criollos are Spaniards born in Mexico. Poole, *Our Lady of Guadalupe*, 1–2.

42. Ibid., 1–2.

43. Ibid., 1–2.

44. Ibid., 2.

45. Ibid., 1–3.

46. Burkhart, "The Cult of the Virgin of Guadalupe in Mexico," 206.

47. González Fernández, Chávez Sánchez, and Guerrero Rosado, *El encuentro de la Virgen de Guadalupe y Juan Diego*, 7.

48. Ibid., 10, 173.

49. Miguel León-Portilla, *Tonantzin Guadalupe: Pensamiento náhuatl y mensaje cristiano en el "Nican mopohua"* (Mexico City: El Colegio Nacional, 2000), 89.

50. Fernández, Sánchez, and Rosado, *El encuentro de la Virgen de Guadalupe y Juan Diego*, 18.

51. Ibid., 19.

52. Ibid., 13.

53. Ibid., 13.

54. Ibid., 51.

55. Ibid., 51.

56. Davíd Carrasco, *Religions of Mesoamerica: Cosmovision and Ceremonial Centers* (San Francisco: HarperSanFrancisco, 1990), 155–56.

57. Alma M. García, ed., *Chicana Feminist Thought: The Basic Historical Writings* (New York: Routledge, 1997), 4–5.

58. Elena Hernández, "La Chicana y 'El Movimiento,'" *Chicanismo* 3, no. 3 (29 April 1972): 6–8.

59. Ana Castillo, "Extraordinarily Woman," in *Goddess of the Americas: Writings on the Virgin of Guadalupe*, ed. Ana Castillo (New York: Riverhead Books, 1996), 75. Death in Mexican thought has a feminine entity and is oftentimes referred to as María Guadaña.

60. The term *curandera* loosely translated into English means "healer."

61. Elizondo, *Guadalupe*, 10.

62. Castillo, "Extraordinarily Woman," 75.

63. Sandra Cisneros, "Guadalupe the Sex Goddess," in Castillo, *Goddess of the Americas*, 46.

64. Ibid., 48.

65. Ibid., 48.

66. Ibid., 49.

67. This essay appears in her anthology entitled *Living Chicana Theory*.

68. Cited in Castillo, "Extraordinarily Woman," 228.

69. Ibid., 227.

70. Ibid., 227.

71. Laura E. Pérez, "Spirit Glyphs: Reimagining Art and Artist in the Work of Chicana *Tlamatinime*," *Modern Fiction Studies* 44, no. 1 (spring 1998): 37.

72. Lara Medina, "Los Espíritus Siguen Hablando: Chicana Spiritualities," in *Living Chicana Theory*, ed. Carla Trujillo (Berkeley: Third Woman Press, 1998), 189–213. Her findings are based on a sample of twenty-two academic and non-academic Chicanas in the San Francisco area.

73. Patrisia Gonzales and Roberto Rodriguez, *Gonzales/Rodriguez Uncut and Uncensored* (Berkeley, Calif.: Ethnic Studies Library Publications, 1997). See also Aída Hurtado, *Voicing Chicana Feminisms: Young Women Speak out on Sexuality and Identity* (New York: New York University Press, 2003), 287–90.

74. Hurtado, *Voicing Chicana Feminisms*, 284. See also Sarah Ramírez, "Borders, Feminism, and Spirituality: Movements in Chicana Aesthetic Revisioning," in *Decolonial Voices: Chicana and Chicano Cultural Studies in the 21st Century*, ed. Arturo J. Aldama and Naomi H. Quiñonez (Indianapolis: Indiana University Press: Bloomington, 2002), 223–42.

75. For further reading on the scientific study of the *tilma*, I recommend José Aste Tönsmann, *El secreto de sus ojos* (Lima: Tercer Milenio, 1998).

7

Voces de Fe

Mexican American *Altaristas* in Texas

Over the past twenty-five years, I have studied the informal and widespread creation and use of domestic altars by Mexican American Catholic women. By definition, an altar marks a sacred site set apart for communication between deities and humans. Another sense of the term suggests that an altar is a threshold or gateway, the meeting place of the sacred and the mundane. In contrast to the formal altars found in churches and temples, a woman's domestic altar is an informal expression of faith and devotion. Consisting of a special grouping of religious and other symbols selected by her, the altar visually represents its maker's personal relationship with the deities, saints, or ancestors she depends upon for help and comfort in her daily life.

Women keep domestic altars in many folk Catholic traditions (including Irish, Italian, Polish, French, Guatemalan, Haitian, and numerous others), but most of what I learned was taught to me by Mexican American *altaristas* (altar makers). The knowledge they imparted served as the basis for my dissertation in folklore, "Mexican American Women's Home Altars: The Art of Relationship" (1990).[1] My study was based on interviews with working-class women who lived in Austin, San Antonio, Laredo, and other places in Texas. The altar tradition was widely practiced; many women thought of it as a necessity. Pointing to her bedroom dresser top altar, one of my consultants, Gloria Rocha, explained: "Everything here. I put it here. All these things are mine. For me and for Her. . . . You don't feel good when you don't have all this. Is like *you* need to eat. *I* need to have that . . . my altar" (emphasis added).

I visited and interviewed numerous altaristas, finally settling on a core group of about twenty. A majority of these women were between sixty and ninety years. Many of them—including Soledad "Chole" Pescina, Micaela Zapata, and Margarita "Maggie" Guerrero—had fled to Texas during the era of the Mexican Revolution of 1910. After crossing the border, these women lived through very difficult times in Texas: Anglo prejudice against Mexicans was virulent; male dominance prevailed; parish churches were segregated; priestly authority was absolute; and folk religious practices, especially women's practices, were discouraged or prohibited by the church.[2] Fiercely to the contrary, women such as Chole Pescina were ardent in their claims for the particularity of women's religious power. They derived this power from their critical role as mothers. For these women, being a mother did not simply constitute a biological fact or a social role. For them, mothering is a kind of sacred relationship that constitutes the ground of all other relationships. One day Chole Pescina told me her view of motherhood: "The woman is valuable. Very valuable. That's why Jesus cried *Dios Madre* [God, My Mother]. It's [mother] a very sublime word. He [Jesus] didn't say *Dios Padre* [God, My Father]. *La mujer vale cosas diferentes que el hombre* [The woman values different things than the man does] (emphasis added)." Restating the biblical story from her point of view, Chole asserted that Christ's cry from the cross affirmed woman's sacred maternal legacy.

At the time I was conducting interviews, relatively little empirical research had been done to reveal the meaning of devotional practices from individual Mexican American women's own point of view. To a certain extent that gap has been filled in recent years, but the voices of those women had rarely been heard by interested outsiders.[3] Perhaps this is why I was never refused an interview by any woman at any time. Women whom I barely knew were immediately open to discussing their *altarcitos* (home altars) with me. I remember coming to the door of the eighty-three-year-old Margarita "Maggie" Guerrero for the first time. Answering my knock, she briefly scrutinized me. I had barely expressed my purpose when she grabbed my arm and drew me into her home laughing and saying "I knew God would send someone, eventually."

Yes, I was drawn in, and it was my ensuing long-term relationships with a number of altaristas that afforded me a rich and complex understanding of the tradition. Over nearly a decade, I returned again and again to visit Chole Pescina, Maggie Guerrero, Petra Castorena, Chelo González, Lala Treviño, Gloria Rocha, and Micaela Zapata; others—such as Bereniece

Alvarado, Guadalupe Salazar, and María Pérez—I saw less often. These women became much more to me than consultants or informants; they became my esteemed teachers.

This chapter dips back into a bygone era of Texan Mexican women's folk religious practices to reembrace the altar tradition through the voices of some of its keepers. These altaristas still have much to say about the relevance of personal devotion for Mexican American women, then and now. Home altars are still kept throughout the United States. New studies of altar makers will reveal new meanings, and this presentation is in part an invitation to young scholars to add further to what is known about a tradition that simply goes on, as it has for generations.

Over the course of my study with these remarkable, generous, and wise altaristas, I developed a feminist interpretation of the altar tradition based upon what they revealed about it. Most significant, I learned that the home altar practice is considered by altaristas to be a women's tradition, passed down by mothers to their daughters, that marks and instrumentalizes maternal and relational values. My work was synchronous with the work of other feminist scholars of that period, writing from various disciplines, who suggested that maternal discourse centers around attachment, affiliation, and relationship.[4] I came to view the home altar as an instrument for engaging the critical importance of this discourse. At the most primary level, keeping an altar serves the integration of religious practice and maternal practice. I argue that through the creation and manipulation of this symbolic system, women engage in an important aspect of subject formation by accruing the benefits of a sacred validation of mothering.

My historical research demonstrates that domestic altar making by women is culturally widespread and continuous over a long period of time—in the West extending back to pre-Christian times. The most ancient domestic altars dedicated by women in old Europe were conceived of as places for receiving and appealing to the maternal act of creation, the distinctive powers of fertility and giving birth. Archaeological evidence from Mexico suggests similar intentions for domestic shrines discovered at sites in Oaxaca and outside Mexico City at Teotihuacán, among others.[5] Even millennia later, Texan Mexican home altars are in a conceptual sense still used to perpetuate the creative power of women's fertility, only that power is reconceived—more abstractly, perhaps—as the power of achieving relationship.

The idea of relationship implicates a set of beliefs and practices (both religious and social) aimed at asserting the primacy of affiliation and connection. Relationship also denotes a concern for legacy and allegiance; the maintenance of relationship affirms ties between the past and the present and projects them into the future. As we shall see, altarcitos are richly significant in the way they visually and artistically model an ideal of good, productive relationships between various distinct domains (secular/sacred; material/spiritual; earth/heaven). In fact, the home altar may be most inclusively defined as a personal, iconic representation of the power of relationship. Additionally, the home altar is an instrument for the perpetuation of productive relationships because it marks the site where communication (the active means of establishing and maintaining relationships) between deities and humans takes place.

The Home Altar and Its Modes of Relationship

Texan Mexican altars are each composed *bricoleur* style (in the style of bricolage) by the matriarch of the family. Critically, the home altar indexes a folk-religion ideal of relationship in its aesthetic of accumulation, layering, condensation, and integration. Items of both a sacred and secular nature are accumulated. On the altar they stand in relation to each other, and in the overall composition each item resonates with all the others; the combination and association of items tend to increase the potency of any individual piece.

Home altars are distinctively populated with sacred and secular body images—statues and pictures depicting the Virgin Mary and saints, holy cards, family photos, and figurines. These are the altar's most important indicators of its relational modus operandi: a reliance on the embodied person as the chief source of knowing and being known. Central to this modus, and centrally placed on the altar, are statues and pictures of the Virgin, Christ, and saints that comprise, in effect, a holy family of images. The altar literally becomes a home on earth for this sacred family. As Petra Castorena explained to me, "I didn't want my saints roaming about all over the place, so I made a home for them here [at the altar]." Or as Micaela Zapata confirmed, "Everyone needs a home. The saints, the Virgin—I have them here. They have a place with me" (figure 1).

These sacred representations are more than masks for religious ideas or beliefs; they have a visible, bodily reality and by being so considered by the altarista, they not only *stand for*, they *act as*. Altar images are imbued with a quality of intervention in the lives of those who venerate them. They intervene by providing a corporeal scheme of orientations and

1. Doña Micaela
Zapata's home
altar to Niño Jesus,
Austin, Texas, 1979.
Photo: Kay Turner.

values that becomes a basis for people to relate to each other over time
and space. Religious images not only reflect but enhance and shape a
woman's own experience and interpretation of social life.[6]

The doctrine of the Incarnation provides an ecclesiastical basis for allowing bodily images of Christ, the Virgin, and the saints to serve as
fitting prototypes for figuring the intervention of embodied godliness in
the life of the believer. Christianity is not only the revelation of the Word
of God, but also of the Image of God disclosed in the God-Man, Jesus.
But the importance of the sacred body image for my consultants was
more than an acceptance of dogma. In the case of home altar use, images
are deinstitutionalized from their representational and doctrinal status
and made more explicitly the relaters or channelers of power in women's
individual, personal lives. Altar makers blur the distinction between the
sacred and the mundane. Women draw sacred images into the realm of
the social and cultural, making them copartners in a process of nurtur-

ing the individual, the family, and the world. Not surprisingly, the most popular images found on Texan Mexican home altars are those of the Blessed Mother in Her Mexican manifestations such as Nuestra Señora de Guadalupe (Our Lady of Guadalupe) and La Virgen de San Juan (the Virgin of San Juan). These heavenly Mother(s) were made the primary allies of earthly mothers. Concerning the importance of Our Lady of Guadalupe, Chole Pescina declared,

> I have my Virgin of Guadalupe [on my altar] because She is the protectoress of all us Mexicans. . . . She is a mother of the best kind for us. . . . [but] the Virgin of Guadalupe doesn't need an altar. The best altar for her is the heart of the Mexican . . . because for the Mexican, She is our Mother.

The kind of intimacy that defines a woman's relationship with an image and who it signifies is cultivated, deepened, and in many ways determined by the image's legacy within her family. In the majority of cases the altar tradition is taught by mothers to daughters, and this teaching is centered on receipt of images down the female line. This teaching often occurs as part of the rite of passage into marriage. As was the case for Casey Covarrúbias, Viola Short, and Lala Treviño, at the time of their weddings each of their mothers gave them a statue of the Virgin and enjoined them to set up an altar for Her in their new homes. Upon marrying, Micaela Zapata received her image of the Niño Jesús from her great-aunt. Gloria Rocha has given her daughter and her Anglo daughter-in-laws images of the Virgin of San Juan so that "she will be a mother for them and helps them be good mothers for their kids" (figure 2).

Heirloom statues or images of the saints distributed from mother to daughter, grandmother to granddaughter, or from aunt to niece constitute a typical pattern of descent for insuring the continuity of the saint's patronage of, and membership in, the family. In my sample, the legacy of relationship thus established was found in the majority of case histories; when multigenerational the legacy extended back in time to the mid-nineteenth century or earlier. Gloria Rocha, for example, has possession of and responsibility for hand-carved and painted *bultos* (statues) of the Holy Family, which belonged originally to her great-great grandmother and were then passed on to her grandmother. The statues then were given to Sra. Rocha's mother, Francisca Rangel (b. 1892), who gave them to Rocha: "She give me the care of these statues. I'm planning to pass it to my daughter." Chole Pescina's statue of Saint Anthony belonged to her great-grandmother, was subsequently brought across the Rio Grande by

2. Doña Rocha's
Virgin of San Juan,
Laredo, Texas, 1986.
Photo: Kay Turner.

her grandmother when she and Chole crossed in 1912, and eventually
passed down the line to her.

Chelo González's image of our Lady of Guadalupe was given as a gift
by her father to her mother. Because she was the eldest daughter, she explained, "My mother told me She was mine." Chelo received her image of
Our Lady of Guadalupe right before her mother died. This act assured a
continuing legacy of relationship between them. Chelo spoke of receiving
the Virgin's image from her mother as *una herencia* (an inheritance): "It's
an inheritance that my mother has left me—also a faith in the Virgin of
Guadalupe that is very great. And I think the day I go, the day I die, I will
give Her to my daughter."

The altar and the images that distinguish it become symbolic of the
intimate bond of affection and trust between mother and daughter. A
charge from the mother to establish an altar or to care for a family saint is
viewed by some as a sacred duty, a way of simultaneously paying homage

to the natal mother and the Holy Mother, as in the example of Vencesuela "Lala" Treviño of San Antonio. At the time I met her in 1985, Sra. Treviño's mother had been dead for over twenty-five years, but in fulfilling *la carga* (the charge) given by her mother to keep candles burning on her altar dedicated to Our Lady of Guadalupe, Lala never failed:

> The thing she dreaded more than anything was that when she died, she was afraid her saints would not have candles. . . . Sometimes for two or three days they aren't lit, but today I bought a new box [of candles]. . . . She left me that charge and I will take it on until I die. . . .

Even though I was always told that the varied images of the Virgin are in fact all the same Mother of God, women expressed particular preferences for one representation over another, usually based on their mother's or grandmother's preference. Bereniece Alvarado of San Antonio received no heirloom images of Guadalupe from her mother, who died when Sra. Alvarado was only eight years old. But Sra. Alvarado did receive a legacy of preference for Our Lady of Guadalupe from her mother: "Like there's only one Virgin. . . . They're all one Virgin, but I have more devotion to Our Lady of Guadalupe. . . . My mother had a lot of devotion to Our Lady of Guadalupe. She had a lot." Bereniece filled her home with images of Guadalupe because this manifestation of the Blessed Mother recalled her own mother. Sra. Alvarado expressed a sense of its personal attraction for her; she said Our Lady of Guadalupe is "more beautiful, more familiar to me."

Ancestral and present-day family photographs are also found on or near the altar. Often propped against a statue, sometimes tucked inside the framed *retrato* (portrait) of a saint or Virgin, or positioned on the wall near the altar, these pictures are an obvious demonstration of the relation the altar maker assigns between her family and the heavenly family. In some instances an altar's sacred images and its heirloom photographic images combine to represent extended familial relationships derived through marriage. Romualda Perez was given her mother-in-law's altar statues and photos as well as her mother's. Sra. Perez was proud of their intermingling on her altar.

Earthly kin are sacralized by their presence on the altar, and heavenly kin are brought into intimate association with the human family that shares this sacred site. Bereniece Alvarado created an altar on her living room mantle that makes this relationship between the two families most explicit. The mantle itself is filled end-to-end with formal portraits of her seven children. Centered above them is a large picture of Our Lady of

Guadalupe illuminated with encircling Christmas tree lights. Parallel to but slightly below Her on the left is a head of Christ, and similarly spaced to the Virgin's right is a crucifix. Pointing to the Virgin, who was positioned to gaze down directly at the children's portraits, Sra. Alvarado told me, "She is as much a mother to them as I am."

Romualda Perez also kept pictures of her children on the altar as a way of inviting heavenly protection for them. Pictures of Gloria Rocha's children have changed from time to time as she petitions the Virgin of San Juan for the various needs of individual members of the family: "I have all my kids' pictures there on my altar and my grandchildren. In other words, I told Her, I leave the picture of my child—that way you can take care, I leave it in your hands. You're the Mother." At different times, Chole Pescina's altar held photos of her godchildren, her godchildren's children, or the children of friends for whom she had prayed.

While it is more often the case that children's pictures are found on the altar surface, ancestral photos of the altar maker's mother and father, in-laws, and grandparents are usually placed above the altar. Without exception, these heirloom photos—ornately framed ovals of glass containing hand-tinted, sepia-toned formal portraits—are positioned at a height that reflects the high status of the elders they portray. As María Pérez explained in pointing to an heirloom portrait of her parents positioned high on the wall above her altar, "I have them there with the Virgin. To show respect and because they are with Her now." Family photos are passed down within the family much like the saints' images, and in many cases the family members portrayed in these photos have made the gift of the saints' images to the current altar maker. That these heirloom photos are raised up reflects the sense of honor given to forbearers; they are remembered with the reverence that makes their place near the altar appropriate. Family history and sacred history are conjoined at the altar site, bearing witness to a lasting heritage of relationships that binds the family together through time, and in spite of it.

Viola Short kept two altars at home, a traditional one dedicated to the Virgin, Christ, and the saints and one dedicated to her daughter Yvette, who died in 1979. Mrs. Short established the second altar—filled with the child's toys, dolls, and photos of her—in remembrance of Yvette, but more than memory was served there. The altar became a place where Mrs. Short kept in communication with Yvette, a place where she spoke to her and received the consolation that Yvette was still with her: "I feel peaceful when I'm near these things. Yes, yes I do. I come over here and I say, 'Baby, here's mommy. I'm just wondering what you went through.' Thinking she's been through this and that. I just want to know like any mother would." At this altar the potency of death's sting, the force of its potential to separate this mother from her daughter, is diminished. The special case of Yvette's altar reflects the general tendency in home altars to provide a place for uniting the living with the dead.

Altars often include anomalous or what might appear to be "inappropriate" objects—stuffed animals, souvenirs, containers filled with shells, newspaper clippings, and so on. But all of these are signs of relationships; each item captures a story connecting it to someone, sometime, or someplace. The altar maker clearly maintains a formal degree of creative independence in assigning highly personal and idiosyncratic symbols to the altar. In so doing, the microcosmic view of the world at her altar becomes even more dramatically *her* view, her idea of both the sacred and secular worlds and their relation. One of my consultants, Aurora Treviño, kept a jar of buttons on her altar. Each one had been removed from items of clothing her children had outgrown; each one metonymically represented a particular child at a particular time. Mrs. Treviño created her altar in a small nook off the kitchen. She said her husband was always after her to "clean it up," but she refused him. She told me emphatically, "This is my place."

The altar practice nourishes and sustains a woman's desire for good and productive relationships both with other humans and with deities. It also symbolically references relationships between what otherwise might be characterized as distinct domains of social, cultural, religious, and personal life. A snapshot of President John F. Kennedy might be tucked inside the framed image of Our Lady of Guadalupe; a statue of San Antonio might be draped with a scapular *and* encircled with a godchild's necklace. On the altar, symbols of distinct domains are not so much juxtaposed as they are integrated into a coherent visual field that marks their interdependence and connection with each other.

At the home altar women remake and reinvent the usefulness of cultural symbols, both sacred and secular, according to their own histories, purposes, needs, desires, and beliefs. Domestic altar making is very much an act of intention invested with individual consciousness and creativity. Among the altaristas I knew, no altar looked the same; nor was it used exactly the same way. The received aspects of the tradition, learned from their mothers and grandmothers, were in each new generation wedded to an *imaginative* impulse.

Faith and the Value of Relationship

Material representations and communicative acts at the home altar are all ultimately "affiliative" in nature. From a purely religious perspective this insistence on affiliation is grounded in a deeply held conception of fe (faith), which is a developed capacity for knowing and being known by the divine, for sharing one's life with the divine, and ultimately for accepting the reality of the divine presence in one's human experience. As Guadalupe Salazar succinctly declared, "If you don't have faith, you're not worth anything." Petra Castorena explained faith in terms of fiercely defending her relationship with the Virgin:

> I say for my part, for everything that happens to me, "*Oh, Virgencita de Guadalupe! Oh, Virgencita de San Juan! Madre Santísima!*" It's only Her I talk to, no one else. My daughter says I'm crazy. Ha! But I say, "No, She's got to listen to me." She does. It's the faith.

The altar tradition promotes particularity of relationship with divine resources; faith is in *someone*—Guadalupe or San Antonio—not in an abstraction. For these women, fe was an affirmation of connection to, and relationship with, divine persons that was predicated upon intimacy and trust, feelings that in turn constituted a kind of knowledge embedded in their intersubjective experience. Repeatedly, faith was viewed by my consultants as an inheritance from their mothers or grandmothers, not only as a tenet from association with the church. Chelo González exemplifies the claim of this inheritance: "My mother had a lot of faith in the Virgin. She left me a faith in the Virgin of Guadalupe that is very big, very big." And Chelo González maintained that the religious faith that inspires good mothering is taught by the mother to her daughter:

> From the time you are a little girl in the house, you are taught these things. . . . The mother is the one who shapes the values of her children. . . . Just as my mother did, I bring my children here to pray with me. . . . If you instill in the children all the good and teach them to feel good about the world, not to feel badly toward anybody . . . if you speak well about the world. . . . They will grow up with that thought. True? All the good. All the best. In order for them to live well.

As Chelo suggested at a different time, the mother is the one who gives physical form to her child, and just as much she "forms the heart" or shapes the values of the child.

Fe is the inheritance given by mother to daughter, just as the altar tradition itself. This sense of the gift of faith was sometimes expressed in elaborate, extended metaphors or parable-like narrations that remarked the union of mothers and daughters with the Blessed Mother. In telling me why Mexican American women keep the altar tradition Maggie Guerrero eloquently expressed its articulation with the relational construct of motherhood:

> *No hay amor tan grande como el de la mamá* [There is no love greater than a mother's love]. From the moment she conceives in the womb, from the moment that thing falls in the womb of that mother, she feels that weight. Even though it be such a little thing—life begins—it begins to grow, it begins to form. When it's in the mother's womb, the woman-to-be is a ball of blood—nothing more. She's not a baby. She's just a ball of blood that trembles with life. For four months she forms, and then she starts to become a little woman. Then the mother begins to know that she is a woman, and time proves it to her. That's why the mother pays no attention to what it costs her to keep us, to have us, and to give us her life, completely. That's why the mother is very valuable, very influential. Oh, the mother. . . . That's why the Most Holy Mother hears her when she wants to ask for a miracle or something. She asks the Holy Virgin saying, "Most Holy Virgin, you who are the Mother of Christ, grant me this with your Son." She prays for us with Him. She asks Him. And there isn't a thing the Mother asks of Him that He won't grant to Her. Because He loves his Mother who gave Him life. (emphasis added)

In Sra. Guerrero's opinion, Christ responds to His Mother's wishes because She gave Him life.[7] The altar tradition acts as a nexus for the intersection of religious practice with maternal practice; the two are in many ways inseparable, but as we note in Maggie's soliloquy, it is largely maternity that impels the necessity of religious practice. For altaristas personal religion and maternity conflate in the purpose of sustaining relationship, of "giving life." The altar tradition specifies a context of personal faith wherein women implement a care perspective. Women use this site as a place to appeal for divine care in initiating, repairing, restoring, and protecting the vitality of human relationships. Chelo González explained the way in which the altar tradition lends itself to her overarching belief in the goodness of life. At the altar, "We gather the strength and the faith to continue living. It's marvelous to continue living, isn't it? It's a marvel. And here we gather faith to continue going on, fighting."

The Language of Giving and Receiving

But how, we might ask, is "faith gathered" at the altar, as Chelo suggested. The final portion of this chapter addresses this question with reference to language and speech use—prayer—at the altar site. Prayer at the altar activates its potential to serve its maker not only as a representation but as an instrument of her desire to achieve relationship. An altar has communication as its raison d'être, and it fully serves its intended purpose only when this visual performance of powerful things is integrated with a powerful display of actions and words. The accumulation of objects is matched by the cumulative effect of spoken words. The image field of the altar posits an ideal of relationship; speech acts performed there bring that idealization into lived reality.[8] The altar possesses both an object-centered aesthetic quality and a subject-centered performance quality, the two of which when integrated together underscore the importance of viewing the altar tradition as a religio-aesthetic *practice*. Speaking at the altar is substantive; it cannot be separated from the other substances (for example, the heat and light of votive candles, the color and beauty of flowers, the beckoning gesture of a saint's image) that together sustain the relationship between a woman and the divine.

The home altar, by definition, marks a site of personal and intimate communication between humans and deities. Communicative exchange at the altar is located in an altarista's desire to fortify her personal allegiance with God and His saints and to enjoy the benefits of such allegiance in the achievement of blessed (i.e., viable and productive) relationships on earth. Here communication is defined as purposive interaction, aimed at perpetuating a necessary cycle of giving and receiving. Language use at the altar is meant to reference not only symbolic giving and receiving but actual giving and receiving. While the altar and its images visually pose the possibility of the interpenetration of human experience and divine presence, language is the means by which the reciprocal relationship between heaven and earth is daily renewed and regenerated. The power of visual images ultimately resides in their representational capacity, but language excites a *carrying* capacity—a way of literally crossing the threshold between heaven and earth. Speech acts carry the complex particulars of a believer's emotions, needs, circumstances, and experiences as these unfold and change in day-to-day life. Communication through verbal expression keeps affiliation active; it carries the relationship along.

The altar is a model of shared power between the human and divine, but it is also an instrument for achieving the actual distribution and exchange of power between the human and the divine. Personified sacred images of the Virgin and saints lend themselves to speech. Images are the visible subjects to whom speech is addressed. Their familiar presence on the altar stimulates the desire to speak; images act as receivers for the transmission of messages sent by the altar maker.

Communication involves the sharing of codes, codes which when learned and transmitted become the basis for shared meanings.[9] Folk religious belief entails the learning of traditional sacred codes, such as formal prayers. Faith asserts the trustworthiness of communication via such codes, which thereby bring invisible deities into dialogue with sentient human beings. Formal prayers—learned orations, novenas, the Rosary, the Our Father, the Hail Mary—remark the deference to divine allies that signals the altarista's openness to God's love and His will. Formal prayers are the speech acts of *giving*, giving *respeto* (respect), acknowledgment of the ultimate superiority of the divine. Informal prayer—petitions, spontaneous outcries, and conversational speech—emphasizes intimacy and need, the language of *receiving*.

Language fuels the visual engine of the altar, making it a kind of "equipment for living" in Kenneth Burke's sense. Burke viewed verbal arts as "strategies for dealing with situations."[10] In creating and using her altar, the altarista compounds both visual and verbal strategies in her attempt to deal with the particular situations of living she encounters. In combination, these two distinct strategies forge an interactive dynamic which is both compelling in affect and potent in effect.

The work of achieving relationship with the divine is accomplished in large part by laboring through language. Such labor is a daily requirement—a source of livelihood in the "economics" of social reproduction. As Petra Castorena insisted,

> Everyday I'm out there praying for this one and that one. It used to be for my kids. I always needed something. And for me, too. I needed the strength to go on living, especially when I was alone [after her marriage ended]. Now I just talk and talk to Her [the Virgin]. . . . Sometimes, I'm out there at five in the morning praying, giving blessings to everyone.

Language work at the altar directs its energies toward the creation and maintenance of beneficial social relationships, and this is accomplished by a regular expenditure of the self in devotion that ensures continuing relationship with those holy figures who make viable social life possible. In fact, *devotion*—from the Latin *voto*, to make an individual vow—distinguishes the purpose of the altar and the activities surrounding it, especially prayer. An altarista's day-to-day life is, for her, most significantly framed by devotional acts. Margarita Guerrero said, "This is what I do everyday. I'm awake and then I feed the puppies. Then I sit here [at the altar in her living room] and say my prayers. That's the way to begin. And at night the way to finish."

Likewise, Chole Pescina arose in the morning and went to her altar to "expose myself to God and give thanks to Him" through prayer. At night before going to bed, she said her "more complete" devotions, which consisted first of memorized orations to her special patrons—San Antonio and Nuestra Señora de Guadalupe—followed by extensive informal "talk with Tonio" [San Antonio], her most beloved saint. From her grandmother Chole learned numerous *oraciones* (orations/prayers), many of which she still recites in her devotions. But as she grew more autonomous in her faith and practice, she began to create her own prayers too: "I don't always say specific prayers. I bless myself. I give thanks to God. But I compose my own prayers. God has given me the license to do so. As long as I accept what He sends me."

Gloria Rocha said her devotions to the Virgin of San Juan everyday, usually in the morning. For her, devotion was the need to speak regularly with the Virgin while in the presence of her image at the altar. Sra. Rocha said,

> I have my place and I pray everyday. . . . Yes, I pray to Mother of God everyday. I have a regular, I have a regular [oration] for Mother of God. . . . This is the one I pray for my three [children]. It is Oración de Una Madre [A Mother's Prayer]. It is for a mother to pray for her kids.

Many years ago Sra. Rocha memorized the Oración de Una Madre from a printed source. This oration is the formal centerpiece of her daily devotions. Sra. Rocha allowed that she doesn't follow a strict routine in her daily prayers. She wants, as she has said, to remain "free to speak from the heart." Still, a basic pattern of devotion has developed over the years.

Upon approaching the altar, Sra. Rocha blesses herself by making the sign of the cross. She lights a candle to the Virgin of San Juan and begins to pray while standing directly in front of Her image. The Padre Nuestro (Our Father) and Ave Maria (Hail Mary) may be said as the first set of prayers, followed by the Oración de Una Madre. These are the routine formal beginnings of her daily devotion. Then Sra. Rocha spends a good part of her devotion simply "talking with" the Virgin. And this kind of talk can occur in the most casual way: "You see my altar is right there in the bedroom. And if I'm don't feel like getting up—well I do get up to light my candle—but then [laughs] I'm just in my bed talking to Her."

At her altar a woman moves beyond the simple viewing of sacred images and begins to encounter them, to use them, to speak to them. She empowers herself with the affirmation of affiliation. There a woman meets her deities and speaks with assurance in their *mutual* ability to change things for the good. The altar becomes an instrument for fulfilling her desires; through speech and gesture, she *performs* the expectation and certainty of having her needs met. The self-created altar becomes a vehicle for self-creation, a place for manipulating and shaping consciousness, for making the world the way the altarista wants the world to be. As Margarita Guerrero affirmed, "Here with my saints and the *Virgencita* I have accomplished many things. I have prayed and they answer me. And always I have made things better . . . for myself and others."

Daily devotion creates an ongoing circuit of contingency between a woman and her saints. Relationship and the terms of relationship are fabricated and refabricated, renewed and revitalized on a day-to-day basis. Devotional acts are, to a great extent, patterned and redundant, but they should not be viewed as passively repetitive, nor as merely obligatory. For acts of devotion ground the believer's relationship with the divine in the continuity of everyday life. Micaela Zapata emphatically and succinctly summarized the importance for her of this grounding: "Everyday I'm here at my altarcito. Everyday. Everyday. Even if I'm sick I still come here. Everyday."

Regular devotion lends itself to the successful production of daily life—to the successful development and productive flow of sacred and social relationships—but this continuity is subject to abridgments caused by physical and emotional crises. The regular flow of life is interrupted by the unforeseen and unavoidable calamities of illness, death, joblessness, estrangements, and separation—in a word, by loss. The ongoing relationship with divine personages is tested by need. *Peticiones* (prayer petitions), specific requests for divine help, are forwarded with the hope and assurance of gaining God's intervention in recovering from loss. A response from God is requested (and expected) in the form of a miracle. Petitions for special help dramatically heighten the terms of intimate relationship between a woman and the divine. Demands for God's specific action in this world constitute the most important proof of empowerment achieved through devotion at the home altar.

But petitions are not made directly to God; they are mediated through the allies—the saints and the Virgin—with whom a woman has developed the most trusting and dependent relationship. Though petitions may be made at any time and in any context, they are offered most often in private devotion at home. Petra Castorena suggested the desirability of petitioning at home: "I couldn't do this at church. I needed to be here where I could say everything. . . . I have always asked at home. That's where I can cry out."

Specific petitions are mediated by *promesas* (promises) or *mandas* (pledges), a designated offer to return a favor to the saint or Virgin, if a request is granted. Petitions, their consequent replies in the form of miracles, and the response to miracles in the form of "paid" promesas constitute the most action-oriented forms of communication between a believer and a holy personage. The language of giving and receiving is validated through acts of giving and receiving. Through these a lifelong bond between heaven and earth is fashioned, a bond of trust.

This enactment of trust at the home altar is the fundamental labor performed there and underscores its importance as a means for actually achieving the goal of intimate relationship with the divine: the movement from problem to solution. The very kinds of requests made through petition are emblematic of a woman's desire to maintain and regenerate the social—especially the familial—world of which she is the primary keeper. Most requests are made in the interest of gaining or regaining the productivity of human relationship: appeals to heal the sick can be so regarded, as can requests for the restoration of estrangements or separations (e.g., the return of a son from wartime service), or the appeal to gain a family home, or the request to insure a joyous union in marriage, or the birth of a healthy child.

All of the women I knew used their altars as a focus for making specific petitions and promises. Gloria Rocha's husband had cancer. She petitioned the Virgin of San Juan for a miracle on his behalf and pledged to make a pilgrimage to the Virgin's shrine in Jalisco if the request was fulfilled. After her husband's recovery she told him,

> Now it's time to go see Her. . . . [because] my mother, the Mother of God, do to me a miracle because he's alive. And the doctors was not expecting him to live. . . . I made Her a promise. . . . And I go to the Church [in Mexico] and pray. I used to go to the church all the time to fulfill my promises. I used to go to the small little village She have. It's Indian. The Church is rough, the floor is rough. . . . But all the time I go on my knees. I go from the door of the church to the altar with candles for Her.

For the fulfillment of less crucial promises, Sra. Rocha gives money to charities or gifts her altar's image of the Virgin with flower bouquets or trinkets of jewelry. But Sra. Rocha maintains that the arduousness of undertaking a pilgrimage to Mexico is the best sign of thankfulness for promises fulfilled. Just as the Virgin works for her, she feels that she must work to express her gratitude. And moreover, this labor must be spent with joy even in the face of difficulties encountered in the pilgrimage journey:

> Let's say I'm promising I'm coming to Mexico to see you [the Virgin]. And suppose I go. Mother of God puts us through many things—. . . heat, there are no restrooms, or many, many things. You know, you say, "Forget it. I'm not going. I want to turn around." . . . When we are just bitching, Mother of God doesn't want that.

Of course, the Virgin takes the most offense at unfulfilled promises. Sra. Rocha says this is one sure cause of what she called a "breakup" in the relationship between a believer and the Mother of God.

Petra Castorena (see figure 3) continually asked the Virgin's intercession: "I have made many promises. There is much that I have asked. And God has conceded to me what I have asked." Señora Castorena's petitions to the Virgin frequently have been on behalf of her children's needs, especially with regard to their bodily care: "[I have made] many, many promises for the children. For their ears, hands, legs. That's when you ask for more—when you are sick or they are sick, so as not to get the knife [need to go the hospital]. The children—you ask and ask for the children." She also has made petitions to protect her children from involvement in bad love relationships and to assist in bringing about a marriage if Sra. Castorena thought the relationship was a good one: "Yes, they get involved with girls who are no good, and I ask the Virgin to make her drift away. When the relationship was good, I asked that it be fulfilled."

Sra. Castorena has echoed Gloria Rocha's claim that one must work to show thanks to the Virgin. Her promesas often have been in the form of a pledge to perform physical labors on the Virgin's behalf:

> I have fulfilled her promises just as She has fulfilled mine. Just as She does it for me, I do it for Her. That's why I have done washing for Her—washing clothes. So I could take Her an offering of my own sweat. I used to wash and iron and [collect the money] in a little purse. And then I went and paid Her my promise.

Gloria Rocha and Petra Castorena view their relationship with the Virgin as a working relationship; they each work to meet the needs of the

3. Petra Castorena's home altar to Our Lady of Guadalupe, Laredo, Texas, 1986. Photo: Kay Turner.

other. Theirs is an exchange of labor, of giving and receiving based in their connected and trusting knowledge and experience of one another.

On Asking

From the altarista's point of view nothing more critically affirms her intimate relationship with sacred persons than the confidence inspired by asking the saints or Virgin to accomplish miracles on her behalf. In fact, prayer at the altar is most widely predicated upon asking. Women affirm their need for recourse to higher powers in solving the problems of daily life, but what are remarkable are the ease and confidence with which asking is accomplished. Requests for divine help are never equated with weakness; rather, asking is at the core of a woman's ability to empower herself through faith. In affirmation of her intimate relationship with the Virgin and saints, "Pedir es una fuerza" (Asking is a source of strength), according to Chole Pescina. The cycle of giving and receiving at the altar is impelled through constant and assertive asking. One asks because one expects to receive. That is the assurance implied in any relationship bounded by commitment, faith, and love.

In her community Chole was considered an expert in the art of asking. From all over central Texas, people came to her, an extended family of petitioners—even strangers—who sought the benefits of her facility in asking favors of San Antonio, the restorer of lost things and the maker of good love matches. Chole's account speaks clearly to the requirement of assertive asking in recounting the story of a man, partially blinded in an accident, who asked her to help him petition San Antonio for help in restoring his eyesight:

> This *milagro* [an amulet like a small pair of eyes cast in silver] for San Antonio belongs to a man who lives in Kyle called Francisco Melendez. He was blinded. They operated on him. As a result he commended himself to San Antonio. He could see only with one eye. They [he and his wife] would come to my house, and I said to them, "Ask San Antonio. He will return the vision of both. *Don't just ask for one. 'He that asks for little deserves nothing'—ask for both.*" We helped him, and here he is. He drives a car and his tractor to work. Francisco Melendez is his name. (emphasis added)

Be bold in professing faith; asking for a little belies the power which faith makes available.

If altaristas readily affirm both their need and desire to ask, they also affirm the sense of power and fulfillment it brings. As Petra Castorena maintained, "The words you pray to God are never returned empty; they are always returned full." She has constantly sought God's "return" through the intercession of the Virgin:

> I stand up to ask Her with my arms raised. How does the saying go: "Whatever you ask I will give it to you." Whatever I need I ask for. . . . I cry out to Her and I ask Her for all I want . . . I asked everything of Her, and I have received. Not always right away, because sometimes She delays in giving. But everything I have asked Her, she has given me. . . . I've always had it [faith]. I'm a little stupid. I don't have much schooling. But I say what I have to say to the Virgin. I ask for what I need. I know my faith in God is great. This is one thing I know. I have never lacked anything.

For Chole Pescina asking San Antonio for help and blessing was never difficult:

It's very easy to ask him. It doesn't cost a thing. . . . He concedes everything to us. All the good things. He's very miraculous. Very, very. What
could one ask him that he couldn't accomplish? We ask him with faith
and he grants us good things.

Faith is the assumption of relationship with the divine, and asking with
faith puts one in the position of receiving the benefit of God's limitless
power through his sacred representatives.

Given the hardships imposed by the socioeconomic position of most
of the altaristas I knew, it is not difficult to understand how asking for a
portion of something "limitless" can provide a strategy for overcoming
the "limits" of this world. Guadalupe Salazar laughed as she explained: the
Virgin "hears our complaints even if no one else does." She went on to say
that God does not mind being pestered by the disenfranchised: "Among
us poor people, we nag Him a lot. We ask and ask God for our health, for
jobs, for food, for lots of things."

The power of asking is usually employed on behalf of family members.
Most women view asking the favor of the saints and the Virgin from
within the frame of their maternal practice. Pointing to the altar, Petra
Castorena explained that she asked God and the Virgin for help in raising
her family when she was young, especially after her husband left her:

The more saints I have, the more I want. It's for all my children. All my
grandchildren, so that God will care for them. . . . Now I have no fear of
dying. [But] in times past I used to say, "Oh dearest God, don't take me.
My children are so young." My children had not married yet. . . . How
could I not believe in God? I used to say, "How will we eat? Who will
give me milk for the kids?" Everything looked difficult. I asked the Virgin
for everything. . . . But now, they've all gone and I'm alone. I tell God,
"I'm ready whenever you want me." Because I've had a family. I've had it
all. What could I ask for now? Now I don't ask for anything.

As a mother, Chelo González relied upon her alliance with Our Lady of
Guadalupe. Together they protected her children:

I want to say that the Blessed Virgin helped me very much in asking God
on behalf of my children. Because they have grown up to be very good.
That has a lot to do with it. It has a lot to do with it. I give Her thanks,
and I never tire of thanking Her. I have great faith. I have always asked
Her. One of my sons was in Vietnam. Many times he escaped being
killed. They had a close call. They were carrying a stretcher; . . . my son
changed places with his partner and his partner got killed. My son told

me, "I don't know the reason I escaped from so many things." And I always told him "It's the Virgin, my son." And he said "Mama, I could always feel your presence, that you were taking care of me." But I told him "No, it wasn't me, my son. It was the Blessed Virgin." I asked Her to take charge of him. And thanks to God, he returned.

The power to ask corresponds with a woman's sense of responsibility for the care of others. The moral discourse articulated at the altar is not founded in church dogma or abstract principles of law, nor in autonomy or individuality. Founded in maternal practice, in the vernacular of care and seeking the well-being of others, this discourse is therefore critically based in a sense of connection and dependence. Margarita Guerrero explained,

For all those years I was a midwife. I was a mother to those mothers. And the Virgin of San Juan was a mother to me and to them. And we asked Her for the babies. I asked Her. I never cut the cord without thanking Her. And I told those mothers to ask the Virgin for their children's needs. For health, you know, for everything. We can depend on Her because She has a mother's heart. She understands us.

These altaristas ascribed great power to prayer and to their competence in praying. As Petra Castorena claimed, "When I pray, I can ask for anything and I feel very satisfied when God gives me what I want." Chole Pescina further explained that prayer at the home altar is necessitated by women's secondary status in the world:

Let me tell you, this [private prayer] is very important for us. For women. The men they should do it, too. But the world was not made for women. You know that. The world was not made for us. I stopped going to church because they [the priests] accused me of witchery. Because the people came to me to ask [pray] for them. I only helped them. I only asked Tonio or Our Lady of Guadalupe. I never charged [a fee]. But a woman who knows the saints is what? A bad one? No, I tell you we need them. And they know that we have the faith.

Chole asserted in no uncertain terms the necessity of Mexican American women's intensive use of the folk-religion system to satisfy their needs, and moreover, she expressed this claim in a scathing critique of male dominance. Chole's critique was bolstered by her sense of righteousness and right relation with San Antonio, a man not of this world but of God.

Mexican American women of this era suffered a great deal of prejudice, and yet their faith and their practice of it yielded a remarkable generosity.

Similar to the findings in Luis León's chapter on *curanderismo* (chapter 12), Chole insisted that the particular powers of help and healing that she cultivated through her relationship with San Antonio should be made available to all who needed them: "San Antonio is for everyone. He doesn't make distinctions; nor do I. I sit here [at her altar] and I ask [pray] for anyone, for everyone." The first *curación* (curing) Chole performed in the United States was for an African American woman whose daughter was ill. For Chole, friendship with others was a source of true richness: "No soy pobre, porque yo tengo amigos. Vale más amistad que mil pesos en mi bolsa" (I'm not poor, because I have friends. Friendship is worth more than a thousand dollars in my purse). And perhaps most important, her experience speaks for many of my consultants in suggesting that relational activity generated and articulated at the altar is not isolated from a woman's total worldview, but rather substantiates a worldview centered in a deep concern for the sociality, interconnection, and life of all things. Summarizing her philosophy of life, Chole said: "What I do here [at the altar] goes out to the world. That we may live together, live with care for others, and learn to appreciate the life that God gives us. That's the greatest thing He gives us. Life. Living together. And we have to guard it and learn to see that it's the same for everyone."

At their home altars, Mexican American women asserted the value of relationship with others. At the altar, the importance they placed on reproduction and regeneration was consistently affirmed and activated through the project of visibly representing and instrumentally perpetuating the power of good relationship with others, both human and divine. The home altar is a table filled with the signs and symbols of a woman's own "gyno-theology"—a theology inherited from the mother but recast and renewed by each daughter—a theology of relationship founded in women's belief in its centrality to religious and social life.

Notes

All of the direct quotes from altaristas are from interviews conducted primarily in Spanish between 1979 and 1988 as part of my dissertation research. Thanks to Andrea Selvera, Nancy Shepherd Dean, and Mary Margaret Návar for help with translation. This article is dedicated *con cariño* to the memory of the altaristas I knew in Texas, most of whom are long deceased.

1. For the full range of my studies in Mexican American women's altar traditions, see Kay Turner, "Mexican American Home Altars: Toward Their Interpretation," in *The Chicano Studies Reader: An Anthology of Aztlán, 1970–2000* (Los Angeles: UCLA Chicano Studies Research Center Publications, 2001), 327–44;

orig. pub. *Aztlán* 13, nos. 1–2 (1982): 309–26; Turner, "The Cultural Semiotics of Religious Icons: La Virgen de San Juan de Los Lagos," *Semiotica* 47 (1983): 317–61; Turner, *Mexican-American Home Altars: The Art of Relationship*, PhD diss. in Folklore and Anthropology, University of Texas, Austin, 1990 (Ann Arbor, Mich.: UMI Dissertation Services, 1990); Turner, *Beautiful Necessity: The Art and Meaning of Women's Altars* (New York: Thames and Hudson, 1999).

2. For sources on twentieth-century Texas Mexican history see Douglas Foley, *From Peones to Politicos: Ethnic Relations in a South Texas Town, 1900–1977* (Austin: University of Texas Press, 1977); David Montejano, *Anglos and Mexicans in the Making of Texas, 1836–1986* (Austin: University of Texas Press, 1987); Manuel Peña, *The Texas-Mexican Conjunto: History of a Working-Class Music* (Austin: University of Texas Press, 1985); Américo Paredes, *With His Pistol in His Hand* (Austin: University of Texas Press, 1958).

3. Personal experience sources on Mexican American women's religious traditions are included in Norma E. Cantú and Olga Nájera Ramírez, eds., *Chicana Traditions: Continuity and Change* (Urbana: University of Illinois Press, 2002); Holly Everett, *Roadside Crosses in Contemporary Memorial Culture* (Denton: University of North Texas Press, 2002); Ana Castillo, *Goddess of the Americas: Writings on the Virgin of Guadalupe* (New York: Riverhead Books, 1996); Jeanette Rodriguez, *Our Lady of Guadalupe: Faith and Empowerment among Mexican-American Women* (Austin: University of Texas Press, 1994); Dore Gardner, *Niño Fidencio: A Heart Thrown Open* (Santa Fe: Museum of New Mexico Press, 1992).

4. "Relational feminism" is broadly characterized by Karen Offen as acknowledging "women's rights as women, including a positive valuation of their difference from men, difference founded in both biological and cultural distinctions between the sexes." It posits that a woman-centered definition of the self is inseparable from the limiting and enriching contexts of body, feeling, relationship, community, history, and the web of life. See Offen, "Defining Feminism: A Comparative Historical Approach," *Signs* 14, no. 1 (autumn 1988): 135–36. The feminist literature on maternal practice, social reproduction, standpoint theory, and relationship and affiliation is extensive. Seminal works that influenced my thinking about Mexican American altars, some of which have been updated and revised in recent years, include Nancy Chodorow, *The Reproduction of Mothering: Psychoanalysis and the Sociology of Gender* (Berkeley: University of California Press, 1978); Sara Ruddick, "Maternal Thinking," *Feminist Studies* 6, no. 2 (1980): 342–66; Mary O'Brien, *The Politics of Reproduction* (London: Routledge and Kegan Paul, 1981); Carol Gilligan, *In a Different Voice* (Cambridge, Mass.: Harvard University Press, 1982); Nancy Hartsock, "The Feminist Standpoint: Developing the Ground for a Specifically Feminist Historical Materialism," in *Discovering Reality: Feminist Perspectives on Epistemology, Metaphysics, Methodology and Philosophy of Science*, ed. Sandra Harding and Merrill B. Hintikka (Dordrecht, Netherlands: D. Reidel Publishers), 283–310; Mary Belenky et al., *Women's Way of Knowing: The Development of Self, Voice and Mind* (New York: Basic Books, 1986). Exemplary sources which interpret and critique this literature specifically

in terms of women's religious practice include Carol Ochs, *Women and Spiritu-ality* (Totowa, N.J.: Rowman and Allanhead, 1983); Diana L. Eck and Deraki Jain, eds., *Cross-cultural Perspectives on Women, Religion and Social Change* (New Delhi: Kali for Women, 1986); Carolyn Walker Bynum, Stevan Harrell, and Paula Richman, eds., *Gender and Religion: On the Complexity of Symbols* (Boston: Beacon Press, 1986). Some relational feminist and standpoint theories were later critiqued by social constructionists as being essentialist and universalist. The theories have been refined and argued with greater particularity in examples such as "Politics and Feminist Standpoint Theories," a special issue of *Women and Politics* 18, no. 3 (1997). Mexican American altars exemplify a way to bet-ter integrate the complexities of essentialist and social constructionist claims as they are made *within* the social. What I found of interest in looking at women's altar traditions through a relational feminist and standpoint lens is that altaristas made essentialist claims about themselves—their sense of religious authority was based in a sense of maternal essentialism. Yet, I think the most fruitful analysis of the tradition is founded in an understanding of the way such essentialist claims were grounded in a practice aimed almost exclusively at improving social liv-ing. I develop these thoughts in other works. This chapter embeds rather than illuminates feminist theories.

5. Sources on early, pre-Christian domestic altars include Marija Gimbutas, *The Goddesses and Gods of Old Europe* (Berkeley: University of California Press, 1982); Marija Gimbutas, *The Language of the Goddess* (San Francisco: Harper and Row, 1989); James Mellaart, *Cätäl Huyuk: A Neolithic Town in Anatolia* (New York: McGraw Hill, 1967); David G. Orr, *Roman Domestic Religion: A Study of Roman Household Deities and Their Shrines at Pompeii and Herculaneum* (PhD diss., University of Maryland, Baltimore, 1972). Sources for preconquest Mexican domestic altars include Kent V. Flannery, ed., *The Early Mesoamerican Village* (New York: Academic Press, 1976); William T. Sanders, *Life in a Classic Village: Proceedings from Oceana Redonda: Teotihuacán* (Mexico City: Sociedad Mexicana de Antropología, 1966), 123–43. See K. Turner, *Mexican American Women's Home Altars* for additional sources and for discussion of continuities in the home altar tradition from pre-Christian into Christian practice.

6. For further information on Catholic saints' images and the doctrine of the Incarnation, see Leonid Ouspensky, "Icon," in *New Catholic Encyclopedia*, vol. 1 (New York: McGraw-Hill, 1967), 324–26. On women and the cult of icons, see Judith Herrin, "Women and the Faith in Icons in Early Christianity," in *Culture, Ideology and Politics: Essays for Eric Hobshawn*, ed. Raphael Samuel and Gareth Stedman Jones (London: Routledge, 1983), 56–83. See Turner, "The Cultural Semiotics of Religious Icons," for a close semiotic reading of the image of La Virgen de San Juan de Los Lagos, an aspect of the Virgin Mary widely venerated in south Texas and northern Mexico.

7. Margarita "Maggie" Guerrero, Consuela "Chelo" Gonzalez, Soledad "Chole" Pescina, and others spoke pointedly of the value of life. As mothers and as "givers of life," they assumed a sacred guardianship over the processes of preg-nancy, birth, and other entailments and entitlements of womanhood. Their be-

lief in women's difference and their personal alliance with the Virgin and saints produced a remarkable independence of thought concerning sex, birth control, abortion rights, and divorce. Few of the women I interviewed adhered to church proscriptions concerning contraception. A telling example of these altaristas' assumption of authority in matters pertaining to sex and reproduction is found in Maggie Guerrero's answer to my question about what she believed concerning the Immaculate Conception. She replied, laughing, "Well, if the Virgin is a virgin then I'm a virgin, and I'm *not* a virgin."

8. In his study of New Mexican *santos*, Thomas Steele mentions the importance of accounting for the analogous relationship between visual and verbal elements in the folk religious system associated with carved and painted images of the saints: "the *santos* are a set of visual commonplaces in which the verbal epithets of the commonplace are replaced by the visual attributes of the *santo*." Steele further suggests that as a group the santos "make up a system that is both pictorial and, because of the legends, prayers, and associations passed down by word of mouth about the vast majority of the saints . . . , also oral." See Thomas J. Steele, SJ, *Santos and Saints: The Religious Folk Art of Hispanic New Mexico*, 2nd ed. (Santa Fe: Ancient City Press, 1982), 84–85.

9. A useful introduction to cultural codes, including language, is found in Edmund Leach, *Culture and Communication* (London: Cambridge University Press, 1976); for an overview of traditional verbal arts, communication, and performance, see Richard Bauman, ed., *Verbal Art as Performance* (Rowley, Mass: Newbury House Publishers, 1977).

10. Kenneth Burke spoke of "literature as equipment for living" and also of the strategic aspect of verbal art in his *The Philosophy of Literary Form: Studies in Symbolic Action* (New York: Vintage Books, 1957), 262, 256.

8

Los Pastores and the Gendered

Politics of Location

"Allí está mi Señora, comadrando en la casa con las otras mujeres" (Over there's my wife, conversing in the house with the other women) responded Miguel to my query about the location of his wife, as he reentered the conversation in which he was engaged with the other men. It was a Sunday afternoon in mid-January, and I was performing with the local troupe of Los Pastores in San Antonio's west side neighborhood. Turning to me once again, he confessed, "Sí, acompañé a mi vieja . . . pero no mas vengo a tomar una cerveza y, quién sabe" (Yes, I accompanied my old lady . . . but I've just come over to have a beer and, who knows) "maybe I'll watch a little."

After a year and a half of fieldwork with the troupe, the difference between men's and women's participation in Los Pastores—a folk-religion drama of the nativity—was still a puzzle. Los Pastores was, until the mid-sixties, an all-male religious performance, and while women were now more prevalent as members of the troupe, men still controlled the performance by deciding who played which roles, reserving the roles of devils for men alone, and determining the places and times of performance.

My initial interpretive thoughts on this situation stemmed from witnessing men standing outside local Catholic churches on Sunday morning, talking quietly while their "señoras" were inside worshipping. Such scenes reproduced what I took to be "traditional" values concerning the role of religion in the Mexican American community of South Texas. But this view could not answer all the questions that arose from the presence of men at performances of Los Pastores. Their participation was too consistent, in all the "wrong" ways, as their joking, bantering, and often

ludic behavior stood in marked contradistinction to women's more outwardly pious presence.

It was, of course, my expectations that were incorrect and which required adjustment, views that stemmed from working in this area for
several years in the pursuit of developing a model of Chicano liberation
theology. That effort produced a variety of serious and important initiatives that attempted to foster a sense of solidarity and justice that moved
local *mexicanos* in San Antonio to action on their own behalf.[1] While the
local ecclesial climate in the early 1970s and 1980s made possible this bold
and important effort—one that fostered a social commitment to the values of justice and charity shaped out of one's personal experience of injustice—the prophetic spirit of this movement waned by the mid-1980s,
giving rise to more conservative influences in the local church hierarchy.

My initial perceptions of Los Pastores—those based on a seemingly divided religious ethos between men and women—appeared to reproduce,
full force, many of the harsh critiques levied against popular religious
practices by social scientists and committed adherents of liberation theology. Although a full-scale evaluation of this issue must be reserved for a
later project, it should be noted that several of the more animated debates
between and among social scientists and theologians revolve around issues of secularization, patriarchy, and the dislocating forces of modernity
as they flatten or erase a sense of solidarity among the practitioners of
popular religion. Social scientists, informed by diverse methodologies
and epistemologies, are often in disagreement among themselves over
the content and function of popular religion, and also in disagreement
with theologians and pastors who find more religious and institutional
concerns to animate them.[2]

Scholars who understand popular religion from a social perspective interpret these expressive forms as either the result of increased secularization or as a response to the various forms of dislocation associated with
modernity.[3] Both of these positions perceive popular religion as emanating from the forces of industrialization, urbanization, and rationalization,
although the first position is clearly seen as the result of community dis-
integration and the second as a creative response to it. In the first group,
increased secularization is viewed as stripping people of any sense of certainty and foundational beliefs, thrusting them into a sea of insecurity,
anxiety, and anomie. Especially for those who have migrated away from
networks of families and associations, popular religion is interpreted as a
remnant of religious practices associated with traditional and communal
lifeways. In the cities, such practices are reproduced at a distance from the

social networks that spawned them, and serve as disjointed efforts at re-producing rural forms of community culture. In the second group, social scientists believe popular religion emerges as an inventive response to the dislocations of modernity, reconnecting people to their cultural origins by rooting them in tradition. Related to this view are those that interpret popular religion as the domain of the poor, thereby providing class-based fodder for the germination of liberationist practices and ideologies.[4]

At a distance from this perspective are scholars influenced by the legacy of Marx, and who see popular religion as the presence of "false practices" that continue to sustain misplaced hopes as well as the depoliticization of the masses.[5] Associated with this concern is the notion that popular religious practices are formulated on prescientific principles that continue to impel its practitioners toward magical beliefs, pitting them against the elite or "rational" forms of institutionalized religion.[6] These criticisms cannot be dismissed easily and weigh heavily on my discussion of soci-ability, to which I will later return.

Criticisms of popular religion which are brought forth by feminists, and especially criticisms of those religious practices influenced by the Catholic tradition, often center on the patriarchal ideologies that inform folk reli-gion and continue to purport limited roles and possibilities for women. In many ways, these criticisms, while distinct from the concerns raised above, resonate with the "false practice" views of certain politically ori-ented scholars. A different aspect of feminist literature concerns the Cult of Mary as expressed through the Virgin of Guadalupe and a host of other Marian incarnations.[7] This perspective reflects on the lives of women by interpreting Guadalupe or other Virgins as powerful and compassionate Christian (and pre-Christian) female deities who intimately understand and empathize with the daily lives of women, especially in their roles as providers, nurturers, and mothers. Relatedly, a number of revision-ist theologies are being written and exercised that seriously take heed of women's lived experience, particularly women burdened by the strictures of poverty, sexism, and racial prejudice. These perspectives, generally re-ferred to as *mujerista* or women's groups, serve to empower women by theologizing through their lived reality of domination and marginaliza-tion.[8]

This said, how are we to understand the social role and place of popu-lar religion today? Do the forces of global capital and migration, uneven and contradictory as they are, continue to shape our understanding of traditional religion in this (postmodern) era? Are issues of gender con-tradictory to those of solidarity? Or more directly, how can Los Pastores invoke notions of sociability when it is steeped in the kind of practices and sentiment (whereby women are viewed by men as *comadrando* [gossip] and men gather to tell the latest *chingaderas* [dirty talk]) that are associated with patriarchy and the spiritualization of poverty and exploitation. The remainder of this chapter explores how women's religious practices and men's carnivalesque devotion serve as a location that mediates politics, gender, and solidarity.

Los Pastores as Ritual and Performance

Los Pastores is a descendant of Spanish medieval nativity plays that depict the exploits of a group of shepherds on their way to Bethlehem. It is part of a genre of folk dramas—known as *pastorelas, coloquios,* or *auto sacramentales*—that are performed, during the Christmas season, entirely in Spanish octosyllabic poetry.

Most versions of the pastorela consist of a cast that includes shepherds, angels, devils, Mary and Joseph, a hermit, a statue of El Niño Dios (the Christ Child), and others. As the narrative begins, the shepherds are keeping watch over their sheep, when the archangel Michael appears to them, announcing the birth of the Messiah. Upon deciding to journey to Bethlehem, bearing offerings for the new Messiah, the shepherds encounter Luzbel (Lucifer) and his legion of devils, who attempt to thwart their efforts in a series of comedic routines. In the end, the archangel defeats Luzbel, banishing him into the dungeons of hell, and the shepherds arrive in Bethlehem offering their humble gifts to the newborn King.

Sixteenth-century Spanish missionaries in the New World used dramatic representation as a didactic device to teach Christian doctrine.[9] For nearly thirty years after the conquest of Mexico, these dramatic religious enactments were common features of Christian worship and evangelization. Some of these dramas included the enactment of the biblical story of Adam and Eve, the Passion, the Feast of Corpus Christi, and Los Pastores.

Father Pedro de Gante is the most well known of the early missionaries who wrote and produced these dramas. He founded the Colegio de San Francisco in Mexico City as a place for teaching arts and crafts and special trades, and he even built a church with an enlarged atrium for staging religious enactments.[10] After the Council of Trent in December 1545, and later with the emergence of the Enlightenment, the teaching of Christian doctrine through dramatic representation was replaced by more rational and philosophical measures. By this time, however, Los Pastores

1. Los Pastores shepherd's play, San Antonio, Texas, 1990s.
Courtesy: Richard Flores.

and other forms of popular religious practice were spreading throughout
Mexico and the southwestern United States, providing a means of self-
evangelization for mestizo communities. In the early 1900s Don Leandro
Granado fled Irapuato, Mexico, for San Antonio, Texas, where he began
organizing performances of Los Pastores in 1913. Today, the troupe he
founded has continued, and Los Pastores is performed each year on the
predominantly Mexican American west side of San Antonio (figure 1).

Members of the troupe begin rehearsing for this event in late September and meet regularly until the end of the performance season in February. The performers are mexicano working-class men and women, both
young and old, who live mostly in the surrounding west-side barrio and
who share a common devotion to El Niño Dios. Each performer has his/
her special story of how—in times of crisis, sickness, and other moments
of human passage—supplications to El Niño Dios were answered in ways
that provided comfort, solace, and miracles. The most vocal is the director, who never fails to tell how El Niño Dios relieved him of his paralysis
after a stroke at a young age.

The most common place for performing Los Pastores is a home on San
Antonio's west side, a place both familiar and familial. Audience members
consist primarily of extended and immediate family members as well as

work associates and neighborhood *comadres* and *compadres* (godmothers and godfathers). For them, the barrio—replete with potholed streets, closely aligned houses, poor street drainage and housing conditions—is a familiar site. Homes are often multifamily dwellings; it is not unusual to find members of at least three generations housed together. While the lack of economic resources forces family members into crowded living conditions, a network of familial support, however meager, is usually available.

At the home, Los Pastores is staged outdoors, beneath a carport or patio if one is large enough, and the performance is visible to passing cars and pedestrians. The main requirement is an area approximately ten feet square, where the *infierno* (hell mouth)—a four-paneled enclosure decorated with demonic icons that houses Luzbel and the other devils—can be placed. Opposite the infierno, about fifteen yards away, is the *nacimiento* (manger), where El Niño Dios is placed. These two items, the infierno and the nacimiento, are provided by the performers.

The Tasks of Ritual Performance

As one of their most important tasks, women construct and decorate a home altar that is situated directly behind the nacimiento. Flowers are arranged, candles lit, and religious statues placed in proper position, serving as a testimony to the gathered community's commitment and devotion to El Niño Dios. While all women of the household participate in this work, it is grandmothers who usually instruct their daughters and granddaughters on how to create an aesthetically pleasing and religiously appropriate altar.

Besides constructing the home altar, the other major task that women of the hosting family provide is a meal that is served to everyone at the end of the performance. Preparation begins several days in advance with the making of tamales and tortillas, and visits to the butcher or the *mercado* (market) for ordering *menudo* (tripe soup) and other items. The major portion of the work begins the morning of the event as beans are washed and prepared, menudo is cut and cooked, masa (cornmeal) and other dishes prepared. Food for thirty to fifty people is the norm. Like other tasks, food preparation is a familial job where everyone from the youngest to oldest assists in some way.

Women serve, in most cases, as mistresses of ceremony, introducing the event and officially beginning the performance. Their discourse in this effort—what I refer to as a form of ritual centering—usually invokes a *promesa*, or ritual promise. It is quite common to hear a woman state: "Hace dos años que hice una promesa al Niño Dios. Si él curara mi mamá, yo prometí tener una pastorela en mi casa. Pues, la salud de mi mamá se mejoró, y me siento feliz que ya llegó este día" (It has been two years since I made a vow to the Christ Child. If He cured my mother, I promised to hold a pastorela in my house. Well, my mother's health improved, and I feel happy that today has arrived).

By centering Los Pastores in such a way, the intimate relationship that forms the core of ritual negotiation, or a dyadic ritual, is made public through a personal narrative. Such introductions build a sense of empathy for the hosts, but, more important, they serve as reflexive narratives that allow those present to recall their own personal experiences of sickness or death or other moments of human crisis. These narratives cease to be an individual invocation, but a means through which the audience engages the experience as one collective body.

The tasks of men are not as actively engaged in the ritual aspects of Los Pastores; they contribute to it in other ways. Before the event, they aid in clearing space, moving furniture and yard furniture, and tidying the performance area. Chairs are usually set out, although it isn't uncommon to find a sofa brought from indoors and situated near the performance area. The day of the event, when the director and several devils arrive in their truck to arrange the infierno, men from the house assist in carrying and placing this heavy structure in its predetermined location. In cold weather, that is, temperatures below forty-five degrees Fahrenheit in South Texas, men gather old lumber or tree branches and fill several barrels for outdoor bonfires, around which they will gather to offset the chill of the evening air.

The role of women in centering has a contradictory role among men, one that pulls the ritual aspects of Los Pastores into the carnivalesque. Before, during, and after performances, men—hosts, guests, and members of the troupe—drink and comport themselves in jocular fashion. The more common type of verbal repartee is what is referred to as chingaderas, verbal screwing around, as men stand by the open fire or sit in the infierno and retell the latest joke. While the tone is definitely quieter during the performance itself, men's ludic behavior throughout stands in marked contrast to that of the women.

The building of the home altar, the preparation of food, the collecting wood and arranging of the infierno are all tasks that incorporate friends and family in their completion and require a commitment of time and effort. Elsewhere, I refer to these tasks as the "gifting of performance."[11]

In brief, cultural performances, especially those structured by ritual elements, are dynamic events that call forth a special commitment on the part of performers and spectators and are marked by a process of gifting and reciprocity. As such, Los Pastores is enacted as a gift: there is no fee charged or expected for a performance in the home, and all requests for a performance are honored, provided scheduling can be accommodated. But gifts, especially those dealing with ritual, must be reciprocated if they are to be efficacious. In Los Pastores, the time, financial resources, and physical labor utilized in building an altar and providing a meal are seen as reciprocal acts to the gift of performance. The labor involved in reciprocal gifts serves to construct a social network, drawing people into forms of human interaction based on their common tasks. As such, the dynamic of performance and reciprocity, or the gifting of performance, is a process through which networks are enacted, facilitating the construction of a familial atmosphere where social conviviality emerges. In this way, the emergent social relations that are constructed or sustained in the gifting of performance leads to a sense of "sociability" and communal interaction that is fundamental for social life.[12] The gifting of performance, therefore, is the reciprocal process of performance and gratitude that engages performers and audience in an event founded on shared communication, social solidarity, and mutual obligation.

It is this sense of sociability that separates performances of Los Pastores in the barrios of San Antonio from other institutional domains of performance, a difference that moves the discussion and interpretation of Los Pastores from performance to the politics of culture.[13] Without repeating previously stated arguments, I would like to note that performances of Los Pastores in other domains reveal shifts in the social relations that construct this event, so as to negate or diminish the process and structure of the gifting of performance discussed above. These shifts are instructive, since they reveal drastically different notions and values from those that make events like Los Pastores important.

As Stuart Hall states, "What matters is the state of play in cultural relations . . . the class struggle in and over culture."[14] But these shifts in social relations constructed through cultural and religious performances have dramatic consequences that result in the negation and diminishing of sociability. That is, shifts in domain not only change social interactions between performers and audience; they also impact the fruits of social interactions and lead to the negation of sociability. Such changes, in essence, fragment the "nutritive social context" that is necessary for the making of sociability, community, and collective practice.[15] The maintenance, continuation, and celebration of events such as Los Pastores that lead to renewed or reinforced senses of community cannot be dismissed and become political acts. Here, Richard Bernstein reminds us that we need to "seize upon those experiences and struggles in which there are still glimmerings of solidarity."[16] This is so, I suggest, because such glimmerings are foundational to community formation and collective identity, which are, in an atomized social sphere, forms and expressions of collective action and power.

And yet, such glimmerings seem to fade from the glare of Miguel's claim: "Sí, acompañé a mi vieja . . . pero no mas vengo a tomar una cerveza y, quién sabe, maybe I'll watch a little." How can Los Pastores be a familial site of sociability at the same time that men's and women's involvement in, participation in, and attitude about this event seemingly contradict each other?

It is clear that Los Pastores appears to reproduce the political and gender "traps" raised by progressive and critical scholars of religion. First, the focus of this event on El Niño Dios and the deep faith and trust indexed by supplications to him resonate with those notions that understand popular religion as a form of "misplaced hopes." This seems plausible when it is known that little direct action is taken by the performers themselves to address politically the apparent social and structural discord that surrounds their community. And, while the majority of the performers and audience members are lower, working-class Chicanos and Chicanas, the question of class solidarity and its subsequent and direct political articulation remains open for discussion.[17] Second, while this ritual performance is conducted by and participated in by women and men, it certainly does not entail the deep, personal, and theological reflection associated with mujerista movements or other pastoral forms of liberation theology that encourage their participants to undertake a critical reevaluation of one's lived social reality.

Gender and the Social

Traditional notions of the division of labor caricature women as responsible for domestic work related to the production and reproduction of the family, be it birthing and caring for children, providing material sustenance, or acting as tradition bearers. This same caricature portrays men as working outside the home, involved in more "physically demanding" labor than women, and directly engaging the wider social arena. Los Pastores mirrors this reality. It is, among other qualities, a "model of" the outside world. Women's responsibility for the domestic chores of cooking, cleaning, and serving all guests reproduces their traditional roles as keepers of the domicile. Likewise, their involvement in building home altars and centering performances through dyadic ritual narratives serves to construct intimacy and a form of nurturance for the gathered familial and familiar social body. Through their labor, women realize the claims of religion by reproducing—physically and socially—the collective group as well as communicating a particular memory and culture for those gathered.

Men's roles, on the other hand, are quite different from women's. In terms of tasks, their traditional roles are reproduced through their responsibility for situating the infierno in an appropriate place, a rather physically arduous job. Men also fill a second role in Los Pastores by maintaining the farcical tradition of public drama through their drinking, joking, and general banter that highlights the tension between ritual and carnival. The license of men to play during this event, while seemingly contradictory to its ritual tones, continues a festive tradition that is reproduced within the drama itself.[18] Men's carnivalesque behavior should not be read as inherently antithetical to popular religion, but perhaps as a measured counterpoint to the antiseptic values of contemporary religious (official) practice where ritual forms have been stripped of their ludic components.

I have described women's and men's roles in Los Pastores in synchronic and descriptive fashion, but what happens when we think of this performance not as an event but as a social and cultural practice engaged in and produced from the larger arena of South Texas society? Let's move from seeing Los Pastores as a "performed" event to a "social" one.[19] In this interpretive shift, our organizing category is no longer the singular roles that constitute each performance but the collective social roles "in production." Los Pastores exists in time and space, not outside it, and as such must also be viewed as dialogically related to its larger social arena. In such a move, the event and roles just described lose their autonomous and individual quality and gain an enlarged sense of reference that situates them in relation to the historical conditions from which they emerge. This is not to erase or negate the gender differences just described, but to read them as socially based, as well as socially reproduced, in history.

In this move to the social, let me invoke the analytical insights of Chandra Mohanty, who calls for a "politics of location" that requires us to move beyond transcendent notions that erase difference and dependence to the experience of real people in concrete places.[20] As a feminist, Mohanty understands the unity of women "not as given, on the basis of natural/psychological commonality," but instead as "something that has to be worked for, struggled towards—in history."[21] As such, an analysis based on the politics of location is concerned with "uncovering alternative, nonidentical histories which challenge and disrupt the spatial and temporal location of a hegemonic history,"[22] and, I would add, social and religious order. In the case of Los Pastores, alternative readings allow us to see beyond the normative strictures of gender roles and the ideology of politics to explore how these particular social and religious actors "disrupt" the common sense norms of history. The result, for my purposes, is to see how women and men remap the space they occupy through the dialogic tension between ritual and carnival, and how such mappings serve to reconfigure common places as sites of struggle and solidarity.

At the level of the social, the gendered roles exhibited in Los Pastores must not be "read" simply as the reproduction of the dominant or traditional divisions of labor discussed earlier, but also as responsive to and engaged with the social location of the gathered collective. That is, ritual practices such as Los Pastores serve a collective enterprise, however indeterminate and fleeting the practices may be; it is these emergent, ritually constituted collectivities that are responsive to the forces of the dominant by "struggling in history."

The roles women enact that result in intimacy and nurturance through the production of food and ritual discourse work for *both* the material and spiritual reproduction of the community. Women reproduce the home as a place constituted through collective action, shared responsibility, and sociability mediated—in this instance—through a religious discourse of copresence with El Niño Dios. By mapping the home in such a way, women locate themselves as active agents in the wider arena of struggle, where forces of displacement—economic, political, or social—attempt to recenter the dominant notions of familial space as real estate, territory, and a market-value commodity. Women's practice, based on shared work and mutual responsibility, reconfigures the values of common and collective work away from the economic values of the market and commodity labor and reenacts it as a central feature of social life rooted in sociability. As such, women's "traditional" roles in Los Pastores serve a critical task by recasting the spatial location of home as one of collective practice that reproduce it as a locus of communal and familial solidarity.

The roles of men must also be read in terms of the social. While they are not as actively engaged in the production of a collective sentiment, they do serve a significant function. Their general carnivalesque attitude—expressed through their drinking and ludic behavior—remaps this location as one of play. Spheres of play, it must be remembered, especially those in the carnivalesque tradition, are highly charged zones where meanings, values, hierarchies, and power are recast, if only temporarily. As Francis Hearn has adeptly shown, capitalism has relegated play to either an obstacle of progress or an activity with little pragmatic, that is, economic, importance.[23] But play cannot be dismissed so summarily, for it remains an important feature of social behavior and practice that, according to Marcuse, is "denied in labor."[24] It is this freedom and the transgressions that emerge from the space it provides, that allow social and religious actors to act "as if" life were otherwise. As Hearn concludes, "through play, protest becomes more than a task, it becomes rejoicing." But, he is quick to stipulate, it must also be "informed by critical discourse."[25]

It is easy to see how the action of men remaps this place as one of ludic behavior: they drink and engage in verbal repartee, all the while standing at a distance from the performance. As such, their labor of fun stands in contradistinction to their lives of wage labor. But where is the critical discourse that informs the repressive counterside of play? Are we to read these verbal transgressions—chingaderas in which men are figuratively screwed by those in authority—as a form of social comment? Yes and no. I do believe—and here I follow José Limón's insightful comments on this point—that men's ludic repartee concerning personal and sexual violations results from a kind of social ambivalence and structural oppression that gets addressed in this manner.[26] But I must also admit that in and of itself and isolated from other aspects of this performance, men's ludic behavior in this event carries little political weight.

But men are not alone. We cannot separate the comportment of men from that of women in this event, but must read their practices in tandem: they contribute to the same set of social practices that serve to remap this location. I contend that the social critique of men's play only emerges when paired with the lived critique of women's work. Together, the gendered roles of men and women enacted in this ritual performance remap the barrio-home event as one constituted by sociability, intimacy, and play. Remapping the home in such a way celebrates a sense of "freedom"—from the displacing forces of labor that separate worker from product, workers from home, homes from social networks, and communities from nations—and serves as an implicit critique of the work-a-day world of "necessity." Sociability, intimacy, and play serve as counterpoised nodes of a performative dialectic whereby men and women construct the home as a place of the "possible"—a location of freedom, if you will—within the "real."

But solidarity is not without struggle, nor without certain forms of contradiction, and I do not wish to imply that men and women in this event are themselves free from hierarchical relations of power and patriarchy. They are not. The weight of the dominant discourse is not equally experienced by men and women; patriarchy has assured us of that. I do suggest, however, that in Los Pastores men and women contribute to the construction of a shared event that situates them to a place on the map, which Mohanty rightly states, is "also a place in history." Whether this place in history develops into a location for freedom that links, through community and conscious building activity with other similar sites of struggle and solidarity, into a movement for freedom beyond the local is unknown. But I am convinced that without the emergence of local sites, enacted in this case through the religious performance of Los Pastores, the shift from local to broader collective struggles will be more difficult to attain.

The debates concerning politics, gender, and the place of popular religion in Mexican American and Latino communities in the United States are complex and multifarious, and they deserve critical attention by scholars of religion. In these discussions popular religion has been caricatured by many as secondary or even tertiary to more active forms of consciousness raising, political awareness, and social action that lead to empowerment. No doubt, as mentioned above, critical discourse is a necessary aspect of all social awareness. But discourse has other modes of articulation beyond the rhetorical. Religious cultural events such as Los Pastores reveal a performative dimension that cannot go unnoticed. More boldly, they serve important and necessary roles in the formation of collective communities and identities. Their dismissal as apolitical remnants of traditional culture would be remiss, while their in-depth investigation might yield—through their articulation of gender and social roles—a nutritive ritual space for collective identity and communal action.

Notes

1. I am referring to the work of the Mexican American Cultural Center, which actively taught and experimented with incorporating Latin American models of liberation theology into a Chicano context. For a brief overview of their mission, see Moises Sandoval, *The Mexican American Experience in the Church: Reflections on Identity and Mission* (New York: Sadlier, 1983); Gilbert Cadena, "Chicanos and the Catholic Church: Liberation Theology as a Form of Empowerment" (PhD diss., University of California, Riverside, 1987).

2. Meredith McGuire raises some critical issues concerning the methodology of research on popular religion in the Latino community. She does so in an essay that is part of a volume on Latino popular religion published for Program for the Analysis of Religion Among Latinos (PARAL), an interdisciplinary research group that has contributed extensively to the study of religion in the Latino community. See her "Linking Theory and Methodology for the Study of Latino Religiosity in the United States Context," in *An Enduring Flame: Studies on Latino Popular Religiosity*, ed. Anthony M. Stevens-Arroyo and Ana María Díaz-Stevens (New York: Bildner Center for Western Hemisphere Studies, 1994), 191–204.

3. For contrasting but relevant views on popular religion and social disloca-tion, see Pablo Richard and Diego Irarrázaval, *Religión y política en América Central: Hacia una nueva interpretación de la religiosidad popular* (San José, Costa Rica: Colección Centroamérica, Departamento Ecuménico de Investigaciones, 1981); Richard R. Flores, *Los Pastores: History and Performance in the Mexican Shepherds' Play of South Texas* (Washington, D.C.: Smithsonian Institution Press, 1995).

4. For a thorough review of this literature from a Latin American perspec-tive, see Gustavo Benavides, "Resistance and Accommodation in Latin Ameri-can Popular Religiosity," in Stevens-Arroyo and Díaz Stevens, *An Enduring Flame*, 37–68.

5. The political critique of popular religion has been most heavily levied by Latin American social scientists and theologians. See Richard and Irarrázaval, *Religión y política en América Central*.

6. For a brief overview of popular religion and its relationship to social-science research, see Ana María Díaz Stevens, "Analyzing Popular Religiosity for Socio-religious Meaning," in Stevens-Arroyo and Díaz, *An Enduring Flame*, 17–36.

7. Jeanette Rodriguez's recent work offers a sociologically informed analysis of the importance of the Virgin of Guadalupe among Chicanas. See *Our Lady of Guadalupe: Faith and Empowerment among Mexican-American Women* (Austin: University of Texas Press, 1994).

8. Ada María Isasi-Díaz provides a provocative and insightful, if not challeng-ing, discussion of mujerista theology among Hispanic women. See her essay, "The Cultural Identity of the Latina Woman: The Cross-Disciplinary Perspec-tive of Mujerista Theology," in *Old Masks, New Faces: Religion and Latino Identi-ties*, ed. Anthony M. Stevens-Arroyo and Gilbert R. Cadena (New York: Bildner Center for Western Hemisphere Studies, 1995), 93–116.

9. One reason that humorous and dramatic representations were so popular during the early colonial period in Mexico was that this ludic form resonated with a similar indigenous tradition. Aztec society maintained casts of travel-ing troubadours and performers who were trained in special schools known as *cuicacalli* and who enacted comic and farcical scenes. For a general historical account of Christian dramatic performance genres during this time, see Flores, *Los Pastores*.

10. For an important and detailed discussion of this material, see José Rojas Garcidueñas, *Autos y coloquios del siglo XVI* (Mexico City: Universidad Nacional Autónoma de México, 1939); Sister Joseph Marie, IHM, "The Role of the Church and the Folk in the Development of the Early Drama in New Mexico" (PhD diss., University of Pennsylvania [English], Philadelphia, 1948).

11. See Richard R. Flores, "Para El Niño Dios: Sociability and Commemorative Sentiment in Popular Religious Practice," in Stevens-Arroyo and Díaz Stevens, *An Enduring Flame*.

12. I am referring to the notion of sociability provided by Georg Simmel. See Kurt H. Wolff, ed., *The Sociology of Georg Simmel* (New York: Free Press, 1950).

13. Los Pastores is performed in two other domains besides the one discussed here: local churches and one of the historic missions for a tourist audience sponsored by the San Antonio Conservation Society. For more analysis of these performance sites and the cultural politics that embed them, see Richard R. Flores, "'Los Pastores' and the Gifting of Performance," *American Ethnologist* 21, no. 2 (1994): 270–85; and Flores, *Los Pastores*.

14. Stuart Hall, "Notes on Deconstructing the Popular," in *People's History and Socialist Thought*, ed. Raphael Samuel (London: Routledge, 1981), 235.

15. José E. Limón, "Western Marxism and Folklore: A Critical Introduction," *Journal of American Folklore* 96 (1983): 34–52.

16. Richard Bernstein, *Beyond Objectivism and Relativism: Science, Hermeneutic, and Praxis* (Philadelphia: University of Pennsylvania Press, 1983), 228.

17. This is not to say politics is absent. For a discussion of Los Pastores as it relates to cultural rights and power, see Richard R. Flores, "Aesthetic Process and Cultural Citizenship: The Membering of a Social Body," in *Claiming Memory, Space and Rights: Struggles for Latino Cultural Citizenship*, ed. Renato Rosaldo, Rina Benmayor, and William Flores (Boston: Beacon Press, in press).

18. The *ermitaño*, of all characters, has special license to interact and poke fun at the devils, and provides a sense of comic relief throughout this event.

19. For a critical discussion of expressive forms and their social production, see Fredric Jameson, *The Political Unconscious* (Ithaca, N.Y.: Cornell University Press, 1981).

20. Chandra Talpade Mohanty, "Feminist Encounters: Locating the Politics of Experience," *Copyright* 1 (1987): 30–44.

21. Ibid., 38.

22. Ibid.

23. Francis Hearn, "Toward a Critical Theory of Play," *Telos* 30 (1976–77): 145–60.

24. Herbert Marcuse, "On the Concept of Labor," *Telos* 16 (summer 1973): 14.

25. Hearn, "Toward a Critical Theory of Play," 148, 160.

26. See José E. Limón, "Carne, Carnales, and the Carnivalesque: Bakhtinian Batos, Disorder, and Narrative Discourses," *American Ethnologist* 16, no. 3 (1989): 471–86.

IV

Mexican American

Religions and Literature

9

The Religious Vision of Gloria Anzaldúa

Borderlands/La Frontera as a Shamanic Space

In *The Darker Side of the Renaissance: Literacy, Territoriality, and Coloniza-tion*, Walter Mignolo credits Gloria Anzaldúa with achieving an interpre-tive breakthrough, a different way of thinking about the complex cultural histories of Latin America. He writes: "Anzaldúa's great theoretical con-tribution is to create a space-in-between *from where* to think rather than a hybrid space *to talk about*, a hybrid thinking-space of Spanish/Latin American and Amerindian legacies as the condition of possibility for Spanish/Latin American and Amerindian postcolonial theories."[1]

Another scholar, Barbara Harlow, in her article "Sites of Struggle: Immigration, Deportation, Prison, and Exile," applauds Anzaldúa's achievement in *Borderlands/La Frontera* as creating a fragmented "hybrid thinking space" where:

> That already complex identity is fragmented further in the bilingual, even trilingual, multigeneric textual composition which disarticulates Anzaldúa's expression—at once intimate and scholarly. The academically footnoted autobiographical narrative of the first half of the book, with its combined sense of fabled past and political present, gives way in the sec-ond part to a more lyrical disquisition on the contradictions of class and race as these are implicated in questions of gender and sexual identity.[2]

And, Renato Rosaldo ends his celebrated book *Culture and Truth: The Remaking of Social Analysis* by crediting Anzaldúa with showing us that "Chicanos have so long practiced the art of cultural blending, 'we' now stand in a position to become leaders in developing new forms of polyglot cultural creativity. . . . The rear guard will become the vanguard."[3] In all these critical works, it is understood that Anzaldúa's great contribution is a very particular view of *la frontera*, the borderlands, as a creative site where the clash and confluence of languages and cultures will allow for the emergence of the "New Mestiza."[4]

We enter into the praise and critical responses to the writings of Gloria Anzaldúa, from the perspective of the study of religion. The categories of "space" and "ecstatic experience" provide valuable means for interpreting her vision of the borderlands with its wounded bodies and psyches, its creative languages and ethnicities. Many scholars and writers have focused on ethnic, gendered, and political elements of the space she describes. But, we believe that the heart of her portrayal of the borderlands is articulated, and must be understood, as a religious vision. In our readings of la frontera, her borderlands is *a shamanic space* where a different quality of knowledge is achieved through ecstatic trance states which inspire the birth of the "New Mestiza."[5] This shamanic space is not incidental or epiphenomenal in her life and writing, but is, in fact, central to her poetic imagery and attempted cultural healing. Though these ecstatic trances have been largely ignored by scholars reading her work, she tells us on the first page and at strategic points throughout the book that a shamanic imagination—with its attention to spiritual journey, songs, and voices of ancestral spirits, psychic injury, and interior healing—informs her entire project.

She writes that her muse Ehecatl, an Aztec wind god who heralded the fertilizing rains, has been "whispering its secret knowledge, the fleeting images of the soul" to her. She tells us that she is preoccupied

> with the inner life of the Self, and with the struggle of that Self amidst adversity and violation; with the confluence of primordial images; with the unique positioning consciousness takes at these confluent streams, and with my almost instinctive urge to communicate, to speak, to write about life on the borders, life in the shadows.[6]

These *shadowy places* in Anzaldúa's thought deserve critical exploration and attention.

We are not claiming that her work is limited to religious meanings and symbols. Anzaldúa is often playing the contrary, "not to be contradicted," political trickster writer, who rebels and throws words of derision in the face of the Anglo/Mexican patriarchy.[7] But, more often and more deeply, her narratives describe trips "underground" where she communicates with the spirit world, where she is alternately assisted, thwarted, or even tortured. It is during these trips that she acquires a religious language that

1. José Cuellar, also known as "Dr. Loco," 2002.
Cuellar holds a PhD in anthropology from UCLA and
teaches Raza studies at San Francisco State University
while performing solo and with several variations of
his award-winning musical group, Dr. Loco's Rockin'
Jalapeño Band. Courtesy: José Cuellar.

allows her to begin to make sense of her waking world.[8] The religious
language she gains from her trance states results in songs and stories told
in the multiple vocabularies of the borderlands. She describes a shamanic
experience (1) fueled by enormous personal suffering, (2) structured by
the capacity for sustained ecstasies, (3) filled with visitations by powerful
spirit forces including the Shadow Beast, Coatlicue, Tlazolteotl, and the
Toad who sips her strength, and (4) deepened by moments of illumination and healing.

Our approach to Anzaldúa's borderlands develops from our interests
in the diverse forms of religious expression born in the hyphen between
Mexican and American culture.[9] In part we are building on Carrasco's
earlier work on the religious dimensions of Rudolfo A. Anaya's *Bless Me,
Ultima*. His essay entitled "A Perspective for a Study of Religious Dimensions in Chicano Experience: *Bless Me, Ultima* as a Religious Text,"
grew out of conversations with another borderlands artist, the cultural
anthropologist José Cuellar (figure 1), also known as "Dr. Loco," about

religion and Chicanos.[10] In what follows we will make linkages between Dr. Loco's musical art and Anzaldúa's religious vision.

The study of Anzaldúa's influential writing and thought supports Carrasco's earlier essay's contention that, contrary to conventional accounts, Christian theology is most commonly not the ultimate concern expressed in the religious life of Mexicans, Chicanos, and Latinos. In Carrasco's interpretation of *Bless Me, Ultima*, he argued that Chicano scholars seemed profoundly "unable to deal with religion outside the normative framework of Christian theology" if they dealt with it at all, which was not often. Following Charles Long's critique of Black theology, he suggested that "even if one is to have a theology, it must arise from religion, something that is prior to theology."[11] In other words, religious experiences and their expressions were part of the fundament of Mexican American and Chicano culture, serve as prior resources for theology and philosophies of religion, and are equally as important in understanding life in the borderlands. It is also our view that while theology and church history are important, we should look with equal interest and care elsewhere—for instance, at Chicano art and literary works—to develop understandings of religious modes of experience and expression that have ordered vital aspects of Chicano history and culture.

Loca-Centric

In this chapter we are following Anzaldúa's practice of weaving scholarship and autobiography together to interpret her borderlands as a shamanic space. Further, we will suggest that her religious vision of the borderlands is not confined by the traditional scholarly categories of *logos* and *muthos* but that she, along with Dr. Loco, have created a creative religious, artistic style we call loco-centric. A deep and long-standing scholarship has explicated the theological power of the category of logos, which refers to "reason," the evocative power of the "word," and the deep "wisdom" residing in the heart of religion. A competing category is that of muthos, or mythos, which refers to the mode of sacred narrative as a major means of communicating and accessing spiritual truth. In Anzaldúa's loca-centric approach she draws upon both logos and mythos, but her shamanic imagination is not limited to or generated from either. Her ability to use multiple languages allows her to create new and constantly evolving mythic histories that serve to make sense of the chaos of life in the hyphen,[12] but the hyphen as a very dynamic tissue of connection. Reference to the lore of Nahuatl-speaking peoples of Mexico can help us illuminate this alternative creativity of loco-centrism. Throughout the Nahua world, sacred powers moved up and down and throughout the cosmos via passageways called *malinalli*. Malinalli (from *malin*, associated with the day sign *ce malinalli* "twisted grass"—coincidentally the source for the name Malinche, the woman who became the translator and lover of Hernán Cortés) were shaped like double helix structures in constant motion. Located in caves, near ponds, or inside of trees, they served as conduits of ancestral and sacred powers streaming through the natural and human world. They were the dynamic passageways between the human and spirit world. In our view, Anzaldúa's religious imagination functions more like a malinalli then as "reason" or "story." Her writing is not logo-centric but loca-centric, with an intelligent and wild tongue, an endlessly working critical mind, and a whirling malinalli spirit focused in her writing to describe a profound crisis of personal and collective identity and to stimulate deeper and ancestral spiritual forces to heal this same crisis.

By terming her writings "loca-centric" we mean that her thought straddles, balances, and shifts lines of vision, plays the ends against the middle—paradoxically critiquing and occupying both—and works to make painful peripheries new centers of interest, power, and signification. This loca-centrism can be alternately self-destructive and self-creative. On the one hand, her loca-centric writings show us how dominant cultures and master narratives work repressively, not only economically and politically but also spiritually, against those who dwell in the borderlands—"en La Frontera." She writes, "I have so internalized the borderlands conflict that sometimes I feel like one [culture] cancels out the other and we are zero, nothing, no one."[13] On the other hand, just as her self is momentarily dissolved by the terrors of life in the borderlands, she draws upon traditions of resistance and puts her untamed tongue and multiple languages to use—creating a new mythic history for la frontera. She uses her ecstatic states to challenge any authority—white, brown, male—even her own authority as a writer. She lapses, into "an awakened dream," a state "of psychic unrest" in which she does battle with herself and heals herself all at once. Her trance states allow her to create a new kind of center, from the "oro del barrio" (literally, the "gold of the barrio")—the contentious narratives and ignored histories of peoples of the borderlands. Like the Aztec singers she admires, she weaves dreams, ecstasies, and obscured histories into spiritual centers for the New Mestiza cosmos.

Loco Excursus Uno

In this loco-centric sense, we are inspired by the work and musical style of José Cuellar, also known as Dr. Loco. His early work with the band Dr. Loco and the Original Corrido Boggie Band, and more recently Dr. Loco's Rockin' Jalapeño Band, is an upbeat version of a Chicano praise of folly and a musical example of malinalli creativity. His repertoire has grown to include a rich variety of borderlands music, including blues, New Orleans jazz, *corridos*, *rancheras*, salsa, *cumbia*, Reggatón, and more. Just consider José Cuellar's stage name as an example of loco-centrism. On the one hand, Dr. Loco's name represents the legitimate, the professional, mode of social existence. His "Dr." resonates with educational and medical skill, publications, knowledge, and healing associated with the official handle. He is university centered and credentialed, and he can move in the reputable realms of society and "higher" education. On the other hand, Dr. Loco affirms the rearranged, the one deemed crazy, the social rebel, the trickster, the clown, the seeker of *other modes* of knowledge, and the disrupter of traditional modes of knowledge. As a "loco" he is socially illegitimate, disreputable, and dangerous whose only real credential is his ability to scandalize and challenge. Taken together, however his name is a "dialogic structure," a kind of malinalli—and anyone who has seen him perform, dance, and play a range of instruments (flute, ocarina, sax, accordion) sees a living "revolving double helix" Chicano dialogue in action. The name and the music with bilingual songs and multiple rhythmic styles, songs such as "I Feel Chingon" (a takeoff of James Brown's "I Feel Good"), "Homegirl de La Misión" (a takeoff on "Girl from Ipanema"), "Chuco Suave," "Muevete," "Las Revolucionarias," and the awesome "Nosotros Venceremos / We Shall Overcome" in Xoca style represent many of the different and opposed voices of Chicano history and experience. He takes these *opposed voices* and brings them into a linked conversation. Listen to his version of the song "Framed" and discover the shamanic symbolism of "La Semilla." And his "Look a Pye Pye" is a loco-centric Chicano menu for curing the blues.

But it is important to note that Dr. Loco's name and musical discourse and Anzaldúa's loca-narratives have many voices, souls, and tones. As Anzaldúa and Loco show, in order to navigate the borderlands Chicanas and Chicanos must play with the vocabularies and languages at hand, including standard English, invented Spanglish, television Spanish, grandparents' Spanish, and the new Spanish/English inventions that are taking place all the time.[14] Anzaldúa writes about this "loco-language" situation when she lists her languages, which include (1) standard English, (2) working-class English and slang, (3) standard Spanish, (4) standard Mexican Spanish, (5) north Mexican Spanish dialect, (6) Chicano Spanish (Texas, Arizona, New Mexico, and California have regional variations), (7) Tex-Mex Spanish, (8) *pachuco* or calo.[15] In different ways, both Anzaldúa's ecstasies and Dr. Loco's music have centers; they have hearts and rhythms which are technically polished, but they are loco, always center and periphery *and the spaces in between*, always critical of authority in order to unmask it and to subvert its limits while performing a new style of creativity.

Intimations of Shamanism and the Borderlands

> Shamanism is a religious phenomenon centered on the shaman, an ecstatic figure believed to have power to heal the sick and to communicate with the world beyond. —ANZALDÚA, *Borderlands/La Frontera*, 19.

Vilmos Dioszegi, in his *Encyclopedia Britannica* article on shamanism, enhances his definition with a description of traits that include (1) sensitive, mercurial, and sometimes troubled individuals who have (2) developed techniques to go into ecstatic trances and communicate with spirits and (3) form relations, including sexual relations with spirit guides who have *chosen* the individual through dreams. This choice by the spirits sometimes involves the torture of the shaman and the breaking of the shaman's resistance, resulting in periods of illness. The shaman uses techniques to (4) periodically go into trance states which may be like death and dismemberment and (5) involve flights of the soul into the underworld or the sky for further instruction or communication. The shaman (6) has instruments such as drums, rattles, or gourds to create songs, broaden language, and lure others into the shamanic imagination.[16]

If we draw on Diosezegi's model to interpret Anzaldúa's "borderlands," the parallels appear immediately. Her extraordinary sensitivity to language, suffering, sounds, sights, and feelings is remarkable. Her narrative of a rich and complex sexuality reflects her suffering and satisfactions. Anzaldúa tells us that the borderlands are places of individual and collective suffering, demanding extraordinary aids. She speaks of the "herida abierta" [open wound] where the Third World grates against the first and bleeds." Her early chapters are framed with descriptions of Mexica spirit guides. Her muse is the ancient Mesoamerican wind god Ehecatl, who whispers to her and helps her to make sense of life in the border-lands, "her home, this thin edge of barbed wire." And, it is the oppressive pain of life in the borderlands that fuels Anzaldúa's constant rediscovery of her flesh-and-blood capacity for rebellion, resistance, and subversion. She articulates all these elements through descriptions of her religious experiences and religious language. She realized early in her life that the "Shadow Beast" possessed her. And that it

> refuses to take orders from outside authorities. It refuses to take orders from my conscious will, it threatens the sovereignty of my rulership. It is that part of me that hates constraints of any kind, even those self-imposed. At the least hint of limitations on my time or space by others, it kicks out with both feet. Bolts.[17]

One authority she bolts from is the church and Marian images that de-fine the good woman as either submissive to her husband or asexual, while the woman who rebels is a *mujer mala*, a bad woman, prostitute, or witch. Her writing not only denies this destructive dual view of women, but also actively explores complex and ambivalent views of femininity, gender, and identity. She writes about the profound fear humans have of the super-natural, what she calls "the divine and the undivine," and about how the feminine is often associated with the undivine. Her prose is populated by images of monsters, hermaphrodites, half-and-half people who possess supernatural powers. In language remarkably resembling Mircea Eliade's discussion of duality in *The Two and the One*, where Mephistopheles and the Androgyne achieve higher states of knowledge, Anzaldúa writes:

> There is something compelling about being both male and female, about having an entry into both worlds. Contrary to some psychiatric tenets, half and halfs are not suffering from a confusion of sexual identity, or even from a confusion of gender. What we are suffering from is an ab-solute despot duality that says we are able to be only one or the other. It claims that human nature is limited and cannot evolve into something better. But I, like other queer people, am two in one body, both male and female. I am the embodiment of the *hieros gamos*, the coming together of opposite qualities within.[18]

The striking similarities between Eliade's prose and Anzaldúa's meditation on her half-and-half identity suggest a conscious use on her part of the religious imagery of the union of grand dualities—of sky and earth, rain and land, male and female, king and queen. Anzaldúa brilliantly employs this image to formulate a spiritual vision of wholeness—a New Mestizaje. She portrays herself in this passage as a person made up of a colossal contradictory union that gives her access to an alternative form of knowledge, what we are calling a "*loca*-centric" form of knowledge.

Narrative descriptions of her techniques to acquire a religious vision continue in her chapter "Entering into the Serpent," where personal encounters with serpents constitute an initiatory ordeal that reveal her personal connection to the Aztec goddess Coatlicue, "Lady of the Serpent Skirt." In the first episode she recounts her mother's warning, "No vayas al escusado en lo oscuro" (Don't go to the outhouse in the dark) because "a snake will crawl into your *nalgas*, make you pregnant."[19] She is in the outhouse and imagines falling through the hole into the excrement below. Her imagined descent into the underworld is followed by her fear of stepping on a big black slithering snake. In the second episode she is actually bitten by a rattlesnake while chopping cotton. Fortunately her boot protects her and absorbs the venom while her shrieking mother dismembers the writhing body of the snake. She describes how, after she buried the rattles of the serpent between the rows of cotton, she took parts of the snake's body to her room and became possessed by the spirit of the serpent.

> That night I watched the windowsill, watched the moon dry the blood on the tail, dreamed rattler fangs filled my mouth, scales covered my body. In the morning I saw through snake eyes, felt snake blood course through my body. The serpent, mi tono, my animal counterpart. I was immune to its venom. Forever immune.[20]

Descriptions of dreams of possession by an animal are common shamanic tropes, especially in many rural communities in Mexico and South America.[21] Anzaldúa goes on to describe many more signs from serpents, leading her to declare, "I look for omens everywhere" because they reveal "the other mode of consciousness [which] facilitates images from the soul and the unconscious through dreams and the imagination." While the experience of possession provides her with the religious insight that the Virgin of Guadalupe was a dismembered Spanish version of Coatlicue, she tells us that "the Catholic Church and other institutionalized religions impoverish all life, beauty, pleasure," inhibiting access to a more profound mode of consciousness.[22] For Anzaldúa, access to a healing transcendent reality is acquired through *la facultad*, the capacity to see in surface phenomena the presences of spirit helpers, goddesses and other counterparts.[23]

Carrasco's Encounter with Shamanic Techniques
and Ecstatic Knowledge

As you will recall, shamanic experience allows the individual to travel in the supernatural world and form relations with gods, demons, spirits of the dead. Mircea Eliade has described this ecstatic knowledge.

The content of these first ecstatic experiences, although comparatively rich, almost always includes one or more of the following themes: dismemberment of the body, followed by a renewal of the internal organs and viscera; ascent to the sky and dialogue with the gods or spirits; descent to the underworld and conversations with the spirits and souls of dead shamans.[24]

The career of the shaman's ecstatic life has been described as commonly beginning with a spiritual crisis and a rupture from society. The lifelong career of the shaman, which may include personal oscillations between severe illness and healing, is often dedicated to service to the community through healing. Davíd Carrasco experienced shamanic loco-centrism firsthand while a graduate student in Chicago.

Loco Excursus Dos:
Carrasco with the Niño Fidencio (in his own words)

While a graduate student at the University of Chicago, I was also a member of the *misión* of El Santo Niño Fidencio Constantino. Every Thursday night, members of the misión, many of whom were undocumented immigrants, would gather for a five- or six-hour séance and healing session in the attic of a Mexican home in the Little Village neighborhood of Chicago. The central force in these gatherings was the spirit/*materia* of Niño José Fidencio Sintora Constantino, the Mexican healer who was born in Guanajuato in 1898 and had lived, preached, healed, and physically died in Espinazo, Nuevo León, a small village in northeastern Mexico, in 1938. According to the stories of this group, Niño Fidencio fell into a deep, mysterious trance; physicians, believing him dead prematurely, autopsied the body. When his spirit, which had traveled to heaven, descended to enter the body, he saw the destruction that had taken place and decided that his surviving spirit would thenceforth enter into numerous *materias*, or people who would communicate Niño Fidencio's healing powers to the needy. In Chicago, there were two *misiones* organized around Niño Fidencio materias who would lead long healing séances each week, and I joined the one located in Little Village.

The healing ceremonies always began when the materia entered an attic room, where we waited quietly, sitting on a few benches. After each of us kissed his hand amidst murmured greetings, he knelt before a home-made altar which, in the beginning of my time in the misión, consisted of a simple table supporting a picture of Niño Fidencio. In it he held a white cat, a bowl with water and eggs, some flowers, and a crucifix. He was always attended by a female assistant. Stimulated somehow by the repeated droning of the "Ave Maria" in Spanish, which sometimes went on for ten minutes, he suddenly fell into an ecstatic fit marked by intense and even violent, though rhythmic physical motions, jerks, and flailings. This ecstatic transition was always climaxed with a piercing scream that announced the descent into his body of Niño Fidencio's spirit. The materia then fell into a gentle, even sweet mood, and was quietly dressed in ritual robes and a hat by an assistant who also served as an interpreter. When he turned around to face us, his kneeling congregation, we could see his eyes rolled back up into his skull and with the whites of his eyes facing us. Then, in a falsetto voice he would announce how he had traveled from the luminous house of God in heaven to bring us blessings, miracles, and proofs of God's love and healing power. What followed, in small variations over the next two years, were intense physical healing rites that involved flowers, eggs, water, branches, massages, slapping, cupping, private audiences and public instructions, jokes, clowning, and occasionally intense smoke and fires.

When certain individuals were suffering what the materia interpreted as spiritual or social danger, a more powerful healing spirit—such as Don Pedrito Jaramillo or El Pluma Roja (an Indian spirit)—would descend more vigorously, sometimes violently, into the materia to carry out specific healings.

At the time I was studying shamanic traditions with Mircea Eliade and Charles Long at the University of Chicago and was able to compare scholarly literature about ecstasy with the trance states, possessions, ecstatic songs, physical manipulations, androgynous symbols, and blessings of the misión that I witnessed each week. In a number of ways, the Niño Fidencio taught us magical techniques for healing our pains, diseases, and broken hearts. He walked on our backs, had us take tea baths, and recite midnight prayers in which we called him into our presence. He manipulated our bones and went into ecstatic trances that often reached a physical ferocity as though to dramatize the suffering forces within us. This combination of scholarly and personal experience at first challenged my Protestant-biased understanding of how religious knowledge, power, and love become accessible in people's lives. As time went on, I came to realize that the Mexican community through these ecstatic practices had alternative ways of expressing its multiple sufferings and to gain access to much needed forms of spiritual succor and healing. This "loco-centric" experience of ecstatic healing in a secret location in an attic in the Mexican neighborhood initiated me into a wider range of religious practices in the Chicano community. I remember in particular the night that the Niño Fidencio "cupped" an area on my back where an illness was residing. (Cupping is a technique of squeezing lemon juice in and on the edges of a glass, lighting in on fire, and quickly placing it on one's body, resulting in a vacuum that bonds the glass to the body and sucks the flesh slightly upward into the glass while at the same time singeing the area.) I was known to the group as a local teacher with credentials, and one woman, seeing me kneeling before the altar with a towel covering the protruding glass on my upper back, said to another, "Ese Senor Davíd es un Maestro, verdad?" Her *camarada* answered, "Sí, los profesores también necesitan el Santo Niño." On this occasion I was a "Dr. Loco." The songs, dances, and healing techniques of Niño Fidencio introduced me to the experience of synesthesia, the union of the senses (the incense, the prayers, the *gritos*, the songs, the body work) as techniques to access a physical experience of the Holy. It was a form of "loco-knowledge."

Shamans and Madness

One question that accompanies many studies of shamanism is the pathological nature of ecstatic initiation: people take magical flights, talk with spirits, go into sustained trances, and uncover other modes of consciousness. Are shamans inhabited by a psychological illness, or profound *locura*? While we are using the term *loca-centric* to describe Anzaldúa's writing, we do not intend to reduce her work to locura. We emphasize that it is precisely her wild serpentine visions that ground her and allow her to produce her creative language that she employs to heal and reconstitute herself in the chaos of la frontera. Scholars of religion have often described shamanism as a "sacred madness" but acknowledge that

> [it is] unacceptable to assimilate shamanism to any kind of mental disease. . . . Like any other religious vocation, the shamanic vocations is manifested by a crisis, a temporary derangement of the future shaman's spiritual equilibrium . . . but the shaman is not only a sick man; he is above all, a sick man who has been cured, who has succeeded in curing

himself. . . . There is always a cure, a control, an equilibrium brought about by the actual practice of shamanism.[25]

Anzaldúa's descriptions of her shamanism tell of her spiritual journey through disequilibrium and the development of a spoken or written poetics that reflect and contain the pain of these ordeals.

The Coatlicue State

Patterns of shamanic ecstasy in Anzaldúa's *Borderlands/La Frontera* are to be found most clearly in the chapters entitled "La *herencia de* Coatlicue/The Coatlicue State" and "*Tlilli, Tlapalli*/The Path of the Red and Black Ink." The chapter on the "Coatlicue State" begins with the crisis of the death of her father. Her mother covers the mirrors in her house so that their souls will not escape to the place where the souls of the dead live. She tells us that she was first visited by the image of Coatlicue when she was two or three. She was "devoured" by the goddess and fell into the underworld. After her trance, the look on her parents' faces at her difference told her she had the "Mark of the Beast" on her and "something deformed with evil inside." Speaking in the third person, she is overcome with a colossal fear she describes in this manner—it is a religious chant, a description of a mythic dismemberment and lost-ness:

> She has this fear that she has no names that she has many names that she doesn't know her names She has this fear that she's an image that comes and goes clearing and darkening the fear that she's the dream work inside someone else's skull She has this fear that if she takes off her clothes shoves her brain aside peels off her skin that if she drains the blood vessels strips the flesh from the bone flushes out the marrow. She has this fear that when she does reach herself turns around to embrace herself a lion's or witch's or serpent's head will turn around swallow her and grin. She has this fear that if she digs into herself she won't find anyone that when she gets "there" she won't find her notches on the trees the birds will have eaten all the crumbs She has this fear that she won't find the way back.[26]

This is the beginning of the Coatlicue State, a rupture in the everyday world where she has lost crucial parts of her self in a form of spiritual dismemberment. She loses her name, skin, brain, flesh, marrow, and, most important, her way home. She tells us that her soul, due in part to a life plagued by a state of *susto*, is frightened out of her body and driven into the underground, a thousand-foot drop into *miktlan* (the lowest level of the Mexica underworld), where she wallows, sinking deeper and deeper. But in the real spirit of a shaman whose dismemberment is only one "half" of her quest, this journey is part of her "increment of consciousness." Listen to her language about the Coatlicue State and the acquisition of knowledge:

> I am again an alien in new territory. And again, and again. It is a dry birth, a breech birth, a screaming birth, one that fights her every inch of the way. . . . It is her reluctance to cross over, to make a hole in the fence and walk across, to cross the river to take that flying leap into the dark, that drives her to escape that force into the fecund cave of her imagination where she cradled in the arms of Coatlicue, who will never let her go. . . . Darkness, my night. There is darkness and there is darkness. . . . In attending to this first darkness I am led back to the mystery of the Origin.[27]

Thus it is precisely when things become their most chaotic and uncertain that Anzaldúa finds comfort and solace in the arms of Coatlicue. And, it is precisely out of this struggle that she acquires a religious language and discovers a wholeness. In her words: "Suddenly *I* feel everything rushing to a center, a nucleus. All the lost pieces of myself come flying from the deserts, and the mountains and the valleys, magnetized toward that center. *Completa.*"[28]

Anzaldúa tells us that "the ability of the story (prose and poetry) to transform the storyteller and the listener into something or someone else is shamanistic. The writer, as shape changer, is a *nahual*, a shaman."[29] And she employs this method in several chapters—telling the story of her vision, infusing it with fantastic elements, and playfully articulating her transformative experience through the use of the "eight languages" that she speaks. Her central technique is revealed to us and to her when she compares herself to a singer, an Aztec singer whose use of *difrasismos* (two words used for a single concept) enabled direct communication with divinities. The key to this communication with supernatural beings is presented in a section entitled "The Shamanic State." She writes:

> . . . I "trance." I used to think I was going crazy or that I was having hallucinations. But now I realize it *is* my job, my calling to traffic in images. . . . When I don't write the images down for several days or weeks or months, I get physically ill. . . . I sometimes get sick when I *do* write. . . . I need to be alone, or in a sensory-deprived state. I plug *up* my ears with

wax, put on my black cloth eye-shades, lie horizontal and unmoving, in a state between sleeping and waking, mind and body locked into my fantasy. I am held prisoner by it. My body is experiencing events. In the beginning it is like being in a movie theater, as pure spectator. Gradually I become so engrossed with activities, the conversations that I become a participant in the drama. I have to struggle to "disengage" or escape from my "animated story," . . . Thought shifts, reality shifts, gender shifts; one person metamorphoses into another in a world where people fly through the air, heal from mortal wounds.[30]

Notice the language of this passage. Anzaldúa's religious vision is dedicated to the healing of the wounds of the borderlands. The Chicano community is a wounded community, and she employs an array of language strategies to try and bring healing through her voices. Here we see a *religious* in-between space that she has inhabited, and that underlies the colonial in-between space that Mignolo applauds.

Critical Thoughts

Let us return to the claim for her success made by Walter Mignolo when he states that she created a "a space in between *from where* to think rather than a hybrid space *to talk about*." This autobiographical hybrid space is indeed a great accomplishment, and we would like to conclude our essay with these reflections on her religious vision.

1. Anzaldúa claims an interior awareness of the Mexica goddess Coatlicue, the colossal "Lady of the Serpent Skirt" who gave birth to the Aztec war god Hummingbird on the Left at the Mountain of the Serpent. While she has made an initial contact with the indigenous traditions that speak of Coatlicue, she has missed several relevant opportunities to study Coatlicue more thoroughly. In 1978, the colossal monolith depicting Coyolxauhqui, the dismembered daughter of Coatlicue, was excavated in Mexico City. Discussions of Coatlicue without a discussion of Coyolxauhqui, her fate, her stone image, and its central meaning in Aztec religious symbolism are problematic given her dedication to this myth cycle and imager.

The moon goddess Coyolxauhqui, "She of the Bells" leads her 400 siblings in an attack against their mother, Coatlicue, to punish her for a magically induced but illegitimate pregnancy. Just as the mother is attacked, a newborn male child, fully grown and adorned for war, immediately attacks his siblings, dismembering Coyolxauhqui, his own sister, and killing most of his other warrior-siblings. This violent event, in which a woman gives birth to an archetypal, patriarchal warrior, became one of the legitimations for mass human sacrifice, including the ritual killing of children and women among the Mexicas.

Imagine what Anzaldúa's creative mind could do with the narrative of this song had she engaged it through the easily accessible accounts and scholarship about this fuller rendition of the "Coatlicue State."[31] Although Anzaldúa is explicitly self-conscious of the fact that she is not an Azteca but a twentieth-century Chicana, we believe that the degree of her accountability to the cultures and traditions she is appropriating is a live and important question. Thus, we would amend Mignolos's claim: while Anzaldúa gives us a model of a "space-in-between" from which to speak about postcolonial realities, her work and those of us who follow her must show a stronger obligation to knowing the parent cultures she is drawing from, lest her and our appropriations turn out to be less a form of cultural resistance and more an unintended artistic and religious form of colonialism.

2. But Anzaldúa's imagination and profound gifts as a writer have provided a powerful model for discussions of Chicana religious experience and expression. The immense popularity of her writings clearly shows that conventional theologies do not necessarily express the religious concerns and imaginations of individuals and communities in the borderlands. For Chicanas and Chicanos, trance states, dreams, stories, snakes, labor, myths, histories, and especially *language*—the many languages of Chicano life—provide an orientation, a power, and an opening to understanding political oppression and liberation that draw on religious realities. Her insistence on the importance of ecstatic knowledge and her open avowal *of* shamanic experiences reveal that the "hybrid space" she occupies is built upon her rich *loca-centric* religious imagination.

3. Anzaldúa is loca-centric. This loca-centrism, both grounded in traditions and critically, wildly rereading and reinventing the traditions in ways that turn misery and oppression into creative insights and new words, is the source of a New Mestizaje. Her religious vision provides a powerful model for understanding the role of religious imaginations in the borderlands as a source of human good within and beyond the Raza (Race) community. And we hope that scholars will begin to take this central feature of her oeuvre seriously and give it the recognition that it deserves.

Notes

1. Walter Mignolo, *The Darker Side of the Renaissance: Literacy, Territoriality, and Colonization* (Ann Arbor: University of Michigan Press, 1995), xiii.

2. Barbara Harlow, "Sites of Struggle: Immigration, Deportation, Prison, and Exile," in *Criticism in the Borderlands: Studies in Chicano Literature, Culture, and Ideology*, ed. Héctor Calderón and José David Saldívar (Durham, N.C.: Duke University Press, 1991), 149–63.

3. Renato Rosaldo, *Culture and Truth: The Remaking of Social Analysis* (Boston: Beacon Press, 1993).

4. Of the many important critical essays interpreting Anzaldúa's work, see, especially, Maria Among Lugones, "On *Borderlands/La Frontera:* An interpretive Essay," *Hypatia* 7, no. 4 (fall 1992): 31–37; Ann Louise Keating, "Myth Smashers, Myth Makers: (Re)Visionary Techniques in the Works of Paula Gunn Allen, Gloria Anzaldúa, and Audre Lorde," in *Critical Essays: Gay and Lesbian Writers of Color*, ed. Emmanuel S. Nelson (New York: Haworth Press, 1993), 73–95; Regenia Gagnier, "Feminist Autobiography in the 1980s," *Feminist Studies* 17, no. 1 (spring 1991): 135–48; Norma Alarcón, "The Theoretical Subject(s) of *This Bridge Called My Back* and Anglo-American Feminism" and Sonia Saldívar Hull, "Feminism on the Border: From Gender Politics to Geopolitics," in Calderón and Saldívar, *Criticism in the Borderlands*, 28–39, 203–20.

5. See Lawrence E. Sullivan's "Sound and Sense: Toward a Hermeneutics of Performance," *History of Religions* 26, no. 1 (1986): 1–33.

6. Gloria Anzaldúa, *Borderlands/La Frontera: The New Mestiza* (San Francisco: Aunt Lute Books, 1987), first page of unpaginated preface.

7. For the trickster tradition reflected phenomenologically in Anzaldúa, see Robert Pelton's study of the West African trickster, including "Not-to-Be-Contradicted" in his *The Trickster in West Africa: A Study of Mythic Irony and Sacred Delight* (Berkeley: University of California Press, 1980).

8. It would be interesting to compare elements of Anzaldúa's narrative with the magical realism of certain Latin American writers. Is she a Chicana "magical realist"?

9. Davíd Carrasco, "Myth, Cosmic Terror, and the Templo Mayor," in *The Great Temple of Tenochtitlán: Center and Periphery in the Aztec World*, ed. Johanna Broda, Davíd Carrasco, and Eduardo Matos Moctezuma (Berkeley: University of California Press, 1986), 124–62. See also Carrasco, "Jaguar Christians in the Contact Zone," in *Enigmatic Powers: Syncretism with African and Indigenous Peoples' Religions among Latinos*, ed. Anthony M. Stevens-Arroyo and Andrés I. Pérez y Mena (New York: Bildner Center for Western Hemisphere Studies, 1995), 69–79. This publication is part of the important book series generated by PARAL, the Program for the Analysis of Religion Among Latinos.

10. Carrasco, "A Perspective for a Study of Religious Dimensions in Chicano Experience: *Bless Me, Ultima* as a Religious Text," *Aztlán: Journal of Chicano Studies* 13, nos. 1 and 2 (1982): 195–21.

11. Charles H. Long, *Significations: Signs, Symbols, and Images in the Interpretation of Religion* (Philadelphia: Fortress Press, 1986), 174.

12. For an appreciation of the diverse and sustained power of the term *logos* as meaning "reason," "word," and "wisdom" among Western scholars of religion, see Jean Pépin, "Logos," in *The Encyclopedia of Religion*, editor-in-chief, Mircea Eliade, 9: 9–15 (New York: Macmillan, 1987). As Kees W. Bolle points out in his article "Myth: An Overview," in 10:261–73, *myth*, mythos, or its Greek root, *l'muthos*, is contrasted with *logos* through its mode as a story or narrative. While Anzaldúa's approach draws upon both logos and mythos, it emerges from a shamanic imagination that is "loco-" or "loca-centric."

13. Anzaldúa, *Borderlands/La Frontera*, 63.

14. Anzaldúa's multiple languages, a more complex linguistic demography, may contribute to a renewal of social democracy as represented in Doris Sommer's comments about code-switching. "This is certainly not an argument for a Tower of Babel that will quake and crumble with the frustrations of incomprehension. Instead I want to defend code-switching as one of Democracy's most effective speech acts, along with translation and speaking English through heavy accents, because they all slow down communication and labor through the difficulties of understanding and reaching agreement." Personal communication.

15. Anzaldúa, *Borderlands/La Frontera*, 16.

16. Vilmos Dioszegi, "Shamanism," *Encyclopedia Britannica*.

17. Anzaldúa, *Borderlands/La Frontera*, 16.

18. Mircea Eliade, *The Two and the One* (Chicago: University of Chicago Press, 1979). Anzaldúa, *Borderlands/La Frontera*, 19.

19. Ibid., 25.

20. Ibid., 26.

21. Ibid., 26. She discusses shamanic visions here.

22. Ibid., 37.

23. Anzaldúa tells us that she saw the actual Aztec statue of Coatlicue in New York City at the Museum of Natural History. However, it is unlikely that the colossal statue of Coatlicue ever traveled to New York City. Mexican archaeologists tell me that what Anzaldúa saw was a plaster replica which, nonethless served to inspire her visions.

24. Mircea Eliade, *Shamanism: Archaic Techniques of Ecstasy*, trans. Willard R. Trask (New York: Bollingen Foundation, 1964), 34.

25. Ibid., xii, 27, 29.

26. Anzaldúa, *Borderlands/La Frontera*, 43.

27. Ibid., 48–49.

28. Ibid., 51.

29. Ibid., 66.

30. Ibid., 69–70.

31. I had the opportunity to introduce the Nobel Laureate in Literature, Toni Morrison, to Coatlicue and her daughter, Coyolxauhqui, in February 1994 when I took her to the Museo del Templo Mayor in Mexico City. Sometime before

that trip, I had recited the song of Coatlicue, Huitzilopochtli, and Coyolxauhqui to Professor Morrison. I was astonished by Morrison's first comment upon seeing the Coyolxauhqui stone, an eleven-foot-in-diameter circular monolith depicting the dismembered goddess with streams of precious blood flowing from her wounds. Morrison, who had obviously been thinking of the story of the murder of Coyolxauhqui by her brother Huitzilopochtli, looked over the railing at the massive sculpture below, paused only briefly, and exclaimed, "There she is, Miss America."

10

Voice and Vision in Chicana Religious Practice

The Literary Re-elaborations of Mary Helen Ponce,

Denise Chávez, and Sandra Cisneros

As U.S. Latino writers work to reverse the melting-pot model of integration into U.S. society, they frequently foreground ethnic cultural markers that distinguish them from mainstream culture. Religious motifs are one such marker that both facilitate narrative memory and serve as totemic signifiers of membership in a group. More important, however, these motifs are frequently part of a larger network of popular Latino religious practice with much broader functions than the mnemonic or totemic. In much contemporary Chicano narrative the religious also emerges as a sense of social ethics and a new moral vision, often quite different from those of orthodox Catholicism. Issues of social justice and the concerns of immigrants, feminists, gays, the landless, and other marginalized groups are articulated within the alternative religious practices narrativized in this new writing.

As part of a brief overview, I would cite the writing of Chicanos such as Demetria Martínez, Lucha Corpi, Ana Castillo, Denise Chávez, Roberta Fernández, Sandra Cisneros, Pat Mora, Mary Helen Ponce, Sylvia López-Medina, John Rechy, Rudolfo Anaya, and Tomás Rivera, along with the Dominican American Julia Alvarez, the Cuban American Cristina García, and the mainland Puerto Rican Judith Ortiz Cofer.[1] In the 1994 novel *Mother Tongue*, for example, Demetria Martínez rearticulates Catholicism and popular Chicano religious imagery in terms of the social concerns of Central American refugees in New Mexico, who themselves had reread the Bible in the mode of liberation theology. In the novel *Alburquerque*,

Anaya shows the connection between popular alternative religious practices that have been preserved in New Mexico since the colonial period, and the land grant violations that occurred after the U.S. takeover in 1848; the lost lands stand in contrast to the sacred earth preserved and revered at Chimayó and the many popular traditions that have survived as the "core of the onion . . . [that] will endure forever."[2] As the characters travel on a Holy Week pilgrimage to Chimayó and the village of Córdova, Anaya ethnographically describes alternative religious practices, such as *promesas* (vows or promises) and *mandas* (vows); the singing of *alabados* (hymns); the bearing of the cross; the carving of *santos* (wooden figures of religious figures); and the semiotic display of discarded crutches, crosses, and baby shoes for the Santo Niño de Atocha and the Black Christ of Esquipulas; these motifs are the semes of a narrative grammar of deep spirituality. Anaya's representation stands in contrast to an opposing set of images he critiques in the text—the tourist photographs and TV news accounts of these Holy Week practices in which people "think it's a show . . . [and] don't know what it means to us."[3]

The description of religious practices in some of these texts involves an ethnographic dimension in which writers embed explanations in the text to aid a variety of "outsiders," who range from the non-Chicano or non-Catholic readers to Chicanos and other Catholics who themselves might be unfamiliar with certain popular religious practices. In *Hoyt Street*, for example, Mary Helen Ponce must not only explain the practice of repaying mandas for those unfamiliar with the alternative Latino practice. She also includes explanations of the pre–Vatican II Catholic liturgies and customs that predominated in her childhood, but are no longer part of the cultural competence of Chicanos and others born after 1960. And Demetria Martínez must explain the alternate Catholicism of liberation theology and its connection to the struggle for social justice in Central America to a heterogeneous group of "outsiders," both Chicano and non-Chicano. There are no privileged readers of these narratives who can be counted on to have "insider" knowledge of every aspect of religious culture in the accounts.[4]

Like many theorists of subculture and popular expression, Orlando Espín has argued that popular religious practice rereads official doctrines and rites, disregarding certain elements and giving a central role to other beliefs, rituals, and behaviors that the official religious hierarchy deemphasizes. Rather than completely abandoning official symbols, popular religion shares motifs, an ethos, and foundational figures and events with orthodox religion.[5] Chicana narrativists engage in a similar rearticulation of Catholicism, emphasizing popular practices and alternatively interpreting mainstream symbols and doctrine. In some cases, writers carry this further, refashioning even the popular practices in light of contemporary social concerns. Writers such as Denise Chávez and Sandra Cisneros reconfigure symbols and practices with both official and popular variations such as the figure of the Virgin of Guadalupe and the novena, as well as popular religious practices such as the *ofrenda* (offering), the *milagrito* (small wooden figures symbolizing a miracle), and the *retablo* (exvoto painting).

Both official religion and popular alternative practices have focused on the body as a site of both control and recuperation. Official Catholicism simultaneously valorizes and devalorizes the body. On the positive end lie the Eucharistic anthropophagous symbolism and valorization of Christ's corporeality, metaphors of community in which members constitute a large social body, and the strong role of the senses in liturgical ceremonies and pedagogical narratives designed early on to draw in illiterate worshipers. If the sacred word could not be read firsthand, visual, auditory, olfactory, tactile, and gustatory means of representation would communicate religious tenets. But the church simultaneously devalorizes the body as the site of sin and self-denial, even as it argues for respect of the body as the figurative "temple of the Holy Spirit."[6]

The three writers I study here emphasize a recuperation of the denied or repressed body in their ample religious imagery. While all five senses come into play in their narrativized religious remembrances, voice and vision predominate, often in transgressive recuperations of official religious verbal and visual culture.

The Seen and the Unseen: The Disrupting Body in Visual Religious Culture

For Mary Helen Ponce, the remembrance of religion is overlain with images of the disrupting body, its refusal, even within the sacred site of the church ceremony, to remain within the social constraints set for it. In *The Wedding*, grotesque eruptions of bodily functions turn the church ceremony inside out, in a parodic, carnivalesque simulacrum in which nature overpowers culture.[7] Ponce's narrative humorously celebrates the persistence of the centrifugal against the official forces that attempt to constrain and control transgression. She disturbs one Chicano literary critic by this irreverent portrayal, and by a parallel instance in the autobiography *Hoyt Street*, when she remembers having to take the public blame for an elderly woman's passing gas in church, a sacrifice of the self—parallel to Christ's that allows the dying woman a modicum of respect.[8] Where Ponce is denied the power of speech as a child (and, by extension, by the critic who would prefer she not write about such inappropriate themes), she will assert her right to do so now as an adult writer, recuperating the word for her own ends. In this adult narrative she dares to utter the unspeakable—words such as *pedo* (fart)—that will highlight the intrusion of the body into the space of the sacred.

The numerous segments on religion in Ponce's *Hoyt Street* attest to the rich community involvement in religious activity in Pacoima, California, in the 1930s and 1940s—both official religious ceremonies and alternative Mexican practices sometimes integrated into the church. A number of Ponce's remembered religious images involve the interplay between the seen and the unseen and the underlying repressed sexuality of some religious display. She describes her pleasurable memories of Holy Week ceremonies, especially the washing-of-the-feet ritual that allowed her the rare opportunity to view the priest's and altar boys' usually concealed feet. Her desire to see the hidden parts of the Other's body is heightened by the excessive clothing of priests and sisters, and she and her classmates— with an excitement parallel to that displayed at the baring of the priest's feet—try unsuccessfully to dislodge the elaborate head covering of one sister on the playground. Ponce elaborates the tension between the seen and unseen again in describing her role in the daily church processions in honor of the Blessed Virgin in May; and, finally, in her account of the covering and uncovering of the church statues in Holy Week, she embeds further sexual innuendo into her account:

> The candles flickered, the bells filled the room, the flowers shone bright. Suddenly Don Crispin, dressed in a spotless white shirt, appeared from inside the sacristy; in his hands was a long pole. He approached the Guardian Angel and lifted the purple covering; then he did the same with all the other statues. . . . I stared at my friends who had been in hiding, delighted with how refreshed and happy they looked. Even Jesus, his bleeding heart still dangling to the side, appeared less sad.[9]

Ponce emphasizes the corporeal and visceral nature of much visual religious display as it oscillates between the seen and the unseen to heighten the religious experience.

Deploying an ethnographic tone with a visually detailed description of customs by an insider addressed to outsiders, Ponce devotes a section to Doña Magda which focuses on alternative religious practices such as *altares*, shrines to nonofficial religious figures, and the repaying of mandas to saints. In addition to wearing numerous medals and scapulars, Doña Magda prays novenas and fulfills mandas in person, in return for "miracles" received. Ponce describes in rich visual detail the three home altars in Doña Magda's bedroom to El Santo Niño de Atocha, La Santísima Virgen del Perpetuo Socorro, and the Virgen de Guadalupe and the numerous votive candles, framed santos, rosaries, and other religious artifacts displayed there. As Turner has argued—for example, in chapter 7 of this volume—the display of visual representations of religious figures on home altars is a deployment of the body as a central metaphor for the relation between the supernatural and the earthly; altars rely on such bodily representations to bring the spiritual and physical realms together. In effect, Doña Magda's statues reinsert bodily representations of holy figures that she has chosen herself into her alternative, nonofficial religious practice.

When Doña Magda's alternative religious practices enter the public visual space of the official Catholic Church, the new priest tries to quash them. As many in the neighborhood watch Doña Magda coming to church on her knees to fulfill the vow she has made for her son's safety in World War II, Father Mueller stops her at the church door, insisting that her custom is out of date. As a result of this rebuff, the parishioners "snea[k] off" to the Los Angeles Placita and the shrine of the Virgen de San Juan de los Lagos in Sunland to engage in their customary alternative religious practices.

But Father Mueller is not an entirely negative figure. A young priest who replaces the elderly Father Juanito, he brings a new energy to Ponce's parish in the late 1940s, playing jazz on the new church organ, displaying a picture of Duke Ellington on his dresser instead of a religious image, and shouting the transgressive phrase "[ó]rale cabrones [hey, brats]" to loud pachucos who have taunted him with the disrespectful interpellation "Orale, Mickey."[10] Ponce reads the image of the new priest through visual signifiers such as his red, stick-out ears and his sunburned skin when he returns from a day at the beach. With ethnographic explanation that will help readers born after 1960 negotiate the text, Ponce focuses on Father Mueller's revival of pre–Vatican II religious cultural practices that had lost viability during World War II. In this transitional moment before the postconciliar reforms, the new priest revives the traditional *cofradías* (confraternities) and organizes parish *jamaicas*, or bazaars, that Ponce describes through visual motifs.

Mueller encourages the young girls to form a Stella Maris confraternity but instead of engaging in charity work in the community, their role is to appear as a group once a month at Sunday Mass.[11] Relegated to this visual role, the girls fight among each other to be in the front of the procession, in effect, to be the one seen first, and march in public display down the church aisle to the front altar where Father Mueller plays the role of the male surveyor, "beam[ing] his approval."[12]

Ponce focuses further on the tension between the seen and unseen, and on the role of the male surveyor in her religious experience, in describing her role in the daily church processions in May. The pleasure of self-display underlies her enjoyment in marching in the procession that "was like being onstage, with the whole town watching."[13] To be selected for the front of the procession afforded the opportunity to be seen by boys; yet this lucky position represented a repressed mode of self-display, a concealed visibility. The lead girl had to look "pious, humble and pure,"[14] with her head veiled like the nuns, the Virgin Mary, and other female saints: "Dressing up to look like the Virgin Mary was fun. Each time I covered my head with a veil I felt holy, special, like a 'little bride,' or even a child saint."[15] Mary Helen practices attaining this ideal vision of herself in the bathroom mirror at home, engaging at a young age in the process Simone de Beauvoir described of women imagining the implicit approbation of an ideal male surveyor when viewing themselves in the mirror.

Ponce's autobiography depends on a rich intertextual system of verbal and visual narratives about religious figures. In "Catechism," Ponce recounts some of the narratives that fascinated her from the book *The Lives of the Saints*. Especially important to her were the stories about female saints which, with a kind of protofeminism, Mary Helen recognized as countertexts to the predominant male figures of the church. Here also, her experience of religious narrative is closely tied to visual representation.

In an intertextual homology that privileges the visual, Ponce allows the physical appearance of the childhood book about the saints to structure her present narrative. In effect, her readerly experience as a child shaped her preferences for certain saints, her views of her own physical appearance, and ultimately the narrative structure of this section of *Hoyt Street*. Her description of *The Lives of the Saints* begins with its cover image—a beautiful rendering of Saint Teresa whose narrative will then become Mary Helen's favorite. Ponce's remembrances are structured through the cover image, much as her childhood reading experience of the book was. In effect, she has her readers first "see" the cover image as she did as a child so that the visual description of Saint Teresa appears first and accounts for one-half of Ponce's narrative about the saint:

> Saint Teresa . . . was my favorite. She had creamy white skin, blue eyes, and rich auburn hair that fell below her slender shoulders in long, thick waves. She wore a pretty blue robe, which I knew was made of silk, over what resembled a white nightgown. . . . On her delicate feet were tiny slippers, which must have been of silk too.[16]

Similarly, this image will structure Mary Helen's self-perception in later years. On her Confirmation day, measuring herself against the idealized saint, she describes her feelings of inadequacy in her ill-fitting white dress, which she has purposely bought a size too small because of embarrassment about her weight: "I wanted to look like St. Teresa of Avila, known as the Little Flower. I felt pious, holy, and fat."[17] Visual description predominates in Ponce's narratives about religious figures, much as it did in the early classes of catechetical instruction that she recounts here. The nuns taught the biblical narratives using large easel pictures of the stories. Ponce's retelling structures itself homologously:

> In the first illustration, Adam and Eve looked young and healthy on their tropical island. In the second picture, Eve ate an apple, while Adam hid behind a branch; at her feet was the slimy snake. Next we saw Eve crying, while a troubled Adam held her hand; in a corner the sly snake smiled. The lesson ended with Eve clinging to Adam, her blue eyes full of fear and her dark hair flying as they fled the Garden of Eden.[18]

Here Ponce's retelling progresses image by image, much as the classroom story had, so that the visual predominates despite the verbal mode of representation. As in other religious practices, both the seen and the unseen, the told and the untold structure these narratives; Mary Helen and her friends, like most "narratees," perform work themselves to fill in the gaps with images from movies and their own oral counternarratives:

> "Gosh, God sure is mean! He chased Adam and Eve from the pretty garden for nothing!"
> "Yeah."
> "Do you think they were kissing?"
> "Hmmmm, maybe. . . ."

Years later Nancy alluded to what Adam and Eve had *really* done but I never believed her. I thought they were a fine-looking couple who had been unfairly treated.[19]

Performative Voice in the Reconfigured Novena

Although Denise Chávez's experimental one-woman play "Novena narrativas y ofrendas nuevomexicanas" deploys many visual signifiers, I would argue that it recaptures voice as its predominant textual strategy, especially in its published form. When performed, the play adds visual bodily display to its strong emphasis on voice as it recuperates the denied or repressed body of official religious culture. In presenting the oral prayers of nine New Mexican women, Chávez eschews for the most part ethnographic explanation that would help to orient outsiders, choosing instead to present the direct locutions of strongly bilingual characters who often employ Chicano slang. So important is an accurate rendering of voice for Chávez that readers without the requisite cultural and linguistic competence are simply out of luck, clearly not the primary addressees of this work. While briefly mentioning that a novena is a nine-day prayer cycle, Chávez seems unconcerned that many of her readers outside of New Mexico will be unfamiliar with this pre–Vatican II religious ceremony, not now practiced by most U.S. Catholics.[20] In effect, Chávez is transforming a religious rite with both traditional and nontraditional characteristics. The preservation to this day of this religious practice in New Mexico despite the official church's canonization of new updated liturgical practices, affords it a nontraditional character, in much the same way that nonofficial pre-Tridentine versions of Christianity survived throughout the colonial period and beyond in the Americas, as Espín and others have argued. Chávez rearticulates the novena prayer cycle within a framework of contemporary feminist concerns and issues of social justice.

The feminist reappropriation turns on the interplay of the public and the private; the public sphere of the patriarchally configured Catholic Church, with its central altar to the male deity, is refigured here as the private home altar honoring the Virgin. The play then relocates this privatized domestic space of worship to another public arena constituted not only by the public performance of the modified religious ritual but also by the nonprivatized, almost communal, use of the altar by the nine women in succession. The altar, a floating signifier, occupies various "home" sites in the play: Esperanza, for example, comes home to check the mail and eat a can of peas for lunch, while the bag lady Corrine talks to the Virgin on an altar in a church that she temporarily uses as a home. This heterogeneous "familia de mujeres" (family of women),[21] each with her transgressive or subcultural character, collectively and to a certain degree counterhegemonically replace the male deity with the *madrecita* (dear mother) figure of the Virgin with whom they are more comfortable. Minda, the seven-year-old victim of paternal child abuse, asks the Virgin not to tell "God the Man" the secret she is about to reveal,[22] while the promiscuous figure Magdalena exhibits a persevering devotion to the Virgin to whom she makes regular pilgrimages. Chávez's text is an important contestation and rereading of official and nonofficial religious practices. As Turner has argued, the home altar reverses the official church altar, "the stage for . . . the central canonical drama of Catholicism . . . the symbolic focusing point of male privilege and authority," allowing women to function to a certain degree as their own priests at home.[23]

Similarly, Chávez's alternative drama opens a discursive space for a number of women to whom the church has previously denied the power to speak. Several transgressive acts enter into the public domain here, among them those of the lesbian Corrine; the nonmonogamous Magdalena; the "marked" Minda, whose father has sexually abused her; the "nativa" *curandera* Juana, with her indigenous religious practices; and the alienated, illiterate teen Pauline, whose tattoos, like Corine's, reappropriate the sacred symbols of the Virgin and Jesus. While adding important transgressive significations to the dominant icons of the church, Chávez allows the subaltern to speak in their own, forbidden language. As Mikhail Bakhtin, Peter Stallybrass and Allon White, and other theorists of subculture have shown, transgressive cultural production is often characterized by hybridity, redeploying elements of the dominant culture precisely as it contests dominant practices.[24]

We might compare her text to previous reappropriations of the Virgin of Guadalupe during Mexico's wars for independence and later by the United Farm Workers of America union in the United States. Like the Indians under the Spanish conquest, as Michel de Certeau reminds us,[25] who subverted the imposed rituals and representations by using them for oppositional ends while outwardly remaining subjugated, "Novena Narrativas" reconfigures with a transgressive approach several religious signifiers while at the same time using them as unifying cultural symbols. It succeeds in combining a series of tactical reappropriations with counterhegemonic interventions in the politics of signification.

Visual-Verbal Hybridity: Fictional Retablos

There are numerous religious motifs in Sandra Cisneros's 1991 *Woman Hollering Creek and Other Stories*, but here I will focus on a central diptych in the collection, "Little Miracles, Kept Promises" and the gateway story that precedes it, "Anguiano Religious Articles. . . ." While voice is the predominant narrative strategy in the two stories, an implicit intertextual "visuality" underlies all of the characters' profoundly oral utterances. Like Chávez, Cisneros does not bother with ethnographic explanation for various "outsider" readers, although through certain real names, she undergirds her writing as that of an insider. As a result, those unfamiliar with the rich visual system underlying these stories function as partially incompetent readers, similar, I would argue, to readers of Joyce's *Ulysses* who are unfamiliar with *The Odyssey*.

The transgressive utterances of the tough-talking woman who enters Anguiano's religious goods store to buy a gift for a sick friend suggest a recuperation of the denied speech of orthodox Catholicism, in which worshipers repeat prescribed liturgical phrases and songs, or children are taught to retell their sins according to the proper rubric of the sacrament of reconciliation. When the "crab ass" owner, as the narrator terms him, tells her loudly in Spanish to leave the store after other customers have come in, the woman argues that he in fact utters ugly speech, given the content of his directive. But along with the orality of the story, visual imagery plays a central role in understanding the owner's actions. Among the numerous popular religious icons the narrator describes are statues of the Virgen de Guadalupe with long fake eyelashes, which make her look, in the narrator's view "*bien* mean, like *los amores de la calle* [streetwalkers]."[26] Although she rejects these statues that make the Virgin look like a streetwalker, the story hints ironically that the owner is performing the same visual reading of her, anxious that she leave because her "streetwalker's" look forms an oxymoronic combination with the religious images in the store.

Like this character, whom the store owner directs to San Fernando Cathedral across the street, readers who turn the page and begin reading "Little Miracles, Kept Promises" are made to "see" the popular religious culture on display in this church in San Antonio, the city where Cisneros now lives.

The story presents twenty-four fictional *ex votos*, that is, *promesas* (vows), made to religious figures in exchange for a favor requested or granted. Again, although the story is entirely constituted by verbal utterances, images such as the display of votive offerings under the crucifix of the Black Christ of Esquipulas in San Fernando Cathedral (figure 1) are the necessary visual intertexts for a competent decoding of the text. The story depends on the larger public visual system of nonofficial religious practices in Latino communities, including such material culture

1. Mementos and *ex votos* at the base of the crucifix of the Black Christ of
Esquipulas, San Fernando Cathedral, San Antonio, Texas, 1998.
Courtesy: Ellen McCracken.

as *retablos*: small paintings of religious figures, or illustrated narrative
scenes with handwritten verbal texts giving visual and verbal testimony to
a miracle received (figure 2); *santos, bultos,* and *milagritos*: carved wooden
religious figures, sometimes with hair, clothing, and jewelry, placed on
home altars or in churches and sometimes carried in public religious processions; and the display at shrines and in churches of synecdochic signs
of "miracles" received, such as crutches, small replications of body parts
(milagritos), photographs, and small notes narrating the favor requested
or granted. Each of these practices has its own embedded narrative, which
overcodes those of Cisneros's fictive petitioners.[27]

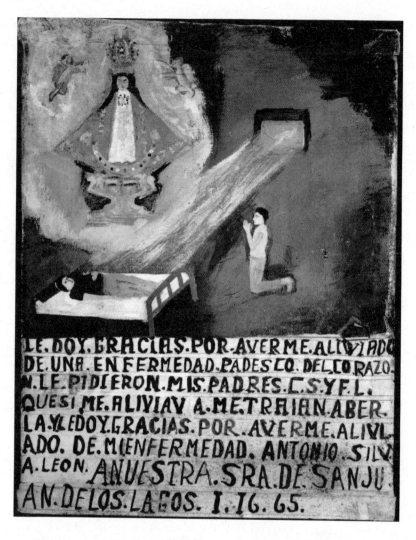

LE.DOY.GRACIAS.POR.AVERME.ALIVIADO
DE.UNA.ENFERMEDAD.PADESCO.DEL.CORAZO
N.LE.PIDIERON.MIS.PADRES.C.S.Y.E.L.
QUESI.ME.ALIVIAV.A.ME.TRAIAN.ABER.
LA.YLEDOY.GRACIAS.POR.AVERME.ALIVL.
ADO.DE.MI.ENFERMEDAD.ANTONIO.SILV.
A.LEON.ANUESTRA.SRA.DE.SANJU.
AN.DELOS.LAGOS.I.I6.65.

2. *Retablo* to La Virgen de San Juan de los Lagos in thanksgiving for curing a heart ailment, 16 January 1965. Courtesy: Ellen McCracken.

3. The Black
Christ of
Esquipulas,
San Fernando
Cathedral, San
Antonio, Texas,
1998. Courtesy:
Ellen McCracken.

Without elaborating on those intertextual narratives here, I would point to some of the images Cisneros's characters allude to: the Black Christ of Esquipulas (figure 3), whose powers of healing in locales as far apart as Guatemala and Chimayó, New Mexico, are believed to be transmitted through material contact with or consumption of sacred earth at the shrine; the Santo Niño de Atocha, patron of travelers and prisoners, for whom believers leave baby shoes to replace those worn out during his nightly journeys of doing good deeds; San Antonio de Padua invoked for finding lost articles, obtaining a husband, and assistance with becoming pregnant and bearing children, and who, like other santos in Latino popular practice, is sometimes "punished" for not granting a favor by being turned to the wall, stood on his head, or put away; San Martín de Porres, from Peru, whose statue occupies a prominent niche in San Fernando Cathedral in San Antonio, the city where Cisneros lives (figure 4); the Virgin of San Juan de los Lagos, whose small triangular statue is often

4. Statue of San Martín de Porres, San Fernando
Cathedral, San Antonio, Texas, 1998.
Courtesy: Ellen McCracken.

brought from her shrine in Jalisco to sites in the U.S. Southwest, such as
the shrine at San Juan, Texas, where Chicanos may pray to her; the popular
curanderos El Niño Fidencio and Don Pedrito Jaramillo, invoked by many
Mexicans in the Southwest; the syncretic Seven African Powers, whose
circular images on a Catholic holy card allows worshipers their choice of
a double decoding of Yoruban gods and Christian saints—Chango or
Santa Barbara, Elegua or San Antonio, Ogún or Saint Peter, Orunla or
Saint Francis; and, most important, the Virgin of Guadalupe, whom the
protagonist Chayo, representing Cisneros herself, recuperates for contemporary feminist ends, much as the Chicana artist Yolanda López does
in her Virgin of Guadalupe series.[28]

While Cisneros's petitioners pray specifically to these and other religious figures, giving testimony in their particularized oral utterances to the social conditions under which they live in the United States, the overarching genre of popular religious culture in this story is the verbal and visual retablo that gives testimony to a miracle. In some cases, as in one retablo from a Mexican immigrant in Compton, California, in 1981, the verbal prayer has narrative gaps and is only a caption to the more fully narrativized visual image that specifies the miracle as the escape from the Immigration and Naturalization Service (INS) at the U.S.-Mexico border. Its vagueness ("I give thanks to the Lord of Mercy for a favor received") entices readers to the fuller narrative information in the illustration. In many other retablos, however, long narrative syntagmas are enchained in the verbal portion, and the resultant orality of the retablo parallels the lengthy verbal utterances of Cisneros' petitioners.[29]

Cisneros extends these popular religious practices to a further dimension of popular recuperation, for now they are also linked to issues of social justice for U.S. Latinos, feminist liberation, and gay oppression. Although the visual intertextual system that undergirds the story is immensely important, the verbal utterances of the characters in the text allow a greater discursive development of social issues than is usually possible in the popular religious practices themselves. For example, one petitioner's request for $253.72 of unpaid wages for "67½ hours that first week and 79 hours the second"[30] offers readers a clear example of the egregiously substandard wages paid to some migrant workers in the United States. Along with the rich narrative detail of this twenty-two-line petition to the Virgencita de Guadalupe, this precise information connects devotion to the Virgin to issues of social justice.

Instead of including photos or illustrations in the story, Cisneros requires supplemental visual work by readers, deploying her skill as a writer to enable us to hear her characters' rich speech. One message thanking Saint Sebastian for helping to get the petitioner's extended family out of his house illustrates this orality: "Here is the little gold milagrito I promised you, a little house, see? And it ain't that cheap gold-plate shit either. So now that I paid you back, we're even, right? Cause I don't like for no one to say Victor Lozano don't pay his debts. I pays cash on the line, bro. . . ."[31] Virgilio Elizondo, former rector of the San Fernando Cathedral in San Antonio, has noted the seriousness with which such promesas or bargains with God are made and repaid: "People know that it requires more than just promising to be good. It requires some action, a sacrifice of sorts, made for God. It requires commitment. You can't just send in a postcard or use your Visa card. It has to be personal."[32] Cisneros's character has developed an elaborate metaphor in praying to San Sebastian in which his in-laws represent the arrows in the saint's chest; he repays his promesa with an expensive milagrito of real gold that gives testimony to his self-sacrifice to keep his end of the bargain and at the same time iconically represents the house now once again his. Cisneros's language enables readers to both hear the character's voice and visualize the images to which he refers.

Cisneros has elaborated a unique visual-verbal hybridity in these two stories, although only verbal signifiers appear on the pages. Underlying the rich orality of the utterances is a particularized system of primarily visual religious intertexts. For readers in possession of or willing to attain the cultural competence the stories demand, the narratives are an intricate imbrication of the verbal and the visual in which popular Latino religious practices are linked to contemporary social issues.

Ponce, Chávez, and Cisneros recuperate the repressed body of official Catholicism in a variety of ways. I have focused here on the interplay of the visual and the oral in these texts as a mode of reclaiming the controlled vision and speech of orthodox religious practice for use in popular and neopopular religious practices. Ponce, Chávez, and Cisneros—along with numerous other contemporary U.S. Latino writers—deploy forbidden speech and repressed vision as a means of reclaiming religion in their struggle for social justice and a new moral vision.

Notes

1. See, for example, Lucha Corpi, "Los Cristos del alma," in *Palabra nueva: Cuentos chicanos*, ed. Ricardo Aguilar et al. (El Paso: Texas Western Press, 1984), 3–12; Ana Castillo, *So Far from God* (New York: W.W. Norton, 1993); Roberta Fernández, "Zulema," *Massachusetts Review* 24, no. 1 (1983): 42–55, rev. version in Fernández, *Intaglio: A Novel in Six Stories* (Houston: Arte Público Press, 1990), 133–54; Sylvia López-Medina, *Cantora* (Albuquerque: University of New Mexico Press, 1992); John Rechy, *The Miraculous Day of Amalia Gómez* (New York: Arcade Publishers, 1991); Tomás Rivera, *And the Earth Did Not Part* (Berkeley: Quinto Sol, 1971); Julia Alvarez, *How the Garcia Girls Lost Their Accents* (Chapel Hill, N.C.: Algonquin Books, 1991); Cristina García, *Dreaming in Cuban* (New York: Knopf, 1992); Judith Ortiz Cofer, *The Line of the Sun* (Athens: University of Georgia, 1989).

2. Demetria Martínez, *Mother Tongue* (Tempe, Ariz.: Bilingual Press, 1994); Rudolfo Anaya, *Alburquerque* (Albuquerque: University of New Mexico Press, 1992), 168.

3. Ibid., 157.

4. Mary Helen Ponce, *Hoyt Street: An Autobiography* (Albuquerque: University of New Mexico Press, 1993); Martínez, *Mother Tongue*.

5. See also the essays in Anthony M. Stevens-Arroyo and Ana Maria Díaz-Stevens, eds., *An Enduring Flame: Studies on Latino Popular Religiosity* (New York: Bildner Center for Western Hemisphere Studies, 1994).

6. Some changes in these negative attitudes are occurring, for example, in the recent development of Catholic ministries of body massage. See Pamela Schaeffer, "Massage an Expanding Healing Ministry," *National Catholic Reporter*, 19 January 1996, 22–23.

7. Ponce, *The Wedding* (Houston: Arte Público, 1989).

8. See Alejandro Morales, "A Chicana Stereotypes Her Own People," *Los Angeles Times Book Review*, 19 November 1989, 10. Morales expressed his reaction to the indelicate scene in *Hoyt Street* in a telephone conversation with me on 9 July 1994. While I understand the concerns of this important Chicano literary critic and creative writer, I offer another reading of the texts here and hope that multiple interpretations from various reading positions continue to flourish.

9. Ponce, *Hoyt Street*, 153–54.

10. Ibid., 265.

11. Ibid., 259.

12. For an important discussion of the concept of the male surveyor, see John Berger, *Ways of Seeing* (London: Penguin, 1972).

13. Ponce, *Hoyt Street*, 162.

14. Ibid., 165.

15. Ibid., 163.

16. Ibid., 190.

17. Ibid., 273.

18. Ibid., 197.

19. Ibid., 198.

20. Chávez notes in an article, "Our Lady of Guadalupe," *New Mexico Magazine* (December 1986): 55–63, that many Catholics in New Mexico pray novenas during the days preceding the feast of the Virgin of Guadalupe on 12 December. This ritual is also observed in Santa Fe in honor of La Conquistadora, "Our Lady of the Conquest."

21. Chávez, "Novena narrativas y ofrendas nuevomexicanas," *Americas Review* 15, nos. 3–4 (1987): 65–72.

22. Ibid.

23. Kay Turner, *Beautiful Necessity: The Art and Meaning of Women's Altars* (New York: Thames and Hudson, 1999).

24. See Mikhail M. Bakhtin, *Rabelais and His World*, trans. Helene Iswolsky (Cambridge: Massachusetts Institute of Technology, 1968); Peter Stallybrass and Allon White, *The Politics and Poetics of Transgression* (Ithaca, N.Y.: Cornell University Press, 1986); Stuart Hall and Tony Jefferson, eds., *Resistance through Rituals: Youth Subcultures in Post-war Britain* (London: Harper Collins Aca-

demic, 1976), 99–102; Angela McRobbie, "Settling Accounts with Subcultures," *Screen Education* 34 (1980): 37–49.

25. Michel de Certeau, *The Practice of Everyday Life*. Translated by Steven Rendall (Berkeley: University of California Press, 1984).

26. Sandra Cisneros, *Woman Hollering Creek and Other Stories* (New York: Random House, 1991), 115.

27. For important studies of some of these alternative religious practices, see José E. Espinosa, *Saints in the Valleys: Christian Sacred Images in the History, Life and Folk Art of Spanish New Mexico* (Albuquerque: University of New Mexico Press, 1960); Thomas J. Steele, S.J., *Santos and Saints* (Santa Fe: Ancient City Press, 1994); George Mills, *The People of the Saints* (Colorado Springs: Taylor Museum, Colorado Springs Fine Art Center, n.d.); Martha Egan, *Milagros: Votive Offerings from the Americas* (Santa Fe: Museum of New Mexico Press, 1991); Eileen Oktavec, *Answered Prayers: Miracles and Milagros along the Border* (Tucson: University of Arizona Press, 1995); Robin Farwell Gavin, *The Traditional Art of Spanish New Mexico* (Santa Fe: Museum of New Mexico Press, 1994); Anita Brenner, "Painted Miracles," *Arts* 15 (January 1929): 11–18; Brenner, *Idols behind Altars* (New York: Biblo and Tannen, 1967), esp. chap. 7; Jorge Durand and Douglas S. Massey, *Miracles on the Border: Retablos of Mexican Migrants to the United States* (Tucson: University of Arizona Press, 1995); Gloria K. Giffords, *Mexican Folk Retablos: Masterpieces on Tin* (Tucson: University of Arizona Press, 1974); Jorge A. González, *Cultura(s)* (Colima, Mexico: Universidad de Colima, 1986); Jorge A. González, *Milagros en la frontera: Los mojados de la Virgen de San Juan dan gracias por su favor* (Mexico City: Secretaría de Relaciones Exteriores, 1991).

28. For discussion of these popular religious practices, see Stephen de Borhegyi, "The Cult of Our Lord of Esquipulas in Middle America and New Mexico," *El Palacio* 61 (1954): 387–401; Stephen de Borhegyi, *El Santuario de Chimayó* (Santa Fe: Ancient City Press for the Spanish Colonial Arts Society, 1956); Elizabeth Kay, *Chimayó Valley Traditions* (Santa Fe: Ancient City Press, 1987); Kay Turner, "The Cultural Semiotics of Religious Icons: La Virgen de San Juan de los Lagos," *Semiotica* 47 (1983): 317–61; Turner, "Because of This Photography: The Making of a Mexican Folk Saint," in Dore Gardner, *Niño Fidencio: A Heart Thrown Open* (Santa Fe: Museum of New Mexico Press, 1992), 120–34; Octavio Romano, "Don Pedrito Jaramillo: The Emergence of a Mexican-American Folk-Saint," PhD diss. (University of California, Berkeley, 1964); Ruth Dodson, "Don Pedrito Jaramillo: The Curandero of Los Olmos," in *The Healer of Los Olmos and Other Mexican Lore*, ed. Wilson M. Hudson (Dallas: Southern Methodist University, 1966; orig. pub. 1951), 9–70; Migene González-Wippler, *Santería: The Religion. A Legacy of Faith, Rites, and Magic* (New York: Harmony Books, 1989).

29. One such retablo reads as follows:

I give infinite thanks to the Holiest Virgin of San Juan de los Lagos for allowing me to return alive to my family's side after a terrible event that occurred during my return to town. I was coming from the United States of America when, just after crossing the border in Chihuahua, I was assaulted on the train by thieves who wanted to take my life and rob me of the money and all that I carried. But they didn't accomplish their goal thanks to the Holiest Virgin. When the bandit struck me with a dagger, an impulse made me defend myself with such force that I broke a glass window with my back and fell backwards outside, landing on the ground so hard that I thought for sure I would lose my life. And if this was not enough, the van that picked me up to bring me to the hospital turned over. This happened on 20 November 1943 at 7:00 in the evening. Antonio Alcaraz, Zacapu, Michoacán. 2–2-49.

Durand and Massey, *Miracles on the Border*, 192, fig. 3.

30. Cisneros, *Woman Hollering Creek and Other Stories*, 120.

31. Ibid., 121.

32. David McLemore, "A Meeting Place with God," *San Jose Mercury News*, 20 April 1996, 12E.

V

Mexican American

Religions and Healing

11

Brown Moses

Francisco Olazábal and Mexican American Pentecostal

Healing in the Borderlands

The story of healing in the Latino community has focused almost exclusively on popular Catholic and metaphysical traditions such as *curanderismo*, Spiritism (*espiritismo*), and Brujería. This is understandable given the rich and historic role that healing plays in these traditions. However, these practices only tell part of the story. This essay refines and expands the story of healing in the U.S. Latino community and argues that the Latino Pentecostal movement has engaged in and popularized the notion of healing for over a century. Despite this fact, we know surprisingly little about this story.

The Latino Pentecostal and Charismatic movements' tremendous emphasis on divine healing is one of the major reasons why adherents of these faiths make up 64 percent of the nation's Latino Protestants. The key to the movement's growth has been its tradition of blending evangelism and healing. Latino Pentecostal evangelists such as Francisco Olazábal (figure 1) conducted large-scale healing services in urban barrios and rural *colonias* (colonies of migrant workers) in order to attract and convert the masses. After participants were converted, he used them to help plant new churches and missions, which institutionalized and spread the practice of mixing healing and evangelism. This religious practice might have been kept localized and marginalized had it not been for his emphasis on constructing indigenous and autonomous Latino churches in almost every location where he conducted large-scale (two weeks in duration or longer) evangelistic campaigns.

1. Francisco Olazábal
portrait, ca. 1925.
Courtesy: Gastón Espinosa.

Contrary to the claims of some scholars, Latino Pentecostals such
as Francisco Olazábal created indigenous and autonomous Protestant
churches throughout the early twentieth century that institutionalized
and transmitted their message and practice of divine healing.[1] He and
Abundio L. López, A. C. Valdez, Luis López, Juan Navarro, Francisco
Llorente, Genaro Valenzuela, Juan Lugo, Roberto Fiero, Matilde Vargas, Carlos Sepúlveda, Leoncia Rosado Rousseau, Aurora Chávez, and
countless others tapped into the preexisting belief in divine healing.
Their emphasis on healing was important because of the direct connection between health and economic survival (and because of the high cost
of medical treatment). A person who was sick or injured could not work
and thus could not support his or her family. In many respects, the Latino Pentecostal community provided a faith-based form of alternative
healing and health practices that addressed physical, spiritual, social, and
emotional issues. In a word, their healing practices tended to be holistic.
This chapter will explore the role of healing through the life and ministry
of Francisco Olazábal, one of the Latino community's most prominent
healing evangelists.

Mexicans, Healing, and the Azusa Street Revival

Francisco Olazábal's decision to mix evangelism and healing was a direct
by product of the Azusa Street Revival in Los Angeles. In 1916, his wife,
Macrina, was healed of a physical ailment after George and Carrie Judd

Montgomery laid hands on her and prayed for her. This traumatic event prompted Olazábal, then an itinerant Methodist minister in San Francisco, to leave the Methodist Church and join the Pentecostal movement and eventually the Assemblies of God (AG). In 1906, the Montgomery's had joined the Pentecostal movement after George had visited William J. Seymour and the Azusa Street Revival in Los Angeles. There he witnessed the revival's practice of mixing healing and evangelism. By the time Olazábal joined the Pentecostal movement, a number of other Latinos were already conducting evangelistic healing work. Thus Olazábal was grafted into a movement that already placed a high premium of mixing healing and evangelism. This emphasis is evident in the numerous testimonies published by Latinos and others in Seymour's *Apostolic Faith Mission* newspaper.[2]

It is significant to note that almost every major reference to Mexicans at the Azusa Street Revival or sister Pentecostal Missions from this period involves healing. The first person allegedly healed at the revival was not an Anglo or a Black, but a Mexican. Shortly after the Apostolic Faith Mission opened, Arthur G. Osterberg, an Azusa Street participant and eyewitness, reported that a Mexican man with a clubfoot was the first person healed at the revival. He stated:

All at once a man who had come in walking haltingly with a clubfoot, got up and went out into the aisle and he was clapping his hands and his face was uplifted. His wife looked at him and pretty soon she followed him. They walked toward the back and then toward the front [of the Mission], and by this time they were walking arm in arm and he [was] clapping his hands and his face [was] uplifted. That must have taken place for four or five minutes, then it quieted down, then he came down with his wife. I noticed when he came up the aisle . . . he wasn't stumbling like he was when he walked into the meeting. I knew something had happened to his foot. . . . For the first time he noticed—he stood there [in the Mission] moving it and then started to walk—then he started to shout "Hallelujah."[3]

This healing left an indelible impression in Osterberg's mind.[4] This miracle "convinced me," he stated, "that there was something different in this [Azusa Street] meeting from any other work I ever attended."[5] Similarly, the famous Mexican American evangelist, A. C. Valdez, reportedly witnessed "many healings" at the mission, including that of his father.[6] Likewise, Abundio López and Rosa López stated that divine healing was part-and-parcel of their ministry inside and outside of the Apostolic Faith

Mission.[7] In a classic example of mixing evangelism and healing, Abundio and Rosa López wrote in 1906:

> We testify to the power of the Holy Spirit in forgiveness, sanctification, and the baptism with the Holy Ghost and fire. We give thanks to God for this wonderful gift, which we have received from Him, according to the promise. Thanks be to God for the Spirit, which brought us to the Azusa Street Mission, the Apostolic Faith, old-time religion. I [and] my wife, on the 29th of last May . . . came for sanctification . . . and [we] thank God for the baptism with the Holy Spirit and fire which I received on the 5th of June, 190[6]. We cannot express the gratitude and thanksgiving which we feel moment by moment for what He has done for us, so we want to be used for the salvation and *healing of both soul and body*. I am a witness of His wonderful promise and *marvelous miracles* by the Holy Ghost, by faith in the Lord Jesus Christ. May God bless you all. (emphasis added)[8]

The Lópezes' blending of healing and evangelism is evident not only at the Azusa Street Revival, but also at other Pentecostal/Charismatic daughter missions in Los Angeles, such as the Pisgah Mission. In January 1909, the Pisgah Mission movement, which placed a heavy emphasis on divine healing, claimed that its work was "spreading rapidly among . . . Spanish and Mexican" Catholics. Leaders attributed Mexican receptivity to divine healing to "immemorial traditions and belief in divine healing." Pisgah leaders claimed that one-fourth of the congregation at one of their missions in Southern California was made up of "Spaniards and Mexicans, among whom are many cripples and deformed."[9] One Pisgah writer reported, "We went among Spanish, French, and colored people, and were rejected but once. We prayed for one lame person . . . and she was healed."[10] At one service in January 1909, fourteen Mexicans came forward for healing. The writer stated that many Mexicans were "afflicted with fearful visitations." Exactly what these "fearful visitations" were is uncertain. Perhaps they refer to the hexes and spells they believed could be cast upon them by *brujas* (witches), *diableras* (satanic witches), Spiritists, and Spiritualists. If this is true, then perhaps some Mexicans sought to use Pentecostalism's emphasis on divine healing and spiritual warfare to restore their health by breaking the power of hexes and other fearful afflictions they believed were brought upon them by malevolent spirits.[11]

Mexican interest in divine healing was neither unique nor transitory. It is the key to understanding the power and attraction of Pentecostalism. Pentecostal evangelistic-healing services—along with personal testimonies from family and friends about healing, spiritual deliverance, and conversion—are part of the reason tens of thousands left the Catholic Church to join the Pentecostal movement in the 1920s and 1930s. This kind of healing and spiritual power offered hope to people unable to pay for proper medical care or the fees that most Spiritists, Spiritualists, and *curanderas* normally charged to perform healing ceremonies, *limpias* (cleansings), or counterspells. Furthermore, many Mexicans and Mexican Americans were reluctant to go to an "American" doctor because they were used to going to village healers in Mexico. Many preferred to take their medical problems to a Mexican Catholic healer such as Don Pedrito Jaramillo, El Niño Fidencio, María Teresa Urrea, and others rather than a modern doctor, who only treated the physical ailment. For example, in Evangeline Hymer's 1923 study of social attitudes among Mexican immigrants in Los Angeles, she found that 42 percent of Mexicans surveyed preferred to take their medical problems to a Mexican healer rather than to an American doctor (20 percent) and that 28 percent reported that they preferred to use Mexican herbs for healing rather than "drug store medicine." She went on to note that among "members of the lower caste . . . faith in divine healing is *still unshaken*."[12]

Many sought out healers not only because this was a long-standing tradition, but also because they believed that bodily healing and the spirit world were intimately related. In the minds of many, there were no accidents in life. All blessings and misfortunes were tied to the supernatural world—for better or worse. Furthermore, there were sicknesses and diseases that a modern "American" doctor could simply never heal. Some people believed that sickness and disease were caused by hexes, curses, spells, and malevolent spirits, not simply by natural ailments. They believed that in order to break the curse or spell of a witch (bruja), a satanic witch (diablera), or a Spiritualist (*espiritualista*), one had to invoke a more powerful spirit. The God of the Pentecostal evangelists, and sometimes the evangelists themselves, was seen as that spirit. Francisco Olazábal and Pentecostalism offered Latinos a new alternative way to challenge and break these spells and other cultural prohibitions in society. This was especially attractive to the poor, who could not afford to pay someone to break the spell, and to women seeking ways to transcend machismo. While Latino converts to Pentecostalism transformed the symbols, source of power, and meaning behind divine healing, they left intact its importance, necessity, and regularity in the Latino consciousness. Although other Latino Evangelical and Mainline Protestant traditions acknowledged that healing was possible, only Pentecostalism made it a central tenet of faith.

Healing was connected not only to the spirit world in the Mexican imagination, but also to practical on-the-ground economic needs. This connection was not accidental. One major study of the Mexican population in Los Angeles in 1920 found that although Mexicans made up only one-twentieth (probably an underestimate) of the population of Los Angeles, they made up one-fourth of all the poverty cases handled by the L.A. County Charities. Significantly, of the top five reasons why Mexicans faced poverty in Los Angeles, the first two were health related—"Acute Illness" and "Chronic Physical Disability." Acute illnesses and chronic physical disabilities left fully one-third (33 percent) of all Mexicans poverty stricken.[13] In light of this fact, it is not difficult to see why thousands converted to Pentecostalism—a religion that promised physical healing and, indirectly, economic hope—as well as many spiritual benefits.

The Struggle for Independence and Autonomy in the U.S.-Mexico Borderlands

Francisco Olazábal was born into a traditional pious Catholic family in El Verano, Sinaloa, Mexico, on 12 October 1886. Although little is known about his father, Juan Olazábal (ca. 1851–1901), we do know that his mother, Refugio Velázquez, was a very devout Catholic. She nurtured Francisco in the rich and poly-vibrant world of Mexican popular Catholicism. From her he learned to recite the Rosary, pray to the saints, venerate Our Lady of Guadalupe, light colorful prayer candles at their home altar, and honor the local priest. Popular Mexican Catholicism taught that sickness and disease were not caused by chance or microbes but rather by evil spirits and spells cast by witches (brujas), Spiritualists, Spiritists, and angry village saints. Olazábal grew up in a world where the supernatural was alive and divine healing was an accepted part of everyday life.[14] There is good reason to believe that he heard stories about the famous contemporary Mexican folk healers such as María Teresa Urrea, from his home state of Sinaloa, and Don Pedrito Jaramillo, from the nearby state of San Luis Postosí.[15]

Francisco Olazábal's spiritual world took a dramatic turn away from popular Mexican Catholicism when, in 1898, his mother converted to Evangelical Protestantism in Mazatlán, Mexico. Her conversion changed her life and prompted her to became a lay Methodist evangelist. Refugio took Francisco on her evangelistic journeys throughout the rugged Sierra Madre mountain range in central Mexico with a Bible in one hand and a rifle in the other. They stayed with hospitable guests, but also often lived off the land and camped just outside of town. Around 1903 Olazábal turned away from his mother's evangelistic ministry and went through a rebellious streak. He traveled north to visit his relatives in San Francisco, California. Caught up in the fantastic stories of faraway exotic places and a chance to earn some silver, he planned to sail the world as a mariner. His plans were abruptly ended after he rededicated his life to Jesus Christ in 1904 through the evangelistic work of George Montgomery, a member of the Christian and Missionary Alliance. After his rededication to Protestant Christianity, he returned to Mexico.[16]

Once back in Mexico, Olazábal returned to the Methodist Church. He attended the Wesleyan School of Theology in San Luis Potosí, Mexico, from 1908 to 1910. There he came under the influence of the Anglo-American Methodist leader F. A. Onderdonk. He was nurtured in the Methodist revivalist tradition through his classes and ministerial internships in local churches and missions. During this time he conducted small-scale evangelistic and revival campaigns in the Mexican states of Durango, San Luis Potosí, and Zacatecas, and across the U.S. border in Texas. As the fires of the Mexican Revolution (1910–20) engulfed the nation, hundreds of thousands of Mexicans fled across the border, including Olazábal. He assumed the pastorate of a small Mexican Methodist Church in El Paso, Texas, in 1911.[17]

While in Texas, Olazábal met an Anglo-American Methodist woman who encouraged him to study at the Moody Bible Institute, her alma mater. The institute was founded by Dwight L. Moody, one of the nation's most famous late nineteenth-century evangelists and revivalists. Following her advice, Olazábal trekked north to Chicago around 1912, where he enrolled. It was here that he developed his English skills and read Bible commentaries; church history; and the history of missions, evangelism, and revivalism. He was profoundly influenced by the writings and ministries of Dwight L. Moody and especially Charles Finney's *Lectures on Revivals of Religion*. This book, which he kept at his bedside, had a profound impact on Olazábal's future ministry. At the institute, he studied under Evangelical leaders and revivalists such as Reuben A. Torrey and James M. Gray. Torrey taught him that the baptism with the Holy Spirit was a necessary part of the Christian life. Yet Torrey differed with Pentecostals (a group he criticized) because he did not believe that tongues was the initial evidence of the baptism with the Holy Spirit, nor that Christians had to speak in tongues to prove they had received the spirit baptism.

After Torrey left Moody to pastor the Church of the Open Door in Los Angeles, he asked Olazábal to leave Moody and minister to the growing

Mexican population in Los Angeles. Olazábal accepted the offer but later ran into conflict with Torrey's teaching that the baptism with the Holy Spirit was a definite experience, because he remained unpersuaded that it added anything important to the Christian life. After parting company with Torrey, Olazábal joined the Spanish-speaking Methodist Episcopal Church in California. In 1914, Olazábal married Macrina Orozco, who came from a family of Protestant ministers in Mexico. Two years later, the Methodist Church ordained Olazábal to the ministry.[18]

The Methodist Episcopal Church leaders claimed that Olazábal was doing "splendid" and "valuable" work in Southern California. He held evangelistic campaigns throughout the greater Los Angeles and Pasadena areas. Concerned about the long-term spiritual well-being of his converts who had no stable place to worship, he also learned how to conduct fund-raising activities among Anglo-Americans—a skill he leveraged to build new churches. He raised thousands of dollars to build a massive new mission-style church in 1915 in Pasadena, California. Shortly thereafter, Olazábal was transferred north, where he was assigned as a circuit preacher in the Methodist tradition for two Spanish churches in San Francisco and Sacramento. His evangelistic, revivalistic, and fund-raising work caught the attention of the Anglo-American bishops who began to whisper about his one day becoming a bishop.[19]

After moving to San Francisco, Olazábal visited George and Carrie Judd Montgomery. To Olazábal's surprise, they had become Pentecostals, a group he often criticized from the pulpit. In 1906, George Montgomery attended the Azusa Street Revival and joined the Pentecostal movement. After initially rejecting the Montgomerys' newfound message, Olazábal was persuaded that the baptism with the Holy Spirit was a second definite experience and a necessary part of the Christian life. He also became convinced that divine healing was available to all who asked in faith. Olazábal's belief was confirmed and put to the test when he, the Montgomerys, and a few other people laid hands on and prayed for his wife who was suffering from a physical ailment. Olazábal claimed that Macrina was healed as a result of their prayers. He soon realized that the combination of speaking in tongues, practicing the spiritual sign gifts (e.g., tongues, healing, spirit baptism, etc.) and his newfound belief in divine healing placed him at odds with some of his Methodist Church colleagues who saw Pentecostals as largely uneducated schismatic competitors. For this reason, he decided to leave the Methodist Church in order to preach the "full Gospel," he later wrote. In response to Methodist criticism of his newfound beliefs, Olazábal stated,

I was blind, but now I see. You cannot make me believe that there is something wrong in my head now, there is rather something right in my heart. . . . I am not going to try and be a bishop in the Methodist Church. I would rather be a humble Pentecostal preacher.[20]

The Methodists were shocked to hear that one of their most promising young evangelists had defected to the Pentecostals. Vernon McCombs, the superintendent of the Spanish-speaking Methodist work, traveled to San Francisco and spent six hours trying to persuade Olazábal to remain in the Methodist Church, even offering him a $2,000-a-year salary plus other bonuses if he would stay. Although he considered the offer, he turned it down because he stated he wanted to be "free" to express himself in ways unacceptable to the Methodist leadership at that time.[21]

Soon after Olazábal left the Methodist Church, he joined the Assemblies of God and received ministerial credentials in 1917. In 1918, Olazábal traveled south to Los Angeles, where he conducted an evangelistic campaign for Alice E. Luce, an emerging leader in the Spanish-speaking AG. After the campaign, he moved to El Paso and opened a Mexican mission to reach the thousands of immigrants streaming across the U.S.-Mexico border. There he conducted a number of evangelistic, healing, and revival services. By 1921 his charismatic personality, ability to heal, and rhetorical gifts led to the conversion of over 400 fellow Mexicanos.[22]

As Olazábal's popularity continued to grow, he ran into conflict with Henry C. Ball and Alice Luce. Reflecting the well-intentioned pious paternalism of their day, Ball tried to take control of the Latin Convention in Victoria, Texas, and dictate its agenda and outcome. He believed that the Mexican Pentecostals in Texas were incapable of organizing and leading their own district within the AG. Although Ball later denied this, internal documents indicate otherwise. Olazábal and a group of ministers (some of them formerly from independent Pentecostal churches) found Ball's attitude toward Mexicans unacceptable. Ball and Luce wrote to the Assemblies of God headquarters accusing Olazábal of instigating trouble and of calling for a separate district under Mexican leadership. There was some truth to the charge. Olazábal did attempt to reform from within what he perceived as Ball's paternalistic and racialized vision of the Mexican Pentecostal movement. As early as 1920, Olazábal laid out a new vision for the Latin District Council and in 1922 began a Bible school under Mexican administration and leadership. He also argued for indigenous Mexican leadership of the fledgling Mexican AG work. As his frustration with Ball and Luce continued to grow, his power base expanded. He criticized Ball and Luce for not keeping their promise to support the Bible school he had started in El Paso and for exaggerating the personal success of their work. Whether or not Olazábal was jealous of their reported success or simply disappointed with their exaggerations is uncertain, although the truth may lay somewhere in between.[23]

The simmering tension erupted into all-out conflict in the fall of 1922, when Ball told the Mexican leaders at the annual convention that despite what he had promised earlier, they could not elect a new president of the Latin District Council until the following year. Most believed that Olazábal would be elected over Ball not only because he was ten years older and had formal seminary training, but also because he was the most respected evangelist in the council. Interpreting the statement as a tactical political move to thwart his election as president and push him to the margins, Olazábal protested the decision. He, Ball, and Luce were summoned to the AG headquarters in Springfield, Missouri, where attempts to reconcile were only temporarily successful. The Anglo-American leadership sided with Ball and Luce. Mexican ministers split over whom to follow. While some—especially the independent Pentecostal ministers that had loosely affiliated with Ball's work—joined Olazábal, those who had converted under Ball's ministry remained loyal to the tall, blonde-haired, blue-eyed Texan.

Isabel Flores stated that they needed a "Brown Moses" to lead them. He proposed that Olazábal lead them to form a new Pentecostal council that would be Mexican led and run. After five years of ministry in the Assemblies of God, Olazábal recognized the racialized politics he now faced. With nine cents in his pocket, Olazábal resigned from the AG in December 1922. When later asked why he resigned, Olazábal stated: "The gringos have control."[24]

Aimee Semple McPherson and the Mexican Billy Sunday

While the controversy raged on, Olazábal accepted Flores's invitation and received Mexican Pentecostal churches and pastors into his new denomination. Although most pastors and churches in the Mexican Assemblies of God Convention decided to remain, a significant number joined Olazábal's new Mexican denomination. On 14 March 1923, the Interdenominational Mexican Council of Christian Churches (Pentecostal) was organized and legally incorporated in the state of Texas. The first completely independent and autonomous Latino Protestant denomination was born. Despite the hardships that Olazábal's new denomination faced, by 1924 it counted over thirty churches, in California, Texas, Arizona, New Mexico, Kansas, Illinois, Michigan, Ohio, Indiana, and Mexico. Despite this separation, Olazábal continued to have warm friendships with many Anglo-American and Mexican pastors in the Assemblies of God and in many other Pentecostal bodies throughout the nation, as evidenced by the scores of invitations to preach in their churches.[25]

While Olazábal had conducted evangelistic healing crusades with the Mexican AG prior to 1923, it was not until after the schism that his healing ministry blossomed and began to take on genuinely national proportions. Olazábal's national healing ministry was ignited by the reported healing of the twelve-year-old deaf-and-dumb daughter of Guadalupe Gómez. Despite the previous healing episodes, he had never performed what was, in the minds of his followers, such a "great" and obvious "miracle." The Church of God leader Homer Tomlinson, one of Olazábal's closest Anglo-American friends, later stated that "from this new beginning his faith for healing and the salvation of souls seemed to take on new proportions."[26]

Empowered by a newfound confidence in God's ability to heal throughout the 1920s Olazábal crisscrossed the nation, preaching evangelism, healing, and revival to thousands of Mexicans in migrant farm labor camps, factories, and inner city barrios. He conducted large-scale evangelistic-healing services in El Paso, San Antonio, East Los Angeles; Boyle Heights (in Los Angeles); Watts; Brownsville; Nogales, Arizona; San Fernando, California; Houston, Texas (figure 2); and in countless other locations. In Los Angeles, his campaigns caught the eye of another former Assemblies of God evangelist and revivalist, Aimee Semple McPherson.

In 1927, the glamorous McPherson was fascinated by the reports she heard from some of her Mexican American parishioners about Olazábal's healing crusades in Los Angeles and Watts. After personally attending his services in Watts, she dubbed Olazábal the "Mexican Billy Sunday." This was a major compliment, as Billy Sunday was the foremost evangelist of their day. Shortly after McPherson preached in his services in Watts, she invited Olazábal and his two Mexican congregations to her 5,000-seat Angelus Temple in Echo Park, Los Angeles. Olazábal's church members attended a number of evening services for several months. At one historic meeting in 1927, McPherson and Olazábal went to the podium, where the theatrical McPherson delivered a sermon entitled "In the Valley of Decision." Olazábal translated her sermon into Spanish. In vintage McPherson style, the sermon was dramatized and illustrated by a team of actors with

2. Francisco Olazábal at Annual Convention, Houston, 1926.
Courtesy: Gastón Espinosa.

theater props. The Mexican congregation was emotionally moved not only by McPherson's theatrics and hospitality but especially by her public blessing on "our Mexican brethren."[27]

McPherson's interest in Olazábal and his movement over the next year prompted her to ask him and the council to merge with her Foursquare Gospel denomination. Olazábal later stated he was flattered, but said the decision to merge had to be decided on by the entire council. He took the idea of a merger to the next national convention, where his Mexican compatriots soundly defeated the proposal. They did not want to submit to Anglo control and, in effect, replace one set of Anglo leaders for another. Olazábal agreed. He related the council's decision to McPherson. She was indignant at what she considered a very generous offer to a Mexican denomination made up of migrant farm laborers, maids, ditch diggers, and the like. She excoriated Olazábal and demanded he return the more than $100 "love offering" she had raised for him at the Angelus Temple. Defiant, Olazábal told McPherson that love offerings are never returned. Angry, McPherson looked at Olazábal and told him to get out of her office and never return. Her dream of merging the two ministries crumbled.[28] Sometime after the conflict with Olazábal, she persuaded one of his music leaders, Anthony Gamboa, to defect to the Foursquare Gospel denomination. He started a rival ministry in 1929 called McPherson Mexican Mission (later El Buen Pastor) just a few blocks away from Olazábal's

3. Francisco Olazábal's Chicago campaign, Palace Opera House, Chicago, 1929. Courtesy: Gastón Espinosa.

Bethel Temple. This conflict helped give birth to the Foursquare's Spanish-speaking work in the United States. El Buen Pastor eventually left the Foursquare and is now an independent Pentecostal Church.[29]

One cannot overestimate the symbolic impact of Olazábal preaching on stage with McPherson in the Angelus Temple. He stood on the platform of one of the largest churches in America with one of the nation's most famous Anglo preachers. In a day when Mexicans were considered cheap labor and cultural outsiders, her praise of Olazábal convinced many of his followers that he was indeed "anointed of God."

As word of Olazábal's healing campaigns spread across the United States, he was invited by a Latino AG minister to speak at the Palace Opera House in Chicago (figures 3 and 4). His evangelistic healing and revival campaigns attracted thousands every night for several weeks. The traffic in human bodies was so great that police had to be called out to control the crowds. He later went on to conduct other evangelistic healing services in Chicago; Joliet, Illinois; Indiana Harbor, Indiana; Houston; Modesto, California; Laredo, Texas; and Mexico City.[30]

4. Francisco Olazábal and Paul Rader worship teams prepare to lead worship at Francisco Olazábal's Chicago evangelistic healing campaign at the Palace Opera House, 1929. Courtesy: Gastón Espinosa.

The Spanish Harlem Revival of 1931

Word of Olazábal's evangelistic healing campaign in Chicago soon spread to New York City. Francisco Paz, an Assemblies of God minister, had attended one of Olazábal's healing services in Chicago and asked him to conduct a similar campaign in New York. In the summer of 1931, Olazábal traveled east to Spanish Harlem for what would become the most important chapter of his life and the birth of his transnational ministry.

"Probably not less than 100,000 different people have attended the Olazábal meetings in New York City since he inaugurated his meetings in New York in August, 1931," one periodical reported (figure 5).[31] Eyewitnesses claimed that despite the humidity and sweltering summer heat, vast throngs attended his services in various locations, including the gigantic Calvary Baptist Church in Brooklyn and later a former synagogue in Spanish Harlem. The large crowds were no accident. Olazábal had his small team of followers distributed 30,000 fliers announcing the healing and revival campaign.[32]

Olazábal's services blazed with drama and power. Despite the grinding poverty the Great Depression was wreaking on the largely Puerto Rican community outside of the church, inside some people claimed to find relief for their aching bodies and souls. The dramatic services followed the same pattern nightly. Olazábal walked onto center stage, led the congregation in a time of rousing singing, preached a twenty-five-minute evangelistic sermon, and then lifted his arms in the air and asked those throughout the church and in the balcony to come down to the front of the church, repent of their sins, and become Born-Again. Thousands answered his call. After the altar call, Olazábal began what many, perhaps most, of the people came for—divine healing. While many turned to a curandera, a Spiritist, or a Spiritualist for healing, others turned to El Azteca or the mighty Aztec, as Olazábal's followers called him.

Yet Olazábal saw healing as a means to an end. He believed that God gave him the ability to heal in order to attract and convert the unconverted and revive the soul of the "back-slidden" Christians. For this reason, he required that anyone seeking healing to fill out a prayer card and have it hole-punched at least five times (representing five nights) before he or she could come forward for prayer, although exceptions were often made for the deathly ill and sick children. This evangelistic strategy forced the person in search of healing to hear the "message of salvation." Ideally, persons would be converted or spiritually revived before they came forward for prayer. While one did not have to convert in order to be prayed for, one did have to agree with him that God was able to heal before he would pray for them.[33]

Olazábal and his followers report that in his 1931 Spanish Harlem campaigns, hundreds of people were healed of major illnesses or medical conditions—such as blindness, tuberculosis, deformity, tumors, heart conditions, rheumatism, deafness—and many other physical ailments and diseases. As at the Azusa Street Revival in Los Angeles more than twenty years earlier, the "relics" of their former life—rosaries, amulets, canes, and crutches—were thrown into a large pile on stage as symbols of God's power to heal. The revival converted thousands to the Pentecostal movement and prompted Olazábal to organize the new mother church of his movement, Bethel Temple, in New York City. They rented and then purchased a former synagogue on 114th Street in Spanish Harlem, just one block away from Robert Orsi's Italian Harlem community on 115th Street. His church had grown from just a handful of members in August 1931 to over 1,500 members by 1932, making it one of the largest churches in New York City. The vast majority of his parishioners were former Catholics,

5. Francisco Olazábal Revival, New York City, September 1931.
Courtesy: Gastón Espinosa.

Spiritists, agnostics, and socialists. Some also came from local mainline Protestant churches.[34]

One famous healing that seized the attention of the people was the story of María Teresa Sapia. Famous in Puerto Rico for her ties to the Puerto Rican underworld, she was reportedly a notorious gambler, gun woman, and rumrunner during Prohibition. Although Sapia was castigated by some as the "worst" woman in Puerto Rico, that was the least of her problems. Asthma and other ailments had whittled her body down to a scant seventy-five pounds. Hopeless, she turned to Olazábal for healing and redemption. At one of Olazábal's healing services, Sapia claimed she was dramatically healed and converted. Immediately she gave up her lifestyle and came to be heralded as the "Mary Magdalene" of Puerto Rico. After her radical conversion to Pentecostalism, she became a loyal supporter and assisted Olazábal at his crusades.[35]

Sapia was not alone in her decision to join Olazábal and the Pentecostal movement. Thousands of women streamed into the movement because it afforded them the chance to go into the ministry and exercise a prophetic voice. No doubt influenced by women such as his mother, Refugio Olazábal, and Carrie Judd Montgomery, Aimee Semple McPherson, Maria Woodworth-Etter, and even Alice Luce, Olazábal allowed women to go into the ministry. Although he did not formally ordain women to the pastoral ministry, he and the council did license and grant them the right

to preach from the pulpit and organize, pastor, and administer churches, and to serve as evangelists and missionaries. Women were not normally allowed to serve communion, perform baptisms, or conduct weddings without a male elder or pastor present, although exceptions were regularly made. Despite these limitations, the council produced a number of very famous female pastors, evangelists, and revivalists, such as María Jiménez—who pastored very large churches in Chicago and El Paso—and evangelists such as María Teresa Sapia, Leoncia Rosado Rousseau, and Julie and Matilde Vargas. Rosado Rousseau went on to cofound the Damascus Christian Church and Matilde Vargas conducted evangelistic services in the Latino community across the United States.[36]

Word of Olazábal's healing services spread rapidly not only through Depression-era Spanish Harlem, but also through New York's Italian and Anglo-American boroughs. It was not long before a growing number of Italians and Anglos began attending regularly. The number of non–Spanish speakers attending Olazábal's services was so large that he began holding English-language services on Monday night and Italian-language services on Thursday evenings and Sunday mornings. Olazábal also regularly ministered in Black Pentecostal churches in Harlem and throughout New York City. His ministry had now crossed linguistic and racial boundaries in a day when white supremacy and segregation dominated the racial and social imagination of many in Anglo-American society.[37]

After Homer Tomlinson, pastor of the Jamaica Tabernacle Church of God, heard about the "miracles" taking place, he invited Olazábal to conduct revival and healing services in his Anglo-American Jamaica Tabernacle Church. Surprised by the offer and eager to make connections with Anglo Pentecostal leaders in New York, Olazábal accepted. For weeks he evangelized and prayed for the sick. Tomlinson proclaimed the campaign an "overwhelming success," as over 800 people were converted. Tomlinson also claimed that "hundreds were healed," including a twenty-four-year-old crippled man who had been paralyzed since his youth.[38]

Olazábal and His Critics

When prominent Anglo Pentecostal leaders such as Robert A. Brown and J. R. Kline asked J. R. Flower and H. C. Ball about Olazábal, they were told that he vilified the Assemblies of God and had "done a great injustice to the work of the Lord." Ball also claimed that his evangelistic work "soon goes to pieces" when his campaigns are over. A few Mexican pastors left the Interdenominational Mexican Council and accused Olazábal of being too heavy handed. Others accused him of authoritarianism. Still others complained that he was too lenient with pastors who had "fallen into sin" or had compromised their Christian testimony.[39] Some of these complaints appear to be true. Despite the large crowds that attended his campaigns, the churches he organized afterward were often just a fraction of the size of the crowds that attended the campaign. Although it does not appear that Olazábal practiced favoritism per se, his ministry style was authoritarian at times. There were instances when he assigned ministers to churches in a part of the country where the minister did not want to serve. Necessity demanded otherwise, he noted. He publicly criticized congregations that did not financially support their pastors. In a day when divorce was grounds for immediate dismissal from the Pentecostal ministry regardless of who instigated it, Olazábal made exceptions. More than once, he allowed a minister who had gone through a divorce to continue in the ministry if the minister's spouse had been in the wrong and initiated the divorce.[40]

Olazábal was also accused of not healing everyone he prayed for. He openly acknowledged this fact. In fact, Frank Olazábal Jr. stated in an interview with the author that his father claimed to heal about 80 percent of those he prayed for. Others were less confident. Puerto Ricans such as Roberto Domínguez and one Anglo-American member of Homer Tomlinson's congregation claimed that despite Olazábal's prayers for healing, they had not been healed. Olazábal responded to these kinds of charges by stating that it was God's prerogative to heal. He was simply a vessel through which God manifested his healing power, nothing more. From a critical reading of the healing testimonies published in Olazábal's *Christian Messenger* magazine, it is clear that a majority of those that claimed healing were women. Furthermore, most of the "healings" were for minor ailments, although a number of people did claim to be healed of tuberculosis, cancer, tumors, blindness, deafness, and terminal diseases. Most doctors would probably categorize many of the "healings" as examples of psychosomatic healings brought about by the power of positive suggestion. Regardless of the reasons, the Latino community's long tradition of folk healing and the fact that most people could not afford a doctor help explain why Olazábal attracted thousands of people to his campaigns across the United States, Mexico, and Puerto Rico.[41]

Puerto Rico "Para Cristo": The Mexican Billy Sunday in Puerto Rico

Despite protests from critics and cynics, news of Olazábal's evangelistic healing crusades spread to Puerto Rico. Soon invitations began to pour in from the island inviting the Mexican American faith healer to hold campaigns in San Juan and Ponce. He responded to one such invitation from the Defenders of the Faith denomination. In 1934 he conducted the first mass Pentecostal, island-wide evangelistic healing and revival crusade in Puerto Rican history. He held services in tents, churches, civic auditoriums, and sports arenas. *El Mundo*, the largest newspaper on the island, dubbed Olazábal the "Mexican Billy Sunday" and claimed that he converted 20,000 people throughout the island.[42]

Olazábal returned to New York City like a triumphant Caesar in the eyes of his Spanish-speaking followers. He quickly realized that the key to his success there was his ability to garner the interdenominational support of Protestant leaders across the island. While at first some denominations opposed his work, by the end of his Puerto Rican campaign, most had been won over by the overwhelmingly positive response of both the press and the masses. Many Protestant ministers, such as Daniel Echevarría (Baptist) and Carlos Sepúlveda (Presbyterian), who had attended the Evangelical Seminary of Puerto Rico, decided to join Olazábal's newly named Latin American Council of Christian Churches.

In 1936, Francisco Olazábal stood at the height of his popularity. He conducted large evangelistic healing services in Puerto Rico, New York

City, Chicago, El Paso, and Edinburg, Texas. Letters arrived from all over the United States, Latin America, and Europe asking him to conduct campaigns. Olazábal began sketching plans to conduct evangelistic-healing services in Spain and Latin America. By that year, he had already sent or had plans to send missionaries and revivalists to Puerto Rico, Cuba, the Dominican Republic, Mexico, Chile, Argentina, Venezuela, Ecuador, and Spain.

The Anglo-American Christian community picked up on Olazábal's ministry. In 1936, the *Christian Herald* magazine and the *Sunday School Times* published articles on his work. Writing for the *Christian Herald*, Spencer Duryee described Olazábal as "The Great Aztec," whose transnational ministry was "one of the most startling stories . . . in modern religious history." He went on to compare Olazábal to the Apostle Paul, John Wesley, David Livingstone, and William Booth. Still others, such as McPherson and the Puerto Rican poet Luis Villaronga, compared him to the famous evangelist, Billy Sunday.[43]

Although Pentecostal in creed, ritual, and practice, Olazábal recognized that his interdenominational evangelistic healing message transcended denominational borders and boundaries. Rather than push his brand of Christianity on people, he would simply invite them to receive the baptism of the Holy Spirit and spiritual gifts when they were ready. While the private Olazábal often said that speaking in tongues was the key to his healing ministry, publicly he stated that he was not Pentecostal, at least not the stereotypical Pentecostal. He was simply "a Christian." This kind of ecumenical-sounding discourse attracted the attention of influential Mainline Protestant leaders such as Robert E. Speer, who agreed publicly to support Olazábal's next Puerto Rican campaign in the spring of 1936.[44]

Olazábal's ministry took a dramatic turn in 1936. Just days before his departure to Puerto Rico, he received devastating news: Speer had decided to withdraw his support. Shocked and disheartened, Olazábal asked his trusted friend Homer Tomlinson why. "Tongues," Tomlinson quietly said. Speer had telephoned Tomlinson and stated that he had just learned that Olazábal "belonged to the 'tongues' people" and therefore had to withdraw his support *immediately*.[45]

Disappointed but not devastated by the loss of Speer's support, Olazábal arrived in Puerto Rico in the spring of 1936 ready to repeat his 1934 campaign. Yet the setback with Speer was nothing compared to what he would experience on the island. Roman Catholic leaders looked at Olazábal as farmers look at an oncoming plague of locusts. They reportedly used their influence with the newspapers to criticize Olazábal and also to persuade them not to announce his campaign or arrival on the island. Some accused him of pocketing $2,000 from his first campaign in 1934—a charge he flatly denied. Some also claimed that he was "a stealer of the sheep of the widow." This criticism was predictable, as he was no fan of Catholicism. Over the years he tended to avoid publicly criticizing Roman Catholicism because he was concerned about alienating his largely Catholic audience—the very people he sought to convert. More devastating than this opposition, however, was the opposition of his Pentecostal and Evangelical colleagues, who were threatened by his growing popularity on the island. They too did not support him, because of the various accusations circulating at the time, and perhaps because of jealousy.

Despite the difficulties he now faced, he continued to hold evangelistic services. In the capital city of San Juan, Olazábal was forced to meet outside the city limits on a racetrack. In Ponce he was denied regular meeting places and had to conduct his meetings at the docks. Frustrated at every turn, he wired his wife in New York and asked her to send his large evangelistic tent to the island to protect the visitors from the drenching tropical rain and scorching sun.[46]

The lack of support from Speer, opposition from the Catholic Church, and criticism from his former Protestant supporters were more than Olazábal could handle. Even before his tent arrived, he boarded a ship and steamed home for New York City, arriving unannounced and without fanfare. According to one report, there on the porch of his home, in front of his close friend Homer Tomlinson, Olazábal wept. With tears streaming down his face, he confided to Tomlinson that he had never been so discouraged. Rejection by the Anglo establishment was hard enough, but to find his fellow Latino Protestant leaders also aligned against him was tremendously painful.[47]

The 1936 Puerto Rico para Cristo campaign marked a sharp turning point in Olazábal's vision. Prior to that campaign, he saw his healing ministry as bridging the racial and denominational divides that fragmented American Protestantism. He now realized that such bridging would be very difficult, if not impossible. Now that the influential Speer knew he was "a tongues speaker," he knew that interdenominational support would be virtually impossible to win from Mainline Protestant denominations. His dream of an interdenominational, transnational, and multiracial evangelistic healing ministry was frustrated by forces beyond his control.

Pentecostal–Roman Catholic Tensions and
the Healing of Southern White Bodies

Although Olazábal's pride and image had been tarnished, he left New York shortly thereafter to begin a new campaign in El Paso, Texas, the place he had begun his transborder ministry in the United States twenty-five years earlier, in 1911. Upon his arrival, he found María Teresa Sapia and his own daughter Martha preparing for the campaign. Olazábal at first had free rein in El Paso, as Catholic leaders were unaware of his arrival. Wasting no time, he secured the enormous city auditorium for his healing services. Thousands of Mexicans poured into the meetings. As with charismatic healers before him, Olazábal's message of hope, healing, and physical and spiritual transformation attracted the masses.[48]

Once Catholic leaders in El Paso found out about Olazábal's campaign, Father Lourdes F. Costa of El Paso began publicly to attack Olazábal in the El Paso newspapers by challenging his claim to heal. Olazábal responded with an equally sharp letter stating that the reason people left the Catholic Church was that it lacked real transformative power.[49] Despite the attempts to silence Olazábal, he reported that many Mexicans were converted and new churches founded as a result of the 1936 El Paso campaign.[50]

No sooner had the El Paso campaign ended, Olazábal and his son Frank, Jr., headed for Cleveland, Tennessee. Olazábal realized that if he was ever going to have an international and multiracial ministry, he needed major financial support and the freedom to travel unrestrained by the cares of administering the council. He was tired and took a second look at the Anglo-American Church of God, which had asked him to join their movement a few years earlier. He realized that while he may not have been able to win the support of Mainline Protestants such as Robert E. Speer, he still could win the support of Pentecostal denominations such as the Church of God.

Reenergized from his recent crusade in El Paso, Olazábal attended the 1936 Church of God Annual Assembly in Cleveland, Tennessee. On 10 September 1936, before an audience of 6,000 white southerners, the somewhat reluctant Olazábal placed his hand on a Bible and swore allegiance to the Church of God. While no formal legal documents had been signed, it was a symbolic gesture of what the Church of God considered an inevitable union. The Church of God was electrified. In one fell swoop they had added an estimated 150 churches, 50,000 people, and Francisco Olazábal. At least so they thought.[51]

"Hundreds Seek Faith Healing" at the Church of God convention, read the headline of the *Chattanooga Times* on 12 September 1936. "More than 700 persons were anointed with oil and prayed for . . . in the annual healing service here tonight before a packed audience that overflowed into three surrounding blocks," the reporter went on to claim. When asked by a newspaper reporter if he was a healer, Olazábal replied by stating "The only thing I know is I am a believer in Jesus . . . [and] that he is the same yesterday, today, and forever."[52] The *Cleveland Daily Banner* reported hundreds of people came "under the spell of Rev. Francisco Olazábal."[53] The response of this southern white crowd to Olazábal's message and healing was overwhelmingly positive. Despite his Spanish accent, or perhaps because of it, thousands of white southerners streamed forward to be healed by the tall Mexican evangelist. Tomlinson claimed that Olazábal prayed for over 1,500 people at the 1936 annual convention. Olazábal made such an impact at the 1936 convention that hundreds of letters continued to pour into the Church of God headquarters for the next two years requesting that Olazábal pray for them.[54]

Olazábal's psychologically devastating setback in Puerto Rico had been softened by his recent campaigns in El Paso and Cleveland. Triumphant in the eyes of his followers, he returned to New York City. Despite his setback with Speer, he had entered the Anglo-American Pentecostal world and had taken center stage. His life and ministry were the embodiment and dream of thousands of other Latinos living in the shadows of Jim Crow America in the 1930s.

Reignited by his recent campaigns in El Paso and Cleveland, Olazábal confidently led 2,000 Latinos in a planned march down New York's Fifth Avenue. Standing six abreast, shouting, praising God, and singing, they boldly waved colorful banners much as Pentecostal and Evangelical Christians do today in the International March for Jesus. They gathered at the plaza at the end of Fifth Avenue and 110th Street for a rally. A rebounding from his recent setbacks, the parade was a powerful symbol that Olazábal and the Latino Pentecostal movement were in Spanish Harlem to stay.[55]

"A Great Oak Has Fallen upon the Mountain":
The Death of Charisma

"Rev. F. Olazábal . . . Dies of Injuries Suffered in Auto Accident" read the *New York Times* obituary on 12 June 1937.[56] Francisco Olazábal was dead. Near Alice Springs, Texas, on his way to an ordination service in Mexico on 1 June, his car skidded off the slippery blacktop surface and turned over. Although critically injured, he was taken to a hospital where he appeared to recover. Then, on 9 June 1937, Olazábal died from internal hemorrhaging. He seemed to know that death was imminent and reportedly dictated a message to his followers. In it he admonished them to continue the work he had started and to keep the Holy Spirit at the center of their ministry. In the minds of his followers, a giant had fallen.

Olazábal's death came as a shock to his followers. On hearing the news, some of his closest friends and followers fainted.[57] In a scene reminiscent of presidents and other national figures, Olazábal's body was placed in a $2,000 gas-vapor-filled casket and taken for display to Houston, New York, Chicago, El Paso, and finally Los Angeles. His lifeless body was placed on public display in his enormous Bethel Temple in the heart of Spanish Harlem for three days. Some estimate that not fewer than 50,000 Latin Americans, Puerto Ricans, Anglo-Americans, and Blacks paid their last respects over the three-day period. Homer Tomlinson eulogized Olazábal before thousands by stating that "a mighty man of God has fallen in the midst of his labors." "A great oak has fallen upon the mountain." Those who had once been healed by the once "mighty Aztec" now looked on in disbelief. On the last day of the memorial, there was a procession of an estimated 20,000 people who walked alongside the hearse, which contained the body of the dead apostle to Latinos. From New York City his body was taken for display to Chicago, then to El Paso, and finally to Los Angeles. In East Los Angeles, the place he called home, thousands of Mexicans, Blacks, and Anglos came from across the Southwest and Mexico to pay their last respects to the Mexican Apostle. His body was laid to rest in Evergreen Cemetery, not far from that of William J. Seymour, the founder of the Pentecostal movement.[58]

With Olazábal's death, the leadership of the Latin American Council of Christian Churches was up for grabs—at least in the minds of the Puerto Rican contingent. Without Olazábal's charisma to hold it together, the movement fragmented along ethnic and regional lines. Miguel Guillén, a Mexican American and the new president, proved unable to rein in the Puerto Rican nationalism surfacing in the council. Members balked at Guillén's ascendancy to the presidency. Many Puerto Ricans were tired of feeling like second-class citizens in the council and resented the Mexican American leadership, which the city-wise Puerto Ricans considered generally ignorant and inferior. A number of key Puerto Ricans and a few Mexican leaders split the council into several warring factions, each championing its own leader. By 1938 the council was in complete disarray and was fighting for its very existence. While everyone preached unity, fragmentation and rebellion spread. As with the schism in 1923, hundreds were confused and not sure which way to turn or whom to follow. The first schism took place in February 1938, with Mexican American Gilberto Díaz breaking away from the council in Chicago. In the fall of 1938, a group of Puerto Ricans under the leadership of Carlos Sepúlveda, Felipe Sabater, and Frank Hernández did the same in New York City. In 1939, Sepúlveda founded the Assembly of Christian Churches (AIC) in New York. No sooner had the Sepúlveda crisis ended, than another erupted when Olazábal's wife, Macrina, Andrés Aguilar, and a number of others decided to leave the council. They took about nineteen churches and missions in 1942. The last major schism prior to 1950 took place in 1947, when Alejandro Leal of Texas broke away with ten churches to found his own denomination. These schisms took their toll on the council and almost destroyed their movement.[59]

The fragmentation of the council made the union between the Latin American Council of Christian Churches and the Church of God impossible. Despite the internal conflict going on in the council, the Church of God continued to move toward consummation of the union. Notwithstanding the generous overtures on the part of the Church of God, there was a general sentiment in the council, from Miguel Guillén on down, that the Church of God really wanted Olazábal and numbers, not rank-and-file Mexicans and Puerto Ricans. This fact, along with the infighting within the council, killed any major movement toward union with the Church of God. Tomlinson's dream of a "grand union" between the two denominations went up in flames.[60]

The Significance and Legacy of Francisco Olazábal

Francisco Olazábal left a lasting mark on Mexican American and Latino Christianity in the United States, Puerto Rico, and Mexico. No single Mexican American religious leader has shaped the history and development of the early Latino Pentecostal movement in North America and the Latin Caribbean as he did. Called the "Apostle Paul to the Latin Americans," Olazábal contributed to the origins or development of at least fourteen denominations.[61] By the time of his death in 1937, he claimed 150 churches and 50,000 followers throughout North America and the Latin Caribbean.[62] The work of Mexican American healing evangelists such as Olazábal helped lay the foundation for the religious reformation currently taking place in the Latino community in the United States and Puerto Rico. It also helps to explain why there are almost 9 million Latino

Protestants in the United States today, 64 percent of whom are Pentecostal or Charismatic.[63] Supporting this seismic shift in Latino religiosity, Andrew Greeley estimates that as many as 600,000 U.S. Latinos may be leaving the Roman Catholic Church every year for Evangelical/Pentecostal Christianity. He argues that almost 1 million U.S. Latinos "defected" from the Roman Catholic Church to Evangelical/Pentecostal Christianity between 1973 and 1989. He calls this "mass defection" "an ecclesiastical failure of an unprecedented proportion."[64] Almost all the scholarship on this shift in Latino religiosity has argued that it is a relatively new, post-1960 phenomenon. As we have seen, this seismic shift actually began in the early twentieth century. The Latino Pentecostal movement in general and the ministry of Francisco Olazábal (1886–1937) in particular served as one stream in the growth of the first nationwide mass conversions from Roman Catholicism to Protestantism throughout the United States, Mexico, and Puerto Rico.

Olazábal was a Latino Pentecostal prophet whose popularity can be attributed to his charisma. After trying to transform the Mexican Assemblies of God from within, Olazábal was pushed to the margins, where he attempted to take control of the movement. The fact that he stood up against Anglo-American leaders and seized control over his own life and movement in Jim Crow America was remarkable in the 1920s and 1930s, an achievement not lost on his followers, who called him the "mighty Aztec" or El Azteca. His authority to evangelize and heal was not dependent solely upon Anglo-American approval, but reportedly came directly from God. He was the Protestant version of famous Catholic folk healers such as El Niño Fidencio, Don Pedrito Jaramillo, and María Teresa Urrea. His ministry tapped into the tremendous emphasis on healing in Latino spirituality and culture. Although his healing ministry was spurred on by his experience of speaking in tongues, it did not fully blossom until after he had broken away from the Assemblies of God. His healing ministry along with his emphasis on church planting, women in ministry, personal evangelism, citywide crusades, and mass-marketing techniques all help explain his ability to attract the masses. These factors helped give birth to one of the first completely transnational Latino Protestant movements in North America and the Latin Caribbean.

Olazábal's prophetic rejection of Anglo-American racism and pious paternalism created a message that would rise again in another Pentecostal leader during the Chicano Movement (1965–75) named Reies López Tijerina, who also had an AG background.[65] Ironically, after Olazábal's death his vision of Christianity was institutionalized and routinized by his followers, who demanded stricter adherence to the letter of Pentecostal doctrine than had Olazábal himself. This transition from charismatic prophet to institutionalization created a period of tremendous conflict and instability and contributed to the fragmentation of the council into a number of smaller denominations or councils (i.e., *concilios*) and scores of independent churches that exist to this day. It is precisely this tendency to produce charismatic prophetic leaders who split off from existing denominations to form their own that has kept the Pentecostal movement constantly fragmenting and spreading almost 100 years after it first erupted onto the stage of world history.

Olazábal's life and work also challenge previous perceptions of Latino Protestantism. Many have argued that Latino Protestants were controlled and manipulated by Anglo-American denominations and leaders. While this certainly was true for some Latino Protestants, his story challenges this stereotype and instead demonstrates that there is also a long tradition of indigenous, independent, and autonomous Latino Protestant churches that are completely run by and for the Mexican American and Latino community. These traditions have created an alternative, self-affirming Latino Protestant subculture in the borderlands that emphasizes healing and personal empowerment. Olazábal's story also demonstrates that the Latino community was more denominationally pluralistic than has hitherto been recognized. Pentecostalism was able to enter the marrow of Mexican American and Latino culture and society precisely because it resymbolized the supernatural worldview of popular Latino Catholicism and metaphysical traditions. In particular, its emphasis on healing resonated with the popular Catholic healing tradition of curanderismo, which Luis León will describe in greater detail in chapter 12. It began to transform the Latino religious marketplace by offering a combinative via media that resonated with select ritual (though not necessarily theological) aspects Latino Catholicism, metaphysical traditions, and Protestantism.

Despite Olazábal's impact on American religious history and Pentecostalism, scholars have overlooked his story. Yet it is important because it demonstrates that the Latino Pentecostal movement and healing began much earlier and was much larger and more indigenous, independent, diverse, and transnational than previously believed. For this reason, his story shatters the biracial view of early Pentecostalism as an essentially a black-and-white story. It also demonstrates that the present growth of Pentecostal healing in the Latino community actually traces its roots back to the early twentieth century, and not the 1960s and 1970s as is often asserted. It further calls on scholars to revise and retell the story of American religions from the periphery, a story of south to north, not just east to west. His story calls on scholars to end the erasure of Mexican Americans and Latinos from the narrative of American religious history and to reimagine and retell it as a North American story. Francisco Olazábal's legacy is evident in thousands of indigenous, independent, and autonomous Latino Pentecostal storefront churches throughout North America and the Latin Caribbean that continue to blend and preach healing, evangelism, and sociocultural empowerment.

Notes

The author wishes to thank Catherine Albanese, Mario T. García, Michael McClymond, Sarah Cline, Colin Calloway, John Watanabe, Robert Gundry, and Rick Pointer for their critical feedback on early drafts of this chapter.

1. When comparing Latinos to African Americans, Barry Kosmin and Seymour Lachman wrote in 1993, "There is no tradition of a separatist or autonomous Hispanic church" in the United States. Kosmin and Lachman, *One Nation under God: Religion in Contemporary Society* (New York: Harmony Books, 1993), 138.

2. A. C. Valdez, with James F. Scheer, *Fire on Azusa Street* (Costa Mesa, Calif.: Gift Publications, 1980); Abundio L. López and Rosa López, "Spanish Receive the Pentecost," *Apostolic Faith* (October 1906); Arthur G. Osterberg, Oral History of the Life of Arthur G. Osterberg and the Azusa Street Revival, interview (transcribed) by Jerry Jensen and Jonathan Perkins, 1966, Assemblies of God Archives.

3. Osterberg, Oral History interview, 12. Nickel stated that this Mexican man's clubfoot had been "completely straightened." Thomas R. Nickel, *Azusa Street Outpouring: As Told to Me by Those Who Were There* (Hanford, Calif.: Great Commission International, 1956, 3rd ed. 1986), 13.

4. Mrs. Knapp, untitled article, *Apostolic Faith*, September 1906, 2; no author, untitled article, *Apostolic Faith*, September 1906, 3.

5. Richard Crayne, *Pentecostal Handbook* (Morristown, Tenn.: Richard Crayne, 1963, 3rd ed., 1990), 228.

6. Valdez, *Fire on Azusa Street*, 27, 34, esp. 39.

7. Abundio L. and López, "Spanish Receive the Pentecost," 4.

8. Ibid., 4.

9. "Work among Spanish," *Pisgah*, January 1909, 11–12.

10. "A Revival in Los Angeles," *Pisgah*, December 1910, 13.

11. "Work among Spanish," *Pisgah*, January 1909, 11–12.

12. Evangeline Hymer, "A Study of the Social Attitudes of Adult Mexican Immigrants in Los Angeles and Vicinity" (MA thesis, University of Southern California, 1923).

13. G. Bromley Oxnam, *The Mexican in Los Angeles: Los Angeles City Survey* (Los Angeles: InterChurch World Movement of North America, 1920), 6, 10, 15.

14. For evidence and a discussion of Mexican popular Catholicism and folk healing, see Robert T. Trotter II and Juan Antonio Chavira, *Curanderismo: Mexican American Folk Healing*, 2nd ed. (Athens: University of Georgia Press, [1981] 1997); Ari Kiev, *Curanderismo: Mexican-American Folk Psychiatry* (New York: Free Press, 1968); William and Claudia Madsen, *A Guide to Mexican Witchcraft* (Mexico City: Minutiae Mexicana, 1972); June Macklin, "*Curanderismo* and *Espiritismo*: Complementary Approaches to Traditional Health Services," in *The Chicano Experience*, ed. Stanley A. West and June Macklin (Boulder, Colo.: Westview Press, 1979), 207–26.

15. Juarez Cano, "El Rev. Francisco Olazábal: Datos biográficos," *El Mensajero Cristiano*, June 1938, 6–8, 12–13; Roberto Domínguez, *Pioneros de pentecostés: Norteamerica y Las Antillas*, vol. 1, 3rd ed. (Barcelona, Spain: Editorial Clie, 1990), 41–42; Luis Villaronga, "¿Quién Es Olazábal?" *El Mundo* (Puerto Rico), 1934, 31; Villaronga, "Datos para la Biografía del Rvdo F. Olazábal," *El Mensajero Cristiano*, October 1938, 5–6; Frank Olazábal Jr., Latino Pentecostal Oral History Project, telephone interview, May 1998, Hanover, New Hampshire.

16. Cano, "El Rev. Francisco Olazábal," 6–8, 12–13; Domínguez, *Pioneros de pentecostés*, 41–42; Villaronga, "¿Quién Es Olazábal?" 31; Villaronga, "Datos para la Biografía del Rvdo F. Olazábal," 5–6.

17. Homer A. Tomlinson, *Miracles of Healing in the Ministry of Rev. Francisco Olazábal* (Queens, New York: Homer A. Tomlinson, 1938), 6; Domínguez, *Pioneros de pentecostés*, 32–35.

18. Domínguez, *Pioneros de pentecostés*, 36.

19. Methodist Episcopal Church, Official Minutes of the Sixty-fourth Session of the California Conference of the Methodist Episcopal Church, Santa Cruz, California, 1916, 26, 34; Methodist Episcopal Church, Official Minutes of the Sixty-fifth Session of the California Conference of the Methodist Episcopal Church, Santa Cruz, California, 1917, 185.

20. Tomlinson, *Miracles of Healing in the Ministry of Rev. Francisco Olazábal*, 6–7; Domínguez, *Pioneros de pentecostés*, 32, 35; Francisco Olazábal, "A Mexican Witness," *Pentecostal Evangel*, 16 October 1920.

21. Tomlinson, *Miracles of Healing in the Ministry of Rev. Francisco Olazábal*, 6–7; Domínguez, *Pioneros de pentecostés*, 32, 35.

22. H. C. Ball, "A Report of the Spanish Pentecostal Convention," *Christian Evangel*, 28 December 1918, 7; Francisco Olazábal, "God Is Blessing on the Mexican Border," *Weekly Evangel*, 1 October 1921, 10; Victor DeLeón, *The Silent Pentecostals* (Taylors, S.C.: Faith Printing Company, 1979), 28–29.

23. J. W. Welch, letter to H. C. Ball, 11 November 1924; H. C. Ball, letter to J. R. Flower, 8 December 1924, personal collection of Gastón Espinosa; Francisco Olazábal, "The Mexican Work at El Paso," *Pentecostal Evangel*, 30 September 1922, 13; Frank Olazábal Jr., Latino Pentecostal Oral History Project; Miguel Guillén, *La Historia del Concilio Latino Americano de Iglesias Cristianas* (Brownsville, Tex.: Latin American Council of Christian Churches, 1991), 83; Latin American Council of Christian Churches, *Seminario del CLADIC 25 Año Aniversario* (Latin American Council of Christian Churches, 1979), 7.

24. H. C. Ball, letter to Pastor J. R. Kline, 7 February 1933, 1–2, personal collection of Gastón Espinosa; Tomlinson, *Miracles of Healing in the Ministry of Rev. Francisco Olazábal*, 7; De Leon, 99.

25. Guillén, *La Historia del Concilio Latino Americano de Iglesias Cristianas*, 93–114.

26. Tomlinson, *Miracles of Healing in the Ministry of Rev. Francisco Olazábal*, 7–8.

27. "La Hermana McPherson en la Carpa de Watts y el Hno. Francisco Olazábal en 'Angelus Temple' de Los Angeles," *El Mensajero Cristiano*, October 1927, 6–8; J. T. A., "Un servicio evangelio para los mexicanos," *El Mensajero Cristiano*, November 1927, 7–8.

28. "La Hermana McPherson en la Carpa de Watts y el Hno. Francisco Olazábal en 'Angelus Temple' de Los Angeles," 6–8; Frank Olazábal Jr., *Revive Us Again!* (Los Angeles: Christian Academic Foundation, 1987), 81; Frank Olazábal Jr., Latino Pentecostal Oral History Project.

29. "La Hermana McPherson en la Carpa de Watts y el Hno. Francisco Olazábal en 'Angelus Temple' de Los Angeles," 6–8; Frank Olazábal Jr., Latino Pentecostal Oral History Project.

30. "Primera Sesión de La Iglesia Interdenominacional de Chicago," *El Mensajero Cristiano*, September 1929, 8–9; "Iglesia De Chicago, IL" and "Testimonios de Sanidad Divina," *El Mensajero Cristiano*, September 1930, 12–16; Tomlinson, *Miracles of Healing in the Ministry of Rev. Francisco Olazábal*, 11.

31. "Cuatro meses con el Rev. Francisco Olazábal en la Ciudad de Nueva York," *El Mensajero Cristiano*, January 1932, 11–12.

32. "Cuatro meses con el Rev. Francisco Olazábal en la Ciudad de Nueva York," 11–12; circular flyer, 1931, in possession of the author.

33. Tomlinson, *Miracles of Healing in the Ministry of Rev. Francisco Olazábal*, 1–2.

34. Ibid., 1.

35. Frank Olazábal Jr., *Revive Us Again!*, 123; Tomlinson, *Miracles of Healing in the Ministry of Rev. Francisco Olazábal*, 12.

36. Gastón Espinosa, "'Your Daughters Shall Prophesy': A History of Women in Ministry in the Latino Pentecostal Movement in the United States," in *Women and Twentieth Century Protestantism*, ed. Margaret Lamberts Bendroth and Virginia Lieson Brereton (Chicago: University of Illinois Press, 2002), 25–48.

37. "Cuatro meses con el Rev. Francisco Olazábal en la Ciudad de Nueva York," 11–12. The KKK reached its apogee in the 1920s, with an estimated 4–5 million men.

38. Homer A. Tomlinson, "Letter to the Pentecostal Evangel," 13 October 1931, personal collection of Gastón Espinosa.

39. Robert A. Brown, letter to H. C. Ball, 13 October 1931, 1–2; H. C. Ball, letter to J. R. Evans, 14 October 1931, 1; J. R. Flower, letter to H. C. Ball, 21 October 1931, 1; H. C. Ball, letter to J. R. Evans, 27 October 1931, 1; J. R. Kline, letter to J. R. Evans, 4 February 1933, 1; J. R. Flower, letter to J. R. Kline, 7 February 1933, 1–2. Copies of letters, in possession of the author.

40. Olazábal Jr., Latino Pentecostal Oral History Project.

41. Domínguez, *Pioneros de pentecostés*, 18.

42. Villaronga, "El Evangelista Olazábal en Río Piedras," *El Mundo* (San Juan, Puerto Rico), 5 May 1934; Guillén, *La Historia del Concilio Latino Americano de Iglesias Cristianas*, 22–131; Spencer Duryee, "The Great Aztec," *Christian Herald* (August 1936): 6.

43. Ernest Gordon, "Revival among Spanish-Speaking," *Sunday School Times*, 24 August 1935, 550–51; Duryee, "The Great Aztec," 5–7; Villaronga, "El Evangelista Olazábal en Río Piedras"; Tomlinson, *Miracles of Healing in the Ministry of Rev. Francisco Olazábal*, 12, 17, 24.

44. Tomlinson, *Miracles of Healing in the Ministry of Rev. Francisco Olazábal*, 16–17; Domínguez, *Pioneros de pentecostés*, 18.

45. Tomlinson, *Miracles of Healing in the Ministry of Rev. Francisco Olazábal*, 17; Domínguez, *Pioneros de pentecostés*, 44.

46. Tomlinson, *Miracles of Healing in the Ministry of Rev. Francisco Olazábal*, 18–19; Domínguez, *Pioneros de pentecostés*, 45–46; "La Campaña Olazábal en Puerto Rico," *El Mensajero Cristiano*, April 1936, 3.

47. Tomlinson, *Miracles of Healing in the Ministry of Rev. Francisco Olazábal*, 18–19.

48. No author, "Campaña Olazábal de El Paso, Texas," *El Mensajero Cristiano*, July 1936, 6, 15; Carlos Sepúlveda, "La Campaña Olazábal en El Paso, Texas," *El Mensajero Cristiano*, August 1936, 6–7; Sepúlveda, "Glorioso servicio de despedida," *El Mensajero Cristiano*, August 1936; Tomlinson, *Miracles of Healing in the Ministry of Rev. Francisco Olazábal*, 19–20.

49. No author, "Campaña Olazábal de El Paso, Texas," 6, 15; Sepúlveda, "La Campaña Olazábal en el Paso, Texas," 6–7; Sepúlveda, "Glorioso Servicio de Despedida"; Tomlinson, *Miracles of Healing in the Ministry of Rev. Francisco Olazábal*, 19–20; Father Lourdes F. Costa, letter to Francisco Olazábal, 9 June 1936; Father Lourdes F. Costa, letter to Francisco Olazábal, 11 June 1936; Rev. Francisco Olazábal, letter to Father Lourdes F. Costa, 13 July 1936. Letters in possession of the author.

50. No author, "Campaña Olazábal de El Paso, Texas," 6, 15; Sepúlveda, "La Campaña Olazábal en El Paso, Texas," 6–7; Sepúlveda, "Glorioso Servicio de Despedida"; Tomlinson, *Miracles of Healing in the Ministry of Rev. Francisco Olazábal*, 19–20; Frank Olazábal Jr., *Revive Us Again!*; Domínguez, *Pioneros de pentecostés*, 280–81.

51. Despite Harold Hunter's inaccurate and denominationally apologetic claim otherwise, in my oral history interview with Frank Olazábal Jr., an eyewitness to the event and the person Hunter cites as evidence of the unification, he stated that his father was surprised by Homer Tomlinson's insistence that he swear allegiance to the Church of God at the convention. Frank Jr. stated rather emphatically that his father had no intention of (or denominational authority for) joining the Church of God prior to his arrival in Cleveland, Tennessee. Furthermore, internal correspondence by A. J. and Homer Tomlinson make clear their frustration that Francisco Olazábal would not consummate the

merger with the Church of God. Frank Olazábal Jr., Latino Pentecostal Oral History Project; Travis Hedrick, *Chattanooga Times*, 12 September 1936, 1, 7; Tomlinson, *Miracles of Healing in the Ministry of Rev. Francisco Olazábal*, 16. Harold D. Hunter and Cecil M. Robeck Jr., *The Azusa Street Revival and Its Legacy* (Cleveland, Tenn.: Pathway Press, 2006), 293.

52. Hedrick, "Hundreds Seek Faith Healing," 1.

53. "Hundreds Pray all Night at Unique Healing Service," *Cleveland Daily Banner*, 12 September 1925.

54. Tomlinson, *Miracles of Healing in the Ministry of Rev. Francisco Olazábal*, 20.

55. Homer Tomlinson, "Big Parade of 2,000 Lead down Fifth Avenue New York City," *White Wing Messenger*, 7 November 1936, 1, 4.

56. "Rev. F. Olazábal, Evangelist Here," *New York Times*, 12 June 1937.

57. "A Mighty Man of God Has Fallen in the Midst of His Labors," *White Wing Messenger*, 3 July 1937, 4.

58. A. D. Evans, "Brother Olazábal Killed in Auto Accident," *White Wing Messenger*, 19 June 1937, 1; "A Mighty Man of God Has Fallen in the Midst of His Labors," 1, 4; Tomlinson, *Miracles of Healing in the Ministry of Rev. Francisco Olazábal*, 23–25; Domínguez, *Pioneros de pentecostés*, 50–56.

59. Guillén, *La Historia del Concilio Latino Americano de Iglesias Cristianas*, 187–300.

60. "Overseer of Latin-American Churches," *White Wing Messenger*, 28 August 1937, 1; Tomlinson, *Miracles of Healing in the Ministry of Rev. Francisco Olazábal*, 26–27; "Miguel Guillén Leaves New York for Another Visit to the Churches," *White Wing Messenger*, 23 April 1938, 1.

61. The fourteen denominations Olazábal directly or indirectly contributed to include (1) the Hispanic United Methodist Church, (2) the Hispanic Districts of the Assemblies of God, (3) the Latin American Council of Christian Churches, (4) the Hispanic International Foursquare Gospel, (5) the Hispanic Church of God of Prophecy, (6) the Defenders of the Faith, (7) the Missionary Church of Christ, (8) the Church of Christ of the Antilles, (9) the Assembly of Christian Churches, (10) the Damascus Christian Church, (11) the Concilio Cristiano Hispano Pentecostés—former Olazábal Council of Christian Churches, (12) Evangelical Assemblies, Inc., (13) the Pentecostal Council of Christian Churches, and (14) the Pentecostal Assembly of Jesus Christ. There are also many other smaller Latino Pentecostal denominations in the United States and in Latin America that trace their roots back to Francisco Olazábal.

62. Villaronga, "¿Quién Es Olazábal?" 31; Duryee, "The Great Aztec," 5–8; Cano, "El Rev. Francisco Olazábal," 6–8, 12–13; Domínguez, *Pioneros de pentecostés*, 41–42.

63. Gastón Espinosa, Virgilio Elizondo, and Jesse Miranda, *Hispanic Churches in American Public Life: Summary of Findings* (Notre Dame, Ind.: Institute for Latino Studies, University of Notre Dame, 2003), 14; Gastón Espinosa, "Changements démographiques et religieux chez les hispaniques des Etats-Unis," *Social Compass: International Review of Sociology of Religion* 51 (2004):

303–20; Gastón Espinosa, "The Pentecostalization of Latin American and U.S. Latino Christianity," *Pneuma: The Journal of the Society for Pentecostal Studies* 26, no. 2 (fall 2004): 262–92.

64. Andrew M. Greeley, "Defections among Hispanics," *America*, 30 July 1988, 61–62. For an update, see Greeley, "Defections among Hispanics (updated)," *America*, 27 September 1997, 12–13.

65. The Chicano Movement (1965–75) was a political-social movement that fought for civil rights against the social and racial indignities many Mexican Americans faced in the United States. Rudy L. Busto, *King Tiger: The Religious Vision of Reies López Tijerina* (Albuquerque: University of New Mexico Press, 2005); Carlos Muñoz Jr., *Youth, Identity, Power: The Chicano Movement* (New York: Verso Books, 1989).

12

Borderlands Bodies and Souls

Mexican Religious Healing Practices in

East Los Angeles

The weathered-looking "Dolores Multiplicadas" has had a hard life.[1] She looks much older than her twenty-four years. "Nothing goes right for me," she gently complains one bright and smoggy fall afternoon at the Sagrado Corazón (Sacred Heart) *botánica* in East Los Angeles. "I came here to see the señora because I heard she was good." Her story is typical of the many patrons who visit this storefront healing center to see the *curandera* Hortencia. They come with great expectations, seeking hope, succor, and power. Punctuated by a pair of gunshots, and unfolding to the rhythms of César Chávez Avenue—families laughing, tacos frying, babies crying, stereos blaring, and Cristina pontificating from her electronic pulpit—Dolores's painful story—combining tragedy, comedy, and struggle—finds mystical affirmation in the charismatic presence of Hortencia the healer, Hortencia the clairvoyant, Hortencia the psychic, Hortencia the prophet, and, above all else, Hortencia, by her own profession, the practicing Catholic.

This study is situated in that paradoxical space—the border that connects yet divides Catholicism and indigenous Mexican ritual, a space between submission and resistance, between hope and despair, between life and death, at the intersections of colonialism, modernity, capitalism, primitivism, the nation, and the self—where desire meets dread, where will meets surrender, where La Virgen de Guadalupe meets the Meso-american mother goddess Tonantzin, where Guadalupe and Tonantzin meet Malinche, and where all coalesce and become La Llorona.[2] The Mexican-derived healing tradition known as *curanderismo* illuminates the conditions of possibility for poor Chicanas/os and Mexicans to heal themselves and their loved ones, to negotiate the suffering and injustice that is for many the quotidian stuff of life. It provides some answers about the alternatives available to Mexicans and other Latinos attempting to overcome the limitations of the material world, to mend the injuries inflicted upon them by the harsh realities of intense late capitalism: it helps Latina and Latino postmoderns bring order to chaos, and wholeness to broken bodies and souls.

Scholars have long argued in the study of religion that people make sense of the anomie that is the phenomenal world through myth and ritual, and that myths and rituals are culturally inflected. The practice of curanderismo offers guidance on a long, less-traveled path to uncover the salient idioms and symbols of Mexican American religious experience, charting the ways in which tradition and discourse have been imagined and reimagined, and the harsh material conditions under which such imaginations were rendered possible.

This study explores one site of curanderismo. It offers an ethnographic account of my own limited perceptions. Over the course of twelve months, and with the help of Lara Medina, I have studied one site of faith and healing in East Los Angeles: the Sagrado Corazón botánica (figure 1). I brought my many years of research on curanderismo to this project. During this period I spoke with and interviewed dozens of the women and men who came to the botánica in search of healing. I listened to and recorded many of their stories. In what follows, I analyze the prominent themes that emerged from these conversations.

The majority of clients at Sagrado Corazón were reluctant to explain exactly what it was they sought, and they were, understandably, unwilling to submit to longer, more personal interviews. I respected people's wishes for privacy, and did not push anyone beyond a first refusal. A study as limited as this can do little more than provide another starting point for future research. Thus, I provide background material and preliminary assessments based on participant observation, and grounded in on-site conversations or interviews. But the wealth of this study comes from the insights of Hortencia herself—just thirty-eight years old. Born in Mexico, she has lived in the United States for eight years. She has four children, the youngest born in September 1999.

1. Sagrado Corazón Botánica, where curanderas purchase their supplies. East Los Angeles. Courtesy: Luis León.

Street Religion

Today's academic understanding of curanderismo would benefit from sustained case studies that probe more deeply into the lives of willing patrons.[3] The multiplication of public sites such as Sagrado Corazón in Chicano barrios within the last ten to fifteen years opens up opportunities for curandera research heretofore unavailable when curanderismo was mostly restricted to private homes and extended kinship networks.

Professor Lara Medina brought Sagrado Corazón botánica to my attention one afternoon while driving down César Chávez Avenue. Earlier I had visited another more traditional curandera who denied me admission to her healing center, which doubled as her private residence. But all are welcome at Sagrado Corazón. People of many faiths visit this storefront religious center. Hortencia does not ask questions of her clients, except what they seek. Though the definitive signs identifying the space point to Catholicism, there is no dogmatic text against which believers measure the accuracy (or inaccuracy) of their lives. This public space is encoded by multiple and multivocal religious symbols drawn from Mexican Catholicism, Aztec, and Native North American traditions, literally creating a hybrid religious text for which the exact meaning is left to the interpretive faculties of the viewer.

When we first entered the center, Hortencia was at the counter tending to some paperwork. After we explained why we were there, I identified myself as a college professor who teaches religion, especially religion in Latino communities. Later, in my first private session with her, I elaborated on my project, explaining that my desire was for her to describe and locate her practice in her own words. She agreed to cooperate without much coaxing. I took up a significant amount of her time over the next year. We collaborated with each other closely on at least a half-dozen sessions. Most often, I would come in on a day she when was seeing other clients; she would tend to me in turn. She read my cards and talked to me as if she were teaching me. She never charged me. At our second meeting I offered to pay her for the time I was taking in one lump sum: $300. This was the only time I managed to offend her. She was obviously hurt, but did not react spitefully. She just asked, rhetorically, how she could accept money from me when I was doing a good work. On a number of occasions, while I was sitting in wait for her, Hortencia would enter the waiting room and instruct the clients to talk openly with me, that it was fine to be honest.

At our first meeting, after I introduced myself, Hortencia did not immediately release my hand. Instead, she held it tightly and looked deep into my eyes. "You're a very passionate person," she said to me in Spanish (she never once spoke a word of English to me). "And because of that," she continued, "you have suffered a lot in love." Lucky guess, I thought, and remained a bit skeptical about this place with a cash register and standard fees for services. Nonetheless, I became a believer in this woman: in her charm, her charisma, and most of all her sincerity. I believe that she believes in the integrity of what she is doing, and that she helps people.

Even though I maintained a hermeneutic of suspicion about the place from the beginning, the devotees who called upon Hortencia right away seemed oddly familiar to me—not for my years of bibliographic research and fieldwork on curanderismo, but because their motivations for being there and their passionate search to encounter and touch the sacred reminded me of the souls who were members of my father's church in East Oakland, La Iglesia de Dios Pentecostal. Like my father's parishioners, and like those attending Catholic Masses in Mexican and other Latino communities, the vast majority of patrons at Sagrado Corazón are women. Women relate to Hortencia not only as an ambassador of the sacred, but as another woman whose experiences of the world are mediated by those things universal to women's embodied experience—especially women who occupy bronze bodies racialized in peculiar ways by North American society.

At Sagrado Corazón, Hortencia is spiritual priestess, guide, muse, mystic—even shamaness—and the clients her followers. In Hortencia's ritual practice, her story and her religious philosophy—a synthesis of Catholicism and, in her own words, "conscience"—the poetics of religious healing are elaborated and manifested.[4] But it is in that uncanny public space itself, Sagrado Corazón, where the narrative of suffering and the drama of healing forcefully unfold and take place. Thus, after a background on curanderismo, this chapter thickly describes the religious ecology of place before weaving the stories together as so many fibers in an organically produced tapestry and local manifestation of the Divine. The narrative turns next to the voice of Hortencia, allowing her perspective to guide the analysis to conclusion.

This study is not so much a modernist ethnography that purports to reveal some scientific facts based on an experimental design, quantitative data, and a set number of interviews. Instead, I approach this project with a desire to know more about this remarkably persistent phenomenon by conversing with devotees at various levels and by treating, reading, and interpreting religiocultural texts in social and historical contexts for what they disclose about curanderismo and, of course, the issues that attend and are produced by it. That is, in synthesizing the narratives of the devotees, I inscribe a context of religious healing; and in my transcription of key parts of my discussions with Hortencia, I create a text of healing. In the conclusion, entitled "Ya No Tengas Susto," I interpret the text and context with the goal of advancing an understanding—a perspective—on religion, North American religions, and especially on Mexican American religious situations and culture.

A Genealogy of Curanderismo

The term curanderismo comes from the Spanish verb *curar*, to heal or to cure. It signifies everything from herbal home remedies to elaborate spiritual, psychic, or symbolic medical operations conducted to unblock clogged arteries and heal diseases such as cancer and AIDS. At its most general, curanderismo is a synthesis of pre-Tridentine Catholicism, Spanish-Moorish medicine, and ancient Mesoamerican medicine and religion.[5] It is a religious and medical nexus articulated in colonialism.

A growing number of hospitals in Latino communities are now conjoining curanderismo practices with conventional medicine.[6] Harmony is possible between religious and conventional healing because of curanderismo's etiology and general philosophy. Though they are faith healers, curanderas believe themselves knowledgeable about human anatomy and physiology and recognize the purely biological maladies that afflict the body. Therefore, curanderas value conventional medicine and routinely refer patients to medical doctors. Yet curanderas are also aware of the high cost of medical care and the financial difficulties visiting a doctor poses to many ethnic Mexicans. Moreover, visiting any U.S. institution, like a hospital, can be a source of great anxiety for undocumented workers in the United States. But mostly curanderas thrive because of their belief that some illnesses affecting the body have supernatural origins, against which medical doctors are powerless. In addition, curanderas provide services such as tarot card readings and spiritual cleansings—*limpias*—that cannot be rendered elsewhere in Mexican American communities.

The foundation of curanderismo is *el don*, or the gift. Each healer believes that his or her curing power is a gift that comes directly from God; in some cases this gift is brokered through a helper spirit, which acts in effect as the healer. If a person is endowed with the gift of healing, she or he will ultimately need to employ that gift in the service of others or suffer general dissatisfaction in life; lack of fulfillment, and in some cases more severe penalties. This sets up an elaborate system of obligation, gift, and exchange: because the healer has received a gift from God, she or he must in turn give healing to those who seek it, and in return the persons who seek healing must gift the healer and others.

Mexican curanderismo traces its roots to ancient Nahua practices, which view the body as composed of both hot and cold properties. Wellness is dependent on maintaining these dichotomous energies in equilibrium. The concept of duality was one of the key organizing factors in Aztec culture. In Aztec thought, the cosmos was divided into various levels of heavens and earth, delineated by complementary dualities: mother and father (corresponding to earth and heavens), female and male, cold and hot, down and up, underworld and heavens, wet and dry, dark and light, night and day, water and fire, and life and death. Many Aztec deities reflected this division, and the highest Aztec god, Ometeotl, was thought to have both feminine and masculine properties. For the Nahuas, the preservation of cosmic order was the highest charge of humanity. Since the body was seen as a microcosm of the cosmos, it too was understood to be divided into complementary dualities.

Just as cosmic disorder was thought to originate in disruptive forces, illness in the body was believed to derive from external stimuli that disrupted the body's equilibrium. Healing procedures sought to restore balance not only to the body but also to the soul. Today curandera healing techniques are designed to restore balance to the body and soul. The focus on the soul derives from both the Aztecs and Spanish Christians and is a premise sympathetic to *espiritualistas* (Mexican spiritualists) and Evangelicals.

The major ailments thought to be responsive to curanderismo are *mal de ojo*, also called *mal ojo* or *ojo* (the evil eye); *biles* (excessive bile); *muina* (anger sickness); *latido* (palpitation or throb); *envidia, mal puesto, salar,* or *maleficio* (a physical disorder caused by envy); *caida de mollera* (fallen fontanel); *empacho* (indigestion); *mal aire* (upper respiratory illness and colds); *susto* (loss of spirit); *desasombro* (a more severe form of spirit loss); and *espanto* (the most serious form of spirit loss).

Susto is the best-studied malady addressed through curanderismo. Dating back to pre-Columbian Mesoamerica, susto is ubiquitous throughout the Latino Americas (including North America). From the earliest Nahuatl rendition loss of soul or susto was associated with the loss of *tonalli,* the "spiritual force sent by the Aztec god *Chneteotl,* the sun; and fire into the human body, giving it character, intelligence, and will. *Tonalli* was concentrated in the head."[7] The Aztecs believed in three vital life forces that corresponded to a triad human soul residing in the head, the heart, and the liver. In this way, a human life could remain animated even after the tonalli escaped from one's head.

Generally, susto is considered to be caused by a severe fright, shock, or encounter with a benign natural spiritual entity. Any experience, relationship, or circumstance that causes distress and fear can result in susto. Spirit loss may have a long incubation period, sometimes as long as several years. Bernardo Ortiz de Montellano has compiled the following symptoms: "restlessness in sleep, listlessness, loss of appetite, weight loss, loss of energy and strength, depression, introversion, paleness, lethargy, and sometimes fever, diarrhea, and vomiting."[8]

Thus, susto is also diagnosed as a loss of vital forces that keep the body in balance. Sudden heat or cold can cause disturbance, as can powerful emotional forces that overwhelm the body and drive away the soul. Diagnosis of susto typically involves checking the patient's pulse. A patient who has all vital forces in balance will demonstrate a normal pulse, whereas an excess of heat will cause the blood to pulsate more rapidly, and the loss of heat, or of tonalli, will slow the pulse rate.

Susto is cured by administering a limpia while calling the soul back to the body. Limpia, or cleansing, is perhaps the most widely practiced curandera healing technique (figure 2). It consists of sweeping the body

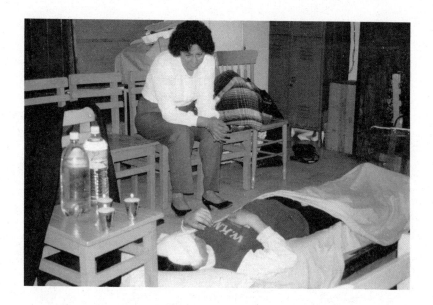

2. A vigilant mother accompanies her son in preparation of a healing.
Courtesy: Luis León.

with a symbolic object, usually held in the left hand of the healer. A limpia is thought to absorb negative energy from the body, driving evil forces into the ritual object used for the sweeping. The most commonly used ritual tool is an egg, a lemon, or a bunch of herbs bound together with a string. Some healers conduct limpias by systematically passing a large crucifix over the body of the supplicant while praying or reciting a Catholic narrative. Customarily, the object used to perform the cleansing is ceremoniously destroyed; most often it is burned.[9]

Sacred Centers

Sagrado Corazón is a small stucco niche in an urban row of continuous structures covered with faded light-blue paint; it is flanked by a barber shop and a restaurant. It is located in Boyle Heights, one of the oldest sections of East Los Angeles and densely populated by mostly Mexican immigrants and Mexican American families.[10] The facade of the building is dominated by a display window and a glass door. In the window is a wide array of products for sale: images of Catholic saints, sprays, powders, herbs, potions, spices, special soaps for baths, candles, incense, and *aguas* (various types of prepared waters). A large hand-painted sign directly outside the entrance reads "love, health, money." The sign further indicates that inside one can obtain card readings and spiritual consultations, as well as fast, effective weight loss without diet or exercise. This is a place where dreams come true.

Upon entering the space one is bombarded by a cacophony of images, creating dissonance and disorientation. Perhaps the dominant sight and sound is a small television located atop a tall bookshelf to the left of the entrance. From there Spanish-language programming blares incessantly. In the left rear of the square floor plan there is a glass counter and display case behind which the clerk sits and watches. She does not typically greet visitors. In fact, she carefully avoids meeting their eyes with hers. At times the clerk is Hortencia's teenage daughter. On the counter there are several upright images of La Virgen de Guadalupe with burning votive candles. On the wall behind the counter hang images of Guadalupe and the saints, and a Sacred Heart. To the right are five white plastic lawn chairs where people wait, often for several hours, to see Hortencia.

She normallly arrives in the morning before ten and typically stays until six or seven in the evening (figure 3). The shop is closed on Sundays. On Tuesdays and Fridays she accepts walk-in clients on a first-come, first-served basis; these days, she explains, possess the most powerful energies. She begins by asking her clients no questions except what they seek. Clients come to the front counter, and the clerk puts their name on a list and tells them the approximate waiting time. On these days Hortencia seldom comes into the shop space. A window in one of her two workrooms in the back affords her a view into the front room. Hortencia's private chambers are partitioned off from the main space by drywall. There are two discrete rooms in the rear of the space that function as Hortencia's workrooms. In one she has a desk, chairs, and a large table that serves as an altar and on which stand a Virgin of Guadalupe, a Sacred Heart of Jesus, and bright candles and incense. Prepared waters line the walls. The second room holds a padded massage table covered with clean white sheets, where Hortencia performs her work as a *sabadora*, or massage therapist.

The bookshelves lining the walls of the front room are packed with sundry merchandise, reflecting the diverse interests and faiths of patrons. In one corner are items that can be purchased in neighborhood markets: shampoo; soap, toothpaste, hair cream, deodorant, and dishwashing and laundry detergent. On the other walls are racks of Mexican spices, fresh herbs, and teas of various kinds. Painted clay images of many official Catholic saints popular in Mexico and elsewhere in Latin America are represented and sold at the botánica. These include especially St. Francis,

3. The curandera Hortencia prepares to perform healing practices in East Los Angeles. Courtesy: Luis León.

El Santo Niño de Atocha, San Martín de Porres, and Santa Barbara. In addition to saints there are replicas of the Buddha, Shango and Eluguia (spiritual entities in Santería), numerous Hindu deities, and various Latin American manifestations of the Virgin Mary, including Los Lagos, Cobra, Caridad, Zapopan, and especially Guadalupe. Perhaps the most striking and prominent saints are those not officially recognized by the Catholic Church, including San Simón, El Niño Fidencio, Juan Soldado, and Don Pedrito Jaramillo. These saints share space and authority with the official Catholic saints without distinction.

Most of the shelves hold a variety of sprays and candles that are labeled according to their functions. Available only in aerosol cans is *tres machos*. This spray is meant to invoke three strong male spirits and is used also in Santería. Mexican espiritualistas often spray tres machos before a ceremony. An espiritualista priestess once commented to me that she enjoys the light floral scent of the spray. But other candles and sprays sold at the center offer more specialized services. Available only in cans is the Uña de Gato, or the Cat's Nail. When I asked what purpose the Uña de Gato spray serves, I was told that it was for general good luck and well-being.

Equally striking also was a large color poster advertising the Uña de Gato spray. On it a robust Latino man sporting a mustache, dark suit, and tie holds the can in his right hand and smiles. Around him float three images: Guadalupe, an Aztec deity, and an image of Jesus Christ.

The brightly colored candles dominated the shelves of the vestibule; there are candles for just about every conceivable type of problem. Candles are encased in colorful glass, and are painted with images and text. One candle reads (in Spanish): "Do as I say, now." This candle is adorned by two images: on one side a man submits to a woman; the other side depicts a woman submitting to a man. There are candles representing each sign of the zodiac; many of the saints and manifestations of the Virgin Mary; Jesus; popular saints; and various wishes, including "Instant money," "Shut your mouth," "Go away," "Protect me from evil," "Work," "Love," "Romance," "Seduction," "Instant luck," "Big money," "Lottery," "Health," and "Power." Here, a person can purchase hope, control, and power. Hortencia prescribes these items to her clients, but she does not earn a commission on their sale. She receives a flat salary from the shop owners. Sagrado Corazón is owned by a group of capitalist investors who also own several of the other botánicas around Los Angeles and employ various curanderos and curanderas. Hortencia was reluctant to speak of the owners. There is no question, however, that Hortencia is the priestess of Sagrado Corazón.

Remaking Myth, Body, and Soul

The Botaníca appeals to many different visitors: some casual clients come only to purchase herbs and spices, while others come to purchase a new lease on life. On days other than Tuesday and Friday, Hortencia sees clients by appointment and tends to the mundane business of the shop—ordering merchandise, balancing bank accounts, and other organizational activities. She prefers to see people during her walk-in hours.

On Tuesdays and Fridays her corazón is filled with a dozen or so people at a time waiting to see her. On a particularly busy day, she sees upward of thirty clients. People are charged according to the service. A basic consultation is $10, but Hortencia regularly adjusts the cost upward or downward according to the services rendered and the patient's means. Typically the customers remain silent while waiting. They survey the walls of merchandise, stare at the television, tend to their children, or read newspapers; on occasion they look up cautiously to examine people as they enter and exit. Privacy is expected.

Visitors come in out of curiosity and browse; others rush in, quickly select some herbs, and go directly to the register to pay. One such customer explained that she was buying special Mexican-grown plants that aid in sleeping, upset stomachs, colds, and general aches and pains.[11] She does not visit the shop for the services offered, but to buy the things she regularly had in Mexico. Speaking for the casual customers, she told of how difficult it was to find these herbs, *medicinas* (medicines), in other stores. "We come here to buy the things that we have grown accustomed to in Mexico."

The patrons at Sagrado Corazón are mostly women, and most have children in tow. Some men come alone or with other male companions. Seldom do women and men come in couples. One twenty-six-year-old man said that he lived alone in the United Sates, working and sending money to his family in Aguas Calientes, Mexico. He was a practicing Catholic who attended Mass weekly and took Communion. Seeking the aid of a curandera generally violated the laws of the Catholic Church as he saw it, but, as he put it, "The Catholic Church does not understand everything, and they are not always correct about everything." His words summed up the position of many of the people I spoke with there. He would not tell me what he sought from Hortencia, but it wasn't a card reading he was after: "I'm here for some other business that I can't tell you."

Many of the men I spoke to at Sagrado Corazón sought help from Hortencia to ease the stresses of separation from their families who remained in Mexico. Numerous men came to Hortencia for extra assistance in finding work. For some, the problem was that, in spite of their best efforts, they had run out of money. Hortencia offered the seekers discernment that uncovered the root of the problem, and solutions to it. To cure the problem she offered them rituals aimed at improving their "auras," which she claimed would eventually lead to finding a job, earning more money, or making their money last longer.

Gerardo Feliz, a strong *güerito* man of twenty-six from Jalisco, Mexico, described a problem of a different nature. He seemed quite nervous while waiting for Hortencia one Friday afternoon. After a brief introductory chat, he told me that he had been visiting Hortencia regularly for about six months; he was there for the fourth time. He sadly recounted the problems with his immediate family back home, "con mi casa" (with my household), he said, and especially with his wife. "In these times a man can no longer count on a woman's fidelity," he confided. He was reluctant to say much more. Hortencia was helping him discern the situation and the proper course of action. He told me he trusted Hortencia and related to her as a son relates to his mother. He had only very cursory and infrequent communication with his mother and had not told her of the family troubles. He believed the problem stemmed at least partially from his absence of almost two years. During his first trip he had been away less than a year, but now he had found a lucrative job as assistant manager of a restaurant; the restaurant owners would not let him go home and return to his job.

The women who visit the center come with similar problems that center on family separation, employment, love, money, and health. Unlike the men, however, they come not only for spiritual aid but also for physical treatments, seeking Hortencia's services as a sabadora, or massage therapist. None of the men I spoke with during my time there called upon Hortencia for massage therapy, though many came for a limpia.

I heard repeated tales of labor exploitation. Many of the undocumented women who patronize Sagrado Corazón work in the United States at menial service jobs, such as house cleaners and seamstresses at sweatshops in downtown Los Angeles. These women told of the long hours they spent toiling for their bosses. After a week or two they would ask for the money they had been promised, only to be told that they would have to wait longer and keep on working. So on it went until, finally, the women realized that they had been deceived and that no money would be paid to them. "What could I do?" they stated in resignation and despair. I suggested Catholic social services or a legal agency in the area. Without fail their response was the same: "But I have no papers, I could be deported." What did they seek, then, from Hortencia? "A consultation and healing." Sagrado Corazón for them was the first step on a new course of action; a new strategy; catharsis and rejuvenation; a renewed sense of dignity, self-worth, and power; a kind of symbolic and spiritual justice, but not vengeance. With ancient Mesoamerican rituals filtered through centuries of Catholic colonialism, innovation, and border crossings, this Hortencia could provide, though somewhat ironically her services could only be rendered for a small fee. Sagrado Corazón is not, by any means, a multinational capitalist corporation nor is Hortencia an owner of Marx's "means of production." And yet, her work and her business are bound up with the exploitive social system and modes of work, compensation, and exchange. She is a dealer in hope.

I noticed mothers at Sagrado Corazón with their teenage gangbanger sons. What did they seek from Hortencia? One mother answered that her son was full of bad energies and needed to be cleansed so that he would be put back on the right path. Her son told me that he needed help so that he could stop "messing up." Why not seek the aid of the church? I asked. "The priest can't do much for him," another mother answered, "just tell him to pray and to stay in school." Was visiting Hortencia against the Catholic religion, I asked. "I don't know," answered one mother. "Maybe it is, but it seems to be the only thing that works."[12]

Leticia, or Letty, a Chicana who is twenty-two years old, told me that she had first come to Hortencia about a year before, for "female problems." Hortencia prescribed a cure that worked. She was back now because she had had increasingly bad luck at her job. "I just quit my job at a restaurant," she explained. "My boss was verbally abusing me. He was calling me dumb and stuff. I couldn't stand it. Now I don't have a job, and my parents have to support me." What could Hortencia do for her? "I feel all dirty, like I've been violated. I'm here because I need a limpia."[13] I asked if she was a Catholic and went to Mass. She responded that she was Catholic but that she seldom went to church, because she found it boring. "I pray to the Virgin at home, you know, Guadalupe, and I come here once in a while."

With Lara Medina I interviewed a group of four Chicanas, including "Dolores Multiplicadas," mentioned at the beginning of this chapter. We spoke in English. Dolores, the eldest, did most of the talking. I asked first how she had learned of Hortencia. She said she had heard of her through friends, who had heard of her through—other friends, "just word of mouth." I asked what she had heard. "That she reads cards, and that she is pretty accurate," she replied. She had started coming in just the last couple of weeks. I asked what it was she sought there.

> Well, it seems that everything goes wrong for me, and in fact she [Hortencia] told me that, that everything goes wrong for me, you know, she said everything in my life goes wrong for me—and it's true. You know, in terms of jobs, relationships, just everything. She told me the truth before I even talked to her.

Her friends had come along to have their cards read but did not want to talk about it. All said that they were Catholics and went to church about every other week.

Dolores is active in a Catholic retreat center, and she was wearing a T-shirt with the center's name on it when we spoke. Lara asked how she combined the work of Hortencia with her Catholicism. She responded that the retreat center was for people who were Catholic but not very active, you know, people who never really felt it. But it is good, really, really good. I was raised Catholic but never really felt it; I wasn't really going much, and I looked around for a while. I was ready to become Christian [she meant Evangelical Christian], but then I got invited to this [Catholic retreat center] and I went; so I was able to accept Catholic back again. Now I understand it, my communion, my confirmation, I know what it's about. I even felt the Holy Spirit too. For me it felt like, it was weird, like I was bouncing off the walls. It was like a high feeling, I mean I don't get high but I guess that's what high feels like. It was really neat, I liked it [laughs].

Lara then asked her how she blended her experience with Hortencia with her experience with the Holy Spirit. Dolores replied: "To tell you the truth, I feel guilty [laughs]." I asked if she thought the Catholic Church was against visiting a curandera. She replied that she believed it was. "Well, because you're messing with other things and not him [points upward]." Her friends looked at her disapprovingly, and she answered their stares with a firm, "Well, it's true." I asked her younger companions if they believed that Sagrado Corazón was Catholic, and if it was okay to go there. "No, it isn't Catholic," one replied. They all agreed. Another companion disagreed and said, "Well, she [Hortencia] believes in Catholicism." To this the other replied, "Well, I know she does but, well, when we have problems we should pray to him [God]."

I asked the younger woman about Guadalupe and whether she prayed to her. Her answer was that she "didn't know much about that." "I don't know much about saints. I really don't. What about you?" she asked Dolores. Dolores said she didn't know about saints either, except for Guadalupe. What did she know, I asked. "Well, if you pray to *her* and everything she'll be there for you." I asked her what she wanted from Hortencia. "I was just curious," she replied, "I wanted to know what was ahead for me. I'm stuck, and I don't know where to go next." "Do you think Hortencia can help to unblock your path?" Lara asked. "We'll see. I don't know, but I hope so."

A Curandera Speaks

Hortencia told me that both Catholics and Evangelicals visit her at the center. The only difference between them, she said, "is that when they get here the Evangelicals are more secretive; they visit me with a bad conscience." Hortencia said this with a touch of contempt, because for her conscience is the key to ethical religious practice. I asked her what she believed the Catholic Church taught about her work at Sagrado Corazón. Without hesitation she responded:

They believe it's bad. Because they themselves believe that no one can do anything but God. And you yourself know that this is against the Catholic religion from whatever aspect you view it. This is against it. But if you yourself are content [*tranquila*] that you are not harming anyone, then it's good, and for that reason I go to Mass. I am satisfied [tranquila] with myself. I'm not going to honor God if I know that I am sinning against him—it's one or the other thing—either you are with God or you are against him. But I am content because I am trying to do good. I try to do only good. I have to maintain my good *conscience*.

Any priest will tell you [that curanderismo is wrong]. My priest back in my village in Mexico would tell me all the time, "Hortencia, you [tú]"—excuse my use of the informal, but that is how he would address me—"you need to change your ways, because if you continue lying to people you are going to die." He himself saw that I could help people. But I *never* myself said that it was I who was helping people. No one can help people without God. I'm not going to go around saying that I am the greatest curandera in the world. I do what I can do to help the people [*la gente*]. And, well, perhaps that is why God, he helps me, because he sees my desire to do the good.

There are people who sometimes come here and say, "I would like this to happen to such and such person." I'm not here for that. If you need to resolve a problem with someone, you know what, just go and have it out with him and that's it, your anger will pass. Why would you want to do harm to the people? That will only work against you yourself.

What I do here is try and help people. People come to me with all sorts of problems. Mostly, people have money problems; they don't have enough money for their families [*casa*]. So, for example, if someone comes to me and says they don't have enough money, I tell them to take a special herb, a one-dollar bill, a [special] small rock, and a red *perejer* [a Mexican herb]. Take a glass of water, and in that water you will put that rock, and that red perejer, and then the dollar. Do you know what a dollar means? Do you have a one-dollar bill, and I'll show you. No? [She moves to the window that opens into the vestibule and calls for Daisy, the receptionist, to bring her a one-dollar bill.] Do you know what religion the dollar bill comes from? Now we are really talking about religion. It comes from the Masons. And why do you think it was the Masons?

Because they wanted to make this the strongest country of all. [She takes the dollar bill, pointing.] This pyramid signifies positive energy. The eye is the eye of the Holy Spirit that you see there. Are you Catholic? I'm Catholic, as I told you, and when you go to Mass you will see the same Holy Spirit symbolized. These are things I'm telling you so that you will learn how things work. Take water, for example. Water is a material [*materia*]. Water is made by God. *Man didn't make water.*

Everything has a mystery. Just like the recitation I was telling you. El perejer, I was telling you, that is a plant that comes from the earth [*la tierra*] that is made by God, not by man. Just like the rocks. The rocks are a materia because they are not made by man but are made from nature [*la naturaleza*]. Okay? When you have four of those rocks it signifies harmony for all. People who know a lot about rocks will tell you that the four roses [*cuatro rosados*] are to create harmony, to bring happiness to your house, and to bring peace. So, *you* take a piece of foundation from your house, with your perejer, and put it in your water with the dollar bill. These are three things that symbolize the earth. It doesn't have to be there more than seventy-two hours. You then put it in the doorway of your house or in the doorway of your business. After three days *you* take the dollar from your water and let it dry in the sun. After it is dry, you put it in your wallet; and that is one way to bring prosperity. Because it is made from things that are purely natural. People don't have to pay in order to be helped. That is one way to help people who come with need.

I asked Hortencia if her practices were religious rituals. She said no, in the sense that rituals for her signified something much bigger, and she then went into a long discourse dissociating her work from the rituals of Afro-Cuban religions such as Santería-inspired animal sacrifices. She forcefully distinguished her work from those who are involved with grave robbing, which "is wrong." She described the practices she prescribes as works, *trabajos*, or as "offerings that you give for your prosperity." I asked her where she learned her work. She replied:

I can't tell you that I learned anything. I had premonitions. How do I explain to you? These are things that *Diosito* can give *you*. It's like a sixth sense. When I want to cleanse [*limpiar*] a person to bring prosperity, I do it with apple and honey, because that will create abundance, and honey will bring good luck. Cinnamon [too] will bring good luck. These are things that come from times long past, ancient times, you know. One doesn't know how one knows these things. I can't explain. I can tell you that my spiritual child [*niño espiritual*] guides me, he tells me what to say, he whispers in my ear.

I was seven years old when I first discovered my gift. It is something *un*explainable. I can tell you that I wouldn't wish it on anyone. Let me tell you that in the first place where I come from is a very small village, and people would say that I had the devil inside of me. Why? Because of the reactions my body would bring. Things would fall when I got a little aggressive. I'm not very aggressive, but a little. My mom would say, "*Don't* ever tell your brothers [*hermanos*] anything," because it could happen. If I would say to *my* sister, "I hope you get hit in your mouth," well, in a little while, she would come with her mouth broken. These are things I cannot explain.

Hortencia related the tragic (*fea*) story about her grandfather, and a premonition she had that if heeded by her family would have prevented the tragedy. She also said that she has revelatory dreams, and she had recently had one in which she was hugging and comforting her mother. The next day she learned that her mother needed surgery. She also claimed that she dreams about earthquakes two or three days before they happen.

I can't explain to anyone because this hurts me and causes great distress [*me mortifica*] inside of me. I identify myself as a curandera, but I don't describe my work with people as curing them, but as helping them. Because there are many things that you can't cure. And you won't fool anyone. If someone comes to me and says, "I have a pain in my chest," the first thing I say to them is "go and see your doctor." It's like the plants, my son [*mi hijo*]. The plants can help you, but over a long period of time. If someone has high blood pressure I can say, "Drink this tea," but if that person has high blood pressure he can have a stroke—he needs to go to the doctor. There are many ways to help people, but a person shouldn't get involved with something in which they don't belong. This is to say that when you come to me to have your cards read I can do that for you because that is what I can do—look a bit at your future, look a bit at your problems to understand what you can do to help yourself, or what I can do to help you resolve your problems. But I won't get involved with things that I have no business in.

Look, that lady who is in the other room, her egg indicated that there was a person who was harming her. You see, your being is one *whole* [*conjunto*]: your body and your spirit. So, if someone hurts your body they also hurt your spirit, and vice versa. Like that lady who is in the other room, what I have to do for her is make sure her spirit is healthy, so that her body will heal. It's a lie, all those, what do they call them, spiritual operations. Or just because they touch you somewhere you've been healed. It has to be someone who has God [*que tenga Dios*]. Yes, sometimes they help. There are people who have that great gift, but there are people who are charlatans, and they take advantage of people. I can tell you about many people who come here complaining about how they went to such-and-such a place and how they got tricked into spending a lot of money. That is not helping someone. When you want to help someone, if you can't help, you tell him that you can't. "Go with your doctor, he will help you." In those cases based on bad luck [*mala suerte*] I can help; and I say, "Yes, I can help"; cleaning your aura or cleaning your spirit—those are things I can do. But to get involved in things I can't do, that would work against me, and the people who are trusting me. I do my work to help people.

Hortencia then told me about a woman who had been through many conventional medical treatments that were ultimately unavailing. The woman could not eat or sleep. She was feeling generally anxious and depressed. Hortencia then took me out to the waiting room where the woman was sitting. She asked the woman to tell me how Hortencia had helped her. The woman said, "I was ill [*asustada*], and the only thing that helped me was Hortencia."

"¡Ya Basta El Susto!"

Sagrado Corazón is a paradox: it is at once an extraordinary and a common place (figure 4). In other words, it is a public locus for the *intersection* of the sacred and the profane. In its extraordinary sense, it is a sacred space where hope abounds and miracles take place. Optimism is in no short supply at Sagrado Corazón. At this storefront botánica, hope and faith are created, nurtured, and packaged as the ability to control life itself, to affect destiny, to turn events in one's favor—all these things and more are available. The idea is relentlessly compelling, a universal in human history: that religious rituals and invisible powers can directly influence our fortunes and bring to us the people and things we desire if *we* offer them the correct prayer and performance.

Claims of divine intervention and power made at Sagrado Corazón are not unlike those made by a Mexican American home-based Catholicism.[14] What differentiates curanderismo and Mexican American popular Ca-

4. Interior of the Sagrado Corazón botánica, East Los Angeles.
Courtesy: Luis León.

tholicism is the cosmogony and function of saints. The saints in Sagrado
Corazón, and in curanderismo generally, include those who are officially
sanctioned by the Catholic Church, but also those who are not counted
among the ranks of the Vatican hierarchy. The second set symbolize,
resonate with, and sacralize a condition of oppression, victimization, and
injustice—and the ambiguous moral choices the poor must often make in
their struggles to survive—to confront and change the susto that poverty
and racism bring.

Take, for example, the saint Jesús Malverde, or (literally) "Jesus Bad
Green." At Sagrado Corazón one can find *many* products that bear his
image and boast his intervention, including aerosol sprays, candles, and
texts. Jesús Malverde is the appellation given to a community-sanctioned
saint who is enshrined in Culiacán, Mexico. Malverde is the patron saint
of drug traffickers. One *corrido* dedicated to him begins: "Jesús Malverde,
angel of the *poor*, I've come to ask you a great big favor."[15] Not only drug
dealers but law-abiding Mexicans and Chicanos make the pilgrimage to

petition the saint who has been named El Narcosanton—the "Big Drug Saint." El Narcosanton arises from a social condition that has pressed people to the limits of their conventional resources. For some who feel they must traffic in drugs or otherwise break the law as a matter of economic necessity, Malverde is the saint of choice. And yet if prayers to Malverde are answered favorably, his devotees will offer devotional dólares not only to Malverde but also to Guadalupe and to official Catholic saints.[16]

But the function of the saints in popular Catholicism and curanderismo is also inflected with cultural understandings and thus changed from the function accorded them by official doctrine. In official Catholicism, saints act only as moral exemplars who point to and act as intercessors to God, praying on behalf of the petitioners. In popular Catholicism and curanderismo, the official saints, spirits of deceased loved ones, and unofficial saints possess power to effect change themselves.[17] Seen in this light, curanderismo is not so much a discrete religious system as it is a logical extension of popular Catholicism: the difference is not one of kind, but of degree. This in part explains how believers can participate in multiple religious practices with little or no cognitive dissonance. Believers who identify as Catholics may also claim multiple religious identities, for each is an extension of a singular religious soul constituted by a core set of beliefs; the beliefs overlap with and extend into practices that may appear at variance with one another but are ultimately all, in effect, derivative.[18]

Additionally, many of the things promised by the mythology of Sagrado Corazón are those also offered by Evangelical and Pentecostal churches. In most Mexican American and other Latino Evangelical circles, religious discourse is translated into native vernaculars, and the grammar of belief, salvation, and blessings is given to local deployments.[19] For these overlapping religious premises, curanderismo can be considered not as isolated from Mexican American Catholicism and Evangelicalism, but as part of a broad network of faith-based mechanisms that enable the poor and the oppressed to navigate the often difficult terrain of their lives. Thus, the question of Sagrado Corazón regards not so much the general beliefs, but the specific idioms and rituals through which these beliefs are expressed and reiterated. In effect, the sensation of the sacred is ubiquitous throughout Latina/o communities, and Sagrado Corazón is but one marker on a continuum where the sacred is routinely imagined (or reimagined) and encountered, conjured, and manifested.

Yet Sagrado Corazón is first and foremost a business. It is a store, a standard marker in the landscape of North American capitalism. Sagrado

Corazón is not an altogether altruistic enterprise that exists solely for the purpose of helping those in need. It is privately owned by entrepreneurs who also own and finance several other botánicas in East Los Angeles. Hortencia and other curanderas are hired by the owners to manage and operate the botánica. Sagrado Corazón is in place to make a profit, and inasmuch as the profit motive dominates the relationships of gift and exchange operative there, Hortencia's work—even if unintentionally—is consistent with corporate capitalism in the United States, since it supports a distinctly capitalist religious sensibility: money buys happiness. A distinction must be drawn, however, between Hortencia's beliefs and practices and the motives of the owners of the shop, who enjoy the most financial gain. Still, with this ordinary business purpose in mind, the many "profane" or secular items (such as dishwashing soap and hair creams) sold alongside the articles that have a distinctively religious purpose are perfectly consistent with the mandate of profit—a divine commandment in the religion of North American capitalism. That both religious and secular items are bought from a wholesale distributor, marked up, sectioned off into discrete display areas, tagged with prices, and sold for profit along with Hortencia's services renders the whole venture less than mystical—unless, of course, one is enchanted by the mystical spectacle of the American marketplace invading the barrio.

Curanderismo was once restricted to private homes and kinship networks. Today it has shifted from the familiar intimate space of home to the public space of commodity consumption. In fact, Mexican American urban religious landscapes are in general experiencing a radical transformation. Currently storefront religions—be they botánicas, spiritualist temples, or Pentecostal churches—compete for space and patrons with grocery stores, movie houses, restaurants, barber shops, and the like. The space of the sacred and the space of the profane, which was for Emile Durkheim so clearly distinguishable, is for Mexican-descent Angelenos increasingly blending into one another, and becoming one fluid mass of capitalist desire.

But there is an assumptive familiarity to storefront religious practice that is utterly logical to postmoderns in East Los Angeles: the ritual of capital exchange. That is, people pay for what they want; when applied to the sacred, the appeal is nonetheless highly rational. People seek the services of a religious specialist as they would seek the services of a doctor, lawyer, electrician, beautician, and the like; and now these services are increasingly offered in the same consumer spaces. If the seeker wants a miracle, then he or she need only shop around for the curandera or curandero with the best reputation (cost, product, or service), visit the practitioner's place of business—which is open and accessible to the public—pay the set fee, and expect results. Why not Christian services? Aren't they available through the same mechanism of exchange?

Curanderismo was once organized predominantly around an elaborate system of gifting.[20] Traditionally the cycle began with the healer, who would recognize his or her gift of healing powers, which came directly from God.

The healer would gift those who sought healing. In turn, the person or persons who received the gift of healing, or whatever divine services they sought, would be obliged to gift the curandera in return, and obliged also to gift others as they had been gifted. El don, the gift, was the principle that once guided social relations in curandera practice. The gift that seekers would offer to healers was never fixed or predetermined; it was at the discretion of the seeker and conformed to whatever means he or she possessed.[21] With the emergence of storefront healing centers, however, this pattern is changing. Market value and laws of supply and demand, together with the costs of maintaining a healing "business," now delimit exchange in curanderismo. The charisma of blessings and gift so central to religious narratives is giving way to the rationale of capitalist ideology. As a result, religious expectations are blended with financial means, and religious spaces serve multiple purposes. Sagrado Corazón, for example, is at once a medical clinic of sorts, a religious article store, a sacred place of magic and devotion, an extension of devotional images and practices fostered by the Catholic Church, and a store that is in business for profit. As such it is the epitome of a postmodern religious place, whose success is found precisely in its ability consistently to transform religious irony and indeterminacy into efficacious social functionality.

For this reason, patrons of Sagrado Corazón come with various needs, usually at moments of crisis. Seekers fall into categories based on frequency of visits and intensity of beliefs: casual and onetime visitors, occasional visitors, and regular clients. As Hortencia claimed, visitors are of all faiths, but they are all Latino, for Hortencia does not speak English. This one common element suggests a core set of beliefs originating and nurtured in aspects of Mexican American and other Latino cultures that get expressed in discrete yet ironically consistent practices. For example, as seen in the previous chapter, the belief that divine healing is possible is held by Latina/o Pentecostals, Catholics, and curanderas, even while it is eschewed as medieval superstition by rational Catholic and Protestant institutions.

It is of no small significance that all the believers in this study who were asked about their faith replied with no uncertainty that they were indeed Catholic. And yet they all also confessed that visiting the Sagrado Corazón botánica (which is how the question was phrased) was contrary to the teachings of Catholic doctrine. But the seekers nonetheless persisted in their visits to see Hortencia. When asked about this seeming contradiction, Hortencia's answer was clear and utterly pragmatic, articulating the perspective of the patrons of Sagrado Corazón: these are matters of personal conscience. And as long as one is convinced that he *or* she is doing good work in the world, there is no need to be burdened by sin in spite of perceived Catholic teachings.

This appeal to conscience is a triumph powerfully narrated in Gloria Anzaldúa's mestiza consciousness. Anzaldúa argues that the definitive characteristic of mestiza consciousness is "a tolerance for contradictions, a tolerance for ambiguity."[22] This consciousness, or soul, is the impulse for physical (or metaphysical), geopolitical, and symbolic boundary transgression: border crossings. As Hortencia and those interviewed confessed, they believed the practice of curanderismo to be contrary to the teachings of the Catholic Church. And yet, they professed also a Catholic identity while concomitantly defying the Catholic Church. Only a "tolerance for contradiction" would enable them to live out this tension. For Anzaldúa, this consciousness emerges from a lifetime of struggle, from experiencing injustice and subsequently transforming pain into tactical maneuvers. In the borderlands, the tragic soul of a poet is nurtured. Thus, Hortencia boldly re-mythologized her world, forcefully assuming poetic license with Catholic narrative. Assuming poetic control over religion when managing one's world—thought narrative and practice—is what I call religious poetics.

In conclusion, I want to suggest that my guides in this study were practicing a type of what I call "religious poetics"—inasmuch as they renarrated religious discourse so that it became more conducive to their struggles. Even those, such as Dolores, who professed a feeling of "guilt" for being at Sagrado Corazón were nevertheless assuming poetic creativity with Catholicism in practice, for Dolores (and others) believes that Catholicism was elastic enough to bend to her needs without breaking.

Although most of the folks I watched and talked with at Sagrado Corazón lacked the vocabulary to describe powerfully what they were doing, in their various ways they, too, participated in producing a fresh religious mythology, or "mythopoesis," insofar as they followed the teachings of Hortencia. Together they deftly delineated an ethics of healing and, even more, an ethics of borderland religions which brought together many disparate elements of a religious life, including Catholicism, memory, and culture in an attempt to survive. At the center of Hortencia's poetic religious ethics lies, in her own words, a commitment to conscience. In her heart and soul she believes that what she is doing is helping people: she appeals to conviction, and that conscience enables her poetics of material salvation and power to forcefully transform lives.

The participants in this study saw the Catholic Church as key to who they were and to who they were becoming. Yet they simultaneously understood the church as a human institution mediating the sacred, and Hortencia as a human who, not so unlike the priests, manifested the divine—both received and disseminated God—and both could work in concert when deploying the sacred in their herculean efforts to survive.[23] For it is in these stories that religious poetics take center stage. Indeed, it is precisely this poetic orientation that helps to explain the popularity and creativity of Luis Valdez's plays, such as *La Pastorela*, as we shall see in chapter 13.

Notes

All names of interviewees in the text are pseudonyms. Unless otherwise noted, all interviews were conducted in Spanish by the author at Sagrado Corazón from June 1998 through September 1999. I thank Lara Medina for her assistance.

1. Dolores Multiplicadas, interview by author, 17 September 1999, East Los Angeles.

2. Tonantzin, in Nahuatl, literally, "our mother," was the symbol of a fertility goddess. Malinche was the Maya concubine and lover of Hernán Cortés. She is known pejoratively as the great traitor of Mexico. La Llorona is the archetypical "weeping woman" in Mexico; she foretells tragedy, transformation, and change. See Octavio Paz, "Sons of La Malinche," in *The Labyrinth of Solitude: Life and Thought in Mexico*, trans. Lysander Kemp (New York: Grove, 1961).

3. Although there is a significant amount of Mexican ethnographic literature in Spanish from case studies conducted over a long period, there is little information in English on curanderismo, and none of the English-language literature adopts a religious studies perspective. For a review of some of this literature, see Robert Trotter and Juan Antonio Chavira, *Curanderismo: Mexican American Folk Healing*, 2nd ed. (Athens: University of Georgia Press, 1997).

4. In what I call "religious poetics," believers renarrate religious discourse through practice, imbuing existing religious doctrines with poetic, contextual meanings. See Luis D. León, *La Llorona's Children: Religion, Life, and Death in the U.S.-Mexican Borderlands* (Berkeley: University of California Press, 2004).

5. On the influence of pre-Tridentine Catholicism in the colonization of Mexico, see Orlando O. Espín, in *The Faith of the People: Theological Reflections on Popular Catholicism* (Maryknoll, N.Y.: Orbis, 1997), 32–62.

6. John Orr and Sherry May, "Religion and Health Services in Los Angeles: Reconfiguring the Terrain," Center for the Study of Religion and American Civic Culture, April 2000, available at http://www.usc.edu/schools/college/crcc/publications/.

7. Davíd Carrasco, *Religions of Mesoamerica: Cosmovision and Ceremonial Centers* (San Francisco: HarperSanFrancisco, 1990), 170.

8. Bernard Ortiz de Montellano, *Aztec Health and Medicine* (New Brunswick, N.J.: Rutgers University Press, 1990), 220.

9. See Trotter and Chavira, *Curanderismo*.

10. Boyle Heights occupies an area of 3.27 square miles. Its population of 55,157 consists of 2 percent African Americans, 4 percent Asian Pacific Islanders, 93 percent Latinas/os, and 1 percent others. Thirty-nine percent of these households earn less than $15,000 per year, and 39 percent earn between $15,000 and $35,000 per year.

11. For an extensive list of Mexican healing herbs, see Annette Sandoval, *Homegrown Healing: Traditional Remedies from Mexico* (New York: Berkeley Books, 1998).

12. This account synthesizes discussion on three occasions; some of the conversation took place in English.

13. This interview was conducted in English.

14. See Jeffrey S. Thies, *Mexican Catholicism in Southern California* (New York: Peter Lang, 1993).

15. Anita Snow, "Drug Dealers Honor Patron Saint," *Santa Barbara New Press*, 4 September 1995.

16. For an extended discussion on this phenomenon, see James Griffith, *Saints and Holy Places: A Spiritual Geography of the Pimería Alta* (Tucson: University of Arizona Press, 1992).

17. See Thies, *Mexican Catholicism in Southern California*.

18. For an extended discussion of this core set of beliefs, see León, *La Llorona's Children*.

19. Manuel Vasquez, "Pentecostalism, Collective Identity, and Transnationalism among Salvadorans and Peruvians in the U.S.," *Journal of the American Academy of Religion* 67, no. 3 (September 1999): 617–36.

20. Here, of course, I draw upon Marcel Mauss's seminal study of rites of gift and exchange, *The Gift: The Form and Reason for Exchange in Archaic Societies* (New York: W.W. Norton, 1990).

21. Trotter and Chavira, *Curanderismo*. See also Eliso Torres, *The Folk Healer: The Mexican-American Tradition of Curanderismo* (Kingsville, Tex.: Nieves Press, 1983).

22. Gloria Anzaldúa, *Borderlands/La Frontera: The New Mestiza*, 2nd ed. (San Francisco, Calif.: Aunt Lute Books, 1999), 79.

23. One model for this kind of work is Karen McCarthy Brown's *Mama Lola: A Vodou Priestess in Brooklyn* (Berkeley: University of California Press, 1991).

VI

Mexican American

Religions and Pop Culture

13

Luis Valdez's *La Pastorela*: *"The Shepherds' Play"*

Tradition, Hybridity, and Transformation

Much of Chicano literature traces its antecedents to European cultural production dating from the sixteenth century. The *copla* and the *décima* in poetry, the *romance* and *canción* in song, and religious dramas in theater are but a few examples. Luis Valdez's video drama *La Pastorela: "The Shepherds' Tale"* (1991) is fundamentally based on the folk play Los Pastores—a Christmas mystery play based on the Spanish *autos sacramentales* imported to America by Franciscan friars in 1524. When Spanish missionary friars arrived in what is now Mexico they resorted to the auto sacramental theatrical performances to instruct the Native American populations on the intricacies of the Catholic faith. Through the spectacle of live theater, the clergy were able to transmit their religious message since they did not speak the Native American languages and the Mesoamerican Indians did not speak Spanish. In this chapter, I analyze Valdez's *pastorela* with respect to traditional as well as postmodern elements and posit that this particular nativity play's evolution and transformation, as well as its hybrid nature, are directly connected to political and ideological issues extant in society. Furthermore, I posit that it is this hybrid position between tradition and modernity that makes Valdez's drama *La Pastorela* a strategic weapon that can be effectively deployed to articulate contemporary political issues and to advocate reforms for social justice via its accepted traditional religious format. Through this strategic maneuvering, Valdez's militancy is attenuated and appears less threatening to more conservative, reactionary forces. The hybrid nature of Chicano artistic expression lends itself well to being used as a tool in combating repressive national and state forces.

The transformations evident in pastorela production and the links these transformations have to power relations adhere to theoretical paradigms posited by Michel Foucault regarding the manner in which discourse is connected to power. Foucault's writings detail the power of discourse and how those in power seek to control it. In his essay on "The Discourse of Language" he asserts:

> In every society the production of discourse is at once controlled, se-lected, organized and redistributed according to a certain number of pro-cedures, whose role is to avert its powers and its dangers, to cope with chance events, to evade its ponderous, awesome materiality.

> In a society such as our own we all know the rules of *exclusion*. The most obvious and familiar of these concerns what is *prohibited*. We know per-fectly well that we are not free to say just anything, that we cannot simply speak of anything, when we like or where we like; not just anyone, finally, may speak of just anything. We have three types of prohibition, cover-ing objects, ritual with its surrounding circumstances, the privileged or exclusive right to speak of a particular subject; these prohibitions inter-relate, reinforce and complement each other, forming a complex web, continually subject to modification.[1]

Foucault further points out that the two major prohibitions are those "dealing with politics and sexuality." Equally important in Foucault's the-ories on discourse, and pertinent to my analysis of the Valdez pastorela, is his view on the importance of history in discursive change. That is to say, particular forms of discourse will be acceptable or unacceptable ac-cording to who is in power at a specific point in time. The French critic's works on the prison system (*Discipline and Punish: The Birth of the Prison*) and on madness (*Madness and Civilization: A History of Madness in the Age of Reason*) delineate how an epoch's archival rules and constraints determine whether particular discourses are classified as normal or mad. Should these discourses be considered abnormal or beyond the pale of society's dictum, there will be attempts to repress and silence them. Pas-torela production falls within this purview of repression, censorship, and silence in certain historical periods and enjoys a modicum of freedom of expression at other points in time.[2]

The Foucauldian concept of "heterotopia" is also important in the anal-ysis of pastorela production. Foucault's notion that we are in an epoch of space, of simultaneity, of juxtaposition, of the near and the far, of the side by side bears out in Luis Valdez's pastorela: all of the above Foucauldian concepts are evident in the video production of the play.[3] Hybridity is evident in the juxtaposition of medieval shepherds with the *vato loco* (gang member type) and his 1955 shiny red Chevy. The medieval devil will appear in several guises, including Hell's Angels and a Middle East sultan with his flying carpet and throng of scantily clad belly dancers.

Valdez's *La Pastorela* can be viewed as a heterotopia in two significant aspects: first, it is a play usually performed in a particular space—a stage (i.e., the San Juan Bautista Mission in California)—and second, it is a video seen through a television screen. Foucault defines both of these spaces, the theater stage and cinema, as heterotopic.

> The heterotopia is capable of juxtaposing in a single real space several spaces, several sites that are in themselves incompatible. Thus it is that the theater brings onto the rectangle of the stage, one after the other, a whole series of places that are foreign to one another, thus it is that the cinema is a very odd rectangle room, at the end of which, on a two-dimensional screen, one sees the projection of a three-dimensional space.[4]

In addition, although Foucault does not explicitly state it, another heterotopic space can be dream space. Dream reality is another reality and is analogous to a mirror (which Foucault does classify as a heterotopic space) in that it too reflects material reality. It can be conceptualized as a Foucauldian countersite where reality can exist at multiple levels—that is, real, phantasmagoric, magical, heavenly, extraterrestrial, and so forth. Valdez's video version of *La Pastorela* begins by depicting everyday farmworker reality, but this reality is soon transposed (about five minutes into the video) into a dream world where fantasy and reality intermix in order to weave the tale of the struggle between good and evil.

I center my analysis on Valdez's video production played on national television in 1991 (although he has been presenting pastorelas in San Juan Bautista, California since the 1970s).[5] My work underscores the long trajectory traveled by this literary text: from European medieval and Spanish colonial periods to the present. This shepherds' play has evolved into various forms since its inception in the Middle Ages in Europe and its importation to the Americas in the sixteenth century. Luis Valdez's version is one in a series of transformations this folk drama has undergone. Valdez will suffuse the theatrical representation of the play with political elements and absurd juxtapositions which situate it within postmodernist parameters. The Chicano playwright will evince at times a subversive view of society; at other times an affirmative stance is taken, particularly when its referent is Mexican American culture and family values.

As pointed out earlier, the autos sacramentales were used as a strategy to Christianize the Native American populations. The religious play *Juicio Final* (*Last Judgment*) was first performed in 1533 and was the first European drama enacted in America; by the end of the decade, at least seven different plays had been staged.

These early missionary plays performed in New Spain soon evolved from religious plays to more secular forms of entertainment. The popular sectors found the dramas extremely pleasing and fairly flexible in structure, so almost immediately changes in these religious plays began to be introduced in spite of the fact that the changes were unacceptable to the clergy and tended to scandalize them. Fray Juan de Zumárraga, first bishop of Mexico, classified the autos sacramentales as too sexually explicit and prohibited their enactment during the 1540s decade.[6] Fortunately for pastorela productions, the bishop died in 1548: with the bishop's demise the plays were performed once again.

The arrival of the Jesuit order in 1572 infused a new life in pastorela production since the Jesuits came to America well versed in literary traditions and with a strong European theatrical background. The term *pastorela* emerged during this period, and the representation of these plays began to surface throughout the various geographic regions of New Spain. Nevertheless, the constant attacks against dramatic productions continued; by 1644 Bishop Juan Palafox de Mendoza in his battle with the Jesuits attacked with great severity the enactment of these dramas. The pastorelas nearly received a deathblow when the Jesuits were expelled in 1767 and denunciations against these dramatic performances appeared, accusing them of being scandalous. In spite of the plays' being banned by the Inquisition, they did not disappear but on the contrary, the character of the devil expanded to include numerous secondary devils—normally the Seven Deadly Sins plus Lucifer and Satan.

It is in the nineteenth century, during the wars of independence that pastorelas became part of the emerging Mexican national landscape and began to be tied to cultural identity. The independence movements (1810–21) of Mexico and other Latin American countries embraced a political ideology derived from the Enlightenment and other revolutionary movements that took place in the eighteenth century in such countries as the United States and France. The pastorela, having been banned under Spanish rule, now exploded as a symbol of national freedom. Once again, a political movement had stimulated the flourishing and expansion of this genre.

The nineteenth century witnessed three different expressions of pastorela production: (1) traditional, religious pastorelas, (2) literary, mainstream theater pastorelas, and (3) urban pastorelas. The character of the hermit was introduced at this juncture, since he is symbolic of the contradictions found in the Catholic Church.

After the Mexican playwright and author Joaquín Fernández de Lizardi's pastorela appeared in 1826, right after the independence movements, an explosion of literary pastorela texts surfaced in the ensuing Christmas seasons. Theaters throughout Mexico City enacted pastorelas or pastorela-derived plays such as *Los hijos de Bato y Bras o travesuras del diablo* (*The Sons of Bato and Bras or the Tricks of the Devil*), written by an anonymous author [1848]; *La pata del diablo* (*The Devil's Foot*), written by Mariano Osorno in 1862; *El diablo predicador o mayor contrario amigo* (*The Preaching Devil or the Worst Contrary Friend*), written by Calizto Dodun y Conde [1888–89].

The three categories of shepherds' plays continued to be popular during the twentieth century, although in Mexico City the urban pastorelas predominated and were characterized by their strong sexual overtone, and by their mordant criticism directed toward the ruling class, the bourgeoisie, and politicians. Mexico City's urban pastorelas zeroed in on the economic problems of the country and the social injustices extant therein. Written mainly for entertainment, with their strong doses of satire and irony explicitly presented, pastorela performances made people laugh. Nevertheless, the social and political criticism was such that the playwright producer and actor of the avant-garde pastorela Tapadeus, Germán Dehesa, in an interview I conducted with him in December 1986, informed me that he was constantly in fear of having his production shut down by government officials.

Since the 1960s, after the noted Mexican playwright Miguel Sabido introduced sophisticated, urban pastorelas in Mexico City, there has been a renaissance of pastorela performances in that metropolitan center as well as throughout Mexico and the Southwest.[7] In 1986, when I first undertook fieldwork on the genre, I was able to collect nine different variants of the shepherds' plays that were on stage in numerous theaters throughout Mexico City. Luis Valdez's play *La Pastorela: "The Shepherds' Tale"* is based on a traditional shepherds' play titled *Los Pastores* found in the American Southwest but, in particular, popular in Texas and New Mexico during the nineteenth century and early twentieth. Both Texas and New Mexico continue to enact pastorela performances every Christmas season.[8] The traditional play depicts the shepherds Lizardo, Bato, Gila, Abelicio, Bartolo, Menapas, Dina, and Melideos tending their sheep when an archangel (Gabriel in some texts and Saint Michael in others) announces the birth of Jesus and directs the shepherds to go worship him at the grotto in Bethlehem. On their journey to the grotto, the *ermitaño* or hermit, representative of the Catholic Church, joins them. Throughout the shepherds' journey, there are appearances by one or more devils, who try to divert them by using various strategies to distract them.

Los Pastores is the most widely diffused liturgical play throughout the Americas; hundreds of variants attest to its popularity.[9] A common structural variation in the drama is found within the tricks the devil plays on the shepherds when trying to intercept their pilgrimage to worship the newborn Child. The devil may use any of the Seven Deadly Sins in tempting the shepherds to forget their quest. As might be expected, the most common Deadly Sins used are Lust, Gluttony, and Greed, that is, sex, food, and money!

Valdez adheres to the traditional structure and plot of the pastorela. His basic plot has the announcement of the birth of Christ given by Saint Michael (played by Linda Ronstadt); the shepherds' journey; the hermit's incorporation in the journey; the devils' machinations in trying to divert the shepherds from their sacred task (the main devil, Osmodeo, is played by the Chicano comic Paul Rodríguez); the battles between minor devils and Saint Michael; the battle between Lucifer and Saint Michael (victory of Good over Evil); the final scene at Bethlehem where the shepherds pay homage to the newborn Jesus.

There are four major strategies through which Valdez (figure 1) subverts the traditional pastorela structure in order to permeate it with an ideology that is congruent with Chicano political positions and demands for social justice and a more equitable society. These strategies include the farmworkers as protagonists, Chicano language registers—that is, code-switching (switching between English and Spanish)—working-class speech, expletives, standard Spanish, standard English, and *caló* (mainly adolescent jive talk or jargon); numerous musical genres; and representation of the devil in a multiplicity of forms: Hell's Angels, a wealthy Californio rancher, a Middle East sultan.

Farmworkers

The Chicano playwright subverts the traditional pastorela structure by incorporating the contemporary farmworker into the plot. In this manner the pastorela is not merely a traditional religious play but becomes a political statement vis-à-vis the exploited farmworker. The issues of poverty are underscored at the inception of the play and will be reiterated

1. Luis Valdez, 1990s.
Courtesy: Luis Valdez.

throughout. The offers by the devils of rich banquets and plentiful food
resonate within the ideological parameters of farmworker exploitation
and poverty in a wealthy society.

Valdez initiates the action on his video with the camera shot of a dreamy
young woman named Gila seated on a hillside near the town of San Juan
Bautista, California. After focusing on the young woman, the camera
proceeds to show a group of migrant farmworkers who are returning
from laboring in the local garlic fields in Gilroy, California. This is a small
agricultural town located in a rich agricultural area near San Juan Bautista
and known as the "Garlic Capital of the World." The workers realistically
present the poverty found in the United States among Mexican Americans and in this manner underscore the political subtext of the play. The
migrant workers' camp further demonstrates through the camera's sharp
eye the poor living conditions under which the farmworkers toil in spite
of being the principal workers in California's multibillion-dollar agricultural industry. Poverty and a life of backbreaking work are evident in the
faces of the workers. The lack of money is underlined when Gila upon returning to her house complains to her mother about the lack of adequate
Christmas presents for the children. The stoic mother chastises the young
girl for her discontent and her complaining.

After this brief interlude in Gila's house, the family proceeds to the mission church in San Juan Bautista to see a pastorela performance (this pastorela is presented every other year in the San Juan Bautista Mission). As Gila sits in a church pew, an object falls from the priest's pulpit and strikes Gila on the head, rendering her unconscious. Valdez uses the same filmic technique present in the classic movie *The Wizard of Oz* (1939), where young Dorothy, the main character, is struck on the head by a flying object and "wakes up" in another reality. Gila, in a similar manner, wakes up in another reality. She is transported from the San Juan Bautista Mission church into the countryside and wakes up as a shepherdess tending sheep with her father and neighbors all dressed as shepherds. Thus the play within a play begins and the pastorela narrative commences, for immediately after Gila wakes up in the bucolic setting of the hills of San Juan Bautista the archangel Saint Michael makes his dramatic appearance and conveys the message to the shepherds about the newborn Jesus.

Valdez's casting of the farmworkers as principal characters in the pastorela contextualizes the play within present working-class conditions. The farmworker as sacred image, as hero, as active agent in helping the forces of Good overcome the forces of Evil redefines his or her role in society. Farmworkers are the subjects, the privileged ones within the frame of the narrative, and are not pathetic objects to be pitied or scorned. Valdez's pastorela is transgressive and subversive because it empowers the downtrodden through an artistic production.

Language

A structural element immediately noticeable in the play is the multiplicity of language registers used. *La Pastorela* is not performed in its original language, that is, Spanish. The play introduces both Spanish and English in the dialogues, and code-switching is particularly evident. Language becomes a subversive element in that the pastorela is performed in the language of the Chicano—a language that has been vilified by hegemonic classes both in the United States and in Spanish-speaking countries. By using Chicano Spanish, English, and a combination of both languages, Valdez is conferring legitimacy to what has been called a "bastardized" language. Gloria Anzaldúa in her book *Borderlands/La Frontera: The New Mestiza* (1987) includes a section titled "Linguistic Terrorism." In this essay Anzaldúa discusses the issue of speaking Chicano English and its harsh consequences:

Deslenguadas. Somos los del español deficiente. We are your linguistic night-mare, your linguistic aberration, your linguistic *mestizaje*, the subject of your *burla*. Because we speak with tongues of fire we are culturally cruci-fied. Racially, culturally and linguistically *somos huérfanos*—we speak an orphan tongue.

Chicanas who grew up speaking Chicano Spanish have internalized the belief that we speak poor Spanish. It is illegitimate, a bastard language. And because we internalize how our language has been used against us by the dominant culture, we use our language differences against each other.[10]

Thus Valdez's use of Chicano English throughout the video affirms the linguistic validity of this form of communication and reaffirms its use as an important element in artistic creations. The language employed in Valdez's drama is not abstract or alienating; it is the voice of the Chicano people who creatively mix Spanish and English—the play being both bi-lingual and bicultural. Within Valdez's forms of linguistic expression is the Foucauldian concept of heterotopia: a multiplicity and "plurivalence" of forms coexisting in a single space. Valdez incorporates the linguistic expressions created and articulated by the Mexican American population and utilizes these expressions as realistic speech acts that aid in the struc-turing of a picaresque-type humor. For example, we hear Gila's mother admonish her daughter: "Some diablo has gotten into you." The code-switching interjects a humorous note and at the same time introduces other cultural elements since the word *diablo* (devil) conveys a series of cultural vectors indicative of the Mexican conceptualization of the devil. Other examples of code-switching include the following:

Bilingual Text	My Translation
1. Oh, *chihuahua*!	1. Oh, darn it!
Here I am in my hermit's cave.	Here I am in my hermit's cave.
2. Help your *comadre* get some *tortillas*.	2. Help your co-mother get some *tortillas*.

(Excerpts from video *La Pastorela*, 1991)

The bilingual expressions function in various ways: two of the most important are to elicit humor and to underscore Hispanic cultural as-pects. In example 1 the term *chihuahua* is a common Mexican expression (a euphemism) for the harsh expletive *chingado*. The term situates the action and speaker within a Mexican and Chicano cultural context being that it is specifically Mexican and Chicano and not Latin American or peninsular Spanish.

The same can be said for example 2, where the words *comadre* and *tortilla* are used as signifiers for Mexican and Chicano culture. In this case there is no direct translation for the word *comadre* (can be loosely translated as "co-mother") or *tortilla*, a type of Mexican corn bread eaten and used as a main ingredient in many Mexican dishes such as *tacos* and *enchiladas*.

Music

A third major strategy through which Valdez incorporates subversive elements is through musical compositions. While traditional pastorelas adhere to religious *villancicos* (Christmas carols), Valdez's text mixes the sacred with the profane, producing various hybrid forms of music. For example villancicos *and* classic rock are played side by side (the classic rock song "Black Magic Woman," recorded by Carlos Santana and his band, is played in one scene). Jazz is also played throughout one major scene in the video production and a villancico is rendered in a jazzy musical style. In this manner, hybridity is manifested through the various musical scores extant in the video production.

Musical compositions range from classical to working class, to middle class and popular culture. We find classical religious music, *conjunto* music (Tex-Mex), bluegrass, rock and roll, Latin American, *nueva canción* and *canciones rancheras* (Mexican rural type songs). This mixture of musical compositions underscores the postmodernist obsession for breaking boundaries between the center and the margin. Nevertheless, within this musical style what predominates are those musical compositions emanating from the working class, from marginalized groups.

The Devil

A fourth strategy used in subverting the traditional religious pastorela structure is through the figure of the devil. The representation of the devil has evolved from a traditional medieval figure; to a baroque devil in the sixteenth and seventeenth centuries; to a romantic, anguished creature of the nineteenth century; and finally to a contemporary postmodernist devil. A heterogeneous mixture of devils appears in Luis Valdez's pastorela, some of which are half human–half animal while others are represented as Hell's Angels! The latter are dressed in Heavy Metal punk attire; that is, they are dressed in black with metal trimming on their shirts and pants. The representation of modern-day evil as Hell's Angels mounted on their Harley Davidson motorcycles produces reactions of both terror and amusement. The characterization of evil in our modern-day society as the Hell's Angels and their appearance as such in modern-day pastorelas are indicative of the flexibility of this genre's structure, a structure which lends itself to easy updating of issues and events. In one pastorela presented in San Diego, California (1999), the devils disguised themselves as three Teletubbies!

While the devils play tricks on the shepherds in their attempt to divert them from their pilgrimage, they are not equivalent to the Mexican trickster figure. In Mexican culture the trickster figure plays tricks on the devil and defeats the devil; such a trickster figure in Hispanic/Mexican culture is Pedro de Urdemalas. The Mexican trickster always defeats the devil with his wit and cunning. In the case of pastorelas, the devils are not clever enough to defeat the shepherds. The shepherds, however, are not the ones that defeat the devil(s); it is the archangel Saint Michael and his angels who accomplish this feat.

Valdez's pastorela has the minor devils represented as Hell's Angels. However, the chief devil, Lucifer (Luzbel), appears in three instances in different costumes. In Lucifer's first appearance he wears a black tuxedo with a black cape and arrives on the scene in a limousine. The image projected is that of wealth and power. In Lucifer's second and third appearance, he is dressed as a nineteenth-century *Californio don* (wealthy, titled, landowning person) and is riding a horse. Here once again we can detect the political agenda resonating within the play. The landowner–*hacendado*–agribusiness rancher–grower as representative of "evil" is within the political, historical parameters of Mexican/Chicano society. The Spanish/Mexican *hacendado* (landowner) has been perceived as "evil" from the perspective of the Indian and the mestizo who suffered under the hacienda peonage system in the Spanish colonial period and under Mexican government in the nineteenth century and early twentieth. Since there are no longer Californio (Spanish/Mexican) landowners, the figure is a signifier for the contemporary California big business farmer against whom César Chávez, the Chicano union organizer, fought so hard. Valdez was intimately involved in the struggle to unionize farmworkers, and his pastorela is within the parameters of the union struggle tradition of the Teatro Campesino. An interesting question arises as to why Valdez did not present Lucifer as a contemporary Anglo grower but chose the extinct Californio rancher. The answer most likely lies in Foucault's theory of discourse and power. Since Valdez's sponsors were probably Anglo-Americans and the national audience targeted is mostly Anglo, the Chicano playwright either self-censored his pastorela or he was pressured into changing the ethnicity of the grower to the now defunct and very dead Californio. Censorship frequently happens to Chicano artists who are too vocal or too graphic in their denunciations of Anglo-American oppression and discriminatory practices. In the *Los Angeles Times* articles quoted previously the authors clearly state that the two figures, Jesus Christ on the cross and Lucifer, are counterposed and that at times these two appear to blend into one. This blending coincides with Luis Valdez's adaptation of Mayan philosophical beliefs of "Tú eres mi otro yo" (You are my other self). The disappearance of the boundary separating good and evil, or between the archetypal figures of Jesus and Lucifer, underscores the postmodernist position of abolishing boundaries between binary structures such as good and evil—the signifier and the signified.

Valdez's *La Pastorela: "The Shepherds' Tale"* encompasses multiple characteristics of postmodernist aesthetics. It is a politically subversive play that aims its critical darts directly at the establishment and at capitalist society and in particular against those forces oppressing the Chicano people.

At the same time, Valdez's drama affirms traditional mores and beliefs such as love for one's family, respect for parents, belief in the tenets of Catholicism—although belief in the devil is not necessarily reaffirmed, since the devils act more as a source of humor and laughter than as horrific figures. Lucifer, in contrast, is representative of capitalism and the evils this system supposedly encompasses: conspicuous consumption, wealth, luxury, and so forth. The Holy Family is not satirized, while the hermit—representative of the Catholic Church—is castigated through parody and satire for his hypocrisy and false humility. Valdez's shepherds' play continues to privilege heterogeneity. It attacks hierarchical structures, such as patriarchy and the false materialistic values of our affluent society, while affirming such Mexican American cultural values as the family and religious belief systems.

As is evident, the pastorela is a folk genre that continues to be performed in Mexico and the United States, both in the traditional religious style and in more contemporary modes. Political forces have been directly instrumental in the evolution of the genre, and its flexible structure makes it appealing to playwrights. Dramatists frequently exercise their creative talents and transform the pastorela plays in order to meet contemporary tastes and to address the issues that concern today's audiences.

Notes

Valdez uses both *Tale* and *Play* interchangeably in the title of his work.

1. Michel Foucault, *The Archaeology of Knowledge and the Discourse on Language* (New York: Pantheon Books, 1972), 216.

2. Ibid. (quote); Foucault, *Discipline and Punish: The Birth of the Prison*; trans. Alan Sheridan (New York: Random House, Vintage Books, 1979); Foucault, *Madness and Civilization: A History of Insanity in the Age of Reason* (New York: Pantheon, 1965).

3. See Michel Foucault, "Of Other Spaces," *Diacritics: A Review of Contemporary Criticism* 16, no. 1 (spring 1986): 22–27.

4. Michel Foucault, "Of Other Spaces," 25.

5. *Los Angeles Times* pt. II, 5, 24 December 1977 and pt. I, 5, 19 December 1985.

6. Ibid.

7. *Los Angeles Times*, pt. III, 5, 24 December 1977 and pt. I, 5, 19 December 1985.

8. For Texas see Richard R. Flores's in-depth study of a popular pastorela performed every Christmas in San Antonio, Texas: *Los Pastores: History and Performance in the Mexican Shepherds' Play of South Texas* (Washington, D.C.: Smithsonian Institution Press, 1995). For New Mexico, I videotaped two pastorelas in Taos and Española in 1989 and have them in my pastorela collection.

9. Rael collected numerous pastorelas and has a detailed study of their diffusion. Juan B. Rael, *The Sources and Diffusion of the Mexican Shepherds' Plays* (Guadalajara: Librería La Joyita, 1965).

10. Gloria Anzaldúa, *Borderlands/La Frontera: The New Mestiza* (San Francisco: Aunt Lute Books, 1987).

LAURA E. PÉREZ

14

Hybrid Spiritualities
and Chicana Altar-Based Art

The Work of Amalia Mesa-Bains

Ranging from atheist, to disaffected Catholic, to a mix of Christian and Jewish, to culturally hybrid forms of spirituality, the work of many post-sixties Chicana feminist artists illuminates the fact that spiritual beliefs and practices generate social and political effects that matter.[1] In academic fields outside of religious studies and anthropology, and in art-world spheres, particularly in the studied nihilism of much of postmodern art and poststructuralist thought, the spiritual and the political remain separated, following assumptions dating to the Enlightenment in the modern Western world—a binary that is clearly one of the last "frontiers" to be deconstructed.[2] For most of the Chicana artists whose work I have studied, and not necessarily in the way spirituality works for the larger Chicana/o and *mexicana/o* communities in the United States, the spiritual is in varying degrees consciously evoked in their art for political effects that are very different from, indeed, the opposite of those sought by the religious discourses of right-wing Christian politicians and religious leaders. Further, a particular kind of spirituality, a culturally hybrid spirituality, is what is most often cited or articulated in the work of more than forty literary, visual, and performance artists from the 1970s through 2000.[3] This hybrid spirituality is indeed a "politicizing spirituality" as Mesa-Bains herself phrased it,[4] and it emphasizes embodiment—that is, spiritual consciousness that is manifest in identifiable, socially mappable bodies and practices, rather than in vague, binary, and abstract notions of goodness, sin, s/Spirit(s), and spirituality. In the artwork of these women, it is the day-to-day practices of spiritual consciousness and its material effects, rather than identification with the dogma and ritual practices of traditional religious institutions, that is of most interest.[5]

What emerges most often as a hybrid notion of the spiritual in the work of the contemporary Chicana artists I have studied claims continuities with cultural traditions alongside, or other than, the dominating Euro-American, Judeo-Christian in a process inadequately described as syncretism, or as "cultural Catholicism."

Apart from the artists' own hereditary ethnic and cultural hybridities or *mestizajes*, the multiethnic and multicultural realities of cities such as Los Angeles, San Francisco, San Antonio, and Houston and of parts of the U.S.-Mexico borderlands, where many Chicana artists of the postmodern, postindustrial era—that is, the 1970s to the present—have been raised or formatively shaped, have allowed for the circulation of a multiplicity of religious worldviews from which to compare received spiritual practices and to attempt to fashion personally and historically meaningful new ones. The receptivity to the unorthodox in the aftermath of the 1960s and that era's criticism of received state, family, and religious institutions have also played their part in shaping Chicana feminist and culturally hybrid spiritualities. When they have looked to the pre-Christian past, feminist Chicana artists have done so in order to imagine a future beyond colonizing, heteronormative patriarchal cultures. In addition to Mesoamerican and North American female deities, some have variously assimilated goddess-spiritualities from around the globe. Others have embraced Eastern spiritualities, such as Buddhism, in their work. Some have studied and incorporated aspects of African diaspora practices and beliefs, such as those of Santería. And many have engaged their ancestral spiritualities of Mesoamerican or North American native peoples or both, whether to rediscover and reinterpret them or to merely nurture them. For many Chicana artists, Native American ancestry is quite direct and living, as in a mother or father of Tepehuan, Chumash, Kickapoo, Nez Percé, or Huichol ancestry. Others may know the Indigenous ancestry of grand- or great-grandparents, but for perhaps most of us, in spite of Indigenous appearance and persistence of non-Western cultural customs, the conscious ties to language and a given Indigenous people have been occluded by imperialist histories of anti-Indigenous racism in both Latin America and the United States, and the silencing, if not the full erasure of, our Indigenous linguistic and other cultural legacies.[6]

In spite of these realities, the myth of the supposedly fervent and uncritical Christian—and more specifically Catholic—religiosity of Mexican and

Mexican American women, continues to be one of the more overworked stereotypes about Latin Americans and U.S. Latina/os that has been extended to contemporary female artists. Robert Henkes, for example, writing about Latina/os in the United States, ventures that

> Devout ties to their faith have led many Latin Americans to depict saintly images, especially the Blessed Virgin Mary and the image of Christ. Women have patterned their lives after the Blessed Mother and have had patron saints intercede for earthly favors. . . . Shrines, chapels and sanctuaries are essential installations of the three-dimensional artist. The world outside of Catholicism may find it difficult to accept these works. Nonetheless, such works are essential for the viewer to understand the position of the Latin American artist in the mainstream of American art.[7]

Confusion between Latin American women in general and artists in particular, and the culturally essentialist conflation of Latin American and U.S. Latina/o cultures aside, it may be that there exists a private collection of devout Catholic artwork by women of Latin American descent in the U.S. during the nineteenth century. The case, however, is far less clear among contemporary, particularly post-1960s, U.S. Latina *or* Latin American women artists. Given that by definition Chicana artists are those who identify as such as a result of the Chicana/o and feminist civil rights movements that emerged in the second half of the 1960s, within the context of other countercultural youth movements. What is soon apprehended by anyone who has studied this work in any depth is the following: First, orthodox Catholicism is rare to begin with among circulating artists post-1965, and second, Christianity in general is no longer such a self-evident fact among these generations. Non-Christian identifications (Indigenous, Jewish, African-diaspora, Eastern, neopagan "Goddess"), not to mention the complications of mixed-"race" and mixed-cultural religiosities are made evident in this artwork. But perhaps most pertinent, Christianity and other systems of traditional religious belief are subjected to a feminist critique of Eurocentric, patriarchal, and heterosexist underpinnings in most of the Chicana, and for this matter other U.S. Latina, contemporary artwork I have seen.[8]

Though Chicana art from the 1960s through the present is not widely known in its breadth and extension, two of the most familiar images in feminist, multicultural, and U.S. Latina/o art publications are, nonetheless, precisely the foundational, feminist critiques of a Eurocentric and patriarchal visual cultural legacy of the Virgin Mary's and Virgin of Guadalupe's representations. From 1972 to 1978, the pioneering Chicana artists Patssi Valdez and ASCO, Ester Hernandez, Yolanda López, and Yreina D. Cervántez, respectively, create a punkish Black Virgin warrior, and working-class, and Frida Kahlo–based Indigenous everyday Chicana "Virgins," all ensconced within the traditional *mandorla* (full-body halo) of sacredness. In so doing, they initiated a tradition that continues to the present in Chicana feminist, Chicano queer, and even straight Chicano aesthetic and spiritual hybridizations and spins of Eurocentric, patriarchal renditions of Mother Mary.[9] Like Virgin Mary / Virgin of Guadalupe Chicana/o iconography and performance representations, altar-based art is one of many meaningful vehicles of expression—and debate—of culturally hybrid and decolonizing forms of spirituality.

On the Altars of Alterity

Contemporary altar art can be traced back to ancient, cross-cultural traditions of altar building and, even more relevantly here, to the multiethnic reality and cultural hybridity of the earliest colonial encounters in the Americas.[10] As a form of domestic religious practice outside of the domain of dominant religiosities, the altar has been a site for the socially and culturally other, the "alter," to express, preserve, and transmit cultural and gender-based religious and political differences.[11] It is no wonder then that the altar installation has become a widespread art form in the last three decades, or that it has been described as a particularly apt late twentieth-century art form that captures the "altar-like reality" of the multiethnic, postmodern, urban cultural world of the United States.[12] Altar installations and altar-inspired art inescapably reference the altar's timeless and cross-cultural spiritual function, whether to sacralize the seemingly profane; to interrogate the spiritual claims and political effects of dominant religious beliefs; to figure the coexistence of the artistic, the spiritual, and the material and thus of the political; or finally, to articulate presently meaningful, hybrid forms of spirituality and spiritually conscious art making. A reading of the function of the altar and religious discourse in Amalia Mesa-Bains' installations, for example, as "replac[ing] the transcendental with the political,"[13] misses the very point of a "politicizing spirituality" that this pioneering altar-installation artist has theorized,[14] and has enacted through her installations.[15] That altar installation and related art forms have inspired Chicana artists can be more precisely connected to the search for, and expression of, alternative spiritualities and alternative art practices, particularly those that are visionary with respect to social justice and transformation.

Latina/o theologians,[16] scholars of feminist spiritualities and practices,[17] queer spiritualities writers,[18] and religion scholars and journalists[19] have observed the relation between, on the one hand, the various civil rights struggles of the 1960s through the present, and, on the other, changing and even new forms of spirituality that have emerged since then. For Chicana/o and other artists, spirituality, politics, and art have been entwined in the radical rethinking and cultural restructuring of the past twenty-five years.[20] The concern with the spiritual in Chicana/o and Latina/o art is surely connected to "resistance and affirmation" of Mexican American and Indigenous cultural differences,[21] wherever these may be relevant to the artist, but it is important to recognize that not all forms of spirituality referred to are culturally native to the artists. Thus, cultural difference in their artwork functions *both* to signal cultural specificity traditionally received *and* to produce culturally relevant visual "thought" about the increasingly globalized, multiethnic, and economically polarized global cities of the present that Saskia Sassen and others have described. The search for (and creation of) more socially relevant spiritual beliefs and practices has characterized the United States since the midsixties and is thus hardly characteristic of U.S. Latina/o artists alone.[22] What *is* different is the source of spiritualities cited, the politics of such drawing, and the possible effects of such inscriptions, given the historical and ongoing marginalized social, political, economic, and cultural status of Chicana/os as inequitably racialized ethnic minorities.

In the United States Latina/os, along with other socially marginalized groups, are at the forefront of newer, socially relevant, and trendsetting forms of both art making and new religiosities. Gruzinski's model of religious visual cultural warfare and mutual cultural appropriations in colonial Mexico are, in fact, as he hopes, useful for understanding urban postmodernity, particularly in the study of contemporary Chicana/o cultural practices.[23] Altar-based and altar-inspired art forms by the artists whose work is studied in the longer version of this essay (in the book *Chicana Art: The Politics of Spiritual and Aesthetic Altarities*)—as well as in the specific work of Amalia Mesa-Bains, to which I will turn in a later section—are constructed in varying degrees through the codes of different, competing, and hybridized visual and religious cultures. Western high-art conventions, for example, may be seen as the language through which those Chicana/o and Mexican American popular cultural beliefs and practices that are rooted in Amerindian or other so-called pagan or Goddess cultures are rephrased. Alternately, the discourse of Western high-art conventions are interrogated through culturally different conventions of "art," beauty, and value that Indigenous, Mexican American, and popular urban or rural classes hold. In perhaps all cases, the spiritualities and political stances expressed in the work reflect the post-1965 search for more meaningful spiritual, artistic, and political practices that continue to this day. Feminist neopagan, goddess spiritualities,[24] Native American beliefs and practices, Mexican American "folk Catholicism,"[25] elements from African-diaspora Santería, decolonizing ethnic-minority discourses, and the critique of the Eurocentrism of mainstream and dominant cultural forms, including those of "high" religion and "high" art—these are all components of the new kinds of cultural hybridity that appear in Chicana art forms that articulate themselves through references to the spiritual.

Domestic or so-called folk artistic and religious cultural practices have traditionally been a terrain of female agency for Indigenous, mestiza women. Thus, the domestic altar has embodied a space of some religious and gender freedom, as well as creativity, for the socially marginalized and oppressed. In this sense, the altar has mediated the social and cultural survival and to some degree the personal empowerment of the *alter*, that is, the socially "other." Kay Turner has written extensively on the altar as a site for the visual recording of familial histories, and has observed the empowerment that domestic *altaristas* (altar makers) derive from control over these histories.[26] Among many of the elderly Mexican and Mexican American subjects whose altars she has studied, she has noted the empowering personal spiritualities that are expressed through their highly personal, religiously unorthodox altars.[27] The preservation of "herstories" appears repeatedly in Chicana art articulated through religious visual culture, as we will see in Mesa-Bains's altars. Though partly articulated through Catholic visual culture, altar installations, like their domestic counterparts, allow for the unorthodox reshaping, appropriation, or rejection of Christian, patriarchal, and heteronormative beliefs.

To some degree, the gender-conscious, politicized spiritualities enacted in Chicana art are part of the "Latino religious resurgence" that Ana María Díaz-Stevens and Anthony Stevens-Arroyo have documented as a movement of religious and social reform, rooted in the Latina/o civil rights struggles of the 1960s.[28] Chicana altar installations and other related art practices that are structured through Christian visual discourses—such as *caja* or *nicho* (niche) work, or *retablos* (ex-voto paintings)—can indeed be accurately read as "Third World" inflections upon Eurocentric Christianity missing in that what they do not fully reject Christianity are still not necessarily circumscribed by it. Amalia Mesa-Bains's early altar to Saint Teresa of Avila, some of Santa Barraza's neo-*retablo* or votive paintings, and some *santos* (wooden sculptures of saints) or Virgin of Guadalupe–inspired work could be read in this way. However, in the work of many Chicana artists, including the other work by the artists mentioned, spiritual beliefs rooted in Indigenous, African-diaspora, Buddhist, or global pagan feminist thought and practice strain the effort to recuperate them into an all-engulfing, "multicultural," but still Eurocentric, patriarchal Christianity.

Chicana/o and other U.S. Latina/o intellectuals, in the fields of both religion and visual arts,[29] along with U.S. Latina/o artists, are radically redefining our understanding of religious and cultural syncretism beyond what is still a Eurocentric idea that vestiges of the precolonial survive as largely incoherent fragments within the engulfing colonial culture. Migene González-Wippler, for example, speaks of syncretism instead as the effect of a logic of discernment on the part of early Santería adherents. To her, Yoruba belief systems allowed the diasporic African communities to carefully screen Christian beliefs, adopting those that seemed compatible. In González-Wippler's view, such refitting and adoption operations are part and parcel of a general, human search for meaning. Such a view cautions us against the "exotifying" tendency to ascribe syncretic processes specifically to Creole cultures, as if syncretism, hybridity, and mestizaje did not occur whenever and wherever different cultural currents come into significant contact. Andrés Pérez y Mena defines syncretism by those cultural differences that cannot be melded into each other, but his emphasis remains, like González-Wippler's, on the cultural simultaneity of Puerto Rican Spiritism, for example, with Christianity. Arturo Lindsay and Gerardo Mosquera, from within the intersecting fields of art and religion, argue—in the anthologies they have respectively edited: *Santería Aesthetics in Contemporary Latin American Art* and *Beyond the Fantastic*—even more forcefully for the predominance of the African-diaspora and Indigenous influences over the culturally European ones in some of the U.S. Latina/o and Latin American art practices they survey. Similarly, in the work of Celia Herrera Rodríguez, Kathleen Alcalá, Yreina Cervántez, or Delilah Montoya, Latin American and U.S. Latina/o Eurocentric notions of hybridity, mestizaje, or religious syncretism are found to be lacking. What their and other artistic practices reveal, rather, is the perdurance of Native American and African-diaspora religious cultural *cores* that have selectively absorbed bits and pieces of the Euro-Christian influence, rather than the other way around.

In this regard, Chicana art practices may not reflect theological or broader Mexican American or U.S. Latina/o perspectives on religiosity and spiritual practice. Most of those works I have studied—and it is a large body—are well beyond arguing from within Christianity, not only because of its patriarchal and heteronormative bent today but, more to the point of the matter, because of an official, institutionalized religious worldview that is found lacking when compared with Indigenous, African-diaspora, Eastern, and European neopagan "animist," non-human-centered, and nondualistic spiritualities. In varying degrees, the works critique the political ideologies manifested in the histories of imperialist, patriarchal, racist, and heteronormative Christian officialdom. At the juncture of discourses of globalization, postcoloniality, poststructuralism, and civil rights, the body of Chicana artists' work I have studied, in the main, offers sustained reflections on what is in fact a more complex picture of hybridized spiritualities whose compass navigates *through*, rather than to, dominant forms of Christianity. If this art work can be taken, in the style of the religion journalists Richard Cimino's and Don Lattin's *Shopping for Faith: American Religion in the New Millennium*, as a present indicator of things to come on a more massive scale, we can expect to move beyond the "Third-Worlding" of a still Eurocentric Christianity.[30] Some of these art practices map, rather, a fundamental restructuring of orthodox Christian dogma that amounts to its demise and cannibalization. Cimino's and Lattin's reports on the Christian interdenominational, culturally pluralistic religious future of the United States would appear, from the perspective of contemporary Chicana art, to be the tip of the iceberg of the great Eurocentric Christian meltdown. This change has come about because the cultural effects of increased globalization include not only the restructuring of religious beliefs and practices; they also include the birth of altogether new forms that are more than simply the uneven mixtures of older forms, and that are more than simply the resurgence of surviving ancient Indigenous forms, in the wake of the cultural contestation and displacement of patriarchal, Eurocentric, heteronormative Christianity.

Altars and Related Art Forms

In a culture where "we find it indescribably embarrassing to mention 'art' and 'spirit' in the same sentence," altar, and related art forms, bring into view the important questions of how our religious beliefs shape and impact our social lives, and what art's role is in all of this.[31] Chicana/o artists transferred the popular, domestic altar into the art installation and related forms at least as early as 1972, when the Galería de la Raza, in San Francisco, started organizing altars with community participation, around the Day of the Dead.[32] Most, if not all, of the visual artists mentioned in the larger study from which this chapter is taken participated in early, pioneering Day of the Dead altar installations and related exhibitions.[33] Some have appeared in mainstream galleries or museums only during such guest installations. Some, like Amalia Mesa-Bains, have achieved a notable degree of success in both mainstream and Latina/o art worlds, through what has thus far been her signature medium, the altar installation. There are, in fact, numerous other excellent artists who have productively worked with the altar and its related forms.[34] I will, however, limit myself here to the altar installations of Amalia Mesa-Bains.

The Altars of Amalia Mesa-Bains

Amalia Mesa-Bains's altar installations are among the earliest and the most sustained exploration of the medium, spanning from 1975 through the present, in more than thirteen major pieces. In terms of women's art in the United States in general, she is considered among "the artists who first brought the women's altar into public settings for consideration of its history, aesthetic attributes, and political force."[35] Her altar installations have been exhibited widely and have received intellectually rich, scholarly consideration. Tomás Ybarra-Frausto and Mesa-Bains herself have been the foremost theorists of Chicana/o and U.S. Latina/o altar installation, more recently joined by the art historian Jennifer González.

In the "Sanctums of the Spirit—The Altares of Amalia Mesa-Bains," for the exhibition catalog of *Grotto of the Virgins*, Tomás Ybarra-Frausto described the evolution of the artist's altar installations in three stages.[36] He saw the initial phase of her work, 1975–80, "revital[ing] an ancient and ongoing devotional expression" within the larger project of cultural reclamation and identity construction of the early Chicana/o Movement, and he noted the theme that would become characteristic of her altar-installation work: historical, cultural, and psychological excavation.[37] Of the altars produced from 1980 through 1985, the Chicano critic and theorist noted that "beyond gender affirmation and validation of Mexican models of female experience, the artist begins cross-cultural investigations of arcane spiritual traditions among women in traditional cultures."[38] Regarding what was then her current work, that of 1986–87, he was again particularly perceptive in observing that "narrative history now becomes a symbolic reflection moving beyond Mexican culture to embrace a cross-cultural assemblage of objects and practices from universal sacred traditions like curanderismo, voodoo, Santeria, and shamanism."[39] He noted the canonization of figures such as the Mexican screen idol Dolores del

Río and the artist Frida Kahlo, who were paid homage as early as 1977 in Mesa-Bains's altars, into a "personal feminist pantheism of goddesses, saints and virgins."[40]

Celeste Olalquiaga interestingly discussed Mesa-Bains's work, and that of other contemporary artists using altar and religious forms, as "third-degree kitsch" art, a postmodern form of art that reinvests kitschy and traditional religious signs with new meanings, and that in drawing upon Latina/o cultural objects contributes to the ongoing transformation of an increasingly globalized visual culture that Latin American immigration to the urban centers of the United States has helped to effect.[41] Mesa-Bains, however, carefully distinguishes between kitsch and the ethnically different notions and functions of *rasquachismo*, or *domesticana*, its Chicana counterpart, out of which Chicana altar installations such as her own emerge.

> Kitsch as a material expression is recuperated by artists who stand outside the lived reality of its genesis. Conversely, *rasquachismo* for *Chicano* artists is instrumental from within a shared barrio sensibility. One can say that kitsch is appropriated while *rasquachismo* is acclaimed or affirmed. *Rasquachismo* is consequently an integral world view that serves as a basis for cultural identity and a sociopolitical movement.[42]

Jennifer González has carefully studied Mesa-Bains's corpus of altar installations, through the second part of her *Venus Envy* trilogy.[43] She describes the artist's practice as a "'memory theater' or *autotopography* . . . which includes signs of a female Mexican lineage, intimate possessions and family snapshots."[44] She observes that

> The artist does not seek to "salvage" the past or to claim a place of "authentic" subjectivity, but to use the signs of a material history to illustrate the intricate and overlapping networks of power that produce any given subject. It is in the tension between these two positions—metaphor and evidence—that her work rests, and so forms a new space in which the ephemeral is made concrete.[45]

The politics of Mesa-Bains's altar work are also well described by Mesa-Bains's own theory of domesticana and *rasquache* (discussed earlier), the sensibility of feminist Chicana art that reclaims cultural practices in the face of their historic social devaluation in Eurocentric culture and that critiques the patriarchal limitations within Mexican and Mexican American culture. The idea of domesticana emphasizes a gendered aesthetic that has developed in the domestic sphere and that "includes home embellishments, home altar maintenance, healing traditions, and personal feminine style or pose."[46] Rather than situating its aesthetic of fragmentation and recombination in the postmodern experience, she situates it in an aesthetic of the impoverished and socially disenfranchised that is specific to Mexican and Mexican American cultures, as a "making do with what's at hand," as Tomás Ybarra-Frausto and Shifra Goldman had described it.[47] The artist clarified that though "making do with what's at hand" is, or was, a historic experience for many Mexican Americans, its conscious use as a style—fragmentation, recombination, accumulation, display, and abundance—by Chicana/o artists is a stance of defiant "resistance and affirmation" of not only the popular, but more specifically, of the "integral world view" (as noted above) of Mexican American urban and working classes "that provides an oppositional identity."[48] This is not only evident in the work of Chicana artists but also in Mexican American pop culture music, as Gastón Espinosa demonstrates in chapter 15, on Tejana music star Selena.

Mesa-Bains's altar installations are not, however, solely cultural practices of ideological resistance to the historic discrimination and oppression of Mexican Americans, and an affirmation of their rural and urban cultures. As feminist works, they appropriate and transform the aesthetic of material accumulation of the domestic altar, yard shrines, and the like, into "an aesthetic of accumulation of experience, reference, memory, and transfiguration."[49] The altar installations of the artist create a space of critical distance through which to simultaneously reexamine the personal, as well as the cultural gendered past of Mexican American women and their female forebears that is symbolized by the domestic altar. Here the ephemerality and changeability of both the home altar and the art installation genre figure history itself; they also figure cultural practices that are not timeless, but rather transformed through such histories. However, it is not an altogether nostalgic perspective, for the losses endured may also be emancipatory with respect to the patriarchal cultures from which Chicanas, in part, descend.

It is from this perspective that I would like to more closely examine Mesa-Bains's tablelike altars that appear in her gallery-sized trilogy of installations, *Venus Envy*. The artist designates each of the parts of the trilogy as a "chapter," in this way emphasizing the character of her artwork as a discursive practice, a "writing" constituted within the larger "library" of global history and effective within it. Thus, the altar in her work is also the desk, where what is offered is a response to the past that inevitably must be a rewriting of it (i.e., though history may repeat itself, histories are never identical). What is transfigured in a profane transubstantiation is an old social text, infused with the spirit of new times, as it is embodied in her work. In this sense, the significance of the vanity table in *Venus Envy I* (figure 1) and the laboratory desk of Sor Juana Inés de la Cruz in *Venus Envy II* (figure 2) partake of this semiotic oscillation between altar and desk, to which are now added vanity table and laboratory. Sor Juana's desk and laboratory, through a make-do-with-what's-at-hand politics of her own, symbolizes the rejection of what was intended for her as a woman in patriarchal, viceregal New Spain: the vanity table and the decorative practices of painting and costuming oneself in the image of male desire. But the vanity table in *Venus Envy I* also functions, in a more positive vein, as a theatrical space that allows for potentially expansive refashioning of identity. Like the religious altar, it is also a place for the care of the self and for the accumulation of personal objects imbued with meaning. In this sense, it is an altar where reverence for the self, and what is important to the self, is cultivated. The richness of possibilities opened up through the exploration and "excavation" of such cultural substitutions and slippages suggests why Mesa-Bains has worked with the altar form so extensively. With *Venus Envy III, Cihuatlampa, the Place of the Giant Women*, the artist has perhaps begun to close her thirty-year study of the altar form and social critique through it.[50] Here, interestingly, the altar does indeed appear to have disappeared. The only table is the archaeology table, figuring both the Foucauldian archaeological search for the genealogies that have shaped her, and the condition of women, in general. The concept of the altar and its twin processes of signifying the presence of the sacred and assuring such presence through sacrifice or homage are dispersed beyond the altar as a specific space symbolizing the divine s/Spirit.

In *Venus Envy III*, Earth, indeed the cosmos, is the vanity table/altar. Strewn upon the gallery space re-created as the heavenly "Cihuatlampa, the Place of the Giant Women," are high heels, perfume garden, vestments, and hand mirror. Women's or "the feminine's" (i.e., in both male and female) body—like the divine—is the seemingly missing but ubiquitous presence, suggesting that what women yearn for is not to be male because they supposedly recognize inherent male superiority (i.e., Freud's idea of "penis envy"). But rather they/we search for our own power, on our own terms, rejecting the devaluation of the female and embracing that which is oversized, excessive, with respect to present-day restrictive conceptions of gender. Further, the trilogy structure of her installation series rephrases the traditional, Christian tripartite altar screen that symbolizes the mystery of the tripartite identity of the God (the Father, the Son, and

1. Amalia Mesa-Bains, Vanity Table, detail, *Venus Envy I*, 1991. Courtesy: Amalia
Mesa-Bains.

2. Amalia Mesa-Bains, Sor Juana's Desk, detail, *Venus Envy II*, 1991.
Courtesy: Amalia Mesa-Bains.

the Holy Ghost). In this way, the *Venus Envy* trilogy calls attention to the three installations as "altars" and to her three "chapters" as a kind of altar-book, that is, as a holy book, a sacred script. If this is so, then her three-part *Venus Envy* has been an effort to reenchant the patriarchal world with an awareness of the sanctity, that is, the intrinsic value of women as reflected in the deity pantheons of ancient cultures, and in the genius of women like Sor Juana, and in the women of one's own family history.[51]

The Alter

At the altar, conditions that appear in mutual opposition are mediated. The absent, the invisible, the disembodied, and the unknowable are invoked and acknowledged. This is an ambiguous zone of coexistence that, we are reminded in this work, is abnormal and normal, sacred and profane. It is no wonder that Chicana artists interested in the intersections of the spiritual, the political, and art should draw, conceptually and formally, upon the altar. Through altars and related forms, Chicana artists bring to visibility that which is disembodied by virtue of its alterity with respect to dominant cultural norms. They call upon an ancient domestic art form to bring to light the perduring and alternative beliefs and practices of those who have historically and unofficially worshipped and communed at altars other than those of the official and the institutional. In the Americas of the last five centuries, those celebrants of other ways of being continue to be marked by gender, sexuality, ethnicity, culture, and other socially weighted "differences." Through altar-based art, Chicana artists succeed in reminding us of the Mayan, indeed perennial and cross-cultural concept, "you are my other self" (*In Laketch*).

Notes

Part of this essay was presented at the American Academy of Religion, 20 November 2001, based on a longer chapter from my book, *Chicana Art: The Politics of Spiritual and Aesthetic Altarities* (Durham, N.C.: Duke University Press, 2007). That chapter studies the altar-based art in installations, drawing, photography, video, writing, and performance art of Carmen Lomas Garza, Santa Contreras Barraza, Patricia Rodríguez, Barbara Carrasco, Patssi Valdez, Lourdes Portillo, Frances Salome España, Rita González, Christina Fernández, Kathy Vargas, Delilah Montoya, and Celia Herrera Rodríguez, in addition to the work of Mesa-Bains examined here. My thanks to Duke University Press for permission to reprint parts of this essay.

1. In daily speech, *spirituality* and *religion*, and their adjective forms, are often used interchangeably, and their dictionary definitions overlap in important ways. It is, however, the difference between them that determines my own choice of the first over the second in describing the loose, unorthodox, or self-fashioned forms of belief and practice that characterize the work I've studied, which is characterized by its "hybrid spiritualities" as opposed to its identification with religious institutions. Thus, I do not describe it as religious art, instead studying its concern with more general spirituality. Under *religion*, the *Oxford English Dictionary* emphasizes membership in religious orders and "action or conduct indicating a belief in, reverence for, and desire to please, a divine ruling power; the exercise or practice of rites or observances implying this"; "a religious duty or obligation"; and "a particular system of faith and worship." "Spirituality" is defined by the *OED* as "the quality or state of being spiritual; spiritual character" and "the body of spiritual or ecclesiastic persons; the spiritual estate of the realm; the clergy." It is the former, broad definition of spirituality that I use throughout this chapter, to refer to a range of beliefs culled from different established faiths, as well as new, self-fashioned forms of belief, worship, and social practice. As I discuss elsewhere, spiritual or religious beliefs are not transparent, timeless universal categories, in spite of the transcendent subject matter to which they

refer. Unlike the claims of revealed divine scriptures, the act of articulating our beliefs and formulating spiritual and religious practices is not necessarily socially or historically transcendent, and therefore reflects our social positioning and interests. The marginalized and demeaned place of Indigenous and African-diaspora beliefs and practices within Christian churches, for example, speak of the earthly interests at play in what gets to count as spiritual. See Ana María Díaz-Stevens and Anthony Stevens-Arroyo and essays in Lindsay (cited later in this note) for detailed discussion of the Eurocentrism of Christianity in the United States. It should be obvious therefore that while Marx's observation that religion is political is clearly at work in my study, his theory of religion as false ideology and "opium of the people" is not taken by me as universal truth, applicable to all spiritual belief and religious systems, across time (via Burger). It is therefore not my interest to study references to the spiritual in Chicana art as manifestations of socially and politically escapist flights whose "measurement" speaks directly to the condition of society. Marx's materialist critique of religion is itself a reflection of his own cultural and historical specificity, and belies a Eurocentric view of what the religious landscape of imperialist and capitalist hegemonic Europe had produced. *Oxford English Dictionary* ([1971] 1979): 410, 425; Díaz-Stevens and Stevens-Arroyo, *Recognizing the Latino Resurgence in U.S. Religion: The Emmaus Paradigm* (Boulder, Colo.: Westview Press, 1998); Arturo Lindsay, ed., *Santería Aesthetics in Contemporary Latin American Art* (Washington, D.C.: Smithsonian Institution Press, 1996); Peter Burger, *Theory of the Avant-Garde*, trans. Michael Shaw (Minneapolis: University of Minnesota Press, 1984; orig. pub. in German, 1974), 4–8.

2. For example, see the later work of Derrida. Jacques Derrida, "Faith and Knowledge: The Two Sources of 'Religion' at the Limits of Reason Alone," in *Religion*, ed. Jacques Derrida and Gianni Vattimo (Palo Alto, Calif.: Stanford University Press, 1998; orig. pub. in French, Editions du Seuil, 1996).

3. For a more extensive discussion of "hybrid spiritualities" and their decolonizing politics and aesthetics, see Laura E. Pérez, "Spirit Glyphs: Reimagining Art and Artist in the Work of Chicana *Tlamatinime*," *Modern Fiction Studies* 44, no. 1 (spring 1998): 36–76.

4. Amalia Mesa-Bains, "Curatorial Statement," in *Ceremony of Spirit: Nature and Memory in Contemporary Latino Art* (San Francisco: Mexican Museum, 1993), 9.

5. There are some strong parallels between this study and a chapter on "orthodox and nonorthodox religious culture" in U.S. Latina writing in McCracken. In describing the work of the Chicana writers Lucha Corpi and Demetria Martínez, for example, McCracken speaks of the "deploy[ment of] politically imbricated religious practices" and in describing the work of Denise Chávez, she says, "it recuperates the denied or repressed body of official religious culture." Another text, by Charlene Villaseñor Black and recent at the time of the original drafting of this chapter, acknowledges that "Chicana visual language, like Chicano Spanish, is multidialectical" but focuses on the uses, including subversions, of "the language of Catholicism in Chicana art." Ellen McCracken, "Remapping

Religious Space: Orthodox and Non-Orthodox Religious Culture," in *New Latina Narrative: The Feminine Space of Postmodern Ethnicity* (Tucson: University of Arizona Press, 1991), 95–149, esp. 105, 127; Charlene Villaseñor Black, "Sacred Cults, Subversive Icons: Chicanas and the Pictorial Language of Catholicism," in *Speaking Chicana: Voice, Power, and Identity*, ed. D. Leticia Galindo and María Dolores Gonzales (Tucson: University of Arizona Press, 1999), 134–74.

6. Gloria Anzaldúa acknowledges the African ancestors of some mexicanos; Ana Castillo, in discussing Hispanic sexist cultural patterns, traces these to the Moorish cultural legacy in the Spanish culture brought to the Americas. The same might be said of a Jewish cultural legacy. The hidden Jewish and Native American legacies of Chicanos are the subject of Kathleen Alcalá's novel *Spirits of the Ordinary*. Recent scholarship has unearthed the African and Asian mestizajes of Latin America, and U.S. Latina/os. In the United States, Chicana/os are further mixed with Puerto Ricans, Italian, Irish, English, Scandinavian, German, Lebanese, East Indians, and U.S. Native peoples, in short with, it seems, everybody. Gloria Anzaldúa, *La Frontera/Borderlands: The New Mestiza* (New York: Aunt Lute Books, 1987); Ana Castillo, *Massacre of the Dreamers: Essays on Xicanisma* (Albuquerque: University of New Mexico Press, 1994), 70–79; Kathleen Alcalá, *Spirits of the Ordinary: A Tale of Casas Grandes* (New York: Harvest, 1998).

7. Robert Henkes, *Latin American Women Artists of the United States: The Works of Thirty-Three Twentieth-Century Women* (Jefferson, N.C.: McFarland and Company, 1999), 233.

8. See Black, "Sacred Cults, Subversive Icons," for a study of the uses of Catholic visual language among some Chicana artists.

9. In performance art, Patssi Valdez, a member of the Los Angeles–based multimedia art group ASCO, performed as a punkish Black Virgin when the group took part in a procession through a Chicana/o East Los Angeles neighborhood on Christmas Eve 1972. Hernández's etching, *La Virgen de Guadalupe Defendiendo los Derechos de los Xicanos/The Virgin of Guadalupe Defending the Rights of the Xicanos*, dates to 1975. López's Guadalupe Series in various media, of which her better-known Guadalupe triptych forms part, is from 1978. Yreina D. Cervántez's watercolor *Homage to Frida Kahlo*, exhibited at the San Francisco Galería de la Raza's groundbreaking Day of the Dead exhibition in honor of Frida Kahlo, then little known in the United States, is from 1978. These pioneering reinterpretations of Virgin of Guadalupe iconography form a small fraction of the growing fascination with gender, spirituality, and the sacred and with cultural power that continues to this day in various media. My own collection of Virgin Mary/Virgin of Guadalupe iconography in visual and performance art includes more than 100 different renditions from the sixties to the present, by artists of different gender and sexual identifications.

10. On the first point, see Kay Turner, *Beautiful Necessity: The Art and Meaning of Women's Altars* (New York: Thames and Hudson, 1999), 8, 25; Robert Farris Thompson, *Face of the Gods: Art and Altars of African and the African Americas* (New York : Museum for African, 1993), 20. On the cultural hybridity

of altars, see William H. Beezley, "Home Altars: Private Reflections of Public Life," in *Home Altars of Mexico,* by Dana Salvo (Albuquerque: University of New Mexico Press, 1997), 92; Serge Gruzinski, *La guerra de las imágenes: De Cristóbal Colón a 'Blade Runner' (1492–2019)* (Mexico City: Fondo de Cultura Económica, [1994] 1995; orig. pub. in French, Paris, Librairie Artheme Fayard, 1990), 50, 185–86.

11. Gruzinski, *La guerra de las imágenes;* Beezley, "Home Altars," 1997; Turner, *Beautiful Necessity,* 20–21, 44.

12. Turner, *Beautiful Necessity;* Celeste Olalquiaga, *Megalopolis: Contemporary Cultural Sensibilities* (Minneapolis: University of Minnesota Press, 1992), 42.

13. Olalquiaga, *Megalopolis,* 49.

14. Mesa-Bains, "Curatorial Statement," 9.

15. Jennifer González' criticism of Olalquiaga is similar: "By overemphasizing the ironic use of material culture in contemporary art, Olalquiaga misses the point that many altar installations, in particular those of Mesa-Bains, do not so much *erase* the religious connotations of the iconography they employ, but rather *redefine* this iconography by producing a hybrid mix of signs." González, "Siting Histories: Material Culture and the Politics of Display in the Work of Fred Wilson, Pepón Osorio, and Amalia Mesa-Bains, 1985–1995" (PhD diss., History of Consciousness, University of California, Santa Cruz, September 1996), 346.

16. See Díaz-Stevens and Stevens-Arroyo, *Recognizing the Latino Resurgence in U.S. Religion.*

17. See Eric Davis, *Techgnosis: Myth, Magic, and Mysticism in the Age of Information* (New York: Harmony Books, 1998); Cynthia Eller, *The Myth of Matriarchal Prehistory: Why an Invented Past Won't Give Us a Future* (Boston: Beacon Press, 2000); Turner, *Beautiful Necessity.*

18. See Randy P. Conner, David Sparks, and Mariya Sparks, *Cassell's Encyclopedia of Queer Myth, Symbol, and Spirit* (London: Cassell, 1997); Christian De la Huerta, *Coming Out Spiritually: The Next Step* (New York: Jeremy P. Tarcher, 1999).

19. See Wade Clark Roof, *A Generation of Seekers: The Spiritual Journeys of the Baby Boom Generation* (San Francisco: HarperSanFrancisco, 1993; reprint. Harper SanFrancisco, 1998); Richard Cimino and Don Lattin, *Shopping for Faith: American Religion in the New Millennium* (San Francisco: Jossey-Bass, 1998).

20. Chicana/a art practices lend particular weight to David Harvey's Marxist reaffirmations regarding the relations between economic and cultural forms, including religious forms. David Harvey, *The Condition of Postmodernity: An Enquiry into the Origins of Social Change* (Cambridge, Mass.: Blackwell, [1989] 1990), 238, 292.

21. Richard Griswold del Castillo, Teresa McKenna, and Yvonne Yarbor-bejarano, eds., *Chicano Art: Resistance and Affirmation, 1965–1985* (Los Angeles: Wight Art Gallery, University of California Press, 1991) is the title of the exhibition catalog edited by Richard Griswold del Castillo, Teresa McKenna, and Yvonne Yarbro-Bejarano. Los Angeles: Wight Art Gallery, University of

California, Los Angeles, 1991. The exhibition was the largest of Chicana/o art until the present, and characterized the period of art it covered as one of "resistance and affirmation."

22. On baby boomer spirituality, see Clark Roof, *A Generation of Seekers*, and the well-documented work of the religion journalists Cimino and Lattin, *Shopping for Faith*, on contemporary religiosity in the United States. For other recent efforts by Euro-American artists and writers to bring a socially relevant, spiritually conscious art practice back into art world discourse, see Alex Grey, *The Mission of Art* (Boston: Shambhala, 1998); Suzi Gablik, *The Reenchantment of Art* (New York: Thames and Hudson, 1991); Deborah J. Haynes, *The Vocation of the Artist* (Cambridge: Cambridge University Press, 1997).

23. Gruzinski argues,

> Los imaginarios coloniales, como los de hoy, practican la descontextualización y el reaprovechamiento, la destructuración y la restructuración de los lenguajes. La mezcla de referencias, la confusión de los registros étnicos y culturales, la imbricación de lo vivido y de la ficción, la difusión de las drogas, la multiplicación de los soportes de la imagen también hacen de los imaginarios barrocos de la Nueva España una prefiguración de nuestros imaginarios neobarrocos o posmodernos, así como el cuerpo barroco en sus nexos físicos con la imagen religiosa anunciaba el cuerpo electrónico unido a sus máquinas, walkmans, videocaseteras, computadoras. . . . Ese mundo de la imagen y del espectáculo es, más que nunca, el de lo híbrido, del sincretismo y de la mezcla, de la confusión de las razas y de las lenguas, como ya lo era en la Nueva España.

> [Colonial imaginaries, like those of today, practice decontextualization and the recycling, destruction, and reconstruction of languages. The mixture of references, the confusion of ethnic and cultural registers, the imbrication of the lived and the fictitious, the diffusion of drugs, the multiplication of the image's supports also make of the baroque imaginaries of New Spain a prefiguration of our neobaroque or postmodern imaginaries, just as the baroque body in its physical links with the religious image announced the electronic body tied to its machines, walkmans, videomachines, computers. . . . That world of the image and spectacle is, more than ever, that of the hybrid, of syncretism and mixture, of the confusion of races and languages, as it already was in New Spain.]

Gruzinski, *La guerra de las imágenes*, 214–15.

24. See Eller's recent criticisms of the fallacies within goddess-centered writing and the scholarship it extrapolates from. Eller, *The Myth of Matriarchal Prehistory*.

25. By definition what is referred to as the folk Catholicism of Mexican and Mexican American communities is the mixture of surviving "pagan" beliefs and practices, but the term privileges the predominance of the Christian over the In-

digenous, and over other cultural strata, such as the secret Jewish culture of the Southwest. The recent flowering of research in U.S. Latina/o theology amply contests such designations as inaccurate and ethnocentric, arguing for a more complex understanding of the effects of Indigenous and African-diaspora derived belief systems, even to the extent of arguing that Eurocentric Christian discourse and practices have been selectively used as vehicles to preserve or appropriately "translate" non-Western systems of belief. See, for example, Díaz-Stevens and Stevens-Arroyo, *Recognizing the Latino Resurgence in U.S. Religion*; Ada María Isasi-Díaz, *Mujerista Theology: A Theology for the Twenty-first Century* (Maryknoll, N.Y.: Orbis Books, 1996).

26. Turner, *Beautiful Necessity*, 40.

27. The feminist scholar Turner points out, throughout patriarchal cultures worldwide, "the home altar . . . has for centuries encoded a visual language through which objects 'speak' to the distinctive concerns of women's 'hidden' culture." Turner's study of the post-1960s, widespread resurgence of the ancient tradition of domestic and artistic altar building in the United States revealed that the former (domestic altar building) is a largely female-based practice, largely rooted in Roman Catholic culture of various ethnicities, and that in Catholic homes, it is mother centered. Turner's rich study reflects on the various forms of power reversals that the practice of keeping domestic altars effect, such as placing the record of family history—and even more specifically, matrilineal history—in women's hands, "mak[ing] men dependent on women for divine intercession in insuring the prosperity and protection of the family," and perhaps most importantly, allowing for women's participation in spiritual expression, particularly given their unequal footing with men in the world's major, patriarchal world religions. Turner, *Beautiful Necessity*, 20–21, 44.

28. Díaz-Stevens and Stevens-Arroyo, *Recognizing the Latino Resurgence in U.S. Religion*.

29. Migene González-Wippler, "Santería: Its Dynamics and Multiple Roots," in *Enigmatic Powers: Syncretism with African and Indigenous Peoples' Religions among Latinos*, ed. Anthony Stevens-Arroyo and Andrés Pérez y Mena (New York: Bildner Center for Western Hemisphere Studies, 1995), 99–111; Isasi-Díaz, *Mujerista Theology*; Lindsay, *Santería Aesthetics in Contemporary Latin American Art*; Gerardo Mosquera, ed., *Beyond the Fantastic: Contemporary Art Criticism from Latin America* (Cambridge, Mass., and London: MIT Press, 1996).

30. Cimino and Lattin, *Shopping for Faith*.

31. Allison Krauss, cited in Grey, *The Mission of Art*, 44.

32. Conversation with the artist René Yáñez (the first, and long-term director of San Francisco's Galería de la Raza), 31 July 2000, telephone interview.

33. See Davalos for a discussion of the politics of exhibition displays, including those of Days of the Dead, at the Mexican Fine Arts Center Museum, in Chicago. Karen Mary Davalos, *Exhibiting Mestizaje: Mexican (American) Museums in the Diaspora* (Albuquerque: University of New Mexico Press, 2001); Davalos, "Exhibiting Mestizaje: The Poetics and Experience of the Mexican Fine Arts

Center Museum," in *Latinos in Museums: A Heritage Reclaimed*, ed. Antonio José Ríos-Bustamante and Christine Marin (Malabar, Fla.: Krieger Publishing Company, 1998).

34. Younger artists, for example, who explore the altar form in mixed-media installations include the sometime performance group The Mexican Spitfires (i.e., Victoria Delgadillo, Elizabeth Delgadillo, and Patricia Valencia) and Pat Gómez, from Los Angeles, and Pilar Agüero, in San Jose, California.

35. Turner, *Beautiful Necessity*, 73.

36. Tomás Ybarra-Frausto, "Rasquachismo: A Chicano Sensibility," in *Chicano Art: Resistance and Affirmation, 1985–1995*, ed. Richard Griswold del Castillo, Teresa McKenna, and Yvonne Yarbro-Bejarano (Los Angeles: Wight Art Gallery, University of California, 1991). This essay was originally published in *Chicano Aesthetics: Rasquachismo*, exhibition catalog, curated by Tomás Ybarra-Frausto, Shifra M. Goldman, and John L. Aguilar (Phoenix: Movimiento Artístico del Río Salado [MARS], 1989).

37. Ibid., 4, 6.

38. Ibid., 9.

39. Ibid., 9.

40. Ibid., 9.

41. Olalquiaga, *Megalopolis*, 52–54.

42. Amalia Mesa-Bains, "*Domesticana*: The Sensibility of Chicana Rasquache," in *Distant Relations/Cercanías Distantes/Clann I Gcéin: Chicano, Irish, Mexican Art and Critical Writing*, ed. Trisha Ziff (Santa Monica, Calif.: Smart Art Press, 1995), 156–63, esp. 157.

43. Jennifer González, "Autotopographies," in *Prosthetic Territories: Politics and Hypertechnologies*, ed. Gabriel Brahm Jr. and Mark Driscoll (Boulder, Colo.: Westview Press, 1995), 133–49.

44. Jennifer González, "Siting Histories," 385.

45. Ibid., 410.

46. Mesa-Bains, "*Domesticana*," 159–60.

47. Ybarra-Frausto, "Rasquachismo."

48. Mesa-Bains, "*Domesticana*," 157.

49. Ibid., 163.

50. Statement by the artist during a presentation of her work, spring 1998, at California State University, Monterey Bay, National Association of Chicana and Chicano Studies Northern Foco Conference.

51. Further discussion of Mesa-Bains's *Venus Envy* trilogy, from the perspective of the giant costumes and figures within it, can be found in Laura E. Pérez, "Writing on the Social Body: Dresses and Body Ornamentation in Contemporary Chicana Art," in *Decolonial Voices: Chicana and Chicano Cultural Studies in the 21st Century*, ed. Arturo J. Aldama and Naomi Quiñónez (Bloomington: Indiana University Press, 2002), 30–63.

15

Mexican Madonna

Selena and the Politics of Cultural Redemption

"To us, Selena has become Santa Selena," Barbara Renard González wrote in *Latina* magazine. "We revere Selena because she, like our *Virgen de Guadalupe*, was a postmodern mestiza who came to remind us who we are."[1] Indeed, González is not alone in her attempt to use religious imagery to reappropriate the twenty-three-year-old Tejana music star gunned down by her manager on 31 March 1995. Selena's tragic death shocked the nation and made her more popular in death than in life (figure 1).

The reaction of the masses to Selena's death carried religious overtones that have, for the most part, been overlooked by scholars of religion and pop culture.[2] This is because she does not fall neatly into the current paradigm of popular religiosity. After all, Selena was a Latin music diva, not a religious leader—right? What does she have to do with religion? Probably very little if we limit its study to traditional religiosity. However, if we expand the study of religion to include pop culture icons, then Latin divas such as Selena may provide scholars with rich insights into the texture of Mexican American religiosity.

This chapter theorizes and explores the relationship between religion and pop culture in the Mexican American community in the United States. Mexican Americans and other Latinos have reimagined, reconstructed, and transformed Selena's life and tragic death into a collective symbol of cultural and political resistance in order to help redeem their subcultural minority status in mainstream Anglo-American society. She has been symbolically resurrected from the dead and reappropriated by youth and elites as a collective symbol and agent of cultural redemption. Her resurrection as a pop culture icon on par in the Latino community

1. Selena altar in chapel at Mi Tierra Restaurant, San Antonio, Texas,
17 November 2004. Courtesy: Ann E. Robson.

with James Dean, Marilyn Monroe, Jim Morrison, Jimmy Hendrix, Elvis Presley, and Kurt Cobain is largely the result of the timing of her death; her reconstruction by the Latino intelligentsia, media, and masses; and her reconstruction as a collective agent and symbol of cultural redemption. She redeems Mexican American and Latino race, gender, class, transnational cultural hybridity, and the U.S.-Mexico borderlands. Her reconstruction reveals the important role of religious symbols, values, and attitudes in Mexican American and Latino pop culture. It also reveals the Mexican American penchant for transforming its seemingly secular cultural heroes into pop culture saints. This is because Mexican American pop culture is rooted in a grounded aesthetic that materializes the sacred and sacralizes the profane in everyday life.[3]

Theorizing Latino Religions and Popular Culture

The aesthetic desire to materialize the sacred and sacralize the profane in everyday life is deeply embedded in the Mexican and Latin American consciousness. It is evident in the artistic and sensory flavor of Latino popular Catholicism and folk healing. This manifests itself in home altars, shrines, healing, and pilgrimage sites, and in the bright colors, smells, bells, holy oil, incense, charms, statues, dramas, plays, festivals, prayer candles, potions, special powders, healing remedies, spirit possession, and ecstatic speech found in popular Catholicism and, to a lesser degree, Spiritualism and some forms of Mexican American Pentecostalism.[4] While many African American and Anglo-American religions share similar ritual beliefs and practices, it is precisely the Mexican and Latin American cultural, artistic, and aesthetic reimagination and rearticulation of these practices that distinguish them from these counterparts. Furthermore, it is the localized subcultural reproduction and manufacture of religious rituals, beliefs, traditions, and practices that make African American religion African American, and Mexican American religion Mexican American.

This chapter departs from previous literature on Mexican American and Latino popular religiosity, which has tended to focus on overtly religious symbols, texts, and practices—including Our Lady of Guadalupe, the home altar tradition, and religious festivals.[5] As important as that focus is in recovering, exploring, and explaining popular religiosity, it has not examined the religious cadence, rhythm, and symbols found in Latino pop culture. This chapter seeks to initiate this discussion and draw attention to this emergent field of study.

In contrast to the traditional study of Latino popular religiosity, the study of Latino religions and popular culture takes its cues from the emerging field of religious and cultural studies in its subjects, methods, theories, and goals. Scholars in this field are interested in studying the religious cadence, meanings, and symbols found throughout Latino pop culture icons, texts, and personalities. They are not interested in the theological correctness or orthodoxy of their subjects or texts, although these are very important to interpreting pop culture.[6] Rather, they are interested in explaining what these religious themes, motifs, and myths reveal about a particular religion and culture. The best place to explore and analyze Latino religions and popular culture is in the commodities produced by the culture industries and masses in Latino pop music, movies, theater, art, fashion, fiction, and magazines.

Before analyzing Selena's relationship to pop culture, we first need to define what we mean by culture. The four most common definitions of culture are (1) that which is well liked by many people, (2) inferior kinds of work, (3) work deliberately setting out to win favor with the people, and (4) work actually made by and for the people themselves.[7] Drawing on the work of Raymond Williams, I interpret popular culture as a particular *way of life* that is made by the people from the commodities produced by culture-generating industries and by the masses.[8]

Since all cultures are socially constructed by elites and the masses from the repertoire(s) provided by the culture industries, they are inherently ideological because they promote particular worldviews. This ideological representation of the world becomes political when it seeks to project its own ideology onto the broader public culture as normative at the expense of another. In this process, it often masks, conceals, or distorts alternative, competing worldviews. This is what Stuart Hall calls the "politics of signification," which is the attempt to win people over to one's own way of seeing the world.[9] The collective process of constructing and projecting one's own ideology onto the public space creates social glue that binds members of the group together in a collective myth. Roland Barthes notes that this myth is almost always (consciously or unconsciously) projected onto the public as universal and objective when it is in fact partial and political.[10] This cuts to the heart of why Mexican Americans and Latinos have reappropriated Selena. They have reimagined and reconstructed her to challenge mainstream cultural myths.

It is precisely this ideological struggle over who shapes the dominant myths of society that lead to social, political, and religious conflict. The attempt on the part of dominant culture(s) to suppress alternative and competing cultures leads to the creation of subcultures that often generate their own countermyths. This process is evident in the unconscious resurrection of Selena as a Latino countermyth to Anglo-America's Elvis and MTV's (Music Television's) Madonna. Although Cathy Schwichtenberg correctly notes that "subcultural identities" are often created in the "struggle over and against the dominant" society, more often than not subcultural identities are also the result of compromise, co-optation, and reappropriation.[11] In short, we need to be careful not to uncritically celebrate countermyths, pop culture, and the "other," because they are often the sites of both cultural resistance and co-optation by the dominant society and its culture industries. More important, the goal of studying religion and pop culture is not simply to superficially identify the acts of resistance, accommodation, and co-optation, but also to unravel what they reveal about religion and popular culture in the community under study.

This theory of cultural redemption is not limited to Latino pop culture icons such as Selena. Although beyond the scope of this paper, one could argue that Martin Luther King, César Chávez, Elvis Presley, James Dean, Madonna, and Kurt Cobain have all been reconstructed by their followers to offer a certain measure of cultural (or subcultural) redemption.[12] Rather than use the notion of redemption in an individual or strictly theological sense, I use it in a collective sense to mean the ability to make good and garner appreciation, tolerance, and acceptance for subcultures deemed as marginal, criminal, or irrelevant by mainstream society.

Selena is a culturally redemptive symbol and text that has been inscribed with meaning by the masses. Her power as a cultural symbol is based on the Latino community's ability to use her to signify and represent the values, attitudes, and traditions of her culture. Selena, like so many other pop culture icons, has been used by members of the Latino subculture to indirectly and perhaps unconsciously expose, challenge, and undermine that way of life that seems in conflict with their own. For this reason, pop culture icons are a threat because they often challenge and redefine what Pierre Bourdieu calls "national distinction" or cultural taste.[13] Subcultures use icons and myths to challenge, redefine, and create new myths, tastes, and notions of good and bad. The icons do this by creating their own poetry, music, drama, and satire. For this reason, pop culture icons are often agents of liberation and redemption for the subculture they represent.

However, we need to avoid the tendency to romanticize or uncritically celebrate pop culture icons solely as agents of resistance and empowerment.

What many people do not realize is that pop culture icons can also be used to keep subcultures subordinate to mainstream society. In short, music, art, drama, and television can create and promote passive rather than active agents of social and political change.

While religion has often been the best example of a cultural force that is used to pacify the masses, it can also be used as a vehicle for political and social empowerment, often when it is created outside the halls of power and the establishment. The most powerful culturally redemptive agents and symbols are those that can be leveraged to transcend cultural boundaries that dice up society. In order to do this, these symbols must have or promote some kind of universal values or sentiment. Religious symbols, terms, and lyrics are some of the most common vehicles for expressing values and attitudes that transcend the social borders and boundaries of their day.

Although many culturally redemptive symbols and agents are secular in nature, some of these agents in the Latino community have been laden with a quasi-religious aura. This is precisely because religion animates and pervades almost every aspect of Latino life and culture. The most powerful examples of this are the countless pictures and statues of Our Lady of Guadalupe and Aztec pyramids that grace the brightly painted walls of barrio liquor stores and *Lowrider Arte* magazine.[14] Unlike the Anglo-American world, the Latino community has never gone through a period of European-style secularization. Religion has been, and still is, one of the most powerful forces shaping the culture. In fact, recent studies have found that more than 99 percent of all U.S. Latinos self-identify either as Christian (93 percent) or as something else, as being of another religion, or as having no one particular religious preference (6.63 percent). Less than one half of one percent (.37 percent) of all U.S. Latinos self-identify as atheist or agnostic.[15]

Reconstructing Mexican American
Pop Culture Icons in the Borderlands

One of the major reasons Selena became more popular in death than in life is that she was in the midst of crossing over the deeply entrenched cultural border between Spanish- and English-speaking America when she was murdered. By the eve of her tragic death, she had been dubbed the "Queen of *Tejano* Music," won the *Tejano* music award for best album, appeared in Spanish-language *telenovelas* (soap operas) and talk shows, performed concerts throughout the Spanish-speaking community in the

U.S. Southwest and in Mexico, and appeared on over a dozen Spanish-language magazine covers for publications such as *Estylo*, *Corazón*, and *TV Novelas*. In short, she was a hot commodity in the Spanish-speaking world on both sides of the U.S.-Mexico border.

Selena's celebrity status in the Spanish-speaking community also set the stage for her phenomenal crossover success in the English-language market. Her success was spurred on by four time-sensitive factors. First, her crossover celebrity status received a boost when she won a Grammy Award for Best Mexican American Album in 1994. Although the award was given for best Mexican American album, it garnered her national media attention. In many respects, her Grammy catapulted her into the English-speaking marketplace. This helped her win a major recording contract with EMI records to produce her now famous English crossover album, *Dreaming of You*. The album was a phenomenal success. Released not long after her death, it has since sold more than 5 million copies. Her total album sales have reached 20 million. For this reason *Billboard Magazine* named her Best-Selling Latin Artist of the Decade (1990s).

A year before her death she began receiving front-page print and media coverage, not only in regional magazines—*Texas Monthly* and *Texas Hispanic*, for instance—also in *Latin Style* and that pop-icon-making magazine the *National Enquirer*. Right after she was killed, her face appeared on the cover of *TIME* and *People* magazines. *TIME* even issued a special commemorative issue in Selena's honor in the Southwest, which quickly sold out at newsstands. This was only the third such commemorative issue in the magazine's history.[16]

Her cameo shot in the Marlon Brando movie *Don Juan de Marco* came out just a month after her untimely demise. And then governor George W. Bush proclaimed Selena's birthday, 16 April 1995, El Día de Selena. Ten years later, in 2005, the Texas House of Representatives issued Resolution H.R. 954 commemorating her death. This gesture added cultural gravitas to her memory in the Latino community.[17] In short, the timing of her Grammy Award; media publicity; crossover appearances in movies, soap operas, and commercials; and recognition as a positive cultural symbol in the Mexican American community all contributed to her larger-than-life popularity.

However, Selena's popularity was not simply a matter of commercial marketing. Although not as timely as the events described above, three other major factors have also contributed to the Selena myth. First, her father, Abraham Quintanilla, and the rest of the family and EMI Records were quick to defend and help perpetuate her memory. They created a

Web site and museum to commemorate Selena and sell memorabilia. Second, the famous Mexican American film producer, Gregory Nava, worked with Mr. Quintanilla to create a sanitized, yet moving popular movie called *Selena*, starring the legendary Mexican American actor Edward James Olmos and a then unknown Puerto Rican actress named Jennifer López. In fact, this movie was López's "big break" and helped launched her career in the movie and music industries. At least three other documentaries have also been made about Selena's life and death. These films and documentaries, perhaps more than any other single factor, have helped immortalize Selena's memory in the Mexican American/Latino consciousness. In addition to the work of her father and film producers, many other would-be Latino and Anglo-American capitalists have taken advantage of her cultural and pop icon status to create innumerable Web sites and to sell "unofficial" Selena memorabilia. She has become the basis for a small but steady cottage industry in the Mexican American/Latino community. The commercial and cultural significance of Selena was best captured by a comment made by the famous Mexican American novelist Sandra Cisneros, who although somewhat critical of Selena was surprised to see her image on a key chain alongside others with images of Jesus Christ and Our Lady of Guadalupe. Cisneros remarked that this was the first time she had ever seen "a Chicana on a keychain that wasn't Our Lady of Guadalupe."[18] This has prompted Cisneros and others to reflect on the cultural significance of Selena for a younger generation of U.S. Latinos/as.

In addition to these factors, the mainstream music industry itself continues to sell Selena's music and generate revenues and by so doing helps perpetuate her memory. The commercial commodification of Selena is not particularly surprising, as similar cottage industries have sprung up for other pop culture icons who met tragic deaths as well, like James Dean, Marilyn Monroe, Jim Morrison, Elvis Presley, Jimmy Hendrix, Jerry Garcia, John Lennon, and Kurt Cobain. Several weeks after Selena's death, Christina Galvan, a Mexican American student at Jefferson Davis High School, Texas, said in a public tribute to Selena that "Now we know how our parents felt when Ritchie Valens died. Selena is Ritchie Valens. She's our John Lennon. She's our Elvis. We'll always miss Selena. There will never be another queen of *Tejano* music."[19] What makes Selena's story different is that she was a young Mexican American *woman* who made it to the top of stardom by singing and affirming both mainstream Anglo and Tejano music. It is precisely her cultural hybridity and real and symbolic location *in* the U.S.-Mexico borderlands (with fans on both sides) which makes her story intriguing.

Yet, timing and commerciality do not alone explain Selena's newfound pop culture celebrity status. Although easy to overlook, it has been precisely Selena's fans and critics—both in the intelligentsia and in working-class and middle-class communities—that have transformed Selena into a national Latino pop culture symbol par excellence. Selena's resurrection from the dead as a powerful symbol of *latinidad* (or Latino/a identity) is due to the fact that she offered her followers cultural redemption. In the process of resurrecting, reconstructing, and reimagining Selena as an agent and symbol of cultural redemption, her followers and detractors have consciously and subconsciously invested her with pop culture gravitas and almost saintlike qualities. This involvement illustrates the Latino community's penchant for engaging in a kind of popular beatification of some of its cultural icons cut down at the height of their careers.

Materializing the Sacred: Beatification, Sacred Centers, and Pilgrimage

Latino agents of cultural redemption are not only often laden with a religious aura; many are granted almost saintlike status. More than one popular figure in Mexican history has been unofficially beatified by the masses. El Niño Fidencio, María Teresa Urrea, Don Pedrito Jaramillo, Juan Soldado, Jesús Malverde, and now even César Chávez have all been raised to the status of folk saint among the millions of Latinos living in the U.S.-Mexico borderlands. In 1995, Selena began a similar journey. This process is not only evident in the shrines, prayers, and popular articles offered up in her memory, but also in the numerous comparisons made between her and the patron saint of Mexico, Our Lady of Guadalupe.[20]

This grounded ascetic desire to materialize the sacred in everyday life is perhaps evident in Selena's popular beatification. Aside from the obvious commercialization evident in Selena dolls, key chains, albums, and clothing, and her use in other brand names, she also has fans whose devotion goes beyond ordinary youthful admiration. Journalists, scholars, and fans alike are quick to point out that she was born on Easter Sunday and was shot in the back in Corpus Christi (Latin, "Body of Christ") by a Judas-like friend on César Chávez's birthday. Her death follows the script of the Christ figure—humble birth, enormous popularity, betrayal, violent death, and immortality.[21] Still others have noted how Mexican Americans

2. Home table altar to Selena in Mi Tierra Restaurant, San Antonio, Texas, November 2005. Courtesy: Arturo Chávez.

and Latinos have created home altars (figure 2) to Selena, offered up food to her image at grave sites during the Día de los Muertos (Day of the Dead) celebration, write poetry to her, and even offer up quasi-prayers to the Tejana.[22] Her image and memory, like those of a saint or goddess, are kept alive not only by commercial vendors seeking a quick buck, but also by devoted fans who function like priestesses and priests directing Selena's parishioners (or followers) through their self-created and self-funded virtual reality Web sites and commercial texts that often function almost as online churches and sacred paraphernalia—albums, posters, photos, lyrics, books, biographies, and movies. Her home in the Molina barrio and enormous memorial along the beach boardwalk in Corpus Christi function like a shrine and pilgrimage center for her fans.[23] Today there are maps that guide pilgrims and tourists alike to the various places where Selena lived, worked, was shot, died, and is buried. The steady stream of attention to Selena prompted one angry Corpus Christi resident to editorialize in a local newspaper: "Our city is named the 'Body of Christ' and Jesus Christ is not getting as much recognition as Selena. This is not Selenaville. Back off!"[24] Talk of "Selenaville" conjures up images of Elvis's "Graceland," although the comparisons are incomplete.

Selena's devotees have granted her almost salvific-like power. However, this power is not literal power or a saving grace but rather figurative and symbolic. She stands as a symbol that "redeems" Mexican Americans and other Latinos by challenging cultural stereotypes projected onto their culture by mainstream Anglo-American society. Reflecting on the cultural significance of Selena for some Latina women, Renard González wrote, "She is gone, but we still listen to her songs and construct altars in her name. We want to be saved, so we continue to elevate her."[25]

The mixing, blending, and fusing of the sacred and profane, saint and sinner is evident in the way that Selena's life, work, and death have been reconstructed by her followers. This reconstruction of Selena as cultural symbol is often laden with language, symbols, events, and an aura that all have quasi-religious properties. For this reason, people should not be surprised that more than one person has transformed Selena the Jehovah's Witness into "Santa Selena," a new symbolic mestiza Guadalupe for the modern Latina.[26] One astute observer of Mexican American culture wrote, "We are in the process of mythifying Selena, getting away from the facts about her life and refining her image to the truth that people believed about her. She has become part of the secular pantheon of saints."[27] This beatific vision of Selena is often linked in some way or another to Our Lady of Guadalupe. In fact, Silvia Pellarolo observes: "it is easy for her Mexican American fans to fuse her memory with the national religious icon par excellence, *la Virgen de Guadalupe*. Whose *morena* skin reflects the carnality of her worshippers."[28] This popular grounded aesthetic beatification process, although more symbolic than real, prompted the sometimes scathing social critic Ilan Stavans's quip, "Many people north and south of the Rio Grande have been engaging in active prayer to *Virgen* Selena, their own Madonna, so that heaven might send some miracles to *la frontera*; more *dolares* . . . or a less condescending attitude towards its idols while they are still alive."[29]

This mythifying and pop culture beatification process was not lost on her relatively devout Jehovah's Witness father, Abraham. It prompted him to state publicly: "Selena would not want that because she believed *worship* should go only to the Creator. Just remember her as a good person who loved life. I don't think Selena would be pleased to be part of any form of *idolatry*" (emphasis added).[30] Jehovah's Witnesses, like other non-Catholic Christian traditions, strictly prohibit the veneration and worship of icons, saints, and human personalities. The fact that Selena and her entire family were Jehovah's Witnesses is ironic, given the strong animus between Mexican American Catholics, Protestants, and Jehovah's

Witnesses, which have on more than one occasion engaged in theological mudslinging and name-calling. In fact, one former member of the band and a Baptist named Pyeatt Dearman remembers engaging in "intense religious discussions" with Selena's father about theology.[31] This fact perhaps explains why Gregory Nava made no reference to Selena's Jehovah's Witness religion in his movie, something uncharacteristic given the rich religious themes and symbols in his previous films *El Norte* and *Mi Familia*.

Despite these differences, many Catholic churches held memorials or other events in her honor. On Selena's birthday not long after her death, some 3,000 people gathered at Johnny Canales's Johnnyland Park for an Easter Mass in memory of Selena. Monsignor Michael Heras of Our Lady of Perpetual Health Catholic Church in Corpus Christi somewhat ironically said,

> Is it coincidence that we celebrate Selena's birthday on the same day we celebrate the victory of Jesus over death? I don't think so. Death was defied forever. That's what this day is about. Forever! The last words of Christ were, "Father, forgive them, for they know not what they do." That is our quote, for it is the only way to make meaning out of senselessness. The most powerful moment came when a group of children came on stage and set free 24 doves, one for each year of Selena's life, to celebrate her "return to the angels."[32]

While some might argue that Selena's connection to the Jehovah's Witness faith appears to have been somewhat ornamental in the years preceding Selena's death, we should keep in mind that she refused to sing many lyrics contrary to her faith. Still, spirituality fell by the wayside during the height of her career, something her father later regretted. He said: "I think, 'What if I hadn't done that? What if we hadn't left the spiritual things aside?' She would have been a dedicated servant of God." He went on to say, "We take life for granted, you know. In our daily hustle to make a living, we forget our spiritual needs. I have no doubt that we'll see Selena again, when she comes with the resurrection." Selena's death led her family to recommit their lives and work to their Jehovah's Witness faith.[33] This is evidenced not only by her father's comments, but also by the fact that her funeral was performed by a Jehovah's Witness elder. Furthermore, after her death her brother, Abraham Jr., when asked about revenge against Yolanda Saldívar, the person who shot Selena, said, "The Bible says that revenge belongs to Jehovah. It is in God's hands now."[34] The Jehovah's Witness translation (The New World Translation) of a favorite scripture verse from Isaiah 25:8 is quoted in English and Spanish on her tombstone. Given Selena's pop culture immortality, it prophetically reads: "He will actually swallow up death forever, and the Sovereign Lord Jehovah will certainly wipe the tears from all faces."

Selena's Jehovah's Witness faith is not as much of an anomaly as one might think in the Mexican American community. Recent studies indicate that the Jehovah's Witnesses are the largest non-Catholic Christian tradition in the United States, with more than 800,000 Latino Jehovah's Witnesses attending more than 2,200 Spanish-language congregations.[35]

"A Star from the HOOD": Redeeming Race

Selena's popular beatification among the masses has contributed to her popularity in the Latino community because it has invested her with a certain moral authority and purity that validate her persona. For this reason, she has been reappropriated as an agent of cultural redemption and an unconscious counternarrative to Anglo-America's blonde-haired, blue-eyed Aryan Madonna.[36] Her followers have reconstructed Selena as a person who redeems her race from obscurity in Anglo-America. Unlike many other Latinos who make it big and then leave the barrio, Selena never left her community or people.

Selena's collective representation and culturally redemptive power are evident in comments by writers, scholars, and youth. Catherine Revilla-Vásquez wrote, "For Mexican Americans, Selena's success became their success. She inspired confidence and ethnic pride. The stage lights that shone on her also reached across to include Mexican Americans by highlighting their language, music, and culture. Her greatest gift was that her talent, beauty, and success empowered all Hispanics."[37] One Latina editorialized in the *Minneapolis Star Tribune*, "She inspired me to return to my roots. . . . I have never been prouder to be Mexican American."[38] Maggie Mendoza captures the attitude of many Mexican American youth when she said: "I'm 15 years old and I really liked Selena's jams. I am from Molina and she was the star from the HOOD. She's full of MEXICAN PRIDE. She was like a flower from Molina's *barrio*. . . . She didn't deserve to get shot. *¡Que Viva Selena!*"[39]

This connection between Selena and barrio youth culture is evident not only in this comment, but also in the fact that her story and image have appeared (and still appear) in numerous editions of the two most popular Latino youth culture magazines on the market today—*Lowrider* and *Latina*—which gave her a full-page description surrounded by the rebozo of Our Lady of Guadalupe. Selena's image is also popping up on an increasing number of barrio wall murals and on the car hoods and doors of lowrider cars in Mexican American barrios and in *Lowrider Arte* magazine and T-shirts. In this respect, Selena's memory has entered the marrow of Mexican American culture and society. She has entered into pop culture immortality like Hernán Cortés, Montezuma, Our Lady of Guadalupe, Miguel Hidalgo, Emilio Zapata, Pancho Villa, César Chávez, Jerry Garcia, and Carlos Santana.

"La Virgen and La Malinche": Reconstructing Latina Femininity

As Selena is one of the few Latina role models available, especially for young U.S.-born Mexican American women, many unconsciously tied their success to hers. In this respect, she represented the collective aspirations of millions of Latino youth and parents who were looking for role models and who struggled with the same issues they faced. Selena's struggle with maintaining her weight, with Spanish fluency, with sexuality and gender roles, and with biculturalism are issues that many Mexican American and Latino youth (male and female) struggle with but are often too embarrassed to talk about with their parents or *familia*. Selena gave these issues a flesh-and-blood voice and a face.

Selena has been reconstructed by the Latino community as a counternarrative on par with other great female Anglo-American stars such as Marilyn Monroe and Madonna.[40] Latinas are quick to point out that Selena's beauty was not tied to dying her hair blond as it was for so many actresses on Spanish-language telenovelas. Although not shy about taking clothing pointers from Madonna's silver-studded bustier, she also let her coal-black hair whisper in the wind and painted her full lips with red-hot lipstick. Picking up on this, Renard González wrote in *Latina* magazine, "She showed us just how beautiful we could be, and she did so without dying her hair Fanta orange or wearing those oppressive blue contacts that make so many of us look like fallen angels. She was a gorgeous *chola morena* who never forgot her *pueblo*."[41]

Selena's followers not only admired her for being a beautiful woman but also because she was a symbol of financial and professional success and independence. Challenging the media image of Mexican American women as maids, dishwashers, and nannies, Selena proved that Latinas could become rich and famous—and on their own terms. She was a business entrepreneur who had just opened up her own clothing store chain, *Selena Etc, Inc., Boutique & Salon*. She worked on her own clothing line, had her own toy doll, and did commercials for Coca-Cola and Syntec. She proved beyond a shadow of a doubt to some women that they could run their own businesses and be their own person. She was also a powerful symbol that women could break through the walls of machismo that seemed to hem them in on so many sides.

Selena was the first woman to break through the glass ceiling of Tejano music, a field dominated almost exclusively by men. Not only did she break the glass ceiling; she became one of its most celebrated artists. This was not only true for Tejano music in the United States, but also in Mexico, where it had a very small following before Selena arrived on the scene. Within just a few short years, Tejano music (called *norteña* in Mexico) went from obscurity to the Mexico City hit parade on radio stations throughout the region. Since Selena's death, norteña music has sold more than one million CDs throughout Mexico. Many see Selena largely responsible for pioneering this trend.[42]

Selena has become a kind of Latina heroine and symbol of empowerment both for working-class teenagers and mothers, and for a few Chicana/o intellectuals. This sentiment has not waned over the years. Selena's influence was not only felt among Latino youth, but also their parents. One Latina mother wrote, "We wanted to have somebody to teach our kids that you can accomplish anything if you try. You want to have someone in your life like that. Selena was that person."[43] Still other Chicana/o intellectuals are dismissive of Selena and what she represents because she was deeply influenced by her father's reported headstrong management style, reportedly became overly commercialized, and allowed herself to fall into the trap of becoming a sex symbol that fed male fantasies and thus indirectly contributed to sexism and the oppression of women.[44] Right or wrong, much of this criticism is driven by the fact that Selena's success was largely achieved without adopting an overtly feminist persona.

However, one could just as easily argue that Selena exercised what amounted to feminist agency by breaking the glass ceiling of Tejano music, starting her own business, and deciding to dress in a sexy manner on stage, despite the conservative Latin American values regarding dress, comportment, and public displays of feminine sexuality. Selena's appeal is largely the result of the fact that her life resonated with the aspirations of ordinary women who want to be respected, accomplished, and sexy. Thus notwithstanding her sexy stage performance, at home she lived a very traditional life as a seemingly faithful wife and obedient daughter.[45] It is precisely this paradox that helps to explain her success and popularity. Renard González captures this paradox in her description of Selena:

> She really was *La Virgen de Guadalupe* and *La Malinche* . . . all wrapped up in one silken *rebozo* [shawl]. She was the Madonna-whore of every Latino male's fantasy. As *La Virgen*, she appeared full of light and grace. . . . As *La Malinche*, she embodied the modern woman, with *pasiones de la carne*, or passions of the flesh.[46]

It was precisely Selena's freedom to be both saint and sinner, sexy stage performer and virtuous wife and devoted daughter that helps explain her success. Despite these dualities (and perhaps because of them), what makes her story intriguing is that her fans inscribed her with almost saint-like qualities of purity. One newspaper reporter commented, "Over and over again, people speak of this immaculate purity that Selena possessed. She was untainted in their eyes, a true Madonna. They contemplate the fact that she was born on Easter and assign holy meaning to the coincidence."[47] Another Mexican American wrote: "we all loved her . . . not just because she was Spanish. She was something pure."[48] One Mexican American girl who was struggling with sexual peer pressure said in a note posted at a Selena memorial, "Please Selena, let me remain a virgin . . . just like you."[49] In poetic verse, one unemployed Mexican American schoolteacher ascribed angelic qualities to Selena.

> Do not cry for me, do not suffer for me
> Remember I love you with all my heart
> I know if you listen and do as I ask
> I will be content because
> I have completed my mission here on my beautiful earth
> I can continue to sing to Our Father in Heaven
> Listen, Heaven does not thunder
> The Sun begins to hide
> Our father has given us a new light
> Look up to Heaven
> The light comes from a divine star
> That lights up all of Heaven
> It is the Angel Selena
> The most beautiful star of the world
> And now of Heaven.
> Goodbye, my lovely Star.[50]

"Ascended to Stardom": Redeeming the Lower Classes

Selena has been reconstructed by the masses to not only redeem Latino race and gender, but the status of working-class Latinos as well. In a recent interview in *Latina* magazine, Ramiro Burr, author of *The Billboard Guide to Tejano and Regional Mexican Music*, stated, "We've never heard a hero like her: A young Latina from a humble background who struggled to get to the top."[51] Despite the fact that *Hispanic Business* magazine claimed that Selena was worth more than $5 million in 1994, she still chose to live in a $44,000 home in the molina barrio in Corpus Christi, Texas.[52] Her Grammy, commercials, short scene in a Marlon Brando film, *Don Juan DeMarco* (1995), and English crossover album, *Dreaming of You*, all demonstrated that Latinos could bridge the class chasm that separated Anglo-America and the Latino community. In a tribute to Selena in *Latina* magazine, Burr wrote, "She is a role model . . . for young *Latinos*. She is frozen atthe age of 23—young, attractive, at the peak of her success. . . . She represents the promise of youth, ambition, honesty, and conviction."[53] More than one Latino unconsciously hoped that Selena could "redeem all of us from second-class citizenship, if she only crossed over enough." Selena has been reconstructed by her fans as a person who had almost Mother Teresa and Virgin Mary–like qualities of self-sacrifice and mercy toward the poor. One elderly Mexican American woman said, "Selena had died because heaven was desperate for another Cherub. . . . [She was a] celestial beauty . . . whose time on earth was spent helping the poor and unattended."[54]

"Redeeming the Borderlands": Redeeming Transnational Cultural Hybridity and *Mestizaje*

Selena's fame and fortune also legitimized and redeemed the Latino community's reality of transnational cultural hybridity and *mestizaje*. Selena's life and music redeemed the U.S.-Mexico borderlands as a creative and even beautiful hybrid cultural space and place. The images of poverty, wetbacks, and drug cartels shooting at DEA (Drug Enforcement Administration) agents were collectively symbolically redeemed if only for a moment by what seemed like a beautiful young flower singing a hybrid form of music that married two cultures—Mexican and American. Selena's reconstruction as an agent and symbol that redeemed cultural hybridity was not lost on her fans and social commentators. A Los Angeles radio host, Amalia González, claimed that Selena sojourned on earth to "unite all creeds and races."[55] Similarly, Stavans wrote, "She ascended to stardom robed in the music of the people—*conjunto, ranchera,* polka, and *cumbia*—the synthesis of everything that others, our conquerors, had scorned." He went on to state, "As long as *la frontera* remains a hybrid territory, hidden from the sight of Anglo America and ignored by the Mexican government, people north and south of the Rio Grande will continue to pray to their new Madonna."[56] Reflecting on Selena's legacy, one disk jockey from Texas said, "Thanks to her *tejanos* are being heard. . . . She put us in the news—and on the front page of *The New York Times*."[57] Selena's success was more than just a glorified plug for Tejano music; on a collective level, she represented thousands of other Latino musicians and artists whose lives, music, and futures still languished in the shadows of the borderlands. Even more important, Selena's Grammy Award and crossover status signaled to her compatriots that Latino musicians could break out of the barrio and into the mainstream. Many soon followed, included Jennifer Lopez, Ricky Martin, and Shakira.

Indeed, Selena's life and music acted as a kind of transnational bridge that connected two seemingly disparate worlds. This transnational bridging is evident in Richard Corliss's observation that Selena "bridged the considerable social chasm between Mexicans who settled in the Southwest and those who stayed at home."[58] Yet Selena did more than just serve as a bridge; her life and work made the *bridge itself* a place to live, work, be, and die. She lived and worked in the U.S.-Mexico borderlands and was one of its most celebrated cultural products. She redeemed the hybrid culture on both sides of the U.S.-Mexico border. Reflecting on Selena's impact in Mexico, the famed Mexican social satirist Guadalupe Loaeza wrote, "All we used to know or care about the border was its problems: drug trafficking, wetbacks and the like. Since Selena's death, it has a new face for us—a bit of fantasy."[59] Writing for *TIME* magazine in Mexico City, Jim Padgett wrote, "Selena's 1995 murder dramatically changed the Mexican music scene. Her global martyrdom gave the capital's snobs an appetite for *norteña*."[60] Selena's life and death became a transnational bridge. What's more, she served as a site and symbol of cultural redemption and empowerment that reached not only into America, but also into the political, cultural, and symbolic heart and soul of Mexico.

Conclusion

Whether or not "Santa Selena" will continue to be reappropriated and reimagined by Latinos in the twenty-first century remains uncertain. However, if the recent coverage of Selena in *Latina* and *Lowrider* magazines is any indication of the future of her cultlike status, then she may be here to stay. In fact, like other pop culture saints, there is good reason to believe that she will continue to function as a source and symbol of resistance, empowerment, and cultural redemption for many years to come.

Notes

1. Barbara Renard González, "¿Santa Selena?" *Latina*, April–May 1997, 83.

2. The notable exceptions to this are Silvia Pellarolo's psychoanalytical interpretation of Selena, "Reviv/s/ing Selena," *Latin American Issues*, no. 14 (1998): 51–76; Karen Anijar, "Selena-Prophet, Profit, Princess," in *God in the Details: American Religion in Popular Culture*, ed. Eric Michael Mazur and Kate McCarthy (New York: Routledge, 2001), 83–101. For an earlier and shorter version of this article, see Gastón Espinosa, "Selena and the Politics of Cultural Redemption," in *U.S. Latino Literatures and Cultures: Transnational Perspectives*, ed. Francisco A. Lomelí and Karin Ikas (Heidelberg: Universitatsverlag C. Winter, 2000), 53–60.

3. For a discussion of material Christianity, see Colleen McDannell, *Material Christianity: Religion and Popular Culture in America* (New Haven, Conn.: Yale University Press, 1995). Also see David Morgan, *Visual Piety: A History and Theory of Popular Religious Images* (Berkeley: University of California Press, 1998).

4. For a discussion of home altars, shrines, pilgrimage sites, and healing in the Mexican American and Latino community, see Kay Turner, "Mexican American Home Altars: Toward Their Interpretation," *Aztlán: A Journal of Chicano Studies* 13, nos. 1–2 (1982): 309–26; Turner, *Beautiful Necessity: The Art and Meaning of Women's Altars* (New York: Thames and Hudson, 1999); Michael Riley, "Mexican American Shrines in Southern Arizona," *Journal of the Southwest* (summer 1992): 206–31; Sam Howarth and Enrique R. Lamadrid, *Pilgrimage to Chimayó: Contemporary of a Living Tradition* (Santa Fe: Museum of New Mexico Press, 1999); William and Claudia Madsen, *A Guide to Mexican Witchcraft* (Mexico City: Minutia Mexicana, 1972); Ari Kiev, *Curanderismo: Mexican-American Folk Psychiatry* (New York: Free Press, 1968); June Macklin, "*Curanderismo* and *Espiritismo*: Complementary Approaches to Traditional Health Services," in *The Chicano Experience*, ed. Stanley A. West and June Macklin (Boulder, Colo.: Westview Press, 1979), 207–26.

5. The best study on home altars is Turner, *Beautiful Necessity*. One of the best books on Latino popular religiosity is Anthony M. Stevens-Arroyo and Ana María Díaz-Stevens, ed., *An Enduring Flame: Studies on Latino Popular Religiosity* (New York: Bildner Center for Western Hemisphere Studies, 1994).

6. Commenting on the Aztec influence on the construction of Our Lady of Guadalupe, one scholar wrote, "Indeed, over time popular religiosity can bestow orthodoxy upon traditions with non-Christian roots" and even make them

"theologically correct." Stevens-Arroyo and Díaz-Stevens, *An Enduring Flame*, 11, 25, 72, 76.

7. John Storey, *An Introduction to Cultural Theory and Popular Culture*, 2nd ed. (Athens: University of Georgia Press, 1998), 2, 7–13.

8. Storey, *An Introduction to Cultural Theory*, 2.

9. Stuart Hall, cited in ibid., 5.

10. Roland Barthes, cited in ibid., 6.

11. Cathy Schwichtenberg, *The Madonna Connection: Representational Politics, Subcultural Identities, and Cultural Theory* (San Francisco: Westview Press, 1993), 3.

12. Ilan Stavans writes, "Elvis, John Lennon, Kurt Cobain, and Jerry Garcia . . . roll over: there's a new kid in the pop star firmament, one who gives voice to the silenced and oppressed." Ilan Stavans, *The Riddle of Cantinflas: Essays on Hispanic Popular Culture* (Albuquerque: University of New Mexico Press, 1998), 5.

13. For more on Bourdieu, see Storey, *An Introduction to Cultural Theory and Popular Culture*, 2, 5–13.

14. The special edition of *Lowrider Arte* magazine is full of images laden with religious symbols and significance. *Lowrider Arte*, February/March 2000.

15. For a discussion of Latino religious affiliation, see Gastón Espinosa, Virgilio Elizondo, and Jesse Miranda, *Hispanic Churches in American Public Life: Summary of Findings* (Notre Dame, Ind.: Institute for Latino Studies, University of Notre Dame, 2003), 14. Also see Gastón Espinosa's "Changements démographiques et religieux chez les hispaniques des Etats-Unis," *Social Compass: International Review of Sociology of Religion* 51 (2004): 303–20.

16. Rick Mitchell, "Selena: In Life, She Was the Queen of *Tejano* Music. In Death, the 23-year-Old Singer Is Becoming a Legend," *Houston Chronicle*, 21 May 1995, 6.

17. One of the most accurate and reliable of the more than one dozen biographies on Selena is Joe Nick Patoski, *Selena: Como la flor* (New York: Boulevard Books, 1997). I take most of the historical and biographical information in this essay about Selena from this biography.

18. As cited in Anijar, "Selena-Prophet, Profit, Princess," 85, who in turns cites the original source as Elaine Liner, "Independent Film on Selena's Impact Airs on PBS," *Corpus Christi Caller-Times*, 13 July 1999. The author has in his possession a photograph of Selena on a key chain next to other key chains with images of Our Lady of Guadalupe and Jesus.

19. Mitchell, "Selena," 6.

20. For more on this see, Gastón Espinosa, "Mexican Madonna: Selena, Religion, and Popular Culture," paper presented at the American Academy of Religion, November 1999, Boston. Also see Barbara Renard González, "¿Santa Selena?"; Stavans, *The Riddle of Cantinflas*; Pellarolo "Reviv/s/ing Selena."

21. Pellarolo, "Reviv/s/ing Selena," 51–76.

22. Jo Ann Zuniga, "Selena Remembered in Day of Dead Altars," *Houston Chronicle*, 20 October 1995, A39; Carlos Miller, "Valley Family Takes Yearly Tradition Seriously," *Arizona Republic*, n.d., available at http://www.azcentral.

com/ent/dead/history/history2.html; Dave Shultz, "Los Días de Los Muertos," 29 November 1998, available at http://www.travelady.com/articles/article-diamuertos.html.

23. Mitchell, "Selena," 6.

24. Patoski, *Selena*, 210–11, 258.

25. Barbara Renard González, "¿Santa Selena?" 83.

26. Ibid., 83; Silvia Pellarolo, "Reviv/s/ing Selena," 51–76; Stavans, *The Riddle of Cantinflas*, 5.

27. As cited in Anijar, "Selena-Prophet, Profit, Princess," 90. Catherine Revilla-Vásquez, "Thank You Selena," *Hispanic* 8, no. 4 (May): 96.

28. Pellarolo, "Reviv/s/ing Selena," 57.

29. Stavans, "Dreaming of You," *New Republic*, 20 November 1995, 24–25.

30. Patoski, *Selena*, 217.

31. Mitchell, "Selena," 6.

32. Ibid.

33. Ibid.

34. Ibid.

35. Espinosa, "Changements démographiques et religieux chez les hispaniques des Etats-Unis."

36. Stavans, *The Riddle of the Cantinflas*, 3–5.

37. As cited in Anijar, "Selena-Prophet, Profit, Princess," 90. Catherine Revilla-Vásquez, "Thank You Selena," 96.

38. As cited in Anijar, "Selena-Prophet, Profit, Princess," 94. Ramiro Burr, "Selena's Impact Still Felt," *Minneapolis Star Tribune*, 31 March 1996, 9F.

39. "¡Que Viva Selena!" means "Long Live Selena!" Anne Hull, "Selena: The Life and Death of an Icon for the New Texas," *St. Petersburg Times*, 20 October 1995, A1, 6.

40. Stavans, *The Riddle of Cantinflas*, 5. Also see Pellarolo, "Reviv/s/ing Selena," 58.

41. Barbara Renard González, "¿Santa Selena?" 83.

42. Jim Padgett, "Border Beat," *TIME*, 24 March 1997; Richard Corliss, "The Legend of Selena," *TIME*, 24 March 1997.

43. Hull, "Selena," A6.

44. Stavans, *The Riddle of Cantinflas*, 5.

45. See Patoski, *Selena*.

46. Renard González, "¿Santa Selena?" 83.

47. Hull, "Selena," A6.

48. Ibid., A1, 6.

49. Stavans, *Riddle of Cantinflas*, 3.

50. Ibid., 3.

51. As cited in Nancy De Los Santos, "Selena Vive," *Latina* (March 2000): 26.

52. Stavans, *The Riddle of Cantinflas*, 6.

53. As cited in De Los Santos, "Selena *Vive*," 223–24, 26–27.

54. Hull, "Selena," A6.

55. As cited in Stavans, *The Riddle of Cantinflas*, 5.

56. Ibid., 9.
57. Stavans, "Dreaming of You," 25.
58. Corliss, "The Legend of Selena."
59. As cited in ibid.
60. Padgett, "Border Beat."

Conclusion

Reflections on Mexican American Religions and Culture

This conclusion explores a number of important themes and insights in Mexican American religion and culture and then reflects on the problems facing the field and areas for future research. The first and most obvious insight is that religion is in the marrow of Mexican American culture and identity. Any scholar, reporter, public policy analyst, trend watcher, or politician seeking to understand Mexican American culture and society must also pay close attention to the critical role that religion plays in shaping the values, worldview, hope, and aspirations of the 30 million people of Mexican ancestry in the United States.

We have seen that religion plays a vital role in helping to shape Mexican American identity. Religion is so intimately tied to Mexican American and Mexican immigrant Catholic identity that being Mexican American and being Catholic are often seen as synonymous. In the minds of many, the two are inextricably linked even if one does not regularly attend church, go to Mass, or perform confession. Home altars, popular plays, student organizations, reconstructions of Our Lady of Guadalupe, Chicano/a art, Chicano/a literature, and even the continuing use of given names such as Jesús, María, Salvador, Milagros, and Guadalupe demonstrate the intrinsic connection between popular Catholicism and Mexican American identity.

Mexican Americans have harnessed and utilized religion as a cultural resource and as a vehicle for social, civic, and political empowerment and protest. As the stories of Católicos por la Raza, César Chávez, Los Pastores, Luis Valdez's Teatro Campesino, and the works of Gloria Anzaldúa, Sandra Cisneros, Mary Helen Poncé, Denise Chávez, and Chicana feminists and artists demonstrate, religious rhetoric, moral authority, and themes have been used to critique Anglo-American society and its capitalist values. They have at the same time also been inextricably caught in its web. Mexican Americans have also used their spirituality and practices to criticize both the institutional Catholic and Protestant traditions and Mexican American patriarchy and sexism. Perhaps most important, they use them to promote a more holistic vision of health and medicine.

This book has spotlighted the important role that religious symbols, rhetoric, and worldviews play outside of the institutional church through art, drama, plays, theater, music, and literature. Religious empowerment is also a prevalent theme in pop culture and in the rapid growth of alternative religious traditions such as Pentecostalism, which has attempted to reach the masses beyond the confines of traditional churches through revivals and evangelistic faith healing services in tents, storefronts, and parks in Mexican American barrios and *colonias* throughout the United States.

Contrary to those interpretations of Mexican American religions that distinguish between institutional and popular religiosity, it is clear that popular religiosity is often in direct and sustained contact, dialogue, and fellowship with institutionally based clergy and churches in the community, even if this contact is sometimes controversial or contested. Thus Mexican American religions are often loosely connected to the institutional church even if they are heavily driven by popular religious practices, traditions, sensibilities, and values.

Despite the fact that Mexican Americans have historically been depicted as almost exclusively Roman Catholic, we have seen that religious pluralism is alive and well. Furthermore, while Roman Catholics make up over 74 percent of people of Mexican ancestry in the United States, the community is nonetheless religiously diverse—with literally hundreds of Protestant, Alternative Christian, metaphysical, occult, and alternative religious traditions competing for the hearts and souls of the people. The dynamic nature of this religious marketplace is evident by simply looking through any phone book in a Mexican American community or by driving through a barrio.

The pluralistic marketplace also helps explain why so many Mexican Americans are religiously eclectic in their spirituality. Some see no contradiction participating in multiple denominations within the same tradition—Protestantism or Pentecostalism, for example—while still others actually combine and blend different religious traditions, such as Catholicism and Spiritualism or aspects of Buddhism. However, it would be an exaggeration to say that all Mexican Americans combine and blend religious traditions, because many do not. Mexican American Pentecostals,

Southern Baptists, Jehovah's Witnesses, Mormons, Seventh-Day Adventists, Muslims, and Jews who have been actively involved (once per week or more) in their churches, synagogues, or mosques over an extended period of time, for example, tend not to combine and blend religious elements from other religions into their new religious identity. While exceptions exist, they tend to prove the rule. The exceptions that do exist are usually among laity, scholars, teachers, and denominational leaders who are encouraged to engage in interreligious dialogue and contact on social and intellectual but not necessarily on theological and spiritual matters. Still, even those that tend not to combine and blend religious traditions bring into their new religious tradition cultural attitudes, practices, and sensibilities from their previous tradition—usually popular Catholicism. This may help explain why the Pentecostal practice of divine healing is so widespread in the Mexican American community, which has a long and established tradition of Catholic healing with *curanderismo*.

The influence of religion is not only evident in the growing religious pluralism in the Mexican American community but also in pop culture, where multiple religious symbols, rhetoric, and traditions are sometimes combined and blended. Many youth blend religious symbols even if they hold strongly to one tradition—whether it is Roman Catholic or Protestantism. This blending of religious symbols is especially evident in Mexican American art, where both young and seasoned artists combine religious symbols and themes from historic, institutional, and popular Catholicism, Mesoamerican art, architecture, and historic leaders; Protestant notions about sin, salvation, and End Times eschatology; and metaphysical and alternative spiritualities complete with angels, demons, and divine-healing herbal remedies. Religious themes are also evident in the work of Mexican American pop music stars (e.g., Carlos Santana's *Shaman* album) and in movies by directors such as Gregory Nava (*El Norte* and *Mi Familia*) and Cheech Marin (*Born in East L.A.*), where popular religious symbols, stories, and imagery pepper the dialogue, humor, and the often fatalistic storyline. In short, the boundaries between what counts as institutional, popular, and pop culture religiosity are not as strongly drawn as some might expect. In fact, the borders are quite porous.

The transnational identity of the Mexican American experience has directly shaped the porous nature of Mexican American religiosity and cultural boundaries. The movement of religious ideas across the U.S. border is not a one-way action driven by white missionaries from the United States to the "heathen" Mexicans south of the border. Today this is more myth than reality. In fact, the border is much more complex, dynamic, pluralistic, and porous than most outside of the community would imagine. Religious ideas, practices, and traditions not only move north to south and east to west, but, historically speaking, south to north—starting in Mexico City and eventually traveling north in the hearts of the millions of Mexican immigrants heading to the United States in search of a fresh start and a new life.

While the immigrants are curious about and interested in exploring Protestantism and other religious systems in the United States, they also bring with them their own versions of popular Catholicism and indigenous Protestantism, Pentecostalism, and metaphysical traditions. The result is that they are not only changing the texture of Mexican American and Latino religiosity, but also what counts for Anglo-American Catholicism, Protestantism, and metaphysical traditions. Images of Our Lady of Guadalupe now adorn many non-Hispanic Catholic churches, and many popular Catholic festivals, feast days, and traditions are increasingly incorporated into the larger American Catholic calendar. Similar trends are taking place among Mexican American Mainline, Evangelical, and Pentecostal Protestants as they make up an increasingly larger share of their respective denomination's numerical growth. This is especially true for denominations such as the Assemblies of God, which would have a flat growth rate were it not for the eight Hispanic and other ethnic districts in the denomination.

The growth of Mexican American Protestantism is shaped in part by immigration and the fact that Protestants emigrate from Mexico to the United States at twice the percentage (15 percent) of the Mexican national population (7.5 percent). Pentecostal denominations birthed in Mexico— for instance, the Apostolic Church of the Faith in Christ Jesus—and with only limited administrative or legal ties to Pentecostalism in the United States, are arriving in Mexican American and Latino barrios and colonias and setting up shop to evangelize the masses. Likewise, indigenous and long-established Mexican American Pentecostal denominations such as the Apostolic Assembly of the Faith in Christ Jesus, Inc., based in Rancho Cucamonga, California, and the Latin American Council of Christian Churches (CONCILIO) based in Brownsville, Texas, continue to send missionaries to Mexico.

These studies reveal that religion serves as a critical cultural and political resource for Mexican American/Chicana women. These women not only create their matriarchal spaces through home altars, but also use the most important symbol of Mexican American Catholic identity—Our

Lady of Guadalupe—as a source of cultural agency, divine hope, and feminist empowerment. Chicana writers and artists use religious rhetoric, symbols, and ideas about equality and freedom represented by Christ to rebel against patriarchal and heterosexual norms projected onto them by Anglo-American and Mexican society. Still other Mexican American women and youth inscribe cultural icons such as Tejana music star Selena with cultural agency and use them to serve as a symbolic counternarrative and as a vehicle for cultural redemption. For these reasons and many others, it is almost impossible to fully understand the experience of working-class Mexican American women throughout the United States without some understanding of the role that religion plays in their daily lives.

Thus, this book demonstrates the contested nature of religious symbols in the Mexican American community. Religious and cultural symbols such as Our Lady of Guadalupe, Selena, and Gloria Anzaldúa—along with characters in Los Pastores, Luis Valdez's *La Pastorela*, and Chicana literature and art—reveal how Mexican Americans have reimagined traditional religious leaders, personalities, symbols, and traditions to suit their own cultural, religious, and political aims. They also spotlight the dynamic nature of Mexican American religiosity.

This book also explores the historical development of the field of Mexican American religions, why the field is important, and how it has changed over the years. The field was shaped by the political activism and writings of union and civil rights leaders such as César Chávez, the theological writings of Chicano scholar-priests such as Virgilio Elizondo, the praxis of scholar-priests such as Gustavo Gutiérrez and Enrique Dussel, and through the work of Chicano writers such as Moises Sandoval. The field was also heavily influenced by a liberationist framework that continues to define the field to the present. The work of anthropologists and historians of religions such as Davíd Carrasco brought new and important theoretical lenses that expanded our understanding of Mexican American religions. These new interpretative frameworks were often done in direct conversation with the first generation of liberationist theologians and scholars. The field developed even further as it expanded to include feminist, gender, and cultural analyses. It also paid greater attention to the theme of religious pluralism and the development of Protestantism, Spiritualism, and other religious traditions.

Taken as a whole, this book highlights the Mexican American practice of materializing the sacred in everyday life. Whether through religious utopian communities, farm union labor movements, student organizations, symbols, home altars, plays, literature, health and healing, art, or pop culture and music, Mexican Americans sacralize the sacred in everyday life in a way that provides meaning and hope for a better tomorrow.

Despite the pluralistic scope and vision of this book, there are still a large number of topics and themes that need further investigation. For example, there is a need for more research on Mexican American Catholicism; Mainline, Evangelical, and Pentecostal Protestantism; Spiritualism/Spiritism; and popular religiosity. While there are one or two books or articles on these topics, in most cases there is still much work to be done. In addition, there is a need for original, critical, scholarly research and analysis from historical, sociological, and theological perspectives on specific religious traditions that serve Mexican Americans such as Jehovah's Witnesses, Southern Baptists, Mormons, Adventists, and Pentecostals, Islam, Judaism, Spiritualism, curanderismo, and *brujería*. There is also a need for creative research and analyses on the role of religious symbols, rhetoric, and worldviews in Mexican American pop music, barrio wall murals, magazines and newspapers, television and *telenovelas*, movies (both Spanish and English), sports, gang life, prison life, interethnic conflicts, and hobbies. There is a need for continued and more focused research on religion and political activism, faith-based community organizing, gender roles, sexuality, and masculinity for all of the major religious traditions in the Mexican American community. Scholars need to conduct more theological research, reflection, and writing on key followers and leaders of specific religious traditions. There is also a need for transdenominational and transreligious sociological and historical research on the topics concerning religion and politics, religion and civic activism, religious beliefs and ethics, religion and youth, religion and children, and religious switching and conversion. There is also a need for more oral history projects to capture the views of people before they pass away and a need for richly detailed ethnographic community studies. Scholars need to conduct further sociological and demographic national survey research on the Mexican American community and examine how it differs, if at all, from other Latino subgroups and the larger Anglo-American and African American populations.

Finally, we believe that the future academic study of Mexican American religions is open for creative and innovative research and theoretical reflection. We hope that this book will serve as a foundation that future scholars can build on in order to take the field in new and exciting directions in the twenty-first century.

Bibliography

Abalos, David. "Reflections on the Creation of Latino Culture in the United States." In *Old Masks, New Faces: Religion and Latino Identities*. Edited by Anthony M. Stevens-Arroyo and Gilbert R. Cadena. New York: Bildner Center for Western Hemisphere Studies, 1995.

Abbott, Carl. *The Metropolitan Frontier: Cities in the Modern American West*. Tucson: University of Arizona Press, 1993.

Abel, Theodore. *Protestant Home Missions to Catholic Immigrants*. New York: Institute of Social and Religious Research, 1933.

Acuña, René. *El teatro popular en Hispanoamérica: Una bibliografía anotada*. Mexico City: Universidad Nacional Autónoma de México, 1979.

Acuña, Rodolfo. *Occupied America: A History of Chicanos*. San Francisco: Canfield Press, 1972.

———. *Occupied America: A History of Chicanos*. 3rd ed. New York: Harper and Row, 1988 [4th ed., New York: Addison Wesley Longman, 2000].

Alarcón, Norma. "The Theoretical Subject(s) of *This Bridge Called My Back* and Anglo-American Feminism." In *Criticism in the Borderlands: Studies in Chicano Literature, Culture, and Ideology*. Edited by Héctor Calderón and José David Saldívar. Durham: Duke University Press, 1991.

Alcalá, Kathleen. *Spirits of the Ordinary: A Tale of Casas Grandes*. New York: Harvest, 1998.

Allen, Robert. *Black Awakening in Capitalist America*. Garden City, N.J.: Doubleday Anchor, 1970.

Alvarez, Julia. *How the Garcia Girls Lost Their Accents*. Chapel Hill, N.C.: Algonquin Books, 1991.

Alves, Rubem. *A Theology of Human Hope*. Washington, D.C.: Corpus, 1969.

Anaya, Rudolfo A. *Alburquerque*. Albuquerque: University of New Mexico Press, 1992.

———. "Aztlán: A Homeland without Boundaries." *Aztlán: Essays on the Chicano Homeland*. Edited by Rudolfo A. Anaya and Francisco Lomelí. Albuquerque, N. Mex.: Academia, 1989.

———. *Bless Me, Ultima*. New York: Warner Books, 1972 [1994].

Anderson, Robert Mapes. *Vision of the Disinherited: The Making of American Pentecostalism*. 2nd ed. Peabody, Mass.: Hendrickson, 1992.

Anijar, Karen. "Selena-Prophet, Profit, Princess." In *God in the Details: American Religion in Popular Culture*. Edited by Eric Michael Mazur and Kate McCarthy. New York: Routledge, 2001.

Anzaldúa, Gloria. *Borderlands/La Frontera: The New Mestiza*. San Francisco: Aunt Lute Books, 1987 [2nd ed., 1999].

———. "Coatlalopeuh: She Who Has Dominion over Serpents." In *Goddess of the Americas, La Diosa de las Américas: Writings of the Virgin of Guadalupe*. Edited by Ana Castillo. New York: Riverhead Books, 1996.

Aquino, María Pilar. "Directions and Foundations of Hispanic/Latino Theology: Toward a Mestiza Theology of Liberation." *Journal of Hispanic/Latino Theology* 1, no. 1 (1993):5–21.

———. "Introduction." In *Religion and Justice: A Reader in Latina Feminist Theology*. Austin: University of Texas Press, 2002.

———. "Latin American Feminist Theology." *Journal of Feminist Studies in Religion* 14 (spring 1998): 94.

———. "Perspectives on Latina's Feminist Liberation Theology." In *Frontiers of Hispanic Theology in the United States*. Edited by Allan Figueroa Deck. Maryknoll, N.Y.: Orbis Books, 1992.

Arcosanti promotional brochure. Scottsdale, Ariz.: Cosanti Foundation, n.d.

ArriveNet Politics Press Release, "Census Bureau: Hispanic Population Passes 40 Million; Number of Elementary School-Age Children in Nation Totaled 36.4 Million." 9 June 2005. Available at http://press.arrivenet.com/pol/article.php/650602.html.

Assmann, Hugo. *Teología desde la praxis de liberación: Ensayo teológico desde América Latina dependiente*. Salamanca, Spain: Sígueme, 1973.

———. *A Theology for a Nomad Church*. Translated by Paul Burns. Maryknoll, N.Y.: Orbis Books, 1975.

Atkinson, Ernest E. *A Selected Bibliography of Hispanic Baptist History*. Nashville: Historical Commission, Southern Baptist Convention, 1981.

Atkins-Vasquez, Jane, ed. *Hispanic Presbyterians in Southern California: One Hundred Years of Ministry*. Los Angeles: Hispanic Commission, Synod of Southern California and Hawaii, 1988.

Austin, Alfredo López. *Tamoanchan, Tlalocan: Places of Mist*. Denver: University Press of Colorado, 1997.

Azevedo, Marcello. *West in Inculturation and the Challenges of Modernity*. Rome: Gregorian University, 1982.

Bach-y-Rita, George. "The Mexican American: Religious and Cultural Influences." In *Mental Health and Hispanic Americans: Clinical Perspectives*, New York: Grune and Stratton, 1982.

Badillo, David A. "The Catholic Church and the Making of Mexican-American Parish Communities in the Midwest." In *Mexican Americans and the Catholic Church, 1900–1965*. Vol. 1. Edited by Jay P. Dolan and Gilberto M. Hinojosa. Notre Dame, Ind.: University of Notre Dame Press, 1994.

Bailey, Ronald, and Guillermo V. Flores. "Internal Colonialism and Racial Minorities." In *Structures of Dependency*. Edited by Frank Bonilla and Robert Girling. Palo Alto, Calif.: Nairobi Press, 1973.

Bañuelas, Arturo, ed. *Mestizo Christianity: Theology from the Latino Perspective*. Maryknoll, N.Y.: Orbis Books, 1995.

Barnes, Linda L., and Susan S. Sered, eds. *Religion and Healing in America*. New York: Oxford University Press, 2005.

Barrera, Mario. *Beyond Aztlán*. Notre Dame, Ind.: University of Notre Dame Press, 1988.

———. *Race and Class in the Southwest: A Theory of Racial Inequality*. Notre Dame, Ind.: University of Notre Dame Press, 1979.

Barrera, Mario, Carlos Muñoz, and Charles Ornelas. "The Barrio as an Internal Colony." In *La Causa Política: A Chicano Politics Reader*. Edited by F. Chris García. Notre Dame, Ind.: University of Notre Dame Press, 1972 and 1974.

Barton, Paul, and David Maldonado, Jr. *Hispanic Christianity within Mainline Protestant Traditions: A Bibliography*. Decatur, Ga.: AETH (Asociación para la Educación Teológica Hispana) Books, 1998.

Bauman, Richard, ed. *Verbal Art as Performance*. Rowley, Mass: Newbury House Publishers, 1977.

Baumann, Greg. Interview by authors. Dolores Mission Parish, 12 November 1998.

Bazán, Nellie, with Elizabeth B. and Don Martínez, Jr. *Enviados de Dios: Demetrio and Nellie Bazán*. Miami: Editorial Vida, 1987.

Beauvoir, Simone de. *The Second Sex*. Translated and edited by H. M. Parshley. New York: Knopf, 1953.

Beezley, William H. "Home Altars: Private Reflections of Public Life." In *Home Altars of Mexico*. By Dana Salvo. Albuquerque: University of New Mexico Press, 1997.

Beirne, Charles J., S.J. *The Problem of Americanization in the Catholic Schools of Puerto Rico*. Río Piedras, Puerto Rico: Editorial Universitaria de la Universidad de Puerto Rico, 1975.

Belenky, Mary, Blythe Clinchy, Nancy Goldberger, and Jill Tarule, eds. *Women's Ways of Knowing: The Development of Self, Voice, and Mind*. New York: Basic Books, 1988.

Belli, Humberto, and Ronald Nash. *Beyond Liberation Theology*. Grand Rapids, Mich.: Baker Book House, 1992.

Benavides, Gustavo. "Resistance and Accommodation in Latin American Popular Religiosity." In *An Enduring Flame: Studies on Latino Popular Religiosity*. Edited by Anthony M. Stevens Arroyo and Ana María Díaz-Stevens. New York: Bildner Center for Western Hemisphere Studies, 1994.

Bernstein, Richard. *Beyond Objectivism and Relativism: Science, Hermeneutic, and Praxis*. Philadelphia: University of Pennsylvania Press, 1983.

Blauner, Robert. "Internal Colonialism and Ghetto Revolt." *Social Problems* (spring 1969): 393–408.

BOCA I, no. 3 (October–November 1998).

Boff, Leonardo, and Clodovis Boff. *Introducing Liberation Theology*. Maryknoll, N.Y.: Orbis Books, 1987.

Bolle, Kees W. "Myth: An Overview." In *The Encyclopedia of Religion*. Editor-in-chief, Mircea Eliade. Vol. 10. New York: Macmillan, 1987.

Bottéro, Jean. *Mesopotamia, Writing, Reasoning and the Gods*. Chicago: University of Chicago, 1992.

Bowman, John S., ed. *Cambridge Dictionary of American Biography*. Cambridge: Cambridge University Press, 1995.

Brackenridge, R. Douglas, and Francisco O. García-Treto. *Iglesia Presbiteriana: A History of Presbyterians and Mexican Americans in the Southwest*. San Antonio: Trinity University Press, 1987.

Brenneis, Brooks, and Samuel Roll. "Dream Patterns in Anglo and Chicano Young Adults." *Psychiatry* 39 (August 1976).

——. "Ego Modalities in the Manifest Dreams of Male and Female Chicanos." *Psychiatry* (May 1975).

Brenner, Anita. *Idols behind Altars*. New York: Biblo and Tannen, 1967.

——. "Painted Miracles." *Arts* 15 (January 1929): 11–18.

Bresette, Linna E. *Mexicans in the United States: A Report of a Brief Survey*. Washington, D.C.: National Catholic Welfare Conference, 1929.

Bryan, C. D. B. *Close Encounters of the Fourth Kind: A Reporter's Notebook on Alien Abduction, UFOs, and the Conference at M.I.T.* New York: Penguin, 1995.

Budde, Michael L. *The Two Churches: Catholicism and Capitalism in the World System*. Durham: Duke University Press, 1992.

Burger, Peter. *Theory of the Avant-Garde*. Translated by Michael Shaw. Minneapolis: [orig. pub. in German, 1974] University of Minnesota Press, 1984.

Burkhart, Louise, M. "The Cult of the Virgin of Guadalupe in Mexico." In *South and Meso-American Native Spirituality: From the Cult of the Feathered Serpent to the Theology of Liberation*. Edited by Gary Gossen H., with Miguel León-Portilla. New York: Crossroad Publishing Company, 1993.

Burke, Kenneth. *The Philosophy of Literary Form: Studies in Symbolic Action*. New York: Vintage Books, 1957.

Burma, John. *Spanish-Speaking Groups in the United States*. Durham: Duke University Press, 1954.

Burns, Jeffery M. "The Mexican American Community in California." In *Mexican Americans and the Catholic Church, 1900–1965*. Edited by Jay P. Dolan and Gilberto M. Hinojosa. Notre Dame, Ind.: University of Notre Dame Press, 1994.

Burr, Ramiro. "Selena's Impact Still Felt." *Minneapolis Star Tribune*, 31 March 1996, 9F.

Busto, Rudy V. *King Tiger: The Religious Vision of Reies López Tijerina*. Albuquerque: University of New Mexico Press, 2005.

——. "The Predicament of *Nepantla*: Chicano/a Religions into the 21st Century." *Perspectives: Occasional Papers*. Hispanic Theological Initiative 1 (fall 1998): 7–20.

Cabrera, Yvette. "Day of the Dead: Cemeteries See Culture Clash." *Woodland Hills Daily News* 31, October 1998, 1, 16.

Cadena, Gilbert. "Chicanos and the Catholic Church: Liberation Theology as a Form of Empowerment." PhD diss., University of California, Riverside, 1987.

Campa, Arthur F. *Spanish Religious Folktheatre in the Southwest*. Albuquerque: University of New Mexico Press, 1943.

——. *Spanish Religious Folktheatre in the Spanish Southwest*. University of New Mexico Bulletin, Language Series. Vol. 5, nos. 1 and 2. Albuquerque: University of New Mexico Press, 1934.

Cantú, Ernesto S., and José Ortega. *Historia de la Asamblea Apostólica de la Fe en Cristo Jesús*. Mentone, Calif.: Sal's Printing Press, 1966.

Cantú, Norma E., and Olga Nájera Ramírez, eds. *Chicana Traditions: Continuity and Change*. Urbana: University of Illinois Press, 2002.

Capps, Walter. *Religious Studies: The Making of a Discipline*. Minneapolis: Fortress Press, 1995.

Carmichael, Elizabeth, and Chloë Sayer. *The Skeleton at the Feast: The Day of the Dead in Mexico*. Austin: University of Texas Press, 1992.

Carrasco, Davíd. "*Cuando Dios y Usted Quiere*: Latinos Studies between Religious Powers and Social Thought." In *Blackwell Reader on Latino Studies*. Edited by Juan Flores and Renato Rosaldo. Oxford: Blackwell Publishers, 2007.

———. "Jaguar Christians in the Contact Zone." In *Enigmatic Powers: Syncretism with African and Indigenous Peoples' Religions among Latinos*. Edited by Anthony M. Stevens-Arroyo and Andrés I. Pérez y Mena. New York: Bildner Center for Western Hemisphere Studies, 1995.

———. "Myth, Cosmic Terror, and the Templo Mayor." In *The Great Temple of Tenochtitlán: Center and Periphery in the Aztec World*. Edited by Johanna Broda, Davíd Carrasco, and Eduardo Matos Moctezuma. Berkeley: University of California Press, 1986.

———. "A Perspective for the Study of Religious Dimensions in Chicano Experience: *Bless Me, Ultima* as a Religious Text." *Aztlán: A Journal of Chicano Studies* 13, nos. 1 and 2 (1982): 195–221.

———. *Quetzalcoatl and the Irony of Empire: Myths and Prophecies in the Aztec Tradition*. Chicago: University of Chicago Press, 1982.

———. *Religions of Mesoamerica: Cosmovision and Ceremonial Centers*. San Francisco: HarperSanFrancisco, 1990.

Carreter, Fernando Lázaro. *Teatro medieval*. Madrid: Odres Nuevos, 1965.

Castañeda, Alfredo. "Traditionalism, Modernism and Ethnicity." In *Chicano Psychology*. Edited by Joe L. Martínez Jr. New York: Academic Press, 1977.

Castañeda, Carlos. *The Teachings of Don Juan: A Yaqui Way of Knowledge*. Berkeley: University of California Press, 1968 [1998].

Castañeda, Carlos E. *Our Catholic Heritage in Texas, 1519–1950*. 7 vols. Austin: Von Boekmann-Jones, 1936–58.

Castillo, Ana. "Extraordinarily Woman." In *Goddess of the Americas: Writings on the Virgin of Guadalupe*. Edited by Ana Castillo. New York: Riverhead Books, 1996.

———. *Massacre of the Dreamers: Essays on Xicanisma*. Albuquerque: University of New Mexico Press, 1994.

———. *So Far from God*. New York: W. W. Norton, 1993.

———. "Virgin Mother Soldier's Whore." In *Massacre of the Dreamers: Essays on Xicanisma*. New York: Plume, 1995.

Castillo, Ana, ed. *Goddess of the Americas: Writings on the Virgin de Guadalupe*. New York: Riverhead Books, 1996.

Cather, Willa. *Death Comes for the Archbishop*. New York: Knopf, 1927.

"Católicos Por La Raza." Document, n.d., in possession of Pedro Arias.

Chávez, Angélico. *The Old Faith and Old Glory: Story of the Church in New Mexico since the American Occupation, 1846–1946*. Santa Fe, N. Mex.: privately printed, 1946.

———. *Our Lady of the Conquest*. Albuquerque: Historical Society of New Mexico, 1948.

Chávez, César. "The Chicano y la Iglesia." *La Verdad* (San Diego), December 1969.

————. "The Mexican American and the Church." *El Grito del Sol* 1, no. 4 (summer 1968): 9–12.

————. "The Mexican American and the Church." In *Voices: Readings from El Grito: A Journal of Mexican American Thought, 1967–1973*. Edited by Octavio I. Romano. Berkeley: Quinto Sol Publications, 1973. As cited in *Prophets Denied Honor: An Anthology on the Hispanic Church in the United States*. Edited by Anthony M. Stevens-Arroyo. Maryknoll, N.Y.: Orbis Books, 1980.

Chávez, Denise. "Novena narrativas y ofrendas nuevomexicanas." *Americas Review* 15, nos. 3–4 (1987): 65–72.

————. "Our Lady of Guadalupe." *New Mexico Magazine*, December 1986, 55–63.

Chávez, John. *The Lost Land: The Chicano Image of the Southwest*. Albuquerque: University of New Mexico Press, 1984.

Chicano Aesthetics: Rasquachismo. Exhibition catalog. Curated by Tomás Ybarra-Frausto, Shifra M. Goldman, and John L. Aguilar. Phoenix: Movimiento Artístico del Río Salado [MARS], 1989.

¡Chicano! The History of the Mexican American Civil Rights Movement, documentary, (episode 1, "Quest for a Homeland"), Los Angeles: National Latino Communications Group, 1996.

Chicano Psychology. 2nd ed. Edited by Joe L. Martínez Jr. and Richard H. Mendoza. San Diego: Academic Press, 1984.

"Christ? Justice, the Catholic Church, and the Chicano Movement." *Explorations in Ethnic Studies* 14, no. 1 (January, 1991): 17–34.

Chodorow, Nancy. *The Reproduction of Mothering: Psychoanalysis and the Sociology of Gender*. Berkeley: University of California Press, 1978.

Cimino, Richard, and Don Lattin. *Shopping for Faith: American Religion in the New Millennium*. San Francisco: Jossey-Bass, 1998.

Cisneros, Sandra. "Guadalupe the Sex Goddess." In *Goddess of the Americas, La Diosa de las Américas: Writings of the Virgin of Guadalupe*. Edited by Ana Castillo. New York: Riverhead Books, 1996.

————. *The House on Mango Street*. Houston: Arte Público Press, 1985.

————. *Woman Hollering Creek and Other Stories*. New York: Random House, 1991.

Clifford, James, and George Marcu. *Writing Culture: The Poetics and Politics of Ethnography*. Berkeley: University of California Press, 1986.

Cole, M. R. *Los Pastores*. Vol. 9. New York: Memoirs of the American Folk-Lore Society, 1907.

Conner, Randy P., David Sparks, and Mariya Sparks. *Cassell's Encyclopedia of Queer Myth, Symbol, and Spirit*. London: Cassell, 1997.

Connor, Steven. *Postmodernist Culture: An Introduction to Theories of the Contemporary*. Cambridge, Mass.: Basil Blackwell, 1989.

Cook, Guillermo. "Protestant Mission and Evangelization in Latin America." In *New Face of the Church in Latin America*. Maryknoll, N.Y.: Orbis Books, 1994.

Corliss, Richard. "The Legend of Selena." *TIME*, 24 March 1997.

Crayne, Richard. *Pentecostal Handbook*. Morristown, Tenn.: Richard Crayne, 1963 [3rd ed., 1990].

Cull, Nicholas, and Davíd Carrasco. *Alambrista and the U.S.-Mexico Border: Film, Music, and Stories of Undocumented Immigrants*. Albuquerque: University of New Mexico Press, 2004.

Culp, Alice Bessie. "A Case Study of the Living Conditions of Thirty-five Mexican Families of Los Angeles with Special Reference to Mexican Children." MA thesis, University of Southern California, Los Angeles, 1921.

Dalton, Frederick John. *The Moral Vision of César Chávez*. Maryknoll, N.Y.: Orbis Books, 2003.

———. "The Moral Vision of César E. Chávez: An Examination of His Public Life from an Ethical Perspective." PhD diss., Graduate Theological Union, Berkeley, 1998.

Davalos, Karen Mary. *Exhibiting Mestizaje: Mexican (American) Museums in the Diaspora*. Albuquerque: University of New Mexico Press, 2001.

———. "Exhibiting Mestizaje: The Poetics and Experience of the Mexican Fine Arts Center Museum." In *Latinos in Museums: A Heritage Reclaimed*. Edited by Antonio José Ríos-Bustamante and Christine Marin. Malabar, Fla.: Krieger Publishing Company, 1998.

Davis, Eric. *Techgnosis: Myth, Magic, and Mysticism in the Age of Information*. New York: Harmony Books, 1998.

Davis, Kenneth. "The Hispanic Shift: Continuity Rather than Conversion." *Journal of Hispanic/Latino Theology* 1, no. 3 (May 1994): 68–79.

Day, Mark. *Forty Acres: César Chávez and the Farm Workers*. New York: Praeger Press, 1971.

Dayton, Donald W. *Theological Roots of Pentecostalism*. Metuchen, N.J.: Scarecrow Press, 1987.

Dear, John. "César Chávez on Voting in the Marketplace." *Pax Christi USA* (winter 1992): 21.

De Borhegyi, Stephen. "The Cult of Our Lord of Esquipulas in Middle America and New Mexico." *El Palacio* 61 (1954): 387–401.

———. *El Santuario de Chimayó*. Santa Fe, N. Mex.: Ancient City Press for the Spanish Colonial Arts Society, 1956.

De Certeau, Michel. *The Practice of Everyday Life*. Translated by Steven Rendall. Berkeley: University of California Press, 1984.

———. "Reading as Poaching." In *The Practice of Everyday Life*. Translated by Steven Rendall. Berkeley: University of California Press, 1984.

Deck, Allan Figueroa. "The Challenge of Evangelical/Pentecostal Christianity to Hispanic Catholicism." In *Hispanic Catholic Culture in the U.S.* Edited by Jay P. Dolan and Allan Figueroa Deck, SJ. Notre Dame, Ind.: University of Notre Dame Press, 1994.

———. *Frontiers of Hispanic Theology in the United States.* Maryknoll, N.Y.: Orbis Books, 1992.

———. "La Raza Cósmica: Rediscovering the Hispanic Soul." *Critic* (Spring 1993).

———. "Latino Theology: The Year of the Boom." *Journal of Hispanic/Latino Theology* 1, no. 2 (February 1994): 51–63.

———. *The Second Wave: Hispanic Ministry and the Evangelization of Culture.* New York: Paulist Press, 1989.

Dehesa, Germán. *Tapadeus.* Live Performance in Mexico City, December 1986.

De la Huerta, Christian. *Coming Out Spiritually: The Next Step.* New York: Jeremy P. Tarcher, 1999.

De la Rosa, Martin. "Iglesia y sociedad en el México de hoy." In *Religión y Política en México.* Mexico City: Siglo Veintiuno Editores, 1985.

De La Torre, Miguel A., and Edwin David Aponte. *Introducing Latino/a Theologies.* Maryknoll, N.Y.: Orbis Books, 2001.

De La Torre, Miguel, and Gastón Espinosa. *Rethinking Latino(a) Religion and Identity.* Cleveland, Ohio: Pilgrim Press, 2006.

Del Castillo, Richard Griswold, Teresa McKenna, and Yvonne Yarboro-Bejarano, eds. *Chicano Art: Resistance and Affirmation, 1965–1985.* Los Angeles: Wight Art Gallery, University of California Press, 1991.

De Leon, Victor. *The Silent Pentecostals.* Taylors, S.C.: Faith Printing Company, 1979.

De Los Santos, Nancy. "Selena *Vive.*" *Latina* (March 2000): 26.

Denis, Manuel Maldonado. *Puerto Rico: A Socio-Historic Interpretation.* New York: Vintage Books, 1972.

D'Epinay, Christian Lalive. *Haven of the Masses: A Study of the Pentecostal Movement in Chile.* London, England: Lutterworth Press, 1966.

Derrida, Jacques. "Faith and Knowledge: The Two Sources of 'Religion' at the Limits of Reason Alone." In *Religion.* Edited by Jacques Derrida and Gianni Vattimo. [Orig. pub. in French, Editions du Seuil, 1996] Palo Alto, Calif.: Stanford University Press, 1998.

De Sahagún, Bernardino. *Historia general de las cosas de la Nueva España.* Vol. 2. Mexico City: Editorial Porrúa, 1969.

Deutsch, Sarah. *No Separate Refuge: Culture, Class, and Gender on an Anglo-Hispanic Frontier in the American Southwest, 1880–1940.* New York: Oxford University Press, 1987.

Díaz, Miguel H. *On Being Human: U.S. Hispanic and Rahnerian Perspectives*. Maryknoll, N.Y.: Orbis Books, 2001.

Díaz-Stevens, Ana María. "Analyzing Popular Religiosity for Socio-religious Meaning." In *An Enduring Flame: Studies on Latino Popular Religiosity*. New York: Bildner Center for Western Hemisphere Studies, 1994.

——. "The Matriarchal Core of Latino Catholicism." *Latino Studies Journal* 4, no. 3 (September 1993): 60–78.

——. *Oxcart Catholicism on Fifth Avenue*. Notre Dame, Ind.: University of Notre Dame Press, 1993.

——. "From Puerto Rican to Hispanic: The Politics of the *Fiestas Patronales* in New York." *Latino Studies Journal* 1, no. 1 (January 1990): 28–47.

Díaz-Stevens, Ana María, and Anthony M. Stevens-Arroyo. *Recognizing the Latino Resurgence in U.S. Religion: The Emmaus Paradigm*. Boulder: Westview Press, 1998.

Dodson, Ruth. "Don Pedrito Jaramillo: The Curandero of Los Olmos." In *The Healer of Los Olmos and Other Mexican Lore*. Edited by Wilson M. Hudson. Dallas: Southern Methodist University, 1966.

——. *The Healer of Los Olmos*. Austin: Texas Folklore Society, 1951.

——. *Tone the Bell Easy*. Dallas: Southern Methodist University Press, 1932.

Dolan, Jay P., and Allan Figueroa Deck, SJ., eds. *Hispanic Catholic Culture in the U.S.: Issues and Concerns*. Notre Dame, Ind.: University of Notre Dame Press, 1994.

Dolan, Jay P., and Jaime R. Vidal, eds. *Puerto Rican and Cuban Catholics in the U.S., 1900–1965*. Notre Dame, Ind.: University of Notre Dame Press, 1994.

Dolan, Jay P., and Gilberto Miguel Hinojosa, eds. *Mexican Americans and the Catholic Church, 1900–1965*. Notre Dame, Ind.: University of Notre Dame Press, 1994.

Donovan, Richard B. *The Liturgical Drama in Medieval Spain*. Toronto: Pontifical Institute of Medieval Studies, 1958.

Ducrue, Benno Iranciscus. *Ducrue's Account of the Expulsion of the Jesuits from Lower California (1767–1769)*. St. Louis: St. Louis University Press, 1967.

Duncan, James, and David Ley. *Place/Culture/Representation*. London: Routledge, 1993.

Dunne, John Gregory. *Delano: Revised and Updated*. New York: Farrar, Straus, and Giroux, 1971.

Durán, Diego. *Historia de las Indias de Nueva España e Islas de la Tierra Firme*. Vol. 1. Mexico City: Porrúa, 1969.

Durand, Jorge, and Douglas S. Massey. *Miracles on the Border: Retablos of Mexican Migrants to the United States*. Tucson: University of Arizona, 1995.

Duryee, Spencer. "The Great Aztec." *Christian Herald* (August 1936): 6.

Dussel, Enrique. *The Church in Latin America, 1492–1992*. Maryknoll, N.Y.: Orbis Books, 1992.

———. *A History of the Church in Latin America: Colonialism to Liberation (1492–1979)*. Translated by Alan Neely. Grand Rapids, Mich.: Wm. B. Eerdmans Publishing Company, 1981.

———. *Método para una filosofía de la liberación: Superación analéctica de la dialéctica hegeliana*. Salamanca, Spain: Ediciones Sígueme, 1974.

Eck, Diana L., and Deraki Jain, eds. *Cross-cultural Perspectives on Women, Religion and Social Change*. New Delhi: Kali for Women, 1986.

Egan, Martha. *Milagros: Votive Offerings from the Americas*. Santa Fe: Museum of New Mexico Press, 1991.

Eliade, Mircea. *The Quest: History and Meaning in Religion*. Chicago: University of Chicago Press, 1984.

———. *Shamanism: Archaic Techniques of Ecstasy*. New York: Bollingen Foundation, 1964.

———. *The Two and the One*. Chicago: University of Chicago Press, 1979.

Elizondo, Virgilio. *Anthropological and Psychological Characteristics of the Mexican American*. San Antonio: Mexican American Cultural Center, 1974.

———. *Beyond Borders: Writings of Virgilio Elizondo and Friends*. Edited by Timothy Matovina. Maryknoll, N.Y.: Orbis Books, 2000.

———. "A Catechetical Response for Minorities." In *Colección mestiza americana*. San Antonio: Mexican American Cultural Center, 1975.

———. "A Challenge to Theology: The Situation of Hispanic Americans." *Catholic Theological Society of America Proceedings* 30 (1975): 163–76.

———. *Christianity and Culture: An Introduction to Pastoral Theology and Ministry for the Bicultural Community*. Huntington, Ind.: Our Sunday Visitor, 1975.

———. "Crisis of Our Times." *Good Tidings* 9 (July–August 1970): 83–90.

———. "Educación religiosa para el méxico-norteamericano." *Catequesis latinoamericana* 4, no. 14 (January–March 1972): 83–86.

———. "Foreword to John Francis Burke." In *Mestizo Democracy: The Politics of Crossing Borders*. College Station: Texas A&M University Press, 2002.

———. *The Future Is Mestizo: Life Where Cultures Meet*. Bloomington, Ind.: Meyer-Stone Books, 1988 [1992].

———. *Galilean Journey: The Mexican-American Promise*. Maryknoll, N.Y.: Orbis Books, [1983] 1994.

———. *Guadalupe: Mother of the New Creation*. New York: Orbis Books, 1998.

———. *La Morenita: Evangelizer of the Americas*. San Antonio: Mexican American Cultural Center, 1980.

———. *Mestizaje: The Dialectic of Birth and Gospel*. San Antonio: Mexican American Cultural Center, 1978.

———. "*Mestizaje* as a Locus of Theological Reflection." In *Mestizo Christianity: Theology from the Latino Perspective*. Edited by Arturo Bañuelas. Maryknoll, N.Y.: Orbis Books, 1995.

———. "Politics, Catechetics, and Liturgy." *Religion Teacher's Journal* 10 (November–December 1976): 30–32.

———. *Religious Practices of the Mexican American and Catechesis*. San Antonio: Mexican American Cultural Center, 1974.

———. "Response to Theological Education and Liberation Theology Symposium." *Theological Education* 16 (autumn 1979): 34–37.

———. *A Search for Meaning in Life and Death*. Manila: East Asian Pastoral Institute, 1971. Also published as *The Human Quest: A Search for Meaning through Life and Death*. Huntington, Ind.: Our Sunday Visitor, 1978, and in Spanish as *Hombre quién eres tú? El enigma del hombre en el tiempo y en el más allá*. Mexico City: Instituto de Pastoral Catequético, 1971.

———. "Theological Interpretation of the Mexican American Experience." *Perkins School of Theology Journal* 29 (fall 1975): 12–21.

Elizondo, Virgilio, and Alan Oddie. "San Antonio International Study Week of Mass Media and Catechetics: A Report." *Living Light* 6 (winter 1969): 67–74.

Elizondo, Virgilio P., and Timothy M. Matovina. *Mestizo Worship: A Pastoral Approach to Liturgical Ministry*. Collegeville, Minn.: Liturgical Press, 1998.

Eller, Cynthia. *The Myth of Matriarchal Prehistory: Why an Invented Past Won't Give Us a Future*. Boston: Beacon Press, 2000.

Employment Security Commission of Arizona. "Pinal County Agricultural Employment Study, September 1956–August 1957." Phoenix: Arizona State Employment Office, 1957.

Englelkirk, John E. "Notes on the Repertoire of the New Mexican Spanish Folktheatre." *Southern Folklore Quarterly* 4 (1940): 227–37.

———. "The Source and Dating of New Mexican Spanish Folk Plays." *Western Folklore* 16 (1957): 232–55.

Espín, Orlando. *The Faith of the People: Theological Reflections on Popular Catholicism*. Maryknoll, N.Y.: Orbis Books, 1997.

———. "Popular Religion as an Epistemology (of Suffering)." *Journal of Hispanic/Latino Theology* 2, no. 2 (November 1994): 66.

———. "The State of U.S. Latino/a Theology: An Understanding." *Perspectivas: Occasional Papers*, Hispanic Theological Initiative 3 (fall 2000): 15–55.

———. "Tradition and Popular Religion: An Understanding of the *Sensus Fidelium*." In *Mestizo Christianity: Theology from the Latino Perspective*. Edited by Arturo J. Bañuelas. Maryknoll, N.Y.: Orbis Books, 1995.

Espín, Orlando, and Miguel Díaz, eds. *From the Heart of Our People: Latino/a Explorations in Catholic Systematic Theology*. Maryknoll, N.Y.: Orbis Books, 1999.

Espinosa, Aurelio M. *España en Nuevo Méjico*. New York: Allyn and Bacon, 1937.

——. "Spanish Folk-lore in New Mexico." *New Mexico Historical Review* 1 (1926): 135–55.

Espinosa, Gastón. "Changements démographiques et religieux chez les hispaniques des Etats-Unis." *Social Compass: International Review of Sociology of Religion* 51 (2004): 303–20.

——. "*El Azteca*: Francisco Olazábal and Latino Pentecostal Charisma, Power, and Faith Healing in the Borderlands." *Journal of the American Academy of Religion* 67, no. 3 (fall 1999): 597–616.

——. "'God Made a Miracle in My Life': Latino Pentecostal Healing in the Borderlands." In *Religion and Healing in America*. Edited by Linda L. Barnes and Susan S. Sered. New York: Oxford University Press, 2005.

——. "The Impact of Pluralism on Trends in Latin American and U.S. Latino Religions and Society." *Perspectivas: Occasional Papers*, no. 7 (fall 2003): 9–55.

——. "Latino Clergy and Churches in Faith-Based Political and Social Action in the United States." In *Latino Religions and Civic Activism in the United States*. Edited by Gastón Espinosa, Virgilio Elizondo, and Jesse Miranda. New York: Oxford University Press, 2005.

——. "Methodological Reflections on Social Science Research on Latino Religions." In *Rethinking Latino Religions and Identity*. Edited by Miguel de la Torre and Gastón Espinosa. Cleveland: Pilgrim Press, 2006.

——. "The Pentecostalization of Latin American and U.S. Latino Christianity." *Pneuma: The Journal of the Society for Pentecostal Studies* 26, no. 2 (fall 2004): 262–92.

——. "Selena and the Politics of Cultural Redemption." In *U.S. Latino Literatures and Cultures: Transnational Perspectives*. Edited by Francisco A. Lomelí and Karin Ikas. Heidelberg: Universitatsverlag C. Winter, 2000.

——. "'Your Daughters Shall Prophesy': A History of Women in Ministry in the Latino Pentecostal Movement in the United States." In *Women and Twentieth-Century Protestantism*. Edited by Margaret Lamberts Bendroth and Virginia Lieson Brereton. Chicago: University of Illinois Press, 2002.

Espinosa, Gastón, Virgilio Elizondo, and Jesse Miranda, eds. *Hispanic Churches in American Public Life: Summary of Findings*. Notre Dame, Ind.: Institute for Latino Studies, University of Notre Dame, 2003.

——. *Latino Religions and Civic Activism in the United States*. New York: Oxford University Press, 2005.

Espinosa, José E. *Saints in the Valleys: Christian Sacred Images in the History. Life and Folk Art of Spanish New Mexico*. Albuquerque: University of New Mexico Press, 1960.

Espinosa, Manuel J. "The Virgin of the Reconquest of New Mexico." *Mid-America* 18 (1936): 79–87.

Fagone, V. "La Religione Popolare in Gramsci." *La civiltá cattólica* 3 (1978): 119–33.

Farwell Gavin, Robin. *The Traditional Art of Spanish New Mexico*. Santa Fe: Museum of New Mexico Press, 1994.

Fernández, Abraham. "History of the Presbyterian Church, U.S.A. among the Spanish-Speaking People of the Southwest." BD thesis, San Francisco Theological Seminary, 1943.

Fernández de Lizardi, José Joaquín. "Pastorela en dos actos." In *Obras: II Teatro*. Mexico City: Centro de Estudios Literarios Universidad Nacional Autónoma de México, 1965.

Fernández, Eduardo. *La Cosecha: Harvesting Contemporary United States Hispanic Theology (1972–1998)*. Collegeville, Minn.: Michael Glazier Books, 2000.

Fernández, José Moreno. "The History and Prospects of Hispanic Methodism in the Southern California-Arizona Conference of the United Methodist Church." PhD diss., Claremont School of Theology, 1973.

Ferriss, Susan, and Ricardo Sandoval. *The Fight in the Fields: César Chávez and the Farmworkers Movement*. New York: Harcourt Brace, 1997.

Findlay, John M. *Magic Lands: Western Cityscapes and American Culture after 1940*. Berkeley: University of California Press, 1992.

Fitzpatrick, Joseph P., S.J., *Puerto Rican Americans: The Meaning of Migration to the Mainland*. Englewood Cliffs, N.J.: Prentice Hall, 1971.

———. *One Church, Many Cultures*. Kansas City, Kans.: Sheed and Ward, 1987.

Flannery, Kent V., ed. *The Early Mesoamerican Village*. New York: Academic Press, 1976.

Flores, Raymond J. "The Socio-Economic Status Trends of the Mexican People Residing in Arizona." MA thesis, Arizona State College, 1951.

Flores, Richard R. "Aesthetic Process and Cultural Citizenship: The Membering of a Social Body." In *Claiming Memory, Space and Rights: Struggles for Latino Cultural Citizenship*. Edited by Renato Rosaldo, Rina Benmayor, and William Flores. Boston: Beacon Press, in press.

———. *Los Pastores: History and Performance in the Mexican Shepherds' Play of South Texas*. Washington, D.C.: Smithsonian Institution Press, 1995.

———. "'Los Pastores' and the Gifting of Performance." *American Ethnologist* 21, no. 2 (1994): 270–85.

———. "Para El Niño Dios: Sociability and Commemorative Sentiment in Popular Religious Practice." In *An Enduring Flame: Studies on Latino Popular Religiosity*. Edited by Anthony M. Stevens Arroyo and Ana María Díaz-Stevens. New York: Bildner Center for Western Hemisphere Studies, 1994.

———. *Reflexiones 1999: New Directions in Mexican American Studies*. Austin: Center for Mexican American Studies, University of Texas, 2000.

Fogarty, Robert S. *Dictionary of American Communal and Utopian History*. Westport, Conn.: Greenwood Press, 1980.

———. "Introduction: 'Paradise Planters.'" In *Dictionary of American Communal and Utopian History*. Westport, Conn.: Greenwood Press, 1980.

Foley, Douglas. *From Peones to Politicos: Ethnic Relations in a South Texas Town, 1900–1977*. Austin: University of Texas Press, 1977.

Foucault, Michel. *The Archaeology of Knowledge and the Discourse on Language*. New York: Pantheon Books, 1972.

———. *Discipline and Punish: The Birth of the Prison*. Translated by Alan Sheridan. New York: Random House, Vintage Books, 1979.

———. *Madness and Civilization: A History of Insanity in the Age of Reason*. New York: Pantheon, 1965.

———. "Of Other Spaces." *Diacritics: A Review of Contemporary Criticism* 16, no. 1 (spring 1986): 22–27.

Foulkes, David. *Dreaming: A Cognitive-Psychological Analysis*. Hillsdale, N.J.: Lawrence Erlbaum Associates, 1985.

———. *A Grammar of Dreams*. New York: Basic Books, 1978.

Freire, Paulo. "Education, Liberation and the Church." *Religious Education* 79 (fall 1984): 527–28.

———. *Pedagogy of the Oppressed: New Revised 20th-Anniversary Edition*. Translated by Myra Bergman Ramos. New York: Continuum Books, 1972 [1994].

Gablik, Suzi. *The Reenchantment of Art*. New York: Thames and Hudson, 1991.

Gagnier, Regenia. "Feminist Autobiography in the 1980s." *Feminist Studies* 17, no. 1 (spring 1991): 135–48.

Galvan, Elias Gabriel. "A Study of the Spanish-Speaking Protestant Church and Her Mission to the Mexican American Minority." PhD diss., Claremont School of Theology, Claremont, Calif., 1969.

Gamio, Manuel. *The Mexican Immigrant: His Life-Story*. Chicago: University of Chicago Press, 1931.

———. *Mexican Immigration to the United States: A Study of Human Migration and Adjustment*. Chicago: University of Chicago Press, 1930.

García, Alma M., ed. *Chicana Feminist Thought: The Basic Historical Writings*. New York: Routledge, 1997.

García, Cristina. *Dreaming in Cuban*. New York: Alfred A. Knopf, 1992.

García, Juan Castañon. "Healer Roles, Society and Healing Efficacy: An Anthropological Essay." *El Grito del Sol* 4, no. 1 (winter 1979): 80–82.

García, Mario T. *Desert Immigrants: The Mexicans of El Paso, 1880–1920*. New Haven: Yale University Press, 1981.

——. *Memories of Chicano History: The Life and Narrative of Bert Corona*. Berkeley: University of California Press, 1994.

——. *Mexican Americans: Leadership, Ideology, and Identity, 1930–1960*. New Haven: Yale University Press, 1989.

——. "Padres: Latino Community Priests and Social Action." In *Latino Religions and Civic Activism in the United States*. Edited by Gastón Espinosa, Virgilio Elizondo, and Jesse Miranda. New York: Oxford University Press, 2005.

Garcíagodoy, Juanita. *Digging the Days of the Dead: A Reading of Mexico's Días de Muertos*. Niwot: University Press of Colorado, 1998.

Garciadueñas, José Rojas. *Autos y coloquios del siglo XVI*. Mexico City: Universidad Nacional Autónoma de México, 1939.

García Montero, Luis. *El teatro medieval: Polémica de una inexistencia*. Granada, Spain: Editorial Don Quijote, 1984.

García-Rivera, Alex. *St. Martín de Porres: The "Little Stories" and the Semiotics of Culture*. Maryknoll, N.Y.: Orbis Books, 1995.

Gardner, Dore. *Niño Fidencio: A Heart Thrown Open*. Santa Fe: Museum of New Mexico Press, 1992.

Gardner, Richard. *¡Grito! Reies Tijerina and the Land Grant War of 1967*. Indianapolis: Bobbs-Merrill, 1970.

Garza, Isidro. "The Development of the Southern Baptist Spanish Speaking Work in California." PhD diss., Golden Gate Baptist Theological Seminary, San Francisco, 1954.

Gates, Henry Louis, Jr. *The Signifying Monkey: A Theory of Afro-American Literary Criticism*. New York: Oxford University Press, 1988.

Geertz, Clifford. *Interpretations of Culture*. New York: Basic Books, 1973.

Gerald, Geary J. *The Secularization of the California Missions*. Washington, D.C.: Catholic University of America, 1934.

Gibson, Delbert Lee. "Protestantism in Latin American Acculturation." PhD diss., University of Texas, Austin, 1959.

Giffords, Gloria K. *Mexican Folk Retablos: Masterpieces on Tin*. Tucson: University of Arizona Press, 1974.

Gilligan, Carol. *In a Different Voice*. Cambridge, Mass.: Harvard University Press, 1982.

Gillmor, Frances. "Los Pastores Number: Folk Plays of Hispanic America—Forward." *Western Folklore* 16 (1957): 229–31.

Gimbutas, Marija. *The Goddesses and Gods of Old Europe*. Berkeley: University of California Press, 1982.

———. *The Language of the Goddess*. San Francisco: Harper and Row, 1989.

Glazer, Nathan. *Ethnic Dilemmas, 1864–1982*. Cambridge, Mass.: Harvard University Press, 1983.

Goizueta, Roberto S. *Caminemos con Jesús: Toward a Hispanic/Latino Theology of Accompaniment*. Maryknoll, N.Y.: Orbis Books, 1995.

———. "U.S. Hispanic Theology and the Challenge of Pluralism." In *Frontiers of Hispanic Theology in the U.S.* Edited by Allan Figueroa Deck, S.J. Maryknoll, N.Y.: Orbis Books, 1992.

Gómez, David F. *Somos Chicanos: Strangers in Our Own Land*. Boston: Beacon Press, 1973.

Gómez-Quiñones, Juan. "On Culture." *Revista Chicano-Riqueña* 5, no. 2 (1977): 29–39.

Gonzales, Patrisia, and Roberto Rodriguez. *Gonzales/Rodriguez Uncut and Uncensored*. Berkeley, Calif.: Ethnic Studies Library Publications, 1997.

González Fernández, Fidel, Eduardo Chávez Sánchez, and José Luis Guerrero Rosado. *El encuentro de la Virgen de Guadalupe y Juan Diego*. Mexico City: Editorial Porrúa, 2001.

González, Jennifer. "Autotopographies." In *Prosthetic Territories: Politics and Hypertechnologies*. Edited by Gabriel Brahm Jr. and Mark Driscoll. Boulder: Westview Press, 1995.

———. "Siting Histories: Material Culture and the Politics of Display in the Work of Fred Wilson, Pepón Osorio, and Amalia Mesa-Bains, 1985–1995." PhD diss., History of Consciousness, University of California, Santa Cruz, September 1996.

González, J. L. "Teología de la liberación y religiosidad popular." *Páginas* 7 (1982).

González, Jorge A. *Cultura(s)*. Colima, Mexico: Universidad de Colima, 1986.

———. *Milagros en la frontera: Los mojados de la Virgen de San Juan dan gracias por su favor*. Mexico City: Secretaría de Relaciones Exteriores, 1991.

González, Justo L. "Characteristics of Latino Protestant Theology." In *Hispanic Christianity within Mainline Protestant Traditions: A Bibliography*. Edited by Paul Barton and David Maldonado Jr. Decatur, Ga.: Asociación para la Educación Teológica Hispana, 1998.

———, ed. *Each in Our Own Tongue: A History of Hispanic United Methodism*. Nashville: Abingdon Press, 1991.

———. *Mañana: Christian Theology from a Hispanic Perspective*. Nashville: Abingdon Press, 1990.

——. *The Theological Education of Hispanics*. New York: Fund for Theological Education, 1988.

González, Nancie L. *The Spanish-Americans of New Mexico: A Heritage of Pride*. Albuquerque: University of New Mexico Press, 1969.

González, Roberto O., and Michael LaVelle. *The Hispanic Catholic in the United States*. New York: Northeast Hispanic Catholic Center, 1985.

González-Wippler, Migene. "Santería: Its Dynamics and Multiple Roots." In *Enigmatic Powers: Syncretism with African and Indigenous Peoples' Religions among Latinos*. Edited by Anthony Stevens-Arroyo and Andrés Pérez y Mena. New York: Bildner Center for Western Hemisphere Studies, 1995.

——. *Santería: Faith, Rites, and Magic*. New York: Harmony Books, 1989.

Gordon, Ernest. "Revival among Spanish-Speaking." *Sunday School Times*, 24 August 1935, 550–51.

Gotay, Samuel Silva. "The Ideological Dimensions of Popular Religiosity and Cultural Identity in Puerto Rico." In *An Enduring Flame: Studies of Latino Popular Religiosity*. Vol. 1. Edited by Anthony M. Steven-Arroyo and Ana María Díaz-Stevens. New York: Bildner Center for Western Hemisphere Studies, 1994.

Grebler, Leo, Joan W. Moore, and Ralph C. Guzman. *The Mexican American People: The Nation's Second Largest Minority*. New York: Macmillan Free Press, 1970.

Greeley, Andrew M. *The American Catholic*. New York: Basic Books, 1977.

——. "Defections among Hispanics." *America*, 30 July 1988, 61–62.

——. "Defections among Hispanics (updated)." *America*, 27 September 1997, 12–13.

——. "Do Catholics Imagine Differently." In *The Catholic Myth*. New York: Charles Scribner's Sons, 1990.

Green, Judith Strupp. "The Days of the Dead in Oaxaca, Mexico: An Historical Inquiry." In *Death and Dying: Views from Many Cultures*. Edited by Richard A. Kalish. Farmingdale, N.Y.: Baywood Publishing, 1980.

Grey, Alex. *The Mission of Art*. Boston: Shambhala, 1998.

Griffith, Beatrice. *American Me*. Boston: Houghton Mifflin Company, 1947.

Griffith, James S. *Folk Saints of the Borderlands: Victims, Bandits, and Healers*. Tucson: Río Nuevo Publishers, 2003.

——. *Saints and Holy Places: A Spiritual Geography of the Pimería Alta*. Tucson: University of Arizona Press, 1992.

Grijalva, Joshua, and Dorothy Grijalva. *Heirs of the Soil*. Atlanta: Home Mission Board, Southern Baptist Convention, 1950.

——. *"A History of Mexican Baptists in Texas 1881–1981."* Dallas: Office of Language Mission, Baptist General Convention of Texas in cooperation with the Mexican Baptist Convention of Texas, 1982.

———. "The Story of Hispanic Southern Baptists." *Baptist History and Heritage* 18, no. 1 (1983): 40–47.

Griswold del Castillo, Richard. *The Los Angeles Barrio, 1850–1890: A Social History*. Berkeley: University of California Press, 1979.

Griswold del Castillo, Richard, and Richard A. García. *César Chávez: A Triumph of Spirit*. Norman: University of Oklahoma Press, 1995.

Groody, Daniel G. *Border of Death, Valley of Life: An Immigrant Journey of Heart and Spirit*. Lanham, Md.: Rowman and Littlefield Publishers, 2002.

Gruzinski, Serge. *The Conquest of Mexico: The Incorporation of Indian Societies into the Western World*. Cambridge: Polity Press, 1993.

Guerrero, Andrés G. *A Chicano Theology*. Maryknoll, N.Y.: Orbis Books, 1987.

Guillén, Miguel. *La Historia del Concilio Latino Americano de Iglesias Cristianas*. Brownsville, Tex.: Latin American Council of Christian Churches, 1982.

Gutiérrez, David G. *Walls and Mirrors: Mexican Americans, Mexican Immigrants, and the Politics of Ethnicity*. Berkeley: University of California Press, 1995.

Gutiérrez, Gustavo. *Teología de la liberación*. Lima: CEP, 1971.

———. *A Theology of Liberation: History, Politics and Salvation*. Edited and translated by Sister Caridad Inda and John Eagleson. Maryknoll, N.Y.: Orbis Books, 1988.

Gutiérrez, Ramón A. *When Jesus Came, the Corn Mothers Went Away: Marriage, Sexuality, and Power in New Mexico, 1500–1846*. Stanford, Calif.: Stanford University Press, 1991.

Hackett, Charles W. *Revolt of the Pueblo Indians of New Mexico and Otermín's Attempted Reconquest, 1680–1682*. 2 vols. Albuquerque: University of New Mexico Press, 1942.

Hall, Stuart. "Notes on Deconstructing the Popular." In *People's History and Socialist Thought*. Edited by Raphael Samuel. London: Routledge, 1981.

Hammerback, John C., and Richard J. Jensen. *The Rhetorical Career of César Chávez*. College Station: Texas A&M University Press, 1998.

Harlow, Barbara. "Sites of Struggle: Immigration, Deportation, Prison, and Exile." In *Criticism in the Borderlands: Studies in Chicano Literature, Culture, and Ideology*. Edited by Héctor Calderón and José David Saldívar. Durham: Duke University Press, 1991.

Harrison, David C. "A Survey of the Administrative and Educational Policies of the Baptist, Methodist, and Presbyterian Churches among Mexican American People in Texas." MA thesis, University of Texas, Austin, 1952.

Hartsock, Nancy. "The Feminist Standpoint: Developing the Ground for a Specifically Feminist Historical Materialism." In *Discovering Reality: Feminist Perspectives on Epistemology, Metaphysics, Methodology and Philosophy of*

Science. Edited by Sandra Harding and Merrill B. Hintikka. Dordrecht, Netherlands: D. Reidel Publishers, 1983.

Harvey, David. *The Condition of Postmodernity: An Enquiry into the Origins of Social Change*. Cambridge, Mass.: Blackwell, [1989] 1990.

Harwood, Thomas. *History of New Mexico Spanish and English Missions of the Methodist Episcopal Church from 1850 to 1910*. 2 vols. Albuquerque: El Abogado Press, 1908, 1910.

Haselden, Kyle. *Death of a Myth: New Locus for Spanish American Faith*. New York: Friendship Press, 1964.

Hassan, Ihab. *The Postmodern Turn: Essays in Postmodern Theory and Culture*. Columbus: Ohio State University Press, 1987.

Hassett, John, and Hugh Lacey. *Towards a Society That Serves Its People: The Intellectual Contribution of El Salvador's Murdered Jesuits*. Washington, D.C.: Georgetown University Press, 1991.

Hayden, Dolores. *Seven American Utopias: The Architecture of Communitarian Socialism, 1790–1975*. Cambridge, Mass.: MIT Press, 1976.

Hayes-Bautista, David. "Mexicans in Southern California." In *The California-Mexico Connection*. Edited by Abraham F. Lowenthal and Katrina Burgess. Stanford, Calif.: Stanford University Press, 1993.

Hayes-Bautista, David, Aída Hurtado, R. Burciaga Valdez, and Anthony C. R. Hernández. *No Longer a Minority: Latinos and Social Policy in California*. Los Angeles: Chicano Studies Research Center, 1992.

Haynes, Deborah J. *The Vocation of the Artist*. Cambridge: Cambridge University Press, 1997.

Hearn, Francis. "Toward a Critical Theory of Play." *Telos* 30 (1976–77): 145–60.

Henkes, Robert. *Latin American Women Artists of the United States: The Works of 33 Twentieth-Century Women*. Jefferson, N.C.: McFarland and Company, 1999.

Hennely, Alfred T. *Liberation Theology: A Documentary History*. Maryknoll, N.Y.: Orbis Books, 1990.

Hernández, Elena. "La Chicana y 'El Movimiento'" *Chicanismo* 3, no. 3 (29 April 1972): 6–8.

Hernández, José. "Hispanics Blend Diversity." In *Handbook of Hispanic Cultures in the United States: Sociology*. Edited by Felix Padilla. Houston: Arte Público Press, 1994.

Hernández-Avila, Inés. "La Mesa del Santo Niño de Atocha and the Conchero Dance Tradition of Mexico-Tenochtitlán: Religious Healing in Urban Mexico and the United States." In *Religion and Healing in America*. Edited by Linda Barnes and Susan S. Sered. New York: Oxford University Press, 2005.

Herrera-Sobek, María. "The Defiant Voice: Gender Conflict in a Mexican-Chicano *Pastorela*. *Gestos* 11 (1991): 63–77.

———. "The Mexican/Chicano Pastorela: Toward a Theory of the Evolution of a Folk Play." In *Feasts and Celebrations*. Edited by Ramón Gutiérrez and Geneviéve Fabré. Albuquerque: University of New Mexico Press, 1995.

Herrin, Judith. "Women and the Faith in Icons in Early Christianity." In *Culture, Ideology and Politics: Essays for Eric Hobshawn*. Edited by Raphael Samuel and Gareth Stedman Jones. London: Routledge, 1983.

Hinojosa, Juan-Lorenzo. "Culture, Spirituality and U.S. Hispanics." In *Frontiers of Hispanic Theology in the U.S.* Edited by Allan Figueroa Deck, SJ. Maryknoll, N.Y.: Orbis Books, 1992.

Hodges, B. A. *A History of Mexican Mission Work Conducted in Synod of Texas*. Waxahachie, Tex.: n.p. 1931.

———. *Our Mexican Missions in Texas*. Waxahachie, Tex.: n.p., 1931.

Holland, Clifton J. *The Religious Dimension of Hispanic Los Angeles: A Protestant Case Study*. South Pasadena, Calif.: William Carey Library, 1974.

Howarth, Sam, and Enrique R. Lamadrid. *Pilgrimage to Chimayó: Contemporary of a Living Tradition*. Santa Fe: Museum of New Mexico Press, 1999.

Hribar, Paul Anthony. "The Social Fasts of César Chávez." PhD diss., University of Southern California, Los Angeles, 1978.

Hull, Anne. "Selena: The Life and Death of an Icon for the New Texas." *St. Petersburg Times*, 20 October 1995, A1, 6.

Hull, Sonia Saldívar. "Feminism on the Border: From Gender Politics to Geopolitics." In *Criticism in the Borderlands: Studies in Chicano Literature, Culture, and Ideology*. Edited by Héctor Calderón and José David Saldívar. Durham: Duke University Press, 1991.

Hunt, Harry T. *The Multiplicity of Dreams: Memory, Imagination, and Consciousness*. New Haven: Yale University Press, 1989.

Hunter, Harold D., and Cecil M. Robeck Jr. *The Azusa Street Revival and Its Legacy*. Cleveland, Tenn.: Pathway Press, 2006.

Hurtado, Juan. *An Attitudinal Study of Social Distance between the Mexican American and the Church*. San Antonio: Mexican American Cultural Center, 1975.

Hymer, Evangeline. "A Study of the Social Attitudes of Adult Mexican Immigrants in Los Angeles and Vicinity." MA thesis, University of Southern California, Los Angeles, 1923.

Hynek, J. Allen. *The UFO Experience: A Scientific Inquiry*. New York: Ballantine Books, 1974.

Igo, John. *Los Pastores: An Annotated Bibliography with an Introduction*. San Antonio: San Antonio College Library, 1967.

Isasi-Díaz, Ada María. "The Cultural Identity of the Latina Woman: The Cross-Disciplinary Perspective of Mujerista Theology." In *Old Masks, New Faces: Religion and Latino Identities*. Edited by Anthony M. Stevens-Arroyo and Gilbert R. Cadena. New York: Bildner Center for Western Hemisphere Studies, 1995.

——. *En la Lucha, In the Struggle: Elaborating a Mujerista Theology*. Minneapolis: Fortress Press, [1993] 2004.

——. *La Lucha Continues: Mujerista Theology*. Maryknoll, N.Y.: Orbis Books, 2004.

——. *Mujerista Theology: A Theology for the Twenty-first Century*. Maryknoll, N.Y.: Orbis Books, 1996.

Isasi-Díaz, Ada María, and Yolanda Tarango. *Hispanic Women: Prophetic Voice in the Church*. Minneapolis: Fortress Press, 1988.

Jameson, Fredric. *The Political Unconscious*. Ithaca, N.Y.: Cornell University Press, 1981.

Jeffrey, David. "Arizona's Suburbs of the Sun." *National Geographic* 152, no. 4 (October 1977): 487–517.

Jenkinson, Michael. *Tijerina: Land Grant Conflict in New Mexico*. Albuquerque: Paisano Press, 1968.

John Paul II, Pope. Address to the Fiftieth General Assembly of the United Nations, New York, 5 October 1996, 14. *Insegnamenti* 18, no. 2 (1995): 741.

Johnson, J. B. "The Allelujahs: A Religious Cult in Northern New Mexico." *Southwest Review of the World* (July 1923): 131–39.

Jones, Arthur. "Millions Reaped What César Chávez Sowed." *National Catholic Reporter*, 7 May 1993, 7.

Jones, Robert C. *The Religious Life of the Mexican in Chicago*. Self-published report, Chicago, 1929.

Jones, Robert C., and Louis R. Wilson. *The Mexican in Chicago*. Chicago: Comity Commission of the Chicago Church Federation, 1931.

Jones Walker, Randi. *Protestantism in the Sangre de Cristos, 1850–1920*. Albuquerque: University of New Mexico Press, 1991.

Kane, Connie M., Ronald R., Pamela Mellen, and Italo Samano. "Differences in the Manifest Dream Content of Mexican, Mexican American, and Anglo American College Women: A Research Note." *Hispanic Journal of Behavioral Sciences* 15, no. 1 (February 1993): 134–39.

Kay, Elizabeth. *Chimayó Valley Traditions*. Santa Fe, N. Mex.: Ancient City Press, 1987.

Keating, Ann Louise. "Myth Smashers, Myth Makers: (Re)Visionary Techniques in the Works of Paula Gunn Allen, Gloria Anzaldúa, and Audre Lorde." In *Critical Essays: Gay and Lesbian Writers of Color*. Edited by Emmanuel S. Nelson. New York: Haworth Press, 1993.

Kelsey, Morton T. *Dreams: The Dark Speech of the Spirit: A Christian Interpretation*. Garden City, N.J.: Doubleday, 1968.

——. *Tongue Speaking: An Experiment in Spiritual Experience*. New York: Waymark Books, 1968.

Kessler, Clive. *Islam and Politics in a Malay State*. Ithaca, N.Y.: Cornell University Press, 1978.

Kibbe, Pauline R. *Latin Americans in Texas*. Albuquerque: University of New Mexico, 1946.

Kienle, John E. "Housing Conditions among the Mexican Population of Los Angeles." MA thesis, University of Southern California, Los Angeles, 1912.

Kiev, Ari. *Curanderismo: Mexican-American Folk Psychiatry*. New York: Free Press, 1968.

Klor de Alva, Jorge. "Aztlán, Borinquen and Hispanic Nationalism in the United States." In *Aztlán: Essays on the Chicano Homeland*. Edited by Rodolfo Anaya and Francisco Lomelí. Albuquerque: University of New Mexico Press, 1991.

——. "Aztec Spirituality and Nahuatized Christianity." In *South and Meso-American Native Spirituality*. Edited by Gary H. Gossen with Miguel León-Portillo. New York: Crossroad Publishing Company, 1993.

——. "California Chicano Literature and Pre-Columbian Motifs: Foil and Fetish." *Confluencia: Revista Hispánica de Cultura y Literatura* 1(1986): 18–26.

——. "Postcolonialization of the (Latin) American Experience: A Reconsideration of 'Colonialism,' 'Postcolonialism,' and 'Mestizaje.'" In *After Colonialism*. Edited by Gyan Prakash. Princeton: Princeton University Press, 1995.

Knowlton, Clark. "Violence in New Mexico: A Sociological Perspective." *California Law Review* 58 (1970): 1053–84.

Köhler, Angelika. "The New World Man: Magical Realism in Rudolfo Anaya's *Bless Me, Ultima*." In *U.S. Latino Literatures and Cultures: Transnational Perspectives*. Edited by Francisco A. Lomelí and Karin Ikas. Heidelberg, Germany: Universitatsverlag C. Winter, 2000.

Kolve, V. A. *Los Pastores (The Shepherds): An Old California Christmas Play*. Translated by María López de Louther. Hollywood, Calif.: Homer H. Boelter, 1953.

Konwlton, Clark. "Violence in New Mexico: A Sociological Perspective." *California Law Review* 58 (1970): 1054–84.

Kosmin, Barry, and Seymour Lachman, *One Nation under God: Religion in Contemporary Society*. New York: Harmony Books, 1993.

Lafaye, Jacques. *Quetzalcóatl and Guadalupe*. Chicago: University of Chicago Press, 1976.

Lara-Braud, Jorge. "Our Spanish-American Neighbors." *The Christian Century* 85, no. 2 (1968): 43–45.

Lawrence, Una Roberts. *Winning the Border: Baptist Missions among the Spanish-Speaking Peoples of the Border*. Atlanta: Home Mission Board, Southern Baptist Convention, 1935.

Leach, Edmund. *Culture and Communication*. London: Cambridge University Press, 1976.

Leddy, Betty. "La Llorona in Southern Arizona." *Perspectives in Mexican American Studies* 1 (1988): 272–77.

Lee, Chu-Fu, and Raymond H. Potvin. "A Demographic Profile of U.S. Hispanics." In *Strangers and Aliens No Longer*. Washington, D.C.: USCC Publications, 1993.

León, Luis D. "César Chávez and Mexican American Civil Religion." In *Latino Religions and Civic Activism in the United States*. Edited by Gastón Espinosa, Virgilio Elizondo, and Jesse Miranda. New York: Oxford University Press, 2005.

———. "Foreword." In *Curanderismo: Mexican American Folk Healing*. 2nd ed. By Robert T. Trotter II and Juan Antonio Chavira. Athens: University of Georgia Press, 1997.

———. *La Llorona's Children: Religion, Life, and Death in the U.S.-Mexican Borderlands*. Berkeley: University of California Press, 2004.

———. "'Soy una Curandera y Soy una Católica': Poetics of a Mexican Healing Tradition." In *Horizons of the Sacred: Mexican Traditions in U.S. Catholicism*. Edited by Timothy Matovina and Gary Riebe-Estrella, SVD (Society of Divine Word). Ithaca, N.Y.: Cornell University Press, 2002.

León-Portilla, Miguel. *Aztec Thought and Culture: A Study of the Ancient Náhuatl Mind*. Translated by Jack Emory Davis. Norman: University of Oklahoma Press, 1963.

———. *Broken Spears: The Aztec Account of the Conquest of Mexico*. Boston: Beacon Press, 1992.

———. *Endangered Cultures*. Dallas: Southern Methodist University Press, 1990.

———. *Los antiguos mexicanos a través de sus crónicas y cantares*. Mexico City: Fondo de Cultura Económica, [1961] 1988.

———. *Tonantzin Guadalupe: Pensamiento náhuatl y mensaje cristiano en el "Nican mopohua."* Mexico City: El Colegio Nacional, 2000.

León-Portilla, Miguel, ed. *Native Mesoamerican Spirituality: Ancient Myths, Discourses, Stories, Doctrines, Hymns, Poems from the Aztec, Yucatec, Quiché-Maya and Other Sacred Traditions*. Translated by Miguel León-Portilla, J. O. Arthur Anderson, Charles E. Dibble, and Munro S. Edmonson. Ramsey, N.J.: Paulist Press, 1980.

Levine, Daniel H. "Liberation Theology, Base Communities, and the Pattern of Change in Latin America." In *Popular Voices in Catholicism*. Princeton: Princeton University Press, 1992.

Levy, Jacques E. *César Chávez: Autobiography of La Causa*. New York: Norton, 1975.

Lewis, Gordon K. *Puerto Rico: Freedom and Power in the Caribbean*. New York: Monthly Review Press, 1963.

Limón, José E. "Carne, Carnales, and the Carnivalesque: Bakhtinian Batos, Disorder, and Narrative Discourses." *American Ethnologist* 16, no. 3 (1989): 471–86.

——. *Dancing with the Devil: Society and Cultural Poetics in Mexican-American South Texas*. Madison: University of Wisconsin Press, 1994.

——. "Western Marxism and Folklore: A Critical Introduction." *Journal of American Folklore* 96 (1983): 34–52.

Lindholm, Charles. *Charisma*. Cambridge, Mass.: Basil Blackwell, 1990.

Lindsay, Arturo, ed. *Santería Aesthetics in Contemporary Latin American Art*. Washington, D.C.: Smithsonian Institution Press, 1996.

Lloyd-Moffett, Stephen R. "The Mysticism and Social Action of César Chávez." In *Latino Religions and Civic Activism in the United States*. Edited by Gastón Espinosa, Virgilio Elizondo, and Jesse Miranda. New York: Oxford University Press, 2005.

London, Joan, and Henry Anderson. *So Shall Ye Reap*. New York: Crowel, 1970.

Long, Charles H. *Significations: Signs, Symbols, and Images in the Interpretation of Religion*. Philadelphia: Fortress Press, 1986.

López, Abundio L., and Rosa López. "Spanish Receive the Pentecost." *Apostolic Faith* (October 1906).

López Austin, Alfredo. *Tamoanchan, Tlalocanh: Places of Mist*. Niwot: University Press of Colorado, 1997.

López-Medina, Sylvia. *Cantora*. Albuquerque: University of New Mexico Press, 1992.

Loya, Gloria Inés. "The Hispanic Woman: Pasionaria and Pastora in the Hispanic Community." In *Frontiers of Hispanic Theology in the United States*. Edited by Allan Figueroa Deck, SJ. Maryknoll, N.Y.: Orbis Books, 1992.

Lucero-White, Aurora, ed. "Coloquio de los Pastores." In *Literary Folklore of the Hispanic Southwest*. San Antonio: Naylor Company, 1953.

——. *The Folklore of New Mexico*. Santa Fe, N.Mex.: Seton Village Press, 1947.

——. "Los Pastores de Las Vegas." MA thesis, New Mexico Normal University, Las Vegas, 1932.

Luckingham, Bradford. *Minorities in Phoenix: A Profile of Mexican American, Chinese American, and African American Communities, 1860–1992*. Tucson: University of Arizona Press, 1994.

Lugones, María. "On Borderlands / La Frontera: An Interpretive Essay." *Hypatia* 7, no. 4 (fall 1992): 31–37.

Luzbetak, Louis J. *The Church and Cultures*. Maryknoll, N.Y.: Orbis Books, 1988.

Machado, Daisy L. *Of Borders and Margins: Hispanic Disciples in Texas, 1888–1945*. New York: Oxford University Press, 2003.

——. "The Writing of Religious History in the United States: A Critical Assessment." In *Hispanic Christianity within Mainline Protestant Traditions: A Bibliography*. Edited by Paul Barton and David Maldonado Jr. Decatur, Ga.: Asociación para la Educación Teológica Hispana, 1998.

Macklin, June. "Curanderismo and Espiritismo: Complementary Approaches to Traditional Health Services." In *The Chicano Experience*. Edited by Stanley A. West and June Macklin. Boulder: Westview Press, 1979.

Madsen, Claudia. *A Study of Change in Mexican Folk Medicine*. New Orleans: Tulane University Middle American Research Institute, 1965.

Madsen, William. *Mexican Americans of South Texas*. New York: Harcourt School, 1973.

Madsen, William, and Claudia Madsen. *A Guide to Mexican Witchcraft*. Claremont, Calif.: Ocelot Press, [1972] 1977.

Maduro, Otto A. *Religion and Social Conflicts*. Maryknoll, N.Y.: Orbis Books, 1982.

Maldonado, David J., ed. *Protestantes/Protestants: Hispanic Christianity within Mainline Traditions*. Nashville: Abingdon Press, 1999.

Malony, H. Newton, and A. Adams Lovekin. *Glossolalia: Behavioral Science Perspectives on Speaking in Tongues*. New York: Oxford University Press, 1985.

Marcuse, Herbert. "On the Concept of Labor." *Telos* 16 (summer 1973): 14.

María y Campos, Armando de, ed. *Pastorelas mexicanas*. Mexico City: Editorial Diana, 1985.

Marie, Sister Joseph, IHM. "The Role of the Church and the Folk in the Development of the Early Drama in New Mexico." PhD diss., University of Pennsylvania [English], Philadelphia, 1948.

Martell-Ortero, Loida. "Women Doing Theology: Una Perspectiva Evangélica." *Apuntes* 14 (1994): 67–85.

Martínez, Demetria. *Mother Tongue*. Tempe, Ariz.: Bilingual Press, 1994.

Matovina, Timothy. *Tejano Religion and Ethnicity: San Antonio, 1821–1860*. Austin: University of Texas Press, 1995.

Matovina, Timothy, and Gerald E. Poyo, eds. *¡Presente! U.S. Latino Catholics from Colonial Origins to the Present*. Maryknoll, N.Y.: Orbis Books, 2000.

Matovina, Timothy, and Gary Riebe-Estrella svd (Society of Divine Word), eds. *Horizons of the Sacred: Mexican Traditions in U.S. Catholicism*. Ithaca, N.Y.: Cornell University Press, 2002.

Matthiessen, Peter. *Sal Si Puedes: César Chávez and the New American Revolution*. New York: Random House, 1969.

Mauss, Marcel. *The Gift: The Form and Reason for Exchange in Archaic Societies*. New York: W.W. Norton, 1990.

Mawn, Benedict J. "Testing the Spirits: An Empirical Search for the Socioeconomic Situational Roots of the Catholic Pentecostal Religious Experience." PhD diss., Boston University, 1975.

McCarthy Brown, Karen. *Mama Lola: A Vodou Priestess in Brooklyn*. Berkeley: University of California Press, 1991.

McCombs, Vernon M. *From over the Border: A Study of the Mexican in the United States*. New York: Council for Women for Home Missions and Missionary Education Movement, 1925.

McCracken, Ellen. "Remapping Religious Space: Orthodox and Non-Orthodox Religious Culture." In *New Latina Narrative: The Feminine Space of Postmodern Ethnicity*. Tucson: University of Arizona Press, 1991.

McDannell, Colleen. *Material Christianity: Religion and Popular Culture in America*. New Haven: Yale University Press, 1995.

McEuen, William. "A Survey of the Mexicans in Los Angeles." MA thesis, University of Southern California, Los Angeles, 1914.

McGowan, John. *Postmodernism and Its Critics*. Ithaca, N.Y.: Cornell University Press, 1991.

McGuire, Meredith. "Linking Theory and Methodology for the Study of Latino Religiosity in the United States Context." In *An Enduring Flame: Studies on Latino Popular Religiosity*. Edited by Anthony M. Stevens-Arroyo and Ana María Díaz-Stevens, eds. New York: Bildner Center for Western Hemisphere Studies, 1994.

McLean, Robert N. "Getting God Counted among the Mexicans." *Missionary Review of the World* (May 1923): 363.

———. *The Northern Mexican*. New York: Home Mission Council, 1930.

McLemore, David. "A Meeting Place with God." *San Jose Mercury News*, 20 April 1996, 1E.

McNamara, Patrick H. "Assumptions, Theories and Methods in the Study of Latino Religion after 25 Years." In *Old Masks, New Faces: Religion and Latino Identities*. Edited by Anthony M. Stevens-Arroyo and Gilbert R. Cadena. New York: Bildner Center for Western Hemisphere Studies, 1995.

———. "Bishops, Priests and Prophecy: A Study in the Sociology of Religious Protest." PhD diss., University of California, Los Angeles, 1968.

———. "Catholicism, Assimilation and the Chicano Movement: Los Angeles as a Case Study." In *Chicanos and Native Americans*. Edited by Rodolfo O. de la Garza, Z. Anthony Kruszewski, and Tomás A. Arciniega. Englewood Cliffs, N.J.: Prentice Hall, 1973.

———. "Dynamics of the Catholic Church from Pastoral to Social Concerns." In *The Mexican American People: The Nation's Second Largest Minority*. Edited by Leo Grebler, Joan W. Moore, and Ralph C. Guzman. New York: Macmillan Free Press, 1970.

McNeil, Norman. *Curanderos of South Texas*. Dallas: Southern Methodist University, 1959.

Medina, Lara. "Broadening the Discourse at the Theological Table: An Overview of Latino Theology 1968–1993." *Latino Studies Journal* 5, no. 3 (September 1993): 10–36.

———. "Communicating with the Dead: Spiritual and Cultural Healing in Chicano/a Communities." In *Religion and Healing in America*. Edited by Linda Barnes and Susan S. Sered. New York: Oxford University Press, 2005.

———. "Los Espíritus Siguen Hablando: Chicana Spiritualities." In *Living Chicana Theory*. Edited by Carla Trujillo. Berkeley, Calif.: Third Woman Press, 1998.

Medina, Lara, and Gilbert R. Cadena. "Días de los Muertos: Public Ritual, Community Renewal, and Popular Religion in Los Angeles." In *Horizons of the Sacred: Mexican Catholic Traditions in U.S. Catholicism*. Edited by Timothy Matovina and Gary Riebe-Estrella, SVD. Ithaca, N.Y.: Cornell University Press, 2002.

Meinig, D. W. *Southwest: Three Peoples in Geographical Change, 1600–1970*. New York: Oxford University Press, 1971.

Mellaart, James. *Cätäl Huyuk: A Neolithic Town in Anatolia*. New York: McGraw Hill, 1967.

Mesa-Bains, Amalia. "ALTARMAKERS: The Historic Mediators." In *Offerings: The Altar Show*. Venice, Calif.: Social and Public Arts Resource Center, 1984.

———. *Ceremony of Memory*. Santa Fe, N.Mex.: Center for Contemporary Arts of Santa Fe, 1988.

———. "Curatorial Statement." In *Ceremony of Spirit: Nature and Memory in Contemporary Latino Art*. San Francisco: Mexican Museum, 1993.

———. "*Domesticana*: The Sensibility of Chicana Rasquache." In *Distant Relations/Cercanías Distantes/Clann I Gcéin: Chicano, Irish, Mexican Art and Critical Writing*. Edited by Trisha Ziff. Santa Monica, Calif.: Smart Art Press, 1995.

Mignolo, Walter. *The Darker Side of the Renaissance: Literacy, Territoriality, and Colonization*. Ann Arbor: University of Michigan Press, 1995.

Míguez Bonino, José. *Doing Theology in a Revolutionary Situation.* Philadelphia: Fortress Press, 1975.

Miller, Rosanna. "The Peralta Land Grant." *Western Association of Map Libraries* 22, no. 2 (March 1991): 121–26.

Mills, George. *The People of the Saints.* Colorado Springs: Taylor Museum, Colorado Springs Fine Art Center, n.d.

Mitchell, Don. *The Lie of the Land: Migrant Workers and the California Landscape.* Minneapolis: University of Minnesota, 1996.

Mitchell, Rick. "Selena: In Life, She Was the Queen of *Tejano* Music. In Death, the 23-year-Old Singer Is Becoming a Legend." *Houston Chronicle,* 21 May 1995, 6.

Mohanty, Chandra Talpade. "Feminist Encounters: Locating the Politics of Experience." *Copyright* 1 (1987): 30–44.

Montejano, David. *Anglos and Mexicans in the Making of Texas, 1836–1986.* Austin: University of Texas Press, 1987.

Montilla, Aida Negrón. *Americanization in Puerto Rico and the Public School System, 1900–1930.* Río Piedras, Puerto Rico: Editorial Edil, 1970.

Moore, Joan W. "Protestants and Mexicans." In *The Mexican American People: The Nation's Second Largest Minority.* Edited by Leo Grebler, Joan W. Moore, and Ralph C. Guzman. New York: Macmillan Free Press, 1970.

Morales, Adam. *American Baptists with a Spanish Accent.* Los Angeles: Judson Press, 1964.

Morales, Alejandro. "Expanding the Meaning of Chicano Cinema: Yo Soy Chicano, Raíces de Sangre, Seguin." *Bilingual Review/La Revista Bilingüe* 10, no. 2–3 (May–December 1983): 121–37.

Morgan, David. *Visual Piety: A History and Theory of Popular Religious Images.* Berkeley: University of California Press, 1998.

Morner, Magnus. *The Expulsion of the Jesuits from Latin America.* New York: Alfred A. Knopf, 1965.

Morrison, Susan Shumate. "Mexico's Day of the Dead in San Francisco, California: A Study of Continuity and Change in a Popular Religious Festival." PhD diss., Graduate Theological Union, Berkeley, Calif., 1992.

Mosquera, Gerardo, ed. *Beyond the Fantastic: Contemporary Art Criticism from Latin America.* Cambridge, Mass., and London: MIT Press, 1996.

Muñoz, Carlos, Jr., *Youth, Identity, Power: The Chicano Movement.* London: Verso Press, 1989.

Nabokov, Peter. *Tijerina and the Courthouse Raid.* Berkeley, Calif.: Ramparts Press, 1969.

Nandy, Ashis. *The Intimate Enemy: The Loss and Recovery of Self under Colonialism.* New York: Oxford University Press, 1983.

Nañez, Alfredo. *History of the Rio Grande Conference of the United Methodist Church*. Dallas: Bridwell Library, Southern Methodist University, 1980.

Nañez, Clotilde. "Hispanic Clergy Wives: Their Contribution to United Methodism in the Southwest, Later Nineteenth Century to the Present." In *Women in New Worlds: Historical Perspectives on the Wesleyan Tradition*. Edited by Hilah F. Thomas and Rosemary Skinner Keller. Nashville: Abingdon Press, 1981.

National Catholic Welfare Conference. *The Spanish-Speaking of the Southwest and West*. Washington, D.C.: National Catholic Welfare Conference, 1943.

Nickel, Thomas R. *Azusa Street Outpouring: As Told to Me by Those Who Were There*. Hanford, Calif.: Great Commission International, 1956 [3rd ed., 1986].

Nieto, Leo D. "The Chicano Movement and the Churches in the United States." *Perkins Journal* 29, no. 1 (1975): 32–41.

Nutini, Hugo. "Pre-Hispanic Component of the Syncretic Cult of the Dead." *Ethnology* 27 (January 1988): 57–78.

———. *Todos Santos in Rural Tlaxcala*. Princeton: Princeton University Press, 1988.

O'Brien, Mary. *The Politics of Reproduction*. London: Routledge and Kegan Paul, 1981.

Ochs, Carol. *Women and Spirituality*. Totowa, N.J.: Rowman and Allanhead, 1983.

Offen, Karen. "Defining Feminism: A Comparative Historical Approach." *Signs* 14, no. 1 (autumn 1988): 135–36, 139, 154–55.

Officer, James E. "Sodalities and Systemic Linkage: The Joining Habits of Urban Mexican Americans." PhD diss., University of Arizona, Tucson, 1964.

Official Catholic Directory. New York: P. J. Kennedy and Sons, 1997.

Oktavec, Eileen. *Answered Prayers: Miracles and Milagros along the Border*. Tucson: University of Arizona Press, 1995.

Olalquiaga, Celeste. *Megalopolis: Contemporary Cultural Sensibilities*. Minneapolis: University of Minnesota Press, 1992.

Orozco, E. C. *Republican Protestantism in Aztlán*. Glendale, Calif.: Petereins Press, 1981.

Orr, David G. *Roman Domestic Religion: A Study of Roman Household Deities and Their Shrines at Pompeii and Herculaneum*. PhD diss., University of Maryland, Baltimore, 1972.

Ortegón, Samuel M. "Mexican Religious Population of Los Angeles." MA thesis, University of Southern California, Los Angeles, 1932.

———. "Religious Thought and Practice among Mexican Baptists of the United States, 1900–1947." PhD diss., University of Southern California, Los Angeles, 1950.

Ortiz, Fernando. *Cuban Counterpoint: Tobacco and Sugar*. New York: Knopf, 1947.

Ortiz Cofer, Judith. *The Line of the Sun*. Athens: University of Georgia, 1989.

Ortiz de Montellano, Bernard. *Aztec Health and Medicine*. New Brunswick, N.J.: Rutgers University Press, 1990.

Osterberg, Arthur G. "Oral History of the Life of Arthur G. Osterberg and the Azusa Street Revival," interview (transcribed) by Jerry Jensen and Jonathan Perkins, Assemblies of God Archives, 1996.

Ouspensky, Leonid. "Icon," in *New Catholic Encyclopedia*, vol. 1. New York: McGraw-Hill, 1967.

Oxnam, Bromley G. "The Mexican in Los Angeles from the Standpoint of Religious Forces of the City." *Annals of the American Academy* 93 (1921): 130–33.

——. *The Mexican in Los Angeles: Los Angeles City Survey*. Los Angeles: Inter-Church World Movement of North America, 1920.

Otto, Rudolf. *Private Myths: Dreams and Dreaming*. Cambridge, Mass.: Harvard University Press, 1995.

Paden, William E. "A New Comparativism: Reply to Panelists." *Method and Theory in the Study of Religion* B-1 (1996): 37–49.

Padgett, Jim. "Border Beat." *TIME*, 24 March 1997.

Padilla, Felix. *Latino Ethnic Consciousness: The Case of Mexican Americans and Puerto Ricans in Chicago*. Notre Dame, Ind.: University of Notre Dame Press, 1985.

Palomar, Margarita. *Pastorelas*. Guadalajara, Mexico: Editorial Conexión Gráfica, 1989.

Paredes, Américo. "Estados Unidos, México y el machismo." *Journal of Inter-American Studies* 9, no. 1(1966): 65–84.

——. *With His Pistol in His Hand*. Austin: University of Texas Press, 1958.

Park, Yong Hak. "A Study of the Methodist Mexican Mission in Dallas." MA thesis, Southern Methodist University, Dallas, 1936.

Patoski, Joe Nick. *Selena: Como la flor*. New York: Boulevard Books, 1997.

Paz, Octavio. *El laberinto de la soledad*. Mexico City: Fondo de Cultural Económica, 1959.

——. "Sons of La Malinche." In *The Labyrinth of Solitude: Life and Thought in Mexico*. Translated by Lysander Kemp. New York: Grove, 1961.

Pearce, T. M. "The New Mexican Shepherds' Play." *Western Folklore* 15 (1956): 77–88.

Pellarolo's, Silvia. "Reviv/s/ing Selena." *Latin American Issues*, no. 14 (1998): 51–76.

Pelton, Robert. "Not-to-Be-Contradicted." In *The Trickster in West Africa: A Study of Mythic Irony and Sacred Delight*. Berkeley: University of California Press, 1980.

Peña, Manuel. *The Texas-Mexican Conjunto: History of a Working-Class Music.* Austin: University of Texas Press, 1985.

Pépin, Jean. "Logos." In *The Encyclopedia of Religion.* Editor-in-chief, Mircea Eliade. Vol. 9. New York: Macmillan, 1987.

Pérez, Laura E. *Chicana Art: The Politics of Spiritual and Aesthetic Altarities.* Durham: Duke University Press, 2007.

———. "Writing on the Social Body: Dresses and Body Ornamentation in Contemporary Chicana Art." In *Decolonial Voices: Chicana and Chicano Cultural Studies in the 21st Century.* Edited by Arturo J. Aldama and Naomi Quiñónez. Bloomington: Indiana University Press, 2002.

———. "El Desorden, Nationalism, and Chicana/o Aesthetics." In *Between Woman and Nation: Nationalisms, Transnational Feminisms, and the State.* Edited by Caren Kaplan, Norma Alarcón, and Minoo Moallem. Durham: Duke University Press, 1999.

———. "Spirit Glyphs: Reimagining Art and Artist in the Work of Chicana *Tlamatinime.*" *Modern Fiction Studies* 44, no. 1 (spring 1998): 36–76.

"Pinal County Arizona: An Industrial and Commercial Summary." Florence, Ariz.: Pinal County Development Board, 1957.

Pitzer, Donald E. *America's Communal Utopias.* Chapel Hill: University of North Carolina, 1997.

Plaskow, Judith, and Carol P. Christ, eds. *Weaving the Visions: New Patterns in Feminist Spirituality.* New York: Harper Collins, 1989.

Polk, Patrick A., Michael Owen Jones, Claudia J. Hernández, and Reyna C. Ronelli. "Miraculous Migrants to the City of Angels: Perceptions of El Santo Niño de Atocha and San Simón as Sources of Health and Healing." In *Religion and Healing in America.* Edited by Linda Barnes and Susan S. Sered. New York: Oxford University Press, 2005.

Ponce, Mary Helen. *Hoyt Street: An Autobiography.* Albuquerque: University of New Mexico Press, 1993.

———. *The Wedding.* Houston: Arte Público, 1989.

Poole, Stafford. *Our Lady of Guadalupe: The Origins and Sources of a Mexican National Symbol, 1531–1797.* Tucson: University of Arizona Press, 1995.

Porte, Philip W., and Fred E. Lukermann. "The Geography of Utopia." In *Geographies of the Mind: Essays in Historical Geography.* New York: Oxford University Press, 1976.

Pred, Allan. *Lost Words, Lost Worlds: Modernity and the Language of Everyday Life in Late Nineteenth-Century Stockholm.* Cambridge: Cambridge University Press, 1990.

Preminger, Alex, ed. *Princeton Encyclopedia of Poetry and Poetics.* Princeton: Princeton University Press, 1965.

Privett, Stephen A., SJ. *The United States Catholic Church and Its Hispanic Members: The Pastoral Vision of Archbishop Robert E. Lucey*. San Antonio: Trinity University Press, 1988.

Pulido, Alberto. "Are You an Emissary of Jesus Christ? Justice, the Catholic Church, and the Chicano Movement." *Explorations in Ethnic Studies* 14, no. 1 (January 1991): 17–34.

———. "Searching for the Sacred: Conflict and Struggle for Mexican Catholics in the Roman Catholic Diocese of San Diego, 1936–1941." *Latino Studies Journal* 5, no. 3 (September 1994): 37–59.

———. *The Sacred World of the Penitentes*. Washington, D.C.: Smithsonian Institution Press, 2000.

Quevedo, Eduardo, Jr. "The Catholic Church in America." *Con Safos* (fall 1968): 11.

Quinn, Anthony. *The Original Sin: A Self Portrait*. Boston: Little, Brown and Company, 1972.

Quoniam, Stephane. "A Painter, Geographer of Arizona." *Environment and Planning D: Society and Space* 6 (1988): 3–14.

Rael, Juan B. *The Sources and Diffusion of the Mexican Shepherds' Plays*. Guadalajara: Librería La Joyita, 1965.

Ramírez, Sarah. "Borders, Feminism, and Spirituality: Movements in Chicana Aesthetic Revisioning." In *Decolonial Voices: Chicana and Chicano Cultural Studies in the 21st Century*. Edited by Arturo J. Aldama and Naomi H. Quiñonez. Bloomington: Indiana University Press, 2002.

Ramírez de Arellano, Annette B., and Conrad Seipp. *Colonialism, Catholicism, and Contraception: A History of Birth Control in Puerto Rico*. Chapel Hill: University of North Carolina Press, 1983.

Ranaghan, Kevin, and Dorothy Ranaghan. *Catholic Pentecostals*. New York: Paulist Press, 1969.

Rankin, Melinda. *Twenty Years among the Mexicans: A Narrative of Missionary Labor*. Cincinnati: Chase and Hall Publishers, 1875.

Reader in Comparative Religion: An Anthropological Approach. 2nd ed., New York: Harper and Row, 1965.

Rechy, John. *The Miraculous Day of Amalia Gómez*. New York: Arcade Publishers, 1991.

Reed-Bouley, Jennifer. "Guiding Moral Action: A Study of the United Farm Workers' Use of Catholic Social Teaching and Religious Symbols." PhD diss., Loyola University, Chicago, 1998.

Renard González, Barbara. "¿Santa Selena?" *Latina*, April–May 1997, 83.

Rendon, Armando. *Chicano Manifesto*. New York: Collier Books, 1971.

"Rev. F. Olazábal, Evangelist Here." *New York Times*, 12 June 1937.

Revilla-Vásquez, Catherine. "Thank You Selena." *Hispanic* 8, no. 4 (May): 96.

Reyes, Ruben. "Prolegomena to Chicano Theology." D.Min. project, Claremont School of Theology, Claremont, Calif., 1974.

Ricard, Robert. *The Spiritual Conquest of Mexico*. Translated by Leslie Byrd Simpson. Berkeley: University of California Press, 1966.

Richard, Pablo, and Diego Irarrázaval. *Religión y política en América Central: Hacia una nueva interpretación de la religiosidad popular*. San José, Costa Rica: Colección Centroamérica, Departamento Ecuménico de Investigaciones, 1981.

Riley, Michael. "Mexican American Shrines in Southern Arizona." *Journal of the Southwest* (summer 1992): 206–31.

Ríos, Elizabeth. "'The Ladies are Warriors': Latina Pentecostalism and Faith-Based Activism in New York City." In *Latino Religions and Civic Activism in the United States*. Edited by Gastón Espinosa, Virgilio Elizondo, and Jesse Miranda. New York: Oxford University Press, 2005.

Ríos, José Muro. *Pastorela de Amozochil*. Guadalajara, Mexico: Gobierno del Estado de Jalisco, 1985.

Rivera, Tomás. *And the Earth Did Not Part*. Berkeley, Calif.: Quinto Sol, 1971.

Robb, J. D. "The Music of *Los Pastores*." *Western Folklore* 16 (1957): 263–80.

Robe, Stanley L. *Coloquio de Los Pastores from Jalisco, México*. Berkeley: University of California Press, 1954.

——. "The Relationship of *Los Pastores* to other Spanish-American Folk Drama." *Western Folklore* 16 (1957): 281–89.

Rodriguez, Jeanette. *Our Lady of Guadalupe: Faith and Empowerment among Mexican-American Women*. Austin: University of Texas Press, 1994.

——. *Stories We Live: Cuentos que vivimos*. New York: Paulist Press, 1996.

Rodríguez, José David, and Loida I. Martell-Otero, eds. *Teología en Conjunto: A Collaborative Hispanic Protestant Theology*. Louisville, Ky.: Westminster, 1997.

Rodríguez, Richard. *Hunger of Memory: The Education of Richard Rodríguez*. Boston: D. R. Godine, 1981.

Rodríguez-Díaz, Daniel R., and David Cortés-Fuentes. *Hidden Stories: Unveiling the History of the Latino Church*. Decatur, Ga.: AETH (Asociación para la Educación Teológica Hispana), 1994.

Roeder, Beatrice. *Chicano Folk Medicine from Los Angeles, California*. Berkeley: University of California Press, 1988.

Rojas, José Vicente. *José Vicente Rojas: God Found Me in Los Angeles*. Hagerstown, Md.: Review and Herald Publishing Association, 1999.

Roll, Samuel. "Chicano Dreams: Investigations in Cross-cultural Research." Southwest Hispanic Research Institute, University of New Mexico, fall 1984.

Roll, Samuel, Richard Hinton, and Michael Glazer. "Dreams of Death: Mexican-Americans vs. Anglo Americans." *Interamerican Journal of Psychology* 8, nos. 1–2 (1974): 111–15.

Romano, Octavio I. "Don Pedrito Jaramillo: The Emergence of a Mexican-American Folk-Saint." PhD diss., University of California, Berkeley, 1964.

———. *Voices: Readings from El Grito*. Berkeley, Calif.: Quinto Sol, 1973.

Romero, Juan, and Moises Sandoval. *Reluctant Dawn: Historia del Padre A. J. Martínez, Cura de Taos*. San Antonio: Mexican-American Cultural Center Press, 1976.

Romero Salinas, Joel. *La pastorela mexicana: Origen y evolución*. Mexico City: SEP Cultura Fondo Nacional para el Fomento de las Artesanías Fonart, 1984.

Romo, Ricardo. *East Los Angeles: History of a Barrio*. Austin: University of Texas Press, 1983.

Roof, Wade Clark. *A Generation of Seekers: The Spiritual Journeys of the Baby Boom Generation*. San Francisco: HarperSanFrancisco, 1993 [1998].

Rosaldo, Renato. *Culture and Truth: The Remaking of Social Analysis*. Boston: Beacon Press, 1989.

Rosales, Arturo F. *¡Chicano! The History of the Mexican American Civil Rights Movement*. Houston: Arte Público Press, 1997.

———. *Testimonio: A Documentary History of the Mexican American Struggle or Civil Rights*. Houston: Arte Público Press, 2000.

Rothstein, Stanley. *Handbook of Schooling in Urban America*. Westport, Conn.: Greenwood Press, 1993.

Ruiz, Vicki. *Cannery Women, Cannery Lives: Mexican Women, Unionization, and the California Food Processing Industry 1930–1950*. Albuquerque: University of New Mexico Press, 1987.

———. *From out of the Shadows: Mexican Women in Twentieth-Century America*. New York: Oxford University Press, 1998.

Sahagún, Fray Bernardino de. *Historia general de las cosas de la Nueva España*. Vol. 2. Mexico City: Editorial Porrúa, 1969 [orig. 1540–85, Spanish].

Saldívar Hull, Sonia. "Feminism on the Border: From Gender Politics to Geopolitics." In *Criticism in the Borderlands: Studies in Chicano Literature, Culture, and Ideology*. Edited by Héctor Calderón and José David Saldívar. Durham: Duke University Press, 1991.

Salpointe, Jean-Baptiste. *Soldiers of the Cross: Notes on the Ecclesiastical History of New Mexico, Arizona, and Colorado*. Banning, Calif.: St. Boniface's Industrial School, 1898.

Salvo, Dana. *Home Altars of Mexico*. Albuquerque: University of New Mexico Press, 1997.

Sánchez, George. *Becoming Mexican American: Ethnicity, Culture and Identity in Chicano Los Angeles, 1900–1945*. New York: Oxford University Press, 1993.

Sánchez, Josue. *Angels without Wings: The Hispanic Assemblies of God Story*. New Braunfels, Tex.: Atwood Printing, n.d.

Sánchez-Walsh, Arlene M. *Latino Pentecostal Identity: Evangelical Faith, Self, and Society*. New York: Columbia University Press, 2003.

Sanders, William T. *Life in a Classic Village: Proceedings from Oceana Redonda: Teotihuacán*. Mexico City: Sociedad Mexicana de Antropología, 1966.

Sandoval, Annette. *Homegrown Healing: Traditional Remedies from Mexico*. New York: Berkeley Books, 1998.

Sandoval, Moises. *Fronteras: A History of the Latin American Church in the USA since 1513*. San Antonio: Mexican American Cultural Center, 1983.

———. *The Mexican American Experience in the Church: Reflections on Identity and Mission*. New York: Sadlier, 1983.

———. *On the Move: A History of the Hispanic Church in the United States*. Maryknoll, N.Y.: Orbis Books, 1991.

San Martín, Beatriz (Vda. de María y Campos), ed. *Pastorelas y coloquios*. Mexico City: Editorial Diana, 1987.

Santos, Richard. "Missionary Beginnings in Spanish Florida, the Southwest and California." In *Fronteras: A History of the Latin American Church in the USA since 1513*. Edited by Moises Sandoval. San Antonio: Mexican American Cultural Center, 1983.

Saragoza, Alex M. "Recent Chicano Historiography: An Interpretive Essay." *Aztlán: A Journal of Chicano Studies* 19, no. 1 (1999): 1–77.

Schepers, Emile Markgraaff. "Voices, Visions and Strange Ideas: Hallucinations and Delusions in a Mexican-Origin Population." PhD diss., Northwestern University, Evanston, Ill., 1974.

Sclabassi, Antonio J. "The Catholic Church and *La Raza*." *La Raza* (January 1970).

Scholes, France V. "Church and State in New Mexico, 1610–1650." *New Mexico Historical Review* 11 (1936): 9–76 and (1940): 78–106.

———. "Documents for the History of New Mexican Missions in the Seventeenth Century." *New Mexico Historical Review* 4 (1929): 195–99.

———. "The First Decade of the Inquisition in New Mexico." *New Mexico Historical Review* 10 (1935): 195–241.

———. *Troublous Times in New Mexico, 1659–1670*. Albuquerque: University of New Mexico Press, 1942.

Schwichtenberg, Cathy, ed. *The Madonna Connection: Representational Politics, Subcultural Identities, and Cultural Theory*. Boulder: Westview Press, 1993.

Segundo, Juan Luis. *The Liberation of Theology*. Translated by John Drury. Maryknoll, N.Y.: Orbis Books, 1976.

Sharpe, Eric J. *Comparative Religion: A History*. La Salle, Ill.: Open Court, 1994.

Simmons, Marc. *Witchcraft in the Southwest: Spanish and Indian Supernaturalism on the Rio Grande*. Lincoln: University of Nebraska Press, 1980.

Smart, Ninian. *The Phenomenon of Religion*. London: Macmillan Press, 1973.

Smith, Clara Gertrude. "The Development of the Mexican People in the Community of Watts." MA thesis, University of Southern California, Los Angeles, 1933.

Smith, Jonathan Z. *Imagining Religion: From Babylon to Jonestown*. Chicago: University of Chicago Press, 1988.

Smith, Rosemary E. "The Work of Bishops' Committee for the Spanish-Speaking on Behalf of the Migrant Worker." MA thesis, Catholic University of America, Washington, D.C., 1958.

Sobrino, Jon. *Christology at the Crossroads: A Latin American Approach*. Translated by John Drury. Maryknoll, N.Y.: Orbis Books, 1978.

Sobrino, Jon, and Juan Hernández Pico. *Theology of Christian Solidarity*. Translated by Philip Berryman. Maryknoll, N.Y.: Orbis Books, 1985.

Soja, Edward. *Postmodern Geographies: The Reassertion of Space in Critical Social Theory*. London: Verso Books, 1989.

Soleri, Paolo. *The Bridge between Matter and Spirit Is Matter Becoming Spirit: The Arcology of Paolo Soleri*. Garden City, N.J.: Anchor, 1973.

Soto, Antonio. *The Chicano and the Church: Study of a Minority within a Religious Institution*. Denver: Marfel Associates, 1975.

Stapleton, Ernest. "The History of the Baptist Missions in New Mexico, 1849–1866." MA thesis, University of New Mexico, Albuquerque, 1954.

"Statement of the Fast for Non-violence." United Farm Workers Organizing Committee, 25 February 1968.

Stavans, Ilan. *The Riddle of Cantinflas: Essays on Hispanic Popular Culture*. Albuquerque: University of New Mexico Press, 1998.

Steele, Thomas J., SJ. *Santos and Saints: The Religious Folk Art of Hispanic New Mexico*, 2nd ed. Santa Fe, N. Mex.: Ancient City Press, 1982.

Stevens-Arroyo, Anthony M. "Cahensly Revisited? The National Pastoral Encounter of America's Hispanic Catholics." *Migration World* 15, no. 3 (fall 1987): 16–19.

———. "The Emergence of a Social Identity among Latino Catholics: An Appraisal." In *Hispanic Catholicism in the U.S.* Vol. 3. Edited by Jay Dolan and Alan Figueroa Deck, SJ. Notre Dame, Ind.: University of Notre Dame Press, 1994.

———. "The Inter-Atlantic Paradigm: The Failure of Spanish Medieval Colonialism of the Canary and Caribbean Islands." *Comparative Studies in Society and History* 35, no. 3 (July 1993): 515–43.

——. "Jaime Balmes Redux: Catholicism as Civilization in the Political Philosophy of Pedro Albizu Campos." In *Bridging the Atlantic: Iberian and Latin American Thought in Historical Perspective*. Edited by Marina Pérez de Mendiola. Albany: SUNY Press, 1966.

——. "Juan Mateo Guaticabanú, September 21, 1946: Evangelization and Martyrdom in the Time of Columbus." *Catholic Historical Review* 82, no. 4 (October 1996): 614–37.

Stevens-Arroyo, Anthony M., ed. *Prophets Denied Honor: An Anthology on the Hispanic Church in the United States*. Maryknoll, N.Y.: Orbis Books, 1980.

Stevens-Arroyo, Anthony M., and Ana María Díaz-Stevens. "Latino Church and Schools as Urban Battlegrounds." In *Handbook of Schooling in Urban America*. Edited by Stanley Rothstein. Westport, Conn.: Greenwood Press, 1993.

Stevens-Arroyo, Anthony M., and Gilbert R. Cadena, eds. *Old Masks, New Faces: Religion and Latino Identities*. New York: Bildner Center for Western Hemisphere Studies, 1995.

——, eds. *An Enduring Flame: Studies on Latino Popular Religiosity*. New York: Bildner Center for Western Hemisphere Studies, 1994.

——. "Puerto Ricans in the United States." In *The Minority Report*. 2nd ed. Edited by Gary and Rosalind Dworkin. New York: Holt Rinehart and Winston, 1982.

——. "Religious Faith and Institutions in the Forging of Latino Identities." In *Handbook for Hispanic Cultures in the United States*. Edited by Felix Padilla. Houston: Arte Público Press, 1993.

Stevens-Arroyo, Anthony M., with Segundo Pantoja, eds. *Discovering Latino Religion: A Comprehensive Social Science Bibliography*. New York: Bildner Center for Western Hemisphere Studies, 1995.

Stevens-Arroyo, Anthony M., and Andrés I. Pérez y Mena, eds. *Enigmatic Powers: Syncretism with African and Indigenous Peoples' Religions among Latinos*. New York: Bildner Center for Western Hemisphere Studies, 1995.

Storey, John. *An Introduction to Cultural Theory and Popular Culture*. 2nd ed. Athens: University of Georgia Press, 1998.

Stowell, Jay S. *The Near-side of the Mexican Question*. New York: Home Missions Council, 1921.

——. *A Study of Mexicans and Spanish Americans in the United States*. New York: Home Missions Council and the Council of Women for Home Missions, 1920.

Stratton, David H. "A History of Northern and Southern Baptists of New Mexico 1849–1950." MA thesis, University of Colorado, 1953.

Sullivan, Lawrence E. "Sound and Sense: Toward a Hermeneutics of Performance." *History of Religions* 26 (1986): 1–33.

Sunseri, Alvin R. *Seeds of Discord: New Mexico in the Aftermath of the American Conquest, 1846–1861.* Chicago: Nelson Hall, 1979.

Swanson, G. E. "Trance and Possession: Studies of Charismatic Influence." *Review of Religious Research* 19 (1978): 1–33.

Sylvest, Edwin E., Jr. "The Hispanic American Church: Contextual Considerations." *Perkins Journal* 29, no. 1 (1975): 22–31.

———. "Hispanic American Protestantism in the United States." In *Fronteras: A History of the Latin American Church in the USA since 1513.* Edited by Moises Sandoval. San Antonio: Mexican American Cultural Center, 1983.

Tafolla, Carmen. "The Church in Texas." In *Fronteras: A History of the Latin American Church in the USA since 1513.* Edited by Moises Sandoval. San Antonio: Mexican American Cultural Center, 1983.

Tatum, Inez. "Mexican Missions in Texas." MA thesis, Baylor University, Waco, Tex., 1939.

Thies, Jeffrey S. *Mexican Catholicism in Southern California.* New York: Peter Lang, 1993.

Thompson, Robert Farris. *Face of the Gods: Art and Altars of African and the African Americas.* New York : Museum for African, 1993.

Tijerina, Reies López. *Hallará fe en la tierra . . . ?* N.p., [1954?].

———. Interview by Rudy V. Busto. Coyote, N. Mex., April 1990.

———. *Mi lucha por la tierra.* Mexico City: Fondo de Cultura Económica, 1978.

Tomlinson, Homer A. "Big Parade of 2,000 Lead down Fifth Avenue New York City." *White Wing Messenger,* 7 November 1936, 1, 4.

———. *Miracles of Healing in the Ministry of Rev. Francisco Olazábal.* Queens, N.Y.: Homer A. Tomlinson, 1938.

Tönsmann, José Aste. *El secreto de sus ojos.* Lima: Tercer Milenio, 1998.

Torres, Eliso. *The Folk Healer: The Mexican-American Tradition of Curanderismo.* Kingsville, Tex.: Nieves Press, 1983.

Touraine, Alain. *Critique of Modernity.* Translated by David Macey. Oxford: Blackwell, 1995.

Traverzo Galarza, David. "Evangélicos/as." In *Handbook of Latina/o Theologies.* Edited by Edwin David Aponte and Miguel A. De La Torre. St. Louis: Chalice Press, 2006.

Trotter, Robert, III, and Juan Antonio Chavira. *Curanderismo: Mexican American Folk Healing.* Athens: University of Georgia Press, 1981 [2nd ed., 1997].

Trujillo, Carla. "La Virgen de Guadalupe and Her Reconstruction in Chicana Lesbian Desire." In *Chicana Lesbians: The Girls Our Mothers Warned Us About.* Berkeley, Calif.: Third Woman Press, 1991.

——. *Chicana Lesbians: The Girls Our Mothers Warned Us About*. Berkeley, Calif.: Third Woman Press, 1991.

Turner, Kay. *Beautiful Necessity: The Art and Meaning of Women's Altars*. New York: Thames and Hudson, 1999.

——. "Because of This Photography: The Making of a Mexican Folk Saint." In *Niño Fidencio: A Heart Thrown Open*. By Dore Gardner. Santa Fe: Museum of New Mexico Press, 1992.

——. "The Cultural Semiotics of Religious Icons: La Virgen de San Juan de Los Lagos." *Semiotica* 47 (1983): 317–61.

——. "Home Altars and the Art of Devotion." In *Chicano Expressions: A New View in American Art*. New York: Latin American Gallery, 1986.

——. "Mexican American Home Altars: Towards the Interpretation." *Aztlán: A Journal of Chicano Studies* 13, nos. 1–2 (1982): 309–26.

——. "Mexican American Home Altars: Toward Their Interpretation." In *The Chicano Studies Reader: An Anthology of Aztlán, 1970–2000*. Los Angeles: UCLA Chicano Studies Research Center Publications, 2001.

——. *Mexican American Home Altars: The Art of Relationship*. PhD diss. in Folklore and Anthropology, University of Texas, Austin, 1990. Ann Arbor, Mich.: UMI Dissertation Services, 1990.

Valdez, A. C., with James F. Scheer. *Fire on Azusa Street*. Costa Mesa, Calif.: Gift Publications, 1980.

Valdez, Luis. *La Pastorela: "The Shepherds' Play."* Video program notes, San Juan Bautista, California, 1989.

——. *La Pastorela: "The Shepherds' Tale."* Video, San Juan Bautista, California: El Teatro Campesino / RSP, produced for PBS's Great Performances Series, 1991. 78 minutes.

——. "The Tale of the Raza." In *Chicano: The Beginnings of Bronze Power*. Edited by Renato Rosaldo, Robert A. Calvert, and Gustav L. Seligmann. New York: William Morrow, 1974.

Valdez, Luis, and Stan Steiner. *Aztlán: An Anthology of Mexican American Literature*. New York: Vintage Books, 1972.

Vasconcelos, José. *La raza cósmica*. Mexico City: Espasa-Calpe Mexicana, 1948.

Vasquez, Manuel. "Pentecostalism, Collective Identity, and Transnationalism among Salvadorans and Peruvians in the U.S." *Journal of the American Academy of Religion* 67, no. 3 (September 1999): 617–36.

Venegas, Sybil. "Day of the Dead in Aztlán: Chicano Variations on the Theme of Life, Death and Self-Preservation." MA thesis, University of California, Los Angeles, 1995.

——. "The Day of the Dead in Los Angeles." Los Angeles: Photography Center, 1990.

Veysey, Laurence. *The Communal Experience: Anarchist and Mystical Counter-cultures in America*. San Francisco: Harper and Row, 1973.

Vidal, Jaime R. "Puerto Rican Catholicism." In *Puerto Rican and Cuban Catholics in the U.S., 1900–1965*. Edited by Jay P. Dolan and Jaime Vidal. Notre Dame, Ind.: University of Notre Dame Press, 1994.

Villaronga, Luis. "El Evangelista Olazábal en Río Piedras." *El Mundo* (San Juan, Puerto Rico), 5 May 1934.

———. "¿Quién Es Olazábal?" *El Mundo* (San Juan, Puerto Rico), 1934, 31.

Villaseñor Black, Charlene. "Sacred Cults, Subversive Icons: Chicanas and the Pictorial Language of Catholicism." In *Speaking Chicana: Voice, Power, and Identity*. Edited by Leticia Galindo and María Dolores Gonzales. Tucson: University of Arizona Press, 1999.

Villaseñor, Victor. *Rain of Gold*. Houston: Arte Público Press, 1991.

Visitor's Guide. *Sunland Visitor Center* 5, no. 2 (spring/summer 1996): 4.

Waldinger, Roger, and Mehdi Bozorgmehr, eds. *Ethnic Los Angeles*. New York: Russell Sage Foundation, 1996.

Walker Bynum, Carolyn, Stevan Harrell, and Paula Richman, eds. *Gender and Religion: On the Complexity of Symbols*. Boston: Beacon Press, 1986.

Walsh, Albeus. "The Work of Catholics Bishops' Committee for the Spanish-Speaking in the United States." MA thesis, University of Texas, Austin, 1958.

Watt, Alan J. "The Religious Dimensions of the Farm Worker Movement." PhD diss., Vanderbilt University, Nashville, Tenn., 1999.

Weatherby, Lela. "A Study of the Early Years of the Presbyterian Work with the Spanish-Speaking People of New Mexico and Colorado and Its Development from 1850–1920." MA thesis, Presbyterian College of Christian Education, 1942.

Weber, David J. *The Spanish Frontier in North America*. New Haven: Yale University Press, 1992.

Weber, Max. *From Max Weber: Essays in Sociology*. Translated by Hans Gerth and C. Wright Mills. 2nd ed. New York: Oxford University Press, 1949.

Weckmann, Luis. *La herencia medieval de México*. Mexico City: Fondo de Cultura Económica, 1995.

Weiner, Annette. *Women of Value, Men of Renown: New Perspectives in Trobriand Exchange*. Austin: University of Texas Press, 1976.

Wiebe, Donald. *The Politics of Religious Studies: The Continuing Conflict with Theology in the Academy*. New York: St. Martin's Press, 1999.

Williams, Peter W. *Popular Religion in America*. Chicago: University of Illinois Press, 1989.

Wilson, Bryan R. "An Analysis of Sect Development." *Sociological Review* 24 (February 1959): 3–15.

Wolff, Kurt H. *The Sociology of Georg Simmel*. New York: Free Press, 1950.

Wright, Robert E. "If It's Official, It Can't Be Popular? Reflections on Popular and Folk Religion." *Journal of Hispanic/Latino Theology* 1, no. 3 (May 1994): 47–67.

Ybarra-Frausto, Tomás. "Rasquachismo: A Chicano Sensibility." In *Chicano Art: Resistance and Affirmation, 1985–1995*. Edited by Richard Griswold del Castillo, Teresa McKenna, and Yvonne Yarbro-Bejarano. Los Angeles: Wight Art Gallery, University of California, 1991.

Contributors

RUDY V. BUSTO is assistant professor of religious studies at the University of California, Santa Barbara. His research interests are Latinos, Asian Americans, and race and religion. He is the author of *King Tiger: The Religious Vision of Reies López Tijerina*.

DAVÍD CARRASCO is the Neil Rudenstine Professor of Latin America Studies at Harvard University. His work focuses on Mesoamerican religions and the religious dimensions of the U.S. Latino experience, including *mestizaje*, the myth of Aztlán, transculturation, and La Virgen de Guadalupe. He has authored or coedited numerous books, including *Religions of Mesoamerica: Cosmovision and Ceremonial Centers* and *Alambrista and the U.S.-Mexico Border: Film, Music, and Stories of Undocumented Immigrants*.

SOCORRO CASTAÑEDA-LILES is a doctoral candidate in sociology at the University of California, Santa Barbara. Her areas of research are sociology of religion, sociology of knowledge, women's studies, and Chicana/o studies. Her PhD dissertation is on U.S. Latino/a interpretations of Our Lady of Guadalupe.

GASTÓN ESPINOSA is assistant professor of religion at Claremont McKenna College. He writes on American and Latino religions, politics, and pop culture. He is the coeditor of *Latino Religions and Civic Activism in the United States*, and, with Miguel De La Torre, of *Rethinking Latino(a) Religion and Identity*.

RICHARD R. FLORES is associate dean of the College of Liberal Arts and professor of anthropology and Mexican American studies at the University of Texas, Austin. His research focuses on critical theory, performance studies, semiotics, and historical anthropology. Flores is the author of *Los Pastores: History and Performance in the Mexican Shepherds' Play of South Texas* and editor of *Reflexiones 1999: New Directions in Mexican American Studies*.

MARIO T. GARCÍA is professor of history and Chicano studies at the University of California, Santa Barbara. He is the author of *Desert Immigrants: The*

Mexicans of El Paso, 1880–1920 and *Mexican Americans: Leadership, Ideology, and Identity, 1930–1960*, and is the editor of *Memories of Chicano History: The Life and Narrative of Bert Corona*. He is presently working on the role of Mexican American activism in the Catholic Church.

MARÍA HERRERA-SOBEK is associate vice-chancellor for diversity, equity, and academic policy and professor of Chicana/o Studies at the University of California, Santa Barbara, where she holds the Luis Leal Endowed Chair in Chicana/o Studies. She is the author of *The Bracero Experience: Elitelore versus Folklore*; *The Mexican Corrido: A Feminist Analysis*; and *Northward Bound: The Mexican Immigrant Experience in Ballad and Song*, and is the coeditor of *Chicana Creativity and Criticism: Charting New Frontiers in Chicana Literature*.

LUIS D. LEÓN is assistant professor of religious studies at Denver University. He is the author of *La Llorona's Children: Religion, Life, and Death in the U.S.-Mexico Borderlands* and an upcoming book on César Chávez.

STEPHEN R. LLOYD-MOFFETT is assistant professor of religious studies at California Polytechnical University at San Luis Obispo. He received his PhD in religious studies from the University of California, Santa Barbara. His research focuses on alternative forms of Christianity, especially the ascetic and mystical traditions.

ELLEN MCCRACKEN is professor of Spanish and Portuguese literatures at the University of California, Santa Barbara. She is the author of *New Latina Narrative: The Feminine Space of Postmodern Ethnicity* and the editor of *Fray Angelico Chávez: Poet, Priest, and Artist*.

LAURA E. PÉREZ is associate professor of ethnic studies at the University of California, Berkeley. Her teaching and research are in contemporary U.S. Latina and Latin American women's writing, Chicana/o literature and visual arts, and contemporary cultural theory. She is the author of *Chicano Art: The Politics of Spiritual and Aesthetic Altarities*.

ROBERTO LINT SAGARENA is assistant professor of religion and American studies at the University of Southern California. His research interests focus on religion in the United States and Mexico, Atlantic world history, religion in the borderlands, and art and ethnic nationalism.

ANTHONY M. STEVENS-ARROYO is professor of Puerto Rican studies at Brooklyn College and founder and director of the Program for the Analysis of Religion Among Latinos (PARAL). He is the coauthor and coeditor of numerous books, including, with Ana María Díaz-Stevens, *Recognizing the Latino Resurgence in U.S. Religion: The Emmaus Paradigm*, and *An Enduring Flame: Studies on Latino Popular Religiosity*; *Old Masks, New Faces: Religion and Latino Identities*; and, *Enigmatic Powers: Syncretism with African and Indigenous Peoples' Religions among Latinos*.

KAY TURNER is adjunct professor in the Department of Performance Studies at New York University and folk arts director at the Brooklyn Arts Council. She is a pioneer in the study of Mexican American women's home altars. She is the author of *Beautiful Necessity: The Art and Meaning of Women's Altars*.

Index

McDonnell, Donald, Fr., as inspiration to Chávez, 23, 112–13
McIntyre, Frances, Cardinal, 7, 137–41, 145
McLean, Robert, 21
McNamara, Patrick, 33; as catalyst in religious studies, 17
McPherson, Aimee Semple, 273–75
MEChA, 127
Medina, Lara, and Our Lady of Guadalupe, 170
Mendoza, Maggie, 371
Mesa-Bains, Amalia, ix, 11, 338–52, 414–15; altar art and, 341–52; alternative spirituality and, 341–45; cultural hybridity and, 338; hybrid spirituality and, 338–39; politics of, 346–48; religiosity and, 340–41; Virgin of Guadalupe/Virgin Mary and, 340–41
Mestizaje, 5, 58, 339; cultural, 339; through marriage, 5; Selena and, 375–76; spirituality of, 338–39
Methodist Episcopal Church, 270
Methodists, Methodism, 265, 269, 271
Mexican American. See Chicanos, Chicanas
Mexican American Cultural Center, 17
Mexico: immigration to United States from, 21; war between United States and, 4, 6, 85
Mexico City, 7, 237
Mignolo, Walter, 223, 237–38
Mohanty, Chandra, 215–16
Montgomery, Carrie Judd, 265, 270
Montgomery, George, 265, 269, 270
Moody, Dwight, 269
Moody Bible Institute, 269
Moore, Joan, 33; as catalyst in religious studies, 17
Morgan, David, 14 n.1
Mormons, Mormonism, 13 n.8, 33, 382, 386; percentage of Latinos of Mexican ancestry as, 20

Mujerista, 32
Muñoz, Carlos, 389
Muslims, 33, 382, 386
Mysticism, 108–12

Nahua, 227
Nebreda, Alfonso, 28
Nepantla, 41, 46 n.8
New Directions in Chicano Religions Conference, 17, 40, 56 n.87
New Mexico, 69, 85, 102; popular Catholicism in, 19
Novels, religion and, 4

Olalquiaga, Celeste, 347
Olazábal, Francisco, 9–10, 19, 263–90; Assemblies of God and, 271; Azusa Street Revival and, 263–67, 270; Bethel Temple and, 277; Catholic background of, 268; Church of God (Cleveland) and, 284–85; conflict of, with Catholicism, 282–84; critics of, 280–81; death of, 285–86; denominational influence of, 287, 294 n.61; El Azteca, 277; Foursquare Church and, 273–74; healing and, 9–10, 263–90; Jamaica Tabernacle Church and, 280; Latin American Council of Churches and, 286–87; Mexican American Pentecostalism and, 263–90; as Mexican Billy Sunday, 273; Mexican leadership and, 268–72; Moody and, 269; in New York, 276–80; Protestantism and, 268–69; in Puerto Rico, 281–83; in Spanish Harlem, 276–80, 285, 286; spiritual worldview of, 268; tongues and, 282, 283; women in ministry and, 278–79
Olmec, 57
Olmos, Edward James, 366
Onderdonk, F. A., 269
Ortegón, Samuel, 22
Ortiz, Fernando, 58
Osterberg, Arthur, 265

Ramírez, Daniel, 31
Ramírez, Ricardo, 27
Razo, Joe, 127, 142, 144
Religion: historic development of, 5; practices and symbols of, as vehicles of activism, 7; traditions of, as vehicles of activism, 7
Religious studies: Chávez and, 23–25; Chicano, and Catholicism, 1–2; Chicano, genealogy of, 17, 20–22; Chicano, history of, 17–43; Chicano and Mexican American, origin of, 43; Chicano, at undergraduate and graduate levels, 3; Latin American influences on, 25–31; phenomenological approach to, 38–39, pluralistic framework of, 32–33; secular interpretation of, 33–34
Renard González, Barbara, 359, 372
Republic of San Joaquín, 102
Reuther, Rosemary Radford, 31
Revilla-Vásquez, Catherine, 371
Ríos, Elizabeth, 32
Rodríguez, Jeanette, 7; Our Lady of Guadalupe and, 7, 154, 158–60
Roman Catholics, Catholicism: Anglo-American institution of, 9; assimilation and, 1, 2, 66–72; body and, 244; Charismatic, 20, 33; Chicano civil rights and, 7, 125–46; churches and socialization of, 33, 66, 81 n.67; colonialism and, 64–72, 81 n.65; curanderismo and, 296–320; healing and, 9–10, 383; in Latino homelands, 60–61; Mexican American identity and, 381, 382; missionaries of, in Southwest, 20; mystical tradition and, 110–12; Our Lady of Guadalupe and, 7, 153–76; percentage of Latinos of Mexican ancestry as, 20, 382; popular Latino, 9, 41, 153–76; rearticulation of, 9; rural survival and, 73; supernatural worldview of, 289; as topic of Mexican American religious study, 1–2, 4, 13 n.8

Romero, Juan, as catalyst in religious studies, 17, 117
Roosevelt, Eleanor, 100
Rosado, José Luis Guerrero, 154; Our Lady of Guadalupe and, 164–66
Rosaldo, Renato, 223
Ruiz, Raúl, 128, 141

Sagarena, Roberto Lint, 8, 223–38
Salazar, Rubén, 146
Saldívar, Yolanda, 370
Salinas, Raul, 130, 134
Salpointe, Jean-Baptiste, 20
San Antonio de Padua, 254
Sánchez, Alfonso, 87
Sánchez, Eduardo Chávez, 154; Our Lady of Guadalupe and, 164–66
Sánchez-Walsh, Arlene, 32
Sandoval, Moises, 4, 13 n.8, 386, 421, 422; as catalyst in religious studies, 17, 27
San Martín de Porres, 254
Santería, 305, 312
Santero, 19
Santo Niño de Atocha, 243, 254
Sapia, María Teresa, 278
Saragoza, Alex, 25, 422
School District of Abington v. Schempp, 1, 3, 46 n.8, 55 n.81; impact of, on Mexican American and Latino religious studies, 3, 38
Sclabassi, Antonio J., 136–37
Schwichtenberg, Cathy, 363
Second General Conference of Latin American Bishops (CELAM), 25–26, 29
Secularization, 8
Selena [Quintañilla Pérez], ix, 5, 11, 359–77, 385, 386; comparison of, with Marilyn Monroe and Madonna, 372; as culturally redemptive symbol, 359, 363–64, 367, 371–72, 375–76; home altars and,

Valle de Paz, 6, 88–102; Arizona City and, 99–100; Biblical imagery and, 91–92; braceros and, 97; collapse of, 94–95; economic context of, 96–97; geographic context of, 99–100, 105 n.31; Pentecostal character of, 95, 98–99

Vatican II, 27, 28, 128, 246, 249
Virgen of San Juan de los Lagos, 254

Wiebe, Donald, 13 n.5, 13 n.7, 18, 39
Williams, Raymond, 362
Wilson, Louis, 21
Wisconsin v. Yoder, 103 n.19

GASTÓN ESPINOSA is associate professor of religious studies
at Claremont McKenna College and Claremont Graduate University.

MARIO T. GARCÍA is professor of history and Chicano studies
at the University of California, Santa Barbara.

Library of Congress Cataloging-in-Publication Data

Mexican American religions : spirituality, activism, and culture / edited by
    Gastón Espinosa and Mario T. García.
        p. cm.
Includes bibliographical references and index.
ISBN 978-0-8223-4098-0 (cloth : alk. paper)—ISBN 978-0-8223-4119-2 (pbk. :
alk. paper)
    I. Mexican Americans—Religion. I. Espinosa, Gastón. II. García, Mario T.
    BR563.M49M49 2008
    270.089'6872073—dc22   2007042560